Technology Diffusion and Adoption:

Global Complexity, Global Innovation

Ali Hussein Saleh Zolait
University of Bahrain, Kingdom of Bahrain

Information Science
REFERENCE

Managing Director:	Lindsay Johnston
Editorial Director:	Joel Gamon
Book Production Manager:	Jennifer Yoder
Publishing Systems Analyst:	Adrienne Freeland
Assistant Acquisitions Editor:	Kayla Wolfe
Typesetter:	Henry Ulrich
Cover Design:	Nick Newcomer

Published in the United States of America by
Information Science Reference (an imprint of IGI Global)
701 E. Chocolate Avenue
Hershey PA 17033
Tel: 717-533-8845
Fax: 717-533-8661
E-mail: cust@igi-global.com
Web site: http://www.igi-global.com

Library of Congress Cataloging-in-Publication Data

Technology diffusion and adoption: global complexity, global innovation / Ali Hussein Saleh Zolait, editor.
    p. cm.
  Includes bibliographical references and index.
  Summary: "This book discusses the emerging topics of information technology and the IT based solutions in global and multi-cultural environments"--
Provided by publisher.
  ISBN 978-1-4666-2791-8 (hbk.) -- ISBN 978-1-4666-2792-5 (ebook) -- ISBN 978-1-4666-2793-2 (print & perpetual access) 1. Diffusion of innovations. 2. Technology transfer. 3. Information technology--Management. I. Zolait, Ali Hussein Saleh, 1972-
  HC79.T4T43995 2013
  303.48'3--dc23
                            2012032557

British Cataloguing in Publication Data
A Cataloguing in Publication record for this book is available from the British Library.

The views expressed in this book are those of the authors, but not necessarily of the publisher.

Table of Contents

Section 2
Global Technology and System Adoption

Section 3
Trends in Digital Divide

Detailed Table of Contents

Section 1
Mobile Application and Network

Chapter 1

    Krassie Petrova, Auckland University of Technology, New Zealand
    Raymond Yiwen Huang, Auckland University of Technology, New Zealand

The mobile Internet is a fast-growing technology that provides access to the traditional stationary (fixed-line) Internet from devices connected to mobile communication networks. It is predicted that the convergence between mobile networks and the fixed-line Internet will be a core feature in the next generation network architecture, achieving fast 'anywhere' Internet access and global mobility management. Applying a case study approach, this paper reviews the New Zealand mobile Internet market mix, competition, and mobile service provision. The key mobile Internet deployment requirements are determined and analyzed in order to identify a set of mobile Internet critical success factors and to investigate the impact of the shift from fixed-line to mobile and wireless Internet data communication infrastructure.

Chapter 2

    Ahmed Sowaileh, Ministry of Justice, Bahrain
    Ali AlSoufi, University of Bahrain, Bahrain

The development of mobile government services in Bahrain is moving slowly, when compared with traditional e-government services. Few informational and transactional services are available on the mobile portal. The complexity of government services prevents their delivery through the limited mobile phone interface. This exploratory research builds a method to tackle service complexity, as well as simplify and streamline the design and development of government services that target mobile devices. Forty government services in Bahrain were analyzed to identify the factors that affect mobile government services. The model was then applied to the sample services, and results were used to develop the target method. The main finding of this research is that the current approach of taking the existing services on the PC portal and implementing them on the mobile portal should be avoided. A better approach is to break down the services into sessions or components and identify opportunities where mobile technologies can be utilized.

Chapter 3

Many organizations attempt to form strategic networked enterprises, yet such strategies are difficult to implement because they are as likely to fail as to succeed. This failure is due to intangible differences and mismatches between partners in tacit knowledge (TK). Despite the various proposed partnership assessment models/tools in the literature, an immediate need exists for a new approach to measure the mismatch in TK across different organizations. This is due to the complex, vague, and uncertain nature of TK attributes. Hence, an instrument for measuring vagueness (imprecise), such as fuzzy linguistic variables, is needed. In this study, the author applies a neuro-fuzzy approach to assess TK fitness in networked enterprises. The results show how differences in TK between partners affect the networked enterprise's performance. Furthermore, the assessment approach reveals the most significant values to adopt and the irrelevant values that must be abandoned to smooth the partnership formation. The proposed model can prevent unexpected conflicts between partners if managed properly.

Chapter 4

Despite the wide usage of multimedia in several applications, research in the field of olfaction is immature in helping humans work and communicate through multi-sensory interfaces, including smell. There is no consistent method of testing user capability of smell. Therefore, smell detection and generation systems are not well integrated into today's multimedia systems. In this paper, the authors propose an odor sensing system with the capability of the discrimination among closely similar 20 different odor patterns and propose an on-line classification method using a handheld odor meter (OMX-GR sensor) and neural network that can be used in different multimedia applications. The proposed system is integrated to enhance the functionality of an online multimedia shopping system that is capable of selling products with visual and auditory senses.

Chapter 5

Research and development is considered a main source of knowledge and innovation in the Gulf countries and Arab region. Therefore, building a Collaborative Research Network (CRN) in the Gulf is necessary for high quality and sustainable research. In this paper, the authors examine the role of CRN in improving Gulf countries' performance in research and innovation. Four objectives have been set: investigate the current situation regarding scientific research and CRN in the Gulf countries, identify factors that influence the building of a CRN, identify the impact and contribution of CRN in improving the Gulf countries' performance, and develop a model. To achieve these objectives, a quantitative method was adopted. A questionnaire was developed and distributed to 100 participants. The current paper presents the first stage of research that investigates the role of building CRN in improving the Gulf countries' performance in research and innovation. The next stage will examine the model of building CRN.

Section 2
Global Technology and System Adoption

Chapter 6

George Ditsa, Tshwane University of Technology, South Africa
Saleh Alwahaishi, Technical University of Ostrava, Czech Republic
Shayma Al-Kobaisi, United Arab Emirates University
Václav Snášel, Technical University of Ostrava, Czech Republic

Culture is thought to be the most difficult to isolate, define, and measure in the adoption and use of IT (Information Technology) (Hassan & Ditsa, 1999). Consequently, the impact of culture on the adoption and use of IT does not feature prominently in Information Systems (IS) literature. As cultural factors are important to the success of IT adoption and use, this research paper examines culture's impact on the adoption and use of IT in the United Arab Emirates (UAE). The results of the study were compared along eight cultural dimensions with a study on the adoption and use of IT in developing and developed countries. The results are also used to identify issues that concern the relationship of culture and IT and their implications for IT adoption and use in the UAE. The study results are further used to suggest ways of bridging the digital divide between the UAE and developed countries.

Chapter 7

Bartholomew Aleke, University of Northumbria, UK
Udechukwu Ojiako, University of Southampton, UK
David Wainwright, University of Northumbria, UK

In this paper, the authors examine the process of diffusion of innovation ICT within agrarian business enterprises operating in developing countries. There is substantial research in the area of Diffusion of Innovation Theory (DoI) and its application to Information Systems (IS) research within organisations. However, in recognition of the conceptual limitations of DoI, researchers have called for the incorporation of aspects of Social Network Theory (SNT) into DoI frameworks. The findings of this research suggest that an understanding of the conceptual basis of innovation is a major driver of successful innovation adoption.

Chapter 8

Muhammad Z. I. Lallmahomed, Universiti Teknologi Malaysia, Malaysia
Nor Zairah Ab. Rahim, Universiti Teknologi Malaysia, Malaysia
Roliana Ibrahim, Universiti Teknologi Malaysia, Malaysia
Azizah Abdul Rahman, Universiti Teknologi Malaysia, Malaysia

In the light of a diverse body of disorganized usage measures available and the difficulty of building a cumulative research tradition, a literature review is conducted on system use in Information Systems (IS) Acceptance through the two main theories of Technology Adoption, the Technology Acceptance Model (TAM), and The Unified Theory of Use and Acceptance of Technology (UTAUT). The authors seek to understand how usage measures are being operationalised and proposed a preliminary classification of those measures that covers system and task aspects of use. A Q-Sort approach was taken to validate the authors' classification scheme and the result indicates high inter-rater agreement. The ensuing classification is meant to help researchers in their choice of system use measures. This review also summarises the arguments for a multi-dimensional measure of use and establishes that omnibus measure such as frequency, volume and use/non-use hold prevalence. Finally, the authors provide recommendations for further research in the area of system use.

Chapter 9

Khaled Saleh Al Omoush, Alzaytoonah University, Jordan
Raed Musbah Alqirem, Alzaytoonah University, Jordan
Amin A. Shaqrah, Alzaytoonah University, Jordan

The purpose of this study is to develop and validate a comprehensive model for the determinants of household Internet adoption through identifying the driving internal beliefs of individuals and the effect of cultural values on behavioral intention to adopt the household Internet among Jordanians. Given the widely recognized effect of cultural values on adoption of Information and Communication Technology (ICT), this study, applying Hofstede's multidimensional framework, investigated the effect of cultural values on the behavioral intention to household Internet adoption in micro level. The empirical examination of the research model indicated that the behavioral intention to household Internet adoption is determined directly by five internal beliefs, including perceived needs, perceived risks, perceived ease of use, perceived resources, and perceived image. The results provide supporting empirical evidence linking most of Hofstede's cultural dimensions to behavioral intention to household Internet adoption. With the exception of power distance, the results showed that collectivism (low individualism), masculinity, long-term orientation, and uncertainty avoidance had significant effects on the behavioral intention to household Internet adoption. The results demonstrated differences in the driving forces and cultural impact on Internet adoption between households and organizations settings.

Chapter 10

Japhet E. Lawrence, University of Kurdistan-Hawler, Iraq

Electronic commerce (EC) has the potential to improve efficiency and productivity in many areas and has received significant attention in many countries. However, there has been some doubt about the relevance of ecommerce for developing countries. The absence of adequate basic infrastructural, socio-economic, socio-cultural, and government ICT strategies have created a significant barrier in the adoption and growth of ecommerce in the Kurdistan region of Iraq. In this paper, the author shows that to understand the adoption and diffusion of ecommerce in Kurdistan, socio-cultural issues like transactional trust and social effect of shopping must be considered. The paper presents and discusses these issues hindering ecommerce adoption in Kurdistan.

    Aroon Manoharan, Kent State University, USA
    Marc Fudge, California State University-San Bernardino, USA
    Marc Holzer, Rutgers University-Newark, USA

This paper highlights the research findings of a digital governance survey conducted in the fall of 2009. The study replicates previous surveys of large municipalities worldwide in 2007, 2005, and 2003. This longitudinal assessment, focused on the assessment of current practices in municipal e-governance by evaluating their official websites. Specifically, the survey analyzed security, usability, content, the type of online services currently being offered, citizen response, and participation through websites established by city governments worldwide. There were significant changes in the top ranking cities when compared to previous studies. Based on the 2009 evaluation of 87 cities, Seoul, Prague, Hong Kong, New York, and Singapore represent the highest performing cities in digital governance. Moreover, there continues to be a divide in terms of digital governance throughout the world; however, this divide, which increased in 2005, decreased in 2009.

    Jianbin Zhang, Wuhan University, China

This study uses the methods of questionnaire and group discussion to conduct field research in A and B towns, which are located in the eastern developed region and the western undeveloped region of China, respectively. According to comparative study on the status of providing public information service for the disadvantaged between A and B towns, the author finds that the public in A town are superior to the ones in B in terms of information literacy, public information service expenditure, and satisfaction rate of public information service. Similarities exist in terms of differences in accessing public information service between town and village, among social groups, and the causes resulting in imbalance of public information service and features of the information-poor's group distribution. The author discusses the differences in development policies between city and village, as well as differences in financial investment of public information service, education, and individual's income level between A and B towns.

    D. P. Goyal, Management Development Institute, India
    Adarsh Garg, Institute of Management and Research, India

Through extensive research into the area of quality management practices, such as ISO (International Standard Organization), Six Sigma has been observed within small and medium-sized enterprises (SMEs). Few empirical studies have reported the application of Six Sigma in SMEs, especially in software developing SMEs. The reasons can be attributed to complex issues associated with Six Sigma, as well as cost and time constraints. This paper assesses the current status of quality management practices in software developing SMEs. A survey-based approach was used to understand the conventional quality management practices in software SMEs. The data was collected from 230 respondents in 23 software developing SMEs in National Capital Region (NCR) of India. The respondents involved all three managerial levels and statistical results reflect the non-realization of quality management practices in software development. The SMEs under study were aware of the importance of quality management practices but had not implemented the same in the organization which is one of the basic requirements for the success of any software.

Section 4
Database and Algorithms Applications

Chapter 14

François Pinet, Cemagref - Clermont Ferrand, France

Myoung-Ah Kang, LIMOS, France

Kamal Boulil, Cemagref - Clermont Ferrand, France

Sandro Bimonte, Cemagref - Clermont Ferrand, France

Gil De Sousa, Cemagref - Clermont Ferrand, France

Catherine Roussey, Cemagref - Clermont Ferrand, France

Michel Schneider, LIMOS, France

Jean-Pierre Chanet, Cemagref - Clermont Ferrand, France

Recent research works propose using Object-Oriented (OO) approaches, such as UML to model data warehouses. This paper overviews these recent OO techniques, describing the facts and different analysis dimensions of the data. The authors propose a tutorial of the Object Constraint Language (OCL) and show how this language can be used to specify constraints in OO-based models of data warehouses. Previously, OCL has been only applied to describe constraints in software applications and transactional databases. As such, the authors demonstrate in this paper how to use OCL to represent the different types of data warehouse constraints. This paper helps researchers working in the fields of business intelligence and decision support systems, who wish to learn about the major possibilities that OCL offer in the context of data warehouses. The authors also provide general information about the possible types of implementation of multi-dimensional models and their constraints.

Chapter 15

Omar Shehab, Staffordshire University, Malaysia

Ali Hussein Saleh Zoliat, University of Bahrain, Bahrain

In this paper, the authors propose a Semantic Search Engine, which retrieves software components precisely and uses techniques to store these components in a database, such as ontology technology. The engine uses semantic query language to retrieve these components semantically. The authors use an exploratory study where the proposed method is mapped between object-oriented concepts and web ontology language. A qualitative survey and interview techniques were used to collect data. The findings after implementing this research are a set of guidelines, a model, and a prototype to describe the semantic search engine system. The guidelines provided help software developers and companies reduce the cost, time, and risks of software development.

The cursive nature of Arabic writing is the main challenge to Arabic Optical Character Recognition developer. Methods to segment Arabic words into characters have been proposed. This paper provides a comprehensive review of the methods proposed by researchers to segment Arabic characters. The segmentation methods are categorized into nine different methods based on techniques used. The advantages and drawbacks of each are presented and discussed. Most researchers did not report the segmentation accuracy in their research; instead, they reported the overall recognition rate which did not reflect the influence of each sub-stage on the final recognition rate. The size of the training/testing data was not large enough to be generalized. The field of Arabic Character Recognition needs a standard set of test documents in both image and character formats, together with the ground truth and a set of performance evaluation tools, which would enable comparing the performance of different algorithms. As each method has its strengths, a hybrid segmentation approach is a promising method. The paper concludes that there is still no perfect segmentation method for ACR and much opportunity for research in this area.

This paper aims to find an effective and efficient information hiding method used for protecting secret information by embedding it in a cover media such as images. Finding the optimal set of the image pixel bits to be substituted by the secret message bits, such that the cover image is of high quality, is a complex process and there is an exponential number of feasible solutions. Two new ant-based algorithms are proposed and compared with other algorithms. The experimental results show that ant colony optimization algorithm can find the solution efficiently and effectively by finding the optimal set of pixel bits in a few number of iterations and with least Mean Square Error (MSE) comparable with genetic and genetic simulated annealing algorithms.

Preface

"Technology Diffusion and Adoption: Global Complexity and Global Innovations" is collection designed for researchers and all educators who are currently researching and would like to know more about, technology and adoption. This collection gives much concern to the global complexity faced by global Diffusion of Innovations (DOI). The global innovations involve much more than computers, systems and solutions to business's problems therefore the abbreviation used for Technology Diffusion - TD - is a plural term to denote the whole range of technologies related to Global Innovations acceptance on the one hand and, on the other, related to global factors impeding adoption. From a global perspective of adoption, the driving forces for IT acceptance and adoption is different from context to context. Notably, researchers' works in the area of IT adoption are all about finding an empirical evidence to answer the most significant question which is: what causes people, organizations, or the entire context to accept or reject IT? There are some situational conditions that may accelerate or slow the acceptance rate among adopters. These situational conditions in some context drive the adopters' decisions in all circumstances and shape their decisions into a voluntary, mandatory or desirable action toward innovation acceptance. This collection comprised four main themes that represent the structure of this book. Several researches grouped under their intended theme. Themes closely reflect some attributes shared among these research papers placed under each theme. The four themes are as follows: mobile applications and networks, global technology and system adoption, trends in digital divide, database and algorithms applications.

Theme one is reserved to present networks and mobile applications adoption, and authors discuss materials pertaining to deployment and success factors for the mobile Internet, tackling m-government service complexity in Bahrain, an intelligent approach to assess tacit knowledge fitness in networked enterprises, the ANN based approach to integrate smell sense in multimedia systems, and lastly, the role of a collaborative research network (CRN) in improving the Arabian Gulf countries' performance in research and innovation.

Petrova and Huang discussed the deployment and success factors for the mobile Internet using a case study of New Zealand context. The researcher conclude that connection or /access pricing remains the main factor influencing the choice of Internet access. It is price driven market in which DSL is likely to retain a dominant position at least until Mobile Internet starts offering a service comparable to DSL. Petrova and Huang argue the convergence between mobile networks and the fixed-line Internet. Also, they conclude that mobile networks will be feature of the next generation network architecture. Evidence brought from the mobile Internet market mix, competition, and mobile service provision in New Zealand. Applying a case study approach, key mobile Internet deployment requirements such as achieving fast *anywhere* Internet access and global mobility management are among critical success factors of mobile networks adoption. Furthermore; these factors will have impact on the transition from fixed-line to mobile and wireless Internet data communication infrastructure. Although the study findings are based on a one country study (New Zealand) the Petrova and Huang believe that these may be applicable to other similar contexts. Also, the researcher open a room for further research and invite researcher to use the set of proposed critical success factors to create a model for empirical investigation including global mobile interconnectivity.

Then, Sowaileh and AlSoufi research the development of mobile government services in Bahraini context in which adoption of e-government is moving very highly. Although, E-government in the context of Bahrain ranked among the top ten e-governments, the application of mobile government is moving slowly when compared with traditional e-government services. Although, there are some of the informational and transactional services which are available on the mobile portal, complexity of government services prevents their delivery through the limited mobile phone interface. There are few exploratory research designed to tackle service complexity, as well as simplify and streamline the design and development of government services that target mobile devices. The study conducted by Sowaileh and AlSoufi to identify the driving forces of mobile government in Bahrain. In this study a sample of forty government services in Bahrain were analyzed to identify the factors that affect mobile government services. The researcher builds a method to suitable for the model which was then applied to the sample services, and results were used to develop the target method. The analysis of 40 government services revealed that attempting to provide large government services as full mobile services is a very difficult task and it should be avoided. Alternatively, this study recommends a method to exploit the benefits of mobile technologies by identifying parts of these services or break them into sessions or components of services where mobile technologies can be utilized. The researchers conclude that the PC portal approach of taking the existing services on the PC portal and implementing them on the mobile portal should be avoided. The researcher open a room for more research on this issue that target services in specific government areas, for example, healthcare, legal system, and disaster prevention and recovery in order to provide deeper details about the government services and identify better opportunities to utilize mobile technologies.

The attempts to integrate European organizations to the global Japanese automotive organizations have resulted on pitfall conflicts because of the differences on tacit values of the two different contexts. Despite of those differences, globalization of the marketplace produce Networked-Enterprises (NE) which facing more and more global issues that are critical for their success. In the field of strategies for networked enterprises Al-Mutawah paid attention to the immediate need for a new approach to measure the mismatch in Tacit Knowledge (TK) across different organizations. He argued that the intangible differences and mismatches between partners in Tacit Knowledge (TK) cause the failure and difficulty to implement such strategies. This is due to the complex, vague, and uncertain nature of TK attributes. Al-Mutawah applies a neuro-fuzzy approach to assess TK fitness in networked enterprises. The results show how differences in TK between partners affect the networked enterprise's performance. Furthermore, the assessment approach reveals the most significant values to adopt and the irrelevant values that must be abandoned to smooth the partnership formation. The proposed model can prevent unexpected conflicts between partners if managed properly.

Although extensive research has been carried out to develop multimedia systems that can capture, store, and reproduce auditory (sound) and visual (sight) in video technology, the smell is the only sense that can be perceived from a long distance but received less attention within the multimedia research area. Al-Bastaki and Al-Mutawah study one of the five well known physiological systems that lies at the core of the human perceptual experience, which is olfactory (smell). Al-Bastaki and Al-Mutawah study attempted to develop multimedia applications and integrate smell sense in multimedia systems to help humans work and communicate through olfactory sensory (smell) interfaces. The study proposed very useful Artificial Neural Network ANN program for on-line odor recognition system, which has a various types of odor samples. The proposed ANN based olfactory system was conceived for the consumer electronic market. It can also be used in other environments such as industrial application to test products like food, beverages, and cosmetic items for process monitoring and quality control. The proposed odor sensing system has the capability of the discrimination among closely similar 20 different odour patterns. Also, it proposes an on-line classification method using a handheld odour meter (OMX-GR sensor) and neural network that can be used in different multimedia applications such as educational applications, real-time safety and security applications. The study recommends future research opportunity based on the need for developing consistent method for testing user's capability of smell. They also develop smell detection and generation systems which are integrated into today's multimedia systems.

The scientific research in the Gulf countries according to Al-Soufi and Al-Ammary is not stable and is experiencing many problems such as funding support, private sectors involvement, quality, and quantity of the researches conducted and their compatibility for the Gulf region. In this topic, Al-Soufi and Al-Ammary recognized the necessity for building a Collaborative Research Network (CRN) to produce high quality and sustainable research that concerning the Gulf countries context. Therefore, researchers work on this study to investigate the current situation scientific research and CRN in the Gulf countries. In addition, they identify factors influencing the building of a CRN, and then look into the impact and contribution of CRN in improving the Gulf countries' performance. Lastly, the researchers work towards developing a CRN model to be adopted as assistant tool in guiding and improving Gulf countries' performance in research and innovation. The researchers in this is study adopted a quantitative method and questionnaire was developed and distributed to a sample of 150 participants from the Gulf countries and comprised of academics and leaders from universities, research centres and R&D. The findings of the research revealed that there are some barriers and inhibitors stand in front of building the CRN in the Gulf countries. The two main inhibitors are absence of the funding and skilful researchers, who can collaborative, manage and monitor the research progress within the CRN. Factors that influence the building of CRN are education system and research centres. The study suggested a set of structured guidelines to help start and operate research networks and encourage the development of a collaborative research network in the Gulf countries. The study's model explains that there are five factors which have a direct impact on building CRN in the Gulf countries. The researcher call for further collaborative research with full support from research centres, educational organizations, and industries to conduct research which designed to bridge the gap in innovation and knowledge building and transfer among Gulf countries. As next stage, researchers invite for further research to test he the model of building CRN.

Theme two, Global Technology and System Adoption, discusses a comparative study of the effects of culture on the deployment of IT, social drivers for ICT diffusion among agrarian business enterprises in Nigeria, preliminary classification of usage measures in IS acceptance studies, the driving internal beliefs of household Internet Adoption and the role of cultural values, and lastly, barriers hindering e-commerce adoption as case study of Kurdistan.

Ditsa et al. highlight that many information technology (IT) projects in developing countries failed because the designs were not sufficiently tailored to those countries' history and industrial traditions. There are problems that cannot be attributed to the technology process, but rather to the cultural differences between designers and the recipients of the technology. Although, cultural factors are important to the success of IT adoption and use, the impact of culture on the adoption and use of IT does not feature prominently in Information Systems (IS) literature. Ditsa *et al.* examine culture's impact on the adoption and use of IT in the United Arab Emirates (UAE) and then the value of each of the eight cultural indices related to IT issues were compared along eight cultural dimensions with values obtained from Australia and West Africa. The study confirms that IT is not culturally neutral and culture may also inhibit true team spirit for system development and use. Most IT products and projects suit cultures with low power distance, low uncertainty avoidance, and long-term time orientation. The researcher suggest ways of bridging the digital divide between the UAE and developed countries and greater understanding of the various dimensions of culture as applied to IT and the people, who use it. This will lead to a more globally acceptable IT products and better choices for IT.

There is substantial research in the area of Diffusion of Innovation Theory (DOI) and its application to Information Systems (IS) research within organisations. The use of ICT by agrarian business enterprises represents an innovative change, especially for Small and Medium Sized Agribusiness Enterprises operating in developing countries. Researchers have different views in the area of agribusinesses diffusion of innovation. The main question used to be asked about whether agribusinesses can appropriately exploit ICT for operational and productivity gains. Aleke *et al.* examine the process of diffusion of innovation ICT among sample of representative agribusiness enterprises in Southeast Nigeria. However, in recognition of the conceptual limitations of DOI, researchers have called for the incorporation of aspects of Social Network Theory (SNT) into DOI frameworks. Researchers conclude that there is a need to re-conceptualise the innovation diffusion process to incorporate more social interactions which represent the cultural imperatives of the people who are expected to adopt the innovation.

Lack of theoretical grounding on how to choose and use measures of system use in behavioural research and different conceptualisations of this construct has further increase the misuse of this variable and lead to diverse results among IS practitioners. This dilemma was given much concern and researched by Lallmahomed *et al.* in an attempt to build cumulative research tradition. The Information Systems (IS) Acceptance literature of two main theories of Technology Adoption, the Technology Acceptance Model (TAM), and The Unified Theory of Use and Acceptance of Technology (UTAUT) were employed by Lallmahomed, *et al.*, to understand how usage measures are being operationalised and proposed a preliminary classification of those measures that help researchers in their choice of system use measures. A Q-Sort approach was taken to validate the authors' classification scheme and the result indicates high inter-rater agreement. The trend established over the selected papers (101 articles) shows researchers' net preference to measure IS usage with frequency, volume of use, and use/non-use. This study summarises the arguments for a multi-dimensional measure of use and establishes collection of measure such as frequency, volume and use/non-use hold prevalence. The researchers call upon other researchers to further extend the developed classification of usage measures. As well as to identify measures that fills under these three dimensions and their relationship with other variables either in upstream or downstream research.

Given the widely recognized effect of cultural values on adoption of Information and Communication Technology (ICT), Al Omoush *et al.*, in a case study concerning the Jordanian context, attempted to develop and validate a comprehensive model for the determinants of household Internet adoption. The researchers tried to identify the driving internal beliefs of individuals and the effect of cultural values on behavioural intention to adopt the household Internet among Jordanians. Hofstede's multidimensional framework was employed at micro level to assess the effect of cultural values on the behavioural intention of Jordanians. The research findings and the empirical model indicated that the behavioural intention to household Internet adoption is determined directly by five internal beliefs including; perceived needs, perceived risks, perceived ease of use, perceived resources, and perceived image. The researchers found an empirical evidence linking most of Hofstede's cultural dimensions to Jordanians' behavioural Intention to household Internet adoption. With the exception of power distance, the results showed that collectivism (low individualism), masculinity, long-term orientation, and uncertainty avoidance had significant effects on the behavioural intention to household Internet adoption. Here in this study, research outcome demonstrated differences in the driving forces and cultural impact on Internet adoption between households and organizations settings.

Lawrence discusses the relevance of e-commerce as well as issues hindering ecommerce adoption for specific region of developing countries in Kurdistan which is part of Iraq. He argues that the absence of adequate basic infrastructural, socio-economic, socio-cultural, and government ICT strategies have created a significant barrier in the adoption and growth of e-commerce in the Kurdistan region of Iraq. The social and cultural characteristics of most part of Kurdistan and the concepts associated with online transaction pose a much greater challenge and act as a major barrier to adoption and diffusion of ecommerce. Also, the researcher highlights that most Kurdish's cultures and practices in the region do not support e-commerce and the conditions for e-commerce still not mature because of lack of confidence in online transactions and technologies. The researcher concludes that the region of Kurdistan lacks universal Internet resource accessibility, lacks the necessary policies and infrastructure that would enable widespread usage of the Internet, unavailability and unreliability of infrastructure, the absence of government policy frameworks. The region lacks of banking facilities, and amenities (such as credit cards). The level of education, the availability of IT skills, and the level of ICT penetration of personal computers and telephone within the society are barriers to the adoption of ecommerce. Also, the researcher concludes that ignorance on the part of possible users about the enormously beneficial potential of e-commerce. The researcher advice for more research to understand the adoption and diffusion of e-commerce in Kurdistan, socio-cultural issues like transactional trust and social effect of shopping that must be considered in the adoption and diffusion of e-commerce.

Theme three, Trends in Digital Divide – reserved to discuss research issues pertaining to the global trends in digital governance, public information service for the disadvantaged in China's towns, and then an empirical study of Indian SMEs software quality initiatives in the IT Sector.

Governments have begun adopting Information Technology (IT) in order to improve their service delivery along with increasing transparency and accountability. In today's era of globalization and networked governance, it is important to thoroughly understand how various regions of the world perform in terms of e-governance. Research by Manoharan et al., focused on the assessment of current practices and trends in municipal e-governance based on a seven-year longitudinal assessment of their official websites worldwide. Specifically, the survey analyzed security, usability, contents, type of online services currently being offered, citizen response, and participation through websites established by city governments worldwide. There were significant changes in the top ranking cities when compared to previous studies. Based on the 2009 evaluation of 87 cities, Seoul, Prague, Hong Kong, New York, and Singapore represent the highest performing cities in digital governance. Moreover, there continues to be a divide in terms of digital governance throughout the world; however, this divide, which increased in 2005, decreased in 2009. Citizen participation is not considered as important with the average score in the category decreasing from 2007 to 2009. As technological capabilities continue to improve, government-to-citizen (G2C) communication does not seem to be moving at the same pace. In fact, it is going in the opposite direction. This finding is surprising especially with the increased use of social media and network applications that have the potential of enhancing communication between government and its constituents. The researchers open a room for future researchers to explore any specific factors associated with organizational changes and political influences which may greatly impact e-governance in municipalities worldwide.

Zhang conducts comparative study in a town chosen to represent the developed region in eastern and a town from the undeveloped region in western of China. The researcher attempts to find the differences and similarities in the process of public information service provided, and discuss the causes of differences and similarities by carrying out comparative study on the situation of providing public information service for the disadvantaged between two representative towns of west and east China. The researcher employs the quantitative approach in which the methods of questionnaire and group discussion conducted in the eastern developed region and the western undeveloped region of China, respectively. The study finds that the public in the town from eastern region are superior to those in the western region in terms of information literacy, public information service expenditure, and satisfaction rate of public information service. Similarities exist in terms of differences in accessing public information service between towns and villages, among social groups, and the causes resulting in imbalance of public information service and features of the information-poor's group distribution. The author discusses the differences in development policies between city and village, as well as differences in financial investment of public information service, education, and individual's income level between towns of the different regions. The researcher reaches at a conclusion that there is a big digital divide gap among the two region and the citizens in the developed areas are superior to the ones in the undeveloped areas in accessing and using public information service in China. The researcher invites researchers interested in this issue to conduct field research in many styles of cities and villages to employ more meticulous and extensive comparative study.

There are several well-established models for software quality assurance, such as the Capability Maturity model Integrated (CMMI), the Software Process Improvement and Capability Determination, and the ISO 9000 norms from the International Standardization Organization, TickIT, and Six Sigma. Goyal and Garg argued that there is a lack of empirical studies which reported the application of Six Sigma in software developing, especially in the small and medium-sized enterprises (SMEs). The researchers present some reasons for that such as complex issues associated with Six Sigma, as well as cost and time constraints. In order to understand the conventional quality management practices in software SMEs, Goyal and Garg research discuss an empirical study of Indian SMEs in the IT sector. Researchers examine the current status of quality management practices in the software quality of initiatives SMEs. A survey-based approach was used to understand the conventional quality management practices in software development. A sample of 230 respondents obtained and the entire respondents come from 23 SMEs of software developing in National Capital Region (NCR) of India. The respondents involved all three managerial levels and statistical results reflect the non-realization of quality management practices in software development. Six Sigma model suggests Define, Measure, Analyze, Improve, and Control (DMAIC) as the basic steps in software assurance. The model is applicable across different industries and has been adopted in software industry and shown encouraging results. Researchers conclude that the investigated SMEs in this study were aware of the importance of quality management practices for the success of any software but the same organizations they did not implemented them as basic requirements. The reason may be attributed to scarcity of resources and project deadlines. Also, majority of the SMEs organizations resist having a quality department. The researchers open a room for scholars to conduct universal research to understand the effect of Six Sigma adoption in the performance of SMEs.

Theme four, Database and Algorithms Applications, presents research to address issues such as the use of OCL to model constraints in data warehouses, semantic search engine, segmentation of Arabic characters, and a study on information hiding using ant colony optimization algorithm.

In the era of ICT, there is an increase in data produced from different sources which create a needed to integrate, group them in information, and store them. Data warehouses are a specific type of database that serves to integrate and analyze data from various sources. In these lines, a valuable study that designed for researchers in the fields of business intelligence and decision support systems, who wish to learn about the major possibilities that OCL offer in the context of data warehouse and to find citations to learn about this formalism in greater detail was conducted by a group of French research team. Pinet *et al.*, study the use of Object Constraint Language OCL to model constraints in data warehouses. They propose an OCL tutorial and show that OCL can be easily used to model constraints in UML-based multi-dimensional models. According to Pinet, *et al.*, OCL could be also considered with the Model Driven Architecture (MDA). When it comes down to it, no real MDA approach including OCL has been implemented for data warehouse. The study provides overviews the recent OO techniques, describing the facts and different analysis dimensions of the data. Researchers provide a survey of the techniques for object-oriented design of multi-dimensional models. Researchers show that they can help system designers to build a data warehouse model and how to use a complementary language called OCL to represent the different types of data warehouse constraints. The researchers call for more new research and works that will allow using this approach in the future.

Creating a database structure considered one component of the system and connecting it with the search engine to facilitate the gathering of components will lead to a complete framework for service oriented architecture. The information retrieval dilemma is that there are huge numbers of classes developed and to reuse these classes it is necessary to reorganize and restructure the retrieval operations to simplify access to these components. A research concerning this issue conducted by Shehab and Zolait tries to address two problems of retrieval from data warehouse, which are how to create a semantic/ intelligent search engine in order to retrieve the software components stored in the database, and then how to store these software components in the database to facilitate the access operations using the search engine to find the required software component. In using the Enterprise Application Integration (EAI), which links the applications within a single organization, this process suffered from a lack of structure by using a point – to – point approach to link the processes. Creating architecture to reuse and integrate the classes will accelerate the development operation and reduce the cost. The study conducted by Shehab and Zolait attempted to propose a Semantic Search Engine, which retrieves software components precisely and uses techniques to store these components in a database, such as ontology technology. The authors use an exploratory study where the proposed method is mapped between object-oriented concepts and Web ontology language. A qualitative survey and interview techniques were used to collect data. Hence, the search engine uses semantic query language to retrieve these components semantically. The findings after implementing this research are a set of guidelines, a model, and a prototype to describe the semantic search engine system. The guidelines are helpful to software developers and companies trying to reduce the cost, time, and risks of software development.

The Arabic language is one of the most structured and served languages, and many other languages adopted the Arabic alphabet with some changes. In a study concerning segmentation of Arabic characters, Zeki *et al.*, argued that despite the fact that Arabic alphabets are used in many languages, Arabic Character Recognition (ACR) has not received enough interests from researchers. In order to fill this gap, researchers provide a comprehensive review of the methods to segment Arabic characters. The proposed segmentation methods are categorized into nine different methods based on techniques used. The researchers discussed the advantages and drawbacks of each method of the nine methods and conclude that most researchers did not report the segmentation accuracy in their research. Instead, they reported the overall recognition rate which did not reflect the influence of each sub-stage on the final recognition rate. Also, the researchers concluded that there is a need for iterative and hybrid segmentation methods that combine between two or more methods. Extra care should be taken when segmenting characters to small segments to avoid over segmentation. The researchers suggested that the field of Arabic Character Recognition (ACR) needs a standard set of test documents in both image and character formats, together with the ground truth and a set of performance evaluation tools, which would enable comparing the performance of different algorithms. As each method has its strengths, a hybrid segmentation approach is a promising method. The chapter concludes that there is still no perfect segmentation method for ACR, therefore this study invites researchers to much opportunity for research in this area.

Awad, in her research "Information Hiding Using Ant Colony Optimization Algorithm" attempted to find an effective and efficient information hiding method that can be used for protecting secret information. She argued that embedding it in a cover media such as images is of high quality and is a complex process. Although, there are many algorithms, researcher studied two ant-based algorithms and find that ant colony optimization algorithm can find the solution efficiently and effectively by finding the optimal set of pixel bits in a few number of iterations comparing to the genetic and genetic simulated annealing algorithms.

Ali Hussein Saleh Zolait
University of Bahrain, Kingdom of Bahrain

Section 1
Mobile Application and Network

Chapter 1
Deployment and Success Factors for the Mobile Internet:
A Case Study Approach

Krassie Petrova
Auckland University of Technology, New Zealand

Raymond Yiwen Huang
Auckland University of Technology, New Zealand

ABSTRACT

The mobile Internet is a fast-growing technology that provides access to the traditional stationary (fixed-line) Internet from devices connected to mobile communication networks. It is predicted that the convergence between mobile networks and the fixed-line Internet will be a core feature in the next generation network architecture, achieving fast 'anywhere' Internet access and global mobility management. Applying a case study approach, this paper reviews the New Zealand mobile Internet market mix, competition, and mobile service provision. The key mobile Internet deployment requirements are determined and analyzed in order to identify a set of mobile Internet critical success factors and to investigate the impact of the shift from fixed-line to mobile and wireless Internet data communication infrastructure.

INTRODUCTION

Current Internet based services are supported by the existing fixed-line telecommunication infrastructure which provides a platform for deploying them. The corresponding business model is build around the assumption that end users while paying for the connection and for data traffic to a telecommunications network to an Internet Service provider (ISP), will have unlimited and free access to the Internet itself. However in the case of supporting users who may want to access Internet–based services through their mobile device (connected to a commercial mobile data network) there may be a need for a new business model to emerge; it will need to include the roles

DOI: 10.4018/978-1-4666-2791-8.ch001

and responsibilities of mobile network operators (MNOs), mobile virtual network operators (MV-NOs) and other mobile network service providers (MNSPs) as collaborators to industry players such as ISPs (Drejer & Skaue, 2007). It is also expected that in the future mobile Internet and fixed-line Internet services will be running on a converged network platform (Blackman, 2006; Schwefel, 2002; Xavier & Ypsilanti, 2007). A number of directions may be followed including the development of Internet-based applications specifically requiring mobile access to the Internet and/or the development of 'anywhere and anytime' mobile Internet services available to both stationary and mobile Internet users (Petrova & Huang, 2007).

With academic research in the area of mobile Internet (MI) focusing mostly on technical issues and user requirements, the requirements and the impact of MI deployment models and the resulting business models have received relatively little attention. This work addresses the gap identified applying a cases study approach. It examines the market directions and their possible impact using a one-country case and analyzes qualitatively data gathered in a series of interviews with key participants in MI market.

The main objectives of the study presented in this paper can be formulated as follows: 1) To identify the critical success factors (CSFs) of MI deployment, and 2) To critically examine the role of MI in extending the functionality of the Internet and facilitating network and technology convergence. Applying a cases study approach, the study looks into the mobile market value chain of service provision and the network and technology convergence process in New Zealand. After determining the key MI deployment requirements, these are analyzed further in order to identify a set of MI critical success factors and to investigate the impact of the shift from fixed-line to mobile and wireless Internet data communication infrastructure.

The rest of the paper is organized as follows: The next section provides a literature and context background and is followed by a methodology section which describes the study approach and presents the main findings. Finally the case data is summarized and used to propose a set of critical success factors for MI deployment and to examine the evolving role of MI. The paper concludes with directions for further research and a brief summary.

BACKGROUND

For the purposes of this research MI is defined as the part of the current Internet that can be accessed from a mobile device connected to a mobile data network (Ghosh, Wolter, Andrews, & Chen, 2005; Roberts & Kempf, 2006). Another term often used when discussing Internet access via mobile and wireless networks is 'anywhere Internet' implying universal Internet coverage, and also the ability to access the Internet regardless of the availability of a stationary computer (e.g. out of the office or the home). Even though universal coverage of fixed-line Internet (extending the communication media to each household or individual user) has not been achieved yet (Webb, 1998) with mobile data networks supporting individual user access to the Internet anywhere within their coverage, 'mobility' has emerged as second dimension of the anywhere Internet. Finally a third dimension related to 'responsiveness' identified in (Cho & Sung, 2007): the network supporting user ability to reply immediately to email and instant messages. The working definition of MI formulated above implies that MI provides a connection to the Internet to users already connected to a mobile data network meeting user demand for mobility and responsiveness, and to a large extent – for coverage, with a focus on the individual user.

To support MI access, mobile devices need to have an appropriate level of computing power such as an intuitive operating systems, processors that can perform complex computations, user friendly interface, extensibility (connecting to external devices), capability to run applications ported from computer platforms, and also a lasting battery (Burkhardt, Henn, Hepper, Rindtorfe, & Schaek, 2002). As mobile phones acquire the functionality needed to carry out formerly performed on computers, and laptop computers acquire mobility features such as the ability to connect to a mobile data network, these devices are gradually converging into a single portable and mobile device able to work with the modern digital mobile networks (Kim, Lee, & Koh, 2005; Vriendt, Laine, Lerouge, & Xu, 2002). This process affects the Internet as a service and application platform which will need meet the communication requirements of mobile data networks. Network interoperability architectures such as XML and WAP aim to bridge the gap between mobile networks and other network topologies, leading eventually to the merging of the mobile and the fixe-line Internet (Bannister, Mather, & Coope, 2003).

The convergence of devices and networks has triggered the convergence of services, with services originally designed for computers now available on mobile devices through MI (Burkhardt et al., 2002). It is expected that in the future MI fixed-line Internet services will be running on a converged network platform and that through MI it would be possible to introduce new services specifically targeting mobile users, e.g. paid content (Kaspar, Seidenfaden, Ortelbach, & Hagnehoff, 2006).

LITERATURE REVIEW

Most MI research is aligned with the trends discussed above and focuses on three main areas: 1) MI protocols and technologies; 2) MI deployment and business models, and 3) MI services adoption and acceptance. Adapting a mobile commerce research classification proposed by Okazaki (2004), the main MI research areas and themes are presented in Table 1 and briefly reviewed below.

PROTOCOLS AND TECHNOLOGIES

Research in mobile network protocols and data technologies drives development. It is aimed at: 1) Iimproving performance, coverage and robustness, and establishing standards for cellular networks (e.g. 3G/4G technologies and standards,) and wireless broadband access such as WiFi (IEEE 802.11), WiMax (IEEE 802.16) (Agrawal & Famolari, 2006; Ghosh et al., 2005; Santhi & Kumaran, 2006; Saugstrup & Henten, 2006; Varshney & Jain, 2007); 2) Developing mobile IP to provide quality of service (QoS), mobility management across large geographical locations and across heterogeneous radio systems, establishing standards for mobile TCP/IP (Bianchi et al., 2003; Dutta et al., 2004 ; Garcia, Rousseau, Berger, Toumi, & Duda, 2003; Leu & Chang, 2003; Paila, 2003; Roberts & Kempf, 2006; Stojcevska

Table 1. Mobile Internet research areas

Area	Description	Themes
Adoption and acceptance	User attitude, acceptance and use of MI services.	• Identifying application and service specific factors influencing intention to use • Applying to MI adoption critical success factors identified in studies on Internet adoption
Deployment and business models	Issues arising from implementing MI protocols and technologies	• Critical success factors • Value chain models • Profit sharing models • Business models
Protocols and technologies	Performance, applicability and interoperability of protocols and technologies enabling MI	• Performance issues; quality of service • Mobility support; global interoperability

& Gusev, 2002; Zhu, Li, & Duan, 2005), and 3) Facilitating network, technology and service convergence processes (Guardini, D'Urso, & Fasano, 2005; Joseph, Lucky, & Mohan, 2006; Lu, 2000; Nikolaou & Zervos, 2006; Shin et al., 2006).

DEPLOYMENT AND BUSINESS MODELS

Although the best-known successful mobile Internet implementation (DoCoMo's iMode in Japan) has attracted significant interest (Baldi & Thaung, 2002; Barnes & Huff, 2003; Jonason & Eliasson, 2001; Okazaki, 2005), research in the areas of MI deployment and business models remains 'scarce' (Okazaki, 2004). However a number of studies are concerned with the impact of MI on business strategies and business models in the telecommunication sector itself (Ballon, 2004; Dodourova; 2003; Kallio, Tinnila, & Tseng, 2006; Palmberg & Bohlin, 2006), and with the general requirements for MI service deployment (Cerf, 2003; Diot, Levine, Lyles, Kassen, & Ballensiefen, 2000).

Soininen (2005) proposed a comprehensive value network model for the mobile Internet industry segments and concluded that a cooperative model of deployment, across the value chains of the different segments, would have a better chance of success as it would bring value to customers and allow for fair profit sharing among actors in the value chain. Viewed from a global perspective MI interconnects networks in countries with different legislative and other regulatory environments (Shin et al., 2006). Drejer and Skaue (2007) suggested that "digital convergence required new forms of collaboration across traditional geographical, organizational and technological boundaries".

With respect to MI deployment and business models in particular geopolitical entities, examples include in Iceland, China and Japan as the focus of case study investigations by Srivastava (2003),

Xiangdong (2001) and Takaaki, Kenji, and Yasso (2003) respectively with the latter also specifying the requirements that may lead to successful MI deployment; a WLAN-based MI deployment case study (Korea) is presented in Choi et al. (2003).

ADOPTION AND ACCEPTANCE

Research in the area focuses on services using MI as a delivery platform (Naruse, 2003) and the interaction with end-users (Chakraborty, Joshi, Finin, & Yesha, 2005). Usability and user acceptance of service discovery protocols and service management arise as important issues (Fodil, 2005; Ryan & Gonsalves, 2005).

MI services may potentially add significant value to users through personalization and customization and fitting in with the mobile user daily lifestyle (Arbanowski et al., 2004; Ho & Kwok, 2003). Of specific interest to research are services utilizing the advanced MI capabilities such as location based mobile services (Jensen, Kligys, Pedersen, & Timko, 2002; Saab & Kabbout, 2002; Soliman, Agashe, Fernandez, & Vayanos, 2000). By adding a mobile dimension to existing applications some MI based services are already gaining popularity – for example mobile television (Knoche & McCarthy, 2005). Frameworks used to investigate stationary Internet services adoption were adapted and applied in a number of studies (Hung, Ku, & Chang, 2003; Lu, Liu, & Yao, 2003; Nysveen, Pedersen, & Thorbjornsen, 2005; Wang, Ku, & Doong, 2007).

Studies of the impact of mobility- or platform-specific features on the intent to adopt a service have identified a variance in the adoption rate for services within specific business domains such as auctioning, banking, auctioning, advertising (Forster & Tang, 2006; Kleijnen, Wetzels, & Ruyter, 2004; Petty, 2003) and within specific usage contexts - such as having a 'free hand' available to operate the mobile device while moving (Kim, Kim, Lee, Chae, & Choi, 2002).

To summarize the assumptions and predictions in the literature reviewed, MI is seen as an infrastructure enabling the connect between Internet services and mobile device users. When MI becomes readily available to and adopted by mobile device users, service providers may be expected to build various types of solutions based on MI, with the purpose of serving the customers' demands. User behavior is a critical success factor in MI deployment (Yamakami, 2003); the QoS characteristics of MI (an essential feature of the MI deployment model) influence users' acceptance and adoption (Bouch, Bhatti, & Kuchinsky, 2000). MI performance features influence strongly MI adoption – for example connection speed, bandwidth. MI is also a key driver of network and technology innovation including the converged network of the future, therefore a successful MI deployment model should be innovative, fit in with the market, and meet customer QoS requirements.

Mobile Internet Deployment: The Case of New Zealand

In New Zealand, information and communication technologies (ICTs) play a major role in national development: In 2005, New Zealand's ICT industry was ranked 17th in a list of 53 countries surveyed (Computerworld, 2006). Broadband demand including mobile access has grown significantly presenting both opportunities and challenges to all industry participants - operators and service providers (Petrova & Parry, 2008).

A range of technologies is used (some examples are provided in Table 2). There are several cellular MNOs. The highest market share belongs to Vodafone who use GSM and are upgrading their network to 3GPP UMTS Radio Access Network (a European W-CDMA standard). Telecom Mobile is the second largest service provider; Telecom has deployed a CDMA network and uses the EVDO Rev 1 technology to provide mobile broadband services in the major cities. Currently Telecom

is launching a XT network which is based on W-CDMA. A relatively new entrant - 2Degrees have built some infrastructure in the main cities and roam onto Vodafone's network elsewhere in the country. MNSPs include Telstra Clear who do not own their own mobile infrastructure but have an MVNO agreement with Telecom, Compass who have an MVNO agreement with Vodafone.

The MI segment allows new entrants and new cooperative models. Similar to markets elsewhere (Soininen, 2005) other entrants at MNSP and MVNO level may be expected in the future. As all industry players are looking to expand, the industry is extremely competitive. MI deployment acts as a link between services providers and end users and therefore MI impact on the market is related to user demand for MI based services, and also on demand for services supported by converged network technologies. Therefore requirements related to mobile market structure, technologies, the regulatory environment, competition, pricing models, and the range of services offered may all be critical to MI deployment.

The New Zealand government recommends investment in a range of infrastructures to encourage competition and to allow the most advantageous use of the spectrum available for mobile / wireless broadband technologies. With its deregulated market and significantly advanced telecommunications sector New Zealand may provide a suitable case background for the inves-

Table 2. MI provision in New Zealand

MI access type	Industry participant type
Cellular Wireless Network	MNOs: Vodafone, Telecom Mobile, 2Degrees; MVNOs (Compass, TelstraClear), MNSPs: Telstra Clear, Woosh Wireless
WiFi - Hotspots	MNO: Telecom Mobile MNSPs: City Link, iPass / T-Mobile, the FON Community
WiMax	ISP: Call Plus / Slingshot MNSPs: NatCom, NZ Wireless

tigation of MI deployment and the convergence processes as industry players compete in offering value to business and individual customers and maximizing the potential of next generation network technologies.

RESESARCH APPROACH AND FINDINGS

The MI deployment requirements and impact were investigated, applying a qualitative and inductive approach and adopting a single case explanatory study strategy with New Zealand as the unit of investigation (Cavana, Delahaye, & Sekaran, 2001; Myers, 2009). The data collected were analyzed in order to address the first research objective and explain the critical role of MI deployment requirements and the role of MI as a factor in network convergence (objective 2). The study involved conducting interviews and collecting data on the management perspectives of MI service providers including the market, service providers, and end users. This section describes the data gathering process and presents the findings.

Data Gathering

General business information collected from journals, magazines and business websites identified the organizations which deploy MI services in the telecommunication and Internet markets. Subsequently five major network operators and Internet service providers in New Zealand offering mobile / wireless broadband were chosen as organizations to include in the study.

Data were gathered through a series of indepth semi structured interviews with high ranking executives from these organizations (two network operators and three ISPs - Table 3). The interviews were conducted in March 2007 and lasted approximately an hour each.

The ten interview questions (listed in Table 4) were designed to elicit insightful information from

experts in the area and were targeted (i. e. focused directly on the case study topic) (Yin, 2003) however additional information exchange also took place where respondents needed an explanation or wanted a point clarified. After the first round of interviews some follow up data gathering was conducted with three of the interviewees in order to refine some of the initial responses and obtain more information.

Data Analysis

The analysis of the data followed a three step approach of reduction, structuring and constructing an explanatory model (Collis & Hussey, 2003; Myers, 2009). First each interview record was reviewed and coded after it was transcribed, and singular statements were extracted from the responses to questions 2, 3, 5, 6, 7, 8, 9, and 10. A total of 217 statements were accumulated. Second the relevant statements (178) were analyzed in order to identify the emerging main points made by interviewees in relation to the possible requirements, drivers and impediments of MI deployment. Finally the case was summarized using categories identified from the literature and used to address the study research objectives.

Table 3. Interviewees

	Business Type	**Position**	**Comment**
P1	Internet Service Provider	General Manager Information Systems	One further email contact
P2	Network Operator	Client Activation Network Inventory Specialist	One further face-to-face contact
P3	Internet Service Provider	Wireless Solution Manager	One further email contact
P4	Network Operator	Marketing Manager – Wireless Office	No further contact
P5	Internet Service Provider	Technical Specialist	No further contact

Table 4. Interview questions

#	Question
Q1	Could you please explain the role of your company in the telecommunication and Internet market? [*an opening question, not used in the data analysis*]
Q2	Could you please briefly describe the telecommunication and Internet market mix in New Zealand?
Q3	Do you think that Internet competition has moved from fixed-lined Internet to mobile / wireless Internet
Q4	Does your company offer or plan to offer MI services? If the answer is yes, could you please briefly describe the service and its deployment? [*commercially sensitive information, not used in the data analysis*]
Q5	In your opinion, what specific requirements does a MI deployment model need to meet in order to fit into the New Zealand market and meet customer expectation?
Q6	Several technologies (for example, mobile networks, WiFi and WiMax) are available to deploy mobile Internet services presently; could you please give me your personal opinion about the strengths and weaknesses of each deployment model?
Q7	Do you think MI will contribute to the convergence of networks, technologies and services? How?
Q8	Could you please describe how MI will deliver end user services based on converged networks and technologies? (For example, cross network, multiple-technologies).
Q9	What would be the most appropriate MI deployment model or solution for the New Zealand market?
Q10	Do you have additional information about this topic? 'Mobile Internet deployment in New Zealand'

This sub section presents the findings grouped in three categories derived form the main areas of MI research identified in the literature review: 1) MI technology choice and future options; 2) MI market structure and impact, and 3) MI customer acceptance and deployment requirements. Some illustrative direct quotes are embedded in the text.

MI Technology Choice and Future Options

Participants agreed that the CDMA technology had several advantages – for example having a potential to be upgraded, and achieving good coverage with a relatively small number of base-stations. However the cost of upgrading would be significant; it was also noted that few applications and services were developed for CDMA handsets. Therefore, despite its present leading position CDMA may not be the best mobile and wireless solution for the future. W-CDMA has similar problems however as a next generation technology it may be more suitable.

Considering WiFi participants agreed that it had better interpretability than other technologies

and most devices were already WiFi enabled. Furthermore, WiFi is relatively fast and secure. However WiFi has limited coverage and may be suitable to provide Internet access in smaller areas such as cafés, offices, and bus stations but is not the most cost- or technology effective solution in deploying MI citywide or nationwide; however a mesh network with global membership (e.g. FON) may provide global WiFi access to MI.

Despite that the next generation technology WiMax was considered as an expensive investment at present it was seen as a potential cost-effective way of deploying mobile services in the future "… it is not cost-effective to deploy WiMax service in New Zealand unless the cost goes down"(P2). Compared to WiFi, WiMax offers a wider coverage (an approx. 60 km range), better performance and may have lower deployment cost due to the small number of base stations required. With WiFi being also affordable to customers, it may "… become the main platform in the Internet space" (P4) competing with CDMA in the medium term and with W-CDMA in the future.

Participants were confident that MI and wireless connectivity were the two most prominent future trends. With respect to the network convergence process three of the participants (P1, P2, P3) also believed that not only MI was contributing to the convergence process but that it was the key opening the door to a converged global network. Most likely the network of the near future will be IP-based: "Within 10 years, the current networks (for example, WiMax, CDMA, and UMTS) will be converged to a single access platform (P4). All devices will be able to connect to the single access platform via a single access protocol suite. With no significant market differentiation between network and service providers, the competition will move towards the area of customer service.

The mobile devices of the future will be multiple-technologies enabled, for example a cell phone will be able to select 'the best' network in a particular area. People will be using a mobile phone to access MI similarly to the way they use computers to connect to the Internet at present: "…as long as the mobile data service are available, Internet services will be also available" (P3). New context-aware commercial services built around user mobility and anywhere-anytime access is bound to emerge however not until the converged network matures. Customer preferences and demands demand preferences will be among the main drives of the process.

MI Market Structure and Impact

Participants agreed that there were two main business models in the ISP market: first the major network operators who own extensive infrastructure and the most of the subscriber market share are the leaders of the front line competition.

A specific feature of the market is the long lasting monopoly of Telecom New Zealand in the DSL market [which was finally broken in 2007 when deregulation legislation was passed]. The smaller ISPs primarily resell services and solutions and may not be actively involved in the front line competition. However,

deregulation and local loop unbundling have offered new opportunities to the network providers who can now offer directly (or resell) alternative solutions to customers. Generally the MI market is considered as strongly competitive with the potential to facilitate the transition from traditional to future business models with accompanying changes in the service range, and in the roles and responsibilities of the MI value chain players.

It was believed that the existing underground infrastructure will not be devalued as mobile and wireless performance is still not able to meet the technical requirements and customer expectations associated with Internet access. It was noted that the cost of investment in building mobile and wireless infrastructure may present a barrier to MI deployment nation-wide as the case country's population is relatively small (around 4 million people, with 75% living in major cities and towns).

According to participants MI market competition may have a strong impact on the future business strategies of the telecommunication companies. For example, P2 commented that "When mobile and wireless technologies are well developed, everything will be wireless and mobile.…and it will happen quickly. Mobile competition really impacts business strategies in the telecommunication sector" while P4 predicted that "WiMax will become the major technology in the Internet space and compete with CDMA and W-CDMA in the near future". Smaller operators may also consider moving towards their own wireless and mobile infrastructure to compete with the large network providers as WiMax may offer "… opportunities to the smaller players in the market and …will become a major competitor with the CDMA technologies"(P5). ISPs will also have to move forward as "Bundling of fixed and mobile is critical for ISPs in the future. In particular, the FMC (Fixed and Mobile Convergence) strategies highlight the opportunity and importance of providing both fixed-line and mobile services" (P5).

MI Customer Acceptance

According to participants user mobility support is the core benefit of MI and may lead to wide future acceptance. 'Mobility' is seen as the compelling reason which may push people to use mobile or wireless broadband: "Fixed-line broadband is always faster, but mobile and wireless broadband is a lot more friendly and usable when people do lots of 'moving' works (i.e. working while also travelling, with fixed-line Internet not available) (P2). The majority of the participants believed that wireless and mobile broadband is definitely the way of future ("… it is exactly the same step from the landline at home to mobile phones" – P1). However the transition may happen later rather than sooner: Lack of performance stability, high consumer cost, price, lack of strong competition among the major market players, and lack of services specifically targeting mobile users were suggested as possible reasons for the slow MI uptake.

It was noted that New Zealand market was price driven and that customers were unlikely to use unaffordable services even if these were good. Cost considerations are often the most important initial decision making factor: "No matter what you offer, you have to have good price" (P1); "Price is the most important feature that an Internet user primarily looks at and compares" (P5). However the quality of the coverage, the bandwidth, the service performance and customer service are likely to be taken into account when customers have a option to use MI access priced similarly to fixed-line Interne. ("While different service providers offer the same level of performance in service, customers would like to compare the price; in contrast, if the service providers are offering service at the same price level, customers will look at the quality of service and performance" – P5). The quality of both Internet service and customer service need to be addressed when developing or deploying an MI technology.

As already mentioned an important issue about MI deployment is meeting the performance benchmarks set by DSL and fiber networks: ("… the most important requirement of mobile Internet is bandwidth…to compete with DSL and fiber, it is required to have larger pipes and higher speed" – P1) therefore a significant investment may be required in order to build a nationwide mobile network. Despite the investment cost MI should be offered at an acceptable price. This emerges as a key requirement in the price driven consumer market as consumers will be likely to take advantage of user mobility support only with an affordable and a relatively fast MI (e.g. using services such as VPN). However both promotion of MI services and educating customers need to be part of the MI deployment strategy - in order to identify to customers which services are supported by MI, and to open the market to specific customer groups such as late Internet adopters ("A mobile Internet deployment model should educate people. For instance, some older people started using computers in the last 10 years and using the Internet in the last 5 years, they felt like using these new technologies because the deployment model had educated them on how to use the technology"- P1). All participants agreed that MI deployment can build on the experiences with the fixed line Internet deployment process, and that in addition to the primary requirement of connection speed, the reliability of the coverage and reliability of the service also needed to be considered. Finally there will be a need to develop flexible pricing and service bundling able to accommodate change in customer demand.

FURTHER ANALYSIS AND DISCUSSION

Deregulation legislation has created an open and competitive market for the fixed-line communication industry segment and has lowered the barriers for new entrants (especially small to medium enterprises). However, as local loop unbundling focuses mainly on fixed-line communication it impacts mostly on fixed-line telephone services and DSL Internet access. With the consumer cost of DSL broadband decreasing as a result of the competition, users tend to prefer fixed-line DSL to other Internet access solutions. Because the mobile market has not been affected strongly by the local loop unbundling, it still maintains an oligopoly status with only a few major mobile service providers competing. Furthermore, because MI and DSL are providing the same set of services [Internet access] with only a modest level of differentiation [mobility versus stability and performance], connection or /access pricing remains the main factor influencing the choice of Internet access. In the price driven market DSL is likely to retain a dominant position at least until MI starts offering a service comparable to DSL.

There is no evidence about the existence of a strong direct competition between MI and fixed line [DSL] Internet. Network service providers offer these two types of Internet access to two distinctly different groups of users: MI is aimed mostly at low Internet-use subscribers while fixed DSL is for high-use subscribers. However considering the fast growth in complex Internet applications and services it is likely that the low Internet-use customer segment will shrink: with the "cost per megabyte" pricing model used by MI service providers consumers have to pay more for MI compared to DSL –based Internet access.

Finally the fixed-line communication infrastructure in New Zealand is almost homogeneous, meaning that subscribers can obtain the same type of services with the same type of physical medium and the same type of device. At the same time the variety in mobile infrastructure makes the MI services offered by service providers incompatible with each other. The current network deployments include CDMA, W-CDMA, WiFi and WiMax, which all have different hardware requirements, and deployment and operational

costs which may contribute to raising the consumer cost even further.

As mentioned earlier the Internet access market in New Zealand is still price driven. Users are generally looking for a suitable service provider considering in their decision making the cost of ownership, running costs, service stability, performance and expected service lifetime, and also customer service, how simple or easy to learn / use is the service. These factors are relevant to both fixed line [DSL] Internet connection and MI, because users are not normally concerned with the type of communication method and medium as long as their expectations are met. Here MI lags behind DSL in terms of cost, stability and performance.

On the other hand, users are likely to appreciate the value added by the defining characteristic of MI i.e. user mobility support. However its importance and potential benefits may be offset by cost considerations. Second mobile devices still cannot utilize the full power of the Internet due to screen size and processing power limitations. Finally users may prefer to use WiFi hotspots for offsite Internet access (rather than MI) as this would be a simple and cheap method with relatively good performance. Therefore, to make MI more competitive in the market, the service should focus on the general requirements and not only on mobility support. However mobile devices and computers are converging and as the cost of high-end mobile devices goes down, this may impact positively customers decisions.

These findings allow addressing the first research objective of the study: To explain the critical role of MI deployment requirements. The critical success factors presented in Table 5 are grouped as market-, service provider-, and user related. Although based on the case data, these CSFs have parallels in the literature and may be applicable globally to deregulated market environments characterized by high-volume broadband usage.

The case data and the findings from the literature review also allow addressing the second

Table 5. Critical success factors for MI deployment

Perspective	Critical Success Factors
Market	1. MI meeting DSL performance as a benchmark 2. A competitive mobile service provider industry segment
Service Providers	3. Commitment to long-term investment in infrastructure and maintenance 4. Competitive pricing model for MI access and usage
Users	5. Cost of use (purchase and ongoing) and cost stability 6. Expected quality of MI access (performance - bandwidth, latency; reliability; ease of use) 7. Expected quality of the MI service (user mobility support, mobile user-specific service characteristics)

objective of the study and gaining an insight into the role of MI in extending the functionality of the Internet and facilitating network and technology convergence. The role of MI may be expected to become more significant with the move to add wireless connectivity to most computing devices including network access. At present MI plays only a supplementary role to fixed-line Internet access methods such as DSL, or fiber optic network. MI provides user mobility support as an "add-on" to the current Internet services and this can be expected to continue for medium- to long term. The evolving technology will eventually make it possible for MI to meet DSL performance levels and become an alternative Internet access method providing the same set of services as fixed-line communication methods, plus user mobility support. MI capability will continue to extend and eventually MI will outperform fixed-line networks in the long term future; market demand will start favoring MI over fixed-line communication and MI will start driving network and platform convergence. The transition to MI becoming the main Internet access method will be facilitated by the ongoing convergence of mobile devices with stationary computer devices and by the technological progress in the area of mobile data technologies.

The proposed set of CSFs may be used to create a model for empirical investigation which may also be broadened to identify issues arising from the global aspects of MI provision and more specifically - global mobile interconnectivity. A better understanding the impact of MI on the telecommunication sector and other industry segments will facilitate research investigating how MI could enable the provision of services such as mobile-government, mobile-health, mobile-banking which may also lead to a better public recognition of MI.

User demand may start also to play a driving role in network and service convergence; customers will expect to be able to access through MI services available on fixed-line Internet, and more. Future Internet services may have multiple interfaces to allow users to chose; a more abstract generic model will be needed to support such service convergence (Yang, Kim, Nam, & Moon, 2004). Services will become more flexible and platform independent and will seamlessly integrate across organizational boundaries (Pedersen & Ling, 2003). In the user acceptance and adoption area it will be needed to investigate and indentify user needs for applications and services which support user mobility, and can be contextualized and localized.

Device and network convergence have so far played a driving role in the development and deployment of MI. As the significance of mobile voice communication decreases compared to data related features (Kumar, 2004), service development on next generation network platforms will place an emphasis on digital data connectivity. Besides voice communication and SMS, MI will inherit all other communication approaches such as instant messaging and email and will serve as a single mobile communication point (Kim, Lee, Lee, & Choi, 2004). Research in the technology area will need to focus on issues related to the transition to a single access network and on compatibility issues.

CONCLUSION

The study aimed to identify the critical success factors of MI deployment, and to critically examine the role of MI in extending the functionality of the Internet and facilitating network and technology convergence. The research work presented here attempts to meet these objectives by adopting a case study approach; MI deployment and market impact were subject to an in depth investigation in the case country (New Zealand). The requirements of a successful MI deployment model were identified through a review of the New Zealand market mix and competition (in which both major and minor players are involved) and based on data gathered from structured interviews with senior executives in five organizations representing the MI market segment in the case. Issues arising from network convergence, mobile device advances, and service demand as related to the transition from fixed-line Internet to MI were identified and the MI deployment requirements were formulated. Although the study outcomes are based on a one country study the authors believe that these may be applicable to other similar contexts. The proposed set of CSFs may be used to create a model for empirical investigation including global mobile interconnectivity.

REFERENCES

Agrawal, P., & Famolari, D. (2006). Mobile computing in the next generation wireless networks. In *Proceedings of the 3rd International Workshop on Discrete Algorithms and Methods for Mobile Computing and Communications* (pp. 32-39). New York, NY: ACM Press.

Arbanowski, S., Ballon, P., David, K., Droegehorn, O., Eertink, H., & Kellerer, W. (2004). I-centric communications: Personalization, ambient awareness, and adaptability for future mobile services. *IEEE Communications Magazine, 42*(9), 63–69. doi:10.1109/MCOM.2004.1336722

Baldi, S., & Thaung, P. P. (2002). The entertaining way to m-commerce: Japan's approach to the mobile Internet – a model for Europe. *Electronic Markets, 12*(1), 6–13. doi:10.1080/101967802753433218

Ballon, P. (2004). Scenarios and business models for 4G in Europe. *Info Emerald, 6*(6), 363–382. doi:10.1108/14636690410568641

Bannister, J., Mather, P., & Coope, S. (2003). *Convergence technologies for 3G networks*. New York, NY: John Wiley & Sons. doi:10.1002/0470860936

Barnes, S. J., & Huff, S. J. (2003). Rising sSun: iMode and the wireless Internet. *Communications of the ACM, 46*(11), 78–84. doi:10.1145/948383.948384

Bianchi, G., Melazzi, N., Chan, P., Holzbock, M., Hu, Y. F., & Jahn, A. (2003). Design and validation of QoS aware mobile Internet access procedures for heterogeneous networks. *Mobile Networks and Applications, 8*(1), 11–25. doi:10.1023/A:1021163526385

Blackman, C. (2006). The public interest and the global, future telecommunications landscape. *Info, 9*(2-3), 6–16.

Bouch, A., Bhatti, N., & Kuchinsky, A. (2000). Quality is in the eye of the beholder: Meeting users' requirements for Internet quality of service. In *Proceedings of the SIGCHI Conference on Human Factors in Computing Systems* (pp. 297-304). New York, NY: ACM Press.

Burkhardt, J., Henn, H., Hepper, S., Rindtorff, K., & Schaeck, T. (2002). *Pervasive computing: Technology and architecture of mobile Internet applications*. Reading, MA: Addison-Wesley.

Cavana, R. Y., Delahaye, B. L., & Sekaran, U. (2001). *Applied business research: Quantitative and qualitative methods*. New York, NY: John Wiley & Sons.

Cerf, V. G. (2003). Requirements for the Internet. In *Proceedings of the 11th IEEE International Requirements Engineering Conference* (pp. 1-2). Washington, DC: IEEE Computer Society.

Chakraborty, D., Joshi, A., Finin, T., & Yesha, Y. (2005). Service composition for mobile environments. *Mobile Networks and Applications, 10*(4), 435–451. doi:10.1007/s11036-005-1556-y

Cho, S., & Sung, M. (2007). Integrative analysis on service quality and user satisfaction of wired and mobile Internet. *International Journal of Management Science, 13*, 79–97.

Choi, Y., Peak, J., Choi, S., Lee, G. W., & Lee, J. H., & Jung, H. (2003). Enhancement of a WLAN-based Internet service in Korea. In *Proceedings of the First ACM International Workshop on Wireless Mobile Applications and Services on WLAN Hotspots* (pp. 36-45). New York, NY: ACM Press.

Collis, J., & Hussey, R. (2003). *Business research: A practical guide*. New York, NY: Macmillan.

Computerworld. (2006). *New Zealand in top half of the information society index*. Retrieved from http://computerworld.co.nz/news.nsf/news/53F6C5B8FD111E42CC25716C001B8BFA?Opendocument&HighLight=2,mobile,broadband,new,zealand

Diot, C., & Levine, B, N., Lyles, B., Kassem, H., & Balensiefen, D. (2000). Deployment issues for the IP multicast service and architecture. *IEEE Network, 14*(1), 78–88. doi:10.1109/65.819174

Dodourova, M. (2003). Industry dynamics and strategic positioning in the wireless telecommunications industry: The case of Vodafone Group. *Management Decision, 41*(9), 859–870. doi:10.1108/00251740310495919

Drejer, A., & Skaue, K. (2007). Keys to the future: New business models in mobile organization. *International Journal of Mobile Learning and Organisation, 4*(1), 375–389. doi:10.1504/IJMLO.2007.016177

Dutta, A., Zhang, T., Madhani, S., Taniuchi, K., Fujimoto, K., & Katsube, Y. (2004). Secure universal mobility for wireless Internet. *Mobile Computing and Communications Review, 9*(3), 45–57. doi:10.1145/1094549.1094557

Fodil, L. (2005). New generation network and services management for converged networks. In *Proceedings of the 1st International Workshop on Broadband Convergence Networks* (pp.1-3). Washington, DC: IEEE Computer Society.

Forster, P. W., & Tang, Y. (2006). Mobile auctions: Will they come? Will they pay? In M. Khosrow-Pour (Ed.), *Proceedings of the IRMA International Conference* (pp. 779-783). Hershey, PA: IGI Global.

Garcia, J. A., Rousseau, F., Berger, G., Toumi, L., & Duda, A. (2003). Quality of service and mobility for the wireless internet. *Wireless Networks, 9*(4), 341–352. doi:10.1023/A:1023647311052

Ghosh, A., Wolter, D. R., Andrews, J. G., & Chen, R. (2005). Broadband wireless access with WiMAx/802.16: Current performance benchmarks and future potential. *IEEE Communications Magazine, 2*(1), 129–136. doi:10.1109/MCOM.2005.1391513

Guardini, I., D'Urso, P., & Fasano, P. (2005). The role of Internet technology in future mobile data systems. *IEEE Communications Magazine, 38*(11), 68–72. doi:10.1109/35.883491

Ho, S. Y., & Kwok, S. H. (2003). The attraction of personalized service for users in mobile commerce: An empirical study. *ACM SIGecom Exchange, 3*(4), 10–18. doi:10.1145/844351.844354

Hung, S. Y., Ku, C. Y., & Chang, C., M. (2003). Critical factors of WAP services adoption: An empirical study. *Electronic Commerce Research and Applications, 2*(1), 42–60. doi:10.1016/S1567-4223(03)00008-5

Jensen, C. S., Kligys, A., Pedersen, T. B., & Timko, I. (2002). Multidimensional data modeling for location-Based Services. In *Proceedings of the 10th ACM International Symposium on Advances in Geographic Information Systems* (pp. 55-61). New York, NY: ACM Press.

Jonason, A., & Eliasson, G. (2001). Mobile Internet revenues: an empirical study of the I-mode portal. *Internet Research: Electronic Networking Applications and Policy, 11*(4), 341–348. doi:10.1108/10662240110402795

Joseph, V. C., Lucky, K. K., & Mohan, R. (2006). SIP as an enabler for convergence in future wireless communication networks. In *Proceedings of the IFIP International Conference on Wireless and Optical Communications Networks* (pp. 5-10). Washington, DC: IEEE Computer Society.

Kallio, J., Tinnila, M., & Tseng, A. (2006). An international comparison of operator-driven business models. *Business Process Management, 12*(3), 281–298. doi:10.1108/14637150610667962

Kaspar, C., Seidenfaden, L., Ortelbach, B., & Hagenhoff, S. (2006). Acceptance of the mobile Internet as a distribution channel for paid content. In M. Khosrow-Pour (Ed.), *Proceedings of the IRMA International Conference* (pp. 68-72). Hershey, PA: IGI Global.

Kim, H., Kim, J., Lee, Y., Chae, M., & Choi, Y. (2002). An empirical study of the use contexts and usability problems in mobile Internet. In *Proceedings of the 35th Annual Hawaii International Conference on System Sciences* (pp. 132-142). Washington, DC: IEEE Computer Society.

Kim, J., Lee, I., Lee, Y., & Choi, B. (2004). Exploring e-business implications of the mobile Internet: A cross-national survey in Hong Kong, Japan and Korea. *International Journal of Mobile Communications, 2*(1), 1–21. doi:10.1504/IJMC.2004.004484

Kim, Y., Lee, J.-D., & Koh, D. (2005). Effects of consumer preferences on the convergence of mobile telecommunications devices. *Applied Economics, 37*, 817–826. doi:10.1080/0003684042000337398

Kleijnen, M. H. P., Wetzels, M., & Ruyter, K. (2004). Consumer acceptance of wireless finance. *Journal of Financial Services Marketing, 8*(3), 206–217. doi:10.1057/palgrave.fsm.4770120

Knoche, H., & McCarthy, J. D. (2005). Design requirements for mobile TV. In *Proceedings of the 7th International Conference on Human Computer Interaction with Mobile Devices & Services*, Salzburg, Austria (pp. 69-76). New York, NY: ACM Press.

Kumar, S. (2004). Mobile communications: Global trends in the 21st century. *International Journal of Mobile Communications, 2*(1), 67–86. doi:10.1504/IJMC.2004.004488

Leu, S.-J., & Chang, R.-S. (2003). Integrated service mobile Internet: RSVP over mobile IPv4&6. *Mobile Networks and Applications, 8*(6), 635–642. doi:10.1023/A:1026074309946

Lu, J., Yu, C. S., Liu, C., & Yao, J. E. (2003). Technology acceptance model for wireless Internet. *Electronic Networking and Applications, 13*(3), 206–222. doi:10.1108/10662240310478222

Lu, W. W. (2000). Compact multidimensional broadband wireless: The convergence of wireless mobile and access. *IEEE Communications Magazine, 38*(11), 119–123. doi:10.1109/35.883500

Myers, M. (2009). *Qualitative research in business & management*. Thousand Oaks, CA: Sage.

Naruse, K. (2003). The survey of the mobile Internet, usage and awareness, study for m-commerce. In *Proceedings of the Symposium on Applications and the Internet Workshops* (pp. 127-130). Washington, DC: IEEE Computer Society.

Nikolaou, N., & Zervos, N. (2006). Wireless convergence architecture: A case study using GSM and wireless LAN. *Mobile Networks and Applications, 7*(1), 259–267.

Nysveen, H., Pedersen, P. E., & Thorbjornsen, H. (2005). Intentions to use mobile services: Antecedents and cross-service comparisons. *Journal of the Academy of Marketing Science, 33*(3), 330–346. doi:10.1177/0092070305276149

Okazaki, S. (2004). New perspectives on m-commerce research. *Journal of Electronic Commerce Research, 6*(3), 160–164.

Okazaki, S. (2005). How do Japanese consumers perceive wireless ads? A multivariate analysis. *International Journal of Advertising, 23*(4), 429–454.

Paila, T. (2003). Mobile Internet over IP data broadcast. In *Proceedings of the 10th International Telecommunications Conference,* Espoo, Finland (pp. 19-24). Washington, DC: IEEE Computer Society.

Palmberg, C., & Bohlin, E. (2006). Next generation mobile telecommunications networks: Challenges to the Nordic ICT industries. *Info, 8*(4), 3–9. doi:10.1108/14636690610676504

Pedersen, P. E., & Ling, R. (2003). Modifying adoption research for mobile Internet service adoption: Cross-disciplinary interactions. In *Proceedings of the 36th Annual Hawaii International Conference on System Sciences* (pp. 10-20). Washington, DC: IEEE Computer Society.

Petrova, K., & Huang, R. (2007). Mobile internet deployment in New Zealand. In S. Krishnamurthy & P. Isaias (Eds.), *Proceedings of the International Association for Development of the Information Society International Conference on e-Commerce* (pp. 337-34). Algarve, Portugal: IADIS.

Petrova, K., & Parry, D. (2008). Mobile Computing Applications in New Zealand. In Yoo, Y., Lee, J.-N., & Rowley, C. (Eds.), *Trends in mobile technology and business in the Asia-Pacific Region* (pp. 153–177). Oxford, UK: Chandos Publishing.

Petty, R. D. (2003). Wireless advertising messaging: Legal analysis and public policy issues. *Journal of Public Policy & Marketing, 22*(1), 71–82. doi:10.1509/jppm.22.1.71.17627

Roberts, P., & Kempf, J. (2006). Mobility architecture for the global Internet. In *Proceedings of the First ACM/IEEE International Workshop on Mobility in the Evolving Internet Architecture,* San Francisco, CA (pp. 23-28). New York, NY: ACM Press.

Ryan, C., & Gonsalves, A. (2005). The effect of context and application type on mobile usability: An empirical study. In *Proceedings of the 28th Australasian Computer Science Conference* (Vol. 38, pp. 116-124).

Saab, S. S., & Kabbout, S. M. (2002). Map-based mobile positioning system: A feasibility study. *ACTA Press, 5*(2), 50–59.

Santhi, K. R., & Kumaran, G. S. (2006). Migration to 4G: Mobile IP based solutions. In *Proceedings of the Advanced International Conference on Telecommunications and International Conference on Internet and Web Applications and Services,* Lisbon, Portugal (pp. 76-84). Washington, DC: IEEE Computer Society.

Saugstrup, D., & Henten, A. (2006). 3G Standards: The battle between WCDMA and CDMA2000. *Info, 8*(4), 10–20. doi:10.1108/14636690610676513

Schwefel, H. (2002). Mobile Internet: Research toy or product vision? In *Proceedings of the IEEE International Symposium on Network Computing and Spplications* (pp. 267-268). Washington, DC: IEEE Computer Society.

Shin, D., Kim, J., Ryu, S., Oh, D., Lee, J., & Kang, M. (2006). Scenario decomposition based analysis of next generation mobile services. In *Proceedings of the 8th International Conference on Advanced Communication Technology* (pp. 403-408). Washington, DC: IEEE Computer Society.

Soininen, M. (2005). Segments of the mobile Internet industry – examples from Finland and Japan. In *Proceedings of the International Conference on Mobile Busines*, Sydney, Australia (pp. 56-62). Washington, DC: IEEE Computer Society.

Srivastava, L. (2003). Boosting broadband in Iceland. *Info, 5*(3), 8–26. doi:10.1108/14636690310698431

Stojcevska, B., & Gusev, M. (2002). Mobile Internet concepts and mobile Internet TCP/IP. *IEEE Computer, 12*(7), 97–105.

Takaaki, K., Kenji, F., & Yasuo, O. (2003). The MIAKO.NET public wireless Internet service in Kyoto. In *Proceedings of the 1ˢᵗ ACM International Workshop on Wireless Mobile Applications and Services on WLAN Hotspots* (pp. 56-63). New York, NY: ACM Press.

Varshney, U., & Jain, R. (2007). Issues in emerging 4g wireless networks. *IEEE Computer, 34*(6), 94–96.

Wang, H.-C., Ku, Y.-C., & Doong, H.-S. (2007). Case study in mobile Internet innovation: Does advertising or acquaintances communication decide Taiwan's mobile Internet diffusion? In *Proceedings of the 40ᵗʰ Annual Hawaii International Conference on System Sciences* (p. 230). Washington, DC: IEEE Computer Society.

Xavier, P., & Ypsilanti, D. (2007). Universal service in an IP-enabled NGN environment. *Info, 9*(1), 15–31. doi:10.1108/14636690710725049

Xiangdong, W. (2001). Mobile communications & mobile Internet in China. *IQTE, 7*(5), 134–225.

Yamakami, T. (2003). Toward understanding the mobile Internet user behavior: A methodology for user clustering with aging analysis. In *Proceedings of the Fourth International Conference on Parallel and Distributed Computing, Applications and Technologies* (pp. 85-89). Washington, DC: IEEE Computer Society.

Yang, D.-H., Kim, S., Nam, C., & Moon, J.-S. (2004). Fixed and mobile service convergence and reconfiguration of telecommunications value chains. *IEEE Wireless Communications, 11*, 42–47. doi:10.1109/MWC.2004.1351680

Yin, R. Y. (2003). *Case Study Research: design and methods*. London, UK: Sage.

Zhu, Z., Li, Z., & Duan, Y. (2005). An active network based hierarchical mobile Internet protocol version 6 framework. In *Proceedings of the International Conference on Wireless Communications, Networking and Mobile Computing* (Vol. 2, pp. 1029-1033). Washington, DC: IEEE Computer Society.

This journal was previously published in the International Journal of Technology Diffusion, Volume 2, Issue 1, edited by Ali Hussein Saleh Zolait, pp. 1-15, copyright 2011 by IGI Publishing (an imprint of IGI Global).

Chapter 2
Tackling M–Government Service Complexity:
The Case of Bahrain

Ahmed Sowaileh
Ministry of Justice, Bahrain

Ali AlSoufi
University of Bahrain, Bahrain

ABSRACT

The development of mobile government services in Bahrain is moving slowly, when compared with traditional e-government services. Few informational and transactional services are available on the mobile portal. The complexity of government services prevents their delivery through the limited mobile phone interface. This exploratory research builds a method to tackle service complexity, as well as simplify and streamline the design and development of government services that target mobile devices. Forty government services in Bahrain were analyzed to identify the factors that affect mobile government services. The model was then applied to the sample services, and results were used to develop the target method. The main finding of this research is that the current approach of taking the existing services on the PC portal and implementing them on the mobile portal should be avoided. A better approach is to break down the services into sessions or components and identify opportunities where mobile technologies can be utilized.

1. INTRODUCTION

The rapid advancements in wireless and mobile technologies combined with the wide spread of mobile phones and the utilization of such an opportunity in e-government services have created a new direction, the mobile government (m-government) (Kushchu & Kuscu, 2003).

Kushchu and Kuscu (2003) define M-government as the strategy and its implementation involving the utilization of all kinds of wireless and mobile technology, services, applications

DOI: 10.4018/978-1-4666-2791-8.ch002

and devices for improving benefits to the parties involved in e-government including citizens, businesses and all governmental units.

With the continuous advancements in wireless technologies and the new opportunities to provide government services through those technologies, m-government seems to be inevitable (Kushchu & Kuscu, 2003; Sadeh, 2002).

However, mobile devices have limitations regarding their small size, limited bandwidth, low memory and storage capacities, low resolution screens, and keyboard restrictions These limitations have made it more difficult to implement services that target such devices than to develop traditional services that target traditional desktop computers (Al-Khamayseh, Hujran, Aloudat, &Lawrence, 2006; Germanakos, Samaras, & Christodoulou, 2005; Mallick, 2003).

Given the availability of the Government Data Network (GDN), the eGovernment Project and the high mobile phone penetration, there is a great opportunity to implement m-government in Bahrain and to exploit the benefits that wireless technologies provide (AlAmer, 2006; EGovernment Authority, 2007; TRA, 2008; CIO, 2007).

The eGovernment portal is a "one stop shop Portal" and is the key service delivery channel for individuals, business, government and visitors, which integrates and provides all types of vital services. It was launched on 23rd, May, 2007, and it's managed by the eGovernment Authority (EGA) as part of Bahrain's national strategy to execute the comprehensive e-government programs (EGovernment Authority, 2010). The services on this portal are directed to the traditional desktop computer interface and they are not customized for access through the limited mobile phone interface.

Bahrain's main e-government channel is the web based eGovernment portal. Since this channel is accessed mainly through personal desktop computers, it will be referred to in this study as the PC portal to distinguish it from the other channels, especially the mobile channel. Other channels include the Mobile portal, the National Call Centre portal and the Common Service Centers. By the end of 2010, there were more than 190 services on the PC portal. The Mobile portal is a channel that hosts services that are customized for access through mobile phones. By the end of 2010 it hosted 45 services (EGovernment Authority, 2010), where most of those services are informational. A detailed list on Bahrain government eServices can be found at the eGovernment portal (www. bahrain.bh), including mobile services.

1.1 Problem Statement

As described earlier in this study, the Mobile portal is far behind the PC portal in terms of maturity and number and types of services. This is clearly justified since the PC portal was implemented before the Mobile portal and since mobile phones are limited in terms of size and bandwidth when compared to desktop computers. Complex services that are easily provided through the PC portal may need more analysis and reengineering before they can be delivered as mobile services (Olmstead, Peinel, & Tilsner, 2007).

However, given the high mobile phone penetration in Bahrain and the advancements in wireless and mobile technologies, a method is needed to overcome the complexity of mobile services and to enable the optimal utilization of m-government to enhance the delivery of e-government services.

This research aims to study the services provided by Bahrain's government organizations in order to find an appropriate method to simplify their delivery as mobile services.

This study is guided by the following research questions:

1. What are the main characteristics of Bahrain's government services and what are the attributes that affect the ability to provide them through the mobile interface?
2. What is the appropriate method to design and implement mobile government services in Bahrain?

The aim of the research questions is to clearly understand the nature and anatomy of government services, and to identify the factors that can facilitate or hinder their implementation as mobile services in order to find solutions to implementation barriers and set guidelines to simplify and streamline the design and development of mobile services.

2. CHALLENGES TO MOBILE SERVICE DESIGN AND DEVELOPMENT

As an exploratory step, 40 services in a number of government organizations in Bahrain were analyzed. This will later be described in more details. Most of the services were already delivered on the PC portal and were not yet delivered on the Mobile Portal. The analysis revealed the following attributes as the most important attributes that affect the ability to convert the services to mobile services:

1. **Amount of Data Entry Required:** For traditional web services, users mainly use desktop computers with large keyboards and input devices to navigate through the services and to enter the required information. This makes it possible to implement services that require the entry of large amounts of information. On the other hand, mobile phones are much smaller and have very small keypads that allow users to input only limited amounts of information. This makes it more difficult to implement mobile services that require the entry of large amounts of information.

2. **Amount of Information to Display:** Desktop computers have large screens allowing the implementation of traditional services that require the display of large amounts of information. Mobile phones have small screens, making it very difficult to implement mobile services that require the display of large amounts of information.

3. **File Attachments:** Desktop computers have larger storage and higher bandwidth than mobile phones. Uploading large file attachments is also easier, faster and cheaper with desktop computers than with mobile phones. This makes it difficult to implement mobile services that require uploading large file attachments. In addition, files are normally created in personal computers first. Files like Word and Excel documents and images cannot be easily edited in mobile phones. People don't normally carry such sensitive files with them in mobile phones for security reasons. This may reduce the possibility of the availability of such files when they are needed in mobile services.

2.1 Possible Options and Alternatives

Although it is more difficult to develop mobile services than to develop traditional services, there are some options and alternatives that can be used to overcome the challenges:

1. **Service-Oriented Architecture (SOA):** The analysis of the government services revealed that many of the required information can be retrieved from other organizations. For example, in many organizations, a service may require the user to enter personal information which is already available in the Central Informatics Organization (CIO). If a service can connect to CIO and retrieve the required information directly from its service, the user would be able to get the required information by just writing the personal ID number and let the integration between the two services perform the rest. This approach can also be used for file attachments. If the required document can be retrieved from another organization's service, uploading the file attachment would not be required. By just writing the official number of the document, it would be possible to retrieve

it automatically from the organization were it is located. SOA makes it possible to link different organizations' services (Antovski & Gusev, 2006).

2. **Multimodal Input and Output:** The small sizes of the mobile phone's keypads and screens hinder the input and output of large amounts of information. Using multimodal input like voice record, speech recognition, barcode reader, camera and touch screen, and multimodal output like audio and video can improve data input and output (Olmstead et al., 2007; Juell-Skielse, 2008).

3. **Summarized Output:** For services that display large amounts of information, if the data can be filtered to display only important data, then it would be easier to deliver such services through the small mobile interface. For example the Case Inquiry service provided by the Ministry of Justice allows lawyers and case parties to inquire about the details of court cases. The large information can easily be filtered to display the most important information such as the next hearing date and time and the summery of the judgment.

4. **Smartphones:** Smartphones are mobile phones that offer more advanced computing ability than normal basic phones (Mallick, 2003). When it is not possible to implement a mobile service that is usable on basic phones, then building the service that work only for smartphones can be one of the implementation options. The problem with this approach is that users who own only basic phones cannot benefit from the service. However, implementing services for smartphones can be a good investment for the future when smartphones get cheaper and the number of people owning them increases.

5. **Mobile Broadband:** Mobile broadband services are Internet access services offered by mobile phone operators and allow higher speed Internet access for mobile phone users (Batelco, 2010). Such broadband services make it easier for users to upload and download larger amount of information than normal services can. However, since broadband services are more expensive than normal services, the number of users who can benefit from them is limited. But like smartphones, taking broadband into consideration may be a good investment for the future.

6. **Short Messaging Service (SMS):** SMS is a text communication service component of mobile communication systems that allow the exchange of short text messages between mobile phone devices (Mallick, 2003). It is considered as a strategic tool for mobile solution development (Bremer & Prado, 2006; Medina, 2009). SMS is already in wide used as a helper to the services on the PC portal to send quick alerts to users.

7. **Multimedia Messaging Service (MMS):** MMS is a communication service component of mobile communication systems that allow the exchange of messages that include multimedia content (Mallick, 2003). It can be used in mobile government services. For example, in Ireland people can use MMS to send photos of criminal suspects to law enforcement agencies (Ghyasi & Kuschu, 2004).

2.2 Session-Based Mobile Service Implementation Model (SB-MSI)

The analysis of 40 government services revealed that attempting to provide large government services as full mobile services is a very difficult task and it should be avoided. Alternatively, this study recommends a method to exploit the benefits of mobile technologies by identifying the parts of services were mobile technologies can be utilized. This section describes a model proposed by this study to simplify the task of identifying places were mobile technologies can be utilized.

The Session-Based Mobile Service Implementation (SB-MSI) model, is based on the conclusion reached in this research that, in order to convert a service into a mobile service, it is better to break the full end-to-end process that constitutes the service, into "sessions" and study the implementation of each session individually rather than studying the implementation of the service as a single entity (Figure 1). For example, the "formation of regulation cases" service provided by the Ministry of Justice is completed in four sessions. Each session can occur in a different date or time as follows:

Session 1 – Case Filing: The customer enters the information required (plaintiffs, defendants, case requests, required documents, etc)

Session 2 – Request Status Inquiry: The customer can log-in anytime to view the status of the request

Session 3 – Case Modification: If any of the required information is missing, the legal researcher notifies the customer through email to log-in to the service and make the required modifications.

Session 4 – Request Finalization and Payment of Fees: If everything is satisfied, the legal researcher finalizes the case and informs the customer. The customer logs in and either accepts or rejects the case. If accepted, the customer makes the payment of the case fees.

This and many other services cannot be implemented as fully mobile services, if they are taken as a whole. However, if they are broken in sessions, and each session is taken individually then the mobile enablement would be enhanced very much as this research proves.

Breaking an end-to-end process of a service into sessions would enable implementing many services into partial mobile services. In the above example, the first and third sessions are difficult to deliver as mobile sessions since they require the user to enter large amounts of information and to upload many file attachments. All other sessions can easily be delivered as mobile sessions. However, it may be possible to reengineer the first and third sessions and provide them as mobile sessions.

The key to studying a session are the attributes that affect its provision through mobile phones and the implementation options related to the attributes.

As mentioned earlier, the most important attributes that were identified during the analysis of Bahrain's government services are the "amount of data entry required", "the requirement of file attachments" and the "amount of information to display".

The implementation options would be:

1. **Service Oriented Architecture (SOA):** Users don't have to upload file attachments or enter large amounts of data if the information can be retrieved through SOA.

2. **File Upload through Mobile Interface (M-UPLOAD):** A session that requires uploading file attachments can be implemented as a mobile session if it is feasible to upload the required documents through mobile phones. For example, if the expected size of the file is very small or if it is acceptable to provide the session for mobile broadband users only.

3. **Information Summery (SUMMERY):** In a session with a large amount of information to display, if it is possible to filter the information and display only small and important information, then the session can be provided as a mobile session.

4. **Multimodal Input and Output (MM-INPUT and MM-OUTPUT):** Mobile phone keypads and screens are small hindering the input and output of large amounts of information. Using multimodal input like voice record, speech recognition, barcode reader, camera and touch screen, and multimodal output like audio and video may improve the ability to enter and display information.

Figure 1. Session-based mobile implementation model (SB-MSI)

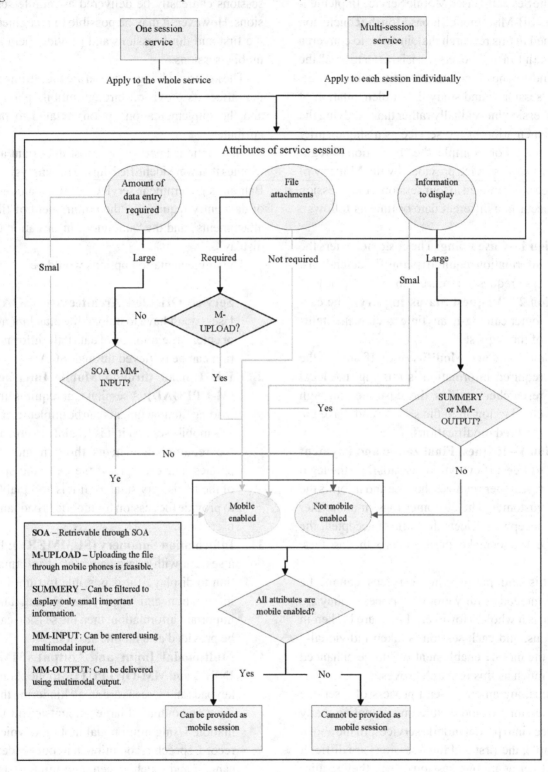

2.3 Service Breakdown Diagram (SBD)

To simplify the analysis of the services, and to easily identify the sessions that are mobile-enabled and the session that are not, and to easily identify the barriers that prevent the implementing mobile sessions, this research introduced the Service Breakdown Diagram (SBD), to describe the results of applying SB-MSI model to the services.

Figure 2 shows an example of applying SBD to the "accreditation validation of certificate" service. Sessions that can be implemented as mobile sessions (mobile-enabled) are in green, and sessions that cannot be implemented as

mobile sessions (non-mobile-enabled) are red. The attributes of each session are listed in boxes above and below the session. There is no difference between the upper and lower boxes. An attribute can be written in any one of them. The attributes are grouped so that they correspond to the flow in SB-MSI model. A flow that leads to a mobile-enabled attribute is green. A flow that leads to a non-mobile-enabled attribute is red. A session is mobile-enabled if all of its attributes are green. If at least one of the attributes is red, then the session is NOT mobile-enabled.

Figure 2. Service breakdown diagram

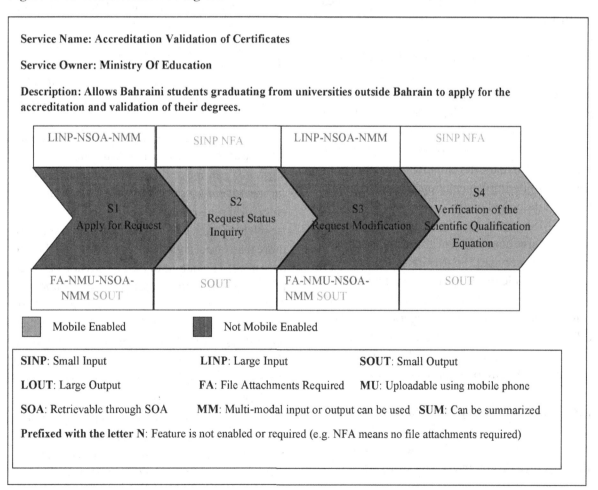

2.4 Research Methodology

Figure 3 shows a general view of the plan that was used to study and analyze the government services in order to streamline their conversion into mobile services.

The first step was to collect a sample of government services. This was provided by the eGovernment Authority (EGA). Out of the 157 implemented and planned service, the documentation of 40 services were selected, which contained important information, such as screen specifications, data input and output, data structures and user manuals. The selection also made sure the diversity of services, in terms of types, size, complexity and also belonging to from different ministries (Table 1).

The thorough analysis of the selected services identified important service attributes and factors that can enable or hinder their provision as mobile services. The results revealed simple services that can be easily implemented as mobile services, and complex services that are difficult to provide through the limited mobile interface. An attempt was made to find a way to reengineer complex services so they can be provided as mobile services. This led to the development of the Session-Based Mobile Implementation (SB-MSI) model that was described earlier.

SB-MSI model was developed to guide and streamline the conversion of government services into mobile services. SB-MSI was then applied to all the sample services, and the resulted SBD's identified the sessions that the services are comprised of and revealed the categories that group different sessions based on their attributes and the difficulty in which they can be designed and implemented as mobile sessions.

2.4.1 Service Analysis Findings

The following sections describe the important findings revealed by the service analysis.

Session Categories

The analysis of the 40 services identified seven categories of sessions that differ in their attributes and the difficulty in which they can be designed and implemented as mobile sessions (Table 2).

The following categories were identified:

1. Informational
2. Search
3. Payment
4. Application for Service
   a. Quick Application or Complaint
   b. Heavy Interactive
5. Application Status Inquiry
6. Application Modification
7. Alerts

Informational sessions have low or no interactivity. They just provide users with the information they request. Implementing informational sessions is straightforward since they require a few or no service re-engineering to be implemented as mobile sessions. Most of them are one-session services.

Search sessions are used to retrieve information based on criteria entered by the user. Two attributes can make them more interactive than *Informational* session. First, they allow users to enter different criteria to filter and summarize search results. Second, users may have to browse more than one search result until they find the one they need. The output of *Search* sessions is often larger than the output produced by *Informational* sessions, especially when users enter general criteria that produce large lists of results. But they are still easy to implement as mobile session since the degree of interactivity they require is low and the search results produced by them are often easy to filter and summarize.

Payment sessions allow users to make payments of their bills or fees of online services they use. They can be stand-alone services, or they can be part of other services that require payment

Figure 3. Service analysis plan

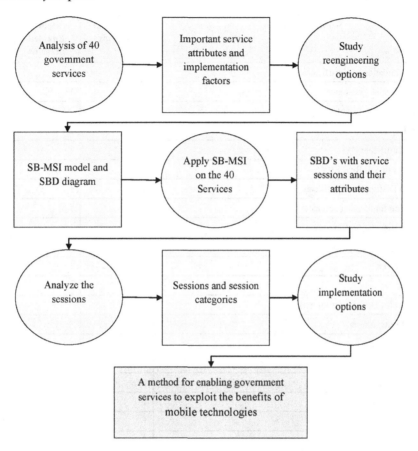

of fees. *Payment* sessions normally require low degree of interactivity and produce small output, which make them easy to implement as mobile sessions. One approach that is already used in some other countries but not yet used in Bahrain to simplify the payment process and to increase the level of security is to charge the customer through the phone bill. For example, in Finland, SMS tickets can be used for Helsinki's public transport system. A user who wishes to order a ticket can easily achieve that by sending a text message and he or she can be billed through his or her regular mobile phone bill. The ticket itself is also delivered to the commuter by SMS (Alampay, 2008). Given the success of this approach in other countries, there is an opportunity to use it in Bahrain.

Application for Service sessions are interactive sessions that allow users to apply for different services online. Information entered by users are stored and manipulated in the backend systems of the service's owner organization. Sessions in this category differ in the size of information they require. There are *Quick Application or Complaint* sessions that are performed in a single step and require the entry of small amounts of information, and there are *Heavy Interactive* sessions that are performed in multiple steps and require users to enter large amounts of information and to upload copies of the required documents. Sessions in this category are the most difficult to implement as mobile sessions. *Quick Application or Complaint* sessions are normally easy to implement as mobile sessions except for those that require uploading file attachments.

Table 1. Services analysis results

	Service Name	Number of Sessions	Mobile Enabled Sessions	Non-Mobile Enabled Sessions
1	Accreditation Validation of Certificates	4	2	2
2	Application for Social Assistance	2	1	1
3	Registration of Clearing Agents	4	2	2
4	Formation of Regulation Cases	4	2	2
5	Issue of Birth Certificate	2	1	1
6	Official Contract to Sell Real Estate	4	2	2
7	Issue of Wealth Distribution Certificate	3	1	2
8	Letter submission for housing services	2	1	1
9	Application for Eid Al-Elm Ceremony	2	1	1
10	Registration of Quran Competitors	2	1	1
11	Apply for Visit eNOC	2	1	1
12	Apply for eVisa	2	1	1
13	Formal Contract for Division of Property	4	2	2
14	Registration of Lawyers	4	3	1
15	Application for Clearing License Exam	1	1	0
16	Request for Copies of Student Certificates and Transcripts	1	1	0
17	Driving License Renewal	1	1	0
18	Bahrain Flights Arrival	1	1	0
19	Court Case Inquiry	1	1	0
20	eWeather	1	1	0
21	Graduates Exam Results	1	1	0
22	Legality of Foreign Workers	1	1	0
23	State Budget	1	1	0
24	View Custom Regulations and Search for Clearing Agents	1	1	0
25	Bahrain Laws	1	1	0
26	Payment of Criminal Order Fines	1	1	0
27	Payment of Traffic Contraventions	1	1	0
28	Payment of Electricity Bill	1	1	0
29	Job Mapping for Job Seekers	1	1	0
30	Tracking of Postal Packages	1	1	0
31	General Complaints of High Consumption of Electricity and Water	2	2	0
32	Electricity and Water Outage/Loss Complaints	2	2	0
33	Pre-Employment Health Check-up	2	2	0
34	Consumer Protection Complaints	2	2	0
35	Health Worker Immunization service	3	3	0
36	Government Directory	2	2	0
37	BCSR Library Reservation	3	3	0
38	Insurance for Job Seekers	4	0	4

continued on following page

Table 1. Continued

	Service Name	Number of Sessions	Mobile Enabled Sessions	Non-Mobile Enabled Sessions
39	Registration in Summer Clubs	2	0	2
40	Flight Project	1	0	1
	Total	**80**	**53**	**27**

Application Status Inquiry sessions enable users to inquire about the status of requests they had applied in earlier sessions, normally *Application for Service* sessions. They may be followed immediately by *Application Modification* sessions or *Payment* sessions. Like the *Informational* category, sessions in this category can easily be implemented as mobile sessions. All the *Application for Service* sessions are followed by *Application Status Inquiry* sessions.

Application Modification sessions allow users to fix incorrect information or add missing information they entered in *Application for Service* sessions. This category often has less interactivity than the *Application for Service* category since the user is normally asked to provide only the missing information and don't have to reenter everything from the beginning. All the *Application for Service* sessions have related *Application Modification* sessions.

Alerts are mainly used to notify users of changes in the status of their application requests. Once the status of a request changes, the service automatically sends a SMS message to alert the user to log-in to the service to view the status of the request and to take the required action (e.g. make the payment). For example, in the Formation of Regulation Cases service, once the legal researcher has finished the preview of the request, the service automatically sends a SMS alerts to notify the applicant if the request is complete or if some of the required information is missing. The user then has to log-in to pay the required fees if the request is accepted, or to provide the missing information if it is not complete. In this research, alerts are considered as helpers to sessions and they are not represented in SBD diagrams. Fortunately, they are already in wide use in most of the services on the PC portal.

Table 2. Services Analysis by Category

Service Category	Number of Sessions	Mobile Sessions	Non-mobile Sessions
Informational	11	11	0
Search	5	5	0
Payment	9	9	0
Quick Application or Complaint	11	11	0
Heavy Interactive	20	0	20
Application Status Inquiry	16	16	0
Application Modification	8	1	7
Total	**80**	**53**	**27**

2.4.2 Results of Applying Session-Based Model on the Services

As shown in Table 1, sixteen of the services that were analyzed were one-session services that can easily be implemented as fully mobile sessions. These services range from simple informational to quick applications and complaints.

"Flight project" service was the only one-session service that could not be implemented as mobile service.

Seven of the services were multi-session services that were fully mobile. All of their sessions can be implemented as mobile sessions. They are mainly quick application services with status inquiry feature.

Only two of the services were multi-sessions that did not have mobile-enabled sessions.

Fourteen of the services were multi-sessions that were partially mobile. Not all of their sessions can be implemented as mobile sessions.

Although 21 sessions out of 40 in the services in Table 1 (raw 1-14) can be implemented as mobile sessions, the existence of one or two non-mobile sessions prevents these services from being fully mobile. If session-based analysis was not used, the sixteen services would not have been implemented as mobile services, meaning that 21 mobile-enabled sessions would have been wasted. Thus, for partially mobile services, this research recommends the use of session-based analysis as an alternative to the current approach of attempting to implement full mobile services.

The service analysis revealed that there are session categories that are easy to implement as mobile sessions. The SBD's revealed a large amount of sessions that are green indicating they are mobile-enabled, even in services that are not fully mobile. Therefore, for such sessions, this research recommends giving the Mobile portal a higher priority than the PC portal. The use of traditional desktop computers for such sessions can be considered as overkill when compared to the use of mobile phones especially that the gap

between the mobile personal computer and the mobile phone has reduced (Ogunleye, 2009). Desktop computers are confined to limited space. Users have to wait until they are in specific places to use the services through the personal computer. In contrast, mobile phones are designed to be carried around by the user and are always "switched on" which let them save users a lot of time and resources and help them perform better and quicker decisions (Carcillo, Marcellin, & Tringale, 2006; Senturk, 2008; Gang, 2007). Personal computers may still be required and a better option for many tasks (like image manipulation and word processing). But for mobile-enabled sessions, mobile phones may be more convenient and they should be given the priority wherever possible.

2.5 Discussion

The first research questions was

What are the main characteristics of Bahrain's government services and what are the attributes that affect the ability to provide them through mobile interface?

To answer this question, 40 government services were taken as case studies and analyzed. The analysis identified the important characteristics of government services and the important attributes that affect their provision as mobile services. To summarize, the following characteristics of government services were identified:

1. A service consists of one or more sessions. Each session can happen in different time or day.
2. There are seven types of sessions; Informational, Search, Payment, Application for Service, Application Status Inquiry, Application Modification and Alerts
3. Sessions differ in complexity according to their attributes and their categories.

4. A service may require information and documents issued by another service.

The service analysis identified the "amount of data entry required", "the requirement of file attachments" and the "amount of information to display" as the most important attributes that affect the ability to provide the government services through the mobile interface.

The second research question was

What is the appropriate method to design and implement mobile government services in Bahrain?

Based on the results of the service analysis and the implementation issues and alternatives explained in the previous sections, this research recommends the following method to design and implement mobile government services in Bahrain:

1. Avoid the current approach of taking the existing services on PC portal and attempting to implement them on the Mobile portal: The current approach works only for fully mobile services. A better approach is to break down the services into sessions or components and identify opportunities in places where mobile technologies can be utilized.

2. Identify mobile opportunities: Study the services and attempt to find opportunities to utilize mobile technologies even in service that cannot be implemented as fully mobile services. The approach proposed by this research is to break down the services into sessions and apply SB-MSI model to each session individually. Other models and approaches can be used if they are applicable.

3. Implement mobile opportunities: Opportunities can be implemented once they are identified. This study recommends giving the priority to the Mobile portal for mobile-enabled sessions. It also recommends the establishment of Service Oriented Architecture (SOA) between government organizations to

reduce the size of the services and increase the number of mobile-enabled sessions. For the same purpose it recommends considering the implementation alternatives explained earlier including multimodal input and output, summarized output, targeting smartphones, targeting mobile broadband, using SMS, using MMS, and using other options and alternatives if applicable. Figure 4 outlines the recommended method.

Figure 4. The method for designing and developing m-government services

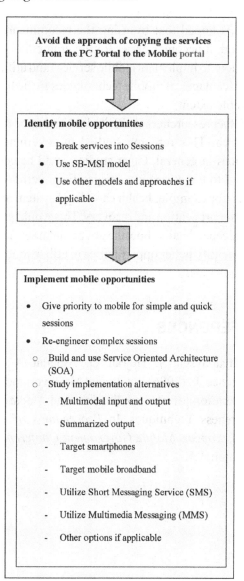

3. CONCLUSION

Implementing mobile services is not as easy and straightforward as implementing traditional services that target personal desktop computers. The services that can be easily implemented on the PC portal may be very difficult to implement on the Mobile portal. This study has developed a method to tackle the complexity of developing mobile government services. The method takes into consideration the limitations of mobile devices and the complexity of government services. It can be used to analyze and reengineer the services to simplify and streamline their delivery through the limited mobile interface.

It is hoped that by using the recommended method, it becomes easier for government organizations to implement mobile services and utilize the advantages of mobile technologies to the best possible extent.

Other researchers are invited to build upon this research. This research studied m-government services in general. Other studies could be conducted to target services in specific government areas, for example, health care, legal system and disaster prevention and recovery. This would provide deeper details about the government services and identify better opportunities to utilize mobile technologies.

REFERENCES

Al-Khamayseh, S., Hujran, O., Aloudat, A., & Lawrence, E. (2006). Intelligent M-Government: Application of Personalization and Location Awareness Techniques. In *Proceedings of the 2nd European Mobile Government Conference*, Brighton, UK.

AlAmer, M. (2006). *Bahrain E-government Project*. Paper presented at the Govtec Exhibition and Conference.

Alampay, E. (2008). *Reporting Police Wrongdoing via SMS in the Philippines*. Retrieved December 12, 2008, from http://www.egov4dev.org/mgovernment/resources/case/text2920.shtml

Antovski, L., & Gusev, M. (2006). M-GOV: The Evolution Method. In *Proceedings of the 2nd European Mobile Government Conference*, Brighton, UK.

Batelco. (2010). *O-net Mobile Broadband*. Retrieved August 21, 2010, from http://www.batelco.com.bh/portal/mobile/mobile_broadband.asp

Bremer, A. A., & Prado, L. A. L. (2006). Municipal m-Services using SMS. In *Proceedings of the 2nd European Mobile Government Conference*, Brighton, UK.

Carcillo, F., Marcellin, L., & Tringale, A. (2006). BlueTo: a location-based service for m-government solutions. In *Proceedings of the 2nd European Conference on Mobile Government*, Brighton, UK.

CIO. (2007). *The Statistics Collection 2007*. Retrieved February 21, 2009, from http://www.cio.gov.bh/StatPublication/02StatisticalAbstract/File/ABS2007/2007-CH02Population.pdf

EGovernment Authority. (2007). *eGovernment Strategy*. Retrieved February 12, 2009, from http://www.e.gov.bh/pubportal/wps/wcm/connect/852031004b96f290b9dfbf13d8048f0c/eGov_Strategy-English.pdf?MOD=AJPERES

EGovernment Authority. (2010). *The eGovernment Portal*. Retrieved December 1, 2010, from http://www.e.gov.bh/

Gang, S. (2007). Transcending e-Government: a Case of Mobile government in Beijing. In *Proceedings of the 1st European Conference on Mobile Government,* Brighton, UK.

Germanakos, P., Samaras, G., & Christodoulou, E. (2005). Multi-channel Delivery of Services: The Road from eGovernment to mGovernment: Further Technological Challenges and Implications. In *Proceedings of the 1st European Conference on Mobile Government,* Brighton, UK.

Ghyasi, A., & Kushchu, I. (2004, June). m-Government Adoption: Cases of Developing Countries. In *Proceedings of the European Conference on e-Government,* Dublin, Ireland.

Juell-Skielse, G. (2008). Pictures and Positioning in Mobile Complaint and Problem Management. In *Proceedings of the mLife 2008 Conference & Exhibitions,* Antalya, Turkey.

Kushchu, I., & Kuscu, H. (2003). From e-government to m-government: Facing the Inevitable. In *Proceedings of the European Conference on e-Government,* Dublin, Ireland.

Mallick, M. (2003). *Mobile and Wireless Design Essentials*. Hoboken, NJ: Wiley.

Medina, I. G. (2009). SMS: a Powerful Tool for Mobile Marketing Communication. In *Proceedings of the mLife 2009 Conference & Exhibitions,* Barcelona, Spain.

Ogunleye, O. S. (2009). Context and Capability: The Future of Small Screen Research and Development in Africa. In *Proceedings of the mLife 2009 Conference & Exhibitions,* Barcelona, Spain.

Olmstead, P. M., Peinel, G., Tilsner, D., Abramowicz, W., Bassara, A., & Filipowska, A. (2007). Usability Driven Open Platform for Mobile Government (USE-ME.GOV). In Kushchu, I. (Ed.), *Mobile Government: An Emerging Direction in E-Government* (pp. 30–59). Hershey, PA: IGI Publishing. doi:10.4018/9781591408840.ch003

Sadeh, N. (2002). *M-commerce: technologies, services, and business models*. New York, NY: John Wiley & Sons.

Senturk, M. (2008). Transformation of Public Places and Social Life by the Impact of Mobile Phones. In *Proceedings of the mLife 2008 Conference & Exhibitions,* Antalya, Turkey.

TRA. (2008). *Telecommunications services indicators in the Kingdom of Bahrain*. Retrieved February 21, 2009, from http://www.tra.org.bh/en/pdf/TelecommunicationsServicesIndicatorsReport301008.pdf

This journal was previously published in the International Journal of Technology Diffusion, Volume 2, Issue 1, edited by Ali Hussein Saleh Zolait, pp. 50-64, copyright 2011 by IGI Publishing (an imprint of IGI Global).

Chapter 3
An Intelligent Approach to Assess Tacit Knowledge Fitness in Networked Enterprises

Khalid A. Al-Mutawah
University of Bahrain, Bahrain

ABSTRACT

Many organizations attempt to form strategic networked enterprises, yet such strategies are difficult to implement because they are as likely to fail as to succeed. This failure is due to intangible differences and mismatches between partners in tacit knowledge (TK). Despite the various proposed partnership assessment models/tools in the literature, an immediate need exists for a new approach to measure the mismatch in TK across different organizations. This is due to the complex, vague, and uncertain nature of TK attributes. Hence, an instrument for measuring vagueness (imprecise), such as fuzzy linguistic variables, is needed. In this study, the author applies a neuro-fuzzy approach to assess TK fitness in networked enterprises. The results show how differences in TK between partners affect the networked enterprise's performance. Furthermore, the assessment approach reveals the most significant values to adopt and the irrelevant values that must be abandoned to smooth the partnership formation. The proposed model can prevent unexpected conflicts between partners if managed properly.

1. INTRODUCTION

Despite becoming a major source of challenges as well as opportunities for many industries, the globalization of the marketplace results Networked-Enterprises (NE) facing more and more global issues that are critical for their success, in particular tacit values conflicts and clashes. For example, the attempts to integrate European organizations to the global Japanese automotive organizations have resulted on pitfall conflicts because of the differences on tacit values between the western

DOI: 10.4018/978-1-4666-2791-8.ch003

management and the Japanese management practices (Smagalla, 2004).

Therefore, assessing tacit values compatibility between partners is a critical and strategic success factor for NE. Nevertheless, current partnerships assessment attributes have included either quantitative indices, such as annual productivity and financial stability (Lorange et al., 1992), or qualitative indices, such as trademark reputation and communication openness (Talluri et al., 1999; Ip et al., 2003). Yet, sometimes evaluation attributes also include subjective indices, such shareholder's favourability, and objective indices, such as corporate image and geographic coverage (Donaldson, 1994; Choi & Hartley 1996; Dacin et al., 1997; Mikhailov, 2002). However, these partnerships assessment models have mainly based on explicit knowledge (EK). EK is disseminated across organizations using physical objects like documents, standard operating procedures, and manual of best practices. This type of knowledge depends on facts, figures, data, and formulas to deliver its contents (Harrison, 1987). EK can be information that are used during the negotiation, coordination and communication processes which are associated with selling price of an item, cost, order quantity, and other tangible data.

On the other hand, tacit knowledge (TK), can be a supplement source of knowledge to optimize partnership assessment process. TK is intangible knowledge that is hidden inside people and represents their individual experiences, culture, beliefs and values (Nonaka & Takeuchi, 1995). Therefore, TK is often learned independently of direct instructions, because this type of knowledge is difficult and sometime impossible to be documented, transferred and shared (Nonaka, 2007).

The main contribution of this research, therefore, is proposing a TK-based model to assess NE performance. The proposed model makes use of the Adaptive Network Based Fuzzy Inference System (ANFIS) that implements a Sugeno fuzzy inference system (Jang et al., 1997).

To construct and validate the model, I used a data set of three organizations from the petrochemical industry where organizations' tacit values (i.e., risk and feedback) are used as inputs to the ANFIS model and the anticipated partnership performance is the output. Furthermore, I applied a resampling method to re-generate an adequate sample for training the proposed ANFIS model. To present this model the paper is divided into seven parts: Section 2 provides a background for the study and definition important terms, Section 3 depicts the instrument used to model TK in this study. Section 4 describes the design of the ANFIS model, Section 5 describes the data used in this study and explains the design of the experiments, Section 6 illustrate the results of the experiments conducted on a petrochemical SC, Section 7 concludes and summarizes the study.

2. BACKGROUND AND MOTIVATIONS

The recent advent on information technologies has overwhelmed decision makers with a large EK base. Consequently, all the incoming EK became a difficult, costly and time consuming task to the extent that decision makers complain of the absents of the right information availability (Feldman & March, 1981). Furthermore, NEs are no longer a simple source of discrete component manufactured based on manufacturer specifications, or a short service provider for a retailer. In contrast, partners are being more responsible for managing the entire network to satisfy the end customers and preserve long-term partnerships (Sako, 1998). Moreover, the use of EK to evaluate NE performance helps making a logical process for making decisions about managing the NE. However, such logical decisions are based on routine and structured information processing, yet the global and dynamics nature of today market expose decision makers to non-routine, unstructured and multiple expertise domain changes in business environment (Holsapple, 2003). This in turn enforces decision makers to depend upon sense-making capabilities for correcting the computational logic of the business and the data it processes. Hence, the same assemblage of data may evoke different responses from different organizations. Hence, partners ought to achieve a level of TK compatibility to decrease any future anticipated conflicts. Therefore, EK alone is inadequate source to evaluate NE performance.

TK can be understood to be knowledge that is embedded in an enterprise's *culture, values, and norms* and it is difficult to share with other enterprises that are not compatible with that particular TK. Nonaka and Takeuchi (1995) introduced the concept of TK in NEs. The study suggested that achieving a level of compatible TK played a vital role in achieving a sustainable innovative process for Japanese manufacturing NEs. An example of the TK approach to transferring knowledge across global organizations is provided by Toyota. When Toyota wants to transfer knowledge of its production system to new employees in a new assembly factory, such as the factory recently opened in Valenciennes, France, Toyota management typically selects a core group of two to three hundred new employees for several months training to work on the assembly line in one of Toyota's existing factories. After several months of studying the production system and working alongside experienced Toyota assembly line workers, the trained workers are sent back to the new factory site where they work alongside all the new employees in the new factory to assure that the TK of Toyota's finely tuned production process is fully implanted in the new factory.

TK defines the fundamental character of the organization, the attitude that distinguishes it from others and creates a sense of identity for the organization. These shared values, however, are a reality in minds of most people throughout the organization (Deal & Kennedy, 1982, p. 23).

3. THE NEURO-FUZZY METHOD

Lotfi Zadeh first developed the mathematical framework that supports fuzzy logic and fuzzy set theory in 1965. Fuzzy sets describe the vagueness, partial truths and greyness inherent in reality. Zadeh (1965) introduced the concept of linguistic variables for the classification of values using words rather than crisp numbers.

An important question that needs to be addressed is "why use fuzzy logic when crisp measurements can be used to assess TK values compatibility"? The answer to this question is that often, crisp precise measurements are not significant in describing reality in particular when the desired value in-between and a precise answer does not necessarily provide the optimal solution (Zimmermann, 1985). Albert Einstein's view of crisp mathematics was, "so far as the laws of mathematics refer to reality, they are not certain. And so far as they are certain, they do not refer to reality" (Kosko, 1990). When the complexity of a system being analysed increases, precise and significant statements about its behaviour are more difficult to make. Real-world problems are so complex, the solutions are not precise, and they are fuzzy (Zadeh, 2008). Furthermore, in time series forecasting the factors that influence the series are so many, that it could hardly be called precise data. It is more realistic to convert the series into fuzzy clusters and use fuzzy set theory in the prediction process than to use crisp data.

In a crisp classification, for a given set A, the function $\mu A(x)$ assumes the Boolean value 1, if x belongs to set A or the value 0 if x does not belong to A, for every element x in the universal set. The value 1 indicates that x belongs to set A. In a fuzzy set, $\mu A(x)$ can assume the value 0.7, a value on the scale 0 to 1, to indicate that x has a high degree of belonging to set A, $\mu B(x)$ can assume the value 0.4 to indicate that x has a low degree of belonging to set B. This means that x can belong to both sets A and B but to a higher degree in A. $\mu A(x)$ and $\mu B(x)$

are the membership values of *x* and the distributions of $\mu A(x)$ and $\mu B(x)$ for all values of *x* are the Membership Function (MFs) of *x*. The value of the MF for a given value of element *x* indicates whether the element belongs to the fuzzy set and to what degree. The development of a MF is the Fuzzification of crisp measurements.

4. FUZZIFICATION PROCESS

Figure 1 shows the complete structure of the proposed fuzzy logic controller. First of all data must be translated into linguistics variables. For example conducting a survey (with five likert scale) using Deal and Kennedy's (1982) model can reveal how partners rate tacit value of risk taking and feedback. The results then can be aggregated for each partner to find the average rating of risk and feedback values. These aggregated values

are then entered separately as fuzzy inputs and translated into linguistic values of "High Risk, Low Risk, Rapid Feedback and Low Feedback", which is called the Fuzzification process. This translation process is achieved via the use of MFs for each TK value (i.e., risk and feedback).

To construct a MF the semantics (interpretation of information content) of the function should be considered, and then the appropriate method for that interpretation should be chosen. For this research I used the Generalized Bell-Shaped MFs (Figure 2). However, based on Deal and Kennedy (1982) model, risk and feedback are both represented by two linguistic values for each. Hence, *Risk* is either high or low, and *Feedback* is either rapid or slow see Figure 2.

Therefore, the crisp value for each TK value (i.e., risk or feedback) is mapped to two linguistic values each of which has a membership degree for the associated TK value. For this reason I used

Figure 1. Structure of the fuzzy logic controller

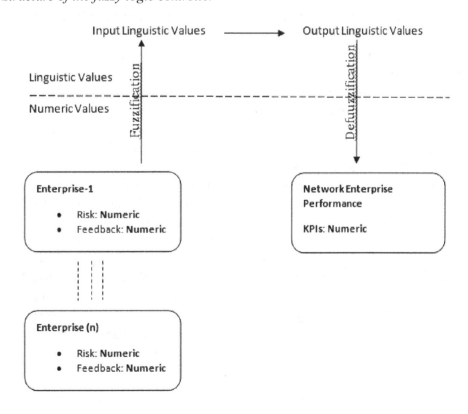

Figure 2. Deal and Kennedy model

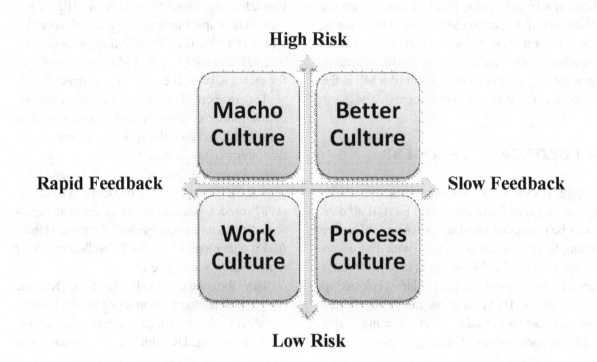

two Generalized Bell Shaped MFs, one decreasing function for measuring *Low* or *slow* linguistic values, and another increasing function for measuring *high* or *rapid* linguistic. These two functions can maintain the monotonically increasing/decreasing characteristics of the five level likert scales. Figure 2 shows the two MFs where, x_i denotes the average of all respondents' judgments for a given TK value i (i.e., risk or feedback). The MF is then calculated according to Equation (1).

$$\mu\left(x_i\right) = \frac{1}{1 + \left|\dfrac{x_i - c}{a}\right|^{2b}} \qquad (1)$$

Where a and b vary the width of the curve and c locates the center.

4.1. Fuzzy Logic Inference Process

The fuzzy inference step identifies the rule that apply to the current situation and compute the value of the output linguistic variables. The computation of fuzzy inference consists of three components: (1) rules aggregation, (2) composition of the rule results, and (3) results aggregation (Ross, 1995).

The rules in Table 1 constructed with helps from domain knowledge experts on assessing TK compatibility. The logical operation between feedback and risk is via "AND" operator. For example, when an organization feedback is *rapid* and risk is *low* then partnership performance is high when the partners TK are compatible with Work culture, performance is low when partners are compatible with Better culture, and performance is medium when partners culture are either compatible with Macho or Process culture.

Table 1. Rules of measuring partners TK values

IF		THEN Performance			
FEEDBACK	**RISK**	**BETTER**	**MACHO**	**PROCESS**	**WORK**
slow	low	Medium	low	high	medium
slow	high	High	medium	medium	low
rapid	low	Low	medium	medium	high
rapid	high	Medium	high	low	medium

- **Rule Aggregation:** The rule aggregation determines the membership value of the complete IF part of the rule. Therefore, if a given rule has multiple antecedents, the fuzzy operator AND or OR is used to obtain a single number that represents the result of the antecedent evaluation. To evaluate the disjunction (i.e., OR operation) of the rule antecedents we used the algebraic sum operation:

$$\mu_{A \cup B}(x) = \mu_A(x) + \mu_B(x) - \mu_A(x) \times \mu_B(x) \tag{2}$$

In contrast the conjunction (i.e., AND operation) uses the product operation:

$$\mu_{A \cap B}(x) = \mu_A \times \mu_B \tag{3}$$

- **Result Composition:** The rule composition uses the membership value of the complete IF part (μ_{IF} support for the precondition) to calculate the membership value of the THEN part (μ_{THEN} support for the consequences). A degree of support (w) is assigned to each rule to reflect its importance relative to other rules in the knowledgebase. The method and conditions to estimate the w is explained later in the extended neuro-fuzzy approach. Furthermore, the support of consequence (μ_{THEN}= THEN part) is calculated via the PROD operator as follows:

$$\mu_{THEN}(Rule(i)) = \mu_{IF}(Rule(i)) \times w \tag{4}$$

- **Result Aggregation:** If more than one rule produces the same output (consequences), an aggregation operation is carried out to aggregate the results of these rules. This aggregation step determines the membership value of each output (consequences). Bounded Sum is used in this research to aggregate the results (Ross, 1995).

4.2. Defuzzification Process

The results of the inference process are linguistic terms describing the performance based on the compatibility level of partners' TK along with its membership degree (μ_{result}). The defuzzification process is responsible for converting the linguistic terms into numerically crisp values that indicate the Key Performance Indicators (KPIs). The KPIs are mapped to a five level likert scale that is collected from the same survey when assessing risk and feedback values. A full illustration is provided afterwards.

4.3. Fuzzification Uncertainty Measure

A further important concept that should be considered when assessing TK compatibility is uncertainty. Since, for any organization, the TK values belong to the fuzzy set to some degree, the fuzzy TK set is also uncertain or vague to some degree. A great variety of measures have been proposed to quantify uncertainty. These measures are classified according to the type of uncertainty they deal with. According to Pal and Bezdek (1999) uncertainty is subdivided into three categories, fuzziness, no specificity and randomness. While fuzziness is addressed by fuzzy sets theory, no specificity is addressed by evidence theory and randomness by probability theory. Fuzzy uncertainty differs from probabilistic uncertainty (randomness) and no specificity in that it deals with situations where the boundaries of the sets under consideration are not sharply defined. Randomness and no specificity are not due to ambiguity regarding set-boundaries but rather are concerned with the belonging of elements or events to crisp sets (Boudraa et al., 2004). As culture sets are perceived as having imprecise boundaries that facilitate gradual transitions from membership to non membership and vice versa, only the type of uncertainty resulting from fuzziness –the lack of sharpness of relevant distinctions – was of interest in this research. In this study a non probabilistic entropy measure based on the MFs of the intersection and union of the set and its complement set is used (Soyer et al., 2007) as follows:

$$H(C) = \frac{1}{n} \sum_{i=1}^{n} \frac{\mu_{C \cap \bar{C}}(x_i)}{\mu_{C \cup \bar{C}}(x_i)} \quad (5)$$

where n denotes the number of TK values in TK type ($n=2$, risk & feedback); x_i is the average of respondents' judgments of an organization for a given TK value i (i.e., risk or feedback) and $\mu(x_i)$ denotes the degree of belongingness of the TK value i to the TK set C. $\bar{C}$ is the complement set of C.

4.4. The Extended Neuro-Fuzzy Architecture

The proposed Fuzzy Inference System (FIS) has utilized human expertise by storing its essential components in a rule base, and performs fuzzy reasoning to infer the overall partnership perfor-

mance. The derivation of *if-then rules* and corresponding MFs depends heavily on the a priori expertise domain knowledge about the partners' TK compatibility and its effects on the partnership performance. However there is no systematic way to transform experiences of knowledge of human experts to the knowledge base of the FIS. There is also a need for adaptability or some learning algorithms to produce outputs within the required error rate. Therefore, we combined the FIS with ANN and used ANFIS to implement Sugeno FIS (Jang et al., 1997).

ANFIS makes use of a mixture of back-propagation to learn the premise parameters and least mean square estimation to determine the consequent parameters. A step in the learning procedure has two parts: In the first part the input patterns are propagated, and the optimal conclusion parameters are estimated by an iterative least mean square procedure, while the antecedent parameters (MFs) are assumed to be fixed for the current cycle through the training set. In the second part the patterns are propagated again, and in this epoch (the presentation of the entire training set to an ANFIS), back-propagation is used to modify the antecedent parameters, while the conclusion parameters remain fixed. This procedure is then iterated. Figure 4 depicts five layers architecture of final produced ANFIS. The functionality of each layer is described.

Layer-1: In Figure 3, there are two groups of nodes in layer 1. The first group includes two nodes that represent the TK values Risk-taking as follows, *High*, and *Low* which are linked by x. The second group includes two nodes linked by y and represent the TK value feedback as follows *Rapid*, and *Slow*. These nodes are equal to the linguistic variables in the original FIS and they serve the partition of the input space. Nodes in this layer are adaptive and the output of each node is defined by a MF of the linguistic value of the input. Herein we used the Generalized Bell Shaped MF as aforementioned

Figure 3. Generalized Bell Shaped MF

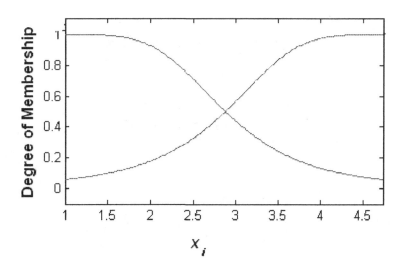

In Equation (1) a_i, b_i and c_i are the premise parameters of the MFs. Therefore, the total premise parameters of layer-1 is **2** (nodes) X **2** (MFs) X **3** (parameters) = **12** premise parameters.

Layer-2: Nodes in layer 2 are fixed nodes labelled according to the type of TK (i.e., B=Better, M=Macho, P=Process, W=Work). The nodes use the conjunction operator to synthesize the information from the previous layer. The product operator is used to multiply all the nodes incoming signals. The outputs, w_j, j=1,...,4 represent the firing strength of each rule. Thus, $O_{j,2}$ is

$$w_1 = \mu_{High}(x) \times \mu_{Slow}(y)$$
$$w_2 = \mu_{High}(x) \times \mu_{Rapid}(y)$$
$$w_3 = \mu_{Low}(x) \times \mu_{Slow}(y)$$
$$w_4 = \mu_{Low}(x) \times \mu_{Rapid}(y)$$

In general any T-norm operators that performs fuzzy AND can be used as the node function in this layer (e.g., min operator).

Layer-3: Nodes in layer 3 labelled **Π** to perform the normalization function of the output signals from layer 2 and this normalization is defined as

$$O_{j,3} = \bar{w}_j = \frac{w_j}{w_1 + w_2 + w_3 + w_4}, \text{j=1,2,3,4}$$

Layer-4: Each node in layer 4 is an adaptive node with the node function defined as

$$O_{i,4} = \bar{w}_i f_i, \text{i=1, 2, 3,4}$$

where f_i is a liner combination of the input variables

$$f_i = p_i x + q_i y + r_i, \text{i=1, 2, 3, 4}$$

where p_i, q_i, and r_i are the coefficients of this liner combination and are the consequence parameters. The number of the consequent parameters in this study is 3(parameters) X 4(linear function) = **12** consequent parameters.

Layer-5: The nodes in layer 5 are a fixed node, which computes the performance level over five Likert scale such that each output represents the TK compatibility effects on partnership performance between NE.

$$O_{i,6} = \sum w_i f_i = \frac{\sum \bar{w}_i f_i}{\sum w_i}$$

Figure 4. ANFIS architecture

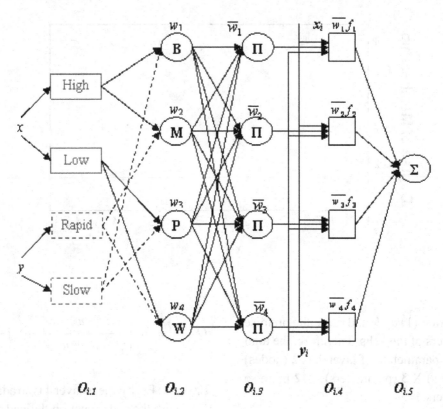

A nonlinear mapping between the independent variables *(x, y)* and the response *z* through ANFIS is achieved by minimizing an error measure *E*, which is defined as

$$E = \sum_{k=1}^{n} \left(z_k - \overline{z}_k \right)^2 \quad (6)$$

where z_k is the desired response for the *k*th observation, $\overline{z}_k$ is the estimate response for the *k*th observation, and n is the total number of observations.

5. DATA SOURCE AND EXPERIMENTS

A random representative sample was obtained from senior management executives from three dominant NEs of a petrochemical industrial network. The sample was not selected from volunteers. Instead, it was carefully arranged so that each participant had a fair chance of selection so that the results could be reliably projected from the sample to the larger population.

A wide diversity of interviewees in government, public, and private sectors were met, who provided different viewpoints of their enterprise. The structure of the chosen NE is vertical with many management levels and a large number of management executives. Having large NE with many management levels would give a variety on responses which is essential for the ANFIS Learning algorithm.

These levels of management were chosen because the decision-making process in many organisations depends fully on these levels of management. Therefore, managers at these levels are either the founder of the TK in their enterprises, or the prospective developer of the current TK to meet their daily tasks expectations, and thus aware of the importance of such factor.

The current study developed a simple questionnaire based on Deal and Kennedy (1982), and Beamon (1999) to measure the NE performance as the following. Resources (*Total cost* and *Return on Investment*), Outputs (*Lead-time* and *Fill rate*), Flexibility (*Volume* and *Product type*).

The data obtained based on two questions associated with two judgments to assess partners' TK compatibility and determine its influence on NE performance. Therefore, the first judgment evaluates the interviewee's TK, while the second judgment evaluates the partner's TK from the interviewee perspective. Specifically, the final instrument asked each participant to respond on five-point scale (not important to very important) of perceived importance to the first question:

1. What is the importance level of (Risk/ Feedback) value on (your enterprise/your partner's enterprise)?

Furthermore, the second question assesses NE performance by asking the respondents to report their perceptions of their NE because of the abovementioned TK values (i.e., risk and feedback) on both their organization and their partner's organization. We used three performance elements to elicit responses on a five scale ranging from 'Greatly deteriorated' (scored as 1) to 'Greatly improved' (scored as 5).

2. How much does the importance level of (Risk/Feedback) TK value on (your enter-

prise/your partner's enterprise) contributes to the improvement of your NE performance (i.e,. Lead-time/fill rate, total cost /ROI, and flexibility on volume/product type)?

I then averaged the three six measures to obtain an index of the NE performance. A simple diagram in Figure 5 is provided to illustrate the data collection approach. Figure 4 shows that the total observation is twelve (i.e., six self evaluation + six partner evaluations), where each observation represents the respondents judgments average. Furthermore, the original sample is drawn from units that perform interactions with partners, thus they can better evaluate partners' TK and the NE performance (e.g., purchasing units, sales units and supplies unit).

5.1. Resampling Strategy

The obtained original sample size was too small (e.g., twelve records) to the extent that the evaluating process of an optimal solution is not convergent. Therefore, I concluded that the sample of data is too poor and inadequate to describe the link between inputs (i.e., TK values) and the output (i.e., NE performance). However, researchers in that case have alternatively relied on "Bootstrapping" - *a very popular statistical resampling technique* - to mange the uncertainty and improve the sample of data with a new pseudo data (Carpenter et al., 1999; Hesterberg et al., 2003). Bootstrapping method has been successfully applied on ANFIS systems in Grosan et al. (2006a, 2006b) and on ANN models (Carney & Cunningham, 1997; Zhang, 1999).

The proposed method uses the bootstrap to generate multiple training sets from a finite sample of data, which are then used to train the ANFIS model. If the training set S consists of N cases, each is assigned a probability of $1/N$, and a new training set, S^A, is assembled by sampling with replacement N times from the original training set,

Figure 5. Data collection structure

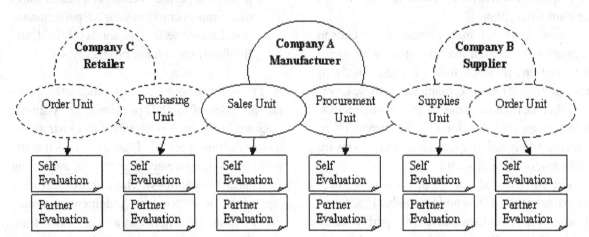

using these probabilities. Some cases in *S* may not appear in *S^A*, while others may appear multiple times. The resampled training set *S^A* is used to train a predictor, the process is repeated, and the results are combined to form a consensus prediction. Bootstrapping represents the most popular technique for constructing predictor ensembles. If the real universe from which the samples are drawn is unknown or inaccessible, one needs to construct an alternative universe that mediates the link between real universe and the samples and includes all known knowledge about the real universe. Basically, bootstrapping method uses the sample data as a population from which repeated samples are drawn.

The original sample size of the petrochemical NE is equal to 12 observations; yet using the bootstrapping resampling method we generated a new data set of size 700 simulated observations. Each observation has two inputs: *risk* average value (numerical: 1-5), *feedback* average value (numerical: 1-5), and one output: *NE performance* average value (aggregation of the six numerical measures: 1-5).

5.2. Design of the Experiment

There are no clear-cut guidelines in the literature to divide the sample into training and test groups. Some researchers advocate a 60–40% split between the training and test samples, whereas others prefer a 75–25% split between the two samples. Accordingly, I divided our data set into a training set of 500 (71.43%) observations and a predict/test set of 200 (28.57%) observations. Further, I used a randomization algorithm to divide the 700 observations into the two sets. To select an observation, I generated a random number using the normal distribution. Then, I tested the final produced ANFIS model with another original sample different from the one used for training to validate the model ability to predict the outcome. Finally I ran a regression analysis to investigate the correlation between the predicted and the actual measured values.

6. RESULTS FROM THE PETROCHEMICAL SUPPLY CHAIN

I conducted the experiments on three level NE each of which has different roles (i.e., supplier, manufacturer, and retailer). For each enterprise I collected data from 240 respondents across 6 function units (Figure 4), yet data is only considered valid when a respondent has spent at least 10 years and is engaged on a senior or above management level. The first half of the responses (120 responses) were averaged together to form an original sample *A* (12 observations) for training step. While the other 120 responses averaged for the validation step (sample *B*).

The main focal enterpise in this NE is *Company A*. *Company A* is one of the largest manufacturers of fertiliser and petrochemicals in the Middle East. *Company A* uses natural gas as a feedstock to produce a wide range of petrochemical products including Urea, ammonia, and methanol. It purchases the natural gas supplies from *Company B* which is a leading natural gas company in the Middle East. However, *Company A* produces petrochemical products according to its retailer (*Company C*) customized requirements. To illustrate the workflow of this NE I studied the production of Urea that is customized for Cattle feedings. The process starts with the natural gas that is considered the best for the production of Ammonia compared with other raw materials such as Naphtha and Coal. Urea is made by mixing liquid Ammonia with a gas called carbon dioxide. A special process turns this liquid into round granules which can then be shipped in bulk cargo containers or packed into polythene bags. Urea can be customized for several uses, such as Fertiliser, Cattle Feed, and Urea Formaldehydes.

6.1. Illustrative Procedure for the Proposed ANFIS Model

The detailed illustrative procedure for the Neuro-fuzzy model is provided as follows:

Step 1: Generate a new sample of data based on the original data (sample A) in Table 2 below using Bootstrapping method (new sample size = 700 observations).

Step 2: Train 71.43% of the new generated sample with the ANFIS model. Then test the model with the reminder 28.57% of the bootstrapped sample. Figure 6(a) shows the convergence of the ANFIS model during the

Table 2. Membership degree of TK values & performance

Observations	Risk	Feedback	μ_{High}	μ_{Low}	μ_{Rapid}	μ_{Slow}	Performance
Observation-1	3.35	3.84	0.675	0.325	0.92	0.08	3.77
Observation -2	3.44	3.49	0.72	0.28	0.745	0.255	3.72
Observation -3	3.95	3.47	0.975	0.025	0.735	0.265	4.07
Observation -4	3.98	4.13	0.99	0.01	1	0	3.53
Observation -5	3.23	1.98	0.615	0.385	0	1	1.89
Observation -6	4.53	2.14	1	0	0.07	0.93	2.02
Observation -7	4.14	1.53	1	0	0	1	1.98
Observation -8	3.81	1.98	0.905	0.095	0	1	2.03
Observation -9	1.98	4.31	0	1	1	0	4.94
Observation -10	2.14	4.19	0.07	0.93	1	0	4.58
Observation -11	1.86	4.49	0	1	1	0	4.92
Observation -12	1.56	4.39	0	1	1	0	4.41

80 epochs training, and the Root Mean Squared Error (RMSE) is minimizing. The RMSE value for the training data was 0.086 and for the test data is 0.095. Figure 6(b) shows different initial step sizes (k=0.01 to 0.09) that influence the speed of ANFIS convergence in each epoch.

Step 3: List and investigate the initial and final MFs for the two inputs (i.e., risk and feedback) during the training process and the testing process (Figure 6). It is interesting to observe that sharp changes in the training data surface around the origin are accounted for by the MFs moving toward the S-shaped (high and rapid) and Z-shaped (low and slow) parameterized MFs. Since the Fuzzification of values are extracted from a theoretically sound five level crisp likert scale, thus theoretically the MFs have maintained the basic characteristics of the crisp likert. Therefore, if x_i is greater than the upper level then it can be inferred that the NE participants must have this TK value without any doubt and the membership

value should be $\mu(x_i)$ =1. Similarly, if $\mu(x_i)$ is smaller than 2, it indicates that the respondents think the most compatible TK does not or weakly have the TK value i (i.e., risk or feedback). So the membership value of $\mu(x_i)$ =0 can be easily assigned. Additionally, a linear MF is assumed for the x_i values between a and b. Thus, the membership degree shows to what extent the organization presents a TK value represented by a particular fuzzy set. By using the MF each TK value is fuzzified. Thus the Final MFs may better utilized the following Equation:

$$\mu\left(x_i\right) = \begin{cases} 0 & if \quad x_i \prec a_i, \\[2em] \dfrac{x_i - a_i}{b_i - a_i} & if \quad a_i \leq x_i \leq b_i \\[2em] 1 & if \quad x_i \succ b_i \end{cases} \tag{7}$$

Figure 6. (a) Training and testing RMSE curves. (b) Training step sizes of MFs

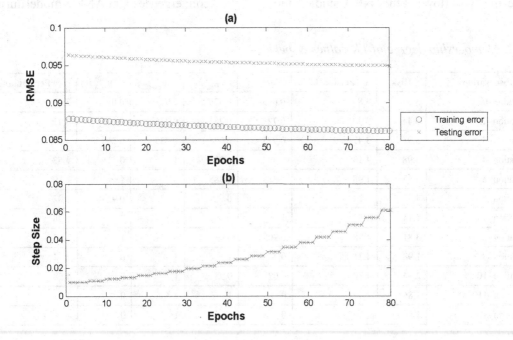

However, MFs for each input should have be symmetric with respect to the characteristics of likert scale, yet due to computing errors and the approximated initial conditions used for bootstrapping both final MFs are semi-symmetric

Step 4: The actual measured (red) and predicted (blue) values for both training data and testing data are essentially the same in Figure 7. The differences between them (green) can only be seen on a much finer scale, as indicated in Figure 8 as "error" calculated by Equation (6). Figure 8 also shows insignificant differences between measured and predicted NE performance where the obtained error is between [-0.298, 0.233].

Step 5: Once the system is trained and tested, one can examine the inputs/output relationships, in an illustrative manner. Figure 8 shows the response of the system when two variables are changed. Figure 9 indicates that the feedback value has larger effects on NE performance than risk-taking. The relationship between feedback and performance is monotonically increasing with high sensitivity around [3.5-5]. In contrast increasing risk-taking value has insignificant effects on performance, in particular when feedback is low.

Step 6: To evaluate the performance of the developed proposed ANFIS model we validate the model using the original sample **B** from the petrochemical NE. The relationship between

Figure 7. Initial and final MFs for both risk and feedback TK values

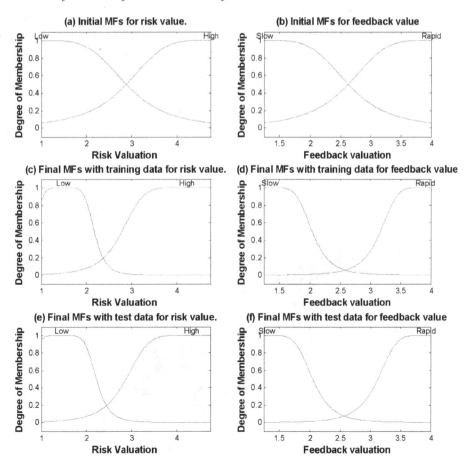

Figure 8. Waveform of the predicted and measured performance using the tested ANFIS

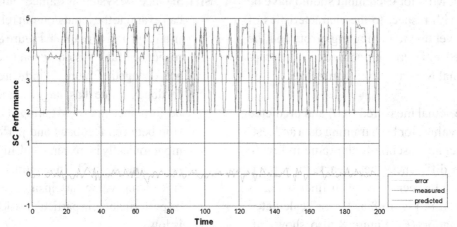

the actual measured performance used for training the ANFIS and the predicted performance are shown in Figure 10. A solid line indicating the line of quality is also shown in the figure. The liner regression method produced the following regression equation:

$$Performance_{\mathrm{Pr}\,edicted} = 1.009 \times Performance_{Actual} \quad (8)$$

Where $Performance_{predicted}$ is the predicted performance level on five likert scale using the ANFIS model and $Performance_{actual}$ is the actual assessed performance on five likert scale by expertise domain knowledge using Deal and Kennedy model (1982). The significant of the above t-test is very high (p<0.0001). Furthermore, the F-test found to be 415.29, for 12 degrees of freedom, which indicates that the overall regression model is highly significant. In fact, the fitted regression model explains 97% of the predicted variations in assessing performance level

Figure 9. Response surface for performance vs. (feedback & risk)

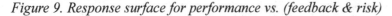

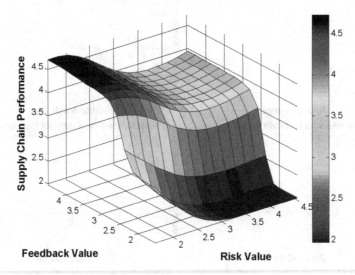

Figure 10. Predicted vs. Actual measured performance using original sample

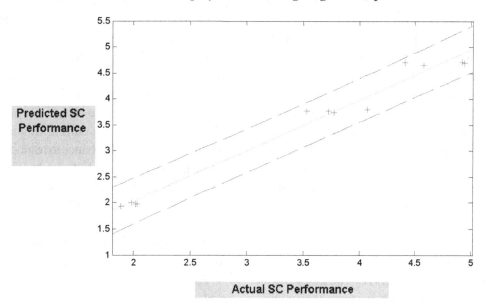

(R²=0.976, Adjusted R²=0.974). The figure also shows how that all the points lie within of the 95% confidence upper and lower bound.

Step 7: We then measure the fuzzy entropy, that may contribute to a more consistent and accurate judgment. This measure reveals the degree of uncertainty inherent in each TK set that we were exposed to in any judgment about these TK set. A value close to one indicates high uncertainty. Based on Equation (5) for Work Culture where $n = \#observations \, X \, \#TK \, values = $ **12 X 2=24**.

$$H(Work) =$$
$$\frac{1}{24}\left[\sum_{i-1}^{24}\left(\frac{\min\{\mu_i(LowRisk);1-\mu_i(LowRisk)\}}{\max\{\mu_i(LowRisk);1-\mu_i(LowRisk)\}}+\frac{\min\{\mu_i(RapidFeedback);1-\mu_i(RapidFeedback)\}}{\max\{\mu_i(RapidFeedback);1-\mu_i(RapidFeedback)\}}\right)\right]$$

$$H(Work) = \frac{1}{24}\left(1.712 + 0.865\right)$$

$$H(Work) = \frac{2.577}{24} = 0.107 = 10.7\%$$

Similarly, the fuzzy entropy of other TK types yields the same results (10.7%), because complement of *Low* risk is *High* risk and complement of *Rapid* feedback is *Slow* feedback. This value implies low uncertainty and thus more accurate judgment about TK values set. Hence, all outcomes from the FIS are considered.

7. CONCLUSION AND FUTURE WORKS

The neuro-fuzzy model performed well in identifying potential TK compatibility between partners to improve performance and, therefore, in minimizing the RMS error in a quite robust way. Overall, neuro-fuzzy models provide significantly a well estimate of the expected performance based on partners' TK compatibility in the illustrated petrochemical NE. In particular, the proposed neuro-fuzzy model has much higher classification accuracy in identifying the strong as well the weak TK values in the petrochemical NE.

The neuro-fuzzy approach makes a substantial contribution to building our understanding of how TK values interact and interrelate with each other to generate a compatible TK that enhances the performance. This outcome of the neuro-fuzzy approach aligns with the noted shortfall in research relating to the assessment of partners' TK in NE to sustain a higher performance. The proposed neuro-fuzzy model has contributed widely on explaining the effects of each NE value on the NE performance. The assessment model can be used as a testing platform where potential partners can assess their TK compatibility prior to establish their long-term NE. The assessment process of all enterprises TK is a time-consuming and costly process that required the participants of all partners, yet the neuro-fuzzy model can provide an accurate prediction of the best TK values or possible changes to achieve a near optimal compatible TK.

Although the results of our findings are preliminary, I believe that this is a good first step in understanding the dynamics of using neuro-fuzzy models in assessing partners' compatibility in NEs. The proposed neuro-fuzzy based TK model can be a supplement to the analytical based EK models to assess partnerships effectiveness. Therefore, in real-world situations, an analyser can easily clarify why a particular performance was outperformed or fall behind other NEs.

Based on the findings reported above, the neuro-fuzzy approach does offer an alternative to other AI techniques because the non-linear prediction function represented by the proposed neuro-fuzzy model provides a better approximation of the NE partners' TK distribution, especially when the distribution is multi-modal like network. Furthermore, ANFIS uses fewer adjustable parameters as compared to the cascade-correlation neural networks and back-propagation multilayer perceptron models. This results in fast convergence to good parameter values that capture the underlying dynamics. Further, ANFIS consists of fuzzy rules that reflect the local experts rather than global generalizations. These local mappings facilitate the minimum disturbance principle that states that the adaptation should not only reduce the output error for the current training pattern but also minimize disturbance to response already learned. This is particularly important for NEs because the environment differ from one industry to another. In addition, ANFIS models offer the advantage of being a linguistically interpretable fuzzy inference system that allows prior knowledge to be embedded in model development.

Finally, researchers and practitioners can explore the design and development of a decision support system that embeds the subjective (judgmental) models based on TK and the objective (analytic) models based on EK to aid the NE partnership formation process in making a decision on the partnerships formation. In the light of the current study, another extension of this research work would be to adopt different models for assessing and modelling TK. An interesting implication for further research is needed on TK values scaling. More research is needed on expanding the range to include more ranges in between, such as a, very high, high, moderate, low, very low risk-taking. Moreover, research on neuro-fuzzy architecture has recently, developed a multi-input-multi-outputs architecture networks (Sheikhzadeh et al., 2008). This can be applied to our assessment model to enable independent measurement for each performance elements. This approach would be of interests to researchers who require the study of the effects of NE compatibility on the performance element separately.

ACKNOWLEDGMENT

We are grateful to the financial support from University of Bahrain who sponsored this research as a part of the King's project to modernise Bahrain's economy and political affairs.

REFERENCES

Beamon, B. M. (1999). Measuring supply chain performance. *International Journal of Operations & Production Management, 19*(3), 275–292. doi:10.1108/01443579910249714

Boudraa, A. A., Ayachi, B., Fabien, S., & Laurent, G. (2004). Dempster--Shafer's basic probability assignment based on fuzzy membership functions. *Electronic Letters on Computer Vision and Image Analysis, 4*(1), 1–6.

Carney, J. G., & Cunningham, P. (1997). The NeuralBag algorithm: Optimizing generalization performance in bagged neural networks. In *Proceedings of the 7th European Symposium on Neural Networks* (pp. 35-40).

Carpenter, J., Goldstein, H., & Rasbash, J. (1999). A non-parametric bootstrap for multilevel models. *Multilevel Modelling Newsletter, 11*, 2–5.

Choi, T. Y., & Hartley, J. L. (1996). An exploration of supplier selection practices across the supply chain. *Journal of Operations Management, 14*(4), 333–343. doi:10.1016/S0272-6963(96)00091-5

Dacin, M. T., Hitt, M. A., & Levitas, E. (1997). Selecting partners for successful international alliances: Examination of US and Korean firms. *Journal of World Business, 32*(1), 3–16. doi:10.1016/S1090-9516(97)90022-5

Deal, T. E., & Kennedy, A. A. (1982). *Corporate cultures*. Reading, MA: Addison-Wesley.

Donaldson, B. (1994). Supplier selection criteria on the service dimension. *European Journal of Purchasing & Supply Management, 1*(4), 209–217. doi:10.1016/0969-7012(95)00009-7

Feldman, M. S., & March, J. G. (1981). Information in organization as signal and symbol. *Administrative Science Quarterly, 26*(2), 171–186. doi:10.2307/2392467

Grosan, C., Abraham, A., & Tigan, S. (2006a). Engineering drug design using a multi-input multi-output neuro-fuzzy system. In *Proceedings of the 8th International symposium on symbolic and numeric algorithms for scientific computing*, Timisoara, Romania (pp. 365-371).

Grosan, C., Abraham, A., Tigan, S., Chang, T. G., & Kim, D. H. (2006b). Evolving neural networks for pharmaceutical research. In *Proceedings of the International Conference on Hybrid Information Technology*, Korea (pp. 13-19).

Harrison, E. F. (1987). *The managerial decision-making process*. Boston, MA: Houghton-Mifflin.

Hesterberg, T., Moore, D. S., Monaghan, S., Clipson, A., & Epstein, R. (2003). *Bootstrap methods and permutation tests*. New York, NY: W. H. Freeman and Company.

Holsapple, C. W. (2003). *Handbook on knowledge management*. Heidelberg, Germany: Springer-Verlag.

Ip, W. H., Huang, M., Yung, K. L., & Wang, D. (2003). Genetic algorithm solution for a risk-based partner selection problem in a virtual enterprise. *Computers & Operations Research, 30*(2), 213–231. doi:10.1016/S0305-0548(01)00092-2

Jang, J.-S. R., Sun, C.-T., & Mizutani, E. (1997). *Neuro-fuzzy and soft computing: A computational approach to learning and machine intelligence*. Upper Saddle River, NJ: Prentice Hall.

Kosko, B. (1990). Fuzziness vs. probability. *International Journal of General Systems, 17*(2), 211–240. doi:10.1080/03081079008935108

Lorange, P., & Roos, J. (1992). *Strategic alliances, evolution and implementation*. Oxford, UK: Blackwell.

Mikhailov, L. (2002). Fuzzy analytical approach to partnership selection in formation of virtual enterprises. *OMEGA International Journal of Management Science, 39*, 393–401. doi:10.1016/S0305-0483(02)00052-X

Nonaka, I. (2007). The knowledge-creating company. *Harvard Business Review, 85*(7-8), 162–171.

Nonaka, L., & Takeuchi, H. (1995). *The knowledge-creating company: How Japanese companies create the dynamics of innovation*. New York, NY: Oxford University Press.

Pal, N. R., & Bezdek, J. C. (1999). Measuring fuzzy uncertainty. *IEEE Transactions on Fuzzy Systems, 2*(2), 107–118. doi:10.1109/91.277960

Ross, T. J. (1995). *Fuzzy logic with engineering applications*. New York, NY: McGraw-Hill.

Sako, M. (1998). The nature and impact of employee 'voice' in the European car components industry. *Human Resource Management Journal, 8*(2), 5–13. doi:10.1111/j.1748-8583.1998.tb00163.x

Sheikhzadeh, M., Trifkovic, M., & Rohani, S. (2008). Adaptive MIMO neuro-fuzzy logic control of a seeded and an un-seeded anti-solvent semi-batch crystallizer. *Chemical Engineering Science, 63*(5), 1261–1272. doi:10.1016/j.ces.2007.07.022

Smagalla, D. (2004). Supply-chain culture clash. *MIT Sloan Management Review, 46*(1).

Soyer, A., Kabak, O., & Asan, U. (2007). A fuzzy approach to value and culture assessment and an application. *International Journal of Approximate Reasoning, 44*(2), 182–196. doi:10.1016/j.ijar.2006.07.008

Talluri, S., Baker, R. C., & Sarkis, J. (1999). A framework for designing efficient value chain network. *International Journal of Production Economics, 62*(1), 133–144. doi:10.1016/S0925-5273(98)00225-4

Zadeh, L. A. (1965). Fuzzy sets. *Information and Control, 8*, 338–353. doi:10.1016/S0019-9958(65)90241-X

Zadeh, L. A. (2008). Is there a need for fuzzy logic? *Information Sciences, 178*(13), 2751–2779. doi:10.1016/j.ins.2008.02.012

Zhang, J. (1999). Developing robust nonlinear models through bootstrap aggregated neural networks. *Neurocomputing, 25*, 93–113. doi:10.1016/S0925-2312(99)00054-5

Zimmermann, H.-J. (1985). *Fuzzy set theory - and its applications*. Boston, MA: Kluwer Academic.

This journal was previously published in the International Journal of Technology Diffusion, Volume 2, Issue 2, edited by Ali Hussein Saleh Zolait, pp. 1-18, copyright 2011 by IGI Publishing (an imprint of IGI Global).

Chapter 4
ANN Based Approach to Integrate Smell Sense in Multimedia Systems

Yousif Al-Bastaki
University of Bahrain, Bahrain

Khalid Al-Mutawah
University of Bahrain, Bahrain

ABSTRACT

Despite the wide usage of multimedia in several applications, research in the field of olfaction is immature in helping humans work and communicate through multi-sensory interfaces, including smell. There is no consistent method of testing user capability of smell. Therefore, smell detection and generation systems are not well integrated into today's multimedia systems. In this paper, the authors propose an odor sensing system with the capability of the discrimination among closely similar 20 different odor patterns and propose an on-line classification method using a handheld odor meter (OMX-GR sensor) and neural network that can be used in different multimedia applications. The proposed system is integrated to enhance the functionality of an online multimedia shopping system that is capable of selling products with visual and auditory senses.

1. INTRODUCTION

The Multimedia systems are widely defined as Multi Sensory systems that convey information about the current state of the real world environment by congregating signals from several receptors in the ears, eyes, and other sense organs. The signals from one side of the body are sent through nerve fibers to the cerebral cortex on the opposite side of the brain, where they are perceived and interpreted in terms of our previous experiences, knowledge, and expectations. The

DOI: 10.4018/978-1-4666-2791-8.ch004

five well known physiological systems that lie at the core of the human perceptual experience are Olfactory (smell), tactile (touch), visual (sight), auditory (sound), and perception of flavor (taste). Nonetheless, extensive research has been carried out to develop multimedia systems that can capture, store and reproduce sound and video with high quality (Paeda et al., 2008; Pfeiffer, Lienhart, & Efflsberg, 2001). However, there are the other three senses, smell, touch and taste that received less attention within the multimedia research area. These senses, in addition to sight and sound, can recreate an environment similar to the real world environment in particular the smell sense. This is because amongst the three other senses the smell is the only sense that can be perceived from a long distance.

Nonetheless, few odor-sensing tools have been proposed in limited applications. This is because of the complexity on designing olfactory system that can perceive different smells for humans with a variety of preferences. Table 1 presents some of these limited applications from the literature.

However, these systems are barely designed to fit on the industrial applications to reduce the cost of productions or prevent risks and hazards when handling toxic gases. Therefore, the implementation cost for these aforementioned olfactory systems is irrational for multimedia systems. In this paper, therefore, we present the design of a low cost odor system that can be employed in a multimedia environment. The odor system proposed in this paper has employed the Artificial Neural Network (ANN) technique of humans brain to discriminate amongst different smells. The organization of the paper is as follows: Section 2 presents a brief description of the human olfactory system and Section 3 provides a summarized overview of ANN techniques. Section 4 presents a justification of the ANN usage in smell sensors. The proposed system is presented in Section 5. The performance evaluation and conclusions are presented in Sections 6.

2. MODELS OF THE OLFACTORY SYSTEM

The goal of much of the research regarding the olfactory system is to understand how individual odors are identified. Many researchers have produced mathematical models of the olfactory

Table 1. Limited applications from previous research

Application	System Specification	Year	Authors
agricultural	Single coated thermistor as the odor sensor	1961	(Moncrieff, 1961)
smell detector	an array of eight electrochemical sensors	1964	(Wilkens & Hartman, 1964)
Electronic nose	pattern recognition techniques	1994	(Gardner & Bartlett, 1994).
polymer gas sensors	an integrated circuit based device that performs data acquisition from a miniature array of 32	1994	(Hatfield, Neaves, Hicks, Persaud, & Travers, 1994)
An Intelligent E-nose	of measuring signals from arrays of resistive and piezoelectric sensor types in the same board	1997	(Dyer & Gardner, 1997)
Robot head that reacts to some smells	A recognition algorithm that uses a look-up table that contains sensor outputs and their derivatives	2001	(Miwa, Umetsu, Takanishi, & Takanohu, 2001)
chemical industry to detect toxic gases and gases without smell	The sensor electronics is based on a scanning version of a vibrating capacitor (Kelvin probe)	2002	(Li & Hopfield, 1989; Mizsei & Ress, 2002)

system. These models often include simulations of the neurobiological information processing systems (biological neural networks). The olfactory information is processed in both the olfactory bulb and in the olfactory cortex. Figure 1 illustrates the main information processing structures within the brain. The olfactory cortex performs pattern classification and recognition of the sensed odors. Once identified, odor information is transmitted to the hippocampus, limbic system, and the cerebral cortex. The connection to the hippocampus explains why odor can sub-consciously evoke memories. Conscious perception of the odor and how to act on the odor takes place in the cerebral cortex (Li & Hopfield, 1989). The mammalian olfactory system uses a variety of chemical sensors, known as olfactory receptors, combined with signal processing in the olfactory bulb and automated pattern recognition in the olfactory cortex of the brain.

3. ARTIFICIAL NEURAL NETWORKS

An artificial neural network (ANN) is an information processing paradigm that was inspired by the way biological nervous systems, such as the brain, process information. The key element of this paradigm is the novel structure of the information processing system. The basic unit of an artificial neural network is the neuron. Each neuron receives a number of inputs, multiplies the inputs by individual weights, sums the weighted inputs, and passes the sum through a transfer function, which can be, e.g., linear or sigmoid (linear for values close to zero, flattening out for large positive or negative values). An ANN is an interconnected network of neurons. The input layer has one neuron for each of the sensor signals, while the output layer has one neuron for each of the different sample properties that should be predicted. Usually, one hidden layer with a variable number of neurons is placed between the input and output layer. During the ANN training phase, the weights

and transfer function parameters in the ANN are adjusted such that the calculated output values for a set of input values are as close as possible to the known true values of the sample properties. It is composed of a large number of highly interconnected processing elements (neurons) working in unison to solve specific problems for this study. It consists of three interconnected layers of neurons (Figure 2). The computing neurons (hidden and output layers) have a non-linear transfer function. In this study sigmoid function was used.

The parameters of the neurons are chosen through a minimization of the output error for a known training set. ANNs, like people, learn by example. An ANN is configured for an application such identifying chemical vapors through a learning process. Learning in biological systems involves adjustments to the synaptic connections that exist between the neurons. This is true of ANNs as well. For the electronic nose, the ANN learns to identify the various chemicals or odors by example. Another advantage of the parallel processing nature of the ANN is the speed performance. During development, ANNs are configured in a training mode. This involves a repetitive process of presenting data from known diagnoses to the training algorithm. This training mode often takes many hours. The payback occurs in the field where the actual odor identification is accomplished by propagating the data through the system which takes only a fraction of a second. Since the identification time is similar to the response times of many sensor arrays, this approach permits real-time odor identification.

Several ANN configurations have been used in electronic noses including back propagation-trained, feed-forward networks; Kohonen's self-organizing maps (SOMs); Learning Vector Quantizers (LVQs); Hamming networks; Boltzmann machines; and Hopfield networks (Erdi & Barna, 1991; Keller, Kouzes, & Kangas, 1994). In this study a Multi-Layered neural network with back-propagation training algorithm, which has generalized delta rule learning is used.

Figure 1. The major processes of the olfactory system

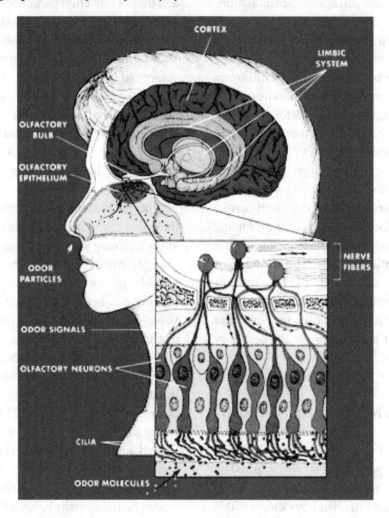

4. ANN BASED ELECTRONIC/ARTIFICIAL NOSES

Electronic/artificial noses are being developed as systems for the automated detection and classification of odors, vapors, and gases. The two main components of an electronic nose are the sensing system and the automated pattern recognition system. The sensing system can be an array of several different sensing elements (e.g., chemical sensors), where each element measures a different property of the sensed odor, or it can be a single sensing device (e.g., spectrometer) that produces an array of measurements for each odor, or it can be

a combination. Each odor presented to the sensor array produces a signature or pattern characteristic of the odor. By presenting many different odors to the sensor array, a database of signatures is built up. This database of labeled odor signatures is used to train the pattern recognition system. The goal of this training process is to configure the recognition system to produce unique mappings of each odor so that an automated identification can be implemented (Erdi & Barna, 1991). The prototype electronic nose, shown in Figure 3, identifies odors from several common household chemicals.

Figure 2. Schematic of an artificial neural network

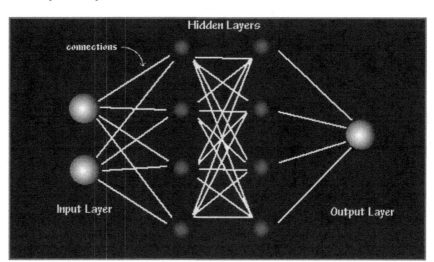

Although each sensor is designed for a specific chemical, each responds to a wide variety of chemical vapors. Collectively, these sensors respond with unique signatures (patterns) to different chemicals. During the training process, various chemicals with known mixtures are presented to the system. Artificial neural networks (ANNs), which have been used to analyze complex data and for pattern recognition, are showing promising results in chemical vapor recognition. When an ANN is combined with a sensor array, the number of detectable odors is generally greater than the number of sensors (Nakamoto, Nakahira, Hiramatsu, & Moriizumi, 2001). Also, less selective sensors which are generally less expensive can be used with this approach. Once the ANN is trained for odor recognition, operation consists of propagating the sensor data through the network. Electronic noses that incorporate ANNs have been demonstrated in the following applications (Bourgeois, Hogben, Pike, & Stuetz, 2003; Nakamoto & Hiramatsu, 2002; Stuetz, Engin, & Fenner, 1998):

- Quality control in the food industry
- Quality control of packaging material
- Medical diagnostics

- Environmental monitoring
- Perfume and aroma industry
- Control of beverages, e.g., wine and beer
- Tobacco industry
- Coffee industry
- Assessment of car interiors

In this study an example shall demonstrate how electronic noses may be used in the Multimedia Systems.

5. THE MONITORING SYSTEM

While the inclusion of visual, aural, and tactile senses into multimedia systems is widespread, the sense of smell has been largely ignored. We have studied a chemical vapor sensing system for the automated identification of chemical vapors. Our prototype chemical vapor sensing system is composed of an array of chemical sensors (usually gas sensors) coupled to an artificial neural network. The artificial neural network is used in the recognition and classification of different odors and is constructed as a standard multilayer feed-forward network trained with the back-propagation algorithm. When a chemical sensor

Figure 3. Prototype of electronic nose

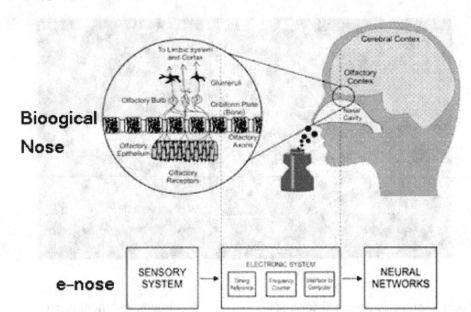

array is combined with an automated pattern identifier, it is often referred to as an electronic or artificial nose. It can be seen in Figure 4, our prototype electronic nose system has been integrated with online shopping systems to identify odors from common household odorants (Perfumes). The current shopping system allow only visual (through images and videos), and audio (sound and video files).

The prototyped ANN was constructed as a multilayer feed-forward network and was trained with the back-propagation of error algorithm by using a training set from the sensor database. This prototype was initially trained to identify odors of 20 different perfumes. This system allows users to obtain the desired data from a particular odorant (perfumes). There are two ways to obtain data by using a handheld odor meter (OMX-GR sensor):

- Real Time Sampling Data
- Memory Sampling Data

The system mainly contains three forms:

1. The first from, shown in Figure 5, allows user to choose among two buttons in which when the user clicks on any one of the buttons an open dialog box well appears (shown in Figure 6), asking the user to enter the name of the file.
2. Real Time sampling form (the second form) shown in Figure 7. It appears when the user chooses the real time sampling data button from the first from.
3. Memory sampling data form (the third form) shown in Figure 8. It appears when the user chooses the Memory sampling data button from the first from.

Finally this is the Artificial Neural Network System, which classifies the data and tests them. The system asks the user to enter some values and input file name, after learning session the system well create four new file, assume that the

Figure 4. On-line monitoring odor sensing system

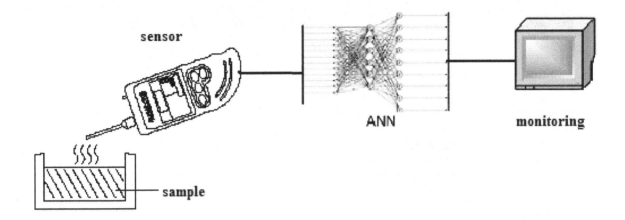

input file name is first_learning.dat, then it well create the following files:

- **First_learning_w.dat**: this file contains the weights.
- **First_learning_v.dat:** this file contains the value.
- **First_learningy.cns:** this file contain the
- **First_learning.err:** this file contains the error.

And for the output generation it well creates:

- **First_learninght.dat:** this file contains the output` of the testing session.

At the beginning the program well ask the user to enter L for learning, O for output generation or 1 to continue from old weights file.

Figure 5. The main form in the sensor program

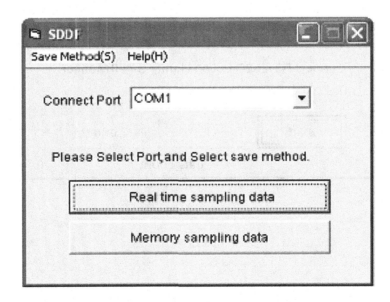

Figure 6. Open dialog box

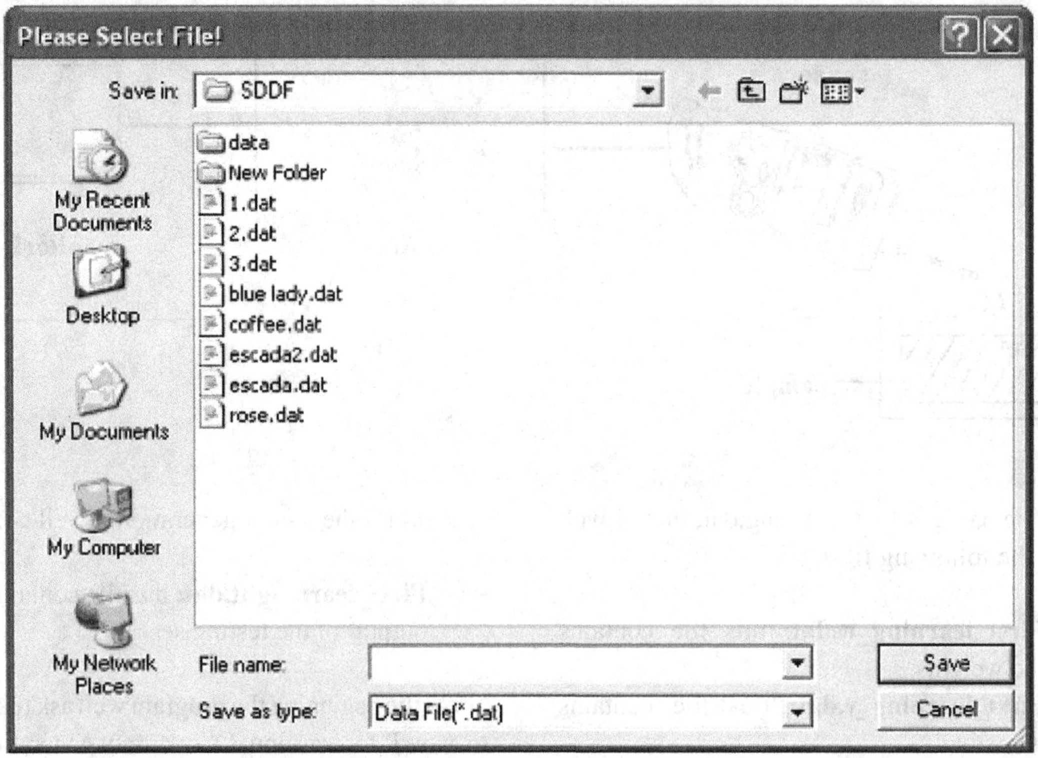

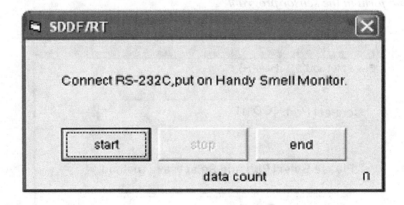

Figure 7. The Real time sampling form

Figure 8. The Memory sampling data form

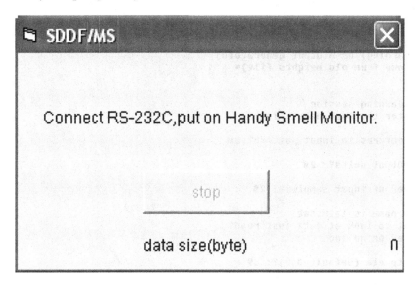

1. If the user chooses learning, the program well asks you to enter the task name that contains data.

   a. Then the user should enter the number of features in each input pattern, which in our case are 30 (each odor contain 30 numbers).

   b. Then the user should enter the number of output units which in our case 20 output (20 odor samples).

   c. Continued by entering the number of input samples, which are also 20 in our case.

   d. The program well search for the file that the user entered & if it found it then it well ask the user if he\she wants to take a look of the data in the file, just to read by entering yes or no.

   e. Then the user should enter the momentum rate value, and it's by default 0.9 and followed by the learning rate Alfa, which is by default 0.7.

   f. Enter the maximum number or iteration, by default its 1000, but its butter to enter a number that is greater than 1000.

   g. Then the program well asks the user to put the number of hidden layers, and a number of layer units for each layer.

   h. The last thing before starting the learning session, the program well ask the user if she\he wants to create an error file or not, if yes press 1 if no press 0.

The learning phase well start and the program well ask the user to wait until it finishes the training (Figure 9).

2. If the user chooses the testing, the program well asks the user if she\he wants to work on a different learning task or not.

After that it well ask the user for the testing input file name, if the user enters a correct file name it well asks the user to enter the number of patterns for processing.

6. CONCLUSION

The proposed ANN based approach addresses a significant limitation of the current Olfactory systems. These systems are designed for specific

Figure 9. The ANN program in the learning session

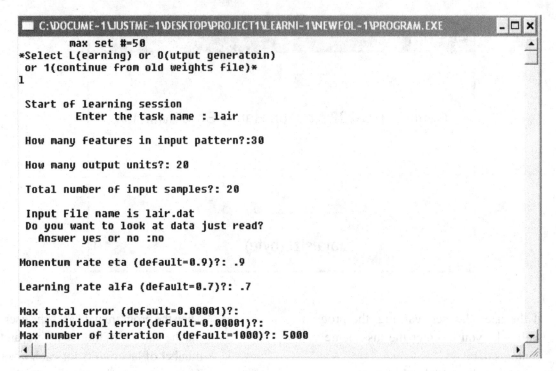

applications with a limited range of odors. However, systems that mimic more of the functionality of the human olfactory system will require a much larger set of sensing elements. In the proposed ANN approach the sensor array "smells" an odor, the sensor signals are digitized and fed into a computer, and the ANN (implemented in software) then identifies the chemical. This identification time is limited only by the response of the chemical sensors, but the complete process can be completed within seconds. The proposed ANN program is very useful for on-line odor recognition system, which has a various types of odor samples. The identified odors can then be transmitted to an odor regeneration system in the future. This feature is one of the most demanded option in the multimedia systems where response time is crucial to synchronize between multisen-

sory interfaces to produce an integrated media outcomes from different human senses.

Further research is planned for studying technical issues and usability on the integration of olfactory information into multisensory interfaces for several applications. The proposed ANN based olfactory system was conceived for the consumer electronic market attempting to integrate the largely absent smell medium, into modern multimedia systems. It can also be used in other environments such as industrial application to test products like food, beverages, and cosmetic items for process monitoring and quality control. Furthermore it can be used to develop multimedia educational applications such as performing chemical experiments to test smells and smoke from potentially dangerous gases in particular for e-learning applications. Moreover, multimedia systems can be implemented to gather information required to enhance real-time safety and security applications in particular for industrial processes where there are many toxic and hazards gases.

REFERENCES

Bourgeois, W., Hogben, P., Pike, A., & Stuetz, R. M. (2003). Development of a sensor array based measurement system for continuous monitoring of water and wastewater. *Sensors and Actuators. B, Chemical*, *88*(3), 312–319. doi:10.1016/S0925-4005(02)00377-5

Dyer, D. C., & Gardner, J. W. (1997). High-precision intelligent interface for a hybrid electronic nose. *Sensors and Actuators. A, Physical*, *62*(1-3), 724–728. doi:10.1016/S0924-4247(97)01546-X

Erdi, P., & Barna, G. (1991). Neurodynamic approach to odor processing. In *Proceedings of the Joint International Conference on Neural Networks*, Seattle, WA (pp. 653-656).

Gardner, J. W., & Bartlett, P. N. (1994). A brief history of electronic noses. *Sensors and Actuators. B, Chemical*, *18*(1-3), 210–211. doi:10.1016/0925-4005(94)87085-3

Hatfield, J. V., Neaves, P., Hicks, P. J., Persaud, K., & Travers, P. (1994). Towards an integrated electronic nose using conducting polymer sensors. *Sensors and Actuators. B, Chemical*, *18*(1-3), 221–228. doi:10.1016/0925-4005(94)87086-1

Keller, P. E., Kouzes, R. T., & Kangas, L. J. (1994). Three neural network based sensor systems for environmental monitoring. In *Proceedings of the IEEE Electro Conference,* Boston, MA (pp. 377-382).

Li, Z., & Hopfield, J. J. (1989). Modeling the olfactory bulb and its neural oscillatory processing. *Biological Cybernetics*, *61*, 379–392. doi:10.1007/BF00200803

Miwa, H., Umetsu, T., Takanishi, A., & Takanohu, H. (2001). Human-like robot head that has olfactory sensation and facial color expression. In *Proceedings of the IEEE International Conference on Robotics and Automation*, Seoul, Korea (pp. 459-464).

Mizsei, J., & Ress, S. (2002). Chemical images by artificial olfactory epithelia. *Sensors and Actuators. B, Chemical*, *83*(1-3), 164–168. doi:10.1016/S0925-4005(01)01035-8

Moncrieff, R. W. (1961). An instrument for measuring and classifying odors. *Journal of Applied Physiology*, *16*(4), 742–749.

Nakamoto, T., & Hiramatsu, H. (2002). Study of odor recorder for dynamical change of odor using QCM sensors and neural network. *Sensors and Actuators. B, Chemical*, *85*(3), 263–269. doi:10.1016/S0925-4005(02)00130-2

Nakamoto, T., Nakahira, Y., Hiramatsu, H., & Moriizumi, T. (2001). Odor recorder using active odor sensing system. *Sensors and Actuators. B, Chemical*, *76*(1-3), 465–469. doi:10.1016/S0925-4005(01)00587-1

Paeda, X. G., Melendi, D., Vilas, M., Garcia, R., Garcia, V., & Rodriguez, I. (2008). FESORIA: An integrated system for analysis, management and smart presentation of audio/video streaming services. *Multimedia Tools and Applications*, *39*(3), 379–412. doi:10.1007/s11042-007-0173-0

Pfeiffer, S., Lienhart, R., & Efflsberg, W. (2001). Scene determination based on video and audio features. *Multimedia Tools and Applications*, *15*(1), 59–81. doi:10.1023/A:1011315803415

Stuetz, R. M., Engin, G., & Fenner, R. A. (1998). Sewage odour measurements using a sensory panel and an electronic nose. *Water Science and Technology, 38*(3), 331–335. doi:10.1016/S0273-1223(98)00559-9

Wilkens, W. F., & Hartman, J. D. (1964). An electronic analog for the olfactory processes. *Journal of Food Science, 29*(3), 372–378. doi:10.1111/j.1365-2621.1964.tb01746.x

This journal was previously published in the International Journal of Technology Diffusion, Volume 2, Issue 3, edited by Ali Hussein Saleh Zolait, pp. 14-23, copyright 2011 by IGI Publishing (an imprint of IGI Global).

Chapter 5

The Role of a Collaborative Research Network (CRN) in Improving the Arabian Gulf Countries' Performance in Research and Innovation

Ali Al-Soufi
University of Bahrain, Bahrain

Jaflah Al-Ammary
University of Bahrain, Bahrain

ABSTRACT

Research and development is considered a main source of knowledge and innovation in the Gulf countries and Arab region. Therefore, building a Collaborative Research Network (CRN) in the Gulf is necessary for high quality and sustainable research. In this paper, the authors examine the role of CRN in improving Gulf countries' performance in research and innovation. Four objectives have been set: investigate the current situation regarding scientific research and CRN in the Gulf countries, identify factors that influence the building of a CRN, identify the impact and contribution of CRN in improving the Gulf countries' performance, and develop a model. To achieve these objectives, a quantitative method was adopted. A questionnaire was developed and distributed to 100 participants. The current paper presents the first stage of research that investigates the role of building CRN in improving the Gulf countries' performance in research and innovation. The next stage will examine the model of building CRN.

DOI: 10.4018/978-1-4666-2791-8.ch005

INTRODUCTION

As a result of the knowledge-based global economy and globalization, knowledge and innovation have become the crucial factors in the development of successful economics (El-Baba, 2006; Bashshur, 2007). Research and development (R&D) is considered as the main source of knowledge and innovation in the Gulf countries and Arab region in general. Therefore, Gulf region's chances for improving their market position and gain a sustainable competitive advantage will be impacted by the lack of research dedicated for their region (El-Baba, 2006). In fact, the current situation of the scientific research and R&D in the Gulf countries is not stable and is experiencing many problems such as funding support, private sectors involvement, quality and quantity of the researches conducted and their compatibility for the Gulf region and alike. Moreover, with continues development in the information technology and communication and the emergent of knowledge economy, the traditional ways of conducting research are changing dramatically. As such, most of the researches nowadays are conducted through multidisciplinary collaborations among research centers, industry and educational institutions. Through such collaborative effort in which stakeholders work together to enhance their understanding of the affected communities, innovation, and knowhow exchanging, sharing and creation can be facilitated (Arab Knowledge Report, 2009; Al-Faham 2006). Consequently, building Collaborative Research Network (CRN) in the Gulf countries is an essential action for building high quality and sustainable research, enabling multidisciplinary research environment and improving the educational system in the Gulf countries (Al-Faham, 2006; Peters & McNeese, 2005).

The current research aims at investigating the role of building CRN in improving the Arabian Gulf Countries' performance in research and innovation. Therefore, the research will be conducted into two stages. In the first stage factors that influence the building of CRN will be identified and the impact of building CRN will be recognized. In the second stage and based on the results of the first stage, a research model for building CRN in the Gulf countries will be developed and examined. The current paper presents the first stage of the research. Four objectives have been set for this stage: investigate the current situation regarding the research and building a CRN in the Gulf countries such as the enablers and inhibitors of building such network, identify factors that influence the building of a CRN, identify the impact and contribution of building a CRN in improving the Gulf countries' performance in research and innovation, and developing a model for building a CRN in the Gulf countries.

This paper consists of eight sections; each section will touch a significant component of this research. The following sections spot the light on the literature review on the current situation regarding the scientific research and R&D in the Gulf countries, the need for building a CRN, factors impacting the building of a CRN, and the impact of building CRN. The research methodology for this study is then illustrated. Description of data analysis is also presented. Finally, the findings of this study are discussed and a conclusion is presented and made ready for the research centers and institutions those intend to participate in building CRN.

THE CURRENT STATUS OF SCIENTIFIC RESEARCH AND R&D IN THE GULF COUNTRIES

Gulf countries are providing vital efforts in developing and improving the scientific research and innovation. However, the level of research and development in these countries is very low compared to some Arabic countries and most others regions of the world (Bashshur, 2007). In fact, the current research environment in the Gulf countries has had a negative impact on the research performance and innovation (Knowledge Report,

2009). R&D endeavors in the Gulf countries are fragmented (El-Baba, 2006). The Arab countries – including the gulf region – have a low ranking in R&D and technology innovation (Sasson, 2007). They actually account for just 0.7% of the total world researchers, although their population account for almost 5% of the total world population (El-Baba, 2006). Moreover, the fund spent by Gulf countries on research and development is very low. They spend less than 50 thousand United States dollars per researchers (El-Baba, 2006) and mostly all research in universities and centers in these countries are sponsored by government (Bashshur, 2007). In addition, in the Gulf countries, the main motivators for conducting a research are the publishing and the promotions which influence the productivity and the performance of the conducted researches (Knowledge Report, 2009). Furthermore, priority of the research and especially the scientific one is given to engineering and technical fields (Bashshur, 2007) rather than to solve problems of society and developing the region economic and community. Finally, the lack of communication and vulnerable relationships between business and industry on one hand, and academic and non-academic research institutions on the other hand, further exacerbate the situation of the research in the Gulf countries (ESCWA, 2005; Alaw, 2008).

THE NEED FOR BUILDING CRN

The globalization has increased the Gulf countries' awareness to the essential need to invest in R&D in many of their sectors such as education (Bashshur, 2007) and industry. Globalization with research, development and innovation as key factors, can offer these countries the opportunities to break through markets, build alliances and make joint ventures (Bashshur, 2007). Therefore, research centers and organizations need to establish a link between the sponsored researches and the community of educational and industrial firms. In addition, they should improve their traditional

ways of conducting researches by making more effective use and integration of ICT in research and development value-adding process. Indeed, there is a need for building a CRN to support the multidisciplinary and multi-institutional approaches as bases for effective promotion of the targeted sector in member countries (ESCWA, 2005). Building CRN will also facilitate the creation of virtual research communities and establish virtual center of excellence to service priority areas for partner institution in the Gulf region (ESCWA, 2005; Plucknett & Smith, 2005). CRN furthermore will play a major role to attract international level of researchers in general, but specifically the migrated Arab talents (Brains), who would still be loyal to their countries but not welling to physically migrate back from western more scientifically advanced countries that have access to huge research resources, i.e., the virtual return of Arab migrated brains.

FACTORS IMPACTING THE BUILDING OF CRN

Building CRN in a region such as the Gulf countries could be challenging. In fact, there are many factors that may impact the building of CRN in the Gulf countries either positively or negatively. In the following sections some of these factors are discussed.

EDUCATIONAL SYSTEM

Educational system in the Gulf countries is considered as one of the main obstacles that may prevent the adoption of CRN. While, there is a shift from education for individual and conventionality to education for creativity innovation and partnership, educational systems in the Gulf countries still follow traditional models (Bashshur, 2007). Most of the universities in the Gulf countries adopt traditional models based on rote learning. Ineffective tools such rote learning focuses on the memorization and avoid the understanding of the subject, as a result, students will not be able to innovate and mix scientific knowledge with practical applications (Al-Rashdan, 2007). Therefore, educational models have failed in the Gulf countries as any other Arab countries, to create qualified scientists capable of tackling the region problems especially those related to the Water and energy and improving public health services (UNESCO, 2010). Moreover, universities' academic staffs constitute the majority of researchers in the Gulf region. However, there are many problems encountered by the researchers in such universities. Academic staff burdened with teaching duties of twice the scope of those of their colleagues in western universities. In most cases they have a load of 10 to 20 hours per week; this is in addition to their other duties such as advising, supervising and participation in different committees. Moreover, there is a lack of clear strategy for the incentives or reward system for full time scientific research, which create insufficient competition environment for faculty members to earn high positions through research and studies (Al-Rashdan, 2007). Therefore, many academic staffs have turned to other professions that realize higher return or join the group of migration from the Arab region (Arab Knowledge Report, 2009). Finally, in most of the universities and academic institutions there are no specific research strategies or policies. Therefore, no clear objectives serving the goal of the university or society are identified and make clear for the researchers (Al-Rashdan, 2007). Consequently, most of the conducted researches in the Gulf region are done without a purpose and the innovative researchers usually work in difficult conditions (Al-Rashdan, 2007).

ORGANIZATIONAL CULTURE AND STRUCTURE

To be part of a collaborative environment, organization needs to be ready for changing and re-culturing. Penny, Ali, Farah, and Smith (2000)

state that "the collaboration needs to be treated with caution in view of potential clashes over values and different interests within a research team." Moreover, traditional nature of research can make research teamwork more difficult and complex (Penny, Ali, Farah, & Smith, 2000). At the level of individual organizations participating in a collaborative networking, changes in culture and practices are needed to enable research networks to "functional boundaries" (El-Baba, 2006). Moreover, the organization should enhance a mutual trust environment and adopt a good reward system; thereby members can participate effectively in the collaborative network. Having such acknowledging and rewarding efforts will also exert into network projects and enhance the productivity of the researchers (El-Baba, 2006). Organizational structure needs also to be flexible and dynamic as the formal or hierarchal organization presents a substantial obstacle for adopting a collaborative network (El-Baba, 2006). Research and development in the Gulf countries may also be constraint by the absence or weakness of the institutional structures, management, policies or lack of staff (Arab Knowledge Report, 2009).

FINANCIAL AND FUNDING POLICIES

Research activity in the Arab region is abnormally low in terms of allocated funds (Bushshur, 2007). The current resources for financing support include: budget for educational scholarships, budget of existing research centers, research budgets of various industrial and government organizations in the region, allocation and commitment from government, and foreign research foundations (Al-Faham, 2006). However, in such developing countries the funded research has long been problematic, with few "success" stories upon their conclusion (Arab Knowledge Report, 2009). A range of reasons for this are that 80% of the fund that is dedicated by the Arab countries for R&D is provided by the government sectors as the private funding account just for 8% (UNESCO, 2010).

The percentage of fund provided by the private sectors in the Gulf countries reached as minimum as 2.2% from the total fund allocated for research. Moreover, there is lack in the cooperation and coordination between the research institutions, economic and business organizations, and educational institutions in funding more productive research and sustainable projects. Furthermore, most of the investments in the Gulf countries made through turnkey contracts which make little provision for technology transfer; hence they do not generate local skilled and knowledgeable employment (Bushshur, 2007).

INFORMATION AND COMMUNICATION TECHNOLOGY (ICT)

The contemporary technology has opened new ways for research and development. The advances in computers and communication technologies have enable many organizations to leverage knowledge and innovation. However, the Gulf countries are still facing a challenge in finding the best ways to optimize the usage of the huge resources offered by ICT and using them effectively (Bashshur, 2007). Gulf countries are immediately called upon to make full use of ICT in their educational system, governmental sectors, private sectors and a like (Bashshur, 2007). ICT can be used to facilitate the collaboration between research institutions and support the multidisciplinary approaches and inter-institutional collaboration (ESCWA, 2005). As such, the emerging powerful systems such as Internet, Intranet, and conferencing systems such as Webex, OOVOO, MS Net meeting, and Skype (specially that they are usually provided free of charge or very low cost) allow people to collaborate and share their complementary knowledge, without constraining them to geographic location and time (Al-Ma'aitah, 2008). Moreover, a portal to host a variety of databases and electronic publications in

the different areas and especially that relevance to academic and enterprise development can be designed and supported by ICTs (ESCWA, 2005). However, adopting ICT in the organization needs to be supported by its structure, arrangements, and information sharing and decision-making processes in order to yield the full benefits of new ICTs (ESCWA, 2005).

GOVERNMENTAL ROLES AND SUPPORT

Although the impact of scientific research on production, economic development and technical progress is noticeable, governments in the Gulf countries do not set accurate policies or define a clear strategic target for scientific research (Alaw, 2008). Governmental and corporate policies are crucial for promoting CRN that aim at enhancing sectoral and national competitiveness. In the Gulf countries the research centers are modest and so are the resources available to drive their cooperation and networking (ESCWA, 2005). Because of the national capabilities of the research centers in the Gulf countries, the role of industry federations and chambers is at most importance (ESCWA, 2005).

ETHICAL ISSUES FOR COLLABORATIVE RESEARCH

Recently, most of the researches are sponsored by different agencies such as government, universities, and private companies; consequently, growing attention is being paid to many ethical issues (Lairumbi, Molyneux, Snow, Marsh, Peshu, & English, 2008). The ethical practices certainly will not ensure good research outcomes. However, lack of ethical considerations or poor ethical practices may result in biased subject selection, poor compliance, duplication of other works, and other factors that may complicate the interpretation of data and impact the quality of research results and its compatibility to the regional environment (Caballero, 2002). According to Lairumbi, Molyneux, Snow, Marsh, Peshu, and English (2008), many ethical aspects are needed to be considered for its "capacity for generating social value locally through the generation of knowledge that can lead to generalize the research results". For instant, there is a contradictory between the need to publish and make results available for public and to keep information confidential and protected by intellectual property rights such as patents (European Commission, 2007). As a result, it has been noticed that many organizations have set a formal agreement between all relevant parties on collaborative network as a way to protect their intellectual property prior to embarking on collaborative research project (ESCWA, 2005). In the Gulf countries situation regarding ethics is very complicated as there are many political restrictions and other impediments. For example there are many restrictions on conducting systematic survey research, the degree to which representative national samples could be drawn, and the extent to which sensitive questions could be asked (Tessler & Jamal, 2006). In addition, in some cases and for certain types of researches, official permission is required and it is sometime necessary to submit survey instruments for review which make conducting research more complex (Caballero, 2002). Besides, research ethics in the Gulf countries are affected by many other factors such as: culture, both national and organizational, social and environmental factors, and economic and political conditions (Caballero, 2002).

THE IMPACT OF BUILDING CRN

CRN is highly relevant to the Arab region and especially the Gulf countries. As a means of collaborative knowledge creation and dissemination, CRN could help these countries in eliminating their impediments and exploiting their opportunities which, in turn, will help in overcoming knowledge

gaps and resources scarcity that are embedded in their environment (El-Baba, 2006). Institutions as well as individuals can benefit from the collaborative research. CRN can increase exchange, cooperation and communication between different institutions and groups working in similar fields (Bushshur, 2007). Consequently, it will allow the researchers to work within a complex cross-nationally environment, establish trust, understanding their roles within a group, and clarifying professional frames and ethical values (Penny, Ali, Farah, & Smith, 2000). Moreover, it can provides opportunities for participants to learn about new methodologies and research approaches, upgrade their skills and strengthen their ability to conduct research designed to overcome constraints and increase their production and leadership skills (Plucknett & Smith, 2005). On the other hand, by the engagement of different stakeholders, a local ownership of a research agenda will be adopted what is relevant to the priorities and needs of the country or region (ESCWA, 2005). As a result the common problems faced by the Gulf countries will be solved and cooperation and resources sharing in the acquisition and dissemination of modern technologies will be promoted among member institutions (ESCWA, 2005), thereby, contributing to enterprise growth and development (Plucknett & Smith, 2005; ESCWA, 2005).

Building a CRN in the Gulf countries will open an opportunity for those researchers around the world in general and the migrated Arab researchers in particular, which do not have capability to travel or migrate back, to fill the capacity gap problem of these countries. On the researcher side, they would not only gain financially, but also they would play as an agent for knowledge transfer from more advanced technological countries to less advanced and more expertise scarce countries, i.e., they would play as Virtual Researchers. In addition, CRN would contribute greatly in the higher education especially PhD programs, where it will bridge the gap of academic supervisors in certain specialized disciplines that a Gulf countries lack expertise. There are many cases, that working students are forced to travel to other western countries to gain their PhD certificates because their specializations are not available or their local universities are not very credible. CRN will help very much in the concept of joint supervision of such candidates. Hence opens up an opportunity for many smart students to pursue their higher studies from their homeland, while they are working.

RESEARCH METHODOLOGY

The current research aims at investigating the role of building CRN in improving Gulf Countries' performance in research and innovation. The current paper introduces a research in progress as it presents the first stage of the research. To achieve the objectives of the first stage, a quantitative method has been adopted. A questionnaire has been developed by the authors for the purpose of the current research. The questionnaire consists of three parts. The first part addresses the demography and personal information. The second part tackles the opinion of the participant regarding some characteristics of the proposed CRN such as types and fields of research that can be conducted and the enablers and inhibitors of building such network. The third part is the main part of the questionnaire as it presents questions on the factors that influence the building of CRN

in the Gulf countries and the impact of building such network in their performance in research and innovation. The study sample is comprised of academics and leaders from universities, research centers and R&D firms among the Gulf countries. One hundred and fifty surveys have been distributed to the selected samples by mail, e-mail or handled to them personally.

DATA ANALYSIS AND RESULTS

The survey instrument provides a response rate of 65% which can be considered as reasonable rate bearing in mind the difficulty in reaching strategic and academic people scattering among the Gulf countries.

Demographic characteristics of the overall participants are presented in Table 1. The results in the table revealed that most of the participants are from educational institution and universities (70%) which consist of three universities and one institute among the Gulf countries.

However, research centers account just for 2.4%. Consequently, it can be noticed that most of the participants are academic staff or researchers in educational institutions or universities (66%) and only 4% are researcher from research centers. Moreover, the results show that most of the participants have Master degrees and above (88%) and more than 10 years of experience in teaching and research (56%).

Table 1. Selected Characteristics of the samples

Partner	%	Partner	%
Public universities	93	Nongovernmental organizations	29
Private universities	73	Industrial sectors	78
Academic research centers	93	Private organizations	36.5
Public administration research centers	68	Research and development firms	76
Governmental organizations	49	International agencies	36

CHARACTERISTICS OF THE PROPOSED CRN

There were 100% positive responses when the participants were asked if they believe that building a CRN in the Gulf countries would benefit the researchers or not. The participants then were asked to identify some characteristics of the proposed CRN such the anticipated partners that should participate in building CRN and types and fields of research that can be conducted within such network. The results are demonstrated in Table 2, Table 3, and Table 4.

The results in Table 2 show that public universities, academic research centers, industrial sectors and R&D firms are identified as the most appropriate partners for CRN (93%, 93%, 78%, and 76%, respectively). Moreover, applied research has been identified by 93% of the participants as the most applicable type of research to be conducted in CRN as seen in Table 3.

According to the fields of research that are suit the Gulf countries, IT and computing research were identified as the most suitable one for the Gulf countries (78%) followed by water and energy, financial and economic, food and nutrition and medical and pharmaceutical researches (59%, 54%, 54%, and 54%, respectively). However, political research recognized to be the least field in which research can be conducted in the Gulf countries.

ENABLERS AND INHIBITORS FOR BUILDING CRN

The participants were asked to identify the enablers and inhibitors of building CRN in the Gulf countries, the results are presented in Table 5 and Table 6.

The results in Table 5 revealed that the main enablers for building CRN in the Gulf countries according to the opinion of most of the participants are the existence of pioneers who are able to manage the idea, make it happen and keep the effort

Table 2. Parties that should participate in CRN

Partner	%	Partner	%
Public universities	93	Nongovernmental organizations	29
Private universities	73	Industrial sectors	78
Academic research centers	93	Private organizations	36.5
Public administration research centers	68	Research and development firms	76
Governmental organizations	49	International agencies	36

Table 3. Types of research that could be conducted in CRN

Type	%
Applied researches	93
Theoretical (pure) researches	73

Table 4. The enablers for building CRN in the Gulf countries

Field	%	Field	%
Agriculture	41	Food and nutrition	54
Business and management	32	Oil and petroleum	49
Water and energy	59	Medical and pharma-ceutical	54
Social and History	7.3	IT and computing	78
Financial and economic	54	political	2.4
Hotels and tourism services	7.3	Environmental research	71

Table 5. The enablers for building CRN in the Gulf countries

Enablers	%
Existence of good national telecommunication infrastructures	51
The support of top management of research institutions	68
The existence of pioneers who were able to manage the idea, make it happen and keep the effort ongoing	71
Willingness of the research institutions to share risk	32
The believe that CRN will have a long term implication for cost saving	44
The believe that CRN will help in knowledge creation and sharing	51
The believe that CRN will stimulate creativity of internal research resources	27
The believe that CRN would help in filling the capacity gaps (expertise) that could exist in GCC research institutions	44

Table 6. The inhibitors for building CRN at gulf countries

Inhibitors	%
Cost productivity differentials	32
Shortage of skills (researchers availability)	63
Shortage of financial resources	63
Confidentiality of research conducted or Un-willingness of sharing knowledge.	41
Exploitation of property rights (copy rights)	24
Legal and political constraints on building CRN partners	44
Lack of disciplinary approach (inexistence of processes and policies to manage the CRN)	41
Lack of ICT standardization (compatibility issues of technology used by CRN partners)	10
The available of few global successful model of CRN	15

ongoing (71%) and the support of top management of research institutions (68%).

However, the results show that the willingness of the research institutions to share risk and the ability of CRN to stimulate creativity of internal research resources are believed to be an enabler for building CRN in the Gulf countries by the minimum percentage of the participants (32% and 27%, respectively). On the other hand, the results in Table 6 clearly presented both shortage of skills and f financial resources as the main inhibitors for building CRN (63% and 63%, respectively). However, lack of ICT standardization (10%) and the available of few global successful models of CRN (15%) have been revealed to emboss less constraint in building CRN in the Gulf countries.

INHIBITORS, FACTORS AND IMPACTS OF BUILDING CRN IN THE GULF COUNTRIES

The participants were asked to provide their own opinion on ten items that were developed to measure some factors that may impact the building of CRN in the Gulf countries. All items were measured on a five-point Likert-scale anchored at both extremes to 1 (strongly disagree) and 5 (strongly agree). The analysis of these items revealed that there are five main factors that may influence positively or negatively the building of CRN as shown in Table 7.

To identify the impact of building CRN in improving the Gulf Countries' performance in research and innovation, twenty one items were developed which are measured on a five-point Likert-scale. The results presented in Table 8 show that quality and quantities of research – building research capacity (78%) and knowledge creation (84%) were identified as the factors that most impact building CRN in the Gulf countries.

DISCUSSION AND CONCLUSION

This paper presents a research in progress as it presented the first stage of the research which aims at investigating the role of building CRN in improving the Gulf countries' performance in research and innovation. The findings of the research revealed that building CRN is essential for enhancing the research capacity and performance in the Gulf countries. Both applied and theoretical research were proposed to be conducted in the field of IT and computing, water and energy, financial and economic, food and nutrition and medical and pharmaceutics. However, to build CRN in the Gulf countries a consideration should be paid to some barriers and inhibitors. One of the main inhibitors is the need for skillful researchers who are able to work collaboratively, manage and monitor the research progress within the CRN. Another inhibitor is the funding. As it has been mentioned before, that there is a need to increase the funding provided for the research and that

Table 7. Factors influence the building CRN at Gulf countries

Factors	Agree	Neutral	Disagree
Educational system and research centers	74%	20%	6%
Financial and funding policies	85%	12%	3%
Organizational culture and structure	78%	17%	5%
Ethical and political issues	39%	37%	24%
ICT infrastructure	68%	24.5%	7.5%

Table 8. The impact of building CRN in Gulf countries

Impact	Agree	Neutral	Disagree
Quality and quantities of research (research capacity)	78%	6%	16%
Researches' satisfactions	76%	14%	10%
Development at community and regional level	75%	6%	19%
Innovation and commercialization of research	76%	19%	5%
Knowledge sharing and creation	84%	13.6%	2.4%

private sector should contribute in the development of the research capacity.

Moreover, the research's findings revealed that the main factors that influence the building of CRN are education system and research centers, financial and funding policies, organizational culture and structure, and information and communication technology infrastructure. Although the findings of the research show a low level of acceptance (39%) of ethical issues to be a critical factor for building CRN, the authors believe that ethical issues need to be considered and its impact in building CRN needs to be evaluated and examined. This is because in the Gulf countries, ethical and political situations are not stable and are challenging. Regarding the impacts of building CRN in the Gulf countries' research performance and innovation, the research findings have revealed five impacts; building research capacity, researchers' satisfaction, innovation, commercialization of

Figure 1. A research model for building CRN in the Gulf countries

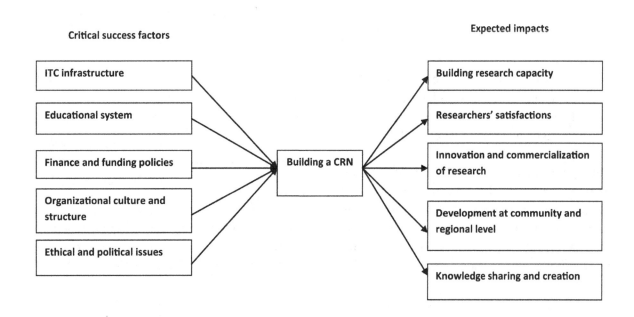

research, development at community and regional level and knowledge sharing and creation.

As a next step for the research, and based on the finding of the first stage, a model for building CRN at Gulf counties has been developed as depicted in Figure 1. The model demonstrates that there are five factors have a direct impact on building CRN in the Gulf countries. Moreover, the figure shows four expected impacts for building such collaborative network. The next stage of the research will examine the model of building CRN to check the existing of such relationships and impact.

Building CRN can be viewed as strategic tools for leveraging information and knowledge sharing, and accessing a greater capacity to innovate, which is imperative for building knowledge societies and economy in the Gulf countries (ESCWA, 2005; El-Baba, 2006). Therefore and as a first steps toward building CRN, Gulf countries should make more emphases on the establishment of research foundations, an effective technology transfer system, sustaining a well established ethical and political strategy to support research and innovation, initiating a mechanism to link research to the industrial sector, and building an integrated Gulf countries research fund (Al-Faham, 2006).

The current research presents a structured set of guidelines to help start and operate research networks in developing countries. It is ultimately intended to encourage the development of a collaborative research network in the Gulf countries. The findings of this research is believed to enhance the awareness of the researcher centers, educational organizations, and industries in the Gulf and other Arab countries and attract their attention to the importance of having CRN in improving research, up skilling their participants, stimulating their nation's ability to conduct research designed to bridge the gap in innovation and knowledge building and transfer.

REFERENCES

Al-Faham, M. (2006, November 14-15). *Networks of international collaboration: key to research advancement.* Paper presented at the Arab World Conference on the Issue and Problems of Scientific Research, Alexandria, Egypt.

Al-Ma'aitah, M. (2008). Impact of using electronic collaborative media on knowledge sharing phase. In *Proceedings of the 7th WSEAS International Conference on System Science and Simulation in Engineering*, Stevens Point, WI (pp. 152-158).

Al-Rashdan, A. (2009). Higher education in the Arab world: hopes and challenges. *Arab Insight*, *2*(6), 77–90.

Alwa, I. (2008). Scientific research in Arab countries- facts and figures (Web log post). *The MEMRI Economic*. Retrieved from http://memrieconomicblog.org/bin/content.cgi?article=91

Bashshur, M. (2007, May 25-26). The impact of globalization and research in Arab states. In *Proceedings of the 2nd Regional Research Seminar for Arab States*, Rabat, Morocco.

Caballero, B. (2002). Ethical issues for collaborative research in developing countries. *The American Journal of Clinical Nutrition*, *76*, 717–720.

El-baba, J. (2006), *Networking research, development and innovation in the Arab countries.* Beirut, Lebanon: United Nation Economic and social commission for Western Asia (ESCWA).

ESCWA. (2005). *Networking research development and innovation in Arab countries (Paper No. E/ESCWA/SDPD/2005/2)*. New York, NY: United Nations.

European Commission. (2007). *Improving knowledge transfer between research institutions and industry across Europe*. Brussels, Belgium: Author.

Lairumbi, G. M., Molyneux, S., Snow, R. W., Marsh, K., Peshu, N., & English, M. (2008). Promoting the social value of research in Kenya: Examining practical aspects of collaborative partnerships using an ethical framework. *Social Science & Medicine, 67*, 734–747. doi:10.1016/j.socscimed.2008.02.016

Penny, A. J., Ali, M. A., Farah, I., Ostberg, S., & Smith, R. L. (2000). A study of cross national collaborative research: reflecting on experience in Pakistan. *International Journal of Educational Development, 20*, 443–455. doi:10.1016/S0738-0593(00)00019-5

Peters, G., & McNeese, R. M. (2008). *Collaborative research in a post-Katrina environment: The facilitation communication and ethical considerations of university researchers.* Retrieved from http://creativecommons.org/licenses/by/2.o/cox.org/content/m17676/1.1

Plucknett, D. L., & Smith, N. J. H. (2005). *The potential of collaborative research networks in developing countries.* Retrieved from http://www,fao.org/wairclocs/ilri/x5443e/x5443eo5.htm

Arab Knowledge Report. (2009). *Toward productive intercommunication for knowledge.* Dubai, UAE: Alghurair Printing.

Sassan, A. (2007, May 24-25). *Research and development in the Arab states: the impact of globalization, facts and perspectives.* Paper presented at the UNESCO Forum on Higher Education, Research and Knowledge, Rabat, Morocco.

Tessler, M., & Jamal, A. (2006). Political attitude research in the Arab world: emerging opportunities, *PSC Online, 39*(3).

UNESCO. (2010). *The current states of scientific around the world.* Paris, France: Author.

This journal was previously published in the International Journal of Technology Diffusion, Volume 2, Issue 3, edited by Ali Hussein Saleh Zolait, pp. 24-35, copyright 2011 by IGI Publishing (an imprint of IGI Global).

Section 2
Global Technology and System Adoption

Chapter 6

A Comparative Study of the Effects of Culture on the Deployment of Information Technology

George Ditsa
Tshwane University of Technology, South Africa

Shayma Al-Kobaisi
United Arab Emirates University

Saleh Alwahaishi
Technical University of Ostrava, Czech Republic

Václav Snášel
Technical University of Ostrava, Czech Republic

ABSTRACT

Culture is thought to be the most difficult to isolate, define, and measure in the adoption and use of IT (Information Technology) (Hassan & Ditsa, 1999). Consequently, the impact of culture on the adoption and use of IT does not feature prominently in Information Systems (IS) literature. As cultural factors are important to the success of IT adoption and use, this research paper examines culture's impact on the adoption and use of IT in the United Arab Emirates (UAE). The results of the study were compared along eight cultural dimensions with a study on the adoption and use of IT in developing and developed countries. The results are also used to identify issues that concern the relationship of culture and IT and their implications for IT adoption and use in the UAE. The study results are further used to suggest ways of bridging the digital divide between the UAE and developed countries.

INTRODUCTION

Technology is believed to be culturally neutral and that the process of development, adoption and use of technology is uniform across countries, once basic economic and political conditions are satis-fied (World Bank, 1994). This review observed that many technology projects, including infor-mation technology (IT), in developing countries failed because the designs were not sufficiently tailored to those countries' history and industrial traditions. There are problems that cannot be

DOI: 10.4018/978-1-4666-2791-8.ch006

attributed to the technology process, but rather the cultural differences between designers of the technology and the recipients. And unlike technologies before it, IT is more of a social system deployed in businesses to do things faster, better and smarter (gaining competitive advantage) (Jessup & Valacich, 2008). It is true culture may not be the only factor that influences the adoption and use of IT. Others such as economy, politics, social factors, and education and skill levels may also be deciding factors.

Hasan and Ditsa (1997, 1999) studied the adoption and use of IT in three regions of widely diverse cultures. They conclude that culture is an important ingredient in the identity of the IT products themselves and influences the impact of IT adoption and use in different cultures. Indeed, a study by Avison and Malaurent (2007) also concludes that cultural differences were the main factors for the failure of the deployment of an ERP system in China. Similarly, Kevin et al. (2007) found that culture has effect on the level of use of built-it-now auctions by sellers.

This research carried out a focused study on the impact of culture on the adoption and use of IT in the UAE. The results were compared along eight cultural dimensions and contrasted with the studies of Hasan and Ditsa (1997, 1999). The results of the study were also used to identify issues of concern for the relationship of culture and IT and their implications for IT adoption and use in the UAE. The study results were further used to suggest ways of bridging the digital divide between the UAE and the developed countries.

The rest of the paper is structured as follows. We first present background definitions of IT, culture and the cultural dimensions used in this study, and the term 'digital divide.' Next, we present the study, in which we outlined the methodology, the data collection methods used, and the three chosen regions for this study. This is followed by how we reduced and displayed the data collected from the study. We then present the application of the results of the study to three issues of culture and IT, followed by discussion and the implications

of the study for the UAE and the IT industry. Finally, we present the limitations of the study, a conclusion and suggestions for further study.

BACKGROUND DEFINITIONS

Information Technology

The term Information Technology (IT) has many connotations in a variety of contexts. We use the term in the context of this paper to primarily mean the development and use of information systems (IS) which are based on computerized hardware and software to support business processes of organizations. Similarly, the term "adoption and use of IT" is used to mean not only the making of decisions to acquire the technology but also its development, implementation and use.

Despite the increase in the development of hardware and software of which the IT is composed of, most of these are still originating from North America, particularly the USA, many of which are from the "silicon valley" in California. Global information systems, such as ERP and SAP, which are used to run businesses worldwide are mainly from the western culture and impose a western way of doing business. More often, the designers and developers of these systems are not aware of the inherent cultural bias that these systems possess. This usually leads to failures of these systems in other cultures (Avison & Malaurent, 2007).

Culture

Culture can be thought of as the beliefs, philosophy, shared values, attitudes, customs, norms, rituals, common practices, and traditions which govern the ways of living of a group of people. Macquarie Dictionary defines the culture of a society as:

The sum total of ways of living built up by a group of human beings, which is transmitted from one generation to another.

Hofstede (1991, p. 5) defines culture as: "the collective programming of the mind which distinguishes the members of one group or category of people from another." More simply, culture is shared values of a particular group of people and culture reflects the core values and beliefs of individuals, which are formed during childhood and reinforced throughout life (Shore & Vankatachalam, 1996). This implies that culture is all pervasive and has a strong influence on all our undertakings. It is not however easy to measure and hence it is a difficult variable to use in a rigorous research.

Hofstede (1991) further looks at the manifestation of culture as symbols, heroes, rituals and values, which he illustrates as the concentric skins of an onion: with symbols forming the outer skin; followed by heroes; rituals; and values as the innermost. Symbols are the most visible attributes of a culture, whereas values form its innermost and deepest manifestations and are difficult to change. Values, according to Hofstede, are broad tendencies to prefer certain states of affairs over others. That is, they are what make a group or a category of people distinguish between good and evil, clean and dirty, beautiful and ugly, natural and unnatural, normal and abnormal, logical and paradoxical, and rational and irrational. According to psychologists, these values are acquired unconsciously at an early age by the individual in a cultural group and are difficult to change in later years of the individual.

National culture is described as the embodiment of the dominant cultures of a nation which distinguishes the citizens of that nation from other nations (Hofstede, 1991). The national facets of culture will include the practices and values as well as language, education, social organization, religion, law, and politics. Strictly speaking, national culture is an integration of the cultures of the societies within that nation: usually with the dominant cultures been seen as the national culture. There are usually strong forces in a nation that

lead to further integration towards: one dominant national language; a national education system; a national army; a national political system; a national market for skills, products and services; and a national representation in sporting events with a strong symbolic and emotional appeal. It is important to note that national culture has a significant impact and influence on corporate (organizational) culture (Hofstede, 1985, 1991).

Schein defines organizational culture as follows:

Organizational culture is the pattern of basic assumptions that a given group has invented, discovered, or developed in learning to cope with its problems of external adaptation and internal integration, and that have worked well enough to be considered valid and therefore to be taught to new members as the correct way to perceive, think, and feel in relation to those problems. (Schein, 1984, p. 3)

Schein's definition above is seen by Avison and Myers (1995) as perhaps having the most influence on IS research into IT and organizational culture. They argue that this definition and other definitions, and the general concept of culture are rather too simplistic. Drawing more on the literature from anthropology they argue that "cultures are contested, ever-changing and emergent, they are invented and re-invented ... through which people create and recreate the worlds in which they live" (Avison & Myers, 1995, p. 52-53). However, the question the authors failed to provide answer to is from where does the "production" of culture start? Certainly, the general view of the concept of culture is that culture is dynamic - ever-changing and emergent - through which people created and recreated their way of living as social beings. The values and other ways of living inherited by the society or group of people will have significant influence on creating and recreating the ways of living of the new generations of a society. Put another way, the metamorphosis of the culture of a society will build on the past ways of living (culture) of the society or group of people.

The Eight Cultural Dimensions

For the purpose of our study we adopted the eight cultural dimensions from Hasan and Ditsa (1999). Brief definitions of the eight dimensions are as follows:

- **Power Distance:** The extent to which the members of a society accept that the power in institutions and organizations is distributed unequally.
- **Uncertainty Avoidance:** The degree to which members of a society feel uncomfortable with uncertainty and ambiguity.
- **Individualism:** Preference for a loosely knit social framework in which individuals take care of themselves and their immediate family as opposed to *collectivism* which is preference for a tightly knit social framework in which individuals expect their relatives or others in their group to look after them in exchange for unquestioning loyalty.
- **Masculinity:** Preference for achievement, heroism, assertiveness and material success as opposed to *feminism* which is preference for relationships, caring and quality of life.
- **Time Orientation:** A measure of people's consideration of the future. Long-term orientation is characterized by people who persevere methodically toward results and save for the future whereas short-term orientation is characterized by people who expect quick results.
- **Monochrony and Polychrony:** *Cultural dimensions describing attitudes towards the use of time in performing tasks.* In Monchronous societies, people focus on issues one at a time and emphasize sched-

ules and procedures for task completion. In Polychronous societies, people perform activities in parallel and focus on task completion rather than adherence to procedures.

- **Context:** *The amount of information that surrounds an event, inextricably bound up with the meaning of that event.* In a high context culture the information surrounding an event is already in the person, and very little is in the coded, explicit, transmitted part of any communication between participants. In low context cultures the mass of information is vested in the explicit code.
- **Polymorphic and Monomorphic:** *Cultural dimensions which relate to the influence of opinion leaders.* In polymorphic cultures, such as traditional villages and farming communities, the expertise of leaders or managers is assumed to span a wide range of issues, whereas in monomorphic cultures, such as modern industrialized societies, a manager's scope is limited to his or her explicit areas of expertise.

In the next section we define *digital divide*, which we envisaged the results of this study will help bridge between the UAE and developed countries.

Digital Divide

There is a growing disparity in the use of IT between the developed and developing countries. While developed countries are harnessing IT to revolutionize their operations of their industries, developing countries, on the other hand, appeared not to have the capabilities or the urge to do so. The disparity which exists in access to and use of IT between countries and between groups within countries is what is referred to today as the *digital divide*. Jessup and Valacich (2008, p. 410) define it as: "the gap between those individuals in our society who are computer literate and have access to information resources like the Internet and those who do not." The growing disparity in the adoption and use of IT also results from the culture of a people as well as the "push" rather than "pull" strategies which results in the ripple effects of widening the gap between the developed and the developing countries in their adoption and use of IT (Ditsa, 2005, 2009). We envisage the results of this study will help bridge the gap between the UAE and developed countries.

THE STUDY

Methodology

The methodology used for this research is both qualitative and interpretive following the model proposed by Miles and Huberman (1984), which incorporates the four phases of: data collection; data reduction; data display; and the verification and drawing of conclusions. The data for analysis was collected from a set of organizations in two emirates (Abu Dhabi and Dubai) of the UAE, which are the largest of the emirates by population and wealth and have the most IT industry in the country. We (the researchers) took particularly care to select, where possible, representatives of the local IT community rather than foreign advisers or members of multinational corporations.

All the data was text-based and comprised of organizational documents and transcripts of semi-structured interviews with IT staff at both managerial and operational levels. In these interviews we recorded answers to specific questions on: the history and use of IT in the organizations; the method of acquisition and development of information systems; and the attitudes of operation and management staff involved in IT. We also recorded any informal discussions that followed. As soon as possible after each interview, a full report was written based on the notes taken. Follow up interviews were conducted as soon as possible

when we felt the need for further explanation of the data collected.

These reports and documents were then analyzed using a process of data reduction with the selection and arrangement of relevant items. We extracted only the data which relates to culture as defined in this paper. The data was arranged along the eight cultural dimensions and is displayed in Table 2 in the next section. An interpretation of the data into generalized issues was made and presented in the concluding sections of the paper.

Data Collection Methods

The data used for this study is descriptive in nature and the method for collecting the data is as follows. Interviews were conducted and observations were made on the adoption and use of IT in three organizations in Al Ain city (in Abu Dhabi emirate where the researchers work and reside), and three each in Abu Dhabi and Dubai cities. We chose at least one government organization in each city. Before the data collection visits, preliminary contacts were made with these organizations. The organizations and interviewees were appropriately informed about our study. For obvious reasons, we agreed to guarantee the anonymity of all the organizations involved in this study.

In each organization, at least one interviewee was selected who had been involved in IT since its first introduction into the organization. Evidence was also taken from the scarce literature of other case studies on the adoption and use of IT in the chosen organizations. Comparisons were then made with the wealth of data on IT in the UAE with that of West Africa and Australia from the study of Hasan and Ditsa (1999).

UAE and the Two Cultural Regions for Comparison in this Study

Based on Hasan and Ditsa's (1999) study which identified three distinct cultural regions using the studies of Hofstede (1983a, 1983b, 1991, 2001) and Hofstede et al. (1990), we replaced the Middle East with UAE for this focused study. The other two regions from Hasan and Ditsa (1999) study are West Africa, which is in the developing world, and Australia, which is a developed country with Western culture.

Australia is one of the developed or industrialized nations which form about 25% of the world population but produce and consume about 12 times more per capita than the Third World countries (ABS, http://www.abs.gov.au/). Australian companies play prominent roles in specialized areas of IT. Most Australian organizations rely on IT for daily operations and strategic decision making. Australian culture is very egalitarian resulting in an extremely low PD and a monomorphic culture where people are only respected for their own area of expertise. Australia culture is also individualistic and masculine. And perhaps being predominantly a nation of immigrants, Australians are generally venturesome and innovative. Per capita, Australia is a world leader in the use of new technologies including IT (Hasan & Ditsa, 1999).

Hasan and Ditsa's (1999) study on the West African region was focused on Ghana based on Hofstede's (1991) cultural study in the region which includes Ghana, Nigeria and Sierra Leone. All the countries in Hosftede's study of the region plus those he did not study were once colonized, except Liberia which was created after the abolition of the slave trade. Ghana, for example, was colonized by the Portuguese, the Spaniards, the Danes, the Dutch, the Germans, the French and lastly the British. The national and organizational administrative structures, languages and educational systems of the countries in this region bear the evidence of the colonial legacies left in them. For example, the official language of Ghana, Gambia, Nigeria and Sierra Leone is English, while the official language of Burkina Faso, Cote d'Ivoire, Senegal and Togo is French. According to Hofstede's (1991) study, the cultures of this region are very similar and despite the colonial rules which brought with them foreign cultures,

the cultural identities of these countries still remain unique. Traditional cultures still permeate organizational cultures. The basic family values with extended family systems still dominate in this region (Hasan & Ditsa, 1999).

In contrast with Australia, the UAE represents an old and perhaps an ancient country, although it is considered young politically. The UAE was a British protectorate known then as Trucial States or Trucial Oman until 1971 when independence was granted and a federation of seven emirates formed the United Arab Emirates. The seven emirates or states are Abu Dhabi, Dubai, Sharjah, Ajman, Umm al-Quwain, Ras al-Khaimah, and Fujairah (Wikipedia, 2011). The largest emirate is Abu Dhabi which is about 86.7 per cent of the total area of the UAE (World Gazetteer, 2011). The current population of the UAE is 7.5 million of which Emiratis (citizens) are only 20 per cent (Abu Dhabi Tourism Authority, 2011). The official religion of the UAE is Islam and the official language is Arabic (Wikipedia, 2011). The UAE, like other countries in the Middle East and the Arab world, has some commonalities of culture, language and religion with countries of Northern Africa, and the other Islamic countries of the Levant and the Arabian Peninsula (Haidar, 1996).

The use of IT in the UAE has grown tremendously in the past few years. Government IT initiatives appear to be towards making the UAE the technology capital of the region. These can be seen in the establishment of educational institutions, the Knowledge Village in Dubai, the Dubai Silicon Valley, and annual fairs such as GITEX and the Global Village to promote IT. The use of IT is widely encouraged in both public and private sectors. Examples are eGovernment initiatives in Dubai and Abu Dhabi, and the police force. The presence in the country of giants in the IT industry (such as Oracle, Dell, IBM, Cisco, and Microsoft) attests to this. This is also evident in the use of IT in the financial and other sectors.

Similar to countries in the West African region, the UAE was once colonized. However, the colonial legacies are not as evident as in the West African region. The culture of the UAE is an Arab culture, which is a blend of traditional tribal, traditional religious and secular cultures that originated from Bedouin and agrarian cultures. The Arab worldview is influenced by Islamic worldview prevails. The diversity in Arab culture which manifested in population density, distribution of wealth and geography predominates. The UAE being one of the oil producing countries in the Arab world and relatively rich, results in a very fast pace of development in the necessary infrastructures to boost its economy. However, in spite of fast pace of development built on the back of mostly western labor, the essence of the Arab culture still predominates in the UAE as in almost all Arab countries (Haidar, 1996).

Haidar (1996) documents vividly the differences between Arab culture and Western culture in the light of science education as follows. Arab worldview understands nature only with reference to God while Western culture does not, which can be attributed to the type of knowledge dominant in each culture. While in Western culture the only knowledge that is valid is the rationale knowledge, in the Arab culture both divine and rationale knowledge are valid. Consequently while Western culture emphasizes scientific thinking, Arab culture accepts metaphysical, scientific thinking as well as other types of thinking such as superstitious, apologetic, and atheoretical thinking. Haidar attributed students' lack of formal reasoning to lack of interaction with scientific and technological culture. Haidar further investigated Emiratis (UAE nationals) and Yemeni prospective science teachers' worldviews in relation to causality and found that the students displayed different types of causal explanations that vary from the scientific explanations to the non-scientific ones.

A dominant patriarchal relation characterized the UAE culture as in Arab culture, which accounts for a one-sided respect (younger to older), dependency and hegemony. UAE culture as in predominant Arab culture also discourages independence of its members and encourages solidarity (collectivism). This system of patriarchal relations should however not be equated to authoritarianism. The patriarchal relations are societal rules blended with compassion. For example, a father directs his son for the son own good not because he wants to exercise his power but to save his son from hard experiences. This concept is similar, but to lesser extent in the West African culture but in contrast with Western culture that encourages independence and individualism. Additionally, in Western culture most communication media depends on reading, whereas Arab culture can be termed to be "verbal" culture where knowledge is transmitted orally. This is similar in West African and in most nonwestern cultures where literacy level is low (Haidar, 1996).

DATA REDUCTION AND DISPLAY

Comparison of the UAE Culture with the Two Cultural Regions in this Study

Values of the eight cultural indices for the UAE are deduced from this study and the literature while those of Australia and West Africa are adapted from Hasan and Ditsa (1999) and verified by representatives from the UAE culture. Table 1 shows values for the three regions.

Summary Cultural Comparison of the Three Regions on the Eight Cultural Dimensions

From the analysis of the data collected in the UAE study, a summary was made of instances where the value of each of the eight cultural indices was related to IT issues and compared with values for Australia and West Africa obtained from Hasan and Ditsa (1999). The results were verified with a representative from the UAE culture. The summary of the results of the three regions are presented in Table 2.

Table 1. Values of the three cultures along the eight cultural dimensions

	AUS	WA	UAE
Power Distance	Low	High	Very High
Uncertainty Avoidance	Moderately Low	Low	High
Individualism vs. Collectivism	Highly Individualistic	Highly Collective	Highly Collective
Masculinity vs. Femininity	Masculine	Feminine	Masculine
Time Orientation	Long-term	Short-term	High Short-term
Monochrony vs. Polychrony	Poly	Mono	Mono?
Context	Low	High	High
Polymorphic vs. Monomorphic	Mono	Poly	Poly

APPLICATION OF THE RESULTS TO THREE ISSUES OF CULTURE AND IT

Hasan and Ditsa (1999) proposed three issues where the cultural significance of IT is critical as follows:

1. **Cultural Identity of IT:** Information Technology is predominantly a Western product, having evolved within it and taking on values of that culture. This may make certain products inappropriate for other cultures.
2. **Cultural Values and IT:** Although based on technology, the success of information systems in organizations is dependent on the activities of people who carry with them a pattern of thinking, feeling and acting which is learnt through their culture. To make most effective use of IT, people should choose a product that supports the work practices determined by their own culture.
3. **Impact of IT on Cultures:** Culture, no matter how firmly it is established, is not static but may be altered by its environment. IT has the power to influence and change a nation's culture. For this reason, those responsible for the introduction of IT in a country or region must be mindful of its social and cultural impact. Computers, and for that matter IT, may be viewed as cultural artifacts which can cause unforeseen long-term social and cultural transformation as the car and telephone have done.

From the results of this study we deduced the relationship between the eight cultural dimensions and the three critical cultural issues significant to IT. Table 3 shows the summary of the deduction.

DISCUSSION AND IMPLICATIONS OF THE STUDY FOR THE UAE

Similarities exist in most of the cultural indices of UAE and West Africa, while there is significant contrast between the cultural indices of UAE and Australia (a Western culture). The seemingly western cultural identity of IT along the eight cultural indices may be due to the origin of IT – the West – where the developers of IT products and IT systems may inadvertently imbued IT with Western culture. The cultural indices of particular interest revealed in this study are the Power Distance, Uncertainty Avoidance, Individualism/ Collectivism, Masculinity / Femininity, Time Orientation, and Monomorphic / Polymorphic dimensions.

The very high power distance that exists in the UAE culture, for example, will most likely prevent IT from penetrating into areas where government and societal structure may feel threatened by the

Table 2. Summary of the cultural comparison of the three regions on the eight cultural dimensions

	AUS	WA	UAE
Power Distance	IT has flourished in this low PD culture as networked organizations develop flatter management structures.	In this high PD culture, IT is often an imposition on organizations from the top without taking advice from IT staff.	A high PD culture where governments seemed to encourage IT use but with concern and control to avoid democratization and lowering of PD.
Uncertainty Avoidance	People here are prepared to take risks and ready to adopt new IT, resulting in successful innovation.	Also prepared to take risks but many unwise and risky projects are undertaken and a lot of incomplete IT projects are observed.	A high UA culture where R&D is near to zero. Well established IT products mostly accepted and usually from western countries.
Individualism vs. Collectivism	The individualist characteristic of this culture is exemplified in the typical solitary image of a dedicated computer programmer.	Here there is a collective attitude towards solving IT problems by teams of IT professionals. This has the potential to produce good IT solutions.	Highly collective, patriarchal dominance and does not encourage independence of members. IT projects mostly initiated by westerners or western trained who are individualistic. Creates problem for IT projects where individualistic approaches are required.
Masculinity vs. Femininity	IT development has been predominantly technical and male oriented. Women are becoming more prominent as the number of less technical positions grows.	Both males and females vie for top jobs in the IT industry and people are more interested in what the technology can do rather than technical details.	Masculine and highly male dominated. Mixed teams (male & female) in the IT industry are rare. Culture does not encourage males and females to mix. This is evident even at university level where males & females are not allowed to mix in a class or see each other. This makes it harder for the females in particular who enter the workforce to adjust.
Time Orientation	Most organizations have a three to five year IT strategies and think reasonably long term.	Short-term planning is prevalent, so that only the results of today determine success and are rewarded.	Short-term orientation resulting in a number of IT projects without adequate maintenance plan including budget allocation. Results of today determine success and are rewarded. With initiatives from westerners IT strategies are beginning to appear in some companies.
Monochrony vs. Polychrony	Modern interactive, multi-tasking systems encourage polychronous work and are popular.	IT professionals prefer completing one job before taking another: a display of monochronous culture.	There is the general tendency to complete tasks without much adherence to schedules and procedures, indicating blend of monochronous/polychronous culture. This is evident in appetite for "turn-key" systems in most organizations.
Context	System developers are good at low level development which requires detail and abstraction.	Interested in getting a system in place without much attention to details.	Preference for high level modern systems without much attention to details once the system can accomplish the task, which is indicative of a high context culture.
Monomorphic vs. Polymorphic	IT management separate from core business resulting in problems of communication: a display of monomorphism.	IT managers are expected to have knowledge of every aspect of IT and the organization: a display of a polymorphic culture.	Expectation of managers to "know it all" to solve all IT issues is apparent – indicating a polymorphic culture which is characterized by the dominant patriarchal relations.

lowering of the power distance by IT. Of particular notice is IT systems that are designed to provide information that should be public knowledge are scarce, although governments, both at federal and emirate levels, seemed to be encouraging IT development and use. Like most of the Arab cultures, the UAE culture in shrouded and strives in secrecy. This results in information scarcity to the extent that information which in Western cultures are supposed to be in public domain,

Table 3. The eight cultural dimensions vs. the three critical cultural issues significant to IT

	Cultural identity of IT	**Cultural Values and IT**	**Impact of IT**
Power Distance	IT designed with inherent low Power Distance (PD) culture.	Some information available through IT may contradict some values high PD cultures and shift power base in society and organizations.	Change in PD from high to low is experienced by the introduction of IT but cannot be ignored in modernization and global competition.
Uncertainty Avoidance	IT is inherently risky and most likely to be developed in low UA cultures and transferred to high UA cultures.	High UA cultures will most likely not have the latest IT to meet competitions from low UA cultures.	Compelling and monumental needs of high UA cultures that IT can solve will result in risk taking leading to lowering UA.
Individualist vs. Collectivist	Traditional IT imbue individualistic approach though some ITs suit collectivism.	IT normally built teams but more individualistic than collective in use.	Empowers individualism in collective cultures encourages dynamism in individualistic cultures.
Masculinity vs. Femininity	IT is characterized by masculinity in development and by femininity in use.	Current IT systems have a blend of both masculinity and femininity cultures.	Modern IT enforcing a blend of both masculinity and femininity.
Time Orientation	Fast changing. Require difficult long-term plan critical to its success. Plan to be flexible for the fast change.	Long-term but flexible plan critical to IT success may pose problem for short-term time orientation cultures.	Fast changing IT compelling flexible long-term planning in anticipation of future requirements.
Monochrony vs. Polychrony	IT exhibits both monochrony and polychrony.	IT exhibits monochronous and polychronous cultures.	Increase in efficiency, effectiveness and job satisfaction.
Context	IT exhibits explicitly in analysis, design and abstraction consistent with a low context culture.	Object oriented approach may suit high context cultures as it is more oriented to objects in the real world and integrates data and process.	IT has imposed its language and mode of operation on all users. It teaches problem solving skills and data abstraction which suits low context cultures.
Polymorphic vs. Monomorphic	Integrated corporate IT systems in use exhibit both polymorphic and monomorphic cultures, while their development requires monomorphism.	Leaders in polymorphic cultures may feel not in control, while those in monomorphic cultures may feel the demand to widen their scope.	Demand on leaders in organization to display both specialized and general knowledge to be successful.

are shrouded in secrecy in the UAE culture. This attribute of the culture makes it difficult for requirements gathering for system development. This attribute also prevents true collaborations between organizations, with the worse perhaps being collaborations between academic institutions and organizations for research purposes. This observation is supported by Haidar (1996). Despite the UAE government initiatives for IT to dominate its work processes at various levels and to make the UAE the technology capital of the region, unless the culture is influenced to lower its power distance, IT adoption and use will still remain a distance from that in the West.

The Uncertainty Avoidance dimension of the UAE culture makes research and development

(R&D) very low. This stems from the lack of research collaborations between academic institutions and organizations due to uncertainty avoidance. The mistrust (or fear) of Western culture penetrating into some organization and societal life may also increase the uncertainty avoidance. Emiratis, like most Arabs, are very private people and will hardly invite "strangers" (including even work colleagues) to their homes. Unless the UAE culture adopts risk taking, which subsequently will lower uncertainty avoidance, well established IT products and systems will continue to be transferred to the UAE – usually from the western countries.

The highly collective nature of the UAE culture makes it hard for independent (individual) work and initiatives. The patriarchal dominance which does not encourage independence of members appears to increase collectivism. Because of the private life nature of the culture too, collectivism with other nationals is also shunned. This may make it hard for Emiratis to engage in collaborative works, such as system developments, with other nationals. The workforce of the country is predominantly foreign with very few Emiratis in the workforce and the IT industry. This in itself makes any collectivism with fellow Emiratis at the workplace difficult. The government noticed this deficiency and launched "Emiratization Program" to get Emiratis to the workforce. Unless this program succeeds, IT projects will mostly be initiated by westerners or western trained who are usually individualistic. Another solution will be to allow expatriate workers who want to take citizenship to do so. Currently, UAE does not allow citizenship for other nationals no matter how long they reside in the country except under extreme circumstances (Bowman, 2008). However, of the total population of the country currently at 7.5 million, the Emiratis are only about one and half million. Citizenship underscores belongings and loyalty to a homeland and plays vital roles in the advancement and prosperity of a nation. Granting citizenship to those expatriate workers who want to will increase the Emirati population and the advancement and prosperity of the country, including the IT industry.

The UAE culture, like most Arab cultures, is masculine and highly male dominated with the females are highly jealously "protected." A female is prohibited from going out without being accompanied by their parents, a brother, or, when married, the husband. Mixed teams (males and females) in the IT industry are rare. The culture does not encourage males and females to mix. This is evident even at university level where males and females are highly separated with all the security necessary to prevent the male and female students from seeing or communicating with one another.

The highly time short-term orientation of the UAE culture makes it hard for a long life cycle of some IT systems. Similar to the West African culture, there is no respect for time in the UAE culture. A number of things are done in ad hoc manner with no long-term plan. This dimension of the culture results in a number of IT projects without adequate maintenance planning including budget allocation. Due to the fast changing nature of IT, flexible long-term planning in anticipation of future requirements must be enforced. The results of today determining success and reward must give way to methodical and strategic approaches to yield long-term results. With initiatives from westerners, IT strategies are beginning to appear in some companies.

From the results and the discussion above, the culture of the UAE can inhibit the flouring of IT in the country and enhance the bridging of the digital divide between the UAE and the developed countries. Of particular concern are six of the eight dimensions mentioned. A conscious attempt should be made to lower the power distance, for example, by: educating and opening up the society; providing common knowledge information in public domains; providing genuine environment for organization-to-organization collaborations and organization-to-research institutions collaborations to encourage R&D. Provision of telecottages to educate the section of the population that is computer illiterate will also go a long way to lower the power distance and the uncertainty avoidance. The "Emiratization Program" should also aim at increasing the number of females in the workforce. The structure of government where each Emirate is highly autonomous and pursuing their individual IT agendas should also be discouraged – since it is leading to duplication of effort while development experiences and information are hardly shared by the emirates. In other words, the national political system needs to be revived and strengthened to take lead in national infrastructure development instead of the current emirate-based infrastructures.

IMPLICATIONS FOR THE IT INDUSTRY

This study confirms that IT is not culturally neutral. There are a number of cultural dimensions that impacts on the success of an IT in a country or region. The IT industry in the UAE in particular and in other parts of world in general should note the cultural identity and values of IT and the cultural impact that it can make when introduced to a country or region. As stated previously, most IT products and systems originate from the West and inherit some Western culture identity and values, sometimes unaware to originators of these IT products and systems. Care should therefore be taken to isolate the cultural differences between the IT and the country or region adopting it. Our study has focused on the UAE culture along eight cultural dimensions with a comparison drawn between a similar culture (West African) and a Western culture (Australian). Of particular interest are six of the eight dimensions mentioned above. Most IT products and projects suit cultures with low power distance, low uncertainty avoidance, and long-term time orientation. As mentioned in the discussion, power distance can also inhibit requirements gathering for systems. Collective cultures which shun "strangers" may also inhibit true team spirit for system development and use.

LIMITATIONS OF THE STUDY

More data is always desirable. It would have been useful to increase the number of organizations in the study and across the seven Emirate of the UAE. These would have required more time and resources, which in the current study were very limited.

CONCLUSION AND SUGGESTIONS FOR FURTHER RESEARCH

This study focused the cultural impact on the adoption and use of IT in the UAE and suggests some areas of the cultural dimensions of the country that can be improved to enhance the flouring of IT in the country and bridge the digital divide between the UAE and the developed countries. This study also confirm previous studies (e.g., Hasan & Ditsa, 1999; Avison & Malaurent, 2007) that cultural impact on IT adoption and use cannot be ignored. Culture is an important ingredient in the identity of the IT products themselves and influences its adoption and use. Problems will arise when there are differences between the culture of an IT product and the culture of its users, as discussed in Tables 2 and 3.

Culture is dynamic, including the UAE culture. IT is also changing fast and its adoption and use continues to expand globally. This study focused on the UAE culture and the existing IT adoption and use in the country at the time of the study. It may be necessary carry further research into the impact of UAE culture on the adoption and use of IT and/or a focused research in one of the countries in the region for comparison. A greater understanding of the various dimensions of culture as applied to IT and the people, who use it, will lead to a more globally acceptable IT products and better choices for IT.

REFERENCES

Abu Dhabi Tourism Authority. (2011). *History & population*. Retrieved June 19, 2011, from http://www.visitabudhabi.ae/en/about.abudhabi/population.aspx

Avison, D., & Malaurent, J. (2007). Impact of cultural differences: A case study of ERP introduction in China. *International Journal of Information Management*, *27*, 368–374. doi:doi:10.1016/j.ijinfomgt.2007.06.004

Avison, D. E., & Myers, M. D. (1995). Information systems and anthropology: an anthropological perspective on IT and organizational culture. *Information Technology & People*, *8*(3), 43–56. doi:doi:10.1108/09593849510098262

Bowman, J. (2008). *UAE flatly rejects citizenship for foreign workers*. Retrieved June 22, 2011, from http://www.arabianbusiness.com/506295-uae-flatly-rejects-citizenship-for-foreign-workers

Ditsa, G. (2005, May 15-18). *Issues of ICTs and development in less developed countries: A case of Africa and a view towards bridging the digital divide*. Paper presented at the Information Resources Management Association Workshop, San Diego, CA.

Ditsa, G. (2009). Trends and challenges facing developing world in adoption and use of ICTs: A view towards bridging the digital divide. *International Journal of Global Business*, *2*(1), 78–100.

Haidar, A. H. (1996). *Western science and technology and the needs of the Arab world*. Paper presented at the Joint Symposium on Traditional Culture, Science & Technology, and Development, Mito, Japan.

Hasan, H., & Ditsa, G. (1997). *The cultural challenges of adopting IT in developing countries: An exploratory study*. Paper presented at the Information Resources Management Association Workshop, Vancouver, BC, Canada.

Hasan, H., & Ditsa, G. E. M. (1999). Impact of culture on the adoption of IT: An interpretive study. *Journal of Global Information Management*, *7*(1), 5–15.

Hofstede, G. (1983a). Dimensions of national cultures in fifty countries and three regions. In Deregowski, J. B., Dziurawiec, S., & Annis, R. C. (Eds.), *Expiscations in cross-cultural psychology* (pp. 335–355). Lisse, The Netherlands: Swets and Zeitlinger.

Hofstede, G. (1983b). National cultures in four dimensions. *International Studies of Management and Organization*, *13*, 46–74.

Hofstede, G. (1985). The interaction between national and organizational value systems. *Journal of Management Studies*, *22*(4), 347–355. doi:doi:10.1111/j.1467-6486.1985.tb00001.x

Hofstede, G. (1991). *Cultures and organisations: Software of the Min*. New York, NY: McGraw-Hill.

Hofstede, G. (2001). *Culture's consequences*. Thousand Oaks, CA: Sage.

Hofstede, G., Neuijen, B., Ohayv, D. D., & Sanders, G. (1990). Measuring organizational cultures: A qualitative and quantitative study across twenty cases. *Administrative Science Quarterly*, *35*, 286–316. doi:doi:10.2307/2393392

Interact, U. A. E. (2009). *Top news stories*. Retrieved July 9, 2011, from http://uaeinteract.com/docs/Expat_numbers_rise_rapidly_as_UAE_population_touches_6m/37883.htm

Jessup, L., & Valacich, J. (2008). *Information systems today: Managing in the digital world*. Upper Saddle River, NJ: Prentice Hall.

Kevin, K. W., Byungjoon, Y., Seunghee, Y., & Kar, Y. T. (2007). The effect of culture and product categories on the level of use of Buy-It-Now (BIN) auctions by sellers. *Journal of Global Information Management*, *15*(4), 1–19. doi:doi:10.4018/jgim.2007100101

Miles, M. B., & Huberman, A. M. (1984). *Qualitative data analysis: A sourcebook of new methods*. Thousand Oaks, CA: Sage.

Schein, E. H. (1984). Coming to a new awareness of organizational culture. *Sloan Management Review, 25*(2), 3–16.

Shore, B., & Vankatachalam, A. (1996). Role of national culture in the transfer of information technology. *The Journal of Strategic Information Systems, 5*(1), 19–35. doi:doi:10.1016/S0963-8687(96)80021-7

Wikipedia. (2011). *United Arab Emirates*. Retrieved July 5, 2011, from http://en.wikipedia.org/wiki/United_Arab_Emirates#cite_note-6

World Bank. (1994). *Lending for industrial technology: Lessons from six countries* (Review No. 70). Retrieved May 20, 2011, from http://lnweb90.worldbank.org/oed/oeddoclib.nsf/DocUNIDView ForJavaSearch/55F1463FA43E535B852567F50 05D8785?opendocument

World Gazetteer. (2011). *Abu Dhabi*. Retrieved August 2, 2011, from http://world-gazetteer.com/wg.php?x=&men=gpro&lng=en&des=gamela n&geo=-265&srt=npan&col=abcdefghinoq&m sz=1500

This journal was previously published in the International Journal of Technology Diffusion, Volume 2, Issue 4, edited by Ali Hussein Saleh Zolait, pp. 12-24, copyright 2011 by IGI Publishing (an imprint of IGI Global).

Chapter 7
Social Drivers for ICT Diffusion among Agrarian Business Enterprises in Nigeria

Bartholomew Aleke
University of Northumbria, UK

Udechukwu Ojiako
University of Southampton, UK

David Wainwright
University of Northumbria, UK

ABSTRACT

In this paper, the authors examine the process of diffusion of innovation ICT within agrarian business enterprises operating in developing countries. There is substantial research in the area of Diffusion of Innovation Theory (DoI) and its application to Information Systems (IS) research within organisations. However, in recognition of the conceptual limitations of DoI, researchers have called for the incorporation of aspects of Social Network Theory (SNT) into DoI frameworks. The findings of this research suggest that an understanding of the conceptual basis of innovation is a major driver of successful innovation adoption.

INTRODUCTION

The use of ICT by agrarian business enterprises represents innovative change, especially for SMAEs operating in developing countries (Rao, 2007; Weick, 2001). It represents innovative change in that it is a significant leap from traditional paper-based methods of business operations such as information sharing. The reality however is that recognition of the capabilities of ICT by *agripreneurs* does not in any form enable efficient and effective diffusion (Rao, 2007): neither does it transform to an automatic enhancement or improvement of productivity, or in fact an acceptance of use by *agripreneurs* (Adrian et al., 2005). Both an enhancement of productivity and a successful diffusion process are highly dependent on effective policy enactment and implementation (Baerenklau & Knapp, 2007).

DOI: 10.4018/978-1-4666-2791-8.ch007

Recognition of the importance of ICT to the agriculture industry has led to policy makers calling for the development of ICT that will facilitate an increase in agriculture productivity (Minten & Barrett, 2008). It is expected that this increase in agribusiness productivity will be translated into national economic development (Omamo & Lynam, 2003). In developing countries, Small and Medium Sized Agribusiness Enterprises (SMAEs) have a substantial role to play in this development. Although the role of agrarian business enterprises in agriculture cannot be over-emphasized (de Lauwere, 2005), its productivity has been compromised by a range of factors. These factors include poor ICT policy formulation and implementation (Diso, 2005) a lack of credit facilities (Jabbar et al., 2002), a high level of illiteracy within the industry (Sabo & Zira, 2009), a changing customer base (Mishili et al., 2009), the lack of access to relevant market information (Awoke & Okorji, 2004), poor supply networks, which restricts their business transactions to within a confined region (Higgins et al., 2008), inadequate infrastructure (Martin & Jagadesh, 2006), and the non-possession of skills relevant to compete in a modern business environment (Weick, 2001). In most cases, all these problems are attributable to under-investment and made more complicated by the deregulation of agricultural markets, increased quality and ethical (*fair trade*) considerations and technology. Developed nations for example invest a considerable amount of their per capita income on research and development, and have a considerably greater number of technicians per capita than the sub-Saharan Africa nations (Rodriguez & Wilson, 2006; Watts & Ashcroft, 2005).

THE RESEARCH PROBLEM

There is a divergent range of scholarly views in the area of agribusinesses diffusion of innovation. For example, questions are being asked about whether agribusinesses can appropriately exploit ICT for operational and productivity gains (Adrian et al., 2005; Cox, 2002; Rao, 2007; Weick, 2001), and what the nature of these gains is (Kirsten & Sartorius, 2002). The situation with agribusinesses is particularly complicated for a number of reasons. For example these categories of agribusinesses entrepreneurs are regarded as highly resistant to change (Adrian et al., 2005). Other scholars (Romani, 2003) have also found that agrarian business enterprises in Africa were prepared to allow ethnic and tribal loyalties to overshadow sound entrepreneurial astuteness. Certainly in the case of Nigeria, matters had not been helped with the passing into law in 1977 of the indigenization decree which represented an apparent attempt by government to 'protect' SMEs from foreign competition. Mishra and Park (2005) observed that SMAEs had little interest in electronic business and online sales technology. In the opinion of Molla et al. (2006), interest and expertise in the use of ICT by SMAEs was sporadic and only tenable in SMAEs operating in developed countries.

This particular research is set in the south-eastern geo-political region of Nigeria called Ebonyi: Ebonyi's capital city is Abakaliki. The area is predominantly rural. With 85% of its workforce working in Agriculture, in comparison to other regions of the country, Ebonyi has the largest proportion of SMAEs in the country (Awoke & Okorji, 2004; Oseni & Winters, 2009). The study is therefore justified for the following reasons. The agriculture industry directly or indirectly employs 60% of the population in Nigeria (Manyong et al., 2005), thus making its profitability essential for the development of the Nigerian economy. However, although the importance of the agriculture industry to the Nigerian economy should not be underestimated, it is still an industry characterized by low efficiencies and productivity (Aleke, 2003; 2010; Aleke et al., 2009). The second justification for the study is that only a limited number of studies have focused on ICT diffusion in agribusiness and the impact of social processes on the process of diffusion in heterogeneous cultural settings.

CONTEXTUALIZATION

Agriculture in Nigeria is to a large extent subsistence-oriented (Aleke, 2010), and dominated by SMAEs (Awoke & Okorji, 2004; Oseni & Winters, 2009). The industry is highly vulnerable to unpredictable weather conditions (Tubiello & Fischer, 2007). Largely, Nigerian agriculture proprietors have been unable to exploit the country's vast agricultural potential due to the undeveloped state of the country's agricultural systems.

Although there has been a diffusion of ICT in Nigeria, its speed lags behind a considerable number of other African countries such as South Africa and Mauritius (Oyelaran-Oyeyinka & La, 2005). It has long been advocated that ICT offers substantial potential for addressing many of the challenges that the Nigerian Agricultural sector is experiencing especially in the area of information exchange and management (Aleke, 2010). For example, locally produced '*Adani*' brand rice from Abakaliki was primarily successfully exported to the Chinese market due to the spearheading of marketing efforts over the Internet. The main advantage delivered by ICT to agrarian business enterprises is an enhancement of competitiveness (Sassenrath et al., 2008). In this respect, ICT does not play a substantially different role in the operations of agrarian business enterprises as either non-agricultural or rural-based firms.

THEORY EXPLORATION

This section sets out the areas of theory underpinning this particular research. Two frameworks form the basis of our study. The first is the diffusion of innovation theory (DoI), while the second is Social Network Theory (SNT). Rogers (1995) first proposed the Diffusion of Innovation Theory (DoI). The theory asserts that the characteristics of an innovation either facilitates or inhibits the innovation's adoption. For this reason, understanding the definition and characteristics of each stage

of the diffusion process, including new policies and procedures, can enable an innovation to be more smoothly implemented; with the potential adopters more easily persuaded to accept change. Numerous scholars such as Spielman et al. (2009) have explored the notion of technology transition and adoption in agriculture by employing DoI as the theoretical foundation. The advantage of utilizing DoI theory to conduct such explorations is that it examines the contextual parameters that precipitate the acceptance of. These parameters may involve the characteristics of the technology, the networks that are employed to communicate information about the technology (process), the profile of the adopters of the technology, and the degree of familiarity between those driving the adoption and the potential adopters. The theory has been broadly applied to areas ranging from the diffusion of new ideas to the diffusion of new machines. In as much as scholars have examined how technology may be diffused in agriculture, few, if any, of emergent studies have actually *operationalized* diffusion theory in agriculture by focusing on *its social dimensions*. The underlying similarities between ICT innovations combined with previous studies of technology innovation diffusion suggest that DoI might provide an explanation for successful innovation and that its social dimension is critical in terms of its long term sustainability.

The diffusion of innovation research domain is not without its critics. Scholars such as Wainwright and Waring (2007), for example, claim that its theories put forward a heterogeneous statement on specific constructs that need to be addressed. For example they highlight that 'enhancements' to the theory appear only to have produced an expanded list of diffusion factors, which at times conflict with each other. Although subject to such criticism, the authors consider the theory adequate within the present research context. There are two major reasons why this is the case. In the first place, the DoI theory was originally conceived within an agricultural context. Secondly, the framework represents the commencement for any research that focuses on utilization of information technology and systems (Prescott & Conger, 1995), within which our study is rooted. In effect, DoI theories represent an acceptable means of exploring the link between agriculture and information technology and information systems (SI/IT).

Our study adopts a three-staged view of the DoI framework which commences with the diffusion decision. Generally, the third stage is where the effect of the maturation of the diffusion process is most likely to impact the sustainability of the diffusion process. It is this stage that we focus our attention on, as our interest lies in gaining an understanding of how successful DoI, possibly informed by a social element, may be realized.

The second theory underpinning this research is social network theory (Adamic & Adar, 2005). Despite the view that formal networking is vital to the viability of SMAEs (Baron & Markman, 2003; Slangen et al., 2004), a number of scholars have found that many SMAEs in Africa do not actively participate in social networks for a number of reasons, including ethnic and tribal loyalties (Romani, 2003). Justification for the incorporation of social network theory (SNT) into the foundations of our study is provided by Hossain and de Silva (2009), who highlight the fact that DoI in its present state lacks a social dimension. There is an expectation that the complexity of the DoI process may serve to enhance research credibility. Because of the numerous perspectives in the field, it is quite difficult to come up with one single exhaustive definition of SNT leading, for example, some scholars focusing on the entrepreneurial dimensions of SNT (Jack, 2010). The reality is that although SNT has attracted heavy usage in the IS/IT arena, it has not gained holistic acceptance among researchers. This may be because of its quantitative origins (Sydow, 2005). Although this is the case, there is a suggestion by some scholars such as Kadushin (2002) that SNT serves as a theoretical basis for characterizing social structures. There are two reasons why this

position has been taken; one, because the social experiences of individuals serve to determine how people interact and are able to build and exist within networks; and second, there are always hierarchies in social networks.

THE RESEARCH METHODOLOGY

One of the key elements of successful research endeavors is the determination of an appropriate choice of research methodology. Often, the choice of methodology may not be necessarily separated from the researcher's own philosophical position. We have highlighted that our research resides at the interface of two conceptual foundations: namely the Diffusion of Innovation Theory and Social Network Theory. Our research is further 'complicated' as it is set within Small and Medium Sized Agribusiness Enterprises (SMAEs), resulting in a need to consider entrepreneurship theories within the context of the agriculture industry. The research is also set within a rural area (Ebonyi) of a developing country (Nigeria), thus leading to the need to incorporate rural development theories into our conceptual foundations. The implication is that the eclectic nature of the study may not be necessarily served by a research philosophy which has its foundations in classical instrumental research methods which are aligned to structured experimentation. Instead, our study may be best served by a philosophical foundation which exhibits a diverse and rich set of theories, within which variables such as morale, judgment formation and an understanding of behaviors may be best understood.

Based on this assessment, in contrast to the positivist paradigm, we adopt a phenomenological research philosophy (*social constructionism*) which focuses on understanding human behavior from the participant's own frame of reference. The basic claim of *social constructionism* is that realities are constructed rather than discovered (Burr, 1995), and that attitudes and behavior are determined by their social setting. It is however recognized that because *social constructionism* is conceptually relative, it is not biased towards any particular picture of reality (Cohen et al., 2004). Data were gathered from semi-structured interviews of 27 SMAE proprietors affiliated with the *Ebonyi State Federation of Cooperatives*. The interviews (Table 4) were designed with particular focus on objective components of the interviewees' experience with business transactions. This included business connections, information communication channels, cluster arrangements into cooperative societies, number of employees and power sharing among employers, government interventions in capacity building, and experiences with intermediaries. We were also interested in gaining an understanding of subjective aspects of innovation diffusion; for example, the reasons why a particular technological innovation was either adopted or discontinued.

To commence template analysis, we created *priori* codes (Table 1) from relevant literature or frameworks. The codes developed *a priori* were meant to represent a test of prediction and therefore served as good pointers when interpreting the data. To assist with the substantial amount of data generated from the interviews, *Atlas.ti* was utilized during data analysis. Coding was organized into high level code clusters. Table 2 shows the *a priori* codes generated from the literature before analyzing the primary document using *Atlas.ti* software, while Tables 3 and 4 show the two code hierarchies and the codes that were developed.

RESEARCH FINDINGS

At this juncture, we draw on 'voices' of the respondents to try and create an understanding of how social dynamics impact on the diffusion of ICT as innovation. For this reason, in order to maintain an element of focus on the main study area, it was felt that a reflection on earlier work on data interpretation put forward by Alvesson and Deetz (2000), which includes intensifying

Table 1. Codes developed a priori

Level One: Ethical Issues in the Research	Level One: Cultural Issues	Level One; Human Interation (ETHICS)	Level One: Relationship Issues	Level One: Security Issues
1. Intellectual Property Rights	1. Change	1. Recruitment and Training	1. Developing Partnership	1. Misuse of Data
2. Electronic Monitoring	2. Assimilation of emerging Technology	Support	2. Virtual Teams	2. Virus/worm Creation
3. Data Utilization Consent	3. Power Asymmetry 4. Implementation and Social Environment	Creativity Cohessiveness	3. Collate Teams 4. Group Cohesion/Adhesion	3. Intranet Abuse 4. Fraud with System Use
4. Morality in Information and Communication Technology Use		2, Leadership	5. Group	stability
		Facilitation		
		3. Motivation Satisfaction	6. Networking 7. Buyer Supplier Linkages	accountability flexibility
		Commitment		5. Standards and Regulation
		4. Social Presence		Certainty
		5. Organizational Championship		

Table 2. Mapping of a priori codes to the literature

S/N	Codes	Related Issues	Literature source
1	Ethics	Intellectual property rights; Electronic monitoring; Data utilization consent; Trust	Crane (2002)
2	Culture	Change; Assimilation of emerging technology; Power asymmetry; Implementation and social environment	Groucutt and Griseri (2005)
3	Human interaction	Recruitment and training; Leadership; Motivation; Social presence; Organizational championship	Kanfer (1990)
4	Relationships	Developing partnership; Virtual teams; Collate teams; Group cohesion/adhesion; Group facilitation; Networking; Buyer/supplier linkages	Castell (2002); Mclean and Wainwright (2008)
5	Security	Mis-use of data; Virus creation; Internet abuse; Fraud within system use; Accountability; Standards and regulation	n/a

interpretation, language sensitivity, historical context and politics, was essential. We recognize that language does not transport meaning outside the context within which it was displayed.

Table 3. Code hierarchies

level-one (high-level) code families	level-two (high-level) code families
1. Awareness	*1. Behavioral*
2. Policy adaptation	*2. Growth and improvement*
3. Business growth	*3. Policy issues*
4. Innovation diffusion factors	*4. Security and risk*
5. Process	*5. Strategy*
6. Products	*6. Relationship and integration*
7. End-user integration	*7. Innovation characteristics*
8. Adopter categories	*8. Cultural antecedent*
9. Networked communities	*9. Communication*
10. Diffusion strategy	*10. Added value*
11. Sustaining innovation	
12. Possible areas of improvement	
13. Return on investment	
14. Diffusion barriers	
15. Uncertainty and trust	
16. Disruptive nature of ICT	
17. Value proposition	

The findings from the semi-structured interviews conducted among representatives of 27 Agribusiness Enterprises in Southeast Nigeria are now presented. In this paper we will focus on findings which relate solely to social imperatives. Four such findings were identified: these are (1) ICT outlook, (2) government policy, (3) cultural antecedents, and (4) information dissemination.

ICT Outlook

We identified general propensity to ICT innovation diffusion as one of the key social drivers for successful ICT innovation diffusion. We found that that some interviewees played a more interactive role during the diffusion process by facilitating greater awareness of the centre and its role in the community. For example, we note that various category of responses. Some of the responses from the innovators interviewed are:

Adoption of measures to stimulate domestic production and broadening the supply base of the economy (Owner-manager XVII).

I prefer information being circulated via electronic media, because it is fast and more accurate. If it is via extension agent, remember information passing from hand to another (Marketing manager II).

Table 4. High level code clusters

Code identity	High level code	Level one code families	Group of codes
AC	Behavioral	Adopter categories	(1) Facilitators, (2) Innovators, (3) Positive attitude, (4) Late majority.
BG	Business Growth and improvement	Business growth	(1) More business opportunity, (2) Enterprise development, (3) Less paper work, (4) Economic growth, (5) Increase in productivity, (6) Competitive advantage.
PA	Policy adaptation	Policy adaptation	(1) Indigenization decree, (2) Unfriendly governmental policy, (3) Deregulation, (4) Just trade, (5) Legislative environment.
UT	Security and risk	Uncertainty and trust	(1) Trialability, (2) Failed diffusion projects, (3) Trust, (4) Societal insecurity, (5) Morality, (6) Internet security.
DS; POI	Strategy	Diffusion strategy Possible area of improvement	(1) Business networking, (2) Access to foreign markets, (3) Business expansion, (4) Change in organizational structure, (5) Product diversification, (6) Connectedness, (7) Manpower to skill labor, (8) Change in business pattern.
NC; EI; PN	Relationship and integration	Networked communities End-user integration Professional networks	(1) Community of practice, (2) Social network, (3) Group activities, (4) Colleagues, (5) ICT team, (6) Affiliations, (7) Collaboration, (8) Cooperative societies, (9) Professional networks.
PS; PT	Innovation characteristics	Process product	(1) Web advertisement, (2) Innovation information brokerage, (3) Internet service provision, (4) Innovation re-invention, (5) e-mail transactions, (6) Virtual team formation, (7) Personal computers, (8) Enterprise personal websites, (9) Mobile phones, (10) Mobile Internet units.
IDF; DT DB	Cultural antecedents	Innovation diffusion factors Disruptive of ICT Diffusion Barriers	(1) Societal norms, (2) Cultural values, (3) Personal exposure, (4) Web services, (5) Accessibility, (6) Finance, (7) Foreign culture, (8) Location of farms, (9) Corruption, (10) Push factors.
AW	Communication	Awareness	(1) Basic education, (2) Social capital, (3) User skills, (4) Background knowledge.
SI; RoI; VP	Added value	Sustaining innovation Return-on-investment Value proposition	(1) Capacity building, (3) Knowledge deployment, (4) Competitive advantage, (5) Technology Fit, (6) More customer density, (7) Maturation, (8) Less paper work, (9) Foster solution, (10) Faster delivery of service, (11) Relative satisfaction, (12) Relative convenience, (13) Vendor and consultancy.

It will give us good competitive advantage, seriously we have started getting more customers as a result of the network participation especially now government has made it compulsory that the farmers must register with insurance companies before they can obtain loan from agric banks (Owner-manager II).

We also found early adopters prepared to take risk…

I visit their websites and get information (Owner-manager XVI).

The people I am transacting with at the moment electronically are those who understand computers but they are so many prospective customers who don't understand what we are doing. So it is a trial really (Owner-manager VI).

This computer business is not a serious change; I don't think it will be (Owner-manager III).

Overall, in line with earlier work by Rogers (1995), we found - as expected - a mix of various adopters. For example, practically all the 27 interviewers had signed up to a dummy social network (*namesdatabase.com*), which we created as part of the study. Only one of the interviewees (*Owner-manager III*) did not sign up. What is of particularly interest is our realization that some of the interviewees had embraced a "mitosis" mindset; for example, we found on some occasions that the early adopters (who generally were more literate and computer-savvy) had set up 'consultancy' services whereby they provided basic support services to the less literate interviewees.

Government Policy

From the interviewees, we found that overall, there was a feeling that

Inconsistency of government policies, power and politics has stopped us from achieving some of our business goals (Commercial manager II).

You know one regime may say this price tags for so product we want something like this and stuff like that then another regime may come and disorganize the previous policies (Farm Secretary I).

The indigenization decree is not helpful to multinational companies that would have been promoting the use ICT here in Nigeria. Our government drove them away with the indigenization decree (Owner-manager IV).

A legislative environment that will support the effective diffusion of the innovation does not exist (Owner-manager I).

Government policy has long been identified as one of the parameters that impact on ICT diffusion (Pande, 2006). In the case of SMAEs in Southeast Nigeria, it was identified that the government's indigenization decree of 1977 had an overall negative impact on ICT diffusion innovation. Over the past years, economic policy in Nigeria has been primarily concerned with structural adjustments programmes (SAP), entrepreneurships, and sector

restructuring. Worryingly, prior to the SAP policy, there had been a silent assumption that the fiscal stringency and monetary stability brought about by such policies may lead to SMAEs becoming more competitive in the country. The reality however is that while there have been conscious efforts to empower small businesses financially through loans, subsidies and grants, in the absence of the ICT center jointly commissioned by the government and UNIDO, very little concrete effort has been made to facilitate the adoption of ICT by agribusinesses in the country (Diso, 2005). Overall, it remains general tacit knowledge that the government's ICT policy will be unrealized (Sanni et al., 2001). Seeing the effect of this particular policy in this particular study suggests that policy interventions and adjustments must be appropriate to the context and should take into account its distinctiveness.

Cultural Antecedents

The interviewees were asked to articulate the state of their current business links before and after the diffusion of the ICT innovation.

In the words of one of the interviewees, such relationships were necessary because;

...no one is a monopoly of knowledge (Owner-manager II).

....yes of course, we do share common knowledge in our meeting. You know that information flows faster informally (Owner-manager I).

The major point of interest is that four of the interviewees did confirm that they had heard about ICT and its use in e-commerce for the first time from colleagues. In their words;

The media is not even accessible here in the remote village as you can see not everybody has television antenna to pick what is said in TV. The crier van is a disturbance because it makes a lot of noise early in the morning (Marketing-manager III)

I have a good rapport with Chyco Farms and I normally chat with the chief executive who happened to be a friend. I detailed him about the implementation of Internet and he promised to link other colleagues so that we can team together and see if we can implement it instead of going about it on [an] individual basis (Head of Technology)

Overall, we found evidence of the existence of a high degree of social collaboration. A substantial number of these groups had been established on account of members' individual initiatives, and only a few of the networks (mainly the larger ones such as ESFC and SASNET) had been set up as part of a wider government initiative. This finding may not be particularly surprising for two reasons. Initially, it is well established that cooperative networks represent good enabling environments for *agripreneurial* activity (Slangen et al., 2004), by their facilitation of learning opportunities (Wasko & Faraj, 2005). The second explanation for the high degree of social activity may be explained by ethnology.

Ebonyi is a state dominated predominantly by the *Igbo* tribe. Earlier work notes possible impact of tribal and ethnic background and orientation towards entrepreneurial behavior (Frederick, 2008; Nnadozie, 2002; Ramachandran & Shah, 1999). For example, the market dominates Igbo culture with traditional daily life revolving mainly around the four-day traditional market cycle (Basden, 1921). Research has already indicated that the *Igbo* worldview also exhibits a relationship-based manifest where lifelong relationships are formed within family, masquerade groups, age grades and titled societies (Henderson, 1966; Jones, 1962; Meek & Arnett, 1938).

Another cultural antecedent emerging from the diffusion of ICT innovation in Ebonyi is empowerment. A substantial number of the interviewees suggested that they explicitly forbade their employees from discussing their business unless they were present. It appeared in most cases that this was due to concerns about commercial confidentiality. There may be a need, however, to highlight that there are plausible *social* reasons for this behavior. The Igbo country is also a society heavily oriented towards authority gained from village assemblies (Meek & Arnett, 1938). Often, although respect is accorded to age (Arth, 1968), Igbo culture is very much orientated towards the empowerment of 'successful' youth. This may have created a situation where some of the older SMAE proprietors, feeling threatened by an educated workforce, sought to prevent the manifestation of networks outside their 'control'.

It remains challenging to allocate quantitative measures on economic activities. Several societies have inherent cultural antecedents that shape their social activities. As relates to our study, the implication of this position is that as already demonstrated in earlier research (Waggoner, 2004), social constructs were found to have had a substantial impact on ICT diffusion innovation in Ebonyi. These social constructs are representative of an *Igbo* culture. For example, during the interviews, concerns were raised by some interviewees that ICT diffusion may disrupt traditional life. One of the interviewees (*Owner-manager IV)* pointed out that the traditional work pattern of the men in the area involved attending to farm business during the day and then family in the evenings. The underlying concern here was that the diffusion of such technology may prove invasive to family life.

Information Dissemination

Another diffusion parameter we explored was communications. Traditionally, communication among the SMAEs took place through personal face-to-face interaction. This approach has also represented the traditional means of agricultural extension services provided by the government (Eze et al., 2006). For example, a resident extension officer is always assigned as a representative of the Ministry of Agriculture. The extension officer, among other roles, serves as the main medium of information. Usually, these extension officers transmit information through two major ways. In the first place, authority is sought through the traditional ruler (*called an Eze or Igwe*) to address the town council through the Town Development Union Forum. This process is augmented with the employment of a town crier operating from a van mounted with a public address system who drives around the village bellowing out information. The process is usually ineffective. In the first place, Town Development Union Forum or village meetings always appear to allocate limited time to agriculture-related matters. Most of these meetings are highly rancorous affairs. In any event they are usually held on a monthly basis which does not facilitate the immediate transmission of information. Secondly, the use of town criers is extremely unpopular due to the noise they generate very early in the morning.

FUTURE MODELS FOR ICT DIFFUSION INNOVATION

The factors identified in this study which influence diffusion of ICT innovation are numerous, and range from environmental to social factors. Among the factors identified, cultural disposition and lack of collaborative mechanisms were highlighted as having a very negative impact on the diffusion process. On the other hand, in line with earlier work by scholars such as Hofstede (1993) (with a focus on culture in this case), the existence of social institutions and cooperative societies was seen to have an extremely positive impact on the diffusion process. One critical element of the *Igbo* worldview which is mentioned is placement of the market place at the centre of community life where people gather after work to socialize and interact with friends.

Sustaining innovative activity will require government and other non-governmental organizations to focus on the provision of targeted support to SMAES, especially in the area of provision of non-existent infrastructure and technology, and the enhancement of social networks. A possible initiative that may enhance the possibility of this objective being achieved is the utilization of ICT data centers which are technology-based community centers that may be used to provide telecommunications and Internet access to SMAES. They are based on the concept of telecenters, and like telecenters, may include single-purpose ICT outlets that provide dedicated communications (local and international telephone connections, computer connections). One such ICT center currently being tried out is the UNIDO-ICT center, a collaborative initiative between UNIDO and the Ebonyi State Government whose daily operations are run by a team of researchers affiliated with the Ebonyi State University. Although there are numerous advantages of the ICT center, it does face challenges. During the months of June and July (the middle of the rainy season), most parts of Ebonyi (especially the rice growing areas) would be subject to heavy flooding. This makes travelling extremely dangerous resulting in most farmers choosing to stay put within their farmhouses. It is likely that during this period the UNIDO-ICT center will be underutilized. One possible means of addressing diffusion challenges during this period may be the deployment of Mobile Internet Units (MIUs).

CONCLUSION

This study identified the dispersive nature of agribusiness influences on ICT innovation diffusion. The findings point to the need to ensure successful ICT innovation diffusion for agrarian business enterprises in Nigeria: there is a need to re-conceptualise the innovation diffusion process to incorporate more social interactions which represent the cultural imperatives of the people who are expected to adopt the innovation.

REFERENCES

Adamic, L., & Adar, E. (2005). How to search a social network. *Journal of Social Networks, 27*, 187–203. doi:10.1016/j.socnet.2005.01.007

Adrian, A., Norwood, S., & Mask, P. (2005). Producers' perceptions and attitudes toward precision agriculture technologies. *Computers and Electronics in Agriculture, 48*(3), 256–271. doi:10.1016/j.compag.2005.04.004

Aleke, B. (2003). *Up-take of e-commerce technologies by small and medium agricultural enterprises*. Unpublished doctoral dissertation, University of Northumbria, Newcastle, UK.

Aleke, B. (2010). *Developing a model for information and communication technology diffusion among small and medium sized agribusiness enterprises in Southeast Nigeria*. Unpublished doctoral dissertation, University of Northumbria, Newcastle, UK.

Aleke, B., Wainwright, D., & Green, G. (2009). Policy issues of e-commerce technology diffusion in Southeast Nigeria: The case of small scale agribusiness. *Northumbria Built and Virtual Environment Working Paper Series, 2*, 39-54.

Alvesson, M., & Deetz, S. (2000). *Doing critical management research*. London, UK: Sage.

Arth, M. (1968). Ideals and behaviour: A comment on Ibo respect patterns. *The Gerontologist, 8*, 242–244. doi:10.1093/geront/8.4.242

Awoke, M., & Okorji, C. (2004). The determination and analysis of constraints in resource use efficiency in multiple cropping systems by small-holder farmers in Ebonyi State, Nigeria. *Africa Development. Afrique et Developpement, 29*(3), 58–69.

Baerenklau, K., & Knapp, K. (2007). Dynamics of agricultural technology adoption: Age structure, reversibility, and uncertainty. *American Journal of Agricultural Economics, 89*, 190–201. doi:10.1111/j.1467-8276.2007.00972.x

Baron, R., & Markman, G. (2003). Beyond social capital: The role of entrepreneurs' social competence in their financial success. *Journal of Business Venturing, 18*(1), 41–60. doi:10.1016/S0883-9026(00)00069-0

Basden, G. (1921). *Among the Ibos of Nigeria*. Dublin, Ireland: Nonsuch Publishing.

Burr, V. (1995). *An introduction to social constructionism*. London, UK: Routledge. doi:10.4324/9780203299968

Castells, M. (2001). *The rise of network society* (2nd ed.). Oxford, UK: Blackwell.

CIA. (2010). *Nigeria- World Factbook*. Retrieved from https://www.cia.gov/library/publications/the-world-factbook/geos/ni.html

Cohen, L., Duberley, J., & Mallon, M. (2004). Social constructionism in the study of career: Accessing the parts that other approaches cannot reach. *Journal of Vocational Behavior, 64*, 407–422. doi:10.1016/j.jvb.2003.12.007

Cox, S. (2002). Information technology: The global key to precision agriculture and sustainability. *Computers and Electronics in Agriculture, 36*(2-3), 93–111. doi:10.1016/S0168-1699(02)00095-9

Crane, A., & Desmond, J. (2002). Societal marketing and morality. *European Journal of Marketing, 36*(5-6), 548–560. doi:10.1108/03090560210423014

de Lauwere, C. (2005). The role of agricultural entrepreneurship in Dutch agriculture of today. *Agricultural Economics, 33*(2), 229–238. doi:10.1111/j.1574-0862.2005.00373.x

Diso, L. (2005). Information technology policy formulation in Nigeria: Answers without questions. *The International Information & Library Review, 37*(4), 295–302. doi:10.1016/j.iilr.2005.10.006

Eze, C. C., Ibekwe, U. C., Onoh, P. J., & Nwajiuba, C. U. (2006). Determinants of adoption of improved Cassava production technologies among farmers in Enugu State of Nigeria. *Global Approaches to Extension Practice*, 2(1), 37–44.

Frederick, H. (2008). Introduction to special issue on indigenous entrepreneurs. *Journal of Enterprising Communities: People and Places in the Global Economy*, 2(3), 185–191. doi:10.1108/17506200810897187

Groucutt, J., & Griseri, P. (2004). *Mastering e-business.* New York, NY: Palgrave Macmillan. Henderson, R. (1966). Generalized cultures and evolutionary adaptability: A comparison of Urban Efik and Ibo in Nigeria. *Ethnology*, 5(4), 365–391.

Higgins, V., Dibden, J., & Cocklin, C. (2008). Building alternative agri-food networks: Certification, embeddedness and agri-environmental governance. *Journal of Rural Studies*, 24(1), 15–27. doi:10.1016/j.jrurstud.2007.06.002

Hofstede, G. (1993). Cultural constraints in management theories. *The Academy of Management Executive*, 7(1), 81–94.

Hossain, L., & de Silva, A. (2009). Exploring user acceptance of technology using social networks. *The Journal of High Technology Management Research*, 20(1), 1–18. doi:10.1016/j.hitech.2009.02.005

Jabbar, M., Ehui, S., & Von Kaufmann, R. (2002). Supply and demand for livestock credit in Sub-Saharan Africa: Lessons for designing new credit schemes. *World Development*, 30(6), 1029–1042. doi:10.1016/S0305-750X(02)00021-9

Jack, S. (2010). Approaches to studying networks: Implications and outcomes. *Journal of Business Venturing*, 25(1), 120–137. doi:10.1016/j.jbusvent.2008.10.010

Jones, G. (1962). Ibo age organization, with special reference to the Cross River and North-Eastern Ibo. *Journal of the Royal Anthropological Institute of Great Britain and Ireland*, 92(2), 191–211. doi:10.2307/2844258

Kadushin, C. (2002). The motivational foundation of social networks. *Social Networks*, 24(1), 77–91. doi:10.1016/S0378-8733(01)00052-1

Kanfer, R. (1990). Motivation theory and industrial and organizational psychology. In Dunnette, M. D., & Hough, L. M. (Eds.), *Handbook of industrial and organizational psychology* (pp. 75–170). Chicago, IL: Rand McNally.

Kirsten, J., & Sartorius, K. (2002). Linking agribusiness and small-scale farmers in developing countries: Is there a new role for contract farming? *Development Southern Africa*, 19(4), 503–529. doi:10.1080/0376835022000019428

Knudson, W., Wysocki, A., Champagne, J., & Peterson, H. P. (2004). Entrepreneurship and innovation in the agri-food system. *American Journal of Agricultural Economics*, 86(5), 1330–1336. doi:10.1111/j.0002-9092.2004.00685.x

Manyong, V. M., Ikpi, A., Olayemi, J. K., Yusuf, S. A., Omonona, B. T., Okoruwa, V., & Idachaba, F. S. (2005). *Agriculture in Nigeria: Identifying opportunities for increased commercialization and investment.* Ibadan, Nigeria: IITA.

Martin, S., & Jagadish, A. (2006, August 25-27). Agricultural marketing and agribusiness supply chain issues in developing economies. In *Proceedings of the New Zealand Agriculture and Resources Economics Society Conference.*

Meek, C., & Arnett, E. (1938). Law and authority in a Nigerian tribe: A study in indirect rule. *Journal of the Royal African Society*, 37(146), 115–118.

Minten, B., & Barrett, C. (2008). Agricultural technology, productivity, and poverty in Madagascar. *World Development, 36*(5), 797–822. doi:10.1016/j.worlddev.2007.05.004

Mishili, F., Fulton, J., Shehu, M., Kushwaha, S., Marfo, K., & Jamal, M. (2009). Consumer preferences for quality characteristics along the cowpea value chain in Nigeria, Ghana, and Mali. *Agribusiness, 25*(1), 16–35. doi:10.1002/agr.20184

Mishra, A. K., & Park, T. A. (2005). An empirical analysis of internet use by US farmers. *Agricultural and Resources Economics Review, 34*(2), 253–264.

Molla, A., Taylor, R., & Licker, P. S. (2006). E-Commerce diffusion in small island countries: The influence of institutions in Barbados. *Electronic Journal on Information Systems in Developing Countries, 28*(2), 1–15.

Nnadozie, E. (2002). African indigenous entrepreneurship: Determinants of resurgence and growth of Igbo entrepreneurship during the Post-Biafra period. *Journal of African Business, 3*(1), 49–80. doi:10.1300/J156v03n01_04

Omamo, S., & Lynam, J. (2003). Agricultural science and technology policy in Africa. *Research Policy, 32*(9), 1681–1694. doi:10.1016/S0048-7333(03)00059-3

Oseni, G., & Winters, P. (2009). Rural nonfarm activities and agricultural crop production in Nigeria. *Agricultural Economics, 40*(2), 189–201. doi:10.1111/j.1574-0862.2009.00369.x

Oyelaran-Oyeyinka, B., & La, K. (2005). Internet diffusion in sub-Saharan Africa: A cross-country analysis. *Telecommunications Policy, 29*(7), 507–527. doi:10.1016/j.telpol.2005.05.002

Pande, R. (2006). Profits and politics: Coordinating technology adoption in agriculture. *Journal of Development Economics, 81*(2), 299–315. doi:10.1016/j.jdeveco.2005.06.012

Prescott, M. B., & Conger, S. A. (1995). Information technology innovations: A classification by IT locus of impact and research approach. *Journal of Data Base for Advances in Information Systems, 26*(2), 20–25.

Ramachandran, V., & Shah, M. (1999). Minority entrepreneurs and firm performance in Sub-Saharan Africa. *The Journal of Development Studies, 36*(2), 71–87. doi:10.1080/00220389908422621

Rao, N. (2007). A framework for implementing information and communication technologies in agricultural development in India. *Technological Forecasting and Social Change, 74*(4), 491–518. doi:10.1016/j.techfore.2006.02.002

Rodriguez, F., & Wilson, E. (2000). *Are poor countries losing the information revolution?* Washington, DC: World Bank.

Rogers, E. M. (1995). *Diffusion of innovations* (4th ed.). New York, NY: Free Press.

Romani, M. (2003). Love thy neighbour? Evidence from ethnic discrimination in information sharing within villages in côte d'ivoire. *Journal of African Economies, 12*(4), 533–563. doi:10.1093/jae/12.4.533

Saho, E., & Zira, D. (2009). Awareness and effectiveness of vegetable technology information packages by vegetable farmers in Adamawa State, Nigeria. *African Journal of Agricultural Research, 4*(2), 65–70.

Sanni, S., Ilori, M., Opaleye, A., & Oyewale, A. (2001). Nigeria's technology policy: Is it adequate in the globalizing world? *Technovation, 21*(4), 237–243. doi:10.1016/S0166-4972(00)00044-4

Sassenrath, G. F., Heilman, P., Luschei, E., Bennett, G. L., Fitzgerald, G., & Klesius, P. (2008). Technology, complexity and change in agricultural production systems. *Renewable Agriculture and Food Systems, 23*(4), 285–295. doi:10.1017/S174217050700213X

Slangen, L., van Kooten, C., & Suchánek, P. (2004). Institutions, social capital and agricultural change in central and eastern Europe. *Journal of Rural Studies, 20*(2), 245–256. doi:10.1016/j.jrurstud.2003.08.005

Spielman, D., Ekboir, J., & Davis, K. (2009). The art and science of innovation systems inquiry: Applications to Sub-Saharan African agriculture. *Technology in Society, 31*(4), 399–405. doi:10.1016/j.techsoc.2009.10.004

Sydow, J. (2005). Managing interfirm networks. In Theurl, T. (Ed.), *Economics of interfirm networks*. Tübingen, Germany: J. C. B. Mohr.

Tubiello, F., & Fischer, G. (2007). Reducing climate change impacts on agriculture: Global and regional effects of mitigation, 2000–2080. *Technological Forecasting and Social Change, 74*(7), 1030–1056. doi:10.1016/j.techfore.2006.05.027

Von Hippel, E. (2006). Horizontal innovation networks: By and for users. *Journal of Research and Development Management, 36*(3), 273–294.

Waggoner, P. (2004). Agricultural technology and its societal implications. *Technology in Society, 26*(2-3), 123–136. doi:10.1016/j.techsoc.2004.01.024

Wainwright, D., & Waring, T. S. (2007). The application and adaptation of a diffusion of innovation framework for information system. *Journal of Information Technology, 22*, 44–58. doi:10.1057/palgrave.jit.2000093

Wasko, M., & Faraj, S. (2005). Why should I share? Examining social capital and knowledge contribution in electronic networks of practice. *Management Information Systems Quarterly, 29*(1), 35–57.

Watts, C., & Ashcroft, L. (2005). ICT skills for information professionals in developing countries: Perspective from a study of the electronic information environment in Nigeria. *IFLA Journal, 31*(1), 146–153.

Weick, C. (2001). Agribusiness technology in 2010: Directions and challenges. *Technology in Society, 23*(1), 59–72. doi:10.1016/S0160-791X(00)00035-X

This journal was previously published in the International Journal of Technology Diffusion, Volume 2, Issue 2, edited by Ali Hussein Saleh Zolait, pp. 19-31, copyright 2011 by IGI Publishing (an imprint of IGI Global).

Chapter 8
A Preliminary Classification of Usage Measures in Information System Acceptance:
A Q–Sort Approach

Muhammad Z. I. Lallmahomed
Universiti Teknologi Malaysia, Malaysia

Roliana Ibrahim
Universiti Teknologi Malaysia, Malaysia

Nor Zairah Ab. Rahim
Universiti Teknologi Malaysia, Malaysia

Azizah Abdul Rahman
Universiti Teknologi Malaysia, Malaysia

ABSTRACT

In the light of a diverse body of disorganized usage measures available and the difficulty of building a cumulative research tradition, a literature review is conducted on system use in Information Systems (IS) Acceptance through the two main theories of Technology Adoption, the Technology Acceptance Model (TAM), and The Unified Theory of Use and Acceptance of Technology (UTAUT). The authors seek to understand how usage measures are being operationalised and proposed a preliminary classification of those measures that covers system and task aspects of use. A Q-Sort approach was taken to validate the authors' classification scheme and the result indicates high inter-rater agreement. The ensuing classification is meant to help researchers in their choice of system use measures. This review also summarises the arguments for a multi-dimensional measure of use and establishes that omnibus measure such as frequency, volume and use/non-use hold prevalence. Finally, the authors provide recommendations for further research in the area of system use.

1. INTRODUCTION

Large investments (Gable et al., 2008) are made by organisations expecting significant improvements in business processes and positive impacts thereof. One of the main criteria for deriving benefits

from those substantial investments is that newly installed Information Systems (IS) are utilised in the correct way. Under or improper utilisation of IS have been the cause of many failures and have been identified as the major factor for the 'productivity paradox' (Agarwal & Prasad, 1998; Sykes et al., 2009; Venkatesh & Davis, 2000).

DOI: 10.4018/978-1-4666-2791-8.ch008

System use, according to Straub et al. (1995) is essential in measuring professional performance, a necessary conduit to derive net benefits and for managers to assess the impact of their systems. Recently, very little attention has been paid to the system use construct itself despite the fact that system usage has been around since the 1970s (Lucas, 1973).

Lack of theoretical grounding (Burton-Jones & Straub, 2006; Straub et al., 1995) on how to choose and use measures of system use coupled with a plethora of unsystematized measures and different conceptualisations (Davis, 1989; Doll & Torkzadeh, 1998) make it difficult to compare research findings and hampers effort to build cumulative research tradition (Straub et al., 1995). The absence of reliable and consistent measures of system use (Petter & McLean, 2009) has further increase the misuse of this variable and lead to diverse results among IS practitioners (Livari, 2002; Rai et al., 2003; Roldan & Leal, 2003). This has lead to calls for further research into measures of system usage (Benbasat & Barki, 2007; Delone & McLean, 2003; Hennington et al., 2009; Straub et al., 1995).

In the absence of proper definitions and conceptualisations of usage measure, researchers have been employing a diverse set of measures, some of which have different conceptualisations but same operationalisations, others were chosen based on previous research and yet others were not even named. This paper builds on the work done by Burton-Jones and Straub (2006) on re-conceptualising system use in order to investigate the current measures of system use being used, to classify the plethora of system use measures being used in an attempt to help researchers in their choice of usage measures. In this research, the researchers have two main questions; first how are measures of system use currently being operationalised in IS acceptance? Second, to what extent can these measures be categorised? In a bid to answer those questions, the researchers summarise the arguments for a multi-dimensional

measures of use and proposed a preliminary taxonomy of usage measures. Considering that system use has been conceptualised into four different domains, this review will be selective, aiming only at the IS acceptance domain using the Technology Acceptance Model and the Unified Theory of Acceptance and Use as underlying framework. This paper is structured as follows: the next section provides a discussion of system use construct and the role it plays in acceptance research as well as a summary of the arguments for a multi-dimensional measure of use. Section 3 explains the chosen methodology for retrieving usage measures from the literature. Section 4 discusses the Q-Sort approach and the findings. Finally, Section 5 provides the limitations, conclusions recommendations for further research.

2. DEFINING SYSTEM USE

The definition of system use itself is problematic as there is no standard definition in the literature. Definition is complicated in the case of system use, as a definition implies the categorisation of a particular construct and setting limits to what is system usage. Currently four main domains in conceptualising this variable has been reported (Burton-Jones & Straub, 2006) namely use in IS success, use for IS acceptance, use in post implementation and use for decision making. Based on these conceptualisation of use, Burton-Jones and Straub (2006) define individual level system use as "an individual user's employment of one or more features of a system to perform a task" (p. 231). Petter and McLean (2009) define system use in the context of IS Success as the "consumption of an IS or its output described in terms of actual or self-reported usage" (p. 161). Straub et al. (1995) define it as "utilisation of Information Technology by individuals, groups or organisations" (p. 1328). This paper will take the view of Burton-Jones & Straub's (2006) definition. Their definition denotes three elements, namely:

a user, a system and task to be carried out. They (Burton-Jones & Straub, 2006, p. 231) argue that any definition must rely on assumptions as follows; (1) "A user is an individual person who employs an IS in a task. This implies that although users are social actors and that it is possible to study user behaviour at a purely individual level. (2) "An IS is an artifact that provides representations of one or more task domains. This implies that ISs provide features that are designed to support functions in those task domain(s)." (3) "A task is a goal-directed activity performed by a user. This implies that task outputs can be assessed in terms of predefined task requirements."

2.1. Acceptance Models

Technology adoption is one of the most mature research areas in the Information System discipline (Brown et al., 2010; Skyes et al., 2009; Straub et al., 1995) with a large number of theories (Brown et al., 2010) that has been developed since the 1980s. The combination of these theories (Venkatesh et al., 2003) focuses on explaining the factors that will lead some individuals or organisations choose to adopt or reject a specific technology. Figure 1 shows the overall model of IS acceptance in its most basic terms. IS acceptance deal with the antecedents of usage denoted in the diagram as individual reactions to technology use. This forms the user's intention to use technology which in turn affects its usage. User's intention to use technology is conceptualised as behavioural intention, which is defined as *"a person's subjective probability*

that he will perform some behaviour" (Fishbein & Azjen, 1975, p. 12). Venkatesh et al. (2003) gives examples of two research streams in the IS acceptance area, namely individual acceptance of technology using intention or usage as a dependent variable (Davis, 1989; Davis et al., 1989), while the other focuses on implementation of IS at the organisational level and task-technology fit (Goodhue & Thompson, 1995; Venkatesh et al., 2003). The dotted line on Figure 1 is the feedback loop from usage that will eventually affect the users' continued intention after having accepted and used the IT artefact in the first place.

Figure 2 depicts a decomposed basic model of IS acceptance that denotes the major constructs involved and their hypothesised relationships based on the works of Doll and Torkzadeh, (1988); Venkatesh et al. (2003) and a thorough review of the literature. Research (Adams et al., 1992; Davis, 1989; Kim et al., 2009; Kwon, 2010; Venkatesh et al., 2003) in the domain of upstream IS acceptance areas deals mainly with factors that will lead an individual to use or intent to use a system and is termed as antecedents or predictors of use. These antecedents are tested against intention and use, where usage is the ultimate dependant variable (Brown et al., 2010; Davis, 1989; Venkatesh & Bala, 2008; Venkatesh et al., 2003). Downstream research intends to find out how usage impacts the organisation or individual (Anandarajan et al., 2002; Bokhari, 2005; Delone & McLean, 2003; Lee et al., 2009; Petter & McLean, 2009) and posits a link between usage and impact derived from that use. Impact, in this case, can mean

Figure 1. Basic concept of acceptance model (adapted from Venkatesh et al., 2003)

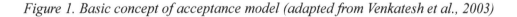

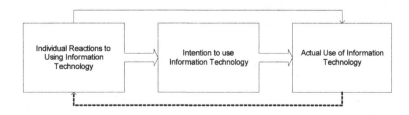

Figure 2. Acceptance to Impact value chain

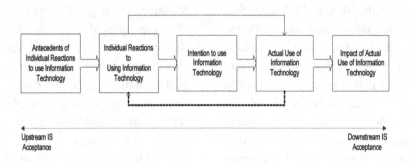

performance, satisfaction or net benefits. Also, based on prior acceptance and usage, users can determined whether they want to continue using the system or reject the system (Battercherjee, 2001). Hence, usage leads to continued use of the system. System use plays the role of an independent variable in downstream research whereas it is a dependant variable in upstream research.

2.2. System Use in IS Acceptance Research

IS acceptance (Venkatesh et al., 2003) is part of a long research tradition that sought to understand how and why individuals adopt and use information technology. Even though, there are no standardise definition of IS acceptance, the recurrent theme in the literature (Davis, 1989; Davis et al., 1989; King & He, 2006; Venkatesh et al; 2003; Yousafzai et al., 2007) has established that the study of IS acceptance refers mainly to the understanding of underlying factors that would cause people to agree and/or disagree to exploit an IS and/or to predict future utilization of an IS (Adams et al., 1992) and/or to improve user adoption of an IS given that user acceptance (Davis, 1993) is a key determinant in the success or failure of an IS. IS Acceptance towards system use mainly refers to the study of factors that cause people to agree to use a particular system, predict and determine determinants that will lead to system use (Davis, 1989; King & He, 2006) where

system use (Venkatesh et al., 2003) is used as a dependant variable and is the ultimate benchmark from which predictors of use will be tested against.

2.3. Technology Acceptance Model (TAM)

A good example of the conceptualisation of system use in IS acceptance is the Technology Acceptance Model (TAM) of Fred Davis. TAM (Davis et al., 1989) is an adaptation of the theory of reasoned action (Fishbein & Ajzen, 1975) which posits that individual behaviour is determined by behavioural intention to perform an action which is itself based on attitude towards performing that action and subjective norms surrounding that particular action.

TAM being an extension of TRA suggests that actual usage of a system is determined by intention to use that system which is itself based on attitudes towards using that system (Figure 3). Attitudes is then affected by perceived usefulness and perceived ease of use.

Perceived usefulness (Davis et al., 1989) refers to the belief that the system will increase one job performance in an organisational setting while perceived ease of use refers to the degree of facility that the prospective user expects of the system. TAM has received a number of modifications over the years; adding additional factors to perceived usefulness and perceived ease of use (Davis & Venkatesh, 1996; Oh et al., 2003; Wixom & Todd,

Figure 3. Theory of reasoned action (adapted from Fishbein & Ajzen, 1975)

```
┌──────────────┐      ┌──────────────┐
│ Beliefs and  │─────▶│ Attitude     │
│ Evaluations  │      │ towards      │
└──────────────┘      │ behaviour    │      ┌──────────────┐      ┌──────────────┐
                      └──────────────┘─────▶│ Behavioural  │─────▶│ Behaviour    │
┌──────────────┐      ┌──────────────┐      │ Intention    │      └──────────────┘
│ Normative    │─────▶│ Subjective   │─────▶└──────────────┘
│ Beliefs and  │      │ Norm         │
│ Motivation   │      └──────────────┘
└──────────────┘
```

2005), extending predictive power of the model (Dishaw & Strong, 1999; Venkatesh et al., 2003). Contextual factors and consequence factors (King & He, 2006) such as gender and perceptual/actual usage respectfully have also been used in extending TAM (Figure 4). Benbasat and Barki (2007), in their criticism of TAM, noted that few researchers have ventured out to really understand the sub-constructs of variables used in TAM. They also note that TAM has been focusing exclusively on explaining system use conceptualised in a simplistic manner while it fails to consider other aspects of usage behaviour such as reinvention and learning.

2.4. Unified Theory of Acceptance and Use of Technology (UTAUT)

TAM is the vanguard model in explaining user acceptance and usage of IT, though not the only model available, e.g., Theory of Planned Behaviour (Ajzen, 1991) and Social Cognitive Theory (Compeau & Higgins, 1995); this abundance of

"Acceptance models" has lead to a variety of competing determinants of user acceptance and usage. In a bid to unify and increase the explanatory power of those models, Venkatesh et al. (2003) developed the Unified Theory of Acceptance and Use of Technology based on 8 prominent models namely the Theory of Reasoned Action (TRA) (Fishbein & Ajzen, 1975), the Technology Acceptance Model (TAM) (Davis, 1989; Davis et al., 1989), the Motivational Model (Davis et al., 1992), the Theory of Planned Behaviour (TPB) (Ajzen, 1991), a model combining the Technology Acceptance Model and the Theory of Planned Behaviour (Taylor & Todd, 1995), the Model of Personal Computer Utilization (MPCU) (Thompson et al., 1991; Triandis, 1977), the Innovation Diffusion Theory (IDT) (Moore & Benbasat 1991; Rogers, 1995), and the Social Cognitive Theory (SCT) (Bandura, 1986; Compeau & Higgins, 1995). During their six month long study, the model was found to outperform all of the eight previous models with an explained variance of 70 percent in user intention to use information technology.

Figure 4. Technology acceptance model (adapted from Davis et al., 1989)

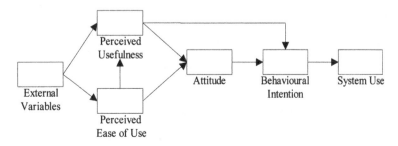

UTAUT (Venkatesh et al., 2003) makes use of 4 predictor variables namely performance expectancy, effort expectancy, social influence, facilitation conditions and 4 moderators of these relationships namely gender, age, experience and voluntariness (Figure 5). Predictor variables were derived from several models, those found to have similar underlying construct and measurement scales were grouped together. Some of these variables were conceptualised under different names such as perceived usefulness in TAM/TAM2 and outcome expectations in SCT among others.

Venkatesh et al. (2003) argues for the insertion of gender and age as mediating variables citing research from Minton and Schneider (1980); Venkatesh and Morris (2000) among others, experience as mediating factor for effort expectancy, social influence and facilitating conditions. According to Levy (1988) the triad of gender, age and experience work together. Further voluntariness of use is expected to mediate social influence only as they were found (Venkatesh et al., 2003) to be non-significant in voluntary context contrary to a mandatory one. As mediators, gender and age have been found to affect the performance expectancy and it was more pronounced among young male workers.

Further, age moderates effort expectancy in older women and those with little experience was also found to be affected while the effect of gender, age, experience and voluntariness was found on social influence in mandatory environments among older women. Moreover, age and experience moderate facilitating conditions especially among workers with experience in the use of technology.

2.5. Importance of a Multi-Dimensional Measure of Use

System use (Straub et al., 1995) albeit being an important conduit to derive net benefits, assess satisfaction and measure adoption of an IT artefact, has received very little theoretical scrutiny (Burton-Jones & Straub, 2006). The literature has no standard measures of use (Hamner & Qazi, 2009) and the plethora of measures may give the wrong conclusion that the current measures of usage are sufficient (Burton-Jones & Straub, 2006). The problem with one-dimensional simplistic measure of use is that it assumes that more usage will lead to more benefits or more usage means high adoption rate and more benefits, this argument is flawed as one-dimensional measures of usage (Doll & Torkzadeh, 1998) may not take

Figure 5. Unified theory of acceptance and use of technology (adapted from Venkatesh et al., 2003)

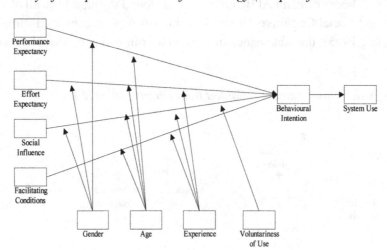

into consideration the context in which systems are used and the nature of that use (Delone & Mclean, 2003).

Further, research (Burton-Jones & Hubona, 2006) assessing the predictive power of TAM on frequency and volume of use shows that TAM better predicts frequency of use rather than volume of use and they conclude that volume of usage is explained by more factors as compared to frequency of use, hence usage measures are much more complex than once thought (Brown et al., 2010; Burton-Jones & Hubona 2006; Hennington et al., 2009). Brown et al. (2010) and Igbaria et al. (1997) used a multi-dimension of use in a bid to improve reliability, following recommendations of Fishbein and Ajzen.

Doll and Torkzadeh (1998) argue that these simplistic measures of system use might be sufficient for upstream research if the goal is only to assess adoption but it should be pointed out that a system might have very high adoption rate, where usage is measured in terms of frequency and volume of use but still not perform as expected. Then in such a scenario, managers would have to identify which part of the system poses problem and make necessary interventions. Hence, using a multi-dimensional measure of usage may alleviate this problem. Moreover, Battacherjee (2001) states that the same variables accounting for pre-acceptance behaviour fail to deal with discontinued use after the user has accepted it and called this phenomenon the "acceptance-discontinuance anomaly." A multi-dimensional measure of use might help to detect such behaviour in advance and help managers, web-site administrators make informed decisions.

The literature dealing with usage often makes the distinction between mandatory and voluntary use. The use of a system is deemed to be a mandatory one when the users have no choice in deciding whether to use the system or not, while in a voluntary context, users have the ability to decide on accepting or rejecting the system. This distinction has serious implications for the adoption and acceptance research as it implies that usage cannot

be used to measure benefits or as a predictor of benefits in a mandatory context as the user would have to use the system anyway, as compared to a voluntary one. Doll and Torkzadeh (1988) argues that voluntary usage can be a measure of success but in mandatory context user satisfaction would be better. Although Delone and McLean (2003); Hartwick and Barki (1994) have argued against it, the authors contend that the user element of usage, may help to alleviate this problem, as knowing the users' lack of interest/affect with the system in a mandatory environment may lead managers to reverse the under-utilisation of those systems.

Moreover, Hennington et al. (2009) found that a multi-dimensional measure of use is necessary in understanding relationship among technology acceptance constructs but cautioned against discarding uni-dimensional ones as they may be useful in certain context. It has also been found that many researchers have used intention to use as a proxy for actual use; these are two different constructs altogether and have different conceptualisations. Hernandez et al. (2009) quotes (Agarwal & Prasad, 1997; Cooper & Zmud, 1990) and states that having an early adoption of the technology does not necessarily lead to benefits, but a sustained use of technology is needed. Further, Rogers (1995) shows that early adoption of a technology has very limited impact on subsequent use of IT. Hence, in order to fully understand the benefits from a technology, it is vital to analyse not only antecedents of use but also usage as well although we acknowledge that in some situations, intention to use might be a better measure of adoption since system use measures are still at its infancy.

2.6. Plethora of System Use Measures

Scholars have argued that the IS literature is filled with usage measures that lack a theoretical background, are disorganised and give the impression that there are adequate measures of use but few researchers have actually shown how this over abundance of usage measures manifest itself through the IS literature. Through our literature review, the reader's attention is drawn to the following examples below in order to explain practically how does this plethora of measures leads to confusion among IS practitioners and why a taxonomy of usage measures is necessary. Researchers have employed a vast array of usage measures, some of these measures have different conceptualisations but same operationalisations for example Karahanna et al. (2006) have conceptualised measures of use as intensity while same conceptualisation is found in Al-Gahtani and King (1999) and Brown et al. (2010) as frequency of use. Duration of use was conceptualised by Venkatesh et al. (2008) but this measure have been operationalised as volume of use in Burton-Jones and Hubona (2006). Scope of use (Karahanna et al., 2006) bears same operationalisation as extent of use (Igbaria et al., 1997). Brown et al. (2010) conceptualised choice as a measure of use and operationlised it by asking about the percentage of time the user choose to use the system while we found about the Alda's-Manzano (2008) and Anderson et al. (2006) have operationalise the same measure of use but with different conceptualisation. Further, the fact that scholars tend to choose measures based on previous articles, this increase the body of disorganised measures such that scholars would think that these are new measures of use while they are not. Other measures of use were not named (Barnett et al., 2007; Bhattacherjee & Sanford, 2009; Konradt et al., 2006). To avoid redundancy of measures and build a cumulative research tradition as suggested by Burton-Jones and Straub (2006) and Straub et al. (1995); a taxonomy of usage measures is the first step to be taken.

3. METHODOLOGY

A literature review on TAM and UTAUT was carried out to retrieve current measures of system use being operationalised. Several databases were searched; Web of Science, EbscoHost, ACM, Science Direct database with keywords 'TAM, Technology Acceptance Model, System use and Usage' and for UTAUT, we repeated the procedure by replacing the keywords with 'UTAUT' and 'Unified Theory of Use and Acceptance of Technology' (Table 1). Articles were retained if they have

1. TAM and UTAUT used in an empirical study.
2. Extension or Addition to TAM and UTAUT but used in empirical study.
3. Have used system use in their study.
4. Have complete and clear empirical data used with system use construct.

The search resulted in 101 articles.

3.1. Classifying Usage Measures

In order to classify usage measures, we adopted a Q-Sort approach. Q-Sort stems from research done by Stephenson (1935) in the 1930s and has been extensively used in social research. Thomas and Watson (2002) state that the first use of Q-sorting in the MIS literature started in the 1980s and has since then gained a foothold in IS discipline. Originally, Q-Sort has been used in psychology to assess personal beliefs and preferences but has been extended to several areas such as psychology, sociology, and marketing. Q-Sort is employed within the Q-Methodology, which is qualitative in nature but also comprises statistical methods to assess the subjectivity of the person's beliefs and is mainly used as an exploratory technique (Watts & Stenner, 2005). Q-Sort is also used to check for reliability (Thomas & Baas, 1992) and is a means of assessing content validity by eliminating measures that does not fit in a particular category. The use of Q-Sort in this paper is to establish whether the current measures of system use fit into our categorisation scheme and establish the inter-rater agreement in line with several researches that has used Q-sort to establish validity of constructs and confirm the structures

Table 1. Articles retained for analysis

Journals	Articles Retained	Journals	Articles Retained
ACM SIGMIS Database	1	Information Resources Management Journal	1
Behaviour & Information Technology	7	Information Systems Research	1
Computer & Education	5	Int. J. Human-Computer Studies	2
Computers in Human Behavior	11	Interacting with Computers	2
Cyber Psychology & Behavior	1	International Journal of Accounting Information Systems	1
The DATA BASE for Advances in Information Systems	4	International Journal of Information Management	2
Decision Sciences	3	International Journal of Man-Machine Studies	1
Decision Support Systems	4	International Journal of Medical Informatics	1
Electronic Commerce Research and Applications	3	Internet Research	2
Expert Systems with Applications	3	Journal of Business Research	1
Government Information Quarterly	2	Journal of High Technology Management Research	1
Group Decision and Negotiation	1	Journal of Information Systems Education	1
Industrial Management & Data Systems	2	Journal of Internet Commerce	1
Industrial Marketing Management	1	Journal of Management Information Systems	2
Information System Frontiers	1	Journal of Organisational Computing and Electronic Commerce	1
Information Systems Journal	1	Journal of the American Society for Information Science and Technology	1
Information & Management	11	Logistics Information Management	1
Information and Software Technology	1	Management Science	3
MIS Quarterly	7	Omega	2
Online Information Review	1	Technology Analysis & Strategic Management	1
Technovation	1	Tourism Management	1
Tsinghua Science and Technology	1		
Total			101

of variables (Moore & Benbasat, 1991; Segars & Grover, 1998).

From the 101 articles, 235 usage measures statements were retrieved. In order to test our categorisation scheme and definitions, the measures of usage were retrieved from the articles in the way they were operationalised and tabled along with the categories. We also provided an "Others/ can't fit" category for measures that coders were unable to sort and to ensure that coders do not force fit usage measures. Examples of usage measures are:

'On average, how frequently do you use computers?'

'How many different applications have you worked with?'

'On average, how much time (in hours) you use collaboration tool.'

Coders were asked to match measures into one of those categories. This approach was taken as it might be easier for the coders due to the large sample of usage measures and it allows for quicker analysis. The definitions of those constructs were given on a separate sheet as well as construct descriptions. During the first trial of the exercise, it was found out that coders had difficulties in sorting measures due to overlapping definitions. This was resolved by amending definitions provided. Coders were chosen from a number of different professions; a secretary, an editor, a physiotherapist and a marketing executive. A range of diverse coders were chosen to ensure that the definitions provided are clear and various perceptions are taken into account (Moore & Benbasat, 1991) and coders were allowed to ask any questions they wanted about the exercise or usage measures.

3.2. Inter-Rater Agreement

Measuring inter-rater agreement was carried using Cohen's kappa (Cohen, 1960). The kappa coefficient (Vanbelle & Albert, 2008; Warrens, 2010) is widely used to measure agreement among nominal variables with similar categories. Cohen's kappa ranges from 0 to 1, where 0 denotes no agreement beyond chance alone while 1 denotes a perfect agreement. Cohen's kappa is calculated as follows:

$$K = P_0 - P_c / 1 - P_c$$

Kappa is defined as the difference between the agreement that was obtained (P_0-P_c) and the agreement that can be obtained by chance alone (1-P_c). Cohen's kappa can only be applied to two coders only while an extended version of

Table 2. Interpretation of kappa (adapted from Landis & Koch, 1977)

Kappa's Value	Agreement	
0.21 - 0.40	Fair	
0.41 - 0.60	Moderate	
0.61 - 0.80	Substantial	
0.81 - 1.00	Almost perfect	

Cohen's kappa by Fleiss (1971), the Fleiss kappa can work with two or more coders. Interpretation of kappa was based on that of Landis and Koch (1977) (Table 2).

4. FINDINGS

The Fleiss kappa for the overall inter-rater agreement was 0.76 (Table 3). Fleiss kappa was calculated manually and was double check using ReCal3, an online utility that calculates reliability coefficients (average pair wise percent agreement, Fleiss kappa, average pairwise Cohen's kappa) for nominal data based on multiple coders, available at http://dfreelon.org/utils/recalfront/recal3/. Although no acceptable pre-defined value exits (Moore & Benbasat, 1991), a score of 0.76 would be deemed to be a substantial agreement (Landis & Koch, 1977) while Moore and Benbasat, (1991) cites (Jarvenpaa, 1989; Todd & Benbasat, 1989; Vasey, 1984) to consider values greater than 0.65 to be acceptable. Cohen's kappa was calculated through ReCal3 and double check using SPSS. Overall 67 percent of the measures of use were

Table 3. Individual measures agreement

Measures	Fleiss Kappa	Interpretation
Use/Non Use	0.58	Moderate agreement
Frequency of Use	0.80	Substantial agreement
Volume of Use	0.85	Almost perfect agreement
Extent of Use	0.67	Substantial agreement
Intensity of Use	0.78	Substantial agreement
Variety of Use	0.83	Almost perfect agreement
Others/Can't Fit	0.61	Substantial agreement
Overall Kappa	0.76	Substantial agreement

Table 4. Inter-coder agreement

Coders	Percent Agreement	Cohen's Kappa
A vs. B	72%	0.65
A vs. C	81%	0.76
A vs. D	82%	0.77
B vs. D	83%	0.78
B vs. C	80%	0.75
C vs. D	89%	0.86
Average	81%	0.76

Table 5. Frequency of measures and percentage classified

Measures of Use	Frequency	Percentage
Use/Non Use	122	13%
Frequency of Use	306	25%
Volume of Use	237	33%
Extent of Use	83	9%
Intensity of Use	132	14%
Variety of Use	46	5%
Others/Can't fit	14	1%

similarly classified by the 4 coders based on our definition while they disagreed upon 33% of the measures. Multiple rounds (Moore & Benbasat, 1991) were not carried out as the sort exhibit high reliability (Segars & Grover, 1998) and the range of usage measures from the articles contain similar operationalisations, thus checking if the coders sorted similar measures in the same categories were possible in 1 round.

Table 4 shows the agreement between the 4 coders based on percentage agreed and kappa statistics. Values were calculated using ReCal3 and SPSS. Average kappa statistics is similar to Fleiss kappa, which shows substantial agreement among coders. Table 5 shows the frequency of usage measures sorted by all 4 coders.

Figure 6 shows the percentage of usage measures employed by articles that used TAM (Davis et al., 1989) and UTAUT (Venkatesh et al., 2003) as their underlying framework, that were categorised by the 4 coders. Over 235 measures, the two main measures of usage that hold prevalence among researches are frequency of use and volume of use. These measures were the first one employed by Davis (1989) and Davis et al. (1989). Thirteen percent of research papers are still employing very lean measures (Burton-Jones & Straub, 2006) such as Use/Non Use to measure usage. Although this might be justifiable in certain circumstances, the 'ultra' lean measure does not tell us much about how the system is being used or which part

Figure 6. Percent of usage measures employed

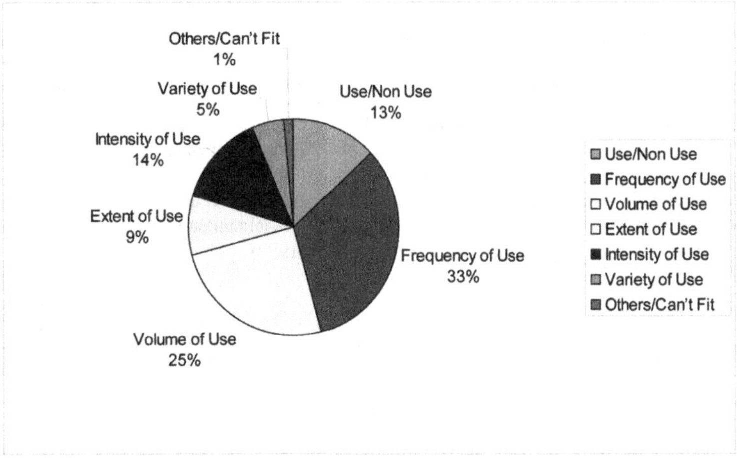

Table 6. Typology and classification of usage measures

		Typology of Usage Measures		
Measures	**Definition**	**Further descriptions**	**Illustrative references**	**Examples**
Use/Non Use	Refers to whether the system is being employed or not.	Use/Non Use is an omnibus measure and is answered by a Yes or No.	Gallego et al. (2008) Kim et al. (2008) Lin (2007)	'Assuming I have access to the system, I intend to use it.' 'I use HFOS so that my work is swift and efficient.' 'I prefer to use online shopping for buying books.'
Frequency of Use	The number of times the system is being used per unit time.	Ask how many times the system were used, measured as daily, monthly or may use a likert scale, e.g., Not all…several times daily Never…Very frequently	Al-Gahtani and King (1999) Brown et al. (2010) Anandarajan et al. (2002) Bhattacherjee and Sanford (2009)	'On average, how frequently did you use spreadsheets while working in the industry?' 'On average, how frequently do you use computers?' 'Self-reported frequency of use was measured on a six-point scale 1 (less than a month) to 6. several times a day 'Number of times you use DMS per week.'
Volume of Use	The amount or length of usage measured in units of time.	Ask how many hours the system has being used, e.g., perceived daily usage measured in hours	Chakraborty et al. (2008) Burton-Jones and Hubona (2006) Brown et al. (2010) Al-Gahtani et al. (2007)	'In the last 2 weeks, I use MSAccess___hours.' 'Please specify how many hours each week you normally spend using email?' 'On average, how much time (in hours) you use collaboration tool.' 'On an average working day, how much time do you spend using computers? (1) Almost never; (2) less than 30 min; (3) from 30 min to 1 h; (4) from 1 to 2 h; (5) from 2 to 3 h; and (6) more than 3 h'
Extent of Use	The number of business tasks or features for which the system/ applications were used.	Ask whether the system/applications was used to complete certain tasks; making decisions, trends, planning budgeting.	Igbaria et al. (1997) Roberts and Henderson (2000)	'For the following job tasks, please indicate whether you use computer to perform each task: (1) Producing Reports (2) Letter and Memos (3) Analysing Problems' 'Participants were asked to respond on a five- point Likert-type scale the extent to which they use the nominated software packages. Responses ranged from 'avoid totally' (1) to 'use to its fullest extent' (4)'
Intensity of Use	The degree of use measured as a percentage or amount of usage in terms on input and output of the system.	Diverse, it can be measured either asking the percentage of system used, messages sent, number of people contacted or pages printed.	Adams et al. (1992) Alda's-Manzano (2008) Anderson et al. (2006) Al-Gahtani and King (1999)	'Usage was measured using the number of messages sent and receive per day.' 'What percentage of your financial operations is done online?' 'Percent of time used.' 'Please indicate your usage level using spreadsheet None-----Extremely Intensive'

continued on following page

Table 6. Continued

Typology of Usage Measures				
Measures	**Definition**	**Further descriptions**	**Illustrative references**	**Examples**
Variety of Use	The number of different applications that is being used.	Ask whether the user uses the different applications, e.g., word processing, email, spreadsheets.	Al-Gahtani and King (1999) Anandarajan et al. (2002) Bhattacherjee and Sanford (2009) Maldonado et al. (2011)	'How many different applications have you worked with?' 'the questionnaire listed ten types of software applications, such as word processing, spreadsheets, database management, graphics, electronic mail, graphics, project management.' 'Number of DMS applications that you currently use:' 'How many different applications of the Peru EDUCA portal have you worked with or used in your studies?'

of the system has better acceptance. 1 percent of measures have been classified as 'Others' as our coders could not sort them in any of the categories; these include measures such as monthly expenses (Turel et al., 2007).

5. LIMITATIONS

The literature review is based on the TAM and UTAUT as underlying framework and thus is limited in that respect. Although, other theories of IS Acceptance are available, they were not added in this review as they stem from a psychology background and can be applied to a diverse set of research domains as compared to TAM and UTAUT that specifically address technology acceptance. Our definition of what constitutes usage is based on Burton-Jones and Straub (2006) article, and from that, it can be seen that the preliminary classification covers areas of system and task aspects of use only.

6. RECOMMENDATIONS AND CONCLUSION

This review has raised a number of issues that might be of interest to future research.

Firstly, five years after the landmark articles from Burton-Jones and Straub (2006) very little progress has been made on the system usage constructs. Majority of scholars are still implementing 'traditional' measures of use, which is frequency and volume of use despite the numerous calls to further enhance our understanding of this variable through better measures of use. Even though several researchers have argued for a multi-dimensional measure of use and based on Burton-Jones and Straub (2006) article which consider usage to be a formative variable, all usage elements, i.e., the system, task and user should be operationalised in order to provide necessary answers to which aspects of the system that are under-utilised and where interventions should be made.

Further, this review also confirms Burton-Jones and Straub (2006) contention that there is still no theoretical discussion of system usage measures five years on. Many researchers ignore to mention the variable, those that discussed it, resume themselves to state the source of the article that they adapted their measures of usage from. The authors join forces with Burton-Jones and Straub (2006) for a better theoretical discussion of usage measures employed. Justifications of usage measures may only be known if each of these conceptualisations of usage is tested in different contexts as they may produce different results in each nomological net and underlying technology being researched instead of being conceptualised as a black box (Benbasat & Barki, 2007).

Although several usage measures fit in the major categories, one aspect of usage was non-existent and that is the user dimension of use. Apart from Burton-Jones and Straub (2006) article, no other articles employed the 'user' aspect of use according to our literature review. Scholars are encouraged to research further the measures of use that might fall under the domain of 'user' and how does these measures fare in their respective nomological network. The development of this preliminary taxonomy of usage measures that can help researchers in choosing measures of use in their respective research and help to clarify measures of use that have appeared in the literature. It also contributes to sort the ever increasing unsystematic plethora of measures that plague the IS literature especially in the IS acceptance. We call upon other researchers to further extend our classification of usage measures (Table 6), as information become even more ubiquitous and complex, novel measures of use may arise.

This paper has used the two main theories employed in IS acceptance, the Technology Acceptance Model (TAM) (Davis, 1989; Davis et al., 1989) and the Unified Theory of Use and Acceptance of Technology (UTAUT) (Venkatesh et al., 2003); a total of 101 articles that have conceptualisation and operationalisation of system use have been reviewed. This taxonomy is one of the first on usage measures being employed in IS acceptance literature. The findings demonstrate the measures that are being used and how they are being used. The evidence shows proof for our taxonomy of usage measures with only 1 percent

of 235 measures that could not be categorise. The trend established over our selected papers shows a net preference to leaner measures of usage with frequency, volume of use and use/non-use. Since usage is based on 3 elements according to Burton-Jones and Straub (2006), further research is required to identify measures under these aspects and their relationship with other variables either in upstream or downstream research.

REFERENCES

Adams, D. A., Nelson, R. R., & Todd, P. A. (1992). Perceived usefulness, ease of use, and usage of information technology: A replication. *Management Information Systems Quarterly*, *16*(2), 227–247. doi:10.2307/249577

Agarwal, R., & Prasad, J. (1997). The role of innovation characteristics and perceived voluntariness in the acceptance of information technologies. *Decision Sciences*, *28*(3), 557–582. doi:10.1111/j.1540-5915.1997.tb01322.x

Agarwal, R., & Prasad, J. (1998). The antecedents and consequences of user perceptions in information technology adoption. *Decision Support Systems*, *22*, 15–29. doi:10.1016/S0167-9236(97)00006-7

Ajzen, I. (1991). The theory of planned behavior. *Organizational Behavior and Human Decision Processes*, *50*(2), 179–211. doi:10.1016/0749-5978(91)90020-T

Al-Gahtani, S. S. (2008). Testing for the applicability of the TAM model in the Arabic context: Exploring an extended TAM with three moderating factors. *Information Resources Management Journal*, *21*(4), 1–26. doi:10.4018/irmj.2008100101

Al-Gahtani, S. S., Hubona, G. S., & Wang, J. (2007). Information technology (IT) in Saudi Arabia: culture and the acceptance and use of IT. *Information & Management*, *44*, 681–691. doi:10.1016/j.im.2007.09.002

Al-Gahtani, S. S., & King, M. (1999). Attitudes, satisfaction and usage: factors contributing to each in the acceptance of information technology. *Behaviour & Information Technology, 18*(4), 277–297. doi:10.1080/014492999119020

Alda's-Manzano, J. N., Ruiz-Mafe, C., & Sanz-Blas, S. (2009). Exploring individual personality factors as drivers of M-shopping acceptance. *Industrial Management & Data Systems, 109*(6), 739–757. doi:10.1108/02635570910968018

Anandarajan, M., Igbaria, M., & Anakwe, U. P. (2002). IT acceptance in a less-developed country: a motivational factor perspective. *International Journal of Information Management, 22*, 47–65. doi:10.1016/S0268-4012(01)00040-8

Anderson, J. E., Schwager, P. H., & Kerns, R. L. (2006). The drivers for acceptance of tablet PCs by faculty in a college of business. *Journal of Information Systems Education, 17*(4), 429–440.

Bandura, A. (1986). *Social foundations of thought and action: A social cognitive theory*. Upper Saddle River, NJ: Prentice Hall.

Barnett, T., Kellermanns, F., Pearson, A., & Pearson, R. (2007). Measuring system usage: Replication and extension. *Journal of Computer Information Systems, 47*(2), 76–85.

Benbasat, I., & Barki, H. (2007). Quo Vadis TAM? *Journal of the AIS, 8*(3), 211–218.

Bhattacherjee, A. (2001). Understanding information systems continuance: An expectation-confirmation. *Management Information Systems Quarterly, 25*(3), 351–370. doi:10.2307/3250921

Bhattacherjee, A., & Sanford, C. (2009). The intention–behaviour gap in technology usage: the moderating role of attitude strength. *Behaviour & Information Technology, 28*(4), 389–401. doi:10.1080/01449290802121230

Bokhari, R. H. (2005). The relationship between system usage and user satisfaction: A meta-analysis. *The Journal of Enterprise Information Management, 18*(2), 211–234. doi:10.1108/17410390510579927

Brown, S. A., Dennis, A. R., & Venkatesh, V. (2010). Predicting collaboration technology use: Integrating technology adoption and collaboration research. *Journal of Management Information Systems, 27*(2), 9–53. doi:10.2753/MIS0742-1222270201

Burton-Jones, A., Detmar, W., & Straub, J. (2006). Reconceptualizing system usage: An approach and empirical test. *Information Systems Research, 17*(3), 228–246. doi:10.1287/isre.1060.0096

Burton-Jones, A., & Hubona, G. S. (2006). The mediation of external variables in the technology acceptance model. *Information & Management, 43*, 706–717. doi:10.1016/j.im.2006.03.007

Chakraborty, I., Hu, P. J.-H., & Cui, D. (2008). Examining the effects of cognitive style in individuals' technology use decision making. *Decision Support Systems, 45*, 228–241. doi:10.1016/j.dss.2007.02.003

Chang, I.-C., Hwang, H.-G., Hung, W.-F., & Li, Y.-C. (2007). Physicians' acceptance of pharmacokinetics-based clinical decision support systems. *Expert Systems with Applications, 33*, 296–303. doi:10.1016/j.eswa.2006.05.001

Chen, J.-L. (2011). The effects of education compatibility and technological expectancy on e-learning acceptance. *Computers & Education, 57*, 1501–1511. doi:10.1016/j.compedu.2011.02.009

Chen, L.-D., Gillenson, M. L., & Sherrell, D. L. (2002). Enticing online consumers: an extended technology acceptance perspective. *Information & Management, 39*, 705–719. doi:10.1016/S0378-7206(01)00127-6

Chen, L.-D., Gillenson, M. L., & Sherrell, D. L. (2004). Consumer acceptance of virtual stores: A theoretical model and critical success factors for virtual stores. *ACM SIGMIS Database, 35*(2).

Cohen, J. A. (1960). Coefficient of agreement for nominal scales. *Educational and Psychological Measurement, 20*(1), 37–46. doi:10.1177/001316446002000104

Compeau, D. R., & Higgins, C. A. (1995). Computer self-efficacy: Development of a measure and initial test. *Management Information Systems Quarterly, 19*(2), 189–211. doi:10.2307/249688

Cooper, R., & Zmud, R. W. (1990). Information technology implementation research: A technological diffusion approach. *Management Science, 36*(2), 123–139. doi:10.1287/mnsc.36.2.123

Dasgupta, S., Granger, M., & McGarry, N. (2002). User acceptance of e-collaboration technology: An extension of the technology acceptance model. *Group Decision and Negotiation, 2*, 87–100. doi:10.1023/A:1015221710638

Davis, F. (1989). Perceived usefulness, perceived ease of use and user acceptance of information technology. *Management Information Systems Quarterly, 13*(3), 319. doi:10.2307/249008

Davis, F. (1993). User acceptance of information technology: system characteristics, user perceptions and behavioral impacts. *International Journal of Man-Machine Studies, 38*, 475–487. doi:10.1006/imms.1993.1022

Davis, F., Bargozzi, R., & Warshaw, P. (1989). User Acceptance of computer technology: A comparison of two theoretical model. *Management Science, 35*(8), 982–1003. doi:10.1287/mnsc.35.8.982

Davis, F. D., Bagozzi, R. P., & Warshaw, P. R. (1992). Extrinsic and intrinsic motivation to use computers in the workplace. *Journal of Applied Social Psychology, 22*(14), 1111–1132. doi:10.1111/j.1559-1816.1992.tb00945.x

Davis, F. D., & Venkatesh, V. (1996). A critical assessment of potential measurement biases in the technology acceptance model: Three experiments. *International Journal of Human-Computer Studies, 45*(1), 19–45. doi:10.1006/ijhc.1996.0040

DeLone, W., & McLean, E. (2003). The DeLone and McLean model of information system success: A ten-year update. *Journal of Management Information Systems, 19*(4), 9–30.

Devaraj, S., & Kohli, R. (2003). Performance impacts of information technology: Is actual usage the missing link? *Management Science, 49*(3), 273–289. doi:10.1287/mnsc.49.3.273.12736

Dishaw, M. T., & Strong, D. M. (1999). Extending the technology acceptance model with task-technology fit constructs. *Information & Management, 36*, 9–21. doi:10.1016/S0378-7206(98)00101-3

Doll, W. J., & Torkzadeh, G. (1988). The measurement of end-user computing satisfaction. *Management Information Systems Quarterly, 12*(2), 259–274. doi:10.2307/248851

Fishbein, M., & Ajzen, I. (1975). *Belief, attitude, intention, and behavior: An introduction to theory and research*. Reading, MA: Addison-Wesley.

Fleiss, J. L. (1971). Measuring nominal scale agreement among many raters. *Psychological Bulletin, 76*, 378–382. doi:10.1037/h0031619

Gable, G., Sedera, D., & Chan, T. (2008). Reconceptualizing information system success: The IS-impact measurement model. *Journal of the Association for Information Systems, 9*(7), 377–408.

Gallego, M. D., Luna, P., & Bueno, S. (2008). User acceptance model of open source software. *Computers in Human Behavior, 24*(5), 2199–2216. doi:10.1016/j.chb.2007.10.006

Gefen, D., & Keil, M. (1998). The impact of developer responsiveness on perceptions of usefulness and ease of use, an extension of the technology acceptance model. *The Data Base for Advances in Information Systems, 29*(2), 35–49. doi:10.1145/298752.298757

Gefen, D., & Straub, D. W. (1997). Gender differences in the perception and use of e-mail: An extension to the technology acceptance model. *Management Information Systems Quarterly, 21*(4), 389–400. doi:10.2307/249720

Goodhue, D., & Thompson, R. (1995). Task-technology fit and individual performance. *Management Information Systems Quarterly, 19*(2), 213–236. doi:10.2307/249689

Gumussoy, C. A., & Calisir, F. (2009). Understanding factors affecting e-reverse auction use: An integrative approach. *Computers in Human Behavior, 25*(4), 975–988. doi:10.1016/j.chb.2009.04.006

Gupta, B., Dasgupta, S., & Gupta, A. (2008). Adoption of ICT in a government organization in a developing country: An empirical study. *The Journal of Strategic Information Systems, 17*(2), 140–154. doi:10.1016/j.jsis.2007.12.004

Hamner, M., & Qazi, R. (2009). Expanding the technology acceptance model to examine personal computing technology utilization in government agencies in developing countries. *Government Information Quarterly, 26*(1), 128–136. doi:10.1016/j.giq.2007.12.003

Hartwick, J., & Barki, H. (1994). Explaining the role of user participation in information system use. *Management Science, 40*(4), 440–465. doi:10.1287/mnsc.40.4.440

Hennington, A., Janz, B., Amis, J., & Nichols, E. (2009). Information systems and healthcare XXXII: Understanding the multidimensionality of information systems use: A study of nurses' use of a mandated electronic medical record system. *Communications of the Association for Information Systems, 25*(25), 243–262.

Hernández, B., Jiménez, J., & Martín, M. J. (2008). Extending the technology acceptance model to include the IT decision-maker: A study of business management software. *Technovation, 28*(3), 112–121. doi:10.1016/j.technovation.2007.11.002

Hernandez, B., Jiménez, J., & Martin, M. J. (2009). Future use intentions versus intensity of use: An analysis of corporate technology acceptance. *Industrial Marketing Management, 38*(3), 338–354. doi:10.1016/j.indmarman.2007.12.002

Hossain, L., & Silva, A. D. (2009). Exploring user acceptance of technology using social networks. *The Journal of High Technology Management Research, 20*, 1–18. doi:10.1016/j.hitech.2009.02.005

Hu, P. J.-H., Chen, H., Larson, C., & Butierez, C. (2011). Law enforcement officers' acceptance of advanced e-government technology: A survey study of COPLINK mobile. *Electronic Commerce Research and Applications, 10*, 6–16. doi:10.1016/j.elerap.2010.06.002

Igbaria, M., Guimares, T., & Davis, G. B. (1995). Testing the determinants of microcomputer usage via a structural equation model. *Journal of Management Information Systems, 11*(4), 87–114.

Igbaria, M., & Livari, J. (1995). The effects of self-efficacy on computer usage. *Omega, 23*(6), 587–605. doi:10.1016/0305-0483(95)00035-6

Igbaria, M., Zinatelli, N., Cragg, P., & Cavaye, A. L. M. (1997). Personal computing acceptance factors in small firms: A structural equation model. *Management Information Systems Quarterly, 21*(3), 279–305. doi:10.2307/249498

Im, I., Hong, S., & Kang, M. S. (2011). An international comparison of technology adoption testing the UTAUT model. *Information & Management, 48*, 1–8. doi:10.1016/j.im.2010.09.001

Jarvenpaa, S. (1989). The effect of task demands and graphical format on information processing strategies. *Management Science, 35*(3), 285–303. doi:10.1287/mnsc.35.3.285

Karahanna, E., Agarwal, R., & Angst, C. M. (2006). Reconceotualising compatibility beliefs in technology acceptance research. *Management Information Systems Quarterly, 30*(4), 781–804.

Karahanna, E., & Limayem, M. (2000). E-Mail and v-mail usage: Generalizing across technologies. *Journal of Organizational Computing and Electronic Commerce, 10*(1), 49–66. doi:10.1207/S15327744JOCE100103

Kijsanayotin, B., Pannarunothai, S., & Speedie, S. M. (2009). Factors influencing health information technology adoption in Thailand's community health centers: Applying the UTAUT model. *International Journal of Medical Informatics, 78*, 404–416. doi:10.1016/j.ijmedinf.2008.12.005

Kim, B. G., Park, S. C., & Lee, K. J. (2007). A structural equation modeling of the Internet acceptance in Korea. *Electronic Commerce Research and Applications, 6*, 425–432. doi:10.1016/j.elerap.2006.08.005

Kim, H.-J., Mannino, M., & Nieschwietz, R. J. (2009). Information technology acceptance in the internal audit profession: Impact of technology features and complexity. *International Journal of Accounting Information Systems, 10*, 214–228. doi:10.1016/j.accinf.2009.09.001

Kim, S. H. (2008). Moderating effects of job relevance and experience on mobile wireless technology acceptance: Adoption of a smartphone by individuals. *Information & Management, 45*(6), 387–393. doi:10.1016/j.im.2008.05.002

Kim, T. G., Lee, J. H., & Law, R. (2008). An empirical examination of the acceptance behaviour of hotel front office systems: An extended technology acceptance model. *Tourism Management, 29*, 500–513. doi:10.1016/j.tourman.2007.05.016

Kim, Y.-M. (2010). The adoption of university library web site resources: A multigroup analysis. *Journal of the American Society for Information Science and Technology*, 979–993.

King, W. R., & He, J. (2006). A meta-analysis of the technology acceptance model. *Information & Management, 43*, 740–755. doi:10.1016/j.im.2006.05.003

Konradt, U., Christophersen, T., & Schaeffer-Kuelz, U. (2006). Predicting user satisfaction, strain and system usage of employee self-services. *International Journal of Human-Computer Studies, 64*, 1141–1153. doi:10.1016/j.ijhcs.2006.07.001

Kwon, O., & Wen, Y. (2010). An empirical study of the factors affecting social network service use. *Computers in Human Behavior, 26*, 254–263. doi:10.1016/j.chb.2009.04.011

Landis, J. R., & Koch, G. G. (1977). The measurement of observer agreement for categorical data. *Biometrics, 33*, 159–174. doi:10.2307/2529310

Lederer, A. L., Maupin, D. J., Sena, M. P., Zhuang, Y., & Abbasi, M. S. (2000). The technology acceptance model and the World Wide Web. *Decision Support Systems, 29*, 269–282. doi:10.1016/S0167-9236(00)00076-2

Lee, S., & Kim, B. G. (2009). Factors affecting the usage of intranet: A confirmatory study. *Computers in Human Behavior, 25*(1), 191–201. doi:10.1016/j.chb.2008.08.007

Lee, S. T., Kim, H., & Gupta, S. (2009). Measuring open source software success. *Omega, 37,* 426–438. doi:10.1016/j.omega.2007.05.005

Lee, Y., Lee, J., & Lee, Z. (2006). Social influence on technology acceptance behavior: Self-identity theory perspective. *The Data Base for Advances in Information Systems, 37*(2), 60–75. doi:10.1145/1161345.1161355

Legris, P., Ingham, J., & Collerette, P. (2003). Why do people use information technology? A critical review of the technology acceptance model. *Information & Management, 40,* 191–204. doi:10.1016/S0378-7206(01)00143-4

Levy, J. A. (1988). Intersections of gender and aging. *The Sociological Quarterly, 29*(4), 479–486. doi:10.1111/j.1533-8525.1988.tb01429.x

Liao, C.-H., & Tsou, C.-W. (2009). User acceptance of computer-mediated communication: The SkypeOut case. *Expert Systems with Applications, 36,* 4595–4603. doi:10.1016/j.eswa.2008.05.015

Lim, K.-S., Lim, J.-S., & Heinrichs, J. H. (2008). Testing an integrated model of e-shopping web site usage. *Journal of Internet Commerce, 7*(3). doi:10.1080/15332860802250336

Lin, C.-P. (2011). Assessing the mediating role of online social capital between social support and instant messaging usage. *Electronic Commerce Research and Applications, 10,* 105–114. doi:10.1016/j.elerap.2010.08.003

Lin, C.-P., & Anol, B. (2008). Learning online social support: An investigation of network information technology based on UTAUT. *Cyberpsychology & Behavior, 11*(3), 268–272. doi:10.1089/cpb.2007.0057

Lin, H.-F. (2007). Predicting consumer intentions to shop online: An empirical test of competing theories. *Electronic Commerce Research and Applications, 6,* 433–442. doi:10.1016/j.elerap.2007.02.002

Lin, M.-J. J., Hung, S.-W., & Chen, C.-J. (2009). Fostering the determinants of knowledge sharing in professional virtual communities. *Computers in Human Behavior, 25*(4), 929–939. doi:10.1016/j.chb.2009.03.008

Lin, T.-C., & Huang, C.-C. (2008). Understanding knowledge management system usage antecedents: An integration of social cognitive theory and task technology fit. *Information & Management, 45*(6), 410–417. doi:10.1016/j.im.2008.06.004

Livari, J. (2002). An empirical test of the DeLone-McLean model of information system success. *The Data Base for Advances in Information Systems, 36*(2), 8–27.

Lu, Y., Deng, Z., & Wang, B. (2010). Exploring factors affecting Chinese consumers' usage of short message service for personal communication. *Info Systems Journal, 20,* 183-208.

Lu, Y., Zhou, T., & Wang, B. (2009). Exploring Chinese users' acceptance of instant messaging using the theory of planned behavior, the technology acceptance model, and the flow theory. *Computers in Human Behavior, 25,* 29–39. doi:10.1016/j.chb.2008.06.002

Lucas, H. (1973). A descriptive model of information systems in the context of the organisation. In *Proceedings of the Wharton Conference on Research on Computers in Organisations* (pp. 27-36).

Lucas, H. C., & Spitler, V. K. (1999). Technology use and performance: A field study of broker workstations. *Decision Sciences, 30*(2), 291–311. doi:10.1111/j.1540-5915.1999.tb01611.x

Luo, M. M., Chea, S., & Chen, J.-S. (2011). Web-based information service adoption: A comparison of the motivational model and the uses and gratifications theory. *Decision Support Systems, 51*(1), 21–30. doi:10.1016/j.dss.2010.11.015

Maldonado, U. P. T., Khan, G. F., Moon, J., & Rho, J. J. (2011). E-learning motivation and educational portal acceptance in developing countries. *Online Information Review, 35*(1), 66–85. doi:10.1108/14684521111113597

Martınez-Torres, M. R., Marın, S. L. T., Garcıa, F. B., Vazquez, S. G., Oliva, M. A., & Torres, T. (2008). A technological acceptance of e-learning tools used in practical and laboratory teaching, according to the European higher education area. *Behaviour & Information Technology, 27*(6), 495–505. doi:10.1080/01449290600958965

Mathieson, K., Peacock, E., & Chin, W. W. (2001). Extending the technology acceptance model: The influence of perceived user resources. *The Data Base for Advances in Information Systems, 32*(3), 86–112. doi:10.1145/506724.506730

Mazman, S. G., & Usluel, Y. K. (2010). Modeling educational usage of Facebook. *Computers & Education, 55*, 444–453. doi:10.1016/j.compedu.2010.02.008

McFarland, D. J., & Hamilton, D. (2006). Adding contextual specificity to the technology acceptance model. *Computers in Human Behavior, 22*, 427–447. doi:10.1016/j.chb.2004.09.009

Minton, H. L., & Schneider, F. W. (1980). *Differential psychology*. Prospect Heights, IL: Waveland Press.

Moon, J.-W., & Kim, Y.-G. (2001). Extending the TAM for a World-Wide-Web context. *Information & Management, 38*, 217–230. doi:10.1016/S0378-7206(00)00061-6

Moore, G. C., & Benbasat, I. (1991). Development of an instrument to measure the perceptions of adopting an information technology innovation. *Information Systems Research, 2*(3), 192–222. doi:10.1287/isre.2.3.192

Ndubisi, N. O., & Jantan, M. (2003). Evaluating IS usage in Malaysian small and medium-sized firms using the technology acceptance model. *Logistics Information Management, 16*(6), 440–450. doi:10.1108/09576050310503411

Ngai, E. W. T., Poon, J. K. L., & Chan, Y. H. C. (2007). Empirical examination of the adoption of WebCT using TAM. *Computers & Education, 48*, 250–267. doi:10.1016/j.compedu.2004.11.007

Oh, S., Ang, J., & Kim, B. (2003). Adoption of broadband internet in Korea: the role of experience in building attitudes. *Journal of Information Technology, 18*(4), 267–280. doi:10.1080/0268396032000150807

Pai, J.-C., & Tu, F.-M. (2011). The acceptance and use of customer relationship management (CRM) systems: An empirical study of distribution service industry in Taiwan. *Expert Systems with Applications, 38*, 579–584. doi:10.1016/j.eswa.2010.07.005

Petter & McLean. (2009). A meta-analytic assessment of the DeLone and McLean IS success model: An examination of IS success at the individual level. *Information & Management, 46*, 159–166. doi:10.1016/j.im.2008.12.006

Pijpers, G. G. M., Bemelmans, T. M. A., Heemstra, F. J., & Monfort, K. A. G. M. (2001). Senior's executive use of information technology. *Information and Software Technology, 43*, 959–971. doi:10.1016/S0950-5849(01)00197-5

Porter, C. E., & Donthu, N. (2006). Using the technology acceptance model to explain how attitudes determine Internet usage: The role of perceived access barriers and demographics. *Journal of Business Research, 59*(9), 999–1007. doi:10.1016/j.jbusres.2006.06.003

Pynoo, B., Devolder, P., Tondeur, J., Van Braak, J., Duyck, W., & Duyck, P. (2011). Predicting secondary school teachers' acceptance and use of a digital learning environment: A cross-sectional study. *Computers in Human Behavior, 27*(1), 568–575. doi:10.1016/j.chb.2010.10.005

Rai, A., Lang, S., & Welker, R. (2002). Assessing the validity of IS success models: An empirical test and theoretical analysis. *Information Systems Research, 13*(1), 50–69. doi:10.1287/isre.13.1.50.96

Roberts, P., & Henderson, R. (2000). Information technology acceptance in a sample of government employees: a test of the technology acceptance model. *Interacting with Computers, 12*(5), 427–443. doi:10.1016/S0953-5438(98)00068-X

Rogers, E. V. (1995). *Diffusion of innovations* (4th ed.). New York, NY: Free Press.

Roldan, J., & Leal, A. (2003). *Adaptation of the Delone and McLean's Model in the Spanish EIS Field.* Retrieved September 1, 2009, from http://business.clemson.edu/ISE/04chap.pdf

Rouibah, K., Hamdy, H. I., & Al-Enezi, M. Z. (2009). Effect of management support, training, and user involvement on system usage and satisfaction in Kuwait. *Industrial Management & Data Systems, 109*(3), 338–356. doi:10.1108/02635570910939371

Saeed, K. A., Abdinnour, S., Lengnick-Hall, M. L., & Lengnick-Hall, C. A. (2010). Examining the impact of pre-implementation expectations on post-implementation use of enterprise systems: A longitudinal study. *Decision Sciences, 41*(4), 659–688. doi:10.1111/j.1540-5915.2010.00285.x

Sánchez, R. A., & Hueros, A. D. (2010). Motivational factors that influence the acceptance of Moodle using TAM. *Computers in Human Behavior, 26*, 1632–1640. doi:10.1016/j.chb.2010.06.011

Sanchez-Franco, M. J. (2006). Exploring the influence of gender on the web usage via partial least squares. *Behaviour & Information Technology, 25*(1), 19–36. doi:10.1080/01449290500124536

Sanchez-Franco, M. J., & Roldan, J. L. (2005). Web acceptance usage model: A comparison between goal directed and experiential users. *Internet Research, 15*(1), 21–48. doi:10.1108/10662240510577059

Sapio, B., Turk, T., Cornacchia, M., Papa, F., Nicolò, E., & Livi, S. (2010). Building scenarios of digital television adoption: a pilot study. *Technology Analysis and Strategic Management, 22*(1), 43–63. doi:10.1080/09537320903438054

Schultze, U., & Carte, T. A. (2007). Contextualizing usage research for interactive technology: The case of car e- tailing. *The Data Base for Advances in Information Systems, 38*(1), 29–59. doi:10.1145/1216218.1216223

Segars, A., & Grover, V. (1998). Strategic information systems planning success: An investigation of the construct and its measurement. *Management Information Systems Quarterly, 22*(2), 139–163. doi:10.2307/249393

Serenko, A. (2008). A model of user adoption of interface agents for email notification. *Interacting with Computers, 20*, 461–472. doi:10.1016/j.intcom.2008.04.004

Sheng, Z., Jue, Z., & Weiwei, T. (2008). Extending TAM for online learning systems: An intrinsic motivation perspective. *Tsinghua Science and Technology, 13*(3), 312–317. doi:10.1016/S1007-0214(08)70050-6

Shih, Y.-Y. (2006). The effect of computer self-efficacy on enterprise resource planning usage. *Behaviour & Information Technology, 25*(5), 407–411. doi:10.1080/01449290500168103

Shin, D.-H. (2009). Towards an understanding of the consumer acceptance of mobile wallet. *Computers in Human Behavior*, *25*, 1343–1354. doi:10.1016/j.chb.2009.06.001

Shin, Y. M., Lee, S. C., Shin, B., & Lee, H. G. (2010). Examining influencing factors of post-adoption usage of mobile internet: Focus on the user perception of supplier-side attributes. *Information Systems Frontiers*, *12*, 595–606. doi:10.1007/s10796-009-9184-x

Stephenson, W. (1935). Technique of factor analysis. *Nature*, *136*, 297. doi:10.1038/136297b0

Stoel, L., & Lee, K. H. (2003). Modeling the effect of experience on student acceptance of web based courseware. *Internet Research*, *13*(5), 364–374. doi:10.1108/10662240310501649

Stone, R. W., Good, D. J., & Baker-Eveleth, L. (2007). The impact of information technology on individual and firm marketing performance. *Behaviour & Information Technology*, *26*(6), 465–482. doi:10.1080/01449290600571610

Straub, D., Limayem, M., & Karahanna-Evaristo, E. (1995). Measuring system usage: Implication for IS theory testing. *Management Science*, *41*(8), 1328–1339. doi:10.1287/mnsc.41.8.1328

Šumak, B., Polančič, G., & Heričko, M. (2010). *An empirical study of virtual learning environment adoption using UTAUT*. Paper presented at the Second International Conference on Mobile, Hybrid, and On-line Learning.

Sun, Y., Bhattacherjee, A., & Ma, Q. (2009). Extending technology usage to work settings: The role of perceived work compatibility in ERP implementation. *Information & Management*, *46*, 351–356. doi:10.1016/j.im.2009.06.003

Sykes, T. A., Venkatesh, V., & Gosain, S. (2009). Model of acceptance with peer support: A social network perspective to understand employees' system use. *Management Information Systems Quarterly*, *33*(2), 371–393.

Szajna, B. (1996). Empirical evaluation of the revised technology acceptance model. *Management Science*, *42*(1), 85–92. doi:10.1287/mnsc.42.1.85

Taylor, S., & Todd, P. A. (1995). Understanding information technology usage: A test of competing models. *Information Systems Research*, *6*(4), 144–176. doi:10.1287/isre.6.2.144

Teo, T. S. H., Lim, V. K. G., & Lai, R. Y. C. (1999). Intrinsic and extrinsic motivation in Internet usage. *Omega*, *27*, 25–37. doi:10.1016/S0305-0483(98)00028-0

Thomas, D. B., & Baas, L. R. (1992). The issue of generalization in q methodology: Reliable schematics revisited. *Operand Subjectivity*, *16*(1), 18–36.

Thomas, D. M., & Watson, R. T. (2002). Q-Sorting and MIS research: A primer. *Communications of the Association for Information Systems*, *8*, 141–156.

Thompson, R. L., Higgins, C. A., & Howell, J. M. (1991). Personal computing: Toward a conceptual model of utilization. *Management Information Systems Quarterly*, *15*(1), 124–143. doi:10.2307/249443

Todd, P. A., & Benbasat, I. (1989). *An experimental investigation of the impact of computer based decision aids on the process of preferential choice*. Kingston, ON, Canada: School of Business, Queen's University.

Triandis, H. C. (1977). *Interpersonal behavior*. Monterey, CA: Brooke/Cole.

Turel, O., Serenko, A., & Bontis, N. (2007). User acceptance of wireless short messaging services: Deconstructing perceived value. *Information & Management, 44*, 63–73. doi:10.1016/j.im.2006.10.005

Van Raaij, E. M., & Schepers, J. L. (2008). The acceptance and use of a virtual learning environment in China. *Computers & Education, 50*, 838–852. doi:10.1016/j.compedu.2006.09.001

Vanbelle, S., & Albert, A. (2009). A note on the linearly weighted kappa coefficient for ordinal scales. *Statistical Methodology, 6*, 157–163. doi:10.1016/j.stamet.2008.06.001

Vassey, I. (1984). *An investigation of the psychological processes underlying the debugging of computer programs* (Unpublished doctoral dissertation). University of Queensland, Brisbane, Australia.

Venkatesh, V., & Bala, H. (2008). Technology acceptance model 3 and a research agenda on interventions. *Decision Sciences, 39*(2), 273–315. doi:10.1111/j.1540-5915.2008.00192.x

Venkatesh, V., Brown, S. A., Maruping, L. M., & Bala, H. (2008). Predicting different conceptualizations of system use: The competing roles of behavioral intention, facilitating conditions, and behavioral expectation. *Management Information Systems Quarterly, 32*(3), 483–502.

Venkatesh, V., & Davis, F. D. (1996). A model of the antecedents of perceived ease of use: development and test. *Decision Sciences, 27*(3), 451–481. doi:10.1111/j.1540-5915.1996.tb01822.x

Venkatesh, V., & Davis, F. D. (2000). A theoretical extension of the technology acceptance model: Four longitudinal field studies. *Management Science, 46*(2), 186–204. doi:10.1287/mnsc.46.2.186.11926

Venkatesh, V., & Morris, M. G. (2000). Why don't men ever stop to ask for directions? Gender, social influence, and their role in technology acceptance and usage behavior. *Management Information Systems Quarterly, 24*(1), 115–139. doi:10.2307/3250981

Venkatesh, V., Morris, M. G., Davis, G. B., & Davis, F. D. (2003). User acceptance of information technology: Toward a unified view. *Management Information Systems Quarterly, 27*(3), 425–478.

Wang, W.-T., & Wang, C.-C. (2009). An empirical study of instructor adoption of web-based learning systems. *Computers & Education, 53*, 761–774. doi:10.1016/j.compedu.2009.02.021

Wang, Y.-S., & Shih, Y.-W. (2009). Why do people use information kiosks? A validation of the unified theory of acceptance and use of technology. *Government Information Quarterly, 26*, 158–165. doi:10.1016/j.giq.2008.07.001

Warrens, M. (2010). Cohen's kappa can always be increased and decreased by combining categories. *Statistical Methodology, 7*, 673–677. doi:10.1016/j.stamet.2010.05.003

Watts, S., & Stenner, P. (2005). Doing Q methodology: theory, method and interpretation. *Qualitative Research in Psychology, 2*, 67–91. doi:10.1191/1478088705qp022oa

Wixom, B., & Todd, P. A. (2005). A theoretical integration of user satisfaction and technology acceptance. *Information Systems Research, 16*(1), 85–102. doi:10.1287/isre.1050.0042

Wu, I.-L., & Wu, K.-W. (2005). A hybrid technology acceptance approach for exploring e-CRM adoption in organizations. *Behaviour & Information Technology, 24*(4), 303–316. doi:10.1080/0144929042000320027

Wu, J.-H., Chen, Y.-C., & Lin, L.-M. (2007). Empirical evaluation of the revised end user computing acceptance model. *Computers in Human Behavior, 23*(1), 162–174. doi:10.1016/j.chb.2004.04.003

Yang, H.-D., & Yoo, Y. (2004). It's all about attitude: revisiting the technology acceptance model. *Decision Support Systems, 38,* 19–31. doi:10.1016/S0167-9236(03)00062-9

Yi, M. Y., & Hwang, Y. (2003). Predicting the use of web-based information systems: self-efficacy, enjoyment, learning goal orientation, and the technology acceptance model. *International Journal of Human-Computer Studies, 59,* 431–449. doi:10.1016/S1071-5819(03)00114-9

Youngberg, E., Olsen, D., & Hauser, K. (2009). Determinants of professionally autonomous end user acceptance in an enterprise resource planning system environment. *International Journal of Information Management, 29,* 138–144. doi:10.1016/j.ijinfomgt.2008.06.001

Yousafzai, S. Y., Foxall, G. R., & Pallister, J. G. (2007). Technology acceptance: a meta-analysis of the TAM: Part 1. *Journal of Modelling in Management, 2*(3), 251–280. doi:10.1108/17465660710834453

Zain, M., Rose, R. C., Abdullah, I., & Masrom, M. (2005). The relationship between information technology acceptance and organizational agility in Malaysia. *Information & Management, 42,* 829–839. doi:10.1016/j.im.2004.09.001

Zhou, T., Lu, Y., & Wang, B. (2010). Integrating TTF and UTAUT to explain mobile banking user adoption. *Computers in Human Behavior, 26,* 760–767. doi:10.1016/j.chb.2010.01.013

APPENDIX
Definition and Description

1. Use/Non Use is defined as whether the system is being employed or not.
    - Description: Use/Non Use is an omnibus measure and is answered by a Yes or No.
2. Frequency of Use is defined as the number of times the system is being used per unit time.
    - Description: It usually asks how many times the system was used, measured as daily/ monthly or may use a likert scale.
3. Volume of Use is defined as the amount or length of usage measured in units of time.
    - Description: It is usually measured as many hours the system has being used.
4. Extent of Use is defined as the number of business tasks or features for which the system/ applications were used.
    - Description: It asks whether the system/applications were used to complete certain tasks; making decisions, trends, planning budgeting.
5. Intensity of Use is defined as the degree of use measured as a percentage or amount of usage in terms on input and output of the system.
    - Description: Diverse, it can be measured either asking the percentage of system used, messages sent, number of people contacted or pages printed.
6. Variety of Use is defined as the number of different applications that is being used.
    - Description: It asks whether the user uses the different applications, e.g., word processing, email, spreadsheets.

This journal was previously published in the International Journal of Technology Diffusion, Volume 2, Issue 4, edited by Ali Hussein Saleh Zolait, pp. 25-47, copyright 2011 by IGI Publishing (an imprint of IGI Global).

Chapter 9
The Driving Internal Beliefs of Household Internet Adoption among Jordanians and the Role of Cultural Values

Khaled Saleh Al Omoush
Alzaytoonah University, Jordan

Raed Musbah Alqirem
Alzaytoonah University, Jordan

Amin A. Shaqrah
Alzaytoonah University, Jordan

ABSTRACT

The purpose of this study is to develop and validate a comprehensive model for the determinants of household Internet adoption through identifying the driving internal beliefs of individuals and the effect of cultural values on behavioral intention to adopt the household Internet among Jordanians. Given the widely recognized effect of cultural values on adoption of Information and Communication Technology (ICT), this study, applying Hofstede's multidimensional framework, investigated the effect of cultural values on the behavioral intention to household Internet adoption in micro level. The empirical examination of the research model indicated that the behavioral intention to household Internet adoption is determined directly by five internal beliefs, including perceived needs, perceived risks, perceived ease of use, perceived resources, and perceived image. The results provide supporting empirical evidence linking most of Hofstede's cultural dimensions to behavioral intention to household Internet adoption. With the exception of power distance, the results showed that collectivism (low individualism), masculinity, long-term orientation, and uncertainty avoidance had significant effects on the behavioral intention to household Internet adoption. The results demonstrated differences in the driving forces and cultural impact on Internet adoption between households and organizations settings.

DOI: 10.4018/978-1-4666-2791-8.ch009

INTRODUCTION

The development of the home ICT has a deep impact on the development of information and knowledge societies (Shan et al., 2008). On the other hand, the family is the natural and fundamental group unit of society and the natural environment to provide the members of the information society. Therefore, the starting point of the information society and dissemination of electronic applications begins from the consolidation of acceptance, access, and usage of the ICT by the families and individuals in their households.

As the Internet gains wider acceptance, information society has begun to emerge and take form. Thus, the vast technological possibilities of the Internet cause the fast progress of the information and knowledge society. The Internet has truly transformed global communication. It is more than just information. The Internet represents a set of services for various subsystems of society, and can be used for very diverse purposes. As a worldwide communications technology, the Internet has a great influence on people's connections to friends, family, and their communities, which provides exchange of the text, graphics, audio and video information and access to the on-line services without boundaries.

The scope of Internet applications is therefore broad, and forces to deliver the Internet resource to households. Thus, the core indicators on acceptance and usage of Internet by households and individuals should be used in parallel with e-business activities and other applications blossom as a starting point of countries that are planning to establish the information and Knowledge society.

In many countries, societies and organizations experience difficulty and even failure in transferring IT into practice. Despite receiving billions of dollars in IT infrastructure, this problem seems to be more severe in Arab countries (Hill et al., 1998; Straub et al., 2001; Loch et al., 2003). In Jordan the ICT sector has grown rapidly during the last years and enormous investments have recently been made. Apart from Jordanian governments,

ICT companies are also making efforts to involve more people in the adoption of their products and services. Although the number of adopters of new ICT products and services is growing, Internet are becoming more accessible, and Internet cafes have sprung up in even small Jordanian cities, there is a considerable ICT adoption gap especially in household Internet connectivity between Jordan and many other countries.

The Jordanian Telecommunications Regulatory Commission (TRC) has announced plan to increase Internet penetration to 50% by 2011. According to official numbers released by the TRC, only 18% of Jordanian households have internet access at the end of 2009 which assures that, things don't go according to plan. Current Jordanian stakeholders such as the government and Internet Service Providers (ISPs), are making a lot of efforts and resources to speed up the adoption of household Internet technology. It seems that these efforts are not being driven sufficiently by an adequate knowledge of the adoption behavior of individuals, the driving internal beliefs of the adopters, and the influence of cultural dimensions on behavioral intention toward entering the Internet to their homes.

On the other hand, the individual adoption of technology has been studied extensively in the workplace or in organizations settings. Recently, some researchers have started to develop models of ICT adaption and usage specifically looking at the household, building on the research of technology adoption in organizations (Oh et al., 2003(. The previous studies on adoption of household technology have offered limited information on the voluntary behavior of individuals, especially in adoption of Internet.

Many studies suggested that the culture of a country or region greatly affects the adoption of a technology through its beliefs and values on modernization and technological development (Straub et al., 1997; Kovacic, 2005; Sundqvist et al., 2005; Erumban & de Jong, 2006; Anandarajan et al., 2003; Gong et al., 2007; Calantone et al., 2006; Park et al., 2007; Srite & Karahanna, 2006;

Myers & Tan, 2002; Veiga et al., 2001; Robichaux & Cooper 1998; Schepers & Wetzels, 2007). In a broader context, and as the initiatives results in failure, cultural barriers to technology transfer between western and other cultures have been well documented (Scheraga et al., 2000; Jensen & Scheraga, 1998; Straub et al., 2001; Hill et al., 1998).

Loch et al. (2003) suggested that if cultural beliefs and attitudes toward Internet were better understood, then the Internet itself might be better adapted to the behavioral patterns of the adopting country, rather than the traditional approach of force-fitting the culture to the technology. Despite their indisputable importance, cultural values have not been sufficiently studied in the diffusion of household Internet. According to Albirini (2006), this may be related to the difficulty involved in capturing the constructs of this field.

Therefore, given this gap in the literature, the present study aims to develop and validate a comprehensive model to discuss the driving internal beliefs and the influence of culture values on household Internet adoption. The results of the present study will be helpful to various stakeholders that pursue the penetration and diffusion of household Internet and home ICTs in general. This research will help regulators, strategies and policies makers in governments and the ISPs to understand the broader issues of household Internet adoption, such as the driving internal beliefs affecting the acceptance and adoption of household Internet technology, and how to employ the cultural dimensions to enhance and facilitate the diffusion of this technology, and minimize the possible barriers, which will be helpful in understanding, stimulating, and facilitating the adoption and usage of household Internet.

THEORETICAL BACKGROUND

In response to the growing importance of IT in the life of societies, organizations, families, and individuals, a considerable body of literature with divested theoretical models has developed in the past few decades to study and provide an explanation of the determinants of IT acceptance, adoption and usage. As pursued in aforementioned studies, there exists a need for a deeper understanding of key determinants which address the direct impact of perceived beliefs and cultural dimensions on behavioral intention to households Internet adoption. Therefore, constructing and validating a comprehensive conceptual model specific to the driving internal beliefs of household Internet adoption and the effect of cultural values necessitates the review, identification and integration of the relevant determinants examined in previous behavioral intention-based models, including the TAM, TPB, U&G Theory, Hofstede's cultural dimensions, and other related works.

THE DRIVING INTERNAL BELIEFS OF HOUSEHOLD INTERNET ADOPTION

IT acceptance and adoption research has postulated many competing models with different constructs terms of adoption determinants to describe almost the same thing. In order to understand of behavioral intention toward IT applications as well as the factors affecting the adoption of such technologies, several models and theories with roots in IT, cultures, psychology, and sociology have been proposed. Furthermore, the authors of these studies have described a variety of constructs or variables may be identified in the other studies as a subset of one or more model.

As whole, the adoption and usage of ICT in the home is different from it in the organizations settings. In the situation where acceptance is voluntary, the most significant question is what causes people to accept or reject IT? (Davis, 1989). IT adoption comprised at one end by voluntary adoption and at the other by mandatory adoption (Venkatesh & Davis, 2000; Venkatesh et al., 2003; Melone, 1990). Voluntary adoption means that the user of specific IT has the freedom to decide whether or not he adopts and uses the technology, such as household Internet. The adoption of household Internet is an active choice made to fulfill diversified informational, social, and psychological needs or wants, and may compete with other media to satisfy users' needs. On the other hand, mandatory adoption means the user does not have this freedom, because he is forced to adopt and use the IT in a way that replaces one or more of his work practices. For example, Brown et al. (2002) and Melone (1990) suggested that employees do not have a decision in regarding IT usage since there are no alternatives, and may choose not to use it voluntarily.

In the last years, researchers have started to develop models using various driving forces of technology adoption specifically looking at the household, building on a large body of research conducted to study workplace adoption in organizational context. The driving forces of IT adoption in traditional acceptance models, such as Theory of Reasoned Action (TRA), Theory of Planned Behavior (TPB), and Technology Acceptance Models (TAM) tailored to examine IT adoption on the job within organizational settings (Venkatesh et al., 2003; López-Nicolás et al., 2008; Choudrie & Dwivedi, 2004; Choudrie & Dwivedi, 2006). Furthermore, many of the supporting research have been conducted in environments where the adoption was mandatory. Thus, this limits the ability of previous theories to be applied in the voluntary choice and behavioral intention of household Internet adoption. However, this problem can be solved by involving Uses and Gratifications (U&G) Theory. U&G inquires into the reasons why people use the media and the gratifications derived from media usage and access. It focuses on the social and psychological motives and needs that explain why people select and use a certain communication technologies (Ruggiero, 2000; Sun et al., 2006; Guo et al., 2009).

Additionally, most of earlier researches on home IT were about hardware, software, and technology standards, which includes all kinds of home information equipments or electronic equipments, such as computers, TV, and cell phones, and home security devices (Choudrie & Dwivedi, 2004; Brown & Venkatesh, 2005; Shan et al., 2008). Far less attention has been paid to families and individuals adoption of the household Internet. The majority of studies conducted to understand Internet related issues were macro and exploratory in nature, without employing the validity measures (Oh et al., 2003; Choudrie & Dwivedi, 2004, 2006; Brown & Venkatesh, 2005; Brown et al., 2009). In addition, most of the previous studies avoided a number of behavioral and social factors that play a critical role in facilitating or impeding the adoption of household Internet subscription, such as perceived risks, perceived resources, and perceived image.

On the other hand, although PC is different to network technologies in terms of alternative choices, periodical cost, durability, and usage, a number of studies (Choudrie and Dwivedi, 2004, 2006; Brown et al., 2009; Dwivedi, et al., 2007) have developed a new models to discuss the adoption and usage of household Internet based on the Model of Adoption of Technology in the Home (MATH). Brown and Venkatesh (2005) derived MATH from the constructs of the decomposed TPB, the Diffusion of Innovation Theory and other studies which is developed to examine users' adoption and usage of PCs within organizational settings (Choudrie & Dwivedi, 2006; Brown et al., 2009).

The term "Internal beliefs" actually derived from Davis's (1989) Technology Acceptance Model (TAM), which represents one of the explanatory models having most influenced the theories of human behaviors (Venkatesh et al., 2003). The core concept of TAM is that internal beliefs and other external variables will drive the individual's intention to use IT, which will ultimately influence actual usage behavior (Davis, 1989). Behavioral intention is defined as the person's subjective probability that he will perform the behavior in question (Fishbein & Ajzen, 1975), and is thus dealing with future behavior. In the context of household Internet adoption, this study refers to the internal beliefs as a household Internet adopter's perception of the needs for Internet in household, potential risks, ease of use, availability of resources, and image that are felt to be true.

THE CULTURAL DIMENSIONS OF HOUSEHOLD INTERNET ADOPTION

Research frequently mention national culture as a profound influential factor on the acceptance, adoption, and behavior of IT usage in each society as a restraining or driving force. There are specific ideas, beliefs, and values of Arab culture and society has an influence on the adoption and transfer of technology from non-Arab cultures to Arab ones. Straub et al. (2001) investigated how cultural impact on the adoption of new technology in the Arab world (Jordan, Egypt, Lebanon, Sudan and Saudi Arabia). He revealed that Arab cultural beliefs are a very strong predictor of resistance to information technology transfer. Loch et al. (2003) investigated the diffusion of the Internet in the Arab world focusing on the role of social norms and technological culturation. Results showed that a strong majority of respondents indicated that Internet acceptance was not without significant reservation. 58 percent disagreed that computers were well-accepted in Arab society and 40 percent disagreed that that the Internet would have a positive impact on the Arab family and community ties. Akour et al. (2006) agreed that the Jordanians had a negative attitude about the social impacts of the Internet and did not want it to replace their traditions, values, and customs of interactions and caring.

Researchers have developed a number of frameworks to classify the cultures of the world in order to understand its impact on the life and behaviors of nations, organizations, and individuals. One of the most well known researchers in the field of culture is Geert Hofstede. IT scholars have frequently referenced the cultural dimensions developed by Geert Hofstede, the most influential researcher on cultural values (Straub et al., 1997;

Kovacic, 2005; Sundqvist et al., 2005; Erumban & de Jong, 2006; Anandarajan et al., 2003; Gong et al., 2007; Calantone et al., 2006; Park et al., 2007; Srite & Karahanna, 2006; Myers & Tan, 2002; Veiga et al., 2001; Robichaux & Cooper 1998; Schepers & Wetzels, 2007).

Furthermore, the cultural dimensions of Hofstede are usable in a non-organizational context (Hofstede, 1991). As a consequence, it seems to be the most useful one in the case of studying the cultural effect on household Internet adoption. Hofstede (1980) suggested a couple of four dimensions to measure culture in the areas of uncertainty avoidance, power distance, individualism, and masculinity based on over 116,000 survey responses in IBM units in approximately 60 countries between 1967 and 1971. The fifth dimension was identified by Michael Bond and was initially called Confucian dynamism. Hofstede added this dimension to his framework, and labeled this dimension long term orientation, which focuses on the degree the society embraces, long-term devotion to traditional, forward-thinking values (Hofsted & Bond, 1988). According to Hofstede's (1980) typology, the Arab countries, including Jordan were classified as having high power distance, high uncertainty avoidance, low individualism, and high masculinity. Such a society may not be ideal for ICT including household Internet adoption and usage (Bagchi et al., 2004; Kovacic, 2005; Erumban & de Jong, 2006; Gong et al., 2007; Straub et al., 1997).

MACRO VS. MICRO CULTURAL LEVEL ANALYSIS

The authors identified different cultural levels or layers with different cultural dimensions. Based on Social Identity Theory, (Straub et al., 2001) has proposed that different layers of culture can influence an individual's behavior, and that each individual is influenced more by certain layers and less by other layers, depending on the situation and their own personal values. Culture has been studied within IS discipline at various levels, including national or macro level, which used in cross-cultural studies, and individual or micro level (Hofstede, 1983; Dorfman & Howell, 1988; Myers & Tan, 2002; Leidner & Kayworth, 2006).

Macro cultural level refers to a set of core values, norms, and practices that a society shares, and shapes the behavior of individuals as well as the whole society (Bagchi et al., 2004; Myers & Tan, 2002). The micro level is referred to as the subjective culture of an individual, which investigates the effects of national culture on individual behavior, and how much an individual takes from the different cultures; even towards opposite direction of his society culture (Dorfman & Howell, 1988; Karahanna et al., 2005).

According to Hill et al. (1998), the cultural beliefs and values of different groups in the hierarchal social structure of Arab society differ markedly in terms of how they construct a meaning for technology in their everyday work and personal lives. Hill et al. (1998) stated that because people from the same country can score differently on the cultural dimensions of Hofstede, researchers need to use individual level measures of culture and not only the country of origin. Straub et al. (2001) and Loch et al. (2003) demonstrated that successful transfer of IT in culturally and socially diverse countries requires an understanding of the micro level beliefs, norms, and actions within the framework of national and international macro-structures. Therefore, this study will examine the effect of cultural values on behavioral intention to household Internet adoption at the micro cultural level of analysis.

FOUNDATIONS OF PROPOSED MODEL AND HYPOTHESES

Since the introduction of technology acceptance models, many researches have been conducted by extending the models, combining it with other

models, and moderating external factors that might affect the constructs in these models. An adapted version of the TAM2 model (Venkatesh & Davis 2000), which integrates social factors, will be used as a guiding theory of our model. TAM2 deals more effectively with the driving forces and adoption decision-making process of individual users when social influence factors may outweigh functional concerns commonly seen in many business decision-making situations (Yang, 2007). Furthermore, the research model postulates several modifications through incorporating additional constructs and variables from TPB, U&G theory, Hofstede's cultural framework, and other related literature.

As "intention" was used to predict actual behavior; including measures of actual usage in the model in practice is relatively unusual (Taylor & Todd, 1995; Horton, et al., 2001; Venkatesh et al., 2003; Straub et al., 1995; Yang & Yoo, 2003). Since this research is concerned with behavioral intention of future adoption, the model gives more attention to the driving internal beliefs, and the expected effect of cultural values on behavioral intention and the future trends toward household Internet subscription, and excludes the behavioral usage construct. Thus, the research model (Figure 1) posits that the behavioral intention to household Internet is influenced directly by five driving internal beliefs, including individual perceived needs, perceived risks, perceived ease of use, perceived resources, and perceived image.

Furthermore, based on the previous studies, the model includes the role of culture, which also theorized to impact directly through five dimensions developed by Geert Hofstede on the behavioral intention to subscribe to the household Internet. The cultural dimensions made up of the degrees of individualism/collectivism, Masculinity, power distance, short/long-time orientation, and uncertainty avoidance.

Below each dimension will be summarized, followed by the related hypotheses.

Figure 1. The Driving Internal Beliefs and Cultural Dimensions Model of Household Internet Adoption

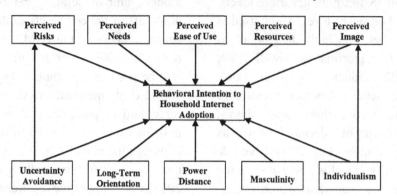

PERCEIVED NEEDS

Adoption theory seeks to explain the process of developing solutions to fulfill a need that begins with an awareness of a need, and ending with adopting and using of the solutions. Furthermore, Motivation theories also posit that an individuals behavior is driven by their needs, and the goal-directed action is to fulfill these needs (Papacharissi & Rubin 2000; Luo et al., 2006; Ruggiero, 2000). A chief tenet of household Internet adoption is that Internet adoption and usage is mostly selective and motivated by self-awareness of the individual's own needs and an expectation that those needs will be satisfied by particular types of technology that give a certain advantage above other already known alternatives.

The study of how and why individuals use media, may offer indications to our understanding about exactly what needs are, where they originate, and how they are satisfied (Ruggiero, 2000). Studies that have focused on this area have found a range of motivations and needs to Internet usage. For example, Korgaonkar and Wolin (1999) established five motivation factors for the Internet users: escapism, information control, interactive control, socialization, and economic motivations. Papacharissi and Rubin (2000) also developed a scale of Internet usage motives that consisted of five primary dimensions, including interpersonal utility, passtime, information seeking,

convenience, and entertainment. Flanagin and Metzger (2001) also identified five dimensions including problem solving, persuading others, relationship maintenance, status seeking, and personal insight. For the purpose of this study, we refer to motivations of household Internet adoption as perceive needs, using the Papacharissi and Rubin (2000) scale of Internet usage motives. Therefore, we hypothesize:

H1: Perceived needs have a positive influence on the behavioral intention to household Internet adoption.

PERCEIVED RISKS

Perceived risk is an important barrier for technology adoption. Kim and Prabhakar (2000) grasped the effect of perceived risk on accepting technology including household Internet by demonstrating that the more perceived risk one has, the less likely he will accept new technology. Since risk is difficult to measure objectively, the literature focuses on users' risk perceptions (Pavlou, 2003; Belanger & Carter, 2008). In this context, perceived risk can be defined as adopter's belief about the potential uncertain negative outcomes from the household Internet (Warkentin et al., 2002; Lee et al., 2007; Kim & Prabhakar, 2000).

Loch et al. (2003) investigated the diffusion of the Internet in the Arab world. Results showed that 46 percent expressed concern that family and community life might be threatened by the internet. As the pervasive appeal of the Internet grows in popularity with youth, parents are beginning to face new concerns and challenges.

Recent research results indicated that people are concerned about unwanted disclosure of private information, or misuse of their information hence invading a user's privacy (Kesh et al., 2002; Brown et al., 2009; Lee et al., 2007). Furthermore, many disturbing, harmful and objectionable materials are freely available to any Internet user. For example, the parents are not sure that the Internet is a safe environment for children from intentionally and accidentally exposure to pornography and violent websites (Isaacs & Fisher, 2008; Chou et al., 2005; Lin et al., 2009).

On the other hand, the Internet offers terrorist groups a powerful instrument, which is increasingly employed by terrorists to continue spreading their propaganda and recruiting new adherents (Anderson, 2003; Conway, 2006; Gray & Head, 2009). A large majority of families in the Arab world would never allow the terrorist groups to affect their children and young people's beliefs and attitudes.

Furthermore, parents are concerned about their children becoming addicted to online activities. Excessive internet usage and spending excessive amounts of time online often associated with a loss of sense of time, and the negative affects on individual's home work and social life, normal function and other aspects of their lives. According to many psychologists, the excessive usage of Internet is now a serious psychological health issue that should be officially recognized as a mental illness, clinical disorder, and constitute behavioral addiction (Chou et al., 2005; Huang & Leung, 2009; Lin et al., 2009; Ni et al., 2009; Lo et al., 2005; Nichols & Nicki, 2004). Internet addiction, like any other kind of addiction is characterized by the compulsive behaviors of the addict in uncontrollable use of the internet for variety of activities ranging from gaming, chatting, shopping, gambling, sexual materials, and excessive use of email. Therefore, we hypothesize:

H2: Perceived risks have a negative effect on the behavioral intention to household Internet adoption.

PERCEIVED EASE OF USE

Perceived ease of use refers to "the degree to which a person believes that using a particular system would be free of effort. This follows from the definition of ease, which refers to freedom from difficulty or great effort. (Davis, 1989) claimed that, an application perceived to be easier to use than another is more likely to be accepted by users. Consumers in the home are less likely to choose an Internet access technology if they perceive it to be complex or not easy to use. This is no less true in developing countries, where perceived ease of use has often been found as a predominant influence on user behavior (Ifinedo, 2006; Brown et al., 2009). Thus, the proposition is as follows:

H3: Perceived ease of use has a positive effect on the behavioral intention to household Internet adoption.

PERCEIVED RESOURCES

Perceived resources refer to an individual's belief that he has the resources needed for adopting and using an information technology (Mathieson et al., 2001). The technology acceptance model has a limitation in assuming that behavioral intention to use IT is volitional, and there are no barriers may prevent an individual from adopting and using an information system if he or she chose to do so (Oh et al., 2003). Ajzen (1991) has added the construct of perceived behavioral control, which includes the individual's beliefs regarding the availability of resources, needed as predictor of behavioral intention, and put forward the TPB framework. Taylor and Todd (1995) and Luarn and Lin (2005) decomposed them into facilitating conditions which reflects the availability of resources needed to engage in a behavior, such as time, money or other specialized resources.

In order to extend the TAM, (Oh et al., 2003; Luarn & Lin 2005; Zhang & Gutierrez, 2007; Dwivedi et al., 2007; Mathieson et al., 2001) has incorporated the construct of perceived resources to predict and explain behavioral intention to use an ICT. Therefore, it is expected that the absence of resources represents barriers may inhibit the formation of behavioral intention to adopt and use household Internet. Thus, this study tests the following hypothesis:

H4: Perceived resources have a positive effect on the on the behavioral intention to household Internet adoption.

PERCEIVED IMAGE

From the perspective of Venkatesh and Davis (2000), image represents the degree to which use of IT is perceived to enhance one's status is one's social system. In the Innovation Diffusion Theory, image is included as an important aspect of relative advantage. For some innovations, the desire to gain social status may be the one of the most important motivations (Lee et al., 2003). Individual household Internet users are likely to be cognizant of the image that they project in their social networks. Many adopt such technology because they believe that these services may help them create, alter or preserve a positive image and social status for themselves within their social setting rather than for addressing a necessity (Teo & Pok, 2003; Yi et al., 2006). Therefore, we hypothesize:

H5: Perceived image has a positive effect on the behavioral intention on the behavioral intention to household Internet adoption.

INDIVIDUALISM/COLLECTIVISM

Hofstede's Individualism dimension refers to the strength of the ties people have to others within the society, and focuses on whether a society is based on loose cooperation of individuals or integrated into groups. On the individualist side, individuals have more loose relationships; everybody has the right of his own opinion, the culture stress on personal achievements and individual rights, and little sharing of responsibility beyond family. On the collectivist side (low individualism), people from birth are integrated into strong, cohesive in groups, often extended families which continue protecting them in exchange for unquestioning loyalty.

Collectivism represents the extent to which people in a society prefer to live as a member of a tight-knit social group rather than live and work independently. Therefore, families in the high collectivism societies are more likely to be motivated to adopt a household Internet as a means of enhancing their status and prestige, or to attract positive attention. Hence, we propose the following hypothesis:

H6: Collectivism (low individualism) has a negative effect on the behavioral intention to household Internet adoption.

H7: There is a positive relationship between collectivism (low individualism) and perceived image of household Internet adoption.

MASCULINITY (MAS)

Masculinity refers to the distribution of roles between the genders, and to how much a society values the traditional man and woman roles. High Masculinity society scores are found in countries where men are expected to be tough, provider, assertive and strong. If women work outside the home, they have separate professions from men. Individuals who perceive economic benefits as a sign of personal success or achievement tend to be more masculine. On the other hand, low Masculinity scores do not reverse the gender roles, and the women's roles are simply blurred. Women and men work together equally across many professions. Furthermore, Femininity stands for a society in which emotional gender roles overlap, where both men and women are supposed to be modest, tender, and concerned with the quality of life. Therefore, we hypothesize:

H8: Masculinity has a negative effect on the behavioral intention to household Internet adoption.

POWER DISTANCE INDEX (PDI)

Power Distance dimension measures the extent to which an unequal distribution of power, wealth, and political authority is accepted, and to which the less powerful members of organizations and institutions (like the family) accept and expect that power is distributed unequally. It suggests that a society's level of inequality is endorsed by the followers as much as by the leaders. Power and inequality are extremely fundamental facts of any society, but some are more unequal than others. Therefore, we propose the following hypothesis:

H9: Power distance has a negative effect on the behavioral intention to household Internet adoption.

LONG-TERM ORIENTATION (LTO)

The fifth dimension is found in the teachings of Confucius, to distinguish the difference in thinking between the East and West. Long-term orientation refers to what extent society adheres to their traditions and values. According to Hofstede's analysis, long-term orientation society is thrift, perseverance, and oriented towards future

rewards. In contrast, short-term orientation society fosters virtues related to the past and present, in particular respect for tradition, protecting one's face, and fulfilling social obligations. Hence, we hypothesize the following:

H10: Long-term orientation has a positive effect on the behavioral intention to household Internet adoption.

UNCERTAINTY AVOIDANCE

Uncertainty Avoidance indicates to the degree to which the members of society feel threatened by uncertain, unknown, ambiguous, or unstructured situations. Uncertainty avoiding cultures try to minimize the possibility of such situations by strict laws and rules, safety and security measures, and on the philosophical and religious level by a belief in absolute truth. People in uncertainty avoiding societies are also more emotional, and motivated by inner nervous energy. The opposite type, uncertainty accepting cultures, are more tolerant of opinions different from what they are used to; they try to have as few rules as possible, and on the philosophical and religious level they are relativist and allow many currents to flow side by side. People within these cultures are more phlegmatic and contemplative, and not expected by their environment to express emotions.

Furthermore, due to the nature of household Internet as a new social and individual worldwide device for communications, exchange formal and informal relations and personal sensitive information in family framework, and the reliability and accuracy of information on Internet, adopters will always experience some level of risk. In essence, they decide to deal with various degrees of uncertainty of the future and the free actions of others. In these uncertain situations, when adopters have to act, risk becomes an important barrier for household Internet adoption (Kim et al., 2008; Lee et al., 2007; Bélanger & Carter, 2008; Garrido & Marina, 2008). Therefore, this study tests the following hypotheses:

H11: Uncertainty avoidance has a negative effect on the behavioral intention to household Internet adoption.

H12: There is a positive relationship between uncertainty avoidance and perceived risks of the household Internet adoption.

RESEARCH METHODOLOGY

The Measurement

The measurement instruments of the driving internal beliefs constructs have long been used in previous research and shown high reliability and validity, therefore, it was reasonable to employ these instruments in this study. Thus, the scales to measure each of the driving internal beliefs constructs in the model were adopted from previous related research (Taylor & Todd, 1995, Pavlou & Fygenson, 2006, Davis, 1989; Papacharissi & Rubin, 2000; Venkatesh & Davis, 2000; Oh et al., 2003; Venkatesh et al., 2003; Belanger & Carter, 2008). Furthermore, consistent with research literature, the measurements of the cultural values constructs were derived from (Srite & Karahanna, 2006; Vitell et al., 2003; Dorfman & Howell, 1988; House et al., 2004; Furrer et al., 2000). Each construct is described in Table 1.

Instrument Development

Survey instrument was developed to examine the driving internal beliefs, behavioral intention, and the effect of cultural values on the household Internet adoption. In order to collect representative data of the target population with limited time and resources, a self-administered questionnaire was considered to be the most appropriate survey instrument in this research. The questionnaire

included a total of 41 questions items representing the eleven constructs identified in Table 1. All questions used a five point Likert-type scale.

Sampling and Questionnaire Distribution

Student sampling has become very common in behavioral intention to IT Adoption and the impact of cultural values research (Devaraj et al., 2002; Srite & Karahanna, 2006; DeLorenzo et al., 2009; Albirini, 2006; ElSaid & Hone, 2005; Moghadam & Assar, 2008). Hofstede and Bond (1988) developed the fifth cultural dimension, based on a study among students in 23 countries around the world. The students are generally younger and more educated; are most affected by other cultures, and represent the most users of Internet in the families and societies. Furthermore, the authors attempted to obtain samples covering various geographic in order to reduce sampling bias caused by user characteristics. Based on that, the questionnaire was distributed in four Jordanians' universities to represent the population at large. Four hundreds and thirty seven printed paper questionnaires were distributed, and a total of 347 questionnaires were returned, representing a response rate of 80%. 19 questionnaires with missing data and incompatible answers were excluded. The remaining 328 questionnaires were used in the statistical analysis.

Data Analysis and Results

Structural Equation Modeling (SEM) using the Partial Least Squares (PLS) technique was used to validate the measures and test the research model and hypotheses. (SEM) permits a simultaneous assessment of the structural component (path model) and measurement component (factor model) in the one model. According to Fornell and Larcker (1981), the PLS method is also more robust since its does not require either a large sample or normally distributed data. In addition, PLS have ability to account for measurement errors for unobserved

Table 1. Constructs and Measurements of Driving Internal Beliefs and Cultural Dimensions of House-hold Internet Adoption Model

Constructs	Variables
Perceived Needs (PN)	- Household Internet provides an easy and cheap access to information or others. - I use the Internet as an information tool to learn about people, places, products and services, news, and scientific materials. - I use the Internet to fulfill needs of affection, inclusion, expression, social interaction, and surveillance. - I use the Internet when there is nothing to do, to occupy idle time, and to relieve boredom.
Perceived Risk (PRI)	- People in my society are concerned about the children accessibility of pornography and violent material on the Internet. - People in my society are concerned about unwanted disclosure of private information, and its subsequent misuse. - The Internet allows the terrorist groups to affect the children and young people's beliefs and attitudes. - The Internet impact on individual's home work, social life, normal function and other aspects of their lives. - The decision of whether to adopt household Internet is risky.
Perceived Ease of Use (PEU)	- I clearly understand how to use the Internet. - Interacting with the Internet does not require a lot of my mental efforts. - Overall, I find the Internet easy to use.
Perceived Resources (PRE)	- It would be within my budget to subscribe to household Internet. - I have the necessary knowledge to use the household Internet. - I have the time needed for using the household Internet
Perceived Image (PI)	- People in my society who adopt the household Internet have more prestige than those who do not. - Having the household Internet is a status symbol in my society.
Behavioral Intention to Household Internet Adoption (BIHIA)	- I predict that I would subscribe and use (or continue use) household Internet in the future. - I intend to subscribe to (or continue my current subscription) household Internet in the future. - I plan to subscribe (or continue my current subscription) to household Internet in the future.
Individualism (IDV)	- Being accepted as a member of a group is more important than being independent. - One has to be loyal to his/her community if one seeks their support and protection. - When one is born, the success or failure one is going to have is already in one's destiny, so one might as well accept. - You should worry more about how your disability would affect your family and relatives than how it would affect you personally.
Masculinity (MAS)	- It is preferable to have a man in high level position rather than a woman. - There are some jobs in which a man can always do better than a woman. - Women are more concerned with social aspects of their job than they are with getting ahead. - It is important for me to have a job which has an opportunity for high earnings.
Power Distance (PD)	- There should be established ranks in society with everyone occupying their rightful place regardless of whether that place is high or low in the ranking. - People having authority should be respected because of their position. - One should always obey the person in authority. - I always conform to my superior's wishes.
Long-term orientation (LTO)	- It is easier to succeed if one knows how to take short-cuts. - Social obligations should be respected regardless of cost. - I believe that the accepted norm in my society is to emphasis on status quo and solving current problems rather than plan for the future. - I believe that people who are successful should take life events as they occur.
Uncertainty Avoidance (UA)	- People should avoid making changes because things could get worse. - It is better to have a bad situation that you know about, than to have an uncertain. - I like to work in a well-defined job where the requirements are clear. - In a situation in which other people evaluate me, I feel that clear and explicit guidelines should be used.

constructs and to examine the significance of structural paths simultaneously (Chin et al., 2003). PLS analysis involves tow steps:

- Assessment of the measurement model, including the reliability and discriminant validity of the measures.
- Assessment of the structural model and hypotheses by examining the path coefficients.

Assessing the Measurement Model

The measurement model was examined for internal consistency, convergent and discriminant validity. Table 2 shows Cronbach's alpha of the research constructs and Rho coefficient. Reliability of constructs is assessed by using the Cronbach's alpha, which reflects the consistency of the measure and the homogeneity of the items in the scale. As shown in Cronbach's Alpha column in the Table 2, all constructs exhibited loading of greater than 0.70. To measure internal consistency, Rho coefficient was used. Unlike Cronbach's alpha, the number of items in the scale does not influence the Rho coefficient. It is influenced by the relative loadings of the items. The Rho coefficient is based on the ratio of construct variance to the sum of construct and error variance. A value greater than 0.50 indicating that the construct variance accounts for at least 50% of the measurement variance (Rivard & Huff, 1988). The Rho coefficients (Table 2) indicate that the construct variances account for 83 to 93% of measurement variances.

Convergent and discriminate validity verifies that items should load higher on their own construct than on the others in the model, and the average variance shared between the constructs and their measures should be greater than the variances shared between the constructs themselves. The factor structure matrix showed that all items load high on their respective constructs (0.70 or more) and lower on other constructs. The square root of the AVE (diagonal elements) was

found to be larger than the correlations (off-diagonal elements) between the constructs (Table 3). Thus, the results exhibit sufficiently strong psychometric properties to support valid testing of the proposed structural model.

Assessing the Structural Model

The structural model in PLS is assessed by examining the path coefficients (standardized betas). The path coefficients indicate the strengths of relationships between constructs. The significance of the path coefficients is assessed by the bootstrap t-values, which should be higher than 2 (Chin, 1998). The PLS path coefficients are shown in Figure 2. According to significant path coefficients, the majority of the hypotheses to the relationships between the model constructs were supported.

Table 4 provides the t values of path coefficients and summarizes hypothesis testing. Overall, the whole model was able to account for 68% of variance in the construct of Behavioral Intention to Household Internet Adoption (BIHIA). It concluded that all driving internal beliefs have strong

Table 2. The Cronbach's alpha and rho coefficient of research constructs

Construct	No. of Items	Cronbach's alpha	Rho
PN	3	0.83	0.85
PRI	4	0.91	0.93
PEU	3	0.89	0.91
PRE	3	0.84	0.89
PI	3	0.90	0.88
BIHIA	3	0.85	0.87
IDV	4	0.88	0.92
MAS	4	0.81	0.87
PD	4	0.78	0.82
LTO	4	0.84	0.87
UA	4	0.79	0.83

Table 3. Variance shared between constructs

Construct	PN	PRI	PEU	PRE	PI	BIHIA	IDV	MAS	PD	LTO	UA
PN	**0.84**										
PRI	0.49	**0.85**									
PEU	0.35	0.14	**0.72**								
PRE	0.42	0.14	0.46	**0.82**							
PI	0.47	0.25	0.13	0.51	**0.74**						
BIHIA	0.37	0.12	0.31	0.57	0.44	**0.96**					
IDV	0.62	0.34	0.42	0.47	0.10	0.78	**0.81**				
MAS	0.56	0.37	0.12	0.55	0.22	0.64	0.26	**0.86**			
PD	0.26	0.10	0.51	0.53	0.32	0.62	0.29	0.49	**0.86**		
LTO	0.12	0.58	0.26	0.56	0.15	0.60	0.18	0.43	0.48	**0.95**	
UA	0.31	0.54	0.54	0.62	0.14	0.89	0.19	0.42	0.41	0.54	**0.91**

positive, direct and significant effect on Behavioral Intention to Household Internet Adoption.

The results indicate that perceived needs (*H1*) has a positive effect on behavioral intention to household Internet adoption with path coefficient of (0.379, p<0.05). This finding is consistent with U&G perspective which posits that the reasons of selecting, adopting, and using specific ICT in the voluntary choice are determined by the awareness of needs and the extent to which the technology helps to fulfill and satisfy their felt needs or wants easily (Ruggiero, 2000; Papacharissi & Rubin, 2000; Luo et al., 2006; Guo et al., 2009). The results also indicate that perceived risks (H2) are a very powerful factor (-0.522, p<0.01), that

negatively affect the behavioral intention to household Internet adoption. The results show that people are concerned about unwanted disclosure of private information, intentionally and accidentally exposure to pornography and violent, the effect of terrorists' propaganda on children and young people's beliefs and attitudes, and the excessive internet usage with a loss of sense of time. Besides of perceived ease of use (*H3*), perceived resources (*H4*) and perceived image (*H5*) contributed significantly to the observed explanatory power of the behavioral intention to household Internet adoption. The path coefficients are 0.203, p<0.01; 0.499, p<0.05; 0.116, p<0.01 respectively. Similar to other related studies

Figure 2. The PLS model results

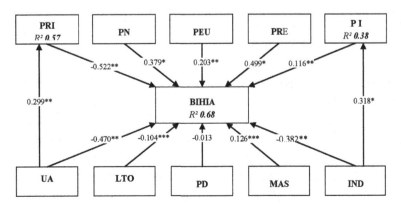

Table 4. Test of hypotheses

Hypothesis	Path		Standardized Path Coefficient	t-Value	The Result
H1	PN	BIHIA	0.379*	6.824	Supported
H2	PRI	BIHIA	-0.522**	-11. 659	Supported
H3	PEU	BIHIA	0.203**	3. 901	Supported
H4	PRE	BIHIA	0.499*	5.201	Supported
H5	PI	BIHIA	0.116**	2.024	Supported
H6	IDV	BIHIA	-0.382**	-7.834	Supported
H7	IDV	PI	0.318*	4.453	Supported
H8	MAS	BIHIA	-0.126***	-0.311	Supported
H9	PD	BIHIA	-0.013	-1.200	Not Supported
H10	LTO	BIHIA	-0.104***	-3.583	Supported
H11	UA	BIHIA	-0.470**	-8.659	Supported
H12	UA	PRI	0.299**	5.202	Supported

Note: *** $p < 0.001$; ** $p < 0.01$; * $p < 0.05$.

(Ajzen, 1991; Oh et al., 2003; Taylor & Todd, 1995; Luarn & Lin, 2005), we found the individual's beliefs concerning the availability of resources (H4) to have a significant positive effect 0.299, $p < 0.05$ on the behavioral intention to household Internet adoption. The results also support the expected positive effect of perceived image (*H5*) with path coefficient of (0.116, $p < 0.01$).

Testing the effect of cultural dimensions on the behavioral intention to household Internet adoption depicted in Figure 2, as suggested by the *t* statistics and path coefficient in Table 4, four of five cultural dimensions paths were significant. The coefficients for collectivism (low individualism) (*H6*), masculinity (*H8*), and uncertainty avoidance (*H11*) dimensions are negative and significant with values of (-0.382, $p < 0.01$) (-0.026, $p < 0.01$), and (-0.470, $p < 0.01$) respectively. The results also support the direct positive effect of long-term orientation on the behavioral intention to household Internet adoption (*H10*), with path coefficient (-0.104, $p < 0.001$).

At the same time, the results show a positive relationship between collectivism and perceived image of household Internet adoption (*H7*), with the path coefficients of (0.318, $p < 0.05$). The results also show that perceived image alone explained 38% of the variance of the behavioral intention to household Internet adoption in collectivism societies, which means that the people with collectivism culture may adopt such technology because they believe that these services may help them create, alter or preserve a positive image and social prestige or status within their society rather than for addressing a necessity, specially with the individual's belief that he has the resources needed for adoption and using household Internet regardless of other internal beliefs and cultural values. Consistent with previous research (Kim et al., 2008; Lee et al., 2007; Bélanger & Carter, 2008; Garrido & Marina, 2008) results also support the positive relationship between Uncertainty Avoidance and Perceived Risks of the household Internet adoption (*H12*) with the path coefficient (0.299, $p < 0.01$). The results show that 57% of the variance in perceived risks is explained by uncertainty avoidance. Inconsistent with our hypothesis (*H9*), power distance does not have a significant effect on the behavioral intention to household Internet adoption. The path coefficient between the two constructs is (-0.382, $p < 0.01$).

The results differ from those of Akour et al. (2006) who examined the impacts of cultural dimensions, perceived ease of use, and perceived usefulness of Jordanian managers' intentions to use the Internet in organization context, regarding power distance, collectivism (low individualism), masculinity, and uncertainty avoidance. The difference between these two results could be due to the difference in the environment of Internet adoption. As whole, the adoption and usage of ICT in the organizational settings is different from it in the home, where acceptance is voluntary social behavior, rather than for addressing a necessity to survival or to achieve competitive advantage. In the case of household Internet adoption, the individuals has the freedom to decide whether or not he utilizes the technology, where the individuals' behavior and decisions are more conditioned by their internal beliefs and cultural values, than the managers in organizations. This conclusion is consistent with the findings of Akour et al. (2006) which reported that Jordanian managers hold double standards toward the Internet. On one hand, they have a negative attitude about the social impacts of the Internet and on the other hand, they perceived the Internet as an important technology to enhance competitiveness, assertiveness, and flexibility for responding fast enough to changing business environments.

CONCLUSION

The Internet represents a set of services for various subsystems of society, and can be used for very diverse purposes. The scope of Internet applications pushes toward delivering the Internet services to households. The Internet technology has some unique idiosyncrasies when it comes to households considering a subscription decision, where adoption is voluntary.

This study aimed to develop and validate a comprehensive model to identify the driving internal beliefs and the effect of cultural values on the adoption of Internet in household. Taking into consideration the specificity of household Internet adoption, and building on extensive review of the technology acceptance frameworks and ICT adoption behavior, five driving internal beliefs were identified. Furthermore, the study employed Hofstede's multidimensional framework to empirically investigate the impact of cultural dimensions, including the levels of power distance, individualism, masculinity, uncertainty avoidance, and long-term orientation.

The findings from this study showed that behavioral intention to household Internet adoption is determined directly by perceived risks, perceived needs, perceived ease of use, perceived resources, and perceived image. The research also found that behavioral intention to household Internet is affected by the levels of individualism, masculinity, long-term orientation, and uncertainty avoidance. The results indicated that people are concerned about unwanted disclosure of private information, intentionally and accidentally exposure to pornography and violent, the effect of terrorists' propaganda on children and young people's beliefs and attitudes, and the excessive internet usage with a loss of sense of time.

This research will help regulators, governments and the telecommunications providers understand the broader issues of household Internet adoption such as the driving internal beliefs, the effect of cultural dimensions affecting the intention to household Internet adoption and usage, which will be helpful in understanding, stimulating, and facilitating the adoption and usage of such technology. On the other hand, understanding the antecedents of adopter perceived risk can provide stakeholders with insights and strategies that they can use to build trust and manage the perceived risks that are inherent in the household Internet adoption.

Despite the comprehensiveness of the proposed model and the empirical support for it, this study leaves as many open questions as it provides answers, which call for additional research. First, although the young students play an important role in forming the decision of Internet adoption in households, it is unclear whether the sample is representative of Jordanians specially the parents, who take the ultimate decision on household Internet adoption in terms of their driving internal beliefs and Hofstede's cultural dimensions. In a collectivism society, Jordanians' children generally live at home with their parents until they get married. Parents are responsible for providing their families with the necessary resources, and they are the ones who have to worry and protect children from the perceived risks on the Internet. Therefore, we recommend that future studies give more attention to the behavioral intention of parents to household Internet adoption.

Second, future research need to investigate the extent to which household Internet adoption is influenced by individuals and national characteristics including educational, social, political, economic and gross national income in comparative research, elaborating a new classification framework for countries and nations. Third, future research will also need to assess the requirements and mechanisms to adapt Internet services and applications to the behavioral patterns of the adopting cultures and nations, giving great consideration to eliminate the fears and threats, rather than continues in the traditional approach of force-fitting the culture to the technology. Finally, it would be valuable to measure and validate the impact of Internet usage on individual's behavior, social interaction, and cultural values of nations in the light of spreading the universal electronic societies, such as Facebook, MySpace, and Twitter.

REFERENCES

Ajzen, I. (1991). The theory of planned behavior. *Organizational Behavior and Human Decision Processes*, *50*(2), 179–211. doi:10.1016/0749-5978(91)90020-T

Akour, I., Alshare, K., Miller, D., & Dwairi, M. (2006). An exploratory analysis of culture, perceived ease of use, perceived usefulness, and internet acceptance: The case of Jordan. *Journal of Internet Commerce*, *5*(3), 83–108. doi:10.1300/J179v05n03_04

Albirini, A. (2006). Cultural perceptions: The missing element in the implementation of ICT in developing countries. *International Journal of Education and Development Using Information and Communication Technology*, *2*(1), 49–65.

Anandarajan, M., Igbariam, M., & Anakwe, U. P. (2002). IT acceptance in a less-developed country: A motivational factor perspective. *International Journal of Information Management*, *22*(1), 47–65. doi:10.1016/S0268-4012(01)00040-8

Anderson, A. (2003). Risk, terrorism, and the Internet. *Knowledge. Technology and Policy*, *16*(2), 24–33. doi:10.1007/s12130-003-1023-7

Bagchi, K., Hart, P., & Peterson, M. F. (2004). National culture and information technology product adoption. *Journal of Global Information Technology Management*, *7*(4), 29–46.

Bélanger, F., & Carter, L. (2008). Trust and risk in e-government adoption. *The Journal of Strategic Information Systems*, *17*(2), 165–176. doi:10.1016/j.jsis.2007.12.002

Brown, I., Letsididi, B., & Nazeer, M. (2009). Internet access in South African home: A preliminary study on factors influencing consumer choice. *The Electronic Journal on Information Systems in Developing Countries*, *38*(2), 1–13.

Brown, S. A., Montoya-Weiss, M. M., & Burkman, J. R. (2002). Do I really have to? User acceptance of mandated technology. *European Journal of Information Systems*, *11*(4), 283–295. doi:10.1057/palgrave.ejis.3000438

Brown, S. A., & Venkatesh, V. (2005). Model of adoption of technology in households: A baseline model test and extension incorporating household life cycle. *Management Information Systems Quarterly, 29*(3), 399–426.

Calantone, R. J., Griffith, D. A., & Yalcinkaya, G. (2006). An empirical examination of a technology adoption model for the context of China. *Journal of International Marketing, 14*(2), 1–27. doi:10.1509/jimk.14.4.1

Chin, W. W. (1998). Issues and opinions on structural equation modeling. *Management Information Systems Quarterly, 22*(1), 7–16.

Chin, W. W., Marcolin, B. L., & Newsted, P. R. (2003). A partial least squares latent variable modeling approach for measuring interaction effects: Results from a Monte Carlo simulation study and an electronic mail emotion/adoption study. *Information Systems Research, 14*(2), 189–217. doi:10.1287/isre.14.2.189.16018

Chou, C., Condron, L., & Belland, J. C. (2005). A review of the research on Internet addiction. *Educational Psychology Review, 17*(4), 363–388. doi:10.1007/s10648-005-8138-1

Choudrie, J., & Dwivedi, Y. K. (2004, August). Investigating the socio-economic characteristics of residential consumers of broadband in the UK. In *Proceedings of the Tenth American Conference on Information Systems* (pp. 1558-1567).

Choudrie, J., & Dwivedi, Y. K. (2006). A comparative study to examine the socio-economic characteristics of broadband adopters and non-adopters. *International Journal of Services and Standards, 3*(3), 272–288.

Conway, M. (2006). Terrorist 'use' of the Internet and fighting back. *International Journal of Information Security, 19*, 9–30.

Davis, F. D. (1989). Perceived usefulness, perceived ease of use, and user acceptance of information technology. *Management Information Systems Quarterly, 13*(3), 319–339. doi:10.2307/249008

DeLorenzo, G. J., Kohun, F. G., Burčik, V., Belanová, A., & Skovira, R. J. (2009). A data driven conceptual analysis of globalization cultural affects and Hofstedian organizational frames: The Slovak republic example. *Issues in Informing Science and Information Technology, 6*, 461–470.

Devaraj, S., Fan, M., & Kohli, R. (2000). Antecedents of B2C channel satisfaction and preference: Validating e-commerce metrics. *Information Systems Research, 13*(3), 316–333. doi:10.1287/isre.13.3.316.77

Dorfman, P. W., & Howell, J. P. (1988). Dimensions of national culture and effective leadership patterns: Hofstede revisited. In McGoun, E. G. (Ed.), *Advances in international comparative management* (*Vol. 3*, pp. 127–149). Greenwich, CT: JAI.

Dwivedi, Y. K., Khan, N., & Papazafeiropoulou, A. (2007). Consumer adoption and usage of broadband in Bangladesh. *International Journal of Electronic Government, 4*(3), 299–313. doi:10.1504/EG.2007.014164

ElSaid, G., & Hone, K. (2005). Culture and e-Commerce: An exploration of the perceptions and attitudes of Egyptian internet users. *Journal of Computing and Information Technology, 13*(2), 107–122. doi:10.2498/cit.2005.02.03

Erumban, A. A., & de Jong, S. B. (2006). Cross-country differences in ICT adoption: A consequence of culture? *Journal of World Business, 41*(4), 302–314. doi:10.1016/j.jwb.2006.08.005

Fishbein, M., & Ajzen, I. (1975). *Belief, attitude, intention and behaviour: An introduction to theory and research*. Reading, MA: Addison-Wesley.

Flanagin, A. J., & Metzger, M. J. (2001). Internet use in the contemporary media environment. *Human Communication Research, 27*(1), 153–181. doi:10.1093/hcr/27.1.153

Fornell, C., & Larcker, D. (1981). Structural equation models with unobserved variables and measurement error. *JMR, Journal of Marketing Research, 18*(1), 39–50. doi:10.2307/3151312

Furrer, O., Liu, B. S.-C., & Sudharshan, D. (2000). The relationships between culture and service quality perceptions: Basis for cross-cultural market segmentation and resource allocation. *Journal of Service Research, 2*(4), 355–371. doi:10.1177/109467050024004

Garrido, N., & Marina, A. (2008). Exploring trust on Internet: The Spanish case. *Observatorio Journal, 2*(3), 223–244.

Gong, W., Li, Z. G., & Stump, R. L. (2007). Global Internet use and access: Cultural considerations. *Asia Pacific Journal of Marketing and Logistics, 19*(1), 57–74. doi:10.1108/13555850710720902

Gray, D. H., & Head, A. (2009). The importance of the Internet to the post-modern terrorist and its role as a form of safe haven. *European Journal of Scientific Research, 25*(3), 396–404.

Guo, Z., Zhang, Y., & Stevens, K. (2009, June). A 'uses and gratifications approach' to understanding the role of wiki technology in enhancing teaching and learning outcomes. In *Proceedings of the 17th European Conference on Information Systems,* Verona, Italy (pp. 2-13).

Hill, C., Loch, K., Straub, D., & El-Sheshai, K. (1998). A qualitative assessment of Arab culture and information technology transfer. *Journal of Global Information Management, 6*(3), 29–38.

Hofstede, G. (1980). *Culture's consequences: International differences in related values.* Thousand Oaks, CA: Sage.

Hofstede, G. (1983). National culture in four dimensions. *International Studies of Management and Organization, 13*(1-2), 46–74.

Hofstede, G. (1991). *Cultures and organizations: Software of the mind.* New York, NY: McGraw-Hill.

Hofstede, G., & Bond, M. (1984). The need for synergy among cross-culture studies. *Journal of Cross-Cultural Psychology, 15*(2), 417–433. doi:10.1177/0022002184015004003

Hofstede, G., & Bond, M. (1988). The Confucius connection: From cultural roots to economic growth. *Organizational Dynamics, 16*(4), 4–21. doi:10.1016/0090-2616(88)90009-5

Horton, R. P., Buck, T., Waterson, P. E., & Clegg, C. W. (2001). Explaining intranet use with the technology acceptance model. *Journal of Management Information Systems, 16*(2), 91–112.

House, R. J., Hanges, P. J., & Javidan, M. (Eds.). (2004). *Culture, leadership, and organizations: The GLOBE study of 62 societies* (pp. 239–281). Thousand Oaks, CA: Sage.

Huang, H., & Leung, L. (2009). Instant messaging addiction among teenagers in China: Shyness, alienation, and academic performance decrement. *Cyberpsychology & Behavior, 12*(6), 675–679. doi:10.1089/cpb.2009.0060

Ifinedo, P. (2006). Acceptance and continuance intention of web-based learning technologies (WLT) use among university students in a Baltic country. *Electronic Journal of Information Systems in Developing Countries, 23*(6), 1–20.

Isaacs, C. R., & Fisher, W. A. (2008). A computer-based educational intervention to address potential negative effects of internet pornography. *Communication Studies, 59*(1), 1–18. doi:10.1080/10510970701849354

Jensen, O. W., & Scheraga, C. A. (1998). Transferring technology: Costs and benefits. *Technology in Society*, *20*(1), 99–112. doi:10.1016/S0160-791X(97)00031-6

Karahanna, E., Evaristo, J. R., & Srite, M. (2005). Levels of culture and individual behavior: An integrative perspective. *Journal of Global Information Management*, *13*(2), 1–20. doi:10.4018/jgim.2005040101

Kesh, S., Ramanujan, S., & Nerur, S. (2002). A framework for analyzing e-commerce security. *Information Management & Computer Security*, *10*(4), 149–458. doi:10.1108/09685220210436930

Kim, D., Derrin, D., & Rao, H. (2008). A trust-based consumer decision-making model in electronic commerce: The role of trust, perceived risk, and their antecedents. *Decision Support Systems*, *44*(2), 544–564. doi:10.1016/j.dss.2007.07.001

Kim, K., & Prabhakar, B. (2000). Initial trust, perceived risk, and the adoption of internet banking. In *Proceedings of the Twenty First International Conference on Information Systems*, Brisbane, Australia (pp. 537-543).

Korgaonkar, P., & Wolin, L. (1999). A multivariate analysis of web usage. *Journal of Advertising Research*, *39*(2), 53–68.

Lee, K. S., Lee, H. S., & Kim, S. Y. (2007). Factors influencing the adoption behavior of mobile banking: A South Korean perspective. *Journal of Internet Banking and Commerce*, *12*(2), 1–9.

Lee, M. S. Y., McGoldrick, P. J., Keeling, K. A., & Doherty, J. (2003). Using ZMET to explore barriers to the adoption of 3G mobile banking services. *International Journal of Retail & Distribution Management*, *31*(6), 340–348. doi:10.1108/09590550310476079

Leidner, D., & Kayworth, T. (2006). A review of culture in information systems research: Toward a theory of information technology culture conflict. *Management Information Systems Quarterly*, *30*(2), 357–399.

Lin, C.-H., Lin, S.-L., & Wu, C.-P. (2009). The effects of parental monitoring and leisure boredom on adolescents' internet addiction. *Adolescence*, *44*(176), 993–1004.

Lo, S.-K., Wang, C.-C., & Fang, W. (2005). Physical interpersonal relationships and social anxiety among online game players. *Cyberpsychology & Behavior*, *8*(1), 15–20. doi:10.1089/cpb.2005.8.15

Loch, K., Straub, D., & Kamel, S. (2003). Diffusing the Internet in the Arab world: The role of social norms and technological culturaltion. *IEEE Transactions on Engineering Management*, *5*(1), 45–63. doi:10.1109/TEM.2002.808257

López-Nicolás, C., Molina-Castillo, F. J., & Bouwman, H. (2008). An assessment of advanced mobile services acceptance: Contributions from TAM and diffusion theory models. *Information & Management*, *45*(6), 359–364. doi:10.1016/j.im.2008.05.001

Luarn, P., & Lin, H. H. (2005). Toward an understanding of the behavioral intention to use mobile banking. *Computers in Human Behavior*, *21*(6), 873–891. doi:10.1016/j.chb.2004.03.003

Luo, M. M.-L., Remus, W., & Chea, S. (2006, August 4-6). Technology acceptance of internet based information system: An integrated model of TAM and U&G theory. In *Proceedings of the Twelfth American Conference on Information Systems*, Acapulco, Mexico (pp. 1139-1150).

Mathieson, K., Peacock, E., & Chin, W. (2001). Extending the technology acceptance model: The influence of perceived resources. *The Data Base for Advances in Information Systems*, *32*(3), 86–112.

Melone, N. P. (1990). A theoretical assessment of the user-satisfaction construct in information systems research. *Management Science*, *36*(1), 76–91. doi:10.1287/mnsc.36.1.76

Moghadam, A. H., & Assar, P. (2008). The relationship between national culture and e-adoption: A case study of Iran. *American Journal of Applied Sciences, 5*(4), 369–377. doi:10.3844/ajassp.2008.369.377

Myers, M., & Tan, F. (2002). Beyond models of national culture in information systems research. *Journal of Global Information Management, 10*(2), 1–19.

Ni, X., Yan, H., Chen, S., & Liu, Z. (2009). Factors influencing internet addiction in a sample of freshmen university students in China. *Cyberpsychology & Behavior, 12*(3), 327–330. doi:10.1089/cpb.2008.0321

Nichols, L. A., & Nicki, R. (2004). Development of a psychometrically sound internet addiction scale: A preliminary step. *Psychology of Addictive Behaviors, 18*(38), 1–4.

Oh, S., Ahn, J., & Kim, B. (2003). Adoption of broadband internet in Korea: The role of experience in building attitude. *Journal of Information Technology, 18*(4), 267–280. doi:10.1080/0268396032000150807

Papacharissi, Z., & Rubin, A. M. (2000). Predictors of internet use. *Journal of Broadcasting & Electronic Media, 44*(2), 175–196. doi:10.1207/s15506878jobem4402_2

Park, J., Yang, S., & Lehto, X. (2007). Adoption of mobile technologies for Chinese consumers. *Journal of Electronic Commerce Research, 8*(3), 196–206.

Pavlou, P. A. (2003). Consumer acceptance of electronic commerce: Integrating trust and risk with the technology acceptance model. *International Journal of Electronic Commerce, 7*(3), 101–134.

Pavlou, P. A., & Fygenson, M. (2006). Understanding and predicting electronic commerce adoption: An extension of the theory of planned behavior. *Management Information Systems Quarterly, 30*(1), 115–144.

Rivard, S., & Huff, S. L. (1988). Factors of success for end-user computing. *Communications of the ACM, 31*(5), 552–561. doi:10.1145/42411.42418

Robichaux, B. P., & Cooper, R. B. (1998). GSS participation: A cultural examination. *Information & Management, 33*(6), 287–300. doi:10.1016/S0378-7206(98)00033-0

Ruggiero, T. E. (2000). Uses and gratifications theory in the 21st century. *Mass Communication & Society, 3*(1), 3–37. doi:10.1207/S15327825MCS0301_02

Schepers, J., & Wetzels, M. (2007). A meta-analysis of the technology acceptance model: Investigating subjective norm and moderation effects. *Information & Management, 44*(1), 90–103. doi:10.1016/j.im.2006.10.007

Scheraga, C. A., Tellis, W. M., & Tucker, M. T. (2000). Lead users and technology transfer. *Technology in Society, 22*(3), 415–425. doi:10.1016/S0160-791X(00)00017-8

Shan, A., Weiyin, R., Peishan, L., & Shoulian, T. (2008). Research of home information technology adoption model. *Homenet and Mobile Terminal, 5,* 10–16.

Srite, M., & Karahanna, E. (2006). The role of espoused national cultural values in technology acceptance. *Management Information Systems Quarterly, 30*(3), 679–704.

Straub, D., Keil, M., & Brenner, W. (1997). Testing the technology acceptance model across cultures: A three country study. *Information & Management, 31*(1), 1–11. doi:10.1016/S0378-7206(97)00026-8

Straub, D., Limayem, M., & Karahanna-Evaristo, E. (1995). Measuring system usage: implications for IS theory testing. *Management Science, 41*(8), 1328–1342. doi:10.1287/mnsc.41.8.1328

Straub, D., Loch, K., & Hill, C. (2001). Transfer of information technology to the Arab world: A test of cultural influence modeling. *Journal of Global Information Management, 9*(4), 6–28. doi:10.4018/jgim.2001100101

Sun, T., Zhong, B., & Zhang, J. (2006). Uses and gratifications of Chinese online gamers. *China Media Research, 2*(2), 58–63.

Sundqvist, S., Frank, L., & Puumalainen, K. (2005). The effects of country characteristics, cultural similarity and adoption timing on the diffusion of wireless communications. *Journal of Business Research, 58*(1), 107–110. doi:10.1016/S0148-2963(02)00480-0

Taylor, S., & Todd, P. A. (1995). Understanding information technology usage: A test of competing models. *Information Systems Research, 6*(4), 144–176. doi:10.1287/isre.6.2.144

Teo, T. S. H., & Pok, S. H. (2003). Adoption of WAP-enabled mobile phones among internet users, omega. *The International Journal of Management Science, 31*(6), 483–498.

Veiga, J. F., Floyd, S., & Dechant, K. (2001). Towards modeling the effects of national culture on IT implementation and acceptance. *Journal of Information Technology, 16*(2), 145–158. doi:10.1080/02683960110063654

Venkatesh, V., & Davis, F. D. (2000). Theoretical extension of the technology acceptance model: Four longitudinal field studies. *Management Science, 46*(2), 186–204. doi:10.1287/mnsc.46.2.186.11926

Venkatesh, V., Morris, M. G., Davis, G. B., & Davis, F. D. (2003). User acceptance of information technology: Toward a unified view. *Management Information Systems Quarterly, 27*(3), 425–478.

Vitell, S. J., Paolillo, J. G. P., & Thomas, J. L. (2003). The perceived role of ethics and social responsibility: A study of marketing professionals. *Business Ethics Quarterly, 13*(1), 63–86.

Warkentin, M., D., Gefen, P. A., Pavlou, P. A., & Rose, G. M. (2002). Encouraging citizen adoption of e-government by building trust. *Electronic Markets, 12*(3), 157–162. doi:10.1080/101967802320245929

Yang, H.-D., & Yoo, Y. (2003). It's all about attitude: Revisiting the technology acceptance model. *Decision Support Systems, 38*(1), 19–31. doi:10.1016/S0167-9236(03)00062-9

Yang, K. C. (2007). Exploring factors affecting consumer intention to use mobile advertising in Taiwan. *Journal of International Consumer Marketing, 20*(1), 33–49. doi:10.1300/J046v20n01_04

Yi, M. Y., Jackson, J. D., Park, J. S., & Probst, J. C. (2006). Understanding information technology acceptance by individual professionals: Toward an integrative view. *Information & Management, 43*(3), 350–363. doi:10.1016/j.im.2005.08.006

Zhang, W., & Guitierrez, O. (2007). Information technology acceptance in the social services context: An exploration. *Social Work, 52*(3), 221–231.

This journal was previously published in the International Journal of Technology Diffusion, Volume 2, Issue 1, edited by Ali Hussein Saleh Zolait, pp. 29-49, copyright 2011 by IGI Publishing (an imprint of IGI Global).

Chapter 10
Barriers Hindering Ecommerce Adoption:
A Case Study of Kurdistan Region of Iraq

Japhet E. Lawrence
University of Kurdistan-Hawler, Iraq

ABSTRACT

Electronic commerce (EC) has the potential to improve efficiency and productivity in many areas and has received significant attention in many countries. However, there has been some doubt about the relevance of ecommerce for developing countries. The absence of adequate basic infrastructural, socio-economic, socio-cultural, and government ICT strategies have created a significant barrier in the adoption and growth of ecommerce in the Kurdistan region of Iraq. In this paper, the author shows that to understand the adoption and diffusion of ecommerce in Kurdistan, socio-cultural issues like transactional trust and social effect of shopping must be considered. The paper presents and discusses these issues hindering ecommerce adoption in Kurdistan.

INTRODUCTION

The number of Internet users around the world has been steadily growing and this growth has provided the impetus and the opportunities for global ecommerce. The literature describes the Internet and ecommerce as an essential part of the development process (Kole, 2000). The environmental contexts and conditions in Kurdistan is not yet conducive to widespread adoption of ecommerce, the region still suffers from disabling deficiencies, scarcities and shortfalls in numerous areas of development.

DOI: 10.4018/978-1-4666-2791-8.ch010

These different characteristics of infrastructural, socio-economic and socio-cultural have created a significant level of variation in the adoption and growth of ecommerce in developing countries, particularly in Kurdistan. Arguably the most salient obstacle to the development of ecommerce in many developing countries is the lack of necessary physical infrastructure particularly a cost-effective telecommunications system (Oxley & Yeung, 2001).

Ecommerce has been predicted to be a new driver of economic growth for developing countries (Humphrey et al., 2003). The opportunities offered by Internet technologies, a necessity for ecommerce has led many to believe that ecommerce will grow rapidly and help developing countries to overcome their problems of exclusion from the world economy and improve the terms of their participation (Odedra-Straub, 2003). It does present great opportunities to business organizations in developing countries to gain greater global access and reduce transaction costs (Kraemer et al., 2002; Humphrey et al., 2003). However, previous research has found that developing countries have not derived the expected benefits from ecommerce (Pare, 2002; Humphrey et al., 2003). Consequently, there is still doubt about how ecommerce will actually lead firms in developing countries to new trading opportunities (Humphrey et al., 2003; Vatanasakdakul et al., 2004).

The obstacles to reaping the benefits brought about by ecommerce are often underestimated. Accessing the Web is possible only when telephones and PCs are available, but these technologies are still in very scarce supply. In addition to this problem, Internet access is still very costly - both in absolute terms and relative to per-capita income in most part of Kurdistan region. While PC prices have fallen dramatically over the last decade, they remain beyond the reach of most individual users and enterprises in Kurdistan. Add to this, the human capital cost of installing, operating,

maintaining, training and support, the costs are beyond the means of many enterprises. There are significant disparities in the level of Internet penetration across parts of Kurdistan, which have profound implications for an individual's ability to participate in ecommerce. Moreover, skilled personnel are often lacking, the transport facilities are poor, and secure payment facilities non-existent in most parts of the region.

Other than the insufficient physical infrastructures, the electronic transaction facilities are deficient and the legal and regulatory framework inadequate. Most consumer markets face severe limitations in terms of connectivity, ability to pay, deliveries, willingness to make purchases on the Web, ownership of credit cards, and access to other means of payment for online purchases and accessibility in terms of physical deliveries. Moreover, the low level of economic development and small per-capita incomes, the limited skills base with which to build ecommerce services (Odedra-Straub, 2003). While Kurdistan has abundant cheap labour, there still remains the issue of developing IT literacy and education to ensure the quality and size of the IT workforce. The need to overcome infrastructural bottlenecks in telecommunication, transport system, electronic payment systems, security, standards, skilled workforce and logistics must be addressed, before ecommerce can be considered suitable for this region.

The objective of this paper is to examine the barriers hindering ecommerce adoption, focusing on technological infrastructures, socio-economic, socio-cultural and the lack of governmental policies as they relate to Kurdistan region. It seeks to identify and describe these issues that hinder the adoption and diffusion of ecommerce in the region. Kurdistan region of Iraq is just like any other developing country where the infrastructures are not as developed as they are in developed countries of U.S., Europe, or some Asian countries, and these infrastructural limitations are significant impediments to ecommerce adoption and diffusion. The next section briefly presents background information about Kurdistan region of Iraq.

A BRIEF BACKGROUND SUMMARY OF KURDISTAN REGION OF IRAQ

This section briefly discusses Kurdistan region which form the background to this study.

The choice of Kurdistan as the context of this study is motivated by the quest to understand why the region is lacking behind in the adoption of ecommerce.

Kurdistan is an autonomous Region of Iraq; it is one of the only regions which have gained official recognition internationally as an autonomous federal entity, with leverages in foreign relations, defense, internal security, investment and governance – a similar setting is Quebec region of Canada. The region continues to view itself as an integral part of a united Iraq but one in which it administers its own affairs. Kurdistan has a regional government (KRG) as well as a functional parliament and bureaucracy. Kurdistan is a parliamentary democracy with a national assembly that consists of 111 seats. It borders Iran to the east, Turkey to the north, Syria to the west and the rest of Iraq to the south. Its capital and seat of Government is the city of Erbil, known in Kurdish as Hewlêr. Erbil is the largest city in Kurdistan, with more than half a million residents and it is the third-largest city in Iraq after Baghdad and Mosul.

Kurdistan is divided into three governorates of Duhok, Erbil and Sulaymaniya. Each of these governorates is divided into districts with a total of 26 districts. Each district is divided into sub-districts. Governorates have a capital city, while districts and sub-districts have district centres. Within the three governorates of Duhok, Erbil and Sulaymaniya the population is 5.5 Million people. Kurdistan has a young population with an estimated 40% of the population being under the age of 15. The Kurdistan region has an increasing urban population with still a significant rural population.

The ethnic make-up of Kurdistan is diverse and includes ethnic Assyrian Christians, Turkmens, Arabs, Armenians, Yezidis, Shabaks and Mandeans next to the Kurdish majority.

The official language of instruction and institutions is Kurdish, which is part of the Iranian linguistic branch of languages. Arabic still has some uses because of its domination under former Iraqi regimes. Kurdistan has a diverse religious population. The dominating religion is Islam, adhered by most of its inhabitants. These include Kurds, Turkmen and Arabs being divided into Sunni and Shia branch of Islam for all of these three ethnic groups. Christianity and Yezidism are adhered to and also Assyrian and Chaldean Christians make up a large minority.

The Kurdistan Region is allowed to have its own foreign relations without referring to Baghdad. Kurdistan houses numerous consulates, embassy offices, trade offices and honorary consulates of countries that want to grow their influence and have better ties with the Kurdistan Regional Government.

The Kurdistan's economy is dominated by the oil industry, agriculture and tourism. Due to relative peace in the region it has a more developed economy in comparison to other parts of Iraq. In 2004, the per capita income was 25% higher than in the rest of Iraq. Kurdistan has a vibrant media and an emerging civil society. The region is fast developing and modest progress is being made in industrialization, housing and transportation. The KRG has invested heavily in education, health, transport, housing, roads and social welfare. The region operates an open-door economic policy; it has opened up to foreign investment, particularly in mineral resources, construction, healthcare and transportation. However, a lot remains to be done in agriculture, banking, insurance, telecommunication etc.

IT INFRASTRUCTURE IN KURDISTAN REGION OF IRAQ: PUBLIC, PRIVATE AND NON-GOVERNMENTAL SECTORS

Until recently the KRG region had a weak IT infrastructure base. With the establishment of the region's Department of Information Technology (DIT), the government has invested heavily in building one of the most robust IT systems of the Middle East region. The IT infrastructure in Kurdistan region of Kurdistan could be divided into the following: (1) Public Sector infrastructure, funded by the government (KRG) (2) Private Sector infrastructure owned by big businesses and SMEs (3) Non-governmental infrastructure owned by development agencies and civil society networks. Our focus is mainly on the first two; however, the last category is also important for instance in terms of synergies for integrated IT solutions. The KRG has adopted an integrated IT Strategy known as "KRG-wide strategy" that includes a robust IT architecture which aims to cater for all sectors of the economy and society.

The key objectives of the infrastructure design include:

- All government entities and offices connected through a secure network.
- Shared infrastructures to serve the entire government
- Communication and productivity applications provided to government employees
- Established IT infrastructure in all government entities.

1. **Public IT Infrastructure:** KRG's IT Infrastructure has evolved in terms of what the government terms as "strategic areas" to achieve its defined Vision for public sector, one capable of creating conducive climate for businesses and entrepreneurship to thrive in the region. The KRG emphasises that the strategy captures the Government

IT Infrastructure needs for the Kurdistan Regional Government (KRG) and its entities and recommends IT infrastructure initiatives to achieve the objectives that have been defined for Government IT Infrastructure earlier. The fundamental goal of KRG's Information Technology (IT) Infrastructure is to make available the KRG IT resources so that the KRG entities can carry out their work efficiently, and in a cost effective manner (KRG, 2011b)

The key components of KRG's integrated IT architecture include: capacity; infrastructure; common applications/datahubs/e-services; private sector; funding; standards and regulations. Each component aims to contribute to the integrated IT architecture of the region (Figure 1)

The role of the IT Infrastructure in the IT Strategy of the KRG is important and significant as it is required to support KRG in delivering business services to customers reliably and securely. Department of IT through KRGIT Strategy project focuses on identifying target reference architectures and the related initiatives to achieve strategic objectives in the area of IT Infrastructure and detailing each of these initiatives. The strategy also outlines the implementation roadmap for these initiatives.

Nevertheless, even though the government's IT plans are robust and strategic, it is important to note some key problems. First, the planned IT is yet to take full course. Many government Departments are still operating out-of-date computers, and most are using computers only for basic functions such as word processing and computations. For instance, there is no dedicated network linking all government departments.

2. **Private Sector Infrastructure:** There are a bourgeoning number of private enterprises in the KRG region. There is no solid data on the number of companies, but it is fair to claim that there are up 50 foreign

Figure 1. The key components of KRG's IT architecture (adapted from KRG, 2011)

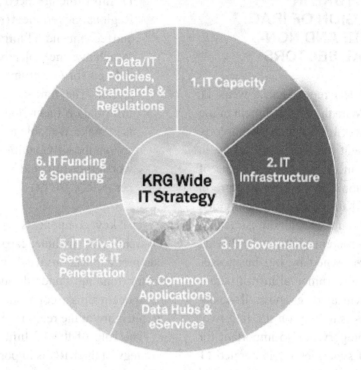

investment firms – operating mainly in the IT; petroleum prospecting, drilling and servicing; construction; housing; hotel; and merchandise sectors among others. Most of these companies – especially subsidiaries of Transnational Companies - have state-of-the-art IT facilities, and networks systems connected to mother companies. The KRG region also has a growing number of SMES operating in diverse business areas of the economy. With the exception of those working on IT solutions, most SMEs are yet to embrace IT, but some are beginning to pick up.

3. **Non-Governmental and Developmental Agencies and their IT Facilities:** There are a number of non-governmental and developmental agencies operating in Iraqi/Kurdistan – such as UN and its subsidiaries; United States Diplomatic Services and, in particular, agencies such as US Agency for International Development (USAID) and Regional Reconstruction Team (RRT); European Diplomatic Missions; International non-governmental organisations such as Red Cross; Mine Advisory Group (MAG) etc – have decent IT services, mostly connected to external networks. There are also local civil society groups that have acquired IT capacity, largely through foreign funding and capacity building programmes.

The study has noted some problems associated with the IT Infrastructure in the KRG region (Table 1). First, there is no synergy or complementarity between the various sector identified above. Second, there is high cost of acquisition and maintenance, particularly because of the remote nature of the region associated with geographic access and transportation. Thirdly, government's strategy for integrated IT solution remains a lip service at the moment; no serious effort has been

Table 1. Private and public IT infrastructure in Kurdistan regions, Iraq

Sector	Examples	Scope of Service/operation
Public	KRG Department of IT; Presidency: Parliament; Ministries; Governorates; Municipalities; Federal agencies operating in the region	• Organisational services • Capacity building for public sector workers and Institutions • Regulation • Funding • Legislations
Private	Multinational Corporations; Small Businesses (SMEs)	• Intra-networking • Inter-Networking • Capacity building • E-commerce
Developmental/Non-governmental	Diplomatic Services Developmental agencies Non-governmental organisations	• Intra-networking • Inter-Networking • Capacity building • Service provision • Philanthropy

made to advance or promote IT in the region. Nevertheless, there is optimism that progress will be made in the coming years.

CASE STUDY: BARRIERS HINDERING ADOPTION OF ECOMMERCE IN KURDISTAN REGION OF IRAQ

The study identified specific infrastructural barriers hindering the adoption of ecommerce in Kurdistan. There is a wide range of reasons why ecommerce adoption is hindered, see Figure 2 for a framework of barriers hindering ecommerce adoption. Reasons vary widely and are most commonly related to these: enabling factors infrastructure (technology, network, availability of ICT skills, qualified personnel); cost factors (costs of ICT equipment and networks); and security and trust factors (uncertainty of payment methods, and legal frameworks), poor distribution logistics, lack of feel-and-touch associated with online purchases, problems in returning products (OECD, 2004).

INFRASTRUCTURAL BARRIERS

The study identified various infrastructural characteristics as barriers hindering ecommerce adoption. Among the most pressing infrastructure limitations are access to telecommunication technology (computers, connectivity, and gateway to Internet), limited bandwidth, which reduces the capacity to handle audio and graphic data; poor telecommunications infrastructures (most of which are still analogue and can only transmit voice) and unreliable electricity supply.

- **Telecommunication:** Ecommerce success relies heavily on a number of technology infrastructures. The majority of developing countries are not ready for ecommerce including Kurdistan, because of their lack of network infrastructure especially among individual users and entrepreneurs. Telecommunication infrastructures are required to connect various regions and parties within a country and across countries. The Internet connections in most part of Kurdistan, particularly in the rural areas are unreliable because of the poor telephone communications and the erratic power supply. In the absence of an adequate basic infrastructure, it is possible that the potential advantages of the use of ecommerce turn into disadvantages.

The outmoded and unreliable telephone connections result in narrow bandwidths offered by many Internet service Providers (ISPs), with consequent low connections. A weak telecommunication infrastructure can cause a concentration of the technology in urban areas, which makes the participation of rural users more difficult. The predominant model for pricing local calls in Kurdistan is the measured service. In other words, the cost of use increases in proportion to the duration of the calls. These costs inevitably affect the use that users can make of the Internet as well as

Figure 2. Framework barriers hindering ecommerce adoption

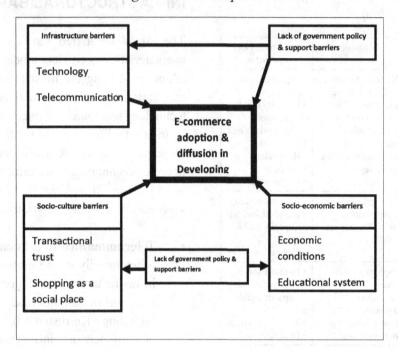

the business model that they will adopt based on its use. Flat-rate ISP pricing and affordable leased lines still do not exist in most part of the region.

Broadband connectivity is a key component in ICT development, adoption and use. It accelerates the contribution of ICTs to economic growth, facilitates innovation, and promotes efficiency. The development of broadband markets, efficient and innovative supply arrangements, and effective use of broadband services require policies that promote effective competition and liberalisation in infrastructure, network services and applications across different technological platforms (OECD, 2004).

- **High Access Cost:** The cost of Internet access makes it inaccessible to most users in Kurdistan region. The monthly connection cost of Internet access far exceeds the monthly income of a significant portion of the population. The cost of accessing the infrastructures also influences the growth of ecommerce. The priority for Kurdistan

is to put in place the necessary infrastructure and a competitive environment and regulatory framework that support affordable Internet access (OECD, 2004). Internet access prices are a key determinant of Internet and ecommerce use by individuals and businesses alike. According to Lawrence and Tar (2010) countries with lower access costs typically have a greater number of Internet hosts, and ecommerce has developed rapidly in countries with unmetered (flat-rate) access.

The availability of a wide range of Internet connections and other communication services, preferably at competitive prices, may affect citizens of Kurdistan decisions to adopt ecommerce and allows users to choose different and appropriate services according to their specific needs (OECD, 2004) and expectations from on-line activities. Broadband speed improves the overall on-line experience for both individuals and businesses, encouraging them to explore more applications and spend more time on line. The basic network infrastructure must be in place for Kurdistan to participate in global ecommerce, although the development of reliable fixed communication networks is an important policy area for ecommerce, especially in this region.

- **Access to Computer Equipment:** There is still a low level of PC penetration in Kurdistan, majority of population lacks the income required to buy PC or have telephone services, especially the low-income and rural populations. The cost of computers and Internet connectivity far surpasses the monthly salary of the average person. For example, average person in Kurdistan neither owns a computer nor has access to a computer connected to the Internet. The prohibitively high cost of computer equipment is seen as one of the barriers to the wide use of computers and subsequent participation in ecommerce. Without computers, one cannot have Internet access and the lack of computers at the individual as well as organisational level therefore becomes a major barrier to accessing the Internet and participating in ecommerce.

A combination of these costs and the high fees charged by telephones companies both contributed to discouraging Internet connectivity and their participation in ecommerce. The necessary infrastructure for such widespread usage simply does not yet exist. Before computer technologies and the Internet in particular, can be used to assist Kurdistan to overcome its problems, the necessary infrastructure and deregulation needs to be firmly in place. However, even with access to the necessary equipment, users will not become active ecommerce participants unless they have reasonable confidence in the integrity of transactions undertaken on-line. The presence of an adequate Internet infrastructure is necessary but not sufficient condition for the development of ecommerce (Oxley & Yeung, 2001).

SOCIO-CULTURAL BARRIERS

The social and cultural characteristics of most part of Kurdistan and the concepts associated with online transaction pose a much greater challenge and act as a major barrier to adoption and diffusion of ecommerce. Most cultures and practices here in the region do not support ecommerce and the conditions are not "ripe" because of lack of confidence in technology and online culture (Efendioglu et al., 2004). Although online transaction are pre-cursors to ecommerce, such as catalogue and telephone sales that have existed in developed countries and have been used by the public for an extended time period (Efendioglu et al., 2004), such systems are new and novel approaches in Kurdistan and is not suitable to the culture and way of doing business. Since the business foundation of ecommerce is based on such a methodology, some of the local cultural characteristics do pose significant challenges for the ecommerce adoption. The study has identified various socio-cultural characteristics as barriers hindering ecommerce adoption, among the most pressing primary cultural barriers are level of trust in institutions, shopping as a social place, limitation on personal contact and language/content.

- **Transactional Trust:** Ecommerce is a radical behaviour that goes contrary to the experience and culture. The move to ecommerce challenges many of the basic assumption about trust. Confidence and trust is an essential requirement for secure electronic trading. The question of trust is even more prominent in the virtual world than it is in the real world. The geographical separation of buyers and sellers, often coupled with a lack of real-time visual or oral interaction, creates a barrier to ecommerce adoption.

Contracts are expected to change and promises may be broken; a strong individual relationship is often the only indispensable ingredient that is required for the implementation of a contract in a normal business transaction. Counterfeiting and distribution of below products is a major problem and further aggravate this lack of transactional trust between parties who do not know each other personally and separated by distance and technology.

The sheer number of people conducting business on the Internet becomes a deterrent. When you find potential partners, do you trust these sellers or buyers to be reliable, their products to have satisfactory quality, and payments to be truthfully carried out? According to Efendioglu et al. (2004), there is no "western honour system" in most developing countries. In the developing world, trust is established and reinforced through family association, repeated personal contact and interaction. The transactional trust and related issues are barriers for conducting online transactions but, are also amplified as a result of cultural characteristics and prevailing legal system.

Developed countries have devised ways of extending the basis for trust through the impartial enforcement of the law and its adaptation to a new technological environment. This is the basis of trust that underpins ecommerce in the developed world. Where legal and jurisdictional institutions are underdeveloped in Kurdistan, businesses find themselves at a disadvantage because of insecurity, whether real or perceived. Therefore, most users are not willing to provide sensitive financial information over the Web. The reluctance to entrust sensitive personal information like credit card numbers to businesses operating on the Web remains strong.

In Kurdistan, many businesses and consumers are still wary of conducting extensive business in cyberspace because of the lack of a predictable legal environment that governs transactions. The lack of a satisfactory redress mechanism in the event of a dispute may strongly hinder online transactions (OECD, 2004). Eurostat (2004) figures clearly show that legal uncertainties constitute, at least in some countries, a significant barrier

to the adoption of ecommerce by entrepreneurs. Legal uncertainty concerning contracts, terms of delivery and guarantees was mentioned as an important barrier to ecommerce purchases.

- **Shopping as a Social Place:** In developing countries, shopping is seen as a social place where friendly conversations between the vendor and the customer. The success of doing business depends heavily on the quality and sometimes the quantity of personal relationships. A strong individual relationship and long term association between the parties provide a sense of community and enhances social bonding. Most of the business is conducted through small enterprises and it is local. A typical company in Kurdistan is a socio-economic entity and not just a pure economic one.

- **Limitation on Personal Contact:** The adoption of ecommerce depends on the cultural and social environment. In Kurdistan, people consider shopping as a recreational activity (Lawrence & Tar, 2010). The idea of buying goods that one cannot see and touch and from sellers thousands of miles away may take some "getting used to" for those who are used to face-to-face transactions, familiarity with the other party, (strong individual relationship and long term association between the parties), and getting satisfaction from winning business negotiations (they are willing to employ a variety of tactics to get the best deal). As one person stated in Lawrence (2002) survey "I like buying over the Internet, but it does not beat going to an actual shop where you can see what you are buying and make sure it's what you want". All of these long standing cultural traits are undermined by and are contrary to the depersonalization associated with ecommerce and business systems designed to sell products online.

The interpersonal relationships with people located at a distance when shopping online is an alien culture to most people here in Kurdistan. The face-to-face contact is irreplaceable, you can't replace going to see people; you can't beat having face-to-face interaction for selling or buying products. The limitation on personal contact as a barrier to ecommerce adoption is a reflection of people here in Kurdistan that prefers more direct and individual contact with their merchants (Lawrence, 2002). In Kurdistan, there is still a suspicion of technology that is perceived to destroy their culture and way of life. It is argued in Lawrence (2002) that the decrease in human interaction with customers could lead to less understanding of the customers' needs, as they are not always able to express comments, criticisms or request for new products while interacting with machines. Most entrepreneurs in developing country rely substantially on personal contact to build confidence with their customers, particularly when the relationship is in the establishment phase.

- **Language/Content:** Language has been identified as a socio-cultural barrier that hinders both access to information and to the Internet and participation in ecommerce. Most people in Kurdistan are illiterates and uneducated people tend to have limited access to information on the web because information is in a language which assumed some degree of education. The less educated and illiterate could not read nor understand the languages that are used to disseminate information on the Internet. Therefore, many people are unaware of how the quality of their lives and their incomes could be improved by skilful use of computer technologies such as the Internet and on-line trading. The issue related to language is important because it is a gateway of information and knowledge transfer in the digital world. English is the primary language used in many western countries where new technologies originate. It is the predominant language for development of IT and ecommerce and it is the main language used on the Web. Language, no doubt, is a barrier to the use of the Internet for most Kurdistan and Arab people who read and writes only Arabic.

SOCIOECONOMIC BARRIERS

Kurdistan needs to address a number of socioeconomic and regulatory barriers before she can participate in electronic commerce. The study identified various socioeconomic characteristics as barriers hindering ecommerce adoption. Among the most pressing are economic condition, educational system, payment systems for enabling transfer of funds, and distribution systems for physical transfer of goods

- **Economic Condition:** The economic condition in developing countries is widely recognized as a major hindrance for ecommerce adoption (Lawrence & Tar, 2010). The GDP and income per capita are common indicators for the economic condition of a country. Since ecommerce relies on some technology infrastructures which are relatively expensive for many developing countries, including Kurdistan. Most developing countries have unfavourable economic condition and are not likely to be involved in ecommerce. For example, the initial and continuing cost of Internet access has dropped in recent years, but it remains a significant barrier to ecommerce adoption in Kurdistan. Consequently, large "entry" and on-going costs are a great disincentive to Internet usage and therefore to the development of ecommerce business both within Kurdistan and for international trade.

The access charge relative to income affects Internet use. Monthly Internet access charges are still very high in most part of Kurdistan. The inequalities in income distribution means the Internet is not affordable for a large proportion of the population in rural areas. The common pattern found across developing countries is the dichotomy between the urban and rural areas in terms of technology use. In urban areas, ICT use is fairly common; while in the rural areas, many small enterprises do not even have computers yet, talk less of Internet access.

- **Resistance to Change:** Resistance to change is one of the most typical drawbacks in any attempts to bring about technological change, and ecommerce is no exception. Decision-makers are used to doing business in a certain way and they do not want to change. "Our system is working, so why change it?" is their attitude, which represents a significant hurdle in itself.

- **Generation Gap:** Many, if not most, CEOs in Kurdistan do not use e-mail for the simple reason that they were not raised in the information age. IT is not a part of their daily routine. This fact is coupled with their mindset of reluctance to invest in IT and their failure to perceive the added value. However, middle-aged managers who are currently in middle management and will rise to top-level management in the next decade are convinced of the benefits of IT and are technologically adept. Therefore, we can be hopeful that the future decision-makers of this region will engage in IT ventures.

- **Educational System:** The poor state of educational system in most part of Kurdistan is seen as barrier to ecommerce adoption. Lack of ICT skills and business skills are widespread impediments to effective adoption of ecommerce. The lack of appropriate IT education is perceived to be a reason why the potential value of computers and the Internet as a means to participate in ecommerce is not appreciated. Lawrence and Tar (2010) report that in most developing countries, school curriculum does not include computer education; there is a need for early computer education in Kurdistan, so that people could become computer literate in school. It is argued that computer literate populations have greater potential to appreciate and participate in ecommerce (Lawrence, 2002). If the Internet is to be of any real benefit to Kurdistan, it must focus primarily on the needs and problems of the majority of populations (i.e., those who are traditionally deprived of education and opportunities for personal and community development). People would have to be comprehensively trained and educated before they could benefit from the advantages offered to them by the Internet and ecommerce.

- **Payment System:** A supportive electronic payments infrastructure is crucial to promote ecommerce, which exposes a key link between ecommerce and the financial foundation of the economy. An institutional environment that facilitates the building of transactional integrity is critical to the development of ecommerce in developing countries (Oxley & Yeung, 2001). This infrastructure makes payment over the Internet possible (through credit, debit, or Smart cards, or through online currencies). It also makes possible the distribution and delivery (whether online or physical) of those products purchased over the Internet to the consumer. Its growth further requires the establishment of reliable and secure payment infrastructures to avoid frauds and other illegal actions. The efficiency of the payments system itself can help or hinder the development of ecommerce.

Few people in Kurdistan have credit cards and most banking sectors here lack a national clearing system and potential customers are suspicious of being cheated (Lawrence & Tar, 2010). In most developing countries users may be unable to purchase online because credit cards are not accepted without a signature (Efendioglu et al., 2004). Additional confirmation via fax is necessary to complete the payment. In addition, in the case of fraud, the credit card holder and not the issuer bears the loss, which makes the customer reluctant to provide information and to use credit cards in an environment where privacy and security issues are not guaranteed. Beyond individual transactions, full efficiency and realization of the benefits of ecommerce depends on rapid authorization, payments, and settlement of accounts. Many developing countries do not have financial institutions or central bank payments mechanisms that are up to this task.

- **Poor Logistical Infrastructure:** Ecommerce relies on efficient logistic infrastructures within a country. In most part of Kurdistan, logistical changes need to occur in order to create an appropriate environment for the effective participation in ecommerce. Inefficiencies in essential services such as postal service along with delivery required in an international transaction can frustrate the success of the transaction itself.

The distribution and delivery systems are key components to developing ecommerce. It is not sufficient to have a name and a product to adopt ecommerce successfully. It is also necessary for an enterprise to have in place the distribution and delivery channels capable of meeting customer expectations. Speed is one of the most important manifestations of ecommerce, overnight delivery, just-in-time processing, 24/7 operations are examples of how much faster and more precisely timed economic activities are in the ecommerce world.

The inefficient distribution and cumbersome delivery systems and the lack of good transport, and postal system are primary obstacles to the growth of ecommerce in Kurdistan. There is a very important link between the effectiveness of the distribution and delivery systems and the incentives for the private sector to innovate and invest in new technology. For example, suppose the private sector spends money on Internet technologies, but cannot get products to customers because of distribution and delivery barriers. Burdensome customs procedures can also further hinder the seamless fulfillment of a cross border ecommerce transaction.

POLITICAL AND GOVERNMENTAL BARRIERS

The poor state of telecommunications infrastructure in Kurdistan is a major barrier hindering the adoption of ecommerce. The lack of telephone lines, low quality, slow speed and high cost of bandwidth and security concerns need to be addressed before users and enterprises in Kurdistan can think of participating in ecommerce. Kurdistan does not have ICT policies to guide the provision of Internet services. No progress is possible in the absence of clear policies and the determined implementation of such policies. The lack of a policy to guide ecommerce expansion is a major hindrance to adoption. Government initiatives are important in the adoption of ecommerce and other ICT in general. They can be in terms of promotion of ICT usage, education and the establishment of adequate regulatory framework for ecommerce. Competition, both for telephone access as well as among ISPs is a key area where government policy can make a difference in access and adoption of ecommerce.

It is very crucial for Governments to ensure an open and competitive telecommunication markets that offer a range of interoperable technological options and network services (particularly broadband) of appropriate quality and price, so that users can choose among various technologies and services for high-speed Internet access. Other issues that are seen as barriers to ecommerce adoption are free trade, the monopoly which national governments exercise over national telecommunications, import duties on IT equipment like hardware and software. The elimination of control and deregulation of telecommunication systems is necessary before a free flow of information and an expanded use of ICT is possible.

Changes in government policy are perceived as being critical to creating an environment for the broad use of the Internet in many sectors of Kurdish economy. The commitment and participation of Government in Internet service provision and the reduction of import duties will lead to the reduction of costs which will in turn make equipment more affordable and encourage connection to the Internet. The Government also urgently needs to formulate information policies that will provide a framework for efficient, widespread and cost-effective use of the Internet. The conditions in most developing countries are sadly not conducive to the widespread, cheap and effective use of the Internet by the majority of citizens (Lawrence & Tar, 2010). There is neither a government policy on Internet provision or on the future of ecommerce nor any comprehensive information policy. The absence of national information policies means that the government is not involved in Internet provision.

CONCLUSION

The Internet is not yet a universally accessible resource in Kurdistan. The region lacks the necessary policies and infrastructure that would enable widespread usage of the Internet. The extent of adoption is hampered by a ranges of obstacles including the unavailability and unreliability of infrastructure, the absence of government policy frameworks, the lack of banking facilities and amenities (such as credit cards), and ignorance on the part of possible users about the enormously beneficial potential of ecommerce. The level of education, the availability of IT skills, the level of penetration of personal computers and telephone within the society hinder adoption of ecommerce.

The Government lacks the necessary policies and infrastructure that would enable widespread adoption, for example the ecommerce technology makes use of the telecommunications infrastructure, whose inadequacy in many parts of Kurdistan (notably in rural areas, where most of the population and a disproportionate share of its poor people live) precludes either telephone or Internet use. Despite the current limitations with the existing infrastructure and other issues related to the economical and socio-cultural conditions. Ecommerce can be an extremely beneficial tool in the development of Kurdistan provided that certain problems are resolved and the government demonstrates that she has the political will to remove the barriers that currently stand in the way of widespread adoption.

REFERENCES

Efendioglu, A. M., Yip, V. F., & Murray, W. L. (2004). *E-Commerce in developing countries: issues and influences*. San Francisco, CA: University of San Francisco Press.

Eurostat. (2004). *E-commerce and the Internet in European businesses*. Retrieved from http://epp.eurostat.ec.europa.eu/cache/ITY_OFFPUB/KS-54-03-889/FR/KS-54-03-889-FR.PDF

Humphrey, J., Mansell, R., Paré, D., & Schmitz, H. (2003). *The reality of e-commerce with developing countries*. London, UK: Media Studies. doi:10.1111/j.1759-5436.2004.tb00106.x

Kole, E. (2000). *African women speak on the Internet: Research report of an electronic survey of African women*. Retrieved from http://www.eldis.org/assets/Docs/13200.html

Kraemer, K. L., Dedrick, J., & Dunkle, D. (2002). *E-Commerce in the United States: Leader or one of the pack? Global B commerce survey, report of results for the United States Centre for Research on Information Technology and Organisations.* Irvine, CA: University of California.

KRG. (2011). *IT infrastructure Erbil.* Kurdistan, Iraq: KRG Department of Information Technology.

Kurdistan. (2011). *The other Iraq.* Retrieved from http://www.theotheriraq.com

Lawrence, J. E. (2002). *The use of Internet in small to medium-sized enterprises.* Unpublished doctoral dissertation, University of Salford, Salford, UK.

Lawrence, J. E., & Tar, U. A. (2010). Barriers to ecommerce in developing countries. *Information. Social Justice (San Francisco, Calif.), 3*(1).

Odedra-Straub, M. (2003). E-Commerce and development: Whose development? *Electronic Journal on Information Systems in Developing Countries, 11*(2), 1–5.

OECD. (2004). Promoting entrepreneurship and innovative SMEs in a global economy: Towards a more responsive and inclusive globalisation. In *Proceedings of the 2nd OECD Conference of Ministers Responsible for Small and Medium-Sized Enterprises (SMEs),* Istanbul, Turkey.

Oxley, J. E., & Yeung, B. (2001). E-Commerce readiness: Institutional environment and international competitiveness. *Journal of International Business Studies, 32*(4), 705–723. doi:10.1057/palgrave.jibs.8490991

Paré, D. J. (2002). *B2B e-commerce services and developing countries: Disentangling myth from reality.* London, UK: London School of Economics and Political Science.

Vatanasakdakul, S., Tibben, W., & Cooper, J. (2004). *What prevent B2B eCommerce adoption in developing countries? A socio-cultural perspective.* Paper presented at the 17th Bled eCommerce Conference eGlobal, Bled, Slovenia.

Wikipedia. (2011). *Kurdistan.* Retrieved from http://en.wikipedia.org/wiki/Kurdistan

This journal was previously published in the International Journal of Technology Diffusion, Volume 2, Issue 2, edited by Ali Hussein Saleh Zolait, pp. 47-59, copyright 2011 by IGI Publishing (an imprint of IGI Global).

Section 3
Trends in Digital Divide

Chapter 11
Global Trends in Digital Governance:
A Longitudinal Study

Aroon Manoharan
Kent State University, USA

Marc Fudge
California State University-San Bernardino, USA

Marc Holzer
Rutgers University-Newark, USA

ABSTRACT

This paper highlights the research findings of a digital governance survey conducted in the fall of 2009. The study replicates previous surveys of large municipalities worldwide in 2007, 2005, and 2003. This longitudinal assessment, focused on the assessment of current practices in municipal e-governance by evaluating their official websites. Specifically, the survey analyzed security, usability, content, the type of online services currently being offered, citizen response, and participation through websites established by city governments worldwide. There were significant changes in the top ranking cities when compared to previous studies. Based on the 2009 evaluation of 87 cities, Seoul, Prague, Hong Kong, New York, and Singapore represent the highest performing cities in digital governance. Moreover, there continues to be a divide in terms of digital governance throughout the world; however, this divide, which increased in 2005, decreased in 2009.

INTRODUCTION

Over the past several years, governments at every level throughout the world have begun adopting information technology in order to improve their service delivery along with increasing transparency and accountability. In today's era of globalization and networked governance, it is important to thoroughly understand how various regions of the world perform in terms of e-governance. This paper highlights the trends in municipal e-governance based on a seven-year longitudinal assessment of municipal websites worldwide. It compares the results of four surveys that evaluate the practice of digital governance in

DOI: 10.4018/978-1-4666-2791-8.ch011

large municipalities. The most recent survey was conducted by a joint international collaboration in the fall of 2009 by Rutgers's E-Governance Institute and the Sungkyunkwan University's Global e-Policy & E-Government Institute. The survey replicated similar research conducted in 2003, 2005 and 2007 (Holzer & Kim, 2005, 2007; Melitski et al., 2005; Carrizales et al., 2006). Apart from identifying the best practices, such regional studies also provide benchmarks for increased performance in e-governance over time, especially for those regions that are still in the earliest stages of development. In this regard, our study provides a critical contribution to the overall literature and research on e-governance.

In addition, comprehensive global studies are needed for a comparative approach in e-governance research. As a methodological tool for such investigation, our survey instrument, with 98 measures and five distinct categorical areas, is one of the most comprehensive indexes, currently in practice for conducting e-governance research. Specifically, we analyzed privacy/security, usability, content of websites, the type of online services currently being offered, and citizen response and participation, through websites established by local city governments.

The format of our paper begins with a review of e-governance literature and why it is important for government to communicate with citizens, thus increasing engagement and participation. Next we explain the research methodology used to examine differences in e-governance practices and applications across the globe. This is followed by the findings from the longitudinal assessment and the regression results. Finally, we conclude with a discussion of the overall findings and its implications for public policy.

LITERATURE REVIEW

E-government is the application of Information and Communication Technologies (ICTs) within government, to optimize its internal and external functions (UNDESA, 2003). E-government also refers to "the delivery of services and information, electronically, to businesses and residents, 24 hours a day, seven days a week" (Norris et al., 2001, p. 5). The Organization of Economic Cooperation and Development (OECD) defines e-government as "the use of information and communication technologies (ICT's), and particularly the Internet, as a tool to achieve better government" (OECD, 2003, p. 22). Bannister (2007) provides a working definition of e-government that includes the use of ICT in the formulation and execution of government and public policy. The use of information technology also expands the possibilities for achieving direct democracy by focusing on transparency and openness. E-governance includes both e-government (delivery of public service) and e-democracy (citizen participation in governance) (Holzer & Kim, 2007). In the development of e-democracy, information disclosures and two-way communication are prerequisites for establishing an informed citizenry and sustaining a high quality of political debate.

According to Barber (2001), ICT tools are more suitable for political communication than the broadcast media and should be exploited to offer electronic delivery of public services, develop communities online and open up numerous possibilities for participation. Lau (2007) states that "good governance" includes modernization and transformation of the public sector, ensuring equity, increasing responsiveness, accountability and participation. When governments fully embrace all the benefits that technology has to offer to public administrators and citizens alike, then improved government performance will follow.

The design of government websites has focused more on informational and transactional e-government applications. The constituents are viewed more as customers than active participants in democratic decision-making (Moon, 2002). Van Nelson et al. (2009) state that the target group of services is varied and highly heterogeneous and government agencies must consider various cultures, skills, political opinions, and disabilities when designing e-government systems. It is critical for internal stakeholders who are responsible for the development and management of government websites to include features that will facilitate participation, and not inhibit it. Facilitating the inclusion of diverse thoughts and ideas helps to promote information sharing and overall improved performance.

'Digital Democracy' is prominent in the e-government literature (Carrizales, 2009) and conceptually, reflects the utilization of technology to increase participation in government. Melitski (2002) defines the participation stage as Internet-driven innovations that improve access of the citizens to government information, services, and equitable participation in government. Schwester (2009) states that digital democracy provides a mechanism through the use of ICT's to reinforce accountability, transparency, and citizen engagement in government activities. According to Paskaleva-Shapira (2006), digital democracy offers potential solutions to leaders for better handling of their responsibilities and invites people to participate in decision-making at the national level and the local communities. With respect to policies, digital democracy offers a mechanism for government agencies to facilitate effective decision-making and improved public policies by transforming relations with citizens, businesses, and other arms of government. To fulfill its mission, Paskaleva-Shapira adds that digital democracy has to reflect transparency, openness, accountability, and inclusiveness. Most importantly, digital democracy must embody the core objectives of public administration - effectiveness, equity and efficiency.

In 2003, out of 19 components of e-government strategy, 25 European Union countries indicated that the two areas needing improvement were equity and extension of the benefits of ICT to as many as possible (Lau, 2007). Recognizing such potential, some municipalities have already begun to practice aspects of e-democracy, including information disclosure, pertaining to government decision-making and mediums for

two-way communication. The case of Seoul's Online Procedures Enhancement for Civil Application (OPEN) system has demonstrated the successful practice of transparency and decreased corruption in government via Internet use (Holzer & Kim, 2007).

However, although researchers agree on the potential of digital governance, little has been written about the state of current e-governance practices worldwide, especially with regard to online citizen participation. That is, to understand better how various world regions differ in terms of e-governance, comprehensive global studies are needed as a basis for comparison. The 2009 Digital Governance in Municipalities Worldwide Survey assessed the practice of digital governance in large municipalities worldwide, replicating our 2003, 2005 and 2007 surveys, and ranked them on a global scale. Because digital governance includes both digital government (delivery of public service) and digital democracy (citizen participation in governance), we analyzed website security, usability, and content; the type of online services currently offered; and citizen response and participation through websites established by municipal governments (Holzer & Kim, 2004, 2005, 2007).

DESIGN AND METHODOLOGY

Our research examined the websites of the largest cities in the 100 most wired nations worldwide. These 100 nations were identified using data from the International Telecommunication Union (ITU), based on the total number of individuals using the Internet in that nation. The largest city by population in each of these nations was then selected for the study and used as a surrogate for all cities in the respective country in examining how the local populations perceive their government online. The study, conducted between August and December 2009, evaluated the official websites of each of these largest cities in their native languages. Of the 100 cities selected, 87 cities were found to have official websites, an increase from 86 cities in 2007 and 81 in 2005. Appendix A lists the municipalities involved in the survey.

To determine the factors impacting e-governance performance, we conducted a factor analysis utilizing variables obtained from the International Telecommunication Union (ITU), the Economist Democracy Index and Human Development Report published by the United Nations Development Program (UNDP). The factor analysis provided the basis for an ordinary least squares (OLS) regression. The descriptive and inferential statistical analyses follow the results of the longitudinal analysis.

E-Governance Survey Instrument

As already pointed out, the Rutgers E-Governance Survey Instrument, with its 98 measures is the most comprehensive index currently in use, for e-governance research. This instrument consists of five components: privacy/security, usability, content, services, and citizen participation. The privacy and security category, examines privacy policies and issues, related to authentication. The usability category involves traditional web pages, forms, and search tools. The content category is addressed in terms of access to contact information,

public documents, multimedia and time-sensitive information, as well as access to the disabled. This study also examines how interactive services allow users to purchase or pay for services as well as apply or register online, for municipal events and services. Finally, the measures for citizen participation consist of examining how local governments are engaging citizens and providing mechanisms for citizen participation in government issues, online. Table 1 summarizes the 2009 survey instrument, and Appendix B presents an overview of the criteria.

For the 2009 research, the survey instrument used 98 measures, of which 43 were dichotomous, and for each of the five e-governance components, the research involved 18 to 20 measures. For non-dichotomous questions, each measure was coded on a four-point scale (0, 1, 2, 3; see Table 2). To avoid the issues of skewing in favor of a particular category while developing an overall score for each municipality, we weighted each of the five categories equally, regardless of the number of questions each contained. The dichotomous measures in the services and citizen participation categories corresponded with the values on the four-point scale of 0 or 3, while the dichotomous measures on privacy and usability corresponded to ratings of 0 or 1 on the scale. To

Table 1. E-governance rerformance measures

E-governance category	Key concepts	Raw score	Weighted score	Keywords
Privacy/ Security	18	25	20	Privacy policies, authentication, encryption, data management, cookies
Usability	20	32	20	User-friendly design, branding, length of homepage, targeted audience links or channels, and site search capabilities
Content	20	48	20	Access to current accurate information, public documents, reports, publications, and multimedia materials
Services	20	59	20	Transactional services - purchase or register, interaction between citizens, businesses and government
Citizen participation	20	55	20	Online civic engagement/ policy deliberation, citizen based performance measurement
Total	98	219	100	

Table 2. E-governance scale

Scale	Description
0	Information about a given topic does not exist on the Web site
1	Information about a given topic exists on the Web site (including links to other information and e-mail addresses)
2	Downloadable items are available on the Web site (forms, audio, video, and other one-way transactions, popup boxes)
3	Services, transactions, or interactions can take place completely online (credit card transactions, applications for permits, searchable databases, use of cookies, digital signatures, restricted access)

ensure reliability, each municipal website was assessed by two evaluators, and in cases where significant variation (+ or − 10%) existed, the websites were analyzed a third time.

LONGITUDINAL FINDINGS AND DISCUSSION

The average e-governance score for municipalities throughout the world is 35.93, an increase from 33.37 in 2007, 33.11 in 2005 and 28.49 in 2003. The top 20 rankings in the survey shows considerable changes compared to the 2007 survey, with only 11 cities retaining their positions in 2009. Seoul ranked 1st with a score of 84.74 of a possible score of 100, followed by Prague in the 2nd position with a score of 72.84. Seoul's website was also the highest ranked in the previous surveys, while Prague moved up significantly from position fifteen in 2007. Hong Kong ranked 3rd with a score of 62.83, followed by New York and Singapore in the 4th and 5th places with scores of 61.10 and 58.81, respectively. The top ranked cities for each continent are Johannesburg (Africa), Seoul (Asia), Prague (Europe), New York City (North America), Sydney (Oceania) and Sao Paolo (South America). Prague replaced Helsinki as the highest ranked city in Europe and Sao Paulo

switched places with Buenos Aires as the highest ranked city in South America. Table 3 ranks the top 20 municipalities and their overall scores.

In the category of privacy and security, the top ranked cities are Seoul, Prague, Vienna, Ho Chi Minh, Bratislava, London and Dubai. The city of Seoul retains the first position from the previous survey with a score of 18.80 of a possible score of 20. Prague ranked 2nd with a score of 16.70 compared to its 19th position in 2007. Vienna improved significantly from 13th ranking in 2007 to 3rd, with a score of 16.0. Similarly Ho Chi Minh has also improved from 24th rank to 4th position, with 14.40. The average score in this category is 5.57, an increase from the previous average of 4.49 in 2007. Among the municipalities evaluated, 18 did not provide any privacy policy online, compared to 26 in 2007. Table 4 summarizes the results for the top 10 municipalities in this category.

Results in usability indicate that the top ranked cities are Prague, Seoul, Bratislava, Singapore and Cairo in the category. The city of Prague ranks highest with a score of 17.62, followed by Seoul and Bratislava in 2nd with a score of 17.50. Excluding Seoul, all cities are new to the top five ranking. The 4th position was shared by Singapore and Cairo with a score of 16.88. The average score in this category is 11.96, with OECD cities' average of 13.39, compared to non-OCED cities' score of 11.28. Table 5 summarizes the results for the top 10 municipalities evaluated in the category.

The average score for all cities in the category of content was 8.21, an increase from 7.63 in 2007. Comparatively, the average score for the top five ranked cities in 2009 is 15.92 and these cities include Seoul, Auckland, Tallinn, Hong Kong and New York. Seoul ranks 1st with a score of 18.20 and Auckland (ranked 30th in 2007) scored 2nd with 16.80 in 2009. Tallinn, also ranked 30th in 2007, has improved to 3rd with a score of 16.40 in 2009. Hong Kong ranked 4th with a score of 14.40 and New York ranked 5th with 13.80. Table

Table 3. Top 20 cities in digital governance (2009)

Rank	City	Overall	Privacy	Usability	Content	Services	Participation
1	Seoul	84.74	18.80	17.50	18.20	19.15	11.09
2	Prague	72.84	16.70	17.62	13.02	13.86	11.64
3	Hong Kong	62.83	11.20	15.31	14.40	13.56	8.36
4	New York	61.10	12.80	13.44	13.80	15.42	5.64
5	Singapore	58.81	6.40	16.88	9.60	15.93	10.00
6	Shanghai	57.41	11.20	11.25	10.00	14.41	10.55
7	Madrid	55.59	11.20	14.38	13.20	13.90	2.91
8	Vienna	55.48	16.00	11.88	12.80	6.44	8.36
9	Auckland	55.28	10.40	14.38	16.80	6.07	7.64
10	Toronto	52.87	12.80	13.00	12.40	8.85	5.82
11	Paris	52.65	12.00	13.13	12.40	7.12	8.00
12	Bratislava	52.51	13.60	17.50	9.20	7.12	5.09
13	London	51.96	13.60	15.00	8.80	9.83	4.73
14	Jerusalem	50.64	8.80	15.63	13.60	11.53	1.09
15	Tokyo	50.59	8.00	14.25	12.40	10.85	5.09
16	Zagreb	50.16	9.60	13.00	12.80	7.12	7.64
17	Ljubljana	49.39	8.00	13.13	11.60	10.85	5.82
18	Lisbon	48.82	8.80	15.00	10.80	9.49	4.73
19	Brussels	48.01	12.00	16.25	11.60	7.07	1.09
20	Johannesburg	47.68	4.00	16.25	8.80	8.81	9.82

Table 4. Results in privacy and security (2009)

Rank	City	Country	Privacy
1	Seoul	Republic of Korea	18.80
2	Prague	Czech Republic	16.70
3	Vienna	Austria	16.00
4	Ho Chi Minh	Vietnam	14.40
5	Bratislava	Slovakia	13.60
5	London	UK	13.60
5	Dubai	UAE	13.60
8	New York	USA	12.80
8	Toronto	Canada	12.80
8	Berlin	Germany	12.80
8	Sydney	Australia	12.80

Table 5. Results in usability (2009)

Rank	City	Country	Usability
1	Prague	Czech Republic	17.62
2	Seoul	Republic of Korea	17.50
2	Bratislava	Slovakia	17.50
4	Singapore	Singapore	16.88
4	Cairo	Egypt	16.88
6	Brussels	Belgium	16.25
6	Johannesburg	South Africa	16.25
6	Bangkok	Thailand	16.25
9	Jerusalem	Israel	15.63
9	Sao Paulo	Brazil	15.63
9	Copenhagen	Denmark	15.63
9	Bucharest	Romania	15.63

Table 6. Results in content (2009)

Rank	City	Country	Content
1	Seoul	Republic of Korea	18.20
2	Auckland	New Zealand	16.80
3	Tallinn	Estonia	16.40
4	Hong Kong	Hong Kong	14.40
5	New York	USA	13.80
6	Jerusalem	Israel	13.60
7	Madrid	Spain	13.20
7	Helsinki	Finland	13.20
9	Prague	Czech Republic	13.02
10	Vienna	Austria	12.80
10	Zagreb	Croatia	12.80
10	Oslo	Norway	12.80
10	Santa Fé de Bogotá	Colombia	12.80

6 summarizes the top 10 municipalities in the content category.

Results in the category of services indicate that the city of Seoul ranks 1st with a score of 19.15, followed by Singapore with a score of 15.93. In the 3rd position is New York with a score of 15.42, followed by Shanghai and Madrid with scores of 4.42 and 13.90 respectively. The average score in this category increased from 5.8 in 2007 to 6.68 in 2009, and more importantly, no city has earned 0 points in this category compared to two in 2005 and three in 2003. However the average score for the top five ranked cities in 2009 is 15.76, a decrease from 16.17 in 2007. Table 7 summarizes the results for the top 10 municipalities evaluated in the services category.

Finally, the citizen participation results indicate that the top five ranked cities are Mexico City, Prague, Bangkok, Seoul and Shanghai. Mexico City ranked 1st with a score of 13.45, a significant improvement from its 42nd position in 2007. In the 2nd position is Prague with 11.64, which also improved from its 36th ranking in 2007. Bangkok retained the 3rd position with a score of 11.27, followed by Seoul in the 4th position with 11.09.

Shanghai, which had ranked 38th with a score of 3.28 in 2007, has received a 5th ranking with a score of 10.55 in 2009. The average score in this category is 3.50, a marginal decrease from 3.55 in 2007. Comparatively, the average score for all the top five cities was much higher at 11.60. Table 8 shows the top 10 municipalities in this category.

Table 7. Results in services (2009)

Rank	City	Country	Services
1	Seoul	Republic of Korea	19.15
2	Singapore	Singapore	15.93
3	New York	USA	15.42
4	Shanghai	China	14.41
5	Madrid	Spain	13.90
6	Prague	Czech Republic	13.86
7	Hong Kong	Hong Kong	13.56
8	Mexico City	Mexico	12.88
9	Tallinn	Estonia	12.20
10	Jerusalem	Israel	11.53

Table 8. Results in citizen participation (2009)

Rank	City	Country	Participation
1	Mexico City	Mexico	13.45
2	Prague	Czech Republic	11.64
3	Bangkok	Thailand	11.27
4	Seoul	Republic of Korea	11.09
5	Shanghai	China	10.55
6	Singapore	Singapore	10.00
7	Johannesburg	South Africa	9.82
8	Vienna	Austria	8.36
8	Hong Kong	Hong Kong	8.36
10	Paris	France	8.00

Discussion of Longitudinal Findings

The following section shows the longitudinal trends in municipal e-governance worldwide based on the findings from the 2003, 2005, 2007 and 2009 evaluations. The overall average score for municipalities surveyed is 35.93, an increase from 33.37 in 2007, 33.11 in 2005 and 28.49 in 2003 (Figure 1). This improvement is a result of the municipalities' increasing use of technology to enhance effectiveness and efficiency.

Among the five categories, the municipalities on average have improved their scores in privacy/ security, content and services, with the most significant improvement being in services. The category of usability continued to record the highest average score, while citizen participation still remains as the category with the lowest average score. Many cities are yet to recognize the importance of involving and supporting citizen participation online. Table 9 highlights these findings.

Descriptive and Inferential Analysis

In order to strengthen the analysis conducted in this research, OLS regression was used to measure the relationship of e-governance to the socio-economic factors prevalent in the 87 nations. These include variables such as Gross Domestic Product (GDP), the number of Internet users and mobile users, level of democracy, and educational level of the citizens. The first variable examined was the nation's GDP, as it is considered an important indicator of a nation's capacity to build and maintain essential infrastructures. An earlier research project by the OECD exploring the impact of technology on the economy found that ICT investments accounted for between 0.5% and 1.3% in GDP growth per capita each year from 1995 to 2000 (Ndou, 2004). Thus, we hypothesize:

Figure 1. Average e-governance scores 2003 – 2009

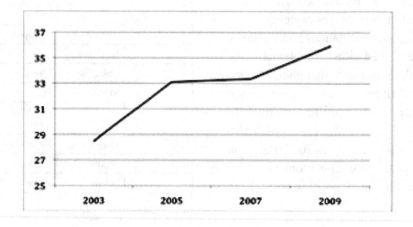

Table 9. Average score by e-governance categories 2003 - 2009

Average Scores	Privacy/ Security	Usability	Content	Service	Citizen Participation
2009	5.57	11.96	8.21	6.68	3.50
2007	4.49	11.95	7.58	5.8	3.55
2005	4.17	12.42	7.63	5.32	3.57
2003	2.53	11.45	6.43	4.82	3.26

H1: Nations with a higher GDP are more likely to earn higher e-governance scores.

Next we include four variables related to nations' capacity pertaining to the use of ICTs by its citizens. Specifically, we were interested in determining whether nations that had a higher number of residents relying upon ICTs to communicate would also have a higher e-governance score. The variables used to assess this relationship were the total number of telephone lines per 100 residents; the number of mobile telephone subscriptions per 100 residents; the number of Internet users per 100 residents; and the number of broadband subscribers per 100 residents. While a great deal of research has examined the relationship between e-government adoption and ICT capacity at the local level of government in particular countries, few studies (Srivastava & Teo, 2006) have analyzed this association globally. Here it is hypothesized that greater the ICT capacity a nation possesses the more likely they are to have a higher e-governance score.

H2: Nations with more telephone lines per 100 residents are more likely to earn higher e-governance scores.
H3: Nations with more cellular subscriptions per 100 residents are more likely to earn higher e-governance scores.
H4: Nations with more Internet users per 100 residents are more likely to earn higher e-governance scores.
H5: Nations with more broadband subscribers per 100 residents are more likely to earn higher e-governance scores.

The third set of variables examined factors from the 2008 Economist Index, which includes the perception of democracy by residents within the nation, its electoral process and pluralism, how well or poorly the government functions, and its political culture. Several studies utilize similar measures to explain the link between citizens' overall perception of government and e-government, as the two concepts are inherently related to trust in government and thus their e-government initiatives (Carter & Belanger, 2005; Parent et al., 2005; Verdegem & Verleye, 2009). Thus, we hypothesize:

H6: Nations whose residents perceive the level of democracy to be high are more likely to earn higher e-governance scores.
H7: Nations whose residents perceive the electoral process and pluralism to be high are more likely to earn higher e-governance scores.
H8: Nations whose residents perceive its functioning of government to be high are more likely to earn higher e-governance scores.
H9: Nations whose residents perceive its political culture to be high are more likely to earn higher e-governance scores.

The last variable we include in our study is the educational index of the selected nations. This variable was utilized in the UNDP Human Development Report in 2009 to assess the mobility of residents in relation to finding schools for their children. According to the UNDP report, movement is likely to enhance educational attainment, especially among children because many families move with the specific objective of having their children attend better or more advanced schools. The report suggests that in many developing nations schools located in rural areas are at a lower quality than they are in developed countries that have more urban centers (UNDP, 2009). Here we hypothesize,

H10: Nations with higher educational levels are more likely to earn higher e-governance scores.

Descriptive Statistics

Our statistical analysis begins in Table 10 where the descriptive statistics are displayed, followed by the regression results in Table 11.

The results of our regression analysis yielded interesting findings. Our first hypothesis, that nations with a higher GDP are likely to earn higher e-governance scores, was found to be significant but the relationship was inverted. In the area of ICT use, the only variable that proved to be a predictor of higher e-governance scores was the number of Internet users per 100 residents. The number of telephone lines, cellular subscriptions, and broadband use were not significant predictors of high levels of e-governance. While factors related to citizens' use of ICT, such as

broadband access, has been seen to impact e-governance in U.S. cities and within other developed nations, it is still not a factor globally. This finding is interesting as it signifies that citizens who use the Internet, and perhaps accept the fact that technology is beneficial to them, are also likely to visit government websites. With regard to the relationship between a person's trust in government and e-governance, the link is still unclear. On the one hand, residents of nations where they perceive the electoral process to be high and view the functioning of government to be effective are more likely to have higher e-governance scores. On the other hand, citizen's perception of democracy and political culture do not have a significant impact on e-governance. Finally, the educational level did not have a significant impact on e-governance implementation.

CONCLUSION

Previous research on government websites has focused primarily on e-governance at the federal, state, and local levels in the United States. Only a few studies have produced comparative analyses of e-governance throughout the world. Our studies in 2003, 2005, 2007 and 2009 have produced

Table 10. Descriptive statistics

Variables	Observations	Mean	SD	Minimum	Maximum
E-gov	87	35.935	14.97	7.78	84.74
GDP (2008)	87	19070.750	20696.96	500	94791.0
Telephone Use	86	27.531	16.50	0.53	64.11
Cellular Use	86	97.050	35.77	27.02	208.65
Internet Use	87	40.631	24.55	4.27	87.84
Broadband Use	87	11.386	11.29	0.01	41.19
Democracy	86	6.422	2.09	0.91	9.88
Electoral Process	86	7.393	3.10	0.00	10.00
Function of Gov	86	6.072	2.21	0.79	10.00
Political Culture	86	6.252	1.71	3.13	10.00
Education Level	85	0.885	0.10	0.49	.99

Table 11. OLS regression model of a country's e-governance score

Variables	Coefficient	T-score
GDP 2008	-.00004963 ***	-4.77
Telephone Use	.1056164	0.77
Cellular Use	.0213468	0.51
Internet Use	.3436677 **	2.84
Broadband Use	.2303952	0.74
Democracy	.477977	0.37
Electoral Process	-2.538564 **	-3.07
Function of Gov	4.651914 ***	4.00
Political Culture	-.6216452	-0.45
Education	27.02746	1.59
_cons	-8.596751	-0.63

$*p < .10, **p < .05, ***p < .001$

findings that contribute to the e-governance literature, particularly in the areas of website privacy/security, usability, content, services, and citizen participation. Our longitudinal analysis highlights the importance of perhaps exploring the digital divide from a different perspective. Contrary to prior expectations, this study indicates that the digital divide is decreasing. This may be the result of society's overall reliance on the use of technology. While it would be extremely naive to suggest that a divide does not exist, our study should move public administrators and policy makers to examine some of the other factors that may impact the digital divide.

The average e-governance score of municipalities continues to increase throughout the world. Our study also shows that significant research and development, capital improvement projects and strategic planning impact information technology capabilities. For example, Seoul continues to rank first in e-governance and their dedication to improving government to citizen communication is unparalleled. Similarly, the city of Prague has also improved its e-governance initiatives based, in large part, due to an increased emphasis on strategic planning to become a leader in e-government. The municipalities' scores in the category of privacy and security indicate that it continues to be viewed as exceptionally important to local governments. The number of cities with an online privacy or security policy in 2009 increased significantly compared to the previous surveys. However, citizen participation is not considered as important with the average score in the category *decreasing* from 2007 to 2009. As technological capabilities continue to improve, government-to-citizen (G2C) communication does not seem to be moving at the same pace. In fact, it is going in the opposite direction. This finding is surprising especially with the increased use of social media and network applications that have the potential of enhancing communication between government and its constituents.

One of the challenges in conducting this study and applying OLS regression to analyze the results was the relatively low number of observations. To address this concern, a time series analysis may be used in future research. The adjusted R square of 0.55, however, indicates that the relationship between the variables is reasonably strong. This is further evidence that future research needs to explore specific factors influencing e-governance in municipalities worldwide. Perhaps factors associated with organizational changes and political influences greatly impact e-governance. Continuing longitudinal analysis will assist in this endeavor as we seek to examine these fluid and dynamic developments and their overall impact on information technology in government.

REFERENCES

Bannister, F. (2007). The curse of the benchmark: An assessment of the validity and value of e-government comparisons. *International Review of Administrative Sciences*, *73*(2), 171–188. doi:10.1177/0020852307077959

Barber, B. R. (2001). The uncertainty of digital politics: Democracy's uneasy relationship with information technology. *Harvard International Review*, *23*, 42–47.

Carrizales, T. (2009). Critical factors in an electronic democracy: A study of municipal managers. *Electronic Journal of E-Government*, *6*(1), 23–30.

Carrizales, T., Holzer, M., Kim, S. T., & Kim, C. G. (2006). Digital governance worldwide: A longitudinal assessment of municipal websites. *International Journal of Electronic Government Research*, *2*(4), 1–23. doi:10.4018/jegr.2006100101

Carter, L., & Bélanger, F. (2005). The utilization of e-government services: Citizen trust, innovation and acceptance factors. *Information Systems Journal*, *15*(1), 5–15. doi:10.1111/j.1365-2575.2005.00183.x

Holzer, M., & Kim, S. T. (2004). *Digital governance in municipalities worldwide*. Newark, NJ: The E-Governance Institute, Rutgers University-Newark and the Global e-Policy e-Government Institute, Sungkyunkwan University.

Holzer, M., & Kim, S. T. (2005). *Digital governance in municipalities worldwide*. Newark, NJ: The E-Governance Institute, Rutgers University-Newark and the Global e-Policy e-Government Institute, Sungkyunkwan University.

Holzer, M., & Kim, S. T. (2007). *Digital governance in municipalities worldwide*. Newark, NJ: The E-Governance Institute, Rutgers University-Newark and the Global e-Policy e-Government Institute, Sungkyunkwan University.

Lau, E. (2007). Electronic government and the drive for growth and equity. In Mayer-Schonberger, V., & Lazer, D. (Eds.), *Governance and information technology* (pp. 39–62). Cambridge, MA: MIT Press.

Melitski, J. (2002). *The world of e-government and e-governance*. Retrieved from http://www.aspanet.org/solutions/egovworld.html

Melitski, J., Holzer, M., Kim, S. T., Kim, C. G., & Rho, S. Y. (2005). Digital government worldwide: An e-government assessment of municipal websites. *International Journal of E-Government Research*, *1*(1), 1–19. doi:10.4018/jegr.2005010101

Moon, M. J. (2002). The evolution of e-government among municipalities: Rhetoric or reality? *Public Administration Review*, *62*(4), 424–433. doi:10.1111/0033-3352.00196

Ndou, V. (2004). E-government for developing countries: Opportunities and challenges. *Electronic Journal of Information Systems in Developing Countries*, *18*(1), 1–24.

Norris, F., Fletcher, P. D., & Holden, S. H. (2001). *Is your local government plugged in? Highlights of the 2000 electronic government survey*. Baltimore, MD: University of Maryland.

OECD. (2003). The case of e-government: Experts from the OECD report: The e-government imperative. *OECD Journal on Budgeting*, *3*(1), 62–96.

Parent, M., Vandebeek, C. A., & Gemino, A. C. (2005). Building citizen trust through e-government. *Government Information Quarterly*, *22*(4), 720–736. doi:10.1016/j.giq.2005.10.001

Paskaleva-Shapira, K. (2006). Transitioning from e-government to e-governance in the knowledge society: The role of the legal framework for enabling the process in the European Union's countries. In *Proceedings of the 7th Annual International Conference on Digital Government Research*, San Diego, CA.

Schwester, R. (2009). Examining the barriers to e-government adoption. *Electronic Journal of E-Government*, 7(1), 113–122.

Srivastava, S. C., & Teo, T. S. H. (2006, December). Determinants and impact of e-government and e-business development: A global perspective. In *Proceedings of the Twenty-Seventh International Conference on Information Systems*, Milwaukee, WI.

United Nations Department of Economic and Social Affairs. (2003). *e-Government readiness assessment survey*. Retrieved from http://unpan1. un.org/intradoc/groups/public/documents/un/ unpan011509.pdf

United Nations Development Programme. (2009). *Human development report-Overcoming barriers: Human mobility and development*. New York, NY: Palgrave Macmillan.

van Velsen, L., van der Geest, T., ter Hedde, M., & Derks, W. (2009). Requirements engineering for e-government services: A citizen-centric approach and case study. *Government Information Quarterly*, 26(3), 477–486. doi:10.1016/j. giq.2009.02.007

Verdegem, P., & Verleye, G. (2009). User-centered e-government in practice: A comprehensive model for measuring user satisfaction. *Government Information Quarterly*, 26(3), 487–497. doi:10.1016/j. giq.2009.03.005

APPENDIX A

Table 12. 100 cities selected by continent (2009)

Africa (16)		
Abidjan (Côte d'Ivoire)*	Dakar (Senegal)*	Luanda (Angola)*
Accra (Ghana)	Douala (Cameroon)*	Lusaka (Zambia)
Algiers (Algeria)*	Harare (Zimbabwe)*	Nairobi (Kenya)
Cairo (Egypt)	Kampala (Uganda)	Tunis (Tunisia)
Cape Town (South Africa)	Omdurman (Sudan)*	
Casablanca (Morocco)	Lagos (Nigeria)	

Asia (25)		
Almaty (Kazakhstan)	Ho Chi Minh (Vietnam)	Riyadh (Saudi Arabia)
Amman (Jordan)	Hong Kong (Hong Kong)	Seoul (Republic of Korea)
Baku (Azerbaijan)	Jakarta (Indonesia)	Shanghai (China)
Bangkok (Thailand)	Jerusalem (Israel)	Singapore (Singapore)
Beirut (Lebanon)	Karachi (Pakistan)	Tashkent (Uzbekistan)
Bishkek (Kyrgyzstan)*	Kuala Lumpur (Malaysia)	Tehran (Iran)
Colombo (Sri Lanka)	Kuwait City (Kuwait)	Tokyo (Japan)
Damascus (Syria)*	Mumbai (India)	
Dubai (United Arab Emirates)	Quezon City (Philippines)	

Europe (35)		
Amsterdam (Netherlands)	Istanbul (Turkey)	Rome (Italy)
Athens (Greece)	Kiev (Ukraine)	Sarajevo (Bosnia and Herzegovina)
Belgrade (Serbia and Montenegro)	Lisbon (Portugal)	Sofia (Bulgaria)
Berlin (Germany)	Ljubljana (Slovenia)	Skopje (TFYR Macedonia)
Bratislava (Slovak Republic)	London (United Kingdom)	Stockholm (Sweden)
Brussels (Belgium)	Madrid (Spain)	Tallinn (Estonia)
Bucharest (Romania)	Minsk (Belarus)	Vienna (Austria)
Budapest (Hungary)	Moscow (Russian Federation)	Vilnius (Lithuania)
Chisinau (Moldova)	Oslo (Norway)	Warsaw (Poland)
Copenhagen (Denmark)	Paris (France)	Zagreb (Croatia)
Dublin (Ireland)	Prague (Czech Republic)	Zurich (Switzerland)
Helsinki (Finland)	Riga (Latvia)	

North America (13)		
Guatemala City (Guatemala)	Panama City (Panama)	San Salvador (El Salvador)
Havana (Cuba)*	Port-au-Prince (Haiti)*	Santo Domingo (Dominican Republic)
Kingston (Jamaica)*	San Jose (Costa Rica)	Tegucigalpa (Honduras)*
Mexico City (Mexico)	San Juan (Puerto Rico)	Toronto (Canada)
New York (United States)		

South America (9)		
Buenos Aires (Argentina)	La Paz (Bolivia)	Santa Fe De Bogota (Colombia)
Caracas (Venezuela)	Lima (Peru)	Santiago (Chile)
Guayaquil (Ecuador)	Montevideo (Uruguay)	Sao Paulo (Brazil)

Oceania (2)		
Auckland (New Zealand)	Sydney (Australia)	

* Official city websites unavailable

APPENDIX B

Table 13. Survey framework

Privacy/ Security	
1-2. Privacy or security statement/policy 3-6. Data collection 7. Option to use personal information 8. Third party disclosures 9. Ability to review personal data records 10. Managerial measures 11. Use of encryption	12. Secure server 13. Use of "cookies" or "Web Beacons" 14. Notification of privacy policy 15. Contact or e-mail address for inquiries 16. Public information in restricted area 17. Nonpublic information for employees 18. Use of digital signatures
Usability	
19-20. Homepage, page length. 21. Targeted audience 22-23. Navigation Bar 24. Site map	25-27. Font Color 30-31. Forms 32-37. Search tool 38. Update of website
Content	
39. Information on location of offices 40. Listing of external links 41. Contact information 42. Minutes of public 43. State code and regulations 44. State charter and policy priority 45. Mission statements 46. Budget information 47-48. Documents, reports, or books	49. GIS capabilities 50. Emergency management or alert mechanism 51-52. Disability access 53. Wireless technology 54. Access in more than one language 55-56. Human resources information 57. Calendar of events 58. Downloadable documents
Service	
59-61. Pay utilities, taxes, fines 62. Apply for permits 63. Online tracking system 64-65. Apply for licenses 66. E-procurement 67. Property assessments 68. Searchable databases 69. Complaints 70-71. Bulletin board on civil applications	72. FAQ 73. Request information 74. Customize the main state homepage 75. Access private information online 76. Purchase tickets 77. Webmaster response 78. Report violations of administrative laws and regulations
Citizen Participation	
79-80. Comments or feedback 81-83. Newsletter 84. Online bulletin board/chat capabilities 85-87. Online discussion forum on policy issues 88-89. E-meetings for discussion	90-91. Online survey/ polls 92. Synchronous video 93-94. Citizen satisfaction survey 95. Online decision-making 96-98. Performance measures, standards, or benchmarks

This journal was previously published in the International Journal of Technology Diffusion, Volume 2, Issue 2, edited by Ali Hussein Saleh Zolait, pp. 32-46, copyright 2011 by IGI Publishing (an imprint of IGI Global).

Chapter 12
Public Information Service for the Disadvantaged in China's Towns:
Case Study of Two Chinese Towns

Jianbin Zhang
Wuhan University, China

ABSTRACT

This study uses the methods of questionnaire and group discussion to conduct field research in A and B towns, which are located in the eastern developed region and the western undeveloped region of China, respectively. According to comparative study on the status of providing public information service for the disadvantaged between A and B towns, the author finds that the public in A town are superior to the ones in B in terms of information literacy, public information service expenditure, and satisfaction rate of public information service. Similarities exist in terms of differences in accessing public information service between town and village, among social groups, and the causes resulting in imbalance of public information service and features of the information-poor's group distribution. The author discusses the differences in development policies between city and village, as well as differences in financial investment of public information service, education, and individual's income level between A and B towns.

INTRODUCTION

Owing to low education and knowledge level and much weaker capacity of identified information, the farmers are short of expenditure consciousness in public information service in China. Meanwhile, because of lacking of effective mechanisms for demand expression, in fact, they enjoy less quantity and lower quality public information service, leading to scarcely meet their basic needs of production and living (Wang, 2009). What's more, in China, many webs don't consider the disableds'

DOI: 10.4018/978-1-4666-2791-8.ch012

needs, page layout, typography, color matching, operating methods and forms of multimedia, etc., which have serious impairment to the disabled (Guo, 2009). That proves preliminary that the public information doesn't meet the disadvantage's needs in China.

In order to understand the status of China town government provides public information service for the disadvantaged, the author conducts field research in A town of the developed region in eastern and B town of the undeveloped region in western of China, hoping to find the differences and similarities in the process of public information service provided, and discuss the causes of differences and similarities by carrying out comparative study on the situation of providing public information service for the disadvantaged between A and B towns.

LITERATURE REVIEW

The discussion of the foreign scholars on public information service for the disadvantaged mainly centers in the study on digital divide (Fuchs, 2009; Aerschot & Rodousakis, 2008; van Deursen & van Dijk, 2009). Christian Fuchs (2009) conducts comparative study by multivariate regression analysis on 126 countries, and contends that income inequality is an important factor to influence Internet usage, and is a main reason for digital divide. Aerschot and Rodousakis (2008) maintain that the digital divide affects low socio-economic status groups in particular; socio-economic factors-especially age and level of education play a role in determining whether a person is an Internet user or non-user. Van Deursen and van Dijk (2009) discuss the equity of public information service from the proposition of digital divide, and argue that digital is bridged by improving digital skills for the use of online public information and services. These study results have been involved the problem of public information service for the disadvantaged, but lacked of in-depth analysis in

terms of communication between government and the public and the measures improved to public information service for the disadvantaged. According to Fuch's study results, in this paper, the author divides the sample group into the high and low income group. According to the study results from Aerschot and Rodousakis, the author emphasizes efforts of education in two towns during the interview. Using the study results from van Deursen and van Dijk, the author designs the twenty-first and twenty-second questions in questionnaire to research the public's information literacy.

China scholars on the study of public information service are mainly from the proposition of macro level, and short of measures study in terms of improving public information service. Li (2008) only discusses the problems and measures of government public information service from the proposition of government information openness, but doesn't involve in the disadvantaged problem. Feng and Zhou (2010) discuss the equity of public information service superficially, and argue that public information management and service should take the public as the center, and emphasize that the public may access and enjoy public information service equity, which requires the means of public information service are diversity, and the content of public information service is rich. Wang (2009) discusses the problems that local government offer public information service for the peasant from the proposition of lacking of effective express mechanism of the peasant's demands, low efficiency decision-making mechanism of public information service supplied from up to down, and lacking of stable funding guarantee mechanism. Xia (2004) discusses diversification of public information service from the interaction relationship between government and the third sector in public information service. These results don't in-depth discuss the causes and measures of the problem of public information service for the disadvantaged. According to the study results from Feng and Zhou, the author designs twenty-fourth question to research the causes of imbalance in public information service; according to study results from Wang, the author designs the seventh and eighth questions in questionnaire and investigates majorly the situation of fund input into public information service during interview in two towns; according to the study results from Xia, the author designs the sixth question in the questionnaire.

METHODOLOGY AND PROCESS

The author particularly chooses A and B towns, which are located in the eastern developed region and in the western undeveloped region of China respectively to conduct field research and comparative study. The author employs questionnaire method to understand the status of two governments offering public information service from the proposition of the public; and employs group discussion method to interview with leaders from financial, civil affairs, education, information construction, social security, propaganda departments, etc. Author holds respectively a group discussion in A and B town, and every time the number of it is ten, in which seven persons are government staffs and three persons are project team members. And author conducts a separate depth interview with leaders of information construction department, by the way of on-spot Q&A to understand the efforts of this two government offering public information service for the disadvantaged.

Survey Location

The basic situation of A town as follows: in 2009, its GDP achieves 24.376 billion ¥ totally, and per capita GDP is 44,124 ¥. This town governmental disposable fiscal revenue is 1.434 billion ¥, the net per capita income of rural residents is 15,195 ¥. The original inhabitants of A town is over 120,000, and the floating population is over 500,000. The number of agricultural population is about 1,100 and the rest is non-agricultural population. In A town, the number of the minimum living security

household is 1,303, the disabled is 1,161, and the number of the disabled from the minimum living security household is 216, what's more, the number of laid-off workers is 1,439 (Ren, 2010).

The town has been at the forefront of the national economy hundred strong towns in the past five years. Its economy is relatively developed, the level of urbanization is relatively high, and information infrastructure is relatively strong, however, before reform and opening up, A town is a small fishing village, and with the help of national policy, it develops rapidly a strong economy town. That is different from the many traditional developed cities, for instance Shanghai city. Therefore, A town has common features of the developed cities in eastern, meanwhile, it also has characteristics of transformation from rural to urban, therefore, it has typical at some extent, and some comparability with traditional country (for instance B town).

The basic situation of B town as follows: in 2009, its GDP achieves 95.76 million ¥ total, and per capita GDP is 4,144 ¥. This town governmental disposable fiscal revenue is 5.389 million ¥, the net per capita income of rural residents is 2,016 ¥. In B town, the number of population is 23,108, and the number of agricultural population is about 22,387 and the rest is non-agricultural population. In B town, the number of the minimum living security household is 2678, the disabled is 598, and the number of the disabled from the minimum living security household is 326, what's more, the number of laid-off workers is 124 (Shen, 2010).

The town is a poor mountain town in the western, its development level of economy is very low, the majority of population is farmer, and information infrastructure construction is relatively low, moreover, information consciousness and skill of the habituates is very low. Therefore, B town has all features of the undeveloped region.

The differences and similarities between town and traditional country in the process of urbanization in public information service could show explicitly by comparing the efforts of two governments in public information service.

Designing Questionnaire and Distribution

In order to guarantee questionnaires' effectiveness, when designing questionnaire, author distributes archives respectively to 45 persons of A and B towns, including 15 persons from high income group, 15 persons from high income group, and 15 persons from the disabled. The findings from the 45 questionnaires as follows: 30 persons choose "rarely" when answering to seventh question, and according to this situation, author adds eighth question to original questionnaire to investigate satisfaction rate of government public information service; 13 persons write "financial investment varies from region to region" behind "others" item when answering to twenty-ninth question, therefore, author adds "financial investment varies from region to region" to twenty-ninth question. The final questionnaire appears in the Appendix. In the questionnaire, from first to third questions aim to survey individual information and they are also the standards of category; from fourth to tenth questions aim to survey the status of government public information service; eleventh and thirteenth questions aim to survey the status of public information service between town and village; twelfth and twenty-first questions aim to survey individuals' information consciousness; twentieth, twenty-second and twenty-third questions aim to survey individuals' information skill; fourteenth and fifteenth questions aim to survey the status of the disabled accessing public information service; sixteenth and eighteenth questions aim to survey the status of the high income group accessing public information service; seventeenth and nineteenth questions aim to survey the status of the low income group accessing public information service; and twenty-fourth question aims to survey the causes of imbalance in public information service.

The method of questionnaires' distribution and withdraw as follows: According to the public's income and health materials supplied by two government departments, project team members distribute and withdraw questionnaires to the high income group, low income group and disabled of two towns. The author uses EXCEL and SPSS statistical analysis software to analyze valid questionnaires (National School of Administration of China project team "The study on public service for information-poor" has three members, in times of distributing questionnaires, every member is responsible for a type group and three members participate in interview with two government staffs together).

Sample Groups

According to the public's income and job materials supplied by two government departments, author divides the public of two towns into the high income group, low income group and disabled group, divides the public of two towns into healthy persons and the disabled. According to report on the work of the A town government in 2010, in 2009, per capita monthly income is 2,042 ¥, therefore, we classify the persons whose monthly income over 2000 ¥ as the high income group and this group is mainly make up of lenders of land or housing and highly paid occupations (for example teachers), and classify the persons whose monthly income under 2000 ¥ as the low income group and this group is mainly make up of persons receiving the minimum living, laid-offs and migrant workers (Ren, 2010). According to report on the work of the B town government in 2010, in 2009, per capita monthly income is 1,012 ¥, we classify the persons whose monthly income over 1000 ¥ as the high income group and this group is mainly make up of non-agricultural populations; and classify the persons whose monthly income under 1000 ¥ as the low income group and this group is mainly make up of farmers, but not all farmers belong to the low income group, and some farmers (for example planters) belong to the high income group (Shen, 2010). The disabled group is different from the healthy persons in accessing and using public information service, because they need some special service channels and apparatus. Therefore, author gives special attention to this group in surveying public information service.

Project team members distribute respectively questionnaires to the high income group, the low income group and the disabled of A town 110,110 and 100, and withdraw respectively valid questionnaires 106,106, and 96, withdrawing rate respectively 96.36%, 96.36%, and 96%. Project team members distribute respectively questionnaires to the high income group, the low income group and the disabled of B town 110,110 and 100, and withdraw valid questionnaires 105,104, and 94, withdrawing rate 94.45%, 94.54%, and 94%, respectively.

RESULTS ANALYSIS

The Public's Information Literacy

Information consciousness and information skill are constituted information literacy. Twenty-first and twenty-second questions in questionnaires aim to survey information quality. Twenty-first ques-

tion "how does your information consciousness?", and the answers of this two towns' three groups seen in Table 1. According to Table 1, although all of this two towns' three groups have some persons lower in information consciousness, in the whole, in A and B towns, the information consciousness of the high income group is higher than the low income group and the disabled. Twenty-second question "how does your information skill?", and the answers of this two towns' three groups seen in Table 2. According to Table 2, this two towns' three groups have some persons lower in information skill, but in A and B towns, the skill of the high income group is generally higher than the low income group and the disabled. In the whole, information consciousness and skill of the high and low income groups in A town are higher than the high and low income groups in B town.

Public Information Service Expenditure

The situations of the high and low income groups in two towns answers to the second question "How about your monthly income?" are seen in Table 3. According to Table 3, the monthly income

Table 1. The status of information consciousness in two towns' three groups

		Very High	Ordinary	Low	Don't Know
A Town	High Income Group	47.17%	26.42%	23.58%	2.83%
	Low Income Group	7.55%	18.87%	62.26%	11.32%
	Disabled	1.04%	10.42%	64.58%	23.96%
B Town	High Income Group	20.95%	52.38%	23.81%	2.86%
	Low Income Group	2.88%	20.19%	57.69%	19.24%
	Disabled	1.06%	10.64%	68.09%	20.21%

Table 2. The status of information skill in two towns' three groups

		Very High	Ordinary	Low	Don't Know
A Town	High Income Group	54.72%	28.31%	16.04%	0.93%
	Low Income Group	8.49%	20.75%	61.32%	9.44%
	Disabled	1.04%	12.50%	67.71%	18.75%
B Town	High Income Group	21.90%	48.57%	25.71%	3.82%
	Low Income Group	1.92%	22.12%	58.65%	17.31%
	Disabled	1.06%	9.57%	70.21%	19.25%

level of the high and low income groups in A town are generally higher than the high and low income groups in B town. Twenty-third question in questionnaire aims to survey the proportion status that the public's monthly expenditure in public information service occupies total monthly expenditure. The answers of the high and low income groups in two towns are seen in Figures 1 and 2. According to Figures 1 and 2, in A and B towns, the proportion of the high income group's

Table 3. The monthly income situation of the high and low income groups in two towns (unit: ¥)

		Under 500	500-1000	1000-1500	1500-2000	2000-2500	2500-3000	Over 3000
A Town	High Income Group					18	23	65
	Low Income Group	2	28	41	35			
B Town	High Income Group			11	51	31	9	3
	Low Income Group	18	86					

Figure 1. The proposition of the high and low income groups' monthly expenditures in public information service occupy total monthly expenditure in A town

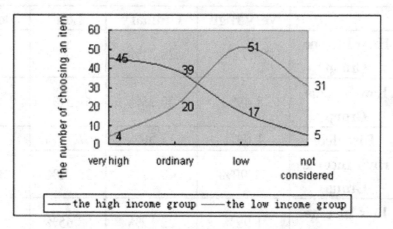

monthly expenditure in public information service occupies total monthly expenditure is higher than the low income group, what's more, the proportion of the high and low income groups' in A town monthly expenditures in public information service occupy total monthly expenditure is higher than the high and low income group in B town. Therefore, we can draw a conclusion that one person's income level is positive correlation with his or her expenditure in public information service approximately.

The Differences in Accessing Public Information Service Between Town and Village

The situation analysis of the public's in A and B towns answering to eleventh question "Do you think accessing to public information service is alike convenient in the town and rural or not?" seen in Table 4. According to Table 4, in A town, rural residents are more difficult than town residents in accessing public information service, and so B town.

Figure 2. The proposition of the high and low income groups' monthly expenditures in public information service occupy total monthly expenditure in B town

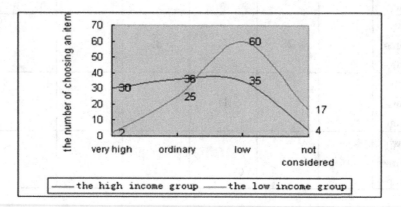

Table 4. The situation of the public's in two towns answering to "accessing to public information service is alike convenient in the town and rural or not?"

		Alike Convenient	The Rural is More Difficult Than the Town	The Rural is More Convenient Than the Town
A Town	High Income Group	15.09%	64.16%	20.75%
	Low Income Group	7.55%	56.60%	35.85%
	Disabled	7.29%	52.08%	40.63%
B Town	High Income Group	5.71%	67.62%	26.67%
	Low Income Group	4.81%	87.50%	7.69%
	Disabled	4.26%	69.15%	26.59%

The Differences in Accessing Public Information Service Among Social Groups

From fourteenth to nineteenth questions in questionnaire aim to survey the differences in public information service among social groups. The situation of the disabled in two towns answering to fourteenth question "Does the government pay attention to the disabled's needs of public information service or not?" seen in Figure 3. According to Figure 3, B town government's attention level to the disabled's needs of public information service is much lower than A town government. The situation of the high and low income groups in two towns answering to sixteenth question "Existing information-poor group in them or not" sees in Table 5. (The information-poor group is that in information society, the social group and persons who have disadvantages in accessing and using information infrastructure and information.) According to Table 5, the high and low income

Figure 3. The situation of two governments pays attention to the disabled's needs of public information service

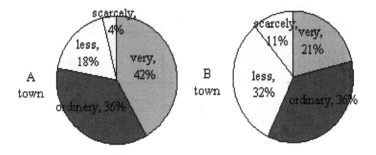

groups generally consider that information-poor group exists in them, and then that shows that the public aren't access and use public information service equally, some persons have disadvantages in accessing and using public information service.

The Causes of Differences in Public Information Service

The twenty-fourth question in questionnaire aims to survey the causes of imbalance in public information service. The situation of the high and low income groups in A and B towns answering to this question are seen in Figures 4 and 5. According to Figures 4 and 5, they generally consider that the causes of imbalance in public information service includes differences in development policies between town and village, differences in financial investment of governments, differences in individuals' education level, differences in individuals' income level, differences in individuals' information quality, and government is short of communication with the public.

Notes

In the two figures, A stands for "differences in development policies between town and village", B stands for "differences in financial investment of governments", C stands for "differences in individuals' education level", D stands for "differences in individuals' income level", E stands for "differences in individuals' information quality", F stands for "government is short of communication with the public", G stands for "others".

Satisfaction Rate of Public Information Service

Seventh and eighth questions in questionnaire aim to survey the status of government offering public information service to the public. The situation of the high and low income groups of two towns answering to seventh question "Do you think government understand your needs before it offering public information service or not?" seen in Table 6. According to Table 6, two governments seldom understand the public's needs of public information service before they offering public information service and A town government is better than B town government. In two towns, the high income group evaluating the efforts of governments is higher than the low income group. The situation of the high and low income groups of two towns answering to eighth question "Do you think government offering public information service meets your needs or not?" seen in Table 7, and according to Table 7, many citizens don't

Table 5. The situation of the high and low income groups in two towns answers to "Existing information-poor group in them or not?"

	Exist in the High Income Group or not		Exist in the Low Income Group or not	
	Yes	No	Yes	No
A Town	71.70%	28.30%	92.45%	7.55%
B Town	80.95%	19.05%	96.15%	3.85%

Figure 4. The situations of the high and low income groups in A town consider that the causes of imbalance in public information service

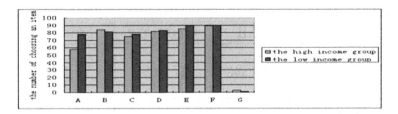

Figure 5. The situations of the high and low income groups in B town consider that the causes of imbalance in public information service

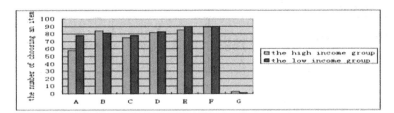

satisfied with public information service offered by government, moreover, the high income group's satisfaction rate is higher than the low income group in two towns.

Taking what's mentioned above, we can draw a conclusion that the public in A town is higher than the public in B town in terms of information literacy, public information service expenditure

Table 6. The situation of the high and low income groups of two towns consider that government understands their needs before it offering public information service

		All	**Ordinary**	**Seldom**	**Never**
A Town	**High Income Group**	10.38%	23.58%	56.60%	9.44%
	Low Income Group	8.49%	19.81%	63.21%	8.49%
B Town	**High Income Group**	7.62%	16.19%	68.57%	7.62%
	Low Income Group	4.81%	11.54%	73.08%	10.57%

Table 7. The situation of the high and low income groups of two towns consider government offering public information service meets their needs

		All	Ordinary	Seldom	Never
A Town	High Income Group	9.43%	27.36%	56.66%	6.55%
	Low Income Group	7.55%	23.58%	63.21%	5.66%
B Town	High Income Group	6.67%	24.76%	60.00%	8.57%
	Low Income Group	5.77%	18.10%	72.12%	4.01%

and satisfaction rate of public information service. In the whole, the public information service level for the disadvantaged of A town is higher than B town government. That difference is basically the same with the different in information development levels between eastern region and western region in China from the proposition of micro. Because the information development level of the developed region of eastern is higher than the undeveloped region of western in China (Zhang, 2008).

DISCUSSION

According to data analyses in fifth part, it's not hard to find that A and B town governments have differences in offering public information service to the disadvantaged. An important discussion point is what causes that differences are.

Difference in Development Policies Between City and Village

Since the foundation of new China, China government applies development strategy of laying particular stress on city and industry (Liu, 2005), many policies and funds pour into the urban rather than the rural, and the rural obtain relatively limited resources. Under its influence, urban residents gain public information service more than rural residents. According to basically situation introduction of A and B towns, we obtain a conclusion that the urbanization and information infrastructure construction in A town are better than B town. This is the reason that the public of A town consider that the difference in accessing public information service between town and country is smaller than the public of B town (Table 3).

The Difference in Financial Investment of Public Information Service

A town's revenue is far higher than B town, and it also largely determines the situation that A town government's expenditure in public information service is necessarily higher than B town. According to the interview between author and director Zhang of information construction office in A town, director Huang of information construction office in B town, financial funds pouring into public information service is more than 500 million ¥ totally from 2002 to 2009 in A town, however, financial funds pouring into public information service is less than 100 million ¥ totally from 2002 to 2009 in B town. The difference in inputs results in difference of the public enjoying public information service in two towns; we can draw a conclusion preliminary that the causes that the public's the satisfaction rate of public information service in A town is higher than B (Tables 5 and 6).

Differences in Education Between A and B Towns

The director Li of education department in A town and director Wang of education department in B town contend that the public's skills accessing and using government public information service are positive correlation with their education levels, what's' more, the improvement of the public's information literacy mainly depends on education's development. The secretary Zhan of financial department in A town introduces that government emphasizes greatly on education's development, the measures employed as follows: first, every year the fiscal budget pouring into education is very high, and the proportion of education investment occupying financial investment from 2006 to 2009 is respectively 20%, 22%, 27%, 25%. Second, the government offers education grant to children from the low income group to ensure them to go to school smoothly, for example,

every year government offer education grant to per university student 7000¥, per senior high school student 3000¥, per junior school student 900 ¥, per pupil 800 ¥.Third, the director Li of education department in A town introduces, government has been conducted information technology education and propaganda for the public ever since 1999, in 2009, 3/4 kindergartens open computer program to enable children to touch computer from an early age. However, according to secretary Li of financial department in B town introduces that due to limited financial income of B town government, the proportion of education investment occupying financial investment from 2006 to 2009 is respectively 2.1%, 2.3%, 2.7%, 3.1%. What's more, the director Li of education department in B town introduces, government has been conducted information technology education and propaganda for the public ever since 2005, In 2009, 1/3 kindergartens in town open computer program, but kindergartens in village don't open computer program. Taking what's mentioned above, we can draw a conclusion that the fiscal budget of A town pouring into education is far higher than B town and A town government conducting information technology education and propaganda for the public is much earlier than B town government. And those are the reasons that the public's information quality in A town is higher than the public in B town (Table 3).

The Difference in Individual's Income Level

According to basic situation introduction of A and B towns, per capita income level in A town is far higher than B town. Moreover, the situation of the high and low income groups answering to second question in questionnaire also reflects this status. Generally speaking, accessing and using public information service need costs, one person' low income level limits his or her expenditure in public information service. That is not hard to understand why the high and low income groups' public information service expenditure in A town are higher than the high and low income groups in B town. What's more, individual's low income level limits his or her expenditure in improving information quality.

What's more, there is still a common worth concerning problem in public information service in A and B towns: the disadvantaged exists in the high income group, owing to relatively low information quality, some high income groups become the disadvantaged in information society. This group needs government's particular attention in offering public information service, because they have differences in needs of public information service from the other disadvantaged, such as the low income group, the disabled and so on.

CONCLUSION AND LIMITATIONS

This paper conducts comparative study on public information service for the disadvantaged in two towns of China, and this paper confirms that the citizens in the developed areas are superior to the ones in the undeveloped areas in accessing and using public information service in China, particularly the disadvantaged. As far as public information service for the disadvantaged is concerned, the scholars' studies on this problem are not in-depth and meticulous. Although author obtains many first-hand materials by field research, owing to limited financial and human resources, the whole study is relatively rough, and the surveyed group is not extensively enough, particularly short of researching and analyzing the effective measures to improve this status. Author will explore this issue more in-depth in the future, meanwhile, not limit to these two towns and try to conduct field research in many styles of cities and villages to employ more meticulous and extensive comparative study.

ACKNOWLEDGMENT

This work is supported by National School of Administration of China.

REFERENCES

Aerschot, L., & Rodousakis, N. (2008). The link between socio-economic background and internet use: barriers faced by low socio-economic status groups and possible solutions. *European Journal of Soil Science*, *21*(4), 317–351.

Feng, H., & Zhou, Y. (2010). The discussion on building public information service system. *Information Studies: Theory & Application*, *7*, 26–31.

Fuchs, C. (2009). The role of income inequality in a multivariate cross-national analysis of the digital divide. *Social Science Computer Review*, *27*(1), 41–58. doi:10.1177/0894439308321628

Guo, J. (2009). The status of the China government website accessibility. *Information Science*, *27*(12), 1802–1805.

Li, X. (2008). The discussion on problems and measures of government public information service. *Business Economics (Cleveland, Ohio)*, *1*, 100–101.

Liu, S. (2005). The current status, causes and reform of urban-rural dual structure in China. *Journal of Chengdu Institute of Public Administration*, *13*(1), 72–74.

Ren, H. (2010). *Report on the work of the A town government in 2010*. Retrieved December 10, 2010, from http://www.humencn.com/news/info.asp?id=51495&classcode=200003

Shen, L. (2010). *Report on the work of the B town government in 2010*. Retrieved December 12, 2010, from http://www.lx.hh.gov.cn/Information-Disclosure.aspx?KindID=0001000300050010

van Deursen, A. J. A. M., & van Dijk, J. A. G. M. (2009). Improving digital skills for the use of online public information and services. *Government Information Quarterly*, *26*(2), 333–340. doi:10.1016/j.giq.2008.11.002

Wang, L. (2009). The study on public information service's supply mechanism of local government. *Information Studies: Theory & Application*, *12*, 41–44.

Xia, Y. (2004). Socaity choice of public information service. *Journal of Library Science in China*, *3*, 18–23.

Zhang, L. (2008). The status analysis and measures of information divide in China. [Natural Science Edition]. *Journal of Henan Institute of Education*, *17*(3), 44–46.

APPENDIX

Questionnaire of Government Public Service for Information-Poor Group

Please you mark option that best meets your actual conditions as "√", and if you can't find answer which is suit for your conditions in questionnaire, please you write out answer behind "others" item. If you are ambiguous about some questions, please ask researcher.

Note

In questionnaire, if the question that doesn't indicate particularly is answered by the high income group, the low income group and the disabled.

1. What is your education level?
   A. Illiteracy
   B. Primary school
   C. Junior high school
   D. High school or secondary
   E. College or university
   F. Graduate

2. How many does your monthly income now?
   A. Under 500￥
   B. 500-1000￥
   C. 1000-1500￥
   D. 1500-2000￥
   E. 2000-2500￥
   F. 2500-3000￥
   G. over 3000￥

3. How does your healthy situation?
   A. Health
   B. Physical disabilities
   C. Visual impairment
   D. Hearing impairment
   E. Others

4. How many the government offering information infrastructure to citizens?(Multiple choices)
   A. Internet
   B. Mobile phone
   C. Fixed line
   D. Radio
   E. Newspapers and magazines
   F. Cable television
   G. Public library
   H. Others

5. Do you think what kind of tools the government used to provide public information service for citizens is more popular? (Multiple choices)
   A. Internet
   B. Mobile phone
   C. Fixed line
   D. Radio
   E. Newspapers and magazines
   F. Cable television
   G. Public library
   H. Others

6. Do you think how many subjects could offer public information service to information-poor? (Multiple choices)
   A. Government
   B. Company
   C. Social organizations

7. Do you think government understand your needs before it offering public information service or not?
   A. All
   B. Ordinary
   C. Seldom
   D. Never

8. Do you think government offering public information service meets your needs or not?
   A. Very
   B. Many
   C. Some
   D. Never

9. Do you think the local government website has the following conditions? (Multiple choices)
   A. Don't have government website
   B. Could enlarge the font
   C. Publish effective consult phone number
   D. Interact with the public

10. Do you think how many the local government affairs hall have facilities? (Multiple choices)
    A. Blind aisle
    B. Disabled channel
    C. Counseling platform
    D. Other convenient facilities

11. Do you think accessing to public information service is alike convenient in the town and rural or not?
    A. Alike convenient
    B. The rural is more difficult than in town
    C. The rural is more convenient than in town

12. Are you understand the Internet to what extent?
    A. Never heard of it

    B.   Heard it but not used

    C.   Understand its basic functions

    D.   Being familiar with it and often surf

    E.   It has been an important part of daily life

13. Do you think what is the important cause of not having internet in local village?

    A.   Have internet

    B.   Terrain is bad for paving cables

    C.   Town government doesn't financial capability

    D.   The government staffs say it will connect Internet some days later

    E.   Internet is not use

14. Do you think government pay attention to needs of the disabled's public information service?(The disabled write it particularly)

    A.   Very

    B.   Ordinary

    C.   A little

    D.   Scarcely

15. Do you think how many factors that barrier you to access public information service? (The disabled writes it particularly, and may choose more than one)

    A.   Out of cry

    B.   Dumb

    C.   Has difficult in walking

    D.   Can't online

    E.   Have difficulty in getting through government's telephone

    F.   Has no money to online

16. Do you think the high income group have information-poor group or not?

    A.   Yes

    B.   No

17. Do you think the low income group have information-poor group or not?

    A.   Yes

    B.   No

18. Do you think how many causes that enable the high income group to became the information-poor group?(The high income group writes it particularly, and may choose more than one)

    A.   Age

    B.   Income level

    C.   Education level

    D.   Information consciousness

    E.   Information skill

    F.   Others

19. Do you think how many causes that enable the low income group to became the information-poor group? (The low income group writes it particularly, and may choose more than one.)

    A.   Age

    B.   Income level

    C.   Education level

    D.   Information consciousness

    E.   Information skill

    F.   Others

20. Do you think how many factors influence your capacity accessing public information service?

    A.   Age

    B.   Income level

    C.   Education level

    D.   Information consciousness

    E.   Information skill

    F.   Others

21. How about your information consciousness?

    A.   Very high

    B.   Ordinary

    C.   Low

    D.   Don't know

22. How about your information skill?

    A.   Very high

    B.   Ordinary

    C.   Low

    D.   Don't know

23. How about the proportion status that your monthly expenditure in public information service occupies total monthly expenditure?

    A.   Very high

    B.   Ordinary

    C.   Low

    D.   Not considered

24. Do you think what are the causes of imbalance in public information service?

    A.   Differences in development policies between town and village

    B.   Differences in financial investment of governments

    C.   Differences in individuals' education level

    D.   Differences in individuals' income level

    E.   Differences in individuals' information quality

    F.   Government is short of communication with the public

    G.   Others

This journal was previously published in the International Journal of Technology Diffusion, Volume 2, Issue 3, edited by Ali Hussein Saleh Zolait, pp. 1-13, copyright 2011 by IGI Publishing (an imprint of IGI Global).

Chapter 13
Software Quality Initiatives:
An Empirical Study of Indian SMEs in the IT Sector

D. P. Goyal
Management Development Institute, India

Adarsh Garg
Institute of Management and Research, India

ABSTRACT

Through extensive research into the area of quality management practices, such as ISO (International Standard Organization), Six Sigma has been observed within small and medium-sized enterprises (SMEs). Few empirical studies have reported the application of Six Sigma in SMEs, especially in software developing SMEs. The reasons can be attributed to complex issues associated with Six Sigma, as well as cost and time constraints. This paper assesses the current status of quality management practices in software developing SMEs. A survey-based approach was used to understand the conventional quality management practices in software SMEs. The data was collected from 230 respondents in 23 software developing SMEs in National Capital Region (NCR) of India. The respondents involved all three managerial levels and statistical results reflect the non-realization of quality management practices in software development. The SMEs under study were aware of the importance of quality management practices but had not implemented the same in the organization which is one of the basic requirements for the success of any software.

1. INTRODUCTION

This research work investigates the application of Six Sigma in software developing small and medium-sized enterprises (SMEs) in India. There are several models for software quality assurance, such as the Capability Maturity model Integrated (CMMI), the Software Process Improvement and Capability dEtermination (SPICE) and the ISO 9000 norms from the International Standardization Organization, TickIT, and Six Sigma. Unfortunately, the successful implementation of such models is usually not feasible.

DOI: 10.4018/978-1-4666-2791-8.ch013

Developing software to meet practical needs with satisfactory levels of quality, within given time period and budget is target of every organization engaged in software development. Software quality may be described as a paradigm that comprises several concepts (McManus, 2000). The first of these concepts relates to defining the software process to be improved. Defining the process means that all the activities to be performed have to be clearly stated, including the order in which they are to be performed and when they are considered complete. The second concept relates to using software processes – to improve the quality of a process it needs to be used on many projects. Quality comes with experience. The third concept is that of metrics, which should be collected to determine if changes incorporated into the process, are really improving. Most of the software development organizations follow best practices of software development, i.e., CMM (CMMI), Six Sigma, ISO 9001, and TickIT.

Six Sigma is more of a philosophy than a model. It concentrates on measuring product quality and improving process engineering. Six Sigma methodology suggests Define, Measure, Analyze, Improve and Control (DMAIC) as the basic steps to process improvement. The model is applicable across the industries. It has also been adopted in software industry and shown encouraging results.

However, it is assumed that the poor adoption of quality management initiatives in SMEs is due to multiple and complex reasons, not just the often stated impediments of cost, time and relative impacts (Gome, 1996). There is also evidence to put forward that quality management programs are not being taken up by SMEs for several reasons, as cited in literature (Husband & Mandal, 1999; Yusof & Aspinwall, 1999; Thomas & Webb, 2003; Antony et al., 2008).

- SMEs find it difficult to distinguish between different quality programs like Six Sigma TQM, ISO and the system that go well with their needs.

- SMEs, due to lack of knowledge, are imprecise about the advantages that one quality intiative has over the other.
- There is misunderstanding that Six Sigma involves voluminous data

Six Sigma approach of quality improvement identifies and removes defects. This approach has many success stories in large organizations which has grossly improved the performance, quality of products and customer loyalty (Antony et al., 2005, 2008; Kumar et al., 2006). However, continuous quality improvement initiatives like Six Sigma is not properly understood by SMEs thus the reason SMEs are yet to implement Six Sigma and hence devoid of the benefits of Six Sigma (Kumar, 2007). It is observed that there are many reasons of non-implementation of Six Sigma in SMEs as cost, time, poor knowledge about the advantage of Six Sigma, better understanding of ISO standards and less evidence of success stories o Six Sigma in SMEs.

The research aims at the study of awareness and implementation of Six Sigma as quality management initiative in software developing SMEs in IT (Information Technology) industry. The Indian IT industry is segmented into IT Services, ITeS-BPO (Information Enabled Services-Business Process Outsourcing), Engineering Services and R&D, Software Products and Hardware. The overall growth rate of these segments is 27.8%. Table 1 shows segregated view of revenue of each segment of IT industry, from 2004-2010. According to NASSCOM (National Association of Software & Services Companies) strategic review 2007, 2008, 2009, 2010, the Indian IT-BPO industry would grow at a CAGR (Compound Annual Growth Rate) of 25% and exports of about US $ 88.1 billion by 2011.

For the research this industry has been chosen because SMEs accounts for more than 15% of India's GDP (Gross Domestic Product), 35% or India's total exports, 95% of total industrial units, 40% of India's industrial output and provides

Table 1. Indian IT industry segmental revenue (2004-10) in US $ billion (NASSCOM)

Segments	FY04	FY05	FY06	FY07	FY08	FY09	FY10	FY11 (EST.)
IT services	10.4	13.5	17.8	23.7	31.0	35.2	39	47.1
IteS-BPO	3.4	5.2	7.2	9.5	12.5	14.8	14.1	17.3
Engineering services and R&D, software products	2.9	3.9	5.3	6.5	8.6	9.5	10	11.7
Total Software and services revenue	16.7	22.6	30.3	39.7	52.0	59.6	63.7	76.1
Hardware	5.0	5.9	7.0	8.2	12.0	12.1	9.4	12.0
Total IT industry	21.6	28.4	37.4	47.8	64.0	71.7	73.1	88.1

direct employment to 29.5 million people. In India IT SMEs are segmented in terms of turnover. 40% of the total companies from North operate with turnovers between less than Rs 10 mn upto Rs 50 mn respectively. 53% of the SMEs in the Southern region have turnovers in the range of Rs 10 – 50 mn. 50% companies in the Eastern region fall in the turnover range of less than Rs 10 mn. In the Western region, 55% companies fall in the bracket of Rs 10 – 50 mn. A major chunk of revenue for the Indian IT industry is earned from exports; however, a divergent trend is noticeable in the case of SMEs in this segment. IT SMEs obtain the maximum of their revenue (65%) from the domestic market with only 35% of revenue coming from exports. SMEs cannot fulfill their potential role because of the various bottleneck factors, which include resource endowments, economies of scale, demand conditions, market size, as well as availability of technology and suitable institutions.

The subsequent sections of research paper are structured so as to have a better understanding of the topic discussed. Section 2 on Research Objectives and Hypotheses describes the basic objectives of the study and four hypotheses are formulated to meet the objectives. A thorough description of the sample selected for the study and the methodology adopted for research has been given in Section 3, i.e., Research Methodology. It includes the type of industry, its products

and services and an overview of Questionnaire-cum-interview research methodology. Section 4 describes the complete analysis of the data which first ranks the important factors for the success of software projects and then frequency distribution and mean of the adoption of best practices of software development and quality initiatives taken by surveyed SMEs has been explained. Section 5 infers the result of the study and reference of all the research papers has been mentioned in Section 6.

2. RESEARCH OBJECTIVES AND HYPOTHESES

The objective of the study is to assess the

1. Awareness of importance of quality management initiatives in software developing SMEs.
2. Status of Six Sigma implementation in software developing SMEs the India.
3. Hindrance factors of implementation of Six Sigma in software developing SMEs in India

On the basis of empirical evidences conducted by previous researchers; and to meet the objectives the following hypotheses are formulated to test the key determinants and quality management initiatives in SMEs.

H1: There is general awareness of importance of product quality and quality management initiatives among software developing SMEs.

H2: Size of the software developing companies positively effects the implementation of Six Sigma as quality Management Initiative.

H3: Cost associated with the software projects has a positive influence on non-implementation of quality management initiatives in SMEs.

H4: Time constraint of software projects negatively effects implementation of quality Management initiatives in SMEs.

3. RESEARCH METHODOLOGY

The organizations selected for the study were Software SMEs of IT industry with head offices located in National Capital Region. Organizations were defined according to total annual turnover and number of employees. In each organization levels of associates, i.e., top level managers, middle level managers, and lower level associates were taken. Strategic level executives included IT professional also. The organizations were Software SMEs of IT industry with head offices located in National Capital Region. Organizations were defined according to total turnover and number of employees. Overall 23 companies participated in this study. Since all were IT companies, they were largely studied to understand the range of services offered by them, market (Domestic and International), diversification to verticals and turnover.

All the participant companies operate in software products besides a few operate in IT services, hardware and ITeS -BPO. It was mandatory for each participating company to offer software products to contribute in this study. Most of the participating companies cater to domestic market with few to international market also. The visibility of accreditation with quality certifications is varying in different companies.

Companies offer different products and services, among which custom application development is the most prevalent service. The participating companies vary in the verticals which include Banking & Financial Services, Manufacturing, Retail & Distribution, Media & Entertainment, Healthcare & Life Sciences, Construction & Infrastructure, Energy & Utilities, Government & Defence, Telecom, Logistics and Travel & Tourism. Table 2 show diversifications to verticals for all the participating companies. Broadly, Companies are into Information systems development with the essence of the IT services also.

Since questionnaire-cum-interview methodology was used for the survey, thus a questionnaire was designed. The questionnaire named Best Practices Questionnaire (BPQ) was designed on the basis of literature survey and input from academia. The questionnaire was first pre-tested on 22 management and IT professionals from the actual sample of respondents for checking its reliability (Cronbach's Alpha test was applied to check the reliability of the scale and the value of the coefficient was more than 0.7 in all the components of the questionnaire set thus indicating the goodness of scale measurement) and content

Table 2. Diversifications to verticals for all the participating SMEs (N=23)

S.No.	Diversification to Verticals	No. of Participating SMEs
1.	Banking & financial services	13
2.	Manufacturing	11
3.	Retail & distribution	11
4.	Health & life sciences	06
5.	Government & defence	09
6.	Media & entertainment	05
7.	Logistics	09
8.	Telecom	05
9.	Consumer goods	05

validity (On an average the questionnaire was found comprehensive and the topic of the research was found appropriate considering the importance of SMEs in current business environment).

4. FINDINGS FROM THE SURVEY

4.1. Success Factors of Software Projects

Developing software to meet functional needs with acceptable levels of quality, within budget, and on schedule, is a goal pursued by every software development organization. Many organizations are adopting the best practices in software development, such as those based on Capability Maturity Model (CMM) (Jalote, 2000), ISO 9001 (Paulk, 1995), or Six Sigma (Pyzdek, 2003). CMM has been one of the most popular efforts in enhancing software quality and reducing development costs (Harter, 2000; Wohlwend & Rosenbaum, 1994; Diaz & Sligo, 1997) McCormick's (2006) opinion summarizes the ideas brilliantly:

What's needed is not a single software methodology, but a rich toolkit of process patterns and 'methodology components' (deliverables, techniques, process flows, and so forth) along with guidelines for how to plug them together to customize a methodology for any given project.

In evaluating information systems effectiveness/ success, DeLone and McLean (1992) proposed a comprehensive software success model which was updated later in 2003. Their study on software success was considered very significant in contributing towards a universal model, which many researchers have employed when looking at the software performance. Attempts have also been made to validate their proposed model (Seddon & Kiew, 1994; Almutairie, 2001; Rai et al., 2002). Studies in software success had given little attention to the antecedent of the software success.

One important antecedent of software success is the product quality. It was envisaged that product quality contributes greatly to the software success of an organization.

Thus, individual responses have been analyzed so as to know the perception of the respondents about enlisted seventeen best practices of software development, as described in Figure 1. It must be emphasized that opinions expressed by the respondents regarding a factors' importance reflect their subjective views, based on their own experience and perception. The respondent experience regarding a particular factor could be either positive or negative.

Customer satisfaction, product quality and user satisfaction are ranked top three software related practices according to the average score. Then, organization level data was used to know the prevalence of these practices. The results are described as follows:

1. Identification of the important factors of software development projects.
2. Ranking the factors so as to know the most important factors.

The success factors considered are shown in Figure 1.

The seventeen factors, selected after literature review and discussion with the practitioners, were then ranked using the average score to know the most important and least significant factors and thus to find the factors for dependent variable. All he factors with average score and ranks have been give in Table 3.

Correlation between all the factors has been given in Table 7 in the Appendix. The study of the Table 3 reflects that

1. Customer requirements (4.158) and product quality (4.115) are the most important factors in developing software, ranked 1st and 2nd respectively. This strongly supports hypothesis H1.

Figure 1. Software development practices for software success

Table 3. Ranking of important factors for success of software projects as tested in selected 23 software SMEs (N=209)

Names of Factors	Average Score	Ranking
Customer requirements	4.158	1
Product Quality	4.115	2
End user Satisfaction	3.986	3
Skill of Team Members	3.933	4
User training	3.928	5
Customer interaction	3.880	6
Project cost	3.766	7
Documentation	3.756	8
Project team	3.727	9
Project deadlines	3.718	10
Development environment	3.689	11
Project management	3.675	12
Project scope	3.646	13
Development technique	3.622	14
Strategic planning	3.593	15
Project size	3.507	16
Project duration	3.469	17

2. End user satisfaction (3.989), skill of team members (3.933), user training (3.928), and customer interaction (3.880) come next in ranking with almost same average score.

3. Documentation (rank 8) is as important and ranked as project cost (rank 7) and project deadlines (rank 10).

4. Project size and duration have less significance as compared to other factors (rank 16 and 17).

5. Development technique and Strategic planning have comparatively low importance (rank 14 and 15) than development environment, project management and scope (rank 11-13).

The ranking of the software development practices reveal that the practices listed in Table 3 are important at low or high level as depicted. 80- 90% of the respondents feel that these software-related practices are important for the success of software projects.

The study of perception of software developing practices depicts that the software practices which have been emerged important after literature review, are significant to the software developing professionals in SMEs. All software related practices are vital to the success and there is universal awareness of significance of these practices across the organizations under study which carry further hypothesis H1.

The data was then analyzed to evaluate the prevalence of the software related practices in selected SMEs. Table 4 summarizes the descriptive findings of adoption of software related best practices.

It is quite evident from the score of 3.52 shows that 87% organization use non-procedural of sometimes procedural method of the project management activity where 91% SMEs on an average have project duration between six to twelve months, average project cost of 10 to 20 lacs, with 10 to 20 developers per project handling 50 to 100 KLOC(Kilo Lines of Code) complex projects.

Nearly 50% of the surveyed SMEs moderately understand customer needs which are the most important emerged factor of software success. 61% SMEs moderately change the chosen technology with controlled user resistance. However project team skills are somewhat between moderate to fairly high.

Deadlines are very vital to any project, but almost all the surveyed organizations have low to fairly low realistic deadlines of software projects as given in Table 4. 40 to 60% quality certification is done in 39% SMEs whereas 61% SMEs go for up to 40% quality certification; which indicates a low adoption of quality initiatives in software projects and holds up H2. From the analysis, it was found that 26.1% of the participating SMEs do not have implemented any kind of quality management initiative and there is non- existence of quality management department even. It has been observed that the poor adoption of quality management initiatives in SMEs is due to many complex reasons, besides the barriers of cost, time (Yusof & Aspinwall, 1999; Thomas & Webb, 2003; Antony et al., 2008). As per the discussion with the software professional in surveyed SMEs it is inferred that

Table 4. Frequency distribution with mean for adoption of best practices of software in SMEs (N=23)

Adoption of Software Practices	1	2	3	4	5	Average Score
Project management activity		2	8	12	1	3.52
Average project duration	8	13	2			1.74
Average project size	15	6	2			1.43
Average allocated project cost	13	9	1			1.48
Average complexity	6	11	5		1	2.13
Understand customer needs			12	7	4	3.65
Change in chosen technology		3	14	6		3.13
Project team sills		1	14	6	2	3.39
Defined scope of the project	1	2	12	7	1	3.22
Defined business needs			10	9	4	3.74
Realistic deadlines	9	10	4			1.78
Sponsorship defined		9	11	3		2.74
Quality certification	4	10	9			2.22
Rework on projects	8	11	2	2		1.91
Repeat order from same customer	6	11	5	1		2.04
Project track progress	4	11	4	4		2.35

(1=<10%;2=11-40%;3=41-60%;4=61-80%;5=>80%)

- Due to lack of knowledge, SMEs are not clear about the advantages that best practices of software development can accrue and thus contribute to the success or otherwise of software.
- SMEs adopt those practices that are sufficient to meet their business needs and thus do not focus on long term quality of softwares.
- SMEs do not want to indulge in lots of statistics pertaining to software engineering practices.

4.2. Quality Management Initiatives

The paramount target of any software developing organization is to produce high-quality software within a stipulated time period. Correctness, maintainability, integrity and usability are the measures of quality whereas quality assurance is the measure of effectiveness and completeness of quality control activities. Today, Six Sigma is the most widely used statistical quality assurance besides SEICMM in the industry which improves organizational performance by identifying and eliminating defects.

ISO9001-2000 is the quality assurance standard that applies to software engineering that helps organizations to ensure their products and services satisfy customer expectations by meeting their specifications.

Table 5 depicts that SMEs do not practice SEICMM or Six Sigma as quality management initiative. Instead some local method of quality assurance is practiced by almost 50% of the organizations. 30% SMEs use ISO 9001:2000 standard and 26% SMEs not at all use any quality management initiatives, thus supporting *H2*. Such a scenario is not acceptable in today's business environment.

4.2.1. Hindrance Factors of Implementation of Six Sigma as Quality Management Initiatives in SMEs

The results of the analysis show that about 43.4% of the responding firms stated that cost issue was one of the hindrance factors to the implementation of Six Sigma as a quality management initiative in participating software developing SMEs as stated in hypothesis H3. Financial resources are the most common barrier of implementation of quality management initiative in SMEs as cited in literature. This was followed by lack of time due to project deadlines H4, lack of knowledge if Six Sigma is applicable to software projects. Further ISO is an accepted standard for and most prevalent quality management practice in SMEs and it is misunderstood that Six Sigma is appropriate for only large sized enterprises as depicted in Table 6.

Table 5. Frequency distribution for quality management initiatives of software projects in SMEs (N=23)

Quality Management Initiatives	Participating SMEs (N=23) Percentage
Six Sigma	0
SEICMM(SEICMMI)	0
ISO9001:2000	30.4
Others(Informal)	43.5
No initiatives	26.1

Table 6. Hindrance factors of implementation of Six Sigma in SMEs

Hindrance Factors of implementation of Six Sigma	Participating SMEs in % Age (N=23)
Cost issue	43.4
ISO is accepted	13.0
Lack of applicability knowledge	08.7
Project deadlines(Time issue)	26.1
Appropriate for large sized enterprises	08.7

Thus it is strongly recommended that SMEs must organize training programs for their employees at all levels to impart knowledge so as they can implement best quality management initiatives for software development. The training programs should be so designed that emphasize on sensitization of the employees first and then on the software development practices. In other words, a mini and simplified version of Software Engineering should be prepared so as to suit the needs of SMEs and softwares effectiveness.

5. CONCLUSION

Six Sigma as a quality management initiative has advanced in large sized organizations but its implementation is still to be materialized in SMEs as depicted from the survey results. There are, in fact, very few studies which have been carried out to explore the realization of quality management initiatives. Majority of the SMEs as compared to large organizations resist having a quality department and quality management practices in the organizations. The reason may be attributed to scarcity of resources and project deadlines. The analysis of the survey findings revealed non-implementation of quality management initiatives despite of the general awareness of importance of these initiatives. Any quality initiative should also be linked to its long term benefit in terms of operational and strategic performance of SMEs. There is significant difference in benefits of Six Sigma and ISO standards irrespective of the size of the firm. This research focuses only on software developing SMEs in NCR of India limiting its generalizability manufacturing SMEs and also excludes micro enterprises, limiting the generalizability of the findings. Future study should focus on performing a universal survey on quality management initiatives in SMEs and understand the effect of implementation of Six Sigma in on performance SMEs.

REFERENCES

Antony, J., Kumar, M., & Labib, A. (2008). Gearing Six Sigma into UK Manufacturing SMEs: An empirical assessment of critical success factors, impediments, and viewpoints of Six Sigma implementation in SMEs. *The Journal of the Operational Research Society, 59*(4), 482–493. doi:10.1057/palgrave.jors.2602437

Antony, J., Kumar, M., & Madu, C. N. (2005). Six Sigma in small and medium sized UK manufacturing enterprises: some empirical observations. *International Journal of Quality & Reliability Management, 22*(8), 860–874. doi:10.1108/02656710510617265

Atkinson, R. (1999). Project management: Cost, time and quality, two best guesses and a phenomenon. *International Journal of Project Management, 17*(6), 337–342. doi:10.1016/S0263-7863(98)00069-6

Brue, G. (2006). *Six Sigma for small business*. Madison, WI: CWL Publishing Enterprises.

Caralli, R. A. (2004). *The critical success factor method: establishing a foundation for enterprise security management* (Tech. Rep. No. CMU/SEI-2004-TR-010). Pittsburgh, PA: Carnegie Mellon University.

Daniel, R. H. (1961). Management data crisis. *Harvard Business Review*, 111–112.

Easterby-Smith, M., Thorpe, R., & Lowe, A. (2003). *Management research – An introduction*. London, UK: Sage.

Fowler, F. J. (2002). *Survey research methods* (3rd ed.). London, UK: Sage.

Gome, A. (1996). Total quality madness. *Business Review Weekly, 18*, 38–44.

Harter, D. E., & Slaughter, S. A. (2003). Quality improvement and infrastructure activity costs in software development: A longitudinal analysis. *Management Science, 49*, 784–800. doi:10.1287/mnsc.49.6.784.16023

Husband, S. G., & Mandal, P. (1999). A conceptual model for quality integrated management in small and medium size enterprises. *International Journal of Quality & Reliability Management, 16*(7), 699–713. doi:10.1108/02656719910286215

Kerlinger, F. N. (1986). Survey research. In Kerlinger, F. N. (Ed.), *Foundations of behavioural research in education*. New York, NY: Holt, Rinehart, and Winston.

Kumar, M. (2007). Critical success factors and hurdles to Six Sigma implementation: The case of a UK manufacturing SME. *International Journal of Six Sigma and Competitive Advantage, 3*(4), 333–351. doi:10.1504/IJSSCA.2007.017176

Kumar, M., & Antony, J. (2008, June 25-27). *Comparing the quality management practices between six sigma and ISO certified SMEs – a survey based approach.* Paper presented at the 13th International Conference on Productivity and Quality Research, Oulu, Finland.

Kumar, M., Antony, J., Singh, R. K., Tiwari, M. K., & Perry, D. (2006). Implementing the lean sigma framework in an Indian SME: A case study. *Production Planning and Control, 17*(4), 407–423. doi:10.1080/09537280500483350

Lee, G. L., & Oakes, I. (1995). The pros and cons of TQM for smaller forms in manufacturing: some experiences down the supply chain. *Total Quality Management Magazine, 6*, 413–426. doi:10.1080/09544129550035341

Lin Yeb-Yun, C. (1999). Success factors of small and medium-sized enterprises in Taiwan: An analysis of cases. *Journal of Small Business Management, 36*(4), 43–56.

Macmanus, J., & Wood-Harper, T. (2007). Software engineering: A quality management perspective. *Total Quality Management Magazine, 19*(4), 315–327.

Snee, R. D. (2004). Six Sigma: the evolution of 100 years of business improvement methodology. *International Journal of Six Sigma and Competitive Advantage, 1*(1), 4–20. doi:10.1504/IJSSCA.2004.005274

Thomas, A. J., & Webb, D. (2003). Quality systems implementation in Welsh small-to-medium-sized enterprises: a global comparison and a model for change. *Journal of Engineering Manufacture, 217*, 573–579. doi:10.1243/095440503321628251

Van der Weile, T., & Brown, A. (1998). Venturing down the TQM path for SME's. *International Small Business Journal, 16*(2), 50–68. doi:10.1177/0266242698162003

Wessel, G., & Burcher, P. (2004). Six Sigma for small and medium-sized enterprises. *Total Quality Management Magazine, 16*(4), 264–272.

ENDNOTES

[1] F1- Strategic planning, F2- Development Technique F3- Project Size F4- Project Duration F5- Project Cost F6- Project Management F7- Project Scope F8- Project Team F9- Skill of team members F10- Development environment F11- Project deadlines F12- Customer interaction F13- Customer requirements F14- End user satisfaction F15- Product Quality F16- User Training F17- Documentation

APPENDIX

Table 7. Correlation between components of important factors[1] of IS project

	F1	F2	F3	F4	F5	F6	F7	F8	F9	F10	F11	F12	F13	F14	F15	F16	F17
F1	1																
F2	.604**	1															
F3	.036	.327**	1														
F4	.149(*)	.303**	.678**	1													
F5	.366**	.350**	.293**	.435**	1												
F6	.177(*)	.365**	.221**	.374**	.703**	1											
F7	.430**	.296**	.105	.467**	.523**	.357**	1										
F8	.267**	.130	.196**	.265**	.563**	.498**	.530**	1									
F9	.264**	.325**	.252**	.224**	.469**	.427**	.493**	.736**	1								
F10	.321**	.053	.177(*)	.386**	.426**	.091	.576**	.487**	.362**	1							
F11	.057	.042	.127	.300**	.508**	.421**	.410**	.515**	.489**	.541**	1						
F12	.090	.137(*)	.126	.233**	.199**	.234**	.367**	.364**	.238**	.334**	.480**	1					
F13	.246**	.087	.184**	.177(*)	.324**	.071	.354**	.331**	.298**	.503**	.413**	.577**	1				
F14	.179**	.195**	.138(*)	.193**	.536**	.366**	.381**	.636**	.660**	.444**	.502**	.416**	.507**	1			
F15	.276**	.221**	.105	.191**	.604**	.338**	.497**	.600**	.608**	.519**	.552**	.433**	.598**	.831**	1		
F16	.275**	.272**	.243**	.370**	.506**	.294**	.609**	.606**	.628**	.560**	.565**	.415**	.439**	.676**	.680**	1	
F17	.117	.183**	.273**	.329**	.459**	.281**	.459**	.571**	.594**	.418**	.523**	.426**	.499**	.664**	.702**	.805**	1

**Significant at 0.01 Level
*Significant at 0.05 Level

This journal was previously published in the International Journal of Technology Diffusion, Volume 2, Issue 4, edited by Ali Hussein Saleh Zolait, pp. 1-11, copyright 2011 by IGI Publishing (an imprint of IGI Global).

Section 4
Database and Algorithms Applications

Chapter 14
Using OCL to Model Constraints in Data Warehouses

François Pinet
Cemagref - Clermont Ferrand, France

Gil De Sousa
Cemagref - Clermont Ferrand, France

Myoung-Ah Kang
LIMOS, France

Catherine Roussey
Cemagref - Clermont Ferrand, France

Kamal Boulil
Cemagref - Clermont Ferrand, France

Michel Schneider
LIMOS, France

Sandro Bimonte
Cemagref - Clermont Ferrand, France

Jean-Pierre Chanet
Cemagref - Clermont Ferrand, France

ABSTRACT

Recent research works propose using Object-Oriented (OO) approaches, such as UML to model data warehouses. This paper overviews these recent OO techniques, describing the facts and different analysis dimensions of the data. The authors propose a tutorial of the Object Constraint Language (OCL) and show how this language can be used to specify constraints in OO-based models of data warehouses. Previously, OCL has been only applied to describe constraints in software applications and transactional databases. As such, the authors demonstrate in this paper how to use OCL to represent the different types of data warehouse constraints. This paper helps researchers working in the fields of business intelligence and decision support systems, who wish to learn about the major possibilities that OCL offer in the context of data warehouses. The authors also provide general information about the possible types of implementation of multi-dimensional models and their constraints.

1. INTRODUCTION

Along with the development of new information and communication technologies, we have seen an increase in data. In order to analyze the data issued from different sources, it is needed to use tools to integrate this information. Data warehouses are a specific type of database that serves to integrate and analyze data from various sources (Calì, Lembo, Lenzerini, & Rosati, 2003). Information stored in different databases can be group together in a data warehouse for combined analysis. De-

DOI: 10.4018/978-1-4666-2791-8.ch014

pending on their requirements, one can load data every week, every month, every year or even less frequently. These data are usually organized in a form that speeds up calculation of indicators. The indicators are made up of aggregated information obtained by aggregation functions such as sum, average, variance, etc. Using data warehouses is therefore important within a decision-making context. For example, a data warehouse containing economic, urban and environmental information will help decision-makers find the best place to establish a new infrastructure. The concept of the data warehouse has great potential for assessing the impact of actions, practices, scenarios and programs (Bimonte, 2010; Mahboubi, Bimonte, Faure, & Pinet, 2010; Nilakanta, Scheibe, & Rai, 2008; Schneider, 2008; Schulze, Spilke, & Lehner, 2007).

We present an example issued from (Trujillo, Palomar, Gomez, & Song, 2001). The *facts* of a data warehouse are the information to analyze (Malinowski & Zimanyi, 2008a). In the example, we consider the facts of the data warehouse to be the product sales of a company in Euros. Each of the company's stores provides these data. In a data warehouse, an analysis results from the use of an aggregation operation (e.g., sum or average) on the facts. In the example, the value of the facts (i.e., the sales) to analyze is the amount of sales. This value is called the *measure*. A possible analysis is the sum of sales calculated by category of product, by store and by month. The result of this analysis can be represented in a cube (Trujillo et al., 2001) (Figure 1). Each dimension of the cube corresponds to a criterion of analysis: type of products, store and month. The cells of the cube are the indicators. They store the sums of sales for each tuple <type of products, store, month>. For instance, in Figure 1, the sum of sales for the tuple <Water, Store 1, December> is 4. In data warehouses, the criteria of analysis are structured in hierarchies called *dimensions*. Figure 2 shows the three dimensions presented by Trujillo et al. (2001). A data warehouse can produce many analyses by combining different levels of dimensions. For example, other cubes could be calculated:

- Sums of sales by city,
- Sums of sales by brand, by city, by year,
- Sums of sales by type, by state, by season, etc.

Note that data warehouses generally support *n*-dimensional cubes. Data can be combined to provide previously unknown causal links. To do so, users can visualize cubes from the data warehouse using tools like OLAP (On-line Analytical Pro-

Figure 1. Example of a data warehouse - cube storing sales by category of products, by store and by month

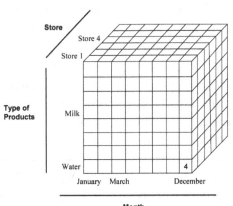

Figure 2. Example of a data warehouse - analysis dimensions

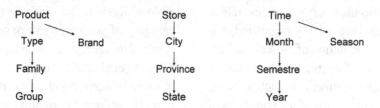

cessing) (Malinowski & Zimanyi, 2006, 2008a). Causal links can also be discerned automatically with data-mining algorithms (Berson & Smith, 1997).

Multi-dimensional models aim to describe the facts and the different analysis dimensions of a data warehouse (Malinowski & Zimanyi, 2008a). Some articles have presented specific methods for formalizing multi-dimensional models. Recent research works propose to use Object-Oriented (OO) approaches such as UML[1] to design data warehouses. Section 2 will briefly overview these recent techniques. We will show that they can help system designers to build a data warehouse model. Section 3 will introduce the Object Constraint Language (OCL) of UML. Until now, this language has been mainly used to model invariant conditions in software and traditional databases (e.g., transactional databases) (Demuth, 2005; Demuth & Hussmann, 1999; Demuth, Hussmann, & Loecher, 2001; Demuth, Loecher, & Zschaler, 2004). The main contribution of this paper (Section 3) is to offer an OCL tutorial and to demonstrate that OCL can be also used to model constraints in multi-dimensional models described in UML. The principal bibliographic references on the subject will be provided here. This article is addressed to researchers working in the fields of business intelligence and decision support systems, who wish to learn about the major possibilities that OCL offer in the context of data warehouse, and to find citations that will allow them to learn about this formalism in greater detail. Section 5 will provide also general information about the possible types of implementation of multi-dimensional models and their OCL constraints.

2. OBJECT-ORIENTED APPROACH FOR DATA WAREHOUSE MODELING

The object paradigm was first popularized through OO programming, then, to a further extent, by formalisms of OO modeling. Alan Kay (winner of the 2003 Turing Award) is considered the father of the OO programming approach. In the early 1990s, several modeling formalisms based on the OO paradigm began to develop; e.g., OMT - Object-Modeling Technique (Rumbaugh, Balaha, Premerlani, Eddy, & Lorensen, 1991) and OOA - Object-Oriented Analysis (Coad & Yourdon, 1991). Unified Modeling Language (UML) would emerge in the second half of the 1990s as the standard for OO modeling (OMG, 2009). In OO, the real world is modeled in terms of object classes. Object classes are linked by associations. An object can encapsulate both data (attributes) and behavior (operations). Unlike in the traditional ER (Entity-Relationship) formalism, the instances (objects) have a unique identity independent of the values of their attributes. Classes of objects can be linked by relationships of generalization / specialization. UML offers modelers the opportunity to use different types of diagrams (e.g., class diagrams, use case, states, and sequence) (Booch, Rumbaugh, & Jacobson, 1999; OMG, 2009).

Several authors have proposed object oriented multi-dimensional models, some of them being based on an extension of UML. Methods very similar, based on ER paradigm can be also found.

The models of Herden (2000), Nguyen, Tjoa, and Wagner (2000), Prat, Akoka, and Comyn-Wattiau (2006), and Trujillo and Palomar (1998) are basic models which incorporate and formalize essential multi-dimensional concepts (fact, dimension, measures, etc.) and offer a number of specific features. The work of Trujillo and Palomar (1998) introduces the notion of cube classes with a set of possible operations to define the analysis. In Herden (2000), a fact class can be aggregated from several others fact classes. A UML profile is suggested. It can be manipulated through an extension of the CASE Tool Rational Rose. The models of Abelló, Samos, and Saltor (2006) and Lujan-Mora, Trujillo, and Song (2006) are much more sophisticated. In Abelló et al. (2006), there are 6 types of nodes in the multidimensional graph. Various types of associations are available. It is possible to change the dimensions of a cube. In Lujan-Mora et al. (2006), typical multidimensional structures are defined through packages. Fourteen stereotypes are suggested for packages, classes, associations and attributes. Each of these two models is supported by a specific UML profile implemented in Eclipse IDE. The correct use of this profile is controlled through the definition of constraints expressed using the Object Constraint Language (OCL). Concerning the design and the implementation of multidimensional systems, various propositions have been made depending on a given context or platform. In Hahn, Sapia, and Blaschka (2000) an environment is suggested which is able to generate the implementation of a star or snowflake multidimensional structure from a conceptual schema. The generation process takes into account the limitations of the OLAP target system (Cognos Powerplay or Informix Metacube). The work of Moody and Kortink (2000) also suggests a method for developing dimensional models from ER schemas. Different options for the resulting schema can be chosen (flat, star, snowflake, constellation). In Prat et al. (2006), a multidimensional structure is derived from a UML schema. The work of Theodoratos, Ligoudistianos and Sellis (2001) addresses the problem of integrating the data from heterogeneous databases and storing it in the repository of the multidimensional structure. In this work, the multidimensional structure is seen as a set of materialized views. So the problem becomes one

of view selection. Different algorithms are proposed and compared for solving it. The work of Mazon and Trujillo (2008) describes how to align the whole data warehouse development process with a Model Driven Architecture framework.

Some proposals of formalization have been introduced to model spatial data warehouses i.e., warehouses that store geo-referenced information (Malinowski & Zimányi, 2008b; Pestana, da Silva, & Bedard, 2005). Several uses of spatial data warehouse are evocated (Bernier, Gosselin, Badard, & Bédard, 2009; Bimonte, 2010; Julien & Rivest, 2009; McHugh, Roche, & Bédard, 2009; Sboui, Salehi, & Bédard, 2010). This type of data warehouses allows displaying the calculated indicators on maps.

3. OCL FOR MODELING DATA WAREHOUSES

The contribution of the present paper is to propose an OCL tutorial (Section 3.1) and to show that OCL can be easily used to model constraints in UML-based multi-dimensional models (Section 3.2).

3.1. OCL Overview

OCL (Object Constraint Language) is a formal language for the expression of constraints applied to UML diagrams (OMG, 2007; Warmer & Kleppe, 1999). It is now an integral part of the UML standard. It is a declarative language: it specifies the conditions that must be met. It is a language without side effects: the assessment of a constraint does not change the state of the system. OCL was designed to be within the reach of information system engineers and designers. The language was developed by a group of IBM scientists around 1995 during a company modeling project. The language has been influenced by Syntropy, an object-orientated language (Cook & Daniels, 1994). An increasing number of information systems designers use this constraint language to complement UML class diagrams to express the invariants of the models for example. In Mandel and Cengarle (1999) and Akehurst and Bordbar, (2001), the possibilities of OCL are studied to express queries; in these articles, the expressivity of the language as a query language is therefore studied. The authors show that by considering the notion of tuples in OCL, the language can support relational algebra. An increasing number of tools use OCL. Nowadays specific plugins are available for Eclipse, Rational Rose and ArgoUML etc. (Klasse Objecten, 2009). Within the context of databases, OCL constraints are modelled at the conceptual level (on the conceptual schema), which massively simplifies their expression.

Here we introduce the general concepts of the OCL language using examples. A constraint may relate to a class (called the constraint context). This paper presents the concept of "invariant" type constraints, which must be met for any class instance. The following examples are based on the UML class diagram in Figure 3. This diagram describes a part of a transactional database.

The following OCL constraint expresses the fact that all employees in the current position of researcher receive a salary of € 2500 or above.

```
context Employee inv:
self.current_position = 'researcher'
implies
self.salary >= 2500
```

This OCL constraint is equivalent to the following (pseudo-)logical formula:

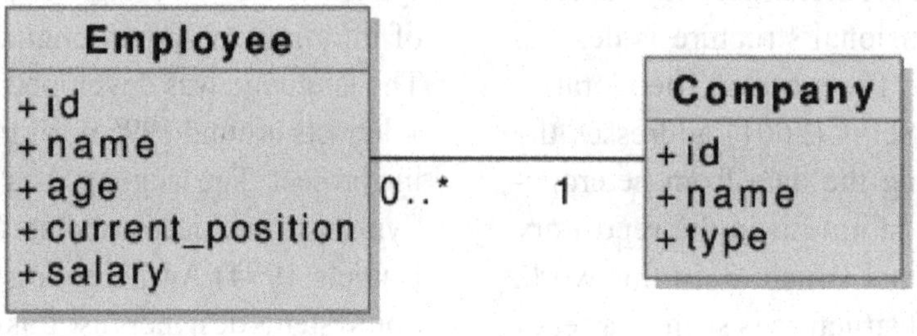

$\forall \text{self} \in \text{Employee (self.current\_position = 're-searcher'} \rightarrow \text{self.salary} >= 2500)$

In OCL, *self* is always an iterator variable which corresponds to a context instance (here the context is the class *Employee*). A constraint must be obeyed for any context instance. The operator *implies* corresponds to the logical implication.

Navigation Among the Classes

Navigation allows constraints to be set which involve different class objects. For example, the following constraint means that small and medium sized enterprises (SMEs) have no more than 499 employees.

```
context Company inv:
self.type = 'SME'
implies
self.Employee->size() <= 499
```

This OCL constraint is equivalent to the following logical formula:

$\forall \text{self} \in \text{Company (self.type = 'SME'} \rightarrow \text{size(self.Employee)} <= 499)$

The attribute *type* is in the *Company* class, and the number of employees is obtained from the instances of the *Employee* class. Navigation is therefore performed between these two classes via the association. Here, *self* corresponds to a

Figure 3. Companies and their staff

company, and *self.Employee* returns a collection containing all the staff of the company *self*. The operation *size()* returns the size of a collection (i.e., the number of objects comprising it).

Operations on the Elements of a Collection

The syntax of an operation relating to the elements of a collection is the following presented in Box 1.where the Boolean expression ⟨expression⟩ is assessed for each of the elements of the ⟨collection⟩. ⟨iterator⟩ is an optional variable which refers to the common element in the ⟨expression⟩. ⟨operation⟩ can be one of the following operations (among others):

1. *forall* represents the universal quantifier which indicates that the Boolean expression must be true for all of the ⟨collection⟩ instances. For example, the fact that all research centre staff are aged at least 18 can be specified.

```
context Company inv:
self.type = 'research centre' implies
self.Employee ->forAll(age>=18)
```

If we represent the constraint in a logical form, we obtain the following:

∀self ∈ Company

(self.type = 'research centre' →

(∀x ∈ self.Employee (x.age>=18)))

2. *exists* represents the existential quantifier which indicates that the Boolean expression must be true for at least an element of ⟨collection⟩. For example, the fact that there is (one or) several researchers in a research centre can be expressed as demonstrated in Box 2.

In a logical form:

∀self ∈ Company

(self.type = 'research centre' →

(∃x ∈ self.Employee | x.current_position='researcher'))

3. *size* returns the number of elements (i.e., the number of objects) of a collection;
4. *select* returns a sub-ensemble of ⟨collection⟩ which only contains elements which verify the ⟨expression⟩. For example, it can be used in a constraint to select staff over 18 by indicating:

```
self.Employee->select(age>=18)
```

allInstances is used to return all the instances in a class. *Employee.allInstances()* returns for example a collection of all the instances of *Employee*. There are a great many other operations applicable to OCL collections (OMG, 2007).

Box 1.

```
⟨collection⟩ -> ⟨operation⟩ ([⟨iterator⟩ |] ⟨expression⟩)
```

Box 2.

```
context Company inv:
self.type = 'research centre' implies
self.Employee->exists(current_position='researcher')
```

3.2. Use of OCL in Multidimensional Models

The main contribution of this section is to demonstrate that OCL can be also used to model constraints in multi-dimensional schemas described in UML. In this section, we present several examples of different types of OCL constraints in a pedagogic manner. All constraints are based on the multidimensional model "Sales" of Figure 4 (represented in UML). It is related to the example introduced in Section 1. The data warehouse allows calculate the sum of sales amount along the different dimensions.

In the present paper, we provide examples of conditions on facts, between facts, on members, between members, about exhaustiveness, and aggregation operations. In the field of data warehouses, a finer classification of OCL constraints

can be found in Boulil, Bimonte, Mahboubi, and Pinet (2010). Note that in our examples, the proposed constraint categories are not necessarily mutually exclusive; in other words, a constraint can be included in several categories.

a) Constraints on Each Fact

This category of constraints aims at controlling the value of each fact. The next constraint indicates that a sale is always greater than zero.

```
context Sales inv:
self.amount > 0
```

The prices of dairy products are usually always less than 50 Euros, as demonstrated in Box 3.

Figure 4. Multidimensional model "Sales"

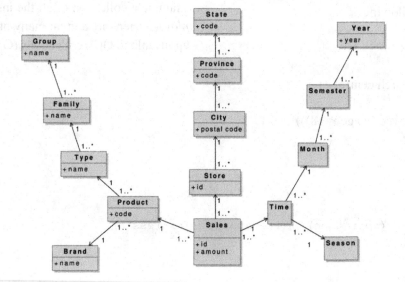

Box 3.

```
context Sales inv:
self.Product.Type.Family.name = 'dairy product'
implies
self.amount < 50
```

b) Constraints Between Facts

These constraints involve two facts or more. This following OCL expression presented in Box 4 allows checking the uniqueness of the fact id.

c) Constraints on Each Member

In the same way of constraints on facts, we now show examples of conditions on members. We indicate that the years included in the data warehouse are all greater than 2000.

```
context Year inv:
self.year >= 2000
```

d) Constraints Between Members

Each product code should be unique, as demonstrated in Box 5.

The next OCL expression indicates that different levels of the dimension "Product" has a member called "Other". All these members are associated.

```
context Product inv:
Product.allInstances()->exists(x|
```

x.Type.name = 'Other' and

x.Type.Family.name = 'Other' and

x.Type.Family.Group.name = 'Other' and

x.Brand.name = 'Other')

e) Exhaustiveness Constraints

These constraints allow checking if all the intended data are stored. For instance, suppose that the only state stored in the data warehouse is "Metropolitan France". In this case, the "Province"

Box 4.

```
context Sales inv:
Sales.allInstances()->forAll(x | x.id <> self.id)
```

Box 5.

```
context Product inv:
Sales.allInstances()->forAll(x | x.code <> self.code)
```

class stores only the administrative departments of Metropolitan France; there are 96 departments. The following OCL presented in Box 6 expression checks if the class contains all the departments.

The first line of the constraint allows indicating the range of values. The second line models that province codes are unique.

f) Constraints on Aggregations

Suppose that the "State" class has an additional attribute called "sum_per_state". This attribute is used to store the pre-calculated sum of sales per state. It is used to improve the performance of the queries. The next constraint defines how this sum is calculated, presented in Box 7.

4. IMPLEMENTATION

4.1. Implementing the Multidimensional Model

Information from the data warehouses are examined interactively using OLAP tools - On-line Analytical Process (Malinowski & Zimányi, 2008b). Among other things, these allow you to view the results of different analyses by selecting the levels of the dimensions required, or by limiting the members involved in an analysis. In some cases, the main results are calculated once and once only; they are usually stored "permanently" directly in the data warehouse, enabling very fast access when examining data.

The main types of OLAP tools are:

- **Relational Olaps (ROLAP):** A ROLAP tool accesses data from the data warehouse which are stored in a relational database. Using this approach, the multidimensional model needs to be converted to a relational model. The two types of relational implementation which are most used are the star schema and the snowflake schema.

- **Multidimensional Olaps:** A MOLAP tool accesses data stored in the form of cubes with n-dimensions which combine the different levels of analysis.

- **Hybrid Olaps (HOLAP):** A HOLAP tool accesses data stored in relational databases and in cubes with n-dimensions.

OLAP tools enable users to carry out specific requests. The results of these requests can be shown in cube form only storing selected data.

OCL provides a platform-independent and generic method to model constraints. It can be interpreted by code engines/compilers to generate code automatically. Some tools allow producing integrity checking mechanisms in different languages (Java, C#, SQL, etc.) from specifications of constraints expressed in OCL (Klasse Objecten, 2009). For instance, OCL2SQL can generate SQL code from OCL constraints (Demuth & Hussmann, 1999; Demuth et al., 2001, 2004); Structured Query Language (SQL) is a language that provides an interface to database systems. The code produced by OCL2SQL can be used to check if a database verifies the constraints or to forbid inserting data that do not verify a constraint; see Demuth and Hussmann (1999) and Demuth et al. (2001) for details. The authors of Boulil et

Box 6.

```
context Province inv:
self.code >= 1 and self.code <= 96 and
Province.allInstances()->forAll(x | x.id <> self.code)
```

Box 7.

```
context State inv:
self.sum_per_state =
self.Province.City.Store.Sales.amount->sum()
```

al. (2010) use OCL2SQL to generate code in the context of data warehouses.

Other implementations of OCL are available (Klasse Objecten, 2009): Octopus, which generates Java expressions based on pre- and post-conditions, Bold for Delphi which can generate SQL code, etc.

4.2. Decision Support Systems

OLAP tools can assist in the decision-making process. Decision-makers can examine the different analyses supplied by the data warehouse to get a complete panorama of the situation. Integrating sources of different data should be able to serve as an aid to decision-making and optimization. The spatial dimension is often important for many decisions: finding a place for installing infrastructures, choosing the best products to sell, optimizing the organization of a company with regard to time and space etc. Data from cubes can be used by optimization algorithms. For example, using environmental data warehouse, it is possible to look for the best positions for a new infrastructure by trying to avoid, to as great a degree as possible, pollution associated with spreading some materials. In addition, this decision may be made by integrating other constraints (surroundings, pollution, etc.). This will mean that other information will need to be integrated within the data warehouse. Similarly, using data from certain cubes, it will be possible to optimize a product delivery service of company by determining precisely how the different operations are organized over time by this service.

Data mining algorithms can be used in data warehouses, still with a view to improving data analysis. By combining data from different sources, it is possible to show the correlations between objects dealt with; for example, show the links between a type of industrial installation and disease. The results of these algorithms can then be stored and shown to decision-makers with the rest of the information from the data warehouse. Summary publications about data mining applied to data warehouses are available (Berson & Smith, 1997).

5. CONCLUSION

Multi-dimensional models allow describing the facts and the different analysis dimensions of a data warehouse (Malinowski & Zimanyi, 2008a). In this paper, we provide a survey of the techniques for object-oriented design of multi-dimensional models. We show that they can help system designers to build a data warehouse model and we present a complementary language called OCL. Until now, OCL has been mainly used to model invariant in software and traditional databases (Demuth, 2005; Demuth & Hussmann, 1999; Demuth et al., 2001, 2004). In this paper, we offer an OCL tutorial and show how OCL can be also used in multi-dimensional models described in UML. The principal bibliographic references on the subject are provided here. This article is addressed to researchers working in the fields of business intelligence and decision support systems, who wish to learn about the major possibilities that OCL offer in the context of data warehouse and to find citations that will allow them to learn about this formalism in greater detail. We also provide the general possible implementation of multi-dimensional models and their OCL constraints.

OCL could be also considered with the Model Driven Architecture (MDA) (Kleppe, Warmer, & Bast, 2003; Mazon & Trujillo, 2008). In practice, no real MDA approach including OCL has been implemented for data warehouse. In this technique, the conceptual multi-dimensional models need to be transformed into different logical schemas and physical schemas. At each transformation step, the OCL constraints of models need also to be converted (from a conceptual representation to a physical representation). We hope that new research works will allow using this approach in the future.

REFERENCES

Abelló, A., Samos, J., & Saltor, F. (2006). YAM2: A multidimensional conceptual model extending UML. *Information Systems*, *31*(6), 541–567. doi:10.1016/j.is.2004.12.002

Akehurst, D. H., & Bordbar, B. (2001). On querying UML data models with OCL. In *Proceedings of the 4th International Conference on the Unified Modeling Language, Modeling Languages, Concepts, and Tools*.

Bernier, E., Gosselin, P., Badard, T., & Bédard, Y. (2009). Easier surveillance of climate-related health vulnerabilities through a web-based spatial olap application. *International Journal of Health Geographics*, *8*(18).

Berson, A., & Smith, S. (1997). *Data warehousing, data mining, and OLAP (data warehousing/data management)*. New York, NY: McGraw-Hill.

Bimonte, S. (2010). A web-based tool for spatio-multidimensional analysis of geographic and complex data. *International Journal of Agricultural and Environmental Information Systems*, *1*(2). doi:10.4018/jaeis.2010070103

Booch, G., Rumbaugh, J., & Jacobson, I. (1999). *The unified modeling language user guide*. Reading, MA: Addison-Wesley.

Boulil, K., Bimonte, S., Mahboubi, H., & Pinet, F. (2010). Vers la définition des contraintes d'intégrité d'entrepôts de données spatiales avec OCL. *Revue des Nouvelles Technologies de l'Information*, *B6*, 121–136.

Calì, A., Lembo, D., Lenzerini, M., & Rosati, R. (2003). Source integration for data warehousing. In *Proceedings of the Conference on Multidimensional Databases: Problems and Solutions* (pp. 361-392).

Coad, P., & Yourdon, E. (1991). *Object-oriented analysis*. Upper Saddle River, NJ: Prentice Hall.

Cook, S., & Daniels, J. (1994). *Designing object systems-object oriented modeling with syntropy*. Upper Saddle River, NJ: Prentice Hall.

Demuth, B. (2005). *The Dresden OCL toolkit and the business rules approach*. Paper presented at the European Business Rules Conference, Amsterdam, The Netherlands.

Demuth, B., & Hussmann, H. (1999). *Using UML/OCL constraints for relational database design* (pp. 751–751). The Unified Modeling Language.

Demuth, B., Hussmann, H., & Loecher, S. (2001). OCL as a specification language for business rules in database applications. In *Proceedings of the International Conference on Unified Modeling Language, Modeling Languages, Concepts, and Tools* (pp. 104-117).

Demuth, B., Loecher, S., & Zschaler, S. (2004, September 15-17). *Structure of the Dresden OCL toolkit*. Paper presented at the 2nd International Fujaba Days MDA with UML and Rule-based Object Manipulation, Darmstadt, Germany.

Hahn, K., Sapia, C., & Blaschka, M. (2000). Automatically generating OLAP schemata from conceptual graphical models. In *Proceedings of the 3rd ACM International Workshop on Data Warehousing and OLAP*, McLean, VA.

Herden, O. (2000). A design methodology for data warehouses. In *Proceedings of the CAISE Doctoral Consortium*, Stockholm, Sweden.

Julien, F. S., & Rivest, S. (2009, October 21-22). *Les analyses relatives au transport maritime: un exemple de géodécisionnel.* Paper presented at the Colloque Géomatique, Montréal, QC, Canada.

Klasse Objecten. (2009). *OCL tools and services web site.* Retrieved from http://www.klasse.nl/ocl

Kleppe, A., Warmer, J., & Bast, W. (2003). *MDA explained.* Reading, MA: Addison-Wesley.

Lujan-Mora, S., Trujillo, J., & Song, I.-Y. (2006). A UML profile for multidimensional modeling in data warehouses. *Data & Knowledge Engineering, 59*(3), 725–769. doi:10.1016/j.datak.2005.11.004

Mahboubi, H., Bimonte, S., Faure, T., & Pinet, F. (2010). Data warehouse and OLAP for environmental simulation data. *International Journal of Agricultural and Environmental Systems, 1*(2).

Malinowski, E., & Zimanyi, E. (2006). Hierarchies in a multidimensional model: From conceptual modeling to logical representation. *Data & Knowledge Engineering, 59*(2), 348–377. doi:10.1016/j.datak.2005.08.003

Malinowski, E., & Zimanyi, E. (2008a). *Advanced data warehouse design: From conventional to spatial and temporal applications.* New York, NY: Springer.

Malinowski, E., & Zimányi, E. (2008b). A conceptual model for temporal data warehouses and its transformation to the ER and the object-relational models. *Data & Knowledge Engineering, 64*(1), 101–133. doi:10.1016/j.datak.2007.06.020

Mandel, L., & Cengarle, M. (1999). On the expressive power of OCL. In *Proceedings of the World Congress on Formal Methods in the Developing of Computer Systems* (pp. 713-713).

Mazon, J. N., & Trujillo, J. (2008). An MDA approach for the development of data warehouses. *Decision Support Systems, 45*, 41–55. doi:10.1016/j.dss.2006.12.003

McHugh, R., Roche, S., & Bédard, Y. (2009). Towards a SOLAP-based public participation GIS. *Journal of Environmental Management, 90*(6), 2041–2054. doi:10.1016/j.jenvman.2008.01.020

Moody, L. D., & Kortink, M. A. R. (2000). From enterprise models to dimensional models: A methodology for multidimensional structure and data mart design. In *Proceedings of the International Workshop on Design and Management of Multidimensional Structures*, Stockholm, Sweden.

Nguyen, T. B., Tjoa, A. M., & Wagner, R. (2000). An object oriented multidimensional data model for OLAP. In H. Lu & A. Zhou (Eds.), *Proceedings of the First International Conference on Web-Age Information Management* (LNCS 1846, pp. 69-82).

Nilakanta, S., Scheibe, K., & Rai, A. (2008). Dimensional issues in agricultural data warehouse designs. *Computers and Electronics in Agriculture, 60*(2), 263–278. doi:10.1016/j.compag.2007.09.009

OMG. (2007). *Unified modelling language: OCL, version 2.0.* Needham, MA: OMG.

OMG. (2009). *Unified modeling language (OMG UML), infrastructure version 2.2.* Needham, MA: OMG.

Pestana, G., da Silva, M. M., & Bedard, Y. (2005). Spatial OLAP modeling: an overview base on spatial objects changing over time. In *Proceedings of the IEEE 3rd International Conference on Computational Cybernetics.*

Prat, N., Akoka, J., & Comyn-Wattiau, I. (2006). A UML-based data warehouse design method. *Decision Support Systems, 42*(3), 1449–1473. doi:10.1016/j.dss.2005.12.001

Rumbaugh, J., Balaha, M., Premerlani, W., Eddy, F., & Lorensen, W. (1991). *Object-oriented modeling and design*. Upper Saddle River, NJ: Prentice Hall.

Sboui, T., Salehi, M., & Bédard, Y. (2010). A systematic approach for managing the risk related to semantic interoperability between geospatial datacubes. *International Journal of Agricultural and Environmental Information Systems, 1*(2). doi:10.4018/jaeis.2010070102

Schneider, M. (2008). A general model for the design of data warehouses. *International Journal of Production Economics, 112*(1), 309–325. doi:10.1016/j.ijpe.2006.11.027

Schulze, C., Spilke, J., & Lehner, W. (2007). Data modeling for precision dairy farming within the competitive field of operational and analytical tasks. *Computers and Electronics in Agriculture, 59*(1), 39–55. doi:10.1016/j.compag.2007.05.001

Theodoratos, D., Ligoudistianos, S., & Sellis, T. (2001). View selection for designing the global Multidimensional structure. *Data & Knowledge Engineering, 39*, 219. doi:10.1016/S0169-023X(01)00041-6

Trujillo, J., & Palomar, M. (1998). An object oriented approach to multidimensional database conceptual modeling. In *Proceedings of the 1st ACM International Workshop on Data Warehousing and OLAP*.

Trujillo, J., Palomar, M., Gomez, J., & Song, I. Y. (2001). Designing data warehouses with OO conceptual models. *IEEE Computer, 34*(12), 66–75. doi:10.1109/2.970579

Warmer, J., & Kleppe, A. (1999). *The object constraint language precise modeling with UML*. Reading, MA: Addison-Wesley.

ENDNOTES

[1] Unified Modeling Language (UML) is a well-known standardized modelling language in the field of object-oriented software engineering.

This journal was previously published in the International Journal of Technology Diffusion, Volume 2, Issue 3, edited by Ali Hussein Saleh Zolait, pp. 36-46, copyright 2011 by IGI Publishing (an imprint of IGI Global).

Chapter 15
Semantic Search Engine and Object Database Guidelines for Service Oriented Architecture Models

Omar Shehab
Staffordshire University, Malaysia

Ali Hussein Saleh Zoliat
University of Bahrain, Bahrain

ABSTRACT

In this paper, the authors propose a Semantic Search Engine, which retrieves software components precisely and uses techniques to store these components in a database, such as ontology technology. The engine uses semantic query language to retrieve these components semantically. The authors use an exploratory study where the proposed method is mapped between object-oriented concepts and web ontology language. A qualitative survey and interview techniques were used to collect data. The findings after implementing this research are a set of guidelines, a model, and a prototype to describe the semantic search engine system. The guidelines provided help software developers and companies reduce the cost, time, and risks of software development.

1. INTRODUCTION

1.1. Project Background

Integration technologies are improved by using the Simple Object Access Protocol (SOAP) which is considered lightweight and is based on XML. This protocol is used for the exchange of information in a distributed systems environment. In addition, the Component Object Model (COM) which is from the Microsoft Windows family, is employed by the developers to re – use software components, and the Remote Method Invocation (Java RMI) enables the programmer to distribute the java technology – base to java technology

DOI: 10.4018/978-1-4666-2791-8.ch015

based applications by invoking java objects from other java virtual machines.

In using the Enterprise Application Integration (EAI), which links the applications within a single organization, this process suffered from a lack of structure by using a point – to – point approach to link the processes. Creating architecture to reuse and integrate the classes will accelerate the development operation and reduce the cost. The guidelines work as a reference point for any companies to increase their productivity. The developers need to find the required object oriented models and integrate them to build the system easily and at a low cost. Creating a database structure which is considered one component of the system and connecting it with the search engine to facilitate the gathering of components will be a complete framework for service oriented architecture. Also, this structure is scalable to enable the developer to integrate the components from other organizations. The service oriented architecture will be used to build new systems by investing the service oriented business model and dividing the system into many partitions. Each partition is called a service. The structure enables the developers to combine one or more services to build their system. Sharing these services enables the software development companies to increase their productivity and build a large system in a short time at low cost. Finally, the information retrieval dilemma is that there are huge numbers of classes developed and to reuse these classes it is necessary to reorganize and restructure the retrieval operations to simplify access to these components. For the developers, it is a challenge to find a class which was built before hiring date and this problem also recurs with the massive amount of components especially when the documentation is very poor. Converting the system development inside the industry media into services is a big shift and it creates new perspectives for reusing these components as a business process model. There are two problems this research tries to solve. The first problem is how to create a search engine which should be semantic/ intelligent in order to retrieve the

software components stored in the database. The second problem is how to store these software components in the database to facilitate the access operations which will lead to using the search engine to find the required software component.

2. LITERATURE REVIEW

The retrieval and integration of existing application components need to deal with connectivity and data exchange to and from those applications. The most contemporary approaches to connecting to a legacy system are Java Connector Architecture and Web Services. And one of the most crucial requirements to offer the services as expected from the applications is by modelling the data exchanges with a Model Business Data such as XML. XML works with object oriented languages to provide "portable information". Even though the applications written in different languages such as Java, VB, or C#, are able to interact with XML, to accomplish the goal of connecting systems the XML specification describes what information is required to complete a transaction and stores this information in its database. Then an XML document is created based on the agreed upon standards. The XML document which uses the agreed upon XML standard is sent to the other side as part of information transition processes. The parser is used to convert the data into the native format of the application side. Juric et al. said "XML is the language that links new tools to legacy applications."

2.1. The Semantic Search Engine Architecture

There are several steps in the Semantic Search engine architecture:

1. Need Resource Description Framework (RDF).
2. Identifying Web Ontology Language (OWL) and mapping operation.

3. Trusting the information using digital signatures.
4. SOA which provide the mechanics of sending commands and receiving results which are services.

XML separates the content from its representation; therefore, it is the most suitable language for a semantic language, and it is also used to add metadata. The computer can understand the world at a specific level. So when the input is human – language text, the goal must be to semantically understand it – perhaps not the full meaning of the words as we imagine, but at least the critical relationships between the input and the real world.

2.2. Ontology Search Engine

The most important concept in implementing a semantic search engine concerns ontology. The dictionary definition of ontology is the metaphysics of the nature of being. However, in the Semantic Search Engine context, a narrower and more precise meaning of casual usage is intended, namely: Computer ontologies are structures or models of known knowledge. This term 'ontology' was used by the Artificial Intelligence (AI) and knowledge representation communities for many years. After that, these communities expanded the concept to include object modeling, XML, and Semantic Web. The original definition of ontology in this new sense is 'a specification of a conceptualization' (Gruber, 1992), but in later analyses, this definition has been expanded as follows:

An ontology is a partial (and explicit) account of a conceptualization... The degree of specification of the conceptualization which underlies the language used by a particular knowledge base varies in dependence of our purposes ... An ontological commitment (is thus) a partial semantic account of the intended conceptualization (Bo Leuf, 2006).

Lee at al. (2007) reported that the keyword search does not suffice for accurately specifying the information required by the user. The idea of using clustering and ontology has raised, however, several weaknesses inherent in these approaches. According to Lee at al. (2007), "The clustering method is not semantic matching and just simple extension of keyword matching. The ontology method requires that users know about ontology concept and select a desired ontology. But it is uncomfortable and hard work to users because they are familiar with keyword based searching."

Lee at al. (2007) proposed a new search engine with cluster – ontology mapping which maps keywords in clusters to ontology classes. They add new algorithms to increase their precision such as ontological pruning which is responsible for removing any web services irrelevant to the user's query among results. Additionally, they add the scoring function to their search engine to sort and capture the level of importance of these intended searched services.

This research devises architecture to represent the operation in the new system as shown in Figure 1 which exhibits all the components included in that search engine. This system consists of six modules: the service module, clustering module, ontology module, mapping module, pruning module and ranking module. These modules are partitioned into the data storing part and searching part.

Figure 1 shows the mapping, pruning, and ranking modules which are involved sequentially in the searching operation. The mapping module will get the keywords as a parameter and return the ontology list which is mapped to the entered keyword. The pruning module is managed by the user when choices are given to the user to select which irrelevant ontologies in the ontology list he wants to remove. After this module is executed, there is a list of search services which are generated and which conform to the users' intention. The last module is the ranking module which

Figure 1. Architecture overview (adapted from Lee et al., 2007)

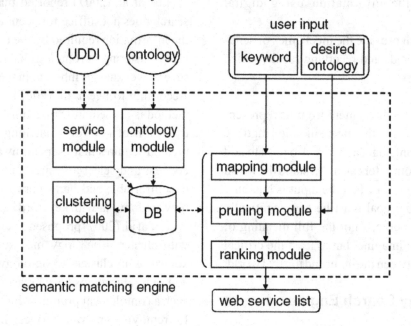

implements the sorting of the ontologies and scores them to output the final result to the user's query.

Sajjan and Shala (2008) proposed a software reuse repository system based on Semantic Wikis. This Semantic Wiki has an underlying model of information described in its pages. This semantic search engine identifies more information about the metadata and how they are related. This information is presented in a formal language such as the Resource Description Framework (RDF) and Web Ontology Language (OWL). Figure 2 exhibits the Semantic Wiki repository system which enables the developer to access and update reusable software artifacts. The Semantic Wiki allows the qualified structure and storage of the software components. Also, it proposes faceted based browsing to enable users to select the component according to certain facets.

2.3. XML Search Engine

The XML search engine is used to query objects in XML documents. Luk et al. (2002) classify the XML search into many types. The first type is the full – text search, which treats XML documents as structured texts and executes a series of algebra query languages on these documents. The second type is to search for information to discard (Filtering). The third is the XML-assisted search, which has several applications: one is to encode loose information to structured information for a semantic search; another is to use XML to translate queries and search results among distributed search engines for search collaboration, or to use XML to facilitate information transformation among different search engines.

Chu-Carroll et al. (2006) propose the utilization of XML fragments to enhance the precision of the semantic search. XML fragments are applied to query, and to realize the functions of conceptualization, restriction and relation, respectively. The conceptualization fragment is to generate a dictionary string to represent a concept; the restriction fragment is to set conditions (string) for XML tags whilst the relation fragment is to show the relationship between two concepts. Syeda-Mahmood et al. (2005) develop a semantic search mechanism consisting of two – step

Figure 2. Semantic Wiki system

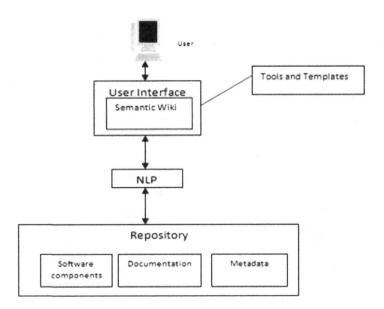

ranking algorithms for ranking an XML schema which depend on cardinality and the similarity of the matched query attributes and the matched repository schema attributes. This search is based on the names and types of attributes.

2.4. New Technologies in the Semantic Search Engine

The semantic search engine requires the involvement of a technique to merge data and the query across data from different sources. RDF is used as a foundation for the semantic Web. The data are stored and represented in different formats such as XML, RDB, and LDAP directories. The powerful technique heralded a new age of data sharing and integration in the shape of RDF (Resource Description Framework). Converting all these mentioned types of data into RDF format is very difficult and expensive to implement and also it is unfeasible for trivial information.

Each resource entity has an identifier which is unique and resolvable. The data resources are represented using RDF and they are connected by

directed edges. Each edge listed in the graph is called a statement which has a subject. Also the edge's label is called a predicate and the object is that which the edge points to. The subject, predicate, and object are referred to as a triple. RDF represents the data in graphical format which contain data and structure. Merging different graphs is a simple operation that involves constructing a set of triples from the graphs.

2.5. Querying RDF with SPARQL

The semantic Web requires the use of a query language and, according to the format provided by using RDF, the suitable query language is SPARQL (Protocol and RDF Query Language) which enables us to query data resources distributed across the Web.

SPARQL has four types of queries:

- **SELECT:** Returns a set of variable bindings that satisfy the query (similar to SQL SELECT). Good for producing data for application consumption.

- **CONSTRUCT:** Returns a graph (a set of RDF statements). Good for retrieving and transforming RDF.
- **ASK:** Returns a Boolean value if a solution to the query exists.
- **DESCRIBE:** Implementation-specific. Takes a resource as input and returns a graph describing that resource.

2.6. Classification Object-Oriented Applications into Domains

The method that the companies used to reuse application's components is called domain analysis; the components which are reused in system development for a particular domain should be identified in domain analysis. A domain is a group of related systems which share common properties. This domain might include a particular application or particular business function. Dividing reuse components into domains makes the practice of software reuse easier to manage. Each domain may include many can cut reusable components to support that domain (McClure, 2009). To define the common usable components which involve the most benefit, these components should be identified using a model–driven approach. The commonalities include common data, common processes, and common system structures. There are two types of semi–automatic training – example, generation algorithms for rapidly synthesizing a domain – a specific Web search engine. The web search engine is used as a method of retrieving information. To increase the quality of the search result it should be a domain based specific search.

Nabeshima et al. (2006) focus on the keyword spice model which is an approach for building a domain–specific search engine. A keyword is a Boolean expression which is used to identify the Web pages belonging to a specific domain. And because there are many Web pages about a specific domain which contain this keyword a lot of pages will be returned as a result of that

search. To solve this problem Nabeshima et al. (2006) came up with refinement algorithms based on semi–automatic training example generation: (i) the sample decision tree based approach, and (ii) the similarity based approach. The formal approach to obtain the information by refining the content of the directory, which is related to the user's desired domain is called the sample decision tree. The second approach is to refine the results of the first approach for some keywords. This experiment shows how the used approaches can be synthesized into a high performance domain–specific search engine with more precision. Nabeshima et al. (2006) said "Our approaches are very effective for the personalization of a general-purpose search engine, and can be a means to cope with the information explosion."

3. RESEARCH METHOD

The quantitative method is used in this research as it is helpful in collecting data and finding the answers to the questions which are not controlled in laboratory environments. Also, qualitative research methods are increasingly being adopted for finer textual data analysis to support a richer, deeper understanding of a study's focus. The survey method and interview techniques are used to collect data about computer-based activities. A comprehensive survey consisting of eight questions in the online version and four questions in the interview type version conducted with other experts in software industry was utilized. As the research focuses on a specific complex field and needs more understanding of many techniques related with Database Design, Artificial Intelligence, Object-Oriented Concepts, Service Oriented Architecture, Search Engines, and many other techniques besides, the collection of information was extremely difficult. This forces the researcher to concentrate on predetermined techniques and deal with them directly trying to show the meaning of terms to make the survey clearer.

Questions were posed to the respective analysts/designers, who work in the software industry fields and who come from different countries, to establish the current situation and the significance of semantic search engines in doing work in terms of time and cost, and with the minimum of effort. The survey comprised three forms; the first form is to be administered directly with the specialists, the second form is the same as the first form but is to be administered online and the last copy is built using the online system.

The first interview was carried out in the MIMOS Company. Two direct interviews were performed with Mr. Khoni Mali who is a project manager in Kompakar Company/ CMMI level 5, And Mr. Nicholas Ruwan who is a project manager in the same company. Also, one survey was administered directly online with a designer who worked in the artificial intelligence field. The online survey was sent by email to many people who are specialists in this field. Additionally, some of these surveys were sent to designers and analysts who work in companies in different countries. The survey aimed to ascertain the degree of willingness and struggle of the developers to extract frequently used code easily. Also, it was arranged in such a manner as to reflect the desire of the developers to implement the system in their industry for many reasons; the first reason is to establish the significance of a proposed system; the second is to ascertain the suitability of the components to achieve these desires. The analysis of the data was conducted by comparing the responses of the various surveys. The questions themselves were formatted in such a way as to facilitate the analyzing process. For example, to obtain precise information the questions were explanation questions and not in multiple choice format to prevent any general information which may not be helpful at the analysis stage.

The nature of the project technically imposes the use of specific research methodology and, according to the results of the research method; the analysis will be implemented to evaluate the possibility of achieving the research objectives. This includes the proposition of the components which are suggested to build the system and how these components are connected to each other. Then, the propositions will be implemented according to the recent technologies used in the semantic search engine and database applications and these components will be implemented for the purpose of evaluation.

Objects Collection System factors are concerned with the storage database, how the application's components are used ontologically, and how the knowledge database is built. One of the important factors used in this system is the SPARQL which is considered as the junction between the database and the semantic search engine and it provides a way of retrieving the required components precisely. The Protégé Knowledge based application will be part of the system and it will be employed to implement the project as will the RDF technology which cooperates as part of the SPARQL and will be taken into consideration as technology to retrieve the graphical information. All these technologies will be assessed during the implementation of the research method.

4. DATA ANALYSIS

Questions are designed to collect information about the factors used in the implementation stage as it is crucial to analyze such factors. The survey responses which were answered by experts gave the data collected more credibility. Data obtained were categorized to deal with each class separately. The first set of data analyzed focused on finding the proper way to be followed in the storage of software components. The second set was to find the search engine that was suitable to retrieve the information stored in the database according to the type of information stored, which were software components. These search engines should be semantic to serve the research purpose. The third group was the improvement of the search engine to make it more semantic and the technique which should be used as well as the division of information into classes as domains can make the searching process more precise. The last division of information was the common way used to retrieve software components and to check whether they are suitable or not. Figure 3 shows the elements of SSE which are under analysis.

4.1. Critical Analysis of Gathered Data

According to the need to implement the Semantic Search Engine some criteria were applied to find the suitability of each factor for the system. These criteria depend on a critical analysis of the information related to integrity, reliability, usability, semantics and complexity. Figure 4 shows the search engine elements and their specifications.

The suitable technologies which will be used in the research guidelines are RDF to store the information semantically, RDF Schema which is very helpful to be a base for the standard vocabulary and business rules, OWL to support RDF by storing the software components ontologically, and SPARQL to retrieve the software components after storing them in the database and to be the base for the SSE. This shows that this research proposal is applicable for the implementation of two functions:

1. Storing the software components semantically using RDF format and OWL to create ontology components.
2. Using the Semantic Search Engine based on the Wiki idea to retrieve the information accurately supported by new technology such as RDF Schema and SPARQL to access these software components precisely.

4.2. Contributions and Theory Implications (SSE System)

This section will show how each step of the process is implemented. Additionally, the format of the code to create each element is presented in detail. Many applications are used to build the ontology components such as the Altova Semantic Works system, the Protégé System, and the SPARQL search engine. This part of the paper will deal with the code insertion and mapping with ontology components and how it will be stored in the knowledge base system.

The first layer in the SSE system is XML which is the standard for the RDF format. This layer has many limitations and the model is started from the Resource Definition Framework as the basis for these guidelines. The RDF specifications include a standard XML serialization format. However, RDF is the data model rather than the serialization so other serializations are also possible and the data can be merged and processed independently of the serialization format chosen (Reynolds et al.,

Figure 3. SSE elements graphical description

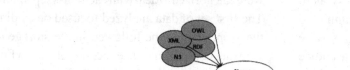
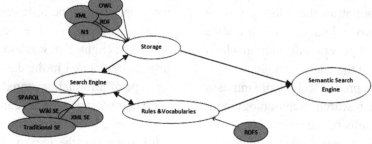

Figure 4. SSE elements traits

	Integrity	Reliability	Usability	Semantic	Complexity
RDF	✓	✓		✓	
RDFS		✓		✓	
XML	✓	✓	✓		
OWL				✓	✓
SPARQL				✓	✓
Traditional SE	n/a		✓		

2005). The guidelines may be divided into three categories; the first is the Database Implementation which means how the software components are stored. The second category is the Service Oriented Architecture which explains the implementation of delivering software components over the Internet as services. The last part is the Search Engine dedicated to achieve the proposal aims.

5. DATABASE IMPLEMENTATION

5.1. Resource Description Framework (RDF)

The first step in the storage operation is how to deal with the program components. Each of the components needs to be formatted in a way that provides common representation which enables the data for the exchange and integration of machine readable information (Reynolds et al., 2005). Through data analysis the findings suggested the use of the RDF format as a suitable technology to store software pieces. RDF represents information by means of atomic, logical statements. These statements take the form of triples: subject,

predicate, and object as seen in Figure 5. RDF can serve as a language to represent knowledge as Meta data about entities in, for example, the business domain. However, this level or layer in the generated model will provide the basic representation for the data.

The Graphical representation of each component in any application or program can be implemented beginning from RDF representation of these components. The example, which is for ATM machine design, explains how to represent the class and its sub classes in a graphical way as shown in Figure 6 and then convert them into RDF format as shown in Figure 7.

5.1.1. RDF Vocabulary Description Language: RDF Schema (RDFS)

For data exchanging, RDF provides a standardized way which supports the distribution and integration of application components from multiple sources. These standards are useful if the applications share a common model of the specific domain. RDF Schema defines the class hierarchies, property hierarchies, and domain and range declaration for properties. There is a

Figure 5. RDF triple

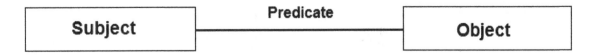

Figure 6. RDF ATM example

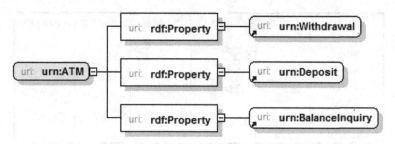

need to access the specific application components required to classify and categorize these components into domains, and this operation will facilitate component seeking and accessing. The proper way to implement domain categorization is by means of RDFS which defines the domain and its affiliated code. The domain's vocabulary is very important to consider as the approach is used to access application components in a very precise way. Therefore, the SSE model proposes the use of specific schema for each domain to express the type of code included in the ontology and this can be implemented by RDF Schema. RDFS facilitates the specification of application-specific ontological domain vocabulary in the form of class and property hierarchies on top of RDF resources. RDFS introduces the concept of a class to define a type of system for RDF. The predicate "rdf:type" is used to specify class membership,

while the predicate "rdfs:subClassOf" is used to state a subclass relationship between two types (Studer & Abecker, 2007). Figure 8 shows how the classes are represented using RDFS.

The semantics of RDFS are implemented by defining the resources in the predicate of RDF as a member of the class "rdfs:Property". In addition, the properties can be organized in a hierarchy using the keyword "rdfs:subPropertyOf" as shown in Figure 9. With the predefined predicates "rdfs:domain" and "rdfs:range", one can define the domain and range for a property.

The example demonstrates how to implement the RDF Schema and how to define the domain using vocabulary description language. This vocabulary description includes a graphic representation of the schema as seen in Figure 10 and RDFS text representation which is added in the Appendix, Figure 22.

Figure 7. RDF language for ATM example

```
1    <?xml version="1.0" encoding="UTF-8"?>
2    <rdf:RDF xmlns:owl="http://www.w3.org/2002/07/owl#" xmlns:rdf="
     http://www.w3.org/1999/02/22-rdf-syntax-ns#" xmlns:rdfs="
     http://www.w3.org/2000/01/rdf-schema#">
3      <rdf:Description rdf:about="urn:ATM">
4        <rdf:Property>
5          <rdf:Description rdf:about="urn:Withdrawal"/>
6        </rdf:Property>
7        <rdf:Property>
8          <rdf:Description rdf:about="urn:Deposit"/>
9        </rdf:Property>
10       <rdf:Property>
11         <rdf:Description rdf:about="urn:BalanceInquiry"/>
12       </rdf:Property>
13     </rdf:Description>
14   </rdf:RDF>
```

Figure 8. RDF schema

Figure 9. RDFS object property presentation

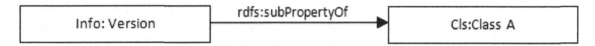

5.1.2. RDFS Semantics

The axiomatic triples and involvement rules that derive new inferred triples leading to the semantics are characteristic of RDFS. To yield the set of all entailed statements for an RDF graph, GRDF, the rules are exhaustively applied to the triples of GRDF together with all axiomatic triples. The following examples give some of these entailment rules and their application to triples.

1. IF GRDF contains (A, rdfs:subClassOf, B) and (C, rdf:type, A)
    THEN derive (C, rdf:type, B)
2. IF GRDF contains (A, rdfs:subClassOf, B) and (B, rdfs:subClassOf, C)
    THEN derive (A, rdfs:subClassOf, C)

Figure 10. Graphical presentation of schema

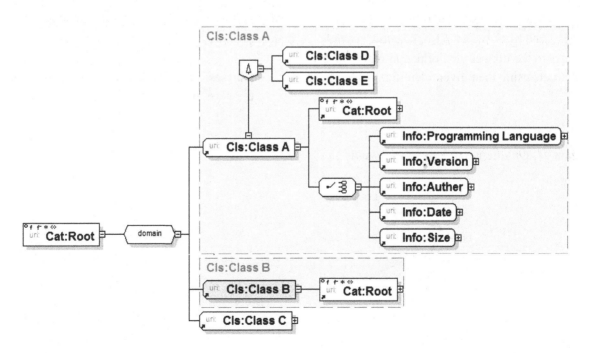

3. IF GRDF contains (B, rdfs:domain, D) and (A,B, C)
    THEN derive (A, rdf:type, D)
4. IF GRDF contains (A, rdfs:range, D) and (A,B,C)
    THEN derive (C, rdf:type, D)

5.1.3. Web Ontology Language (OWL)

"The Web Ontology Language (OWL) is a language for defining and instantiating Web ontologies. Ontology is a term borrowed from philosophy that refers to the science of describing the kinds of entities in the world and how they are related. OWL ontology may include descriptions of classes, properties and their instances. Given such ontology, the OWL formal semantics specifies how to derive its logical consequences" (Smith et al., 2004). OWL describes the code in a semantic ontological way. A set of XML namespace declarations enclosed in an opening rdf:RDF tag defines the standard component of an ontology which provides a much more readable presentation.

In this layer, the developer will use the OWL namespace to define the component location which is considered the basic step in preparing the application components to the SOA layer to be accessed by the users. Also, it is now possible to refer to the classes we defined in other OWL constructs using their given identifier.

This layer is responsible for defining the classes and instances, as well as the property declaration of each class, subclass, and instance implemented in the OWL layer. The properties include ObjectProperty, DatatypeProperty, rdfs:subPropertyOf, rdfs:domain, and rdfs:range. Additionally, many other characteristics are included in this layer to provide more semantic value to the application code in the form of semantic, transitive, and functional properties. Also, the restrictions and cardinality will be defined in this layer to prepare for the next layer which is the Code Layer. Figure 11 shows the design for the classes. See also the ontology (OWL) file in the Appendix, Figure 23, and how it is used to store the code components.

5.1.4. Object Oriented and Ontology Concept Mapping

The cornerstone for achieving SSE is extracting the Object Oriented Concepts and reflecting them by applying ontology mapping. The structure of Object Oriented Programming (OOP) depends on certain principles, and fortunately most of these concepts can be implemented using Web Ontology Language. This section deals with the OOP and how mapping is carried out with ontology concepts.

*   **Classes:** In OOP, the first component is the class which is considered the template

Figure 11. Ontology components hierarchy

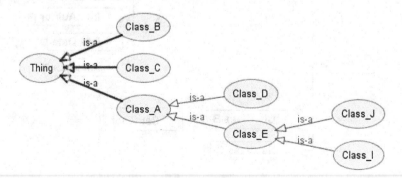

for each Object. To represent these classes ontologically as in Figure 12, the user defines these classes which are subclasses of root class owl: Thing. A class may contain individuals, which are instances of the class, and other subclasses. The OWL text demonstrates how to represent the classes ontologically.

- **Properties:** A property is a binary relation that determines class characteristics. They are attributes of instances and sometimes act as data values or links to other instances. There are two types of properties: data type and object properties. Data type properties are relations between instances of classes and RDF literals (Schema). Object properties are relations between instances of two classes. Data type property can be represented in OOP as attributes of the class and represented ontologically as in Figure 13. The Appendix (Figure 23) includes the ontology code which represents the Data type property and how it can map into OOP.

The object property is represented in OOP as the nature of properties between the classes such as, for example, is a, has a, subClassOf and so on as represented in Figure 14 which shows how the object oriented associations can be implemented ontologically.

- **Instances:** Instances are individuals that belong to the classes defined. A class may have any number of instances. Instances are used to define the relationship among different classes. In OOP, the instance can be implemented by the keyword *constructor.* The instance here is not intended to define the initial value of any object in the memory but it will be specific to the code included in the class among ontology components. However, the instances using ontology will be used to define the distinct object instantiated from each class. Figure 15 displays the instance representation in an ontological way.
- **Operations:** OWL supports various operations on classes and these operations can be invested in OOP. One of these operations is the cardinality which can be implemented ontologically by declaring the range of instances in a specific domain and this can be reflected in the nature of object oriented concepts.

5.1.5. Ontology Code Involvement

In this step, the concrete code will add to the ontology components. The domain of the class will define the code type involved through the service provided by previous layers and the subclasses will be automatically within the super class domain. For each class there is an object property which

Figure 12. Classes Stored using OWL

```
Namespace(=<http://www.Semantic_Search_Engine/2010/1/OOP&OntologyConcepts.owl#>)
Namespace(rdfs=<http://www.w3.org/2000/01/rdf-schema#>)
Namespace(owl2xml=<http://www.w3.org/2006/12/owl2-xml#>)
Namespace(OntologyConcepts=<http://www.Semantic_Search_Engine/2010/1/OOP&OntologyConcepts.owl#>)
Namespace(owl=<http://www.w3.org/2002/07/owl#>)
Namespace(xsd=<http://www.w3.org/2001/XMLSchema#>)
Namespace(rdf=<http://www.w3.org/1999/02/22-rdf-syntax-ns#>)

Ontology(<http://www.Semantic_Search_Engine/2010/1/OOP&OntologyConcepts.owl
// Class: http://www.Semantic_Search_Engine/2010/1/OOP&OntologyConcepts.owl#Class_A
Declaration(Class(Class_A))
)
// Generated by the OWL API (version 2.2.1.1138) http://owlapi.sourceforge.net
```

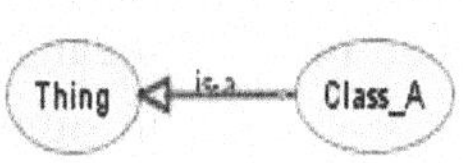

Figure 13. Ontology code

```
<owl:Class rdf:ID="Class_A">
    <rdfs:subClassOf rdf:resource="&owl;Thing"/>
    <rdfs:subClassOf>
        <owl:Restriction>
            <owl:onProperty rdf:resource="#Auther"/>
            <owl:hasValue rdf:datatype="&xsd;string">Omar Shehab</owl:hasValue>
        </owl:Restriction>
    </rdfs:subClassOf>
    <rdfs:subClassOf>
        <owl:Restriction>
            <owl:onProperty rdf:resource="#Description"/>
            <owl:hasValue rdf:datatype="&xsd;string"
                >For Research Purposes</owl:hasValue>
        </owl:Restriction>
    </rdfs:subClassOf>
    <rdfs:subClassOf>
        <owl:Restriction>
            <owl:onProperty rdf:resource="#Programming_Language"/>
            <owl:hasValue rdf:datatype="&xsd;string">C#</owl:hasValue>
        </owl:Restriction>
    </rdfs:subClassOf>
    <rdfs:subClassOf>
        <owl:Restriction>
            <owl:onProperty rdf:resource="#Version"/>
            <owl:hasValue rdf:datatype="&xsd;float">1.1</owl:hasValue>
        </owl:Restriction>
    </rdfs:subClassOf>
</owl:Class>
```

Figure 14. Domain definition

```
<owl:ObjectProperty rdf:ID="object_A">
    <rdf:type rdf:resource="&owl;FunctionalProperty"/>
    <rdfs:domain rdf:resource="#Class_A"/>
    <rdfs:range>
        <owl:Restriction>
            <owl:onProperty rdf:resource="#object_A"/>
            <owl:hasValue rdf:resource="#Class_A"/>
        </owl:Restriction>
    </rdfs:range>
</owl:ObjectProperty>
```

will involve the concrete code. By accessing the class investing RDFS in the semantic search engine, the user should be able to see the hierarchal classes and choose the suitable class with the domain which is already selected during criteria determination in the SSE. This hierarchy can be presented in a graphical way.

5.2. Service Oriented Architecture

SOA establishes an architectural model that aims to enhance the efficiency, agility, and productivity of an enterprise by positioning services as the primary means through which solution logic is represented in support of the realization of the strategic goals

Figure 15. Object Instances using ontology

```
<!-- http://Instance.owl#Instance_1 -->

<owl:Thing rdf:about="#Instance_1">
    <rdf:type>
        <owl:Restriction>
            <owl:onProperty rdf:resource="#Instance"/>
            <owl:allValuesFrom rdf:resource="#Class_A"/>
        </owl:Restriction>
    </rdf:type>
    <Instance rdf:resource="#Instance_1"/>
</owl:Thing>
```

associated with service-oriented computing. It is very important to view and position SOA as an architectural model that is agnostic to any one technology platform. SOA will consider the platform for delivering the application components. Each component uploaded to that platform should be given an ID number to define the owner and for logic processing.

The auto generation included in the traditional web service development process includes using an existing component as the basis for web services, and using the development tools to derive a contract that mirrors the component interface, and the auto generated web service contract which represents the implemented web service.

The SOA techniques will be used for information exchange such as messaging, WSDL, and SOAP. Figure 16 shows the general structure for information transitioning.

5.3. Semantic Search Engine

5.3.1. SPARQL Protocol and RDF Query Language

In 2004, the RDF Data Access Working Group (part of the Semantic Web Activity Group) released a first public working draft of a query language for RDF, called SPARQL. SPARQL is a W3C Candidate Recommendation (Pérez et al., 2009). Essentially, SPARQL is a graph-matching query language. Given a data source D, a query consists of a pattern which is matched against D, and the values obtained from this matching are processed to give the answer. The data source D to be queried can be composed of multiple sources.

A SPARQL query consists of three stages. The pattern matching stage, which includes several interesting features of pattern matching of graphs, like optional parts, a union of patterns, nesting, filtering (or restricting) values of pos-

Figure 16. Web service transitioning

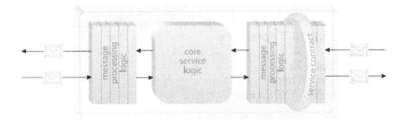

sible matching, and the possibility of choosing the data source to be matched by a pattern. The solution modifiers, which once the output of the pattern has been computed (in the form of a table of values of variables), allows the modification of these values applying classical operators like projection, distinction, order, limit, and offset. Finally, the output of a SPARQL query can be of different types: yes/no queries, selections of values of the variables which match the patterns, construction of new triples from these values, and descriptions of resources.

This project is concerned with building the query using a systematic way and based on the conversion between natural language processing and SPARQL and vice versa. The translation of natural language into SPARQL simplifies the operation of accessing the application component easily. SPARQL is drawn in the Semantic Search Engine in a vertical direction among the RDF, RDFS, OWL, Code, and SOA to illustrate that the query language can work on an RDF triple using algebraic formalization. Also, SSE will invest the schema built by the RDFS to create the query, which helps in obtaining the data precisely. The semantic part of the query when it deals with the ontology layer to retrieve the code, is involved in the upper code layer to retrieve the components over the SOA layer.

The template represents the SPARQL formalization as shown in Figure 17.

5.3.2. Structured Natural Language Processing

In the area of linguistic engineering and Structured Natural Language (SNL), this research deals with ideas about the content and structure of static knowledge sources. A popular idea is adding search and browsing support to ontology editing environments. For instance, Protégé supplies the Query Interface, where one can state the query by selecting some options from a given list of domains, concepts and relations. Advanced users can type a query using a formal language such as SPARQL. The Ontology-based question answering system translates generic natural language queries into SPARQL. For example, Querix relies on clarification dialogues with users. Natural language processing is a huge area and it is not feasible to depend on it in this system for limitation reasons.

5.4. Semantic Search Engine Model

The guidelines for the project implementation are discussed in greater detail to give an idea about how the suggested system should be. This system is a client-server application, the requirement for which is the Protégé System which is included in the server side. The other requirement in this system is the SPARQL query builder and this should be part of the search engine in the client

Figure 17. SPARQL formalization

```
PREFIX owl: <http://www.w3.org/2002/07/owl#>
PREFIX rdfs: <http://www.w3.org/2000/01/rdf-schema#>
PREFIX rdf: <http://www.w3.org/1999/02/22-rdf-syntax-ns#>

#List all of the properties associated with a specific type of resource
SELECT DISTINCT ?predicate
WHERE {
  ?s ?predicate ?o.
  #Insert type uri here...
  ?s a <INSERT-TYPE-URI>.
}
```

side. The Protégé system will provide the ability to convert the application components into ontology components. This mapping operation is implemented with the help of TBox and ABox techniques built into the Protégé system.

ABox and TBox are used to describe two different types of statements in ontologies. TBox "terminological components" are a vocabulary associated with a set of ABox facts. TBox statements describe a system in terms of controlled vocabulary. On the other hand, ABox "assertion components" are a fact associated with a terminological vocabulary within a knowledge base.

The converting of Object Oriented components into ontology components will be implemented manually and this needs sufficient understanding of the concepts and the mapping operation.

Storing the components will be done by the client and it will send them to the server so the mapping operation should implemented by the user. Once the component is stored in the database, then it will be given a unique ID number by the Protégé system and this will make these components available over the Internet as services using the SOA platform. Figure 18 shows the Semantic Search Engine System which includes both the client and server sides.

This Model was presented for examination and this is the last updated version of the model for the system. It has been examined by experts and the testing operation will be discussed in the following sections.

Figure 18. Semantic search engine model

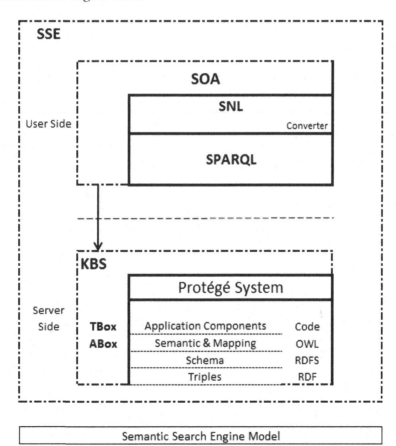

Semantic Search Engine Model

---

6. PROTOTYPE

This section deals with creating a prototype which shows the Semantic Search Engine activities and how it works. As the system is a client–server application, it consists of the client side which is the Search Engine and the server side, the storage system which is the Protégé System. The user side application (Search Engine) will be represented using the Prototype system and, on the other hand, the server side will use the Protégé System. The prototype and semantic search engine model were tested many times and some modifications implemented to the model according to the comments of the specialists from different companies who participated in this research project.

6.1. Ontology Storage and Mapping

This section aims to explain how the system stores the application components semantically using the ontology system. All the important steps in storing the components can be represented physically using the Protégé system. The storing of application components will be implemented manually using the Protégé System, which is free. There are some other systems, which can be used to implement the same functionality as the Protégé system such as the Alegrograph and TopBraid Composer systems. Figure 19 shows the main page of the Protégé system, which represents the active ontology.

Figure 19 shows the annotations of each class, the title of the class and some ontology metrics such as the number of classes. We can mention here the namespace ontology of the active class in the OWL function and the syntax rendering

Figure 19. Protégé main page

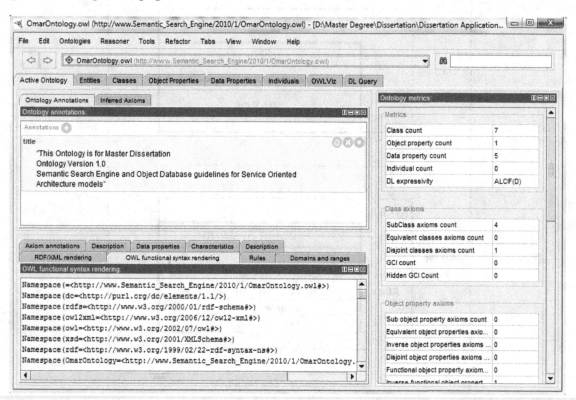

section. Specifications for the class such as the author, Programming Language, version, etc. are displayed for each selected class. This stage is very important in the mapping operation because it is when the user starts to store the component and writes the description for that component and determines how it is related with the other peers.

Figure 20 shows a very important stage in the storage operation which involves the code inside each ontology component. Figure 20 is a concrete code which itself carries the meaning of abstract, interface, or class. However, these concrete pieces of software are inserted inside the ontology in an operation called "Code Mapping".

Figure 20 shows that the relations between the classes are presented according to the association type such as has_a, is_a, and some rules and vocabulary. This gives some clarification about the mapping operation and how it is implemented manually.

6.2. Prototype

The semantic search engine system prototype includes a text box to enter the application components that the user is looking for. However, as discussed earlier, the natural language processing is not enough to find the components precisely so the text should be converted into a structural format. The SPARQL has two advantages, the first of which is that it is considered compatible with the RDF and RDF Schema to retrieve the information. The second is the ability to convert the natural text into a structured format. This idea is applied and proven by some vendors such as Querix and SPARQL Editor. However, some features should be changed to make the SPARQL Editor suitable for the application components collection system. The search engine depends on OWL components, RDF Schema, and RDF. These mechanisms should be generated automatically through the semantic search engine to help the use in SPARQL writing and this will help in

Figure 20. Code insertion

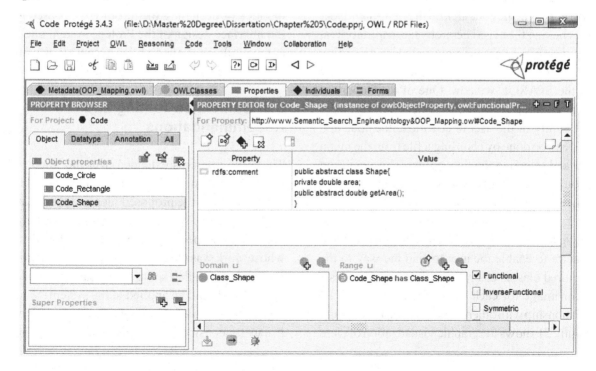

locating the component more precisely. One of the most important features in the SSE system is the graphical representation of each component and the relationships between these components.

The SPARQL tab in the Semantic Search Engine system shows how the natural text can be converted into SPARQL language and that many other selections can be implemented to improve the search operation. The prefixes can be used to implement a semantic search and that will lead to the accurate retrieval of the information. Some selections such as the programming language used, the author, and the version are considered one of the RDF Schema formats which is already built inside each of the ontology components. The search can be performed according to the domain that the user is looking in to limit the search to a specific area. This can be done by clicking the Domain button.

After making the query required, the SSE can display the hierarchy of classes in a tree view menu which leads the user to obtain the required information. For each selected class all the subclasses will be displayed and as the user selects or checks the specific class, the code inserted inside the ontology will appear in the code area on the right-hand side. By clicking the class Hierarchy tab in the tab area, the user can select the required class according to the search operation implemented previously in the SPARQL window. One of the important things related to Service Oriented Architecture is the ability of the user to download the code and this can be done by choosing a file from the menu bar and selecting the save option. This operation should be used in E-business operations such as payment over the Internet.

For usability reasons and to facilitate the navigation over classes, SSE includes a graphical feature to enable the user to find the way to the required classes easily. In addition, it provides a clear image for each class and the nature of its relationship with other classes in the same domain. Figure 21 shows the graphic visualization of class

hierarchy. The type of relation is retrieved from the relation with the ontology itself, and this information will be provided by the designer who will be responsible for the storing of the application components in the database on the server side. According to the Protégé system, most of the relation is "has-a" which is represented as "is-a" in the graphical way as shown in Figure 21 but as the object oriented classes consist of many other types of relations, it is convenient to define the relation type in ontology components and also cardinality which will render the data meaningful.

6.2.1. Prototype Description

The Semantic Search Engine Prototype illustrates how the application components can be collected using the system. However, many other facilities can be added to the system to make the information retrieval operation more precise and make it easier to access pieces of software. The prototype is built using visual C# to facilitate the interface building and it also gives the researcher the ability to make the semantic search engine prototype more compatible with other similar products. Also, the idea of designing this prototype is based on the interface design of the Protégé system due to compatibility reasons and also because they work together to achieve the SSE or the research goal.

6.3. Guidelines Testing and Recommendations

The testing process extended over the stages of research implementation and the field study. The ability to apply the proposed idea and the reality started to grow. Additionally, through meetings held with the specialists, designers, and analysts whose work was closely related to the topic area, it was proposed that some modifications and adjustments should be applied to the system. Since the deliverables of this research are guidelines, it can be considered as one of the testing ap-

Figure 21. Visual appearance of classes

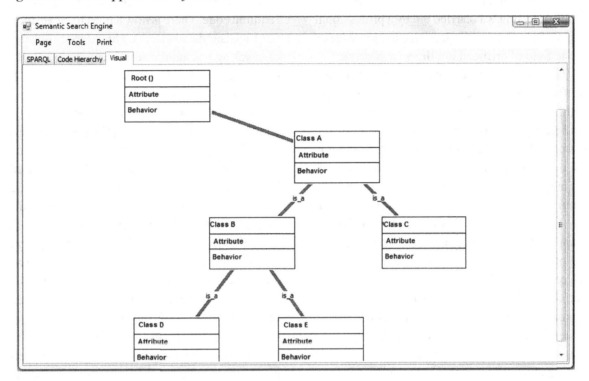

proaches for the deliverables. The deliverables of this research are the guidelines and prototype of the Semantic Search Engine which is dedicated to collecting software pieces offered and spread over the Internet. The testing operation is very important to evaluate whether the system proposed is applicable or not, how the steps were designed to implement the system and which techniques were used. These guidelines were presented for testing at two levels; the preliminary level and the secondary level. Through these two levels many modifications were made to the guidelines to make them clearer and more applicable. The process of evaluation gave credibility to the work. The testing form prepared includes a simple description of the system guidelines to decrease the time required to read the information. Also, to make the ideas clearer the explanation of the system goals and technique used are discussed through the testing process.

The explanation of each step and the technique used there it were tested by specialists who work in the fields of artificial intelligence and semantics. Also, the mapping operation between the object oriented and ontology concepts required the input from specialists who were interested in both areas. The first testing was implemented in the MIMOS Company which is a Malaysian company with CMMI level 5 which has a department concerned with knowledge based systems. Testing was carried out continuously throughout the research. MIMOS was visited three times beginning from the information collection stage and ending with the guidelines testing. The support from the specialists and Senior Staff Researcher in MIMOS helped the researchers a great deal to implement the guidelines testing. The second round of testing was conducted in U.C.T.I University College with the help of a lecturer in the Application's Cluster who has experience in the artificial intelligence field as well as having experience in natural language processing techniques. The third and final round of testing was carried out by a professional in U.C.T.I University College who had knowledge in the field of artificial intelligence systems.

The steps explained started from how to create RDF and how this technique should be exploited in this research, which is very important to clarify sufficiently as it is considered the basis for the system. The most important part of the system is the ontology and there is a discussion as to how the mapping should be implemented. This section required more clarification and a specialist in object oriented concepts is needed to simplify the mapping understanding. Until this stage the testing process was clear enough to deal with. When the code section is discussed, it very important to define clearly the code insertion process and how it should be carried out manually using the Protégé system. After this step, the theory of SPARQL and language processing is well known in that field (artificial intelligence). Also, the service oriented architecture was under discussion in the testing process which is considered to be the business part of the project.

7. CONCLUSION AND FUTURE TRENDS

This research introduces a solution to help programmers to find parts of programs in an easy and reliable way. The continuous development processes led the researcher to find a suitable approach to assist developers to reduce the effort needed in writing their code. In addition, this research helps the industrial software field to reduce the time and cost needed to develop any system by means of finding any piece of code as a service over SOA. Usually, the developers in the companies depend on the Internet to find the code they need to build their systems. Due to the increases in code complexity, surfing the Internet using traditional search engines such as

Google or Yahoo is no longer sufficient to get the required code. There is now a need to create more advanced modern systems. This research depends on creating a semantic search engine to help the developers in their code searching process. In addition, one of the big issues in this research is how to store the software components in the database in a way that enables the user to retrieve the information precisely. These factors constitute the hypothesis of this study which is discussed. The research produced guidelines and a model for a system that achieved the proposed goals. These guidelines are the steps needed to explain the techniques required to implement the system.

The guidelines of the project are delivered according to the data collected. The stages needed to implement the semantic search engine were clarified and the SSE System model was carried out. Proposal problems raised at the beginning of this research were solved using specific techniques such as the ontology approach to store the software components in the database using mapping concepts. Also, the search engine problem is solved using SPARQL and Domain Schema. The model represents an SSE system and how the components interact with each other through the Client – Server System.

The goal of the research is for the loosely coupled components, which include the functions required, to be organized and offered to the developers in the form of service(s). From the academic perspective, it will help the researcher to use this research as a reference to build or convert any system to a service using a protocol defined in this research. Also, from the industrial perspective, it will guide companies to invest in successful areas when the development becomes easy to use with existing services. Also, from the business angle, these guidelines will help companies to reduce their cost, time, and the risks associated with development and enable them to estimate the cost of implementation in an effective manner. The challenge is to use an existing concept, which is the Service–Oriented Architecture, and adapt this concept to be a cornerstone in the research with other components such as the database, search engine and other tools used to complete the project. To meet this challenge, creating a set of guidelines as a protocol will make the implementation easier and applicable in many fields.

For future research, it is very important to develop a system that can help to create ontology components automatically which can help the users who do not have high levels of knowledge in this area and also to reduce the time needed to store software components in the database. Also, it will enable the client side to achieve all such work as uploading the code automatically and this will assist the Service Oriented Architecture to use this method as a business model and to achieve competitive advantage.

Due to the lack of experience encountered in survey implementation the results included some degree of uncertainty. The Semantic Search Engine has some limitations. On the server side, the storing of ontology components and OOP – OWL Mapping should be implemented manually. This makes the process more time consuming and may involve some mistakes during the code insertion. Also, this process needs specialists with high levels of experience who know how to deal with object-oriented concepts and ontology concepts. On the other hand, the client side, which is the search engine, requires some understanding of SPARQL language and related concepts. The limitation of formal text processing simplifies the system work, but it makes interaction with the system more complex. Also, some of the ontology system processes should be transferred from the server side to the client side for the sake of functionality such as the graphical representation of ontology components.

REFERENCES

Chu-Carroll, J., Prager, J., Czuba, K., Ferrucci, D., & Duboue, P. (2006). Semantic Search via XML Fragments: A high-precision approach to IR. In *Proceedings of the 29th Annual International ACM SIGIR Conference on Research and Development in Information Retrieval*, Seattle, WA (pp. 445-452).

Euzenat, J., & Shvaiko, P. (2007). *Ontology matching*. Berlin, Germany: Springer-Verlag.

Lee, D., Kwon, J., Yang, S. H., & Lee, S. (2007). Improvement of the recall and the precision for semantic web services search. In *Proceedings of the 6th IEEE/ACIS International Conference on Computer and Information Science* (pp. 763-768).

Luk, R. W., Leong, H. V., Dillon, T. S., Chan, A. T., Croft, W. B., & Allan, J. (2002). A survey in indexing and searching XML documents. *Journal of the American Society for Information Science and Technology*, *53*(6), 415–437. doi:10.1002/asi.10056

McClure, C. (2009). Reuse finds common ground - software reuse - Forum - Column. *Software Magazine*. Retrieved August 1, 2009, from http://findarticles.com/p/articles/mi_m0SMG/is_n6_v15/ai_17028302/

Nabeshima, H., Miyagawa, R., Suzuki, Y., & Iwanuma, K. (2006). University of Yamanashi rapid synthesis of domain-specific web search engines based on semi-automatic training-example generation. In *Proceedings of the IEEE/WIC/ACM International Conference on Web Intelligence*.

Pedrycz, W. (2005). *Knowledge-based clustering from data to information granules*. New York, NY: John Wiley & Sons. doi:10.1002/0471708607

Pérez, J., Arenas, M., & Gutierrez, C. (2009). Semantics and complexity of SPARQL. *ACM Transactions on Database Systems, 34*(3), 16–45. doi:10.1145/1567274.1567278

Reference Framework Report, S. O. A. (2007). *Enhancing the enterprise architecture with service orientation.* CBDI Journal.

Reynolds, D., Thompson, C., Mukerji, J., & Coleman, D. (2005). *Digital Media Systems Laboratory: An assessment of RDF/OWL modelling.* Retrieved from http://www.hpl.hp.com/techreports/2005/HPL-2005-189.pdf

Sajjan, G. S., & Shala, L. A. (2008). Using semantic wikis to support software reuse. *Journal of Software, 3*(4), 1–8.

Schmidt, D. C., & Fayad, M. E. (1997). Lessons learned: Building reusable OO frameworks for distributed software. *Communications of the ACM, 40*(10), 85–87. doi:10.1145/262793.262810

Shashidhar, A., Raman, S. M., & Moorthy, M. (2010). *Protégé RDF(s)-DB Backend Plugin.* Retrieved March 4, 2010, from http://protege.stanford.edu/

Smith, M. K., Welty, C., & McGuinness, D. L. (2004). *OWL Web Ontology Language Guide.* Retrieved November 12, 2009, from http://www.w3.org/TR/2004/REC-owl-guide-20040210/

Studer, R., Grimm, S., & Abecker, A. (Eds.). (2007). *Semantic web services concepts, technologies, and applications.* New York, NY: Springer. doi:10.1007/3-540-70894-4

Sun Microsystems. (2004). *Java™ Remote method invocation specification.* Retrieved from http://java.sun.com/j2se/1.5/pdf/rmi-spec-1.5.0.pdf

Syeda-Mahmood, T. G., Shah, L. Y., & Urban, W. (2005). Semantic search of schema repositories. In *Proceedings of the Special Interest Tracks and Posters of the 14th International Conference on World Wide Web*, Chiba, Japan (pp. 1126-1127).

Todd, N., & Szolkowski, M. (2003). Locating Resources Using JNDI (Java Naming and Directory Interface). In Todd, N., & Szolkowski, M. (Eds.), *JavaServer Pages Developer's Handbook.* Indianapolis, IN: Sams.

Weisfeld, M. (2009). *The object-oriented thought process* (3rd ed.). Upper Saddle River, NJ: Pearson Education.

Wirfs-Brock, R., & McKean, A. (1999). *Objects design.* Reading, MA: Addison-Wesley.

Yung, W. (2007). *Bring existing data to the Semantic Web, Expose LDAP directories to the Semantic Web with SquirrelRDF.* Retrieved from http://www.ibm.com/developerworks/xml/library/x-semweb.html

APPENDIX

Figure 22. Code example

```xml
<?xml version="1.0" encoding="UTF-8"?>
<rdf:RDF xmlns:owl="http://www.w3.org/2002/07/owl#" xmlns:rdf="http://www.w3.org/1999/02/22-rdf-syntax-ns#"
xmlns:rdfs="http://www.w3.org/2000/01/rdf-schema#">
        <rdf:Description rdf:about="Cls:Class%20A">
                <rdf:type>
                        <rdf:Description rdf:about="http://www.w3.org/2000/01/rdf-schema#Class"/>
                </rdf:type>
                <rdfs:subClassOf>
                        <rdf:Description rdf:about="Cls:Class%20D"/>
                </rdfs:subClassOf>
                <rdfs:subClassOf>
                        <rdf:Description rdf:about="Cls:Class%20E"/>
                </rdfs:subClassOf>
                <owl:oneOf rdf:parseType="Collection">
                        <rdf:Description rdf:about="Info:Programming%20Language"/>
                        <rdf:Description rdf:about="Info:Version"/>
                        <rdf:Description rdf:about="Info:Auther"/>
                        <rdf:Description rdf:about="Info:Date"/>
                        <rdf:Description rdf:about="Info:Size"/>
                </owl:oneOf>
        </rdf:Description>
        <rdf:Description rdf:about="Cat:Root">
                <rdf:type>
                        <rdf:Description rdf:about="http://www.w3.org/2002/07/owl#ObjectProperty"/>
                </rdf:type>
                <rdfs:domain>
                        <rdf:Description rdf:about="Cls:Class%20A"/>
                </rdfs:domain>
                <rdfs:domain>
                        <rdf:Description rdf:about="Cls:Class%20B"/>
                </rdfs:domain>
                <rdfs:domain>
                        <rdf:Description rdf:about="Cls:Class%20C"/>
                </rdfs:domain>
        </rdf:Description>
        <rdf:Description rdf:about="Cls:Class%20B">
                <rdf:type>
                        <rdf:Description rdf:about="http://www.w3.org/2000/01/rdf-schema#Class"/>
                </rdf:type>
        </rdf:Description>
        <rdf:Description rdf:about="Cls:Class%20C">
                <rdf:type>
                        <rdf:Description rdf:about="http://www.w3.org/2002/07/owl#Class"/>
                </rdf:type>
        </rdf:Description>
        <rdf:Description rdf:about="Cls:Class%20D">
                <rdf:type>
                        <rdf:Description rdf:about="http://www.w3.org/2002/07/owl#Class"/>
                </rdf:type>
        </rdf:Description>
        <rdf:Description rdf:about="Cls:Class%20E">
                <rdf:type>
                        <rdf:Description rdf:about="http://www.w3.org/2002/07/owl#Class"/>
                </rdf:type>
        </rdf:Description>
        <rdf:Description rdf:about="Info:Programming%20Language">
                <rdf:type>
                        <rdf:Description rdf:about="http://www.w3.org/2002/07/owl#Thing"/>
                </rdf:type>
        </rdf:Description>
        <rdf:Description rdf:about="Info:Version">
                <rdf:type>
                        <rdf:Description rdf:about="http://www.w3.org/2002/07/owl#Thing"/>
                </rdf:type>
        </rdf:Description>
        <rdf:Description rdf:about="Info:Auther">
                <rdf:type>
                        <rdf:Description rdf:about="http://www.w3.org/2002/07/owl#Thing"/>
                </rdf:type>
        </rdf:Description>
        <rdf:Description rdf:about="Info:Date">
                <rdf:type>
                        <rdf:Description rdf:about="http://www.w3.org/2002/07/owl#Thing"/>
                </rdf:type>
        </rdf:Description>
        <rdf:Description rdf:about="Info:Size">
                <rdf:type>
                        <rdf:Description rdf:about="http://www.w3.org/2002/07/owl#Thing"/>
                </rdf:type>
        </rdf:Description>
</rdf:RDF>
```

Figure 23. Code example

```
<?xml version="1.0"?>

<!DOCTYPE rdf:RDF [
  <!ENTITY owl "http://www.w3.org/2002/07/owl#" >
  <!ENTITY swrl "http://www.w3.org/2003/11/swrl#" >
  <!ENTITY swrlb "http://www.w3.org/2003/11/swrlb#"
>
  <!ENTITY xsd
"http://www.w3.org/2001/XMLSchema#" >
  <!ENTITY rdfs "http://www.w3.org/2000/01/rdf-
schema#" >
  <!ENTITY rdf "http://www.w3.org/1999/02/22-rdf-
syntax-ns#" >
  <!ENTITY protege
"http://protege.stanford.edu/plugins/owl/protege#" >
  <!ENTITY xsp "http://www.owl-
ontologies.com/2005/08/07/xsp.owl#" >
]>
<rdf:RDF
xmlns="http://www.Semantic_Search_Engine/Ontology
&amp;OOP_Mapping.owl#"

xml:base="http://www.Semantic_Search_Engine/Ontolo
gy&amp;OOP_Mapping.owl"
  xmlns:rdfs="http://www.w3.org/2000/01/rdf-
schema#"
  xmlns:swrl="http://www.w3.org/2003/11/swrl#"

xmlns:protege="http://protege.stanford.edu/plugins/owl/
protege#"
  xmlns:xsp="http://www.owl-
ontologies.com/2005/08/07/xsp.owl#"
  xmlns:owl="http://www.w3.org/2002/07/owl#"
  xmlns:xsd="http://www.w3.org/2001/XMLSchema#"
  xmlns:swrlb="http://www.w3.org/2003/11/swrlb#"
  xmlns:rdf="http://www.w3.org/1999/02/22-rdf-syntax-
ns#">
  <owl:Ontology rdf:about=""/>
  <owl:Class rdf:ID="Class_Circle">
    <rdfs:subClassOf rdf:resource="#Class_Shape"/>
  </owl:Class>
  <owl:Class rdf:ID="Class_Rectangle">
    <rdfs:subClassOf rdf:resource="#Class_Shape"/>
  </owl:Class>
  <owl:Class rdf:ID="Class_Shape">
    <rdfs:comment
rdf:datatype="&xsd;string"></rdfs:comment>
  </owl:Class>
  <owl:ObjectProperty rdf:ID="Code_Circle">
    <rdf:type rdf:resource="&owl;FunctionalProperty"/>
    <rdfs:domain rdf:resource="#Class_Circle"/>
    <rdfs:comment rdf:datatype="&xsd;string"
      >public class Circle extends Shape{
        double radius;
        public Circle(double r) {
        radius = r;
        }
        public double getArea() {
        area = 3.14*(radius*radius);
        return (area);
        }
}</rdfs:comment>
    <rdfs:range>
      <owl:Restriction>
        <owl:onProperty
rdf:resource="#Code_Circle"/>
        <owl:hasValue
rdf:resource="#Class_Circle"/>
      </owl:Restriction>
```

```
    </rdfs:range>
  </owl:ObjectProperty>
  <owl:ObjectProperty rdf:ID="Code_Rectangle">
    <rdf:type rdf:resource="&owl;FunctionalProperty"/>
    <rdfs:domain rdf:resource="#Class_Rectangle"/>
    <rdfs:comment rdf:datatype="&xsd;string"
      >public class Rectangle extends Shape{
        double length;
        double width;
        public Rectangle(double l, double w){
        length = l;
        width = w;
        }
        public double getArea() {
        area = length*width;
        return (area);
        }
}</rdfs:comment>
    <rdfs:range>
      <owl:Restriction>
        <owl:onProperty
rdf:resource="#Code_Rectangle"/>
        <owl:hasValue
rdf:resource="#Class_Rectangle"/>
      </owl:Restriction>
    </rdfs:range>
  </owl:ObjectProperty>
  <owl:FunctionalProperty rdf:ID="Code_Shape">
    <rdf:type rdf:resource="&owl;ObjectProperty"/>
    <rdfs:domain rdf:resource="#Class_Shape"/>
    <rdfs:comment rdf:datatype="&xsd;string"
      >public abstract class Shape{
        private double area;
        public abstract double getArea();
}</rdfs:comment>
    <rdfs:range>
      <owl:Restriction>
        <owl:onProperty
rdf:resource="#Code_Shape"/>
        <owl:hasValue
rdf:resource="#Class_Shape"/>
      </owl:Restriction>
    </rdfs:range>
  </owl:FunctionalProperty>
</rdf:RDF>
```

This journal was previously published in the International Journal of Technology Diffusion, Volume 2, Issue 3, edited by Ali Hussein Saleh Zolait, pp. 47-71, copyright 2011 by IGI Publishing (an imprint of IGI Global).

Chapter 16
Segmentation of Arabic Characters:
A Comprehensive Survey

Ahmed M. Zeki
University of Bahrain, Bahrain

Mohamad S. Zakaria
Universiti Kebangsaan Malaysia, Malaysia

Choong-Yeun Liong
Universiti Kebangsaan Malaysia, Malaysia

ABSTRACT

The cursive nature of Arabic writing is the main challenge to Arabic Optical Character Recognition developer. Methods to segment Arabic words into characters have been proposed. This paper provides a comprehensive review of the methods proposed by researchers to segment Arabic characters. The segmentation methods are categorized into nine different methods based on techniques used. The advantages and drawbacks of each are presented and discussed. Most researchers did not report the segmentation accuracy in their research; instead, they reported the overall recognition rate which did not reflect the influence of each sub-stage on the final recognition rate. The size of the training/testing data was not large enough to be generalized. The field of Arabic Character Recognition needs a standard set of test documents in both image and character formats, together with the ground truth and a set of performance evaluation tools, which would enable comparing the performance of different algorithms. As each method has its strengths, a hybrid segmentation approach is a promising method. The paper concludes that there is still no perfect segmentation method for ACR and much opportunity for research in this area.

1. INTRODUCTION

The Arabic language is one of the most structured and served languages. It comes as the fifth of the most used languages (as a first language) after Chinese, Hindi, Spanish and English. It is spoken as a first language by nearly 350 million people around the globe, mainly in the Arab countries, which is about 5.5% of the world population (the world population is estimated at 6.44 billion in July 2005) (CIA, 2005). However, almost all Muslims (close to ¼ of the world population) can read Arabic script as it is the language of the Holy Qur'an.

DOI: 10.4018/978-1-4666-2791-8.ch016

The Arabic script evolved from a type of Aramaic, with the earliest known document dating from 512 AD. The Aramaic language has fewer consonants than Arabic (Burrow, 2004). The old Arabic was written without dots or diacritics. The dots were first introduced by Yahya bin Ya'mur (died around 746 AD) and Nasr bin Asim (died around 707 AD), students of Abu Al-Aswad Al-Du'ali (died around 688 AD) who introduced the diacritics to prevent the Qur'an from being misread by Muslims (Al-Fakhri, 1997). Figure 1 shows a sample of an old manuscript of a sentence written without dots or diacritics.

Due to the Islamic conquests, the use of Arabic language extended in the 7th and 8th centuries from India to the Atlantic Ocean (Al-Fakhri, 1997). Consequently, many other languages adopted the Arabic alphabet with some changes. Among those languages are Jawi, Urdu, Persian, Ottoman, Kashmiri, Punjabi, Dari, Pashto, Adighe, Baluchi, Ingush, Kazakh, Uzbek, Kyrgyz, Uygur, Sindhi, Lahnda, Hausa, Berber, Comorian, Mandinka, Wolof, Dargwa, and few others. Figure 2 shows samples of some of the above mentioned languages. However, it must be mentioned that some of those languages are currently using Latin characters, but in general, people can still read the Arabic script. It is also worth mentioning that the United Nation adopted Arabic in 1974 as its sixth official language (Strange, 1993).

Despite the fact that Arabic alphabets are used in many languages, Arabic Character Recognition (ACR) has not received enough interests from researchers. Little research progress has been achieved as compared to the one done on Latin or Chinese. It has almost only started in 1975 by Nazif (1975), while the earlier research efforts in Latin may be traced back to the middle of the 1940s. However, due to a lack of computing power, no significant work was performed until the 1980s. Recent years have shown a considerable increase in the number of research papers related to ACR.

The rest of this paper is organized as follows: the next section will introduce the Arabic Character Recognition in general. Section 3 will discuss the challenges faced by researchers attempting to segment Arabic characters. Section 4 reviews the methods used in segmenting the Arabic characters. Those methods are categorized under nine different categories based on the techniques used. The paper then ends with a discussion and conclusion.

2. ARABIC CHARACTER RECOGNITION

Character recognition is a major field in the area of pattern recognition which has been the subject of much research in the past four decades. The ultimate goal of any character recognition system is to simulate the human reading capabilities. A character recognition system is a program designed to convert a scanned document, which is seen by the computer as an image, into a text document that can be edited (Zeki & Ismail, 2002).

Character recognition systems can contribute tremendously to the advancement of the automation process and can improve the human computer interaction in many applications, including office automation, automatic mail routing, check verification, library archives, documents identifications,

Figure 1. The Arabic sentence "زادكم في الخلق بسطة فاذكروا" *written without dots*

Figure 2. Samples of languages which use the Arabic alphabets

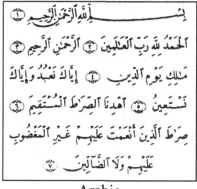

Arabic

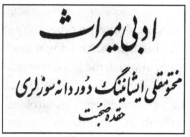

Urdu

هرکه نامُخت از گذشت روزگار
نیز ناموزد ز هیچ آموزگار

Persian

ادبی میراث

Ottoman

e-books production, invoice and shipping receipt processing, subscription collections, vehicle license plate recognition, signature verification, machine processing of forms, questionnaire processing, exam papers processing, and a large variety of banking, business, and data entry applications (Amin et al., 1996; Khorsheed, 2002). Most of those applications are valuable since most of the text we are interested in recognizing is already in printed form (Al-Badr & Mahmoud, 1995).

Arabic OCR solutions available in the market are still far from being perfect (Kunungo et al., 1999). There are several reasons led to this poor result. Among them are: the lack of standardization, the availability of adequate Arabic Databases (DBs), electronic dictionaries, language corpus, and programming tools as well as the emergence of well-established benchmark test procedures. There exists a lack of adequate support and enjoying a less opportune environment in terms of funding and coordination, also no strong research groups

are available. Finally, no specialized conference or symposium has been conducted so far. More important is the cursive nature of Arabic writing (Alshebeili et al., 1997; Khorsheed, 2002; Zeki & Zakaria, 2004).

The different approaches covered under the general term "character recognition" fall into either the online or offline category, each having its own hardware and recognition algorithms. In online character recognition systems, the computer recognizes the symbols as they are drawn. Offline recognition is performed after the writing or printing is completed (Amin, 1997), which means that the temporal information of the text is lost. Other complexity that an offline recognition system has to deal with is the lower resolution of the document. Hence, in terms of simplicity, it is much easier to segment and recognize the online handwriting than the offline machine printed words.

Character recognition systems differ widely in how they acquire their input (online versus offline), in the mode of writing (handwritten versus machine-printed), in the restriction on the fonts (single font versus omnifont) they can recognize, and in the connectivity of text (isolated characters versus cursive words). When it comes to the method of use, the issue becomes whether to segment or not to segment, to segment into characters or into primitives, and to segment during the recognition stage or before.

In a typical OCR system for cursive script, input characters are read and digitized by an optical scanner. Each character is then located and segmented, and the resulting matrix is fed into a preprocessor for smoothing, noise reduction, size normalization and other preprocessing stages (Amin, 1997). This approach is known as an analytical approach, in which the word is segmented into smaller classifiable units such as characters, pseudo-characters, graphemes, or strokes. It is clear how difficult this approach is, especially in the case of handwritten script. However, the advantage of this approach is that it can be used to recognize infinitely large vocabularies (Hashemi et al., 1995).

To avoid the difficult and computationally costly segmentation stage, researchers came out with another approach known as a holistic (or global) approach, in which the recognition is globally performed on the whole representation of words and with no attempt to identify characters individually, hence, it is also known as segmentation-free approach. This approach depends highly on a predefined lexicon which acts as a look-up dictionary (Khorsheed & Clocksin, 1999). Therefore, it is used when the number of words to be recognized is limited (e.g., written numbers on checks, city names, and PDA commands). This approach was originally introduced for speech recognition (Amin, 1996). However, this approach is out of the scope of this survey. For more details on the holistic approach see Al-Badr and Haralick (1992, 1998). Figure 3 shows the major processes in a typical offline Arabic OCR system.

3. CHALLENGES IN SEGMENTING ARABIC CHARACTERS

Several efforts have been devoted to the recognition of cursive script but so far it is still a challenge to researchers. Segmentation methods for cursive and machine printed Latin text have been studied extensively. The effort and techniques deemed necessary for recognizing isolated Arabic characters are not fundamentally different from those used for Latin OCR, but the wider variability of the Arabic character shapes needs more attention (Jambi, 1991). Although some methods for cursive Latin might carry over to Arabic, in general, they are insufficient for segmenting Arabic text (Mostafa, 2004).

Character segmentation and classification, especially for handwritten Arabic characters, depend largely on contextual information, and not only on the topographic features extracted from these characters (Hamid, 2001). Analysis of cursive scripts requires structural description to recognizing Arabic characters, the segmentation of characters within the word, and the detection of individual features.

Amin (2002) stated that this is not a problem unique to computers; even human beings, who possess the most efficient optical reading device (eyes), have difficulty in recognizing some cursive scripts and have an error rate of about 4% on reading tasks in the absence of context. These errors are mainly due to the variation in shapes related to the writing habits, styles, education, social environment, health, psychological situation, and other conditions affecting the writer. Other technical factors may include the writing instrument, writing surfaces, scanning algorithms, and machine recognition algorithms used (Amin & Mari, 1989).

No matter which algorithm is used in the segmentation, it must be derived from the nature of cursive connection in Arabic text (Al-Waily, 1989). Hence, an in-depth understanding of the characteristics of the Arabic script is necessary

Figure 3. Block diagram showing the major processes in an offline Arabic OCR system

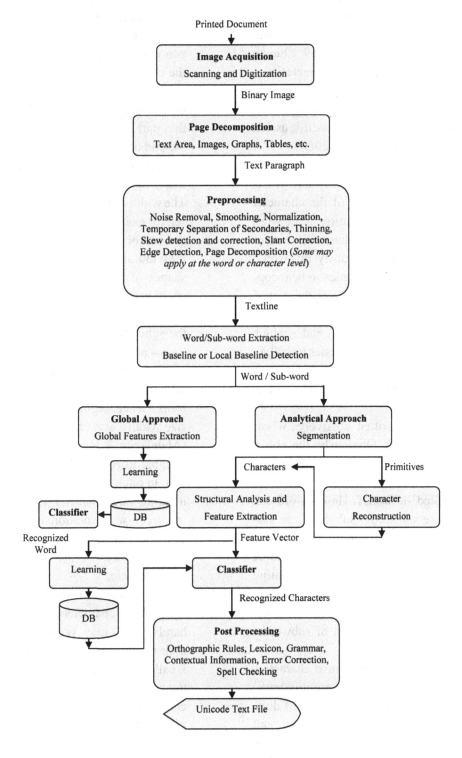

for the development of an OCR system. This knowledge helps in selecting the best technique to be used and may also lead to the development of new techniques (Amin & Mari, 1989; Cheung et al., 2001). Therefore, only those characteristics of Arabic script that heavily influence the process of segmentation and affect its results accuracy are presented here. A more comprehensive discussion can be found in Zeki and Zakaria (2004).

1. Arabic is written from right to left. It has 28 characters. The shape of the character varies according to its position in the word (Table 1). Each character has either two or four different forms. Obviously, this would increase the number of classes to be recognized from 28 to 112. However, there are 6 characters that can only be connected from the right. These are: ز,ر,ذ,د,ا, and و, which will reduce the number of classes to 100. In addition to the 28 characters, there are some supplementary characters such as ء and ى.

Arabic is always written cursively. Words are separated by spaces. Obviously, the above six characters, if appeared in a word, will cause the word to be divided into blocks of connected components called subwords. Thus a word can have one or more subwords. Subwords are also separated by spaces, but usually shorter than the ones between words. So, this issue needs to be considered in ACR systems to avoid segmenting a word into two subwords. Examples of words in which all characters are connected: مجيد ,فسيكفيكهم خليل . Examples of words consist of subwords: طريق, شهادة, ورود .

As it is obvious in Table 1, most characters share the same primary body and are differentiated solely by the location and number of dots. Hence, Arabic text is far more sensitive to "salt and pepper" noise and speckle noise than are Latin character based languages (Trenkle et al., 2001).

2. Arabic characters are normally connected on an imaginary line called baseline, as shown in Figure 4. This line is as thick as a pen point and much less than the width of the character beginning (Romeo-Pakker et al., 1995). So, there is a thin part at the end of a connected character, detection of this thin part is a necessary condition to define the end of a connected character; however, it is not sufficient because some characters like س have thin parts in their middle as well.

3. The width of an Arabic character is variable, see for example ك and ا . They differ also in height, for instance: د and ل . Furthermore, the width and height vary across the different shapes of the same character in different positions in a word. It is maximal either when the character is situated at the end of the subword or when it is isolated, e.g., ب vs. -ب- and ح vs. -ح- . Furthermore, the connection strokes between characters have different lengths and heights for different fonts. Hence, segmentation based on a fixed size width —also called pitch segmentation (Abdelazim & Hashish, 1989) — is not applicable to Arabic. It is worth mentioning that, in pitch segmentation, an error in segmenting one character is likely to cause incorrect segmentation of the following characters in the same word (Al-Yousefi & Upda, 1992). Figure 5 illustrates this characteristic.

4. Arabic script is written in many fonts and styles. Some characters, especially in Arabic handwriting, may vertically overlap with their neighboring characters forming what is called "ligatures" (Amin, 1996), in which, the second character may starts before the end of the first one or even before the beginning of it in a horizontal scanning as shown in Figure 6. Ligatures are often font-dependent (Khorsheed, 2002), and it is estimated that ligatures occur at least 10 times in every 100 subwords (Hamid & Haraty, 2001).

Table 1. Shapes of Arabic characters in different positions

Character Name		Final	Medial	Initial	Isolated
Alif	ألف	ـا	ـا	ا	ا
Ba'	باء	ـب	ـبـ	بـ	ب
Ta'	تاء	ـت	ـتـ	تـ	ت
Tha'	ثاء	ـث	ـثـ	ثـ	ث
Jeem	جيم	ـج	ـجـ	جـ	ج
H'a'	حاء	ـح	ـحـ	حـ	ح
Kha'	خاء	ـخ	ـخـ	خـ	خ
Dal	دال	ـد	ـد	د	د
Th'al	ذال	ـذ	ـذ	ذ	ذ
Ra'	راء	ـر	ـر	ر	ر
Zai	زاي	ـز	ـز	ز	ز
Seen	سين	ـس	ـسـ	سـ	س
Sheen	شين	ـش	ـشـ	شـ	ش
S'ad	صاد	ـص	ـصـ	صـ	ص
Dhad	ضاد	ـض	ـضـ	ضـ	ض
T'a'	طاء	ـط	ـطـ	طـ	ط
Dh'a'	ظاء	ـظ	ـظـ	ظـ	ظ
'Ain	عين	ـع	ـعـ	عـ	ع
Ghain	غين	ـغ	ـغـ	غـ	غ
Fa'	فاء	ـف	ـفـ	فـ	ف
Qaf	قاف	ـق	ـقـ	قـ	ق
Kaf	كاف	ـك	ـكـ	كـ	ك
Lam	لام	ـل	ـلـ	لـ	ل
Meem	ميم	ـم	ـمـ	مـ	م
Noon	نون	ـن	ـنـ	نـ	ن
Ha'	هاء	ـه	ـهـ	هـ	ه
Waw	واو	ـو	ـو	و	و
Ya'	ياء	ـي	ـيـ	يـ	ي
Supplement Characters					
Connected Ta'	تاء مربوطة	ـة			ة
Hamza	همزة				ء
Alif Maqsura	ألف مقصورة	ـى			ى

Figure 4. The baseline (Arabic transparent font)

257

Figure 5. Arabic characters have different heights and widths

1.

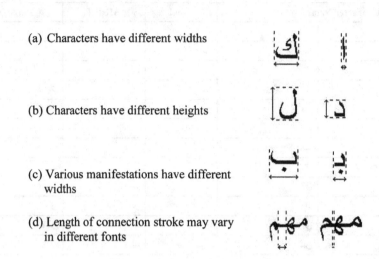

    (a) Characters have different widths

    (b) Characters have different heights

    (c) Various manifestations have different widths

    (d) Length of connection stroke may vary in different fonts

However, the only compulsory ligature is ال while all others are optional (Zeki & Zakaria, 2004). Majority of researchers dealt with the ligature as one single character, although that will increase the number of classes (Haj-Hassan, 1990). Figure 6 illustrates this concept.

Artistic (calligraphy) is another style of Arabic typing, usually full of ligatures, overriding, overlapping, and characters are usually elongated in a decorative way as the one shown in Figure 7. Obviously, this feature makes it difficult to determine the boundaries of the characters even for human. It is worth mentioning that recently there are attempts to generate such fonts by computers (Sakkal, 2002).

5. The strokes of some characters like س or ش are omitted in some fonts or handwriting styles as shown in Figure 8. Dots may appear as two separated dots, touched dots, hat or as a stroke.

6. There are only three characters that represent vowels; و, ا and ي. However, there are other shorter vowels represented by diacritics in the form of overscores or underscores. Use of diacritics is sometimes important to show the correct pronunciation and meaning. For example, the word معلم, if written without diacritics —also out of context— will confuse the reader between three different pronunciations and meanings: مُعَلِّم (Mu'allim) which means teacher, مُعَلَّم (Mu'allam) which means taught or trained, and مَعْلَم (Ma'lam)

Figure 6. Considering the ligature as one character

Figure 7. Arabic calligraphy "وعد الله الذين آمنوا وعملوا الصالحات لهم مغفرة وأجر عظيم"

which means milestone or landmark. Note that some diacritics (Fatha ˒, Dhamma ˒and Kasra) may appear above/below Hamza (ء) and Shadda ().

Madda (~) is used usually with character ا, i.c., آ . There are some other rules that need to be considered such as the Sukoon (˚) is never associated with any other diacritics on the same character. Such rules are very useful in detecting recognition errors. Figure 9 shows the use of the most common diacritics.

In general, a cursive word is recognized through a hierarchical analysis, i.e., a word is decomposed into subwords, subwords into letters, and letters

Figure 8. The strokes of س *are omitted in some fonts*

$$سيف = حـ ـيفـ$$

into primitives made of strokes (Amin & Mari, 1989). Hence, segmentation can be defined as the process of dividing a word into classifiable units to be passed to a recognition stage. Those units could be characters, combination of characters or small strokes (graphemes or primitives). The selection of the type and number of units has direct consequences on the recognition performance (Al-Fakhri, 1997). Segmentation is one of the most crucial, hardest, and time-consuming phases. It represents the main challenge in any ACR system, even more than the recognition process itself (Jambi, 1991). It is considered as the main source of recognition errors. A poor segmentation process leads to mis-recognition or rejection (Obaid, 1998) as incorrectly segmented characters are unlikely to be recognized correctly (Sari et al., 2002).

As it is so difficult and with a great influence on the final recognition rate, many researchers tried to avoid this stage by assuming that characters are

Figure 9. The use of the most common diacritics

عَنَّا   تَشْكُرُونَ   آبَاؤُكُم   كَأَحَدٍ   مَسْجِدٌ

كَبِيرٌ   قَوْلاً   أُولَئِكَ   أَوْلِيَاؤُكُم   مَعْرُوفٌ

already segmented (Alherbish & Ammar, 1998; Fayek & Al Basha, 1992) or treated the whole word as a recognition unit (Al-Badr & Haralick, 1992; Khorsheed & Clocksin, 2000). Dealing with isolated Arabic characters is not practical, except in cases were characters are already isolated such as mathematical formulas (El-Sheikh, 1990). In the early attempts of ACR system development, Parhami and Taraghi (1981) claimed that the segmentation problem was beyond those days' capabilities. Some attempts went even to the extent of proposing new fonts to generate an Arabic script instead of the cursive one whereby the characters can be segmented with simple vertical white cuts to help in automatic document understanding (Abuhaiba, 2003 & Nouh et al., 1980). Moreover, the constrained character recognition is not applicable to Arabic text because of the connectivity property and characters may overlap in domain (Altuwaijri & Bayoumi, 1994).

As mentioned earlier, segmenting online handwriting is always easier than offline because the time dimension exists in online systems. Based on this fact, Abuhaiba and Ahmed (1993) attempted to restore the temporal information in order to use the techniques designed for online systems. It is also generally accepted that segmentation of a typeset Arabic text is harder than that of a typewritten text. This is mainly due to ligatures and character overlapping. However, recognizing handwritten Arabic text is even harder (Alshebeili et al., 1997).

As the document may contain, in addition to the text, other objects such as figures, it becomes an essential to any OCR system to distinguish between textual and non textual components. The document is decomposed into text areas, text lines, words, and subwords, until we reach the level of classifiable characters, ligatures, or graphemes. Some preprocessing stages are assumed done before the segmentation stage. These stages may include noise removal, page orientation (Zeki & Zakaria, 2005), skew detection and correction, and others. Some methods, especially those based on the projection profile, assume that the Arabic text to be well aligned. This can be assured by the Arabic text image acquisition process, and if necessary, a pre-process for skew correction can be included (Zheng et al., 2004). In this paper, it is assumed that the document is substantially text or the text areas have already been identified using methods such as the one proposed by Hadjar and Ingold (2003). Page decomposition is a sub-field of document analysis. Document analysis studies the structure of documents and the identification of the different logical parts in documents (Khorsheed, 2002).

3.1. Line Segmentation

The process of line segmentation aims to separate the pairs of consecutive lines in the text. The process is based on the analysis of the horizontal projection profile of the text, in which, the number of black pixels is found for each row of the image. This number is big at the baseline of each text line. Then the gaps between the text lines are identified by a full row or rows of pixels with zero value as shown in Figure 10. The identified rows are then checked top down to determine the top and bottom of each text line (Fakir et al., 1999). This process should consider the dots above and below the characters; otherwise, they might be isolated as separate lines, giving wrong results. In the case of diacriticized text the line segmentation should also consider the distance allowed between lines compared with the distance between diacritics and characters themselves (El-Dabi et al., 1990).

When the lines are not regularly spaced and upper or lower overstrokes are overlapping, some researchers calculated the mean value of these projections which allows locating the lowercase writing area. The detection of each line starts inside this area and follows the contour of words to avoid overlapping (Romeo-Pakker et al., 2005).

3.2. Word Segmentation

The segmentation of lines into words is achieved simply by detecting spaces between them on their projection on a horizontal axis (Haj-Hassan, 1990) as illustrated in Figure 11. As mentioned earlier, the Arabic words may consist of subwords which are also separated by spaces; hence, the process of word segmentation could also isolate them. Therefore, in order to avoid that, it is worth mentioning that the spaces between subwords are usually shorter than those between words. Haj-Hassan (1990) stated that the minimal space between 2 words is always bigger than the maximum space between subwords. Fakir et al. (2000) estimated the space between words to be half of the text line height. Contour tracing can also be used to extract

Figure 10. The horizontal projection of an Arabic paragraph

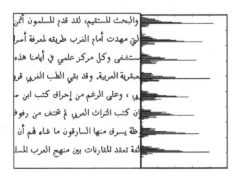

words and subwords. For more details on word segmentation, see for example (Cheung et al., 1997a). In case of confusion, the use of dictionary or spell checker becomes necessary.

Overlapping of adjacent Arabic characters in the same word forms ligatures. Moreover, it is possible in some fonts and handwriting that subwords overlap on each other as well. As a consequence of this kind of overlapping, the vertical projection profile will not indicate a gap between words or subwords as illustrated in Figure 11. However, this problem can be solved easily by tracing the contour (El-Sheikh & Guindi, 1988) as far as the characters are not touching; otherwise, separating them is not a straightforward process. This problem was ignored in most researches because recognition has been implemented on printed text or on handwritten characters with no overlapping (Jambi, 1991). El-Dabi et al. (1990) proposed a method to segment touching characters by finding what is called the cutting edge, however, the method requires that the character is recognized first in order to proceed with the segmentation.

Furthermore, the segmentation is much more difficult than recognition. Humans can easily segment the Arabic word into characters; however, it is not yet an easy task for computers. Recently, this feature was used in filling online forms to tell computer from humans, it works by generating a sequence of characters in different orientations with randomly distributed strokes over the image. The technique was implemented, for instance, by MSN to avoid auto-registration for hotmail accounts and showed 19% drop in daily registration (Simard et al., 2003).

4. ARABIC CHARACTER SEGMENTATION METHODS

Human can easily segment an Arabic word into characters. However, it is not easy to segment it directly into perfect characters by the computer.

Figure 11. Word segmentation using vertical projection profile. Notice the overlapped characters (the projection is constructed after eliminating the secondaries).

Producing perfect characters for the segmentation process is not always possible such as in the case of ligatures or destroyed characters. Therefore, three types of output may come out from the segmentation process: characters, strokes (i.e., parts of a character) and combination of two characters or more. Figure 12 illustrates this concept. It shows the word سبالم, in which, the characters م and ب are perfectly segmented, while the combination of ل and ا is segmented as one character ال. It is even worst in the case of س which has been segmented into three parts.

Hence, two strategies have been applied for segmenting Arabic characters –direct and indirect segmentations (Mostafa, 2004; Abuhaiba et al., 1998; Bushofa & Spann, 1997a, 1997b). In the direct segmentation strategy, the word is segmented directly into letters by applying some rules that attempt to identify all the character segmentation points. On the other hand, in indirect segmentation strategy, a word is segmented into smaller units called strokes which are extracted by finding certain features in the character, such as starting points, ending points, points of sudden change in curvature, cusps, open curves, closed curves, and others (Al-Fakhri, 1997). Those strokes are then recombined to form characters. The advantage of the second approach is that it is easier to find a set of potential connection points than to find the actual connection points directly (Khorsheed & Clocksin, 1999). However, this approach is usually more expensive because it

may lead to over-segmentation in which the process of recombining the strokes to form a character might be very complex.

The process of character segmentation is identified as the cause of recognition errors, and hence a low recognition rate (Khorsheed & Clocksin, 1999). As such, many algorithms' developers prefer to follow the indirect segmentation approach (Almuallim & Yamaguchi, 1987; Hassibi, 1994; Fehri & Ben Ahmed, 1994).

Several attempts to segment the Arabic word into characters can be found in the literature. The work of Parhami and Taraghi (1981) followed by the work of Amin and Masini (1982) were the first attempts to segment the Arabic characters. Since those days, several methods have been proposed. In early attempts, vertical projection was employed for this purpose. Later trend was to obtain the skeleton of the word and trace it systematically searching for proper segmentation points (Obaid & Dobrowiecki, 1997). This method was followed by attempts to segment the words by tracing the contour and upper distance function. Neural networks, line adjacency graph, and morphological operations were also used. There were also attempts to segment while or after recognition.

However, those methods can be categorized into two approaches generally: explicit and implicit approaches (Amin, 1996). In the explicit approach, also known as dissection segmentation (Cheung et al., 2001) words are explicitly or ex-

Figure 12. Three types of segmentation output

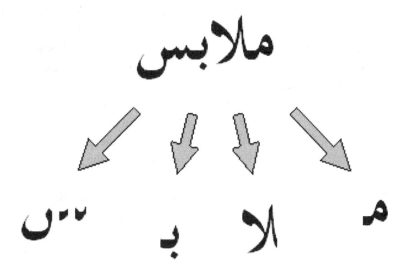

ternally segmented into characters or primitives which are then recognized individually. Contextual high level knowledge (lexical, syntactic or semantic knowledge) is then used to ensure the proper word identification. This approach is usually more expensive due to the increased complexity of finding optimum segmentation points. In the implicit approach, characters are segmented while being recognized, hence, it is also called recognition-based segmentation or straight-segmentation. This type of segmentation is usually designed with rules that attempt to identify all the character's segmentation points. Many rules must be constructed manually to achieve good accuracy. In general, the higher the number of rules, the higher the recognition rate that is to assure a wider coverage of the variability of writing styles (Amin, 2001).

In this paper, segmentation methods are comprehensively reviewed and categorized based on the techniques used. The following are the techniques found to cover all segmentation algorithms proposed so far in the literature. In the next sub-sections they will be discussed in details including their advantages and shortcomings. The techniques are:

1. Methods based on Projection Profile
2. Methods based on Character Skeleton
3. Methods based on Contour Tracing
4. Methods based on Template Matching
5. Methods based on Neural Networks
6. Methods based or Hidden Markov Models
7. Methods based on Line Adjacency Graph
8. Methods based on Morphological Operations
9. Recognition-based Segmentation Methods

4.1. Methods Based on Projection Profile

The aim of the projection method is to simplify drastically a system of character recognition by reducing 2D information into 1D. Historically this method appeared in the early stage of OCR (Mori et al., 1999). It works better with printed documents, especially with fonts which do not form ligatures such as 'Arabic Transparent' and 'Simplified Arabic'. However, for fonts like 'Traditional Arabic' which contains many ligature forms, it does not perform well and even worst with handwritten text. Figure 13 shows an Arabic sentence written in different fonts. Notice the ligatures in the third statement, while the fifth one shows a fixed-width font.

These methods are based on the fact that the connection stroke between characters is always of less thickness than other parts of the word. In these methods, the vertical and horizontal projections of the image are obtained.

The horizontal projection is defined as:

$$h(i) = \sum_j p(i,j) \tag{1}$$

and the vertical projection as:

$$v(j) = \sum_i p(i,j) \tag{2}$$

where p is the pixel value (0 or 1), i is the row number, and j is the column number.

The horizontal projection is useful in separating the lines and detection of text baseline, while the vertical ones are used to segment words, subwords and characters. Figure 14 through Figure 17 shows the horizontal and vertical projection profiles of

an Arabic sentence after removing the secondaries. The longest spike in Figure 16 represents the baseline. The baseline thickness is determined by computing the thickness of the longest spike, taking the most repeated column-height (Timsari & Fahimi, 1996), or considering the position of loops as a reference as they are always close to the baseline (Figure 17) (Olivier et al., 1996).

Among other basic information that can be computed from the projection profile are the width, height and number of connected components (subwords) (Al-Yousefi & Upda, 1992).

Haj-Hassan (1990) conducted an unsupervised training prior to the segmentation process. He used the thickness and length of the characters as two main criteria in the segmentation process. To allow tolerance in the size of characters, he defined all measures relatively to the height of the line. He studied the projection profile and came out with some interesting observations that help a lot in segmenting words into characters. Among them are:

Figure 13. An Arabic sentence written in different fonts

وآمنوا بما نزل على محمد وهو الحق من ربهم كفر عنهم سيئاتهم وأصلح بالهم[1]

وآمنوا بما نزل على محمد وهو الحق من ربهم كفر عنهم سيئاتهم وأصلح بالهم[2]

وآمنوا بما نزل على محمد وهو الحق من ربهم كفر عنهم سيئاتهم وأصلح بالهم[3]

وآمنوا بما نزل على محمد وهو الحق من ربهم كفر عنهم سيئاتهم

وأصلح بالهم[4]

و امنوا بما نزل على محمد وهو الحق من ربهم كفر

عنهم سيناتهم و أصلح بالهم[5]

[1] Arabic Transparent Font
[2] Simplified Arabic Font
[3] Traditional Arabic Font (Naskh)
[4] Akhbar MT Font
[5] Simplified Arabic Fixed Font

Figure 14. Horizontal and vertical projections: An Arabic sentence

أحد ضحايا التدخين

- The characters generally begin with a distinctive-shape, so there is always a thick part at the beginning of the projection of a character on a horizontal axis.
- The length of subwords composed of two characters only, is always more than the maximal length of isolated characters.
- The minimal length of a connected character, the maximal length of an isolated character, or a character at the end of a subword can be defined.

However, we found that these finding are not very accurate at least in some cases. For instance, the word ام consists of two characters and still thinner than the letter س in the isolated form, which contradicts with the second finding.

In projection profile methods, the common process practiced by many researchers is to isolate the secondaries before obtaining the vertical and the horizontal projections as they will affect the projection profile too much (refer to Figures 14 and 15). The secondary parts include the dots, Hamza, and diacritics that are associated with some characters (Al-Yousefi & Upda, 1992). The temporary elimination of the secondaries and recognizing them separately reduces the number of classes to be recognized from 100 to 64 and achieves better correlation between character shapes (Jambi, 1992).

The isolation process of the characters into primary and secondary parts is based on the fact that the basic shapes of Arabic characters are simple and the secondaries are typically placed either above or below the characters. However different fonts (as well as handwriting) place them a little differently in relation to the primary parts, and consequently, the recognition process is made more complicated (Al-Yousefi & Upda, 1992). Once the primary body of the character is recognized, it is associated with the corresponding eliminated dot (if exists) to determine the final class of the character (Hashemi et al., 1995). Detailed work on the elimination of the secondaries can be found in Al-Yousefi and Upda (1992), Nouh et al. (1988), Omar et al. (2000), and Fahmy and El-Messiry (2001).

The application of projection profile methods varies. A simple application takes the minimum baseline thickness to separate the characters (Altuwaijri & Bayoumi, 1994; Timsari & Fahimi, 1996; Sadiq-Hussain & Sarsam, 1998) while more sophisticated ones use rules to further enhance the process. For example, Parhami and Taraghi (1980) segmented the subword into characters by identifying a series of potential connection points on the baseline. Potential connection points are points at which line thickness changes from or to the thickness of the baseline, provided that there is a single segment in a column of pixels.

Figure 15. Horizontal and vertical projections: Secondaries are eliminated

احد صحايا السدحس

Figure 16. Horizontal and vertical projections:Horizontal projection

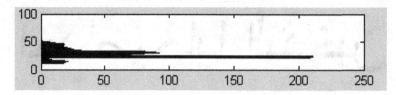

However, the system is heavily font dependent, and fonts of smaller point size will result in less accuracy (Abuhaiba, 2003), and although it uses some rules to keep characters at the end of a sub-word intact, the segmentation process is expected to give incorrect results in some cases (e.g., س) (Abuhaiba et al., 1994).

A similar approach of Parhami and Taraghi (1981) was followed by Moalla et al. (2002) except that the search for vertical projection is made in the middle and lower zones. In case of over-segmentation, a set of rules were used to regroup the strokes. Hammami and Berkani (2002) used a similar method but considered the number of vertical transitions 0–1 or 1–0 for each column in the subword in order to find the boundaries of the characters. Fewer rules were set to avoid over-segmentation. The method was designed for printed text and considered ligatures as one character. However, it fails in case of overlapping (Zidouri et al., 2005). The segmentation rate reported was 98.6%.

A similar approach is also followed by Pal and Sarkar (2003) to segment printed Urdu text into characters, whereby, a text line is scanned vertically. If in one vertical scan two or less object pixels are encountered then the scan is denoted by 0, otherwise the scan is denoted by the number of object pixels in that column. Then if in the vertical projection there exist a run of at least K_l consecutive 0's, then the midpoint of that run is considered as the segmentation point (K_l is determined from the experiment). In case of subword overlapping, this method does not work properly, and hence, each subword is labeled and dealt with separately. The reported segmentation rate was 96.9%.

Amin and Mari (1989) used the Average Value (*AV*) of the vertical projection instead of the simple vertical projection. *AV* is defined as:

$$AV = \frac{\sum_{j=1}^{N_C} C_j}{N_C} \qquad (3)$$

where N_C is the number of columns, and C_j is the number of black pixels of the j_{th} column.

The connectivity point will show the least sum of the average value (*AV*). As the above formula over-estimated the number of connectivity points, rules based on the height and width of the characters were applied to avoid over-segmentation. For instance, the width of the boundary should not be very small and there should be a quick change in the vertical projection in the neighborhood

Figure 17. Horizontal and vertical projections: Vertical projection

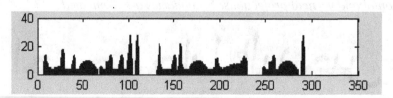

of the potential boundary (Zheng et al., 2004). Another rule is set to consider the long shape of many characters at the end of a word (Amin & Mari, 1989).

The average value method of Amin and Mari (1989) was tested on just a few words and there were no reports about its performance. According to Abuhaiba (2003), the method has inherent ambiguity and deficiencies due to interconnectivity of Arabic text. It also depends heavily on a predefined threshold value related to the character width (Amin, 1996). However, the method seems to be widely accepted, hence, adopted by many researchers (Altuwaijri & Bayoumi, 1994; Al-Yousefi & Upda, 1992; Amin & Masini, 1986; Amin & Al-Fedaghi, 1991; Amin, 1991; Cheung et al., 1997b, 1998; Abuhaiba, 2003).

Ymin and Aoki (1996) segmented the Uygur printed script. They extracted first the vertical projection to search for all potential segmentation points only in the upper zone. Then, those points are verified based on character-width and topological features such as loops. The reported segmentation rate was 93%.

In the work of Zheng et al. (2004), those subwords consisting of one character were excluded first as they do not need to be segmented. Nevertheless, the algorithm used to exclude those single characters was not able to detect all of them correctly. Furthermore, it was also not explained how to count the number of characters in each subword. The vertical projection is then scanned to search for points near the baseline where they changes from low to high values. Those points are considered beginning of characters whereas those points of change from high to low values are the end of characters. Then, some rules are used to verify those potential segmentation points. The method was only tested on non-overlapping fonts and segmentation rate of 94% was reported.

Nawaz et al. (2003) and Sarfraz et al. (2003) used the vertical projection of the middle zone instead of the projection of the entire word. They identified four text line zones, i.e., the upper, middle, baseline and lower zones. The baseline zone is the one with the highest density of black pixels, any zone just above the baseline and twice the thickness of the baseline is the middle zone. The vertical projection of the middle zone is created. A fixed threshold is used for segmenting the word into characters. Whenever the value of the vertical projection of the middle zone is less than two third of the baseline thickness, the area is considered a connection area between two characters. Any area follows the connection area with a larger value is considered as the start of a new character, as long as the profile is greater than one third of the baseline. The method was designed for the recognition of the Naskh font. This method may still oversegments characters such as س as it is not significantly different from the standard technique of the methods based on projection profile. However, the authors tried to resolve this problem in the recognition stage. Unfortunately, they didn't report the segmentation rate.

Fakir et al. (1999) also used the vertical projection profile of the middle zone. Nevertheless, the difference is that they used a fixed threshold to segment the word into characters. From the threshold level, the algorithm searches for the break along the vertical projection profile. However, the middle zone and the threshold value were not defined clearly. The same method was used again later by the authors but was followed by an isolation of the secondaries (Fakir et al., 2000).

Altuwaijri and Bayoumi (1995) constructed the vertical projection for each subword excluding the pixels of the baseline and secondaries. Potential segmentation points are then determined using the minimum projection values and verified by some rules which are designed to avoid over-segmentation.

The previous methods were designed to segment the Arabic printed characters. The method developed by Fahmy and Al Ali (2001) and Al-Ma'adeed (2001) was devoted to segment handwritten text. The maximum and minimum peaks are found from the vertical projection.

The word is then segmented into vertical strips (frames). The boundaries of the strips are then defined to be the midpoints between adjacent maximum / minimum pairs. To ensure that the frames are of proper widths, the very short ones are eliminated and the long ones are divided into shorter and the separation point is chosen to be a portion of the character height. Then, each frame will be divided into three horizontal areas; one below the baseline and two above, from which features will be extracted. However, the results are not perfect; for instance, a character such as ط is divided into two frames.

El-Sheikh and Guindi (1988) used a variant of the vertical projection by calculating the distance between the extreme points of intersection of the contour with a vertical line, i.e., the sum in each column is not the total number of pixels. For each subword the average vertical distance h_{av} is calculated and if it is less than a certain threshold, then a silent region is detected. Two conditions were set: the segmentation points should be on the baseline, and that no secondaries should be detected above or below the silent regions. To avoid unreasonably high distance values resulted from connected overlapped characters, extreme points greater than a certain threshold are rejected.

With slight modification, the same idea was used in Hashemi et al. (1995). Due to imperfections in the scanning process, the derived baseline may be x–pixels far from the actual one. So, segmentation points should be sought in an area x–wide around the detected baseline. If the detected character width is greater than its maximum expected value, the algorithm should be restarted with a decreased window width and an increased height threshold which will result in an earlier detection of the segmentation point. Characters could be separated at different points and generate different shapes which would be alleviated by appending black pixels to both ends of each character. Once a character boundary is detected, a maximum of L pixels will be added to the separated character as long as h_{av} remains

less than a certain threshold. This condition is devised to generate similar shape and size for the same character isolated from different words. In addition, if the remaining of the word is less than a pre-assigned value M wide, the letter would be left attached to the figure, to prevent undesired segmentation of a single character (especially those ending the words). The authors claimed that all characters were segmented with no errors and the method is devised to overcome all the deficiencies of earlier methods while being cautious about computational effort. They also claimed that the method is applicable to any kind of typed text, even if characters are overlapped or highly declined. A performance of 99.7% was reported.

El Gowely et al. (1990) determined the starting point of the character by locating a point where the count of black pixels is greater than the count of the previous point, and then the scan will proceed until the count of black pixels becomes less than a certain ratio of the pixels count of the previous point. The scan line now has passed the main part of the character and this point is recorded and given the name "conversion point". If no such point is detected, the algorithm will record the point at which the count of pixels is zero as the character ending point. The algorithm will continue to search for a point on the character vertical histogram, where the count of black pixels is greater than a certain ratio of the count of the previous point indicating both the beginning of the next character, and the end of the current character. According to the authors, this method was designed to segment multifont Arabic words text. They also reported that this method produces some expected errors which are dealt with during the recognition stage.

In Abdelazim and Hashish (1988, 1989) the technique of traversing the energy curve is used. It is a technique borrowed from the area of speech recognition to discriminate the spoken utterance from the silence background. However, practically it does not differ from the techniques based on the vertical projection. In Allam (1994, 1995) the segmentation occurs at vertical lines present the transition from a column having all the black pixels inside the baseline to a column having pixels outside the baseline.

Ben Amara and Ellouze (1995) used the vertical projection profile to estimate the boundaries of the characters which were further enhanced by calculating the maximum number of black segments in a line of pixels from the upper line of the middle stage over a distance of 1.5 of the height of the textline. Each character must have only one black segment except for few (characters found at the end of a subword or in isolated form and for characters like س and all characters having a loop in their shape which may have more than one black segment). For these characters, a threshold value depending on the horizontal width of writing has to exist between two successive segments. While for the other set of characters, the width of the last character is examined, if it is shorter than that of the average value of a character width, the segmentation process is halted. They reported a 99–100% segmentation rate was reported for fonts without characters overlapping, while for fonts with overlapping or handwritten, the segmentation rate was much lower than this figure.

Tolba and Shaddad (1990) slightly modified the vertical projection definition by multiplying each pixel value by the factor $|k^h|$,

$$G(k) = \sum_{i=0}^{N} p(i,j) \cdot \left| k^h \right| \qquad (4)$$

where h is the height from the baseline, $k = 0,1,2,$ ..., etc., and N is the maximum number of rows.

This multiplication has the effect of magnifying the distance from baseline so that points far from the baseline would not be considered as connection points (Al-Badr & Mahmoud, 1995). The values of the segmentation parameter $G(k)$ are small at the connection strokes. $G(k)$ is computed from right to left and compared continuously with predetermined threshold values. When the value of the parameter is less than the threshold, the investigated region is considered a connection stroke. When the value of the parameter increases, the beginning of the following letter starts. When $k = 2$, G found to give the best results as the letter strokes go far from the baseline. This helps in detecting the thin-identifiers of the Arabic letters. The advantage of this method is that it does not require removing the secondaries, but it expected to separate the single character into many parts then a recombination process must be applied after the segmentation. However, it gives better results when neglecting the secondaries.

A special type of vertical projection is the upper distance function, which is the set of the highest points in each column. For each upper distance function, Kurdy and Joukhadar (1992) determined the baseline of each subword. Then the distance between the baseline and the top of this subword is measured. Finally, one of three tokens (up, middle and down) is given to each point. The tokens are related to the vertical distances between the baseline and the top of this column of each point and the vertical distance of the previous point. Using a grammar, they then parse the sequence of tokens of a subword to find the connection points (Al-Emami, 1988). The same method was adopted by Kurdy and AlSabbagh (2004), and Azmi and Kabir (2001) in which the neighboring points having the same label make a path. If a path satisfies some conditions, such as length of the path is larger than 1/3 of the writing thickness, the last point of the path is marked as a potential segmentation point.

The segmentation rate reported in Azmi and Kabir (2001) was 99%. The researchers reported that the advantage of this method is that the character can be obtained completely in a single piece, hence, the number of different shapes is minimal, and this facilitates the recognition. They also reported that this kind of method is insensitive to scale, slight distortions (rotation and misalignment) and limited noise. It also tolerates any degree of overlapping as it uses the upper contour. It is very fast, and has several sorts of feedback (there is correction to the estimated size and other parameters). Moreover, it is multi-font and multi-style (Kurdy & AlSabbagh, 2004).

From the above review, we can conclude that the segmentation methods based on the calculation of the vertical projection histogram depend greatly on the determination of the baseline which is not an easy task especially in the case of Arabic handwriting. They are independent of the shape, size or font of characters as long as the font contains no overlapping. They are best suited for machine printed characters.

Those projection profile methods proved inadequate for segmenting overlapping characters or handwritten script because the connection strokes are often short and not along the baseline due to such data frequently contain undulations and shifts in the baseline, baseline-skew variability and inter-line distance variability. In many cases, the potential segmentation points will be placed within a character rather than between characters. Moreover, this approach will not work effectively for skewed characters (e.g., Italic style). Special treatment in a later stage is required to separate overlapped characters and to recombine the strokes resulted due to over-segmentation. This conclusion is in agreement with Amin and Mari (1989), Sadiq-Hussain and Sarsam (1998), Walker (1993), and Zahour et al. (2001).

4.2. Methods Based on the Character Skeleton

In character recognition, the essential information about a shape is stored in its skeleton (Abuhaiba et al., 1994). Khorsheed and Clocksin (1999) claimed that extracting segments from the skeleton graph is more reliable than finding the actual connection points in a word. In general, many algorithms have been proposed to extract skeletons, but those specifically designed for Arabic text are Tellache et al. (1993), Altuwaijri and Bayoumi (1995, 1998), and Cowell and Hussain, (2001). Figure 18 shows an example of an Arabic word and its skeleton.

Figure 18. The word محمد and its skeleton

Khorsheed and Clocksin (1999) segmented the skeleton into strokes. Each stroke commences and terminates with a feature point. A feature point could be an end point, branch point or cross point. Other structural features are also computed such as segment length and curvature. In a method developed by El-Khaly and Sid-Ahmed (1990), the baseline of the thinned word is found first, and then only those columns that have no pixels above or below the baseline are considered in finding the segmentation points. The segmentation point will be in the middle of the connection segment.

Almuallim and Yamaguchi (1987) also detected the baseline of the thinned word. Then the words are segmented into strokes. The extraction of a stroke is made by finding out its start point. The search for the start point is done just around the baseline, and then the curve is traced until a point which is inferred to be the stroke end point is reached. An end point can be a branch point, a cross point, a line end or a point with sudden change in the curvature (up or down) after a horizontal motion near the baseline. During the segmentation process, if the current stroke is connected to the next stroke then the difference between the y–coordinate of the connection point and the current baseline is calculated. If it happened that this difference was bigger than a certain threshold, then the baseline is adjusted and given the value of the average of the y–coordinates of the connection points found so far.

To avoid over-segmentation, they attempted to define strokes so that the number of the strokes of a word becomes as small as possible, considering at the same time the easiness of strokes to be extracted and classified, and their appropriateness to represent Arabic handwritten words. They also tried to eliminate insignificant parts of curves, and also to overcome the problem of the noise caused by the thinning process of the word image. However, with all these attempts, the method still produces errors.

In Al-Emami (1988), Goraine and Usher (1989), and Guraine et al. (1992) works, a similar approach is followed whereby the thinned word is segmented into principal strokes (i.e., strings of coordinate pairs) and secondary strokes (i.e., additions to the principal ones) according to the following classification:

- Connection point: a pattern pixel that has only two neighbors.
- Feature point: either a line end (i.e., a pattern pixel with only one neighbor) or a junction (i.e., a pattern pixel with three neighbors);
- Stroke: a string of pixels between two successive feature points.

The start point is found first, and then the curve is traced using a 3×3 window to determine the end point and to identify the stroke. The algorithm imposes the condition that the direction of the curve between two consecutive sampled points does not exceed a certain threshold angle.

In Amin and Al-Sadoun (1992) and Al-Sadoun and Amin (1995) the authors traced the thinned word from right to left using a 3×3 window to identify potential points for segmentation. Then, a binary tree is constructed and the skeleton is represented using Freeman code (1961). Each node of the binary tree describes the shape of the corresponding part of the subword. The binary tree is smoothed to minimize the number of nodes by eliminating the empty nodes, minimize the Freeman code string, and to eliminate or minimize any noise in the thinned image. Finally, the binary tree is segmented into subtrees such that each subtree describes a character using primitives including lines, loops, and double loops. Some rules were set to ensure the correct boundaries of characters such as: long horizontal segment signals the end of the current character, and the existence of loops or a long vertical segment are regarded as the beginning of a character. The algorithm can be applied to any font and size of Arabic text, in addition, it can be applied to handprinted text and permits the overlay of characters (Amin et al., 1996); however, due to the erosion experienced in the image, some of the characters were not segmented properly. The method was adopted in Amin (2001). One advantage of this method is that the identification of the baseline becomes unnecessary since the subword is described by a binary tree, hence, saving processing time (Amin & Al-Sadoun, 1992).

Jambi (1991) constructed the vertical projection of the thinned word where dots were removed. The start and end points of characters are determined from the vertical projection; these points could be actual points or just candidates. The actual start point is determined if there is a change from 0 to non-zero, while the actual end point is determined if there is a change from non-zero to 0. The candidate start point is determined if there is a change from 1 to a greater value, while the candidate end point is determined if there is a change from a higher value to 1. Due to the different width of Arabic characters, it is not easy to avoid over-segmentation, however, some inconsistencies can be detected easily such as having two consecutive ends, but some are still difficult to be determined such as س which has two actual and six candidate starting and ending points. Applying this method will segment the tail of س when appear at the end of a word or in isolated form. This method was adopted in Abandah and Khedher (2004). This method needs further processing in the presence of vertical overlaps.

Atici and Yarman-Vural (1997) also traced the skeleton of subwords to identify key feature points mainly by searching for local minima. A few rules were set to verify whether they are segmentation points or not. Abuhaiba (1996) and Abuhaiba et al. (1998) converted the skeleton of a word into straight-line approximations from which the temporal information is restored. The cursive strokes are then segmented into small parts called tokens. A token is either a single isolated vertex representing a dot, a single vertex representing a loop, or a sequence of consecutive vertices which connect links such that each of the start and end vertices of the sequence is either a terminal vertex or an intersection vertex. The tokens of a stroke are recombined to meaningful strings of tokens.

Mostafa (2004) proposed an adaptive rule-based segmentation algorithm based on the general structural relationship of the Arabic text. The main rule used is that "most characters start with, and end before a T–junction on the baseline." A T–junction occurs when the drawing of the character goes up or down the baseline. This holds for all character shapes at the middle and the end of a word, however, few characters such as س and ص have more than one T–junction with the baseline and should need a special treatment. Structural features strokes, dots, loops, curves, character relative width and height, baseline relative position – are extracted from the skeleton using some rules. Finally, the characters are segmented by grouping its components, e.g., loops with their strokes (e.g., ص_). Dots are used to help in the grouping process. The method is noise-independent, omni-font and omni-size. However, the method was tested on 'Simplified Arabic' font only and the reported segmentation accuracy was 96.5%.

Zidouri et al. (2005) scanned the skeleton (with no secondaries) from right to left to find a band of horizontal pixels having length greater than or equal to the width of the smallest character. Then the vertical projection is found, if no pixel is encountered, a vertical line is drawn as a guide for segmentation. The procedure is repeated for all rows. As a result, an image with several guide bands is obtained. Features are extracted from each guide band, a set of rules is then designed to select from and correct the guide bands. However, the method suffers from the problem of overlap-ping and ligatures which is left to the recognition phase to deal with.

Among the drawbacks of the methods based on the extracted skeleton, is that different thinning algorithms may produce different thinned characters. Moreover, the thinning process might alter the shape of the character, especially in the case of poor quality characters. Some of the common problems encountered during the thinning process include the elimination of vertical notches in some characters and elimination of secondary characters. These modifications make the segmentation of thinned characters a difficult task. This conclusion is in agreement with Amin (2001) and Cowell and Hussain (2001).

4.3. Methods Based on Contour Tracing

The set of boundary pixels or the contour includes important information of an object (Khorsheed, 2002). Figure 19 shows an Arabic sentence and its contour.

Segmentation is also achieved by tracing the outer contour of a given word. The segmentation method used in the SARAT system (Segmentation And Recognition of Arabic printed Text) (Margner, 1992) was based on the outer contour of the main body of the words. First, the start and the end points of the upper contour are determined. Then, a segmentation of the upper contour into parts is made having a curvature of the same sign. Starting with a positive curvature, for example, the change to a negative curvature will finish this segment and start with a new one. In another word, wherever the outer contour changes sign a character is segmented.

Al-Ohali (1995) built his method based on the fact that "each character is formed of a high followed by a low or flat contour". Therefore, whenever, the contour starts to rise, this indicates a potential segmentation point. The method was tested on printed Arabic scripts written in Naskh font only; however, it is not perfect and produces errors.

Sari et al. (2002) proposed a method known as Arabic Character Segmentation Algorithm (ACSA) to segment Arabic handwritten text by detecting the local minima of the lower contour. The baseline is detected first, then, the subwords and secondaries are extracted using the contour tracing. Using horizontal projection, three zones are determined for each subword; namely, upper, median and lower zones. Topological features such as turning points, holes, zigzag, ascenders and descenders are extracted. The segmentation point is defined as a local minimum in the lower outer contour. A set of rules is designed to validate the segmentation points. The reported segmentation rate was 86%. The algorithm suffers from over-segmentation in cases of characters like س and from under-segmentation in cases of ligatures. The authors claimed that their method does not need slant correction.

Bushofa and Spann (1997b) traced the upper contour from left to right and searched for angles between two peak points above the baseline. A local maximum is considered a peak if its value is greater than a threshold value (baseline + t, t is found experimentally to be 1/6 of the distance between the top and the baseline). The value of the contour starts to fall until it reaches a minimum point. If this minimum is lower than the threshold value then it is considered as a segmentation point provided that it is followed by another peak point. If no peak is found after finding a minimum point, this minimum point is neglected. Furthermore, if two or more minimum points are found between two points and all of them satisfy the threshold condition then the point nearest to the first point and closest to the baseline is taken as the segmentation point.

The local minima of the traced contour are also detected in Miled and Ben Amara (2001). The different minima are then joined together to form frontiers between tracing's zones. Accordingly, the points of intersection with the existing extensions are localized. These points are called Horizontal Segmentation Points (HSP). A set of shapes that might appear in the middle zone is defined. The upper contour of the middle zone is then traced and the obtained segmentation points are called Vertical Segmentation Points (VSP).

In Romeo-Pakker et al. (1995), Olivier et al. (1996), and Miled et al. (1997), the local minima of the upper contour are also detected to find Primary Segmentation Points (PSP), from which only the Decisive Segmentation Points (DSP) are chosen based on the following rules:

1. The PSP is eliminated if a loop is detected below it.
2. The line thickness for this PSP must be smaller than a threshold ($\alpha \times$ average line thickness).
3. If there are several DSPs in the same segmentation area, the nearest candidate to the baseline is selected.

The overall segmentation rate reported was 97.41%.

Gillies et al. (1999) proposed two methods to find the local minima, the first one uses Formula (5), such that the segmentation point occur at locations where the objective function $f(x)$ achieves a local minimum,

Figure 19. An Arabic sentence and its contour

$$f(x) = \text{Max}(B - Top(x), 0) + \text{Max}(Bottom(x) - B, 0) \tag{5}$$

where $Top(x)$ is the y–coordinate of the topmost pixel in column x of the component, $Bottom(x)$ is the y–coordinate of the bottommost pixel in column x of the component, and B is the y–coordinate of the nominal baseline in the normalized line image (y–coordinates increases downward).

The same formula is adopted in Jin et al. (2005) followed by structural rules to merge oversegmented characters and over 99% segmentation rate was reported.

The second method looks for local minima in the y–coordinate while tracing the top half of the contour around the component. Unlike the first method, this method can trace parts of the stroke which are in the shadow from an overhanging part of the stroke. The two methods often produce identical or near identical segmentation points. If the segment produced is very small in width (less than 4 pixels) that segmentation point is discarded. The result is a list of image components called atomic segments. The atomic segments are combined using Viterbi algorithm in groups of two to five consecutive atomic segments. The complete set of segments is passed to the recognition module.

In Trenkle et al. (2001), a chain code is extracted from the traced contour. The contour curvature is computed at each point along the chain, and a set of features are obtained. As this is an over-segmentation approach, the small strokes are combined in groups using Viterbi algorithm.

Mostafa and Darwish (1999) traced the upper contour of handwritten words searching for local minima, and at the same time traced the lower contour searching for local maxima. The determination of local minima and maxima are based on the negative and positive slopes. These points are marked as potential segmentation points. A matching process between upper and lower potential segmentation points is performed in order to obtain the minimum number of non-overlapping potential segmentation points for each word. The algorithm achieved 97.7% correct segmentation. Among the advantages of this method, as reported by the authors, is that it does not require the existence of a single baseline for the whole line or even for parts of the word; it is a writer independent and does not require any learning procedures. Also, the problems of segmenting overlapping and overhanging characters are completely surmounted. Furthermore, it can effectively split touching characters.

El-Bialy et al. (2000) and Kandil and El-Bialy (2004) observed that the connection strokes are formed of two parallel lines. Hence, the contour is traced searching for this phenomenon. However, not only the connection strokes are formed of two parallel lines but also some other parts of the word. To overcome this problem, only columns having the two pixels in predefined middle zone are considered. The authors claimed that the method works for multiple font and size and can tolerate some skewness in the line.

Methods based on contour tracing avoid all problems resulted from the thinning process because it analyzes the structural shape of characters as they have been scanned. However, they are affected by noise on the contour, hence the contour need to be smoothed first.

4.4. Methods Based on Template Matching

Template matching is one of the earliest techniques used in image processing. Bushofa and Spann (1995, 1997a) proposed an algorithm that searches for the occurrence of an angle formed by the joining of two characters which occurs at the baseline. Once the baseline is found, the algorithm proceeds by scanning the image from right to left over this baseline using a 7×7 window and examining the neighborhood of the central pixel. The central pixel is taken to be the candidate pixel for segmentation if the pattern is found. Few rules are set to avoid segmenting inside a hole.

However, template matching is not a suitable technique for handwritten character recognition due to the extreme variations and possibilities in the writing of cursive characters (Abuhaiba et al., 1994). Its success in finding the proper angle depends very heavily on the noise in the image (Bushofa & Spann, 1997a).

4.5. Methods Based on Neural Networks

The principle idea here is that, features are extracted first and then verified using Neural Networks (NNs). The only work found to use neural networks for segmenting the Arabic text was by Hamid (2001) and Hamid and Haraty (2001), in which a conventional method was used to scan the handwritten text, extract connected blocks of characters, generate topographic features, and then generate potential segmentation points for the connected blocks, then these points are verified using a NN. To train the NN, the potential points will be manually classified into valid and invalid points and store them in a file together with their features, which is then fed into an error back-propagation NN. A generalized feed-forward multi-layer NN was used to validate the segmentation points. Then the error between the desired and actual output can be determined, and passed backwards through the network. Based on these errors, weight adaptations are calculated, and errors are passed to a previous layer, continuing until the first layer is reached. The error is thus propagated back through the network.

A positive value indicated that a point is a valid segmentation point; while a negative value indicated that a point should be ignored. The segmentation rate reported was 69.72%. These errors were attributed to ligatures and characters with miss located secondaries. Moreover, characters such as س, ش, and ض are never being segmented correctly.

4.6. Methods Based on Hidden Markov Models

Hidden Markov Models (HMMs) are a method of modeling systems with discrete, time dependant behavior characterized by common, short time "processes" and transitions between them. To use HMMs for handling Arabic text, the 2D problem of text image must be converted into 1D problem. This is implemented by scanning the line of text from right to left column by column (after eliminating the secondaries) to extract features. The invariant moment is used to extract the features. HMMs are then fed with the features. To build a system that is able to handle an Arabic font with M different characters (or ligature), M different HMMs are needed, each of which represents one character. All models are initialized using a single bitmap that contains the complete set of ligatures of the used Arabic font. The system is trained first then tested. The system was tested on two fonts and achieved 99% accuracy (Gouda & Rashwan, 2004).

Segmentation methods based on HMMs are still new. Not many researchers have explored them extensively yet. They could be a potential work as they use softcomputing. However, one limitation can be observed is that HMMs require number of HMMs equivalent to the number of classes, which definitely increases the complexity of the method.

4.7. Methods Based on Line Adjacency Graph (LAG)

Elgammal and Ismail (2001) proposed a graph-based framework for the segmentation of Arabic Text. The method is based on the topological relation between the baseline and the line adjacency graph (LAG) representation of the text which is a graph consisting of nodes representing horizontal runlengths. Any two runlengths lying on adjacent scan lines and overlapping with each other have an edge connecting their corresponding nodes.

The process of building a LAG representation for a textline yields a set of subwords. Therefore the process of word isolation is done at the same time the LAG is constructed. A connected component of the LAG may correspond to a dot combination, a diacritic, an isolated character or a subword consisting of several characters. Each LAG component is either intersects with the baseline, i.e., subwords, or either above/below the baseline.

The LAG for each subword is then transformed into another graph which is homomorphic to the LAG (called compressed LAG c-LAG) and has minimum number of nodes. The nodes of the c-LAG are labeled as path or junction. The relation between the c-LAG nodes and the baseline is very important in feature extraction phase and in pseudo-character extraction. To find subgraphs corresponding to pseudo-character, first the c-LAG is traversed starting from any path node that is above the baseline until a junction node that is labeled as inside the baseline is reached. The traversed nodes constitute a subgraph that they call a script. A Junction node labeled as inside the baseline is the break point between scripts. Another rule that is applied when extracting scripts from the c-LAG is that a loop must be contained inside and should not be segmented between different scripts.

The algorithm was robust in case of characters connected at the baseline level while those connected below or over the baseline caused failure for the segmentation.

4.8. Segmentation Methods Based on Morphological Operations

As mentioned earlier, almost all Arabic characters are connected on the baseline; therefore, applying morphological operations (Motawa et al., 1997), such as closing followed by opening, will segment the word into several segments. The beginning of the character preserves most of the significant information required to identify the character. Vertical or semi-vertical strokes which might represent the start, end or a transition to another character (or subword) are found by singularities. On the other hand, regularities contain the information required for connecting a character to the next character. Hence, these regularities are the candidates for segmentation.

Singularities are found by applying an opening to the word image, while regularities are found by subtracting the singularities from the original image. All regularities are tested by scanning them from right to left. Segmentation points should happen at regularities. Regularities are classified to either long or short based on their relative width to the word, e.g., word aspect ratio. The authors noticed that segmented words written by different writers were consistent. The algorithm was able to correctly segment words with every segment containing one character. However, in other experiments, the algorithm segmented two characters in the same segment. The segmentation rate reported was 81.88%.

Timsari and Fahimi (1996) used morphological hit-or-miss transformation to segment the characters. Having the input words described in terms of some pre-defined patterns. The system knowledge-base, holding descriptions for all characters, is searched for possible matches. Finding a match ends in the recognition of a character. The authors claimed that this approach is proved to be fast and reliable in practice. However, no recognition rate was given.

Methods based on morphological operations are not enough to segment the characters if not supported by other techniques.

4.9. Recognition-Based Segmentation Methods

Unlike the previously discussed methods which were considered as explicit segmentation methods, the recognition-based method is an implicit one (Abo Samra et al., 1997). In the explicit segmentation (or dissection segmentation), words are explicitly or externally segmented into characters or pseudo-characters which are then recognized individually. Contextual high level knowledge (lexical, syntactic or semantic knowledge) is then used to ensure the proper word identification. Explicit approach is usually more expensive due to the increased complexity of finding optimum word hypotheses (Cheung et al., 2001). While, in the implicit methods, characters are segmented while being recognized, hence, it is also called recognition-based segmentation or straight-segmentation. The basic principle of this approach is the use a mobile window of variable width to provide the tentative segmentations which are confirmed (or not) by the classification (Cheung et al., 2001). In other words, the system searches the image for components that match classes in its alphabets (Khedher & Abandah, 2002).

In El-Dabi et al. (1990) and Ramsis and El-Dabi (1988), the invariant moments are calculated and checked against the feature space of the font. If a character is not found, another column is appended to the underlying portion of the word and moments are calculated and checked again. This process is repeated until a character is recognized or the end of the word is reached. However, as the system is not always able to recognize all characters, which implied that all succeeding characters in that subword would not be processed, backup scanning algorithm is triggered when such a blockage happened (Khorsheed, 2002). To accelerate the recognition process the scanning can be done from both ends (Khorsheed & Clocksin, 2000). The method allowed the system to handle overlapping and to isolate the connecting baseline between connected characters. This method seems to be limited to the recognition of typewritten fonts; furthermore, it is font dependent and sensitive to pattern variations. Also, the system uses intensive computations to compute the required accumulative moments. No figures are reported regarding the system recognition rate and efficiency (Abuhaiba et al., 1994; Abuhaiba, 2003). A similar method is used in Abdelazim et al. (1989) but without calculating the moments. In Auda and Raafat (1993) a similar approach is used in which slices are added to a window and a

feature vector is fed into neural networks trying to recognize the character first before the segmentation. The reported segmentation rate was 83%.

Walker (1993) used a spacio-temporal approach which performs segmentation and recognition simultaneously. As the word is read column by column from right to left, the contour is extracted and represented by two polynomials. Coefficients of these polynomials are then compared to a database containing the coefficients of previously learned characters. For each set of learned coefficients, a cost function is applied and an error calculated. If this error falls below a chosen threshold (for a particular learned character), the image portion is considered to be recognized. This image portion is removed from the overall image the process repeated until all characters have been recognized.

Mosfeq (1996) applied the concept of centering to segment the characters in which a character is correctly segmented if it appeared in the centre of a large window, regardless of what else appeared in that window.

In Zidouri et al. (2003) and Zidouri (2004), the Minimum Covering Run (MCR) expression is used to represent the character by a number of strokes. MCR of a region of a binary image is the minimal combination of the runlength encoding in both horizontal and vertical directions. The features of those strokes are used to build reference prototypes for recognition by matching. The separation of words into characters is done automatically once characters composing parts are successfully identified and a correct match is found.

Harba and Li (1996) followed the same method but using parallel Digital Learning Networks (DLN) to achieve both segmentation and recognition concurrently. At the beginning of a subword, each DLN will look at a portion of the subword, and will decide which character class the unknown character belongs to. The same procedure is repeated from the left. The middle characters are next considered, and identified in the same manner.

As can be noticed from the above discussion, the recognition-based segmentation approach aims at overcoming the classical segmentation serious problems. Hence, no accurate character segmentation path is necessary. In principle, any of the first seven approaches can be used here as far as it has some recognition capabilities (Cheung et al., 2001).

5. DISCUSSION AND CONCLUSION

In this paper, the segmentation problem of Arabic characters is presented and studied thoroughly. The methods proposed in the literature were classified into nine different groups based on the techniques used. The first seven techniques are considered as explicit segmentation methods, while the ninth one is an implicit one. However, theoretically, the ninth method may apply to any of the first seven techniques with some recognition capabilities. In addition to what has been presented earlier in this chapter, various issues related to the problem of segmentation and further comments are given in this section.

The selection of the method has an impact on the technique to be used in later stages such as feature extraction and recognition. For example, the method developed by Almuallim and Yamaguchi (1987) can only be associated with the strokes vector sequence techniques and cannot be applied to other forms of shape discrimination (El-Khaly & Sid-Ahmed, 1990). Furthermore, different segmentation methods may produce different characters. This problem degrades the classifier performance. It is proposed in Zeki and Zakaria (2004), Hashemi et al. (1995), and Bushofa and Spann (1995, 1997a) that segmentation methods should be designed to isolate the characters from their beginning and not from the middle of the connection stroke. This ensures that the segmentation is carried out in the right place so that no extra fragments or divided characters are generated, and therefore, reducing the number of shapes

of most of the characters to two instead of four, and consequently, reducing the overall number of classes to be recognized in the recognition stage (Bushofa & Spann, 1997a).

The other problem is attributed to the use of topographic features as the characters can be segmented differently depending on whether you look at them separately, in a word, or even in a sentence (Hamid & Haraty, 2001). This is very clear in the case of handwritten text. The existence of ligatures is another challenge in Arabic character recognition. Most segmentation methods proposed so far either does not deal with overlapping characters or propose a computationally intensive method for this case (Hashemi et al., 1995).

To measure the performance of any ACR system, we need to assess how successful the system is in overcoming the obstacle of cursiveness and context-sensitivity (Khorsheed & Clocksin, 1999). Unfortunately, because the segmentation is just an intermediate stage, most of the researchers did not report the segmentation accuracy in their research, but instead reported the overall recognition rate which does not reflect the influence of each sub-stage on that final recognition rate. The speed, which is another important performance aspect, was neglected in almost all proposed methods.

When designing a segmentation method it is important to assume small variations in the input characters (Abuhaiba et al., 1994). However, in unconstrained character writing (e.g., handwriting), large variations in the characters' shapes are expected. This fact implies that a system based solely on geometric or statistical features is not expected to be practical. The reason is that the system will be usually font and designer dependent and may not tolerate large variations in character writing.

Touched characters may result from poorly scanned images or in handwritten documents. They may belong to the same or different word. Segmenting of touched characters is a very complicated task as they may touch at any vertical or horizontal level. This problem was neglected in almost all research papers. Bushofa and Spann (1997) attempted to segment touched characters by tracing the lower contour.

In online systems, the segmentation process is much easier as the time dimension exists. Temporal information restoration is useful and will allow the use of online techniques for offline systems.

Setting rules to enhance the segmentation accuracy is almost unavoidable. Sophisticated rules have been proposed in many methods; however, a general rule cannot apply for segmenting all characters (Mostafa, 2004). The orthographic rules, which are rules about how text is printed, must also be considered (LaPre et al., 1996). For example, there are letters that never appear after each other (e.g., letter س never followed by ش in Arabic) or at the beginning of a word (e.g., ى). Statistical studies on the occurrence of such letters, ligatures or size of words/subwords, as in Khedher and Abandah (2002), must be conducted. Such information will be of a great benefit in correcting the segmentation errors.

We (humans) extensively utilize context in reading that quite often we do not even realize that we have read a misspelled word correctly (Mostafa et al., 1999). Applying contextual techniques such as semantical information, string correction algorithms, linguistic information, lexicon, spell checkers and information about character frequencies and locations of secondaries, are believed to have a great potential for detecting and correcting recognition errors, and hence, increasing the segmentation and recognition accuracy. For example, Fehri and Ben Ahmed (1994) tried to identify the beginning and the last characters of the word while the middle part is treated subsequently. Adopting some of those tools at an early stage is believed to give better performance. Amin and Al-Fedaghi (1991) reported that applying such post processing techniques increased the recognition rate by 7%.

The use of thresholding of the word histogram to detect and eliminate the connection strokes or thresholding on the word outer contour needs a-priori information about the average size of the character in the page. This will not work for omnisize character recognition where different character sizes can exist on the same text line (El-Bialy et al., 2000).

From the above review, it seems that, in general, only a limited test data of font-specific and noise-free was used for testing some of the published algorithms. The size of the training/testing data must be large enough to generalize the algorithm performance (Al-Fakhri, 1997). The reported segmentation rates were generally high which may not reflect the performance of the systems if a larger set of data was used (Al-Badr & Mahmoud, 1995; LaPre et al., 1996). The field of ACR crucially needs a standard set of test documents in both image and character formats, together with the ground truth and a set of performance evaluation tools. This would truly enable comparing the performance of different algorithms.

This work concluded that there is a need for iterative and hybrid segmentation methods that combine between two or more methods. Extra care should be taken when segmenting characters to small segments to avoid over-segmentation. It might be much more difficult to recombine the small strokes to form a character. Dividing the words into a big number of strokes will be complicated where each stroke will take the same process that a character takes (e.g., feature extraction, classification, recognition). The efficiency of these techniques is relatively high but on the other hand, the recognition time increases, where recognition time of character is approximately equal to the time of recognition of a stroke multiplied by the number of strokes (Abd El-Gwad et al., 1990). This method is particularly more appropriate for recognizing handwritten text where character boundaries are often ambiguous (LaPre et al., 1996).

As such, it is concluded that no perfect and error-free segmentation technique is available yet. Extensive research need to be conducted in this area. Further research in the segmentation of Arabic character will strive towards improving

279

the accuracy, speed, and reducing the amount of manual interaction. To improve the mentioned measures, hybrid segmentation approach becomes a promising method.

REFERENCES

Abandah, G. A., & Khedher, M. Z. (2004). *Printed and handwritten Arabic optical character recognition – initial study (Tech. Rep.)*. Amman, Jordan: University of Jordan.

Abd El-Gwad, A., Salem, M., Abou Shadi, F. E. Z., & Arafat, H. (1990, June 16-21). Automatic recognition of handwritten Arabic characters. In *Proceedings of the 10th International Conference on Pattern Recognition*, Atlantic City, NJ.

Abdelazim, H., & Hashish, M. (1988). Arabic reading machine. In *Proceedings of the 10th Saudi National Computer Conference*, Riyadh, Saudi Arabia (pp. 733-743).

Abdelazim, H., Mousa, A., Salih, Y., & Hashish, M. (1989, October 21-24). Arabic text recognition using a partial observation approach. In *Proceedings of the 12th National Computer Conference*, Riyadh, Saudi Arabia (pp. 427-437).

Abdelazim, H. Y., & Hashish, M. A. (1989, May 8-12). Automatic reading of bilingual typewritten text. In *Proceedings of the Conference on Very Large Scale Integration and Microelectronic Applications in Intelligent Peripherals and their Interconnection Networks*, Hamburg, Germany (Vol. 2, pp. 140-144).

Abo Samra, G., Jambi, K., Al-Barhamtoshy, H., Amer, R., & Al-Bidewi, I. (1997). A comprehensive algorithm for segmenting handwritten Arabic scripts in off-line systems. In *Proceedings of the 17th National Computer Conference*, Saudi Arabia (pp. 1-13).

Abuhaiba, I. (1996). *Recognition of off-line handwritten cursive text* (Unpublished doctoral dissertation). Loughborough University, Loughborough, UK.

Abuhaiba, I. (2003). A discrete Arabic script for better automatic document understanding. *The Arabian Journal for Science and Engineering, 28*(1), 77–94.

Abuhaiba, I. (2003). Arabic font recognition based on templates. *The International Arab Journal of Information Technology, 1*(0), 33–39.

Abuhaiba, I., & Ahmed, P. (1993). Restoration of temporal information in off-line Arabic handwriting. *Pattern Recognition, 26*(7), 1009–1017. doi:10.1016/0031-3203(93)90002-E

Abuhaiba, I., Holt, M. J. J., & Datta, S. (1998). Recognition of off-line cursive handwriting. *Computer Vision and Image Understanding, 71*(1), 19–38. doi:10.1006/cviu.1997.0629

Abuhaiba, I., Mahmoud, S., & Green, R. (1994). Recognition of handwritten cursive Arabic characters. *IEEE Transactions on Pattern Analysis and Machine Intelligence, 16*(6), 664–672. doi:10.1109/34.295912

Al-Badr, B., & Haralick, R. (1992). Recognition without segmentation: using mathematical morphology to recognize printed Arabic. In *Proceedings of the 13th National Computer Conference*, Riyadh, Saudi Arabia (pp. 813-829).

Al-Badr, B., & Haralick, R. (1998). A segmentation-free approach to text recognition with application to Arabic text. *International Journal on Document Analysis and Recognition, 1*(3), 147–166. doi:10.1007/s100320050014

Al-Badr, B., & Mahmoud, S. (1995). Survey and bibliography of Arabic optical text recognition. *Signal Processing, 41*(1), 49–77. doi:10.1016/0165-1684(94)00090-M

Al-Emami, S. (1988). *Machine recognition of handwritten and typewritten Arabic characters* (Unpublished doctoral dissertation). University of Reading, Reading, UK.

Al-Fakhri, F. (1997). *On-line computer recognition of handwritten Arabic text* (Unpublished master's thesis). Universiti Sains Malaysia, Penang, Malaysia.

Al-Ma'adeed, S. (2001). An off-line cursive Arabic handwriting recognition system. In *Proceedings of the ACS International Conference on Computer Systems and Applications.*

Al-Ohali, Y. (1995). *Development and evaluation environment for typewritten Arabic character recognition* (Unpublished master's thesis). King Saud University, Riyadh, Saudi Arabia.

Al-Sadoun, H., & Amin, A. (1995). A new structural technique for recognizing printed Arabic text. *International Journal of Pattern Recognition and Artificial Intelligence, 9*(1), 101–125. doi:10.1142/S0218001495000067

Al-Waily, R. (1989). *A study on preprocessing and syntactic recognition of hand-written Arabic characters* (Unpublished master's thesis). University of Basrah, Basrah, Iraq.

Al-Yousefi, H., & Upda, S. S. (1992). Recognition of Arabic characters. *IEEE Transactions on Pattern Analysis and Machine Intelligence, 14*(8), 853–857. doi:10.1109/34.149585

Alherbish, J., & Ammar, R. A. (1998). High-performance Arabic character recognition. *Journal of Systems and Software, 44*(1), 53–71. doi:10.1016/S0164-1212(98)10043-2

Allam, M. (1994). Arabic character recognition. In *Proceedings of the SPIE Conference on Document Recognition* (Vol. 2181, pp. 351-359).

Allam, M. (1995). Segmentation versus segmentation-free for recognizing Arabic text. In *Proceedings of the SPIE Conference on Document Recognition II* (Vol. 2422, pp. 228-235).

Almuallim, H., & Yamaguchi, S. A. (1987). Method of recognition of Arabic cursive handwriting. *IEEE Transactions on Pattern Analysis and Machine Intelligence, 9*(5), 715–722. doi:10.1109/TPAMI.1987.4767970

Alshebeili, S. A., Nabawi, A. A., & Mahmoud, S. A. (1997). Arabic character recognition using 1-D slices of the character spectrum. *Signal Processing, 56*(1), 59–75. doi:10.1016/S0165-1684(96)00150-8

Altuwaijri, M., & Bayoumi, M. (1994, May 30-June 2). Arabic text recognition using neural networks. In *Proceedings of the IEEE International Symposium on Circuits and Systems*, London, UK (Vol. 6, pp. 415-418).

Altuwaijri, M., & Bayoumi, M. (1995, December 17-21). A new recognition system for multi-font Arabic cursive words. In *Proceedings of the 2nd IEEE International Conference on Electronics, Circuits and Systems*, Amman, Jordan (pp. 298-303).

Altuwaijri, M., & Bayoumi, M. (1995. April 28-May 3). A new thinning algorithm for Arabic characters using self-organizing neural network. In *Proceedings of the IEEE International Symposium on Circuits and Systems*, Seattle, WA (Vol. 3, pp. 1824-1827).

Altuwaijri, M., & Bayoumi, M. (1998). A thinning algorithm for Arabic characters using ART2 neural network. *IEEE Transactions on Circuits and Systems II: Analog and Digital Signal Processing, 45*(2), 260–264. doi:10.1109/82.661669

Amin, A. (1991). Recognition of Arabic hand-printed mathematical formulae. *The Arabian Journal for Science and Engineering, 16*(4B), 532–542.

Amin, A. (1997). Arabic character recognition. In Bunke, H., & Wang, P. S. P. (Eds.), *Handbook of character recognition and document image analysis* (pp. 397–420). Singapore: World Scientific.

Amin, A. (2001). Segmentation of printed Arabic text. In *Proceedings of the International Conference on Advances in Pattern Recognition* (pp. 115-126).

Amin, A. (2002, August 6-9). Structural description to recognizing Arabic characters using decision tree learning techniques. In *Proceedings of the Joint IAPR International Workshops on Structural, Syntactic, and Statistical Pattern Recognition*, Windsor, ON, Canada (pp. 152-158).

Amin, A., & Al-Fedaghi, S. (1991). Machine recognition of printed Arabic text utilizing natural language morphology. *International Journal of Man-Machine Studies, 35*(6), 769–788. doi:10.1016/S0020-7373(05)80160-9

Amin, A., & Al-Sadoun, H. (1992, August 30-September 3). A new segmentation technique of Arabic text. In *Proceedings of the 11th International Conference on Pattern Recognition: Methodology and Systems*, The Hague, The Netherlands (Vol. 2, pp. 441-445).

Amin, A., Al-Sadoun, H., & Fischer, S. (1996). Hand-printed Arabic character recognition system using an artificial network. *Pattern Recognition, 29*(4), 663–675. doi:10.1016/0031-3203(95)00110-7

Amin, A., & Mari, J. F. (1989). Machine recognition and correction of printed Arabic text. *IEEE Transactions on Systems, Man, and Cybernetics, 19*(5), 1300–1306. doi:10.1109/21.44052

Amin, A., & Masini, G. (1982). Machine recognition of Arabic cursive words. In *Proceedings of the SPIE 26th International Symposium on Instrument Display, Application of Digital Image Processing IV*, San Diego, CA (Vol. 359, pp. 286-292).

Amin, A., & Masini, G. (1986). Machine recognition of multifonts printed Arabic texts. In *Proceedings of the 8th International Conference on Pattern Recognition*, Paris, France, (pp. 392-395).

Atici, A. A., & Yarman-Vural, F. T. (1997). A heuristic algorithm for optical character recognition of Arabic script. *Signal Processing, 62*(1), 87–99. doi:10.1016/S0165-1684(97)00117-5

Auda, G., & Raafat, H. (1993, September 14-17). An automatic text reader using neural networks. In *Proceedings of the Canadian Conference on Electrical and Computer Engineering* (Vol. 1, pp. 92-95).

Azmi, R., & Kabir, E. (2001). A new segmentation technique for omni-font Farsi text. *Pattern Recognition Letters, 22*, 97–104. doi:10.1016/S0167-8655(00)00086-6

Ben Amara, N., & Ellouze, N. (1995, August 14-16). A robust approach for Arabic printed character segmentation. In *Proceedings of the 3rd International Conference on Document Analysis and Recognition*, Montreal, QC, Canada (Vol. 2, pp. 865-868).

Burrow, P. (2004). *Arabic handwriting recognition* (Unpublished master's thesis). University of Edinburgh, Edinburgh, UK.

Bushofa, B. M. F., & Spann, M. (1995). Segmentation and recognition of printed Arabic characters. In *Proceedings of the 6th British Machine Vision Conference* (Vol. 2, pp. 543-552).

Bushofa, B. M. F., & Spann, M. (1997a). Segmentation and recognition of Arabic characters by structural classification. *Image and Vision Computing, 15*(3), 167–179. doi:10.1016/S0262-8856(96)01119-5

Bushofa, B. M. F., & Spann, M. (1997b, July 2-4). Segmentation of Arabic characters using their contour information. In *Proceedings of the 13th International Conference on Digital Signal Processing*, Santorini, Greece (Vol. 2, pp. 683-686).

Central Intelligence Agency (CIA). (2005). *The CIA world fact book*. Retrieved December 3, 2005, from https://www.cia.gov/library/publications/the-world-factbook/

Cheung, A., Bennamoun, M., & Bergmann, N. W. (1997). A new word segmentation algorithm for Arabic script. In *Proceedings of the 4th Conference on Digital Imaging Computing, Techniques and Applications*, Auckland, New Zealand (pp. 431-435).

Cheung, A., Bennamoun, M., & Bergmann, N. W. (1997). Implementation of a statistical-based Arabic character recognition system. In *Proceedings of the IEEE Region 10 Annual Conference on Speech and Image Technologies for Computing and Telecommunications*, Brisbane, Australia (Vol. 2, pp. 531-534).

Cheung, A., Bennamoun, M., & Bergmann, N. W. (1998, October 11-14). A recognition-based Arabic optical character recognition system. In *Proceedings of the IEEE International Conference on Systems, Man, and Cybernetics*, San Diego, CA (Vol. 5, pp. 4189-4194).

Cheung, A., Bennamoun, M., & Bergmann, N. W. (2001). An Arabic optical character recognition system using recognition-based segmentation. *Pattern Recognition, 34*(2), 215–233. doi:10.1016/S0031-3203(99)00227-7

Cowell, J., & Hussain, F. (2001, July 25-27). Thinning Arabic characters for feature extraction. In *Proceedings of the IEEE Conference on Information Visualization*, London, UK (pp. 181-185).

El-Bialy, A. M., Kandil, A. H., Hashish, M. A., & Yamany, S. M. (2000). Arabic OCR: toward a complete system. In *Proceedings of the SPIE Conference on Document Recognition and Retrieval VII*, San Jose, CA (Vol. 3967, pp. 42-51).

El-Dabi, S. S., Ramsis, R., & Kamel, A. (1990). Arabic character recognition system: a statistical approach for recognizing cursive typewritten text. *Pattern Recognition, 23*(5), 485–495. doi:10.1016/0031-3203(90)90069-W

El Gowely, K., El Dessouki, I., & Nazif, A. (1990, June 21). Multi-phase recognition of multi font photoscript Arabic text. In *Proceedings of the 10th International Conference on Pattern Recognition*, Atlantic City, NJ (Vol. 1, pp. 700-702).

El-Khaly, F., & Sid-Ahmed, M. A. (1990). Machine recognition of optically captured machine printed Arabic text. *Pattern Recognition, 23*(11), 1207–1214. doi:10.1016/0031-3203(90)90116-3

El-Sheikh, T. S. (1990, March 19-22). Recognition of handwritten Arabic mathematical formulas. In *Proceedings of the UK Information Technology Conference*, Southampton, UK (pp. 344-351).

El-Sheikh, T. S., & Guindi, R. M. (1988). Computer recognition of Arabic cursive scripts. *Pattern Recognition, 21*(4), 293–302. doi:10.1016/0031-3203(88)90042-8

Elgammal, A. M., & Ismail, M. (2001, September 10-13). A graph-based segmentation and feature extraction framework for Arabic text recognition. In *Proceedings of the 6th International Conference on Document Analysis and Recognition*, Seattle, WA (pp. 622-626).

Fahmy, M. M. M., & Al Ali, S. (2001). Automatic recognition of handwritten Arabic characters using their geometrical features. *Journal of Studies in Informatics and Control, 10*(2).

Fahmy, M. M. M., & El-Messiry, H. (2001). Automatic recognition of typewritten Arabic characters using Zernike moments as a feature extractor. *Studies in Informatics and Control Journal, 10*(3), 48-51.

Fakir, M., Hassani, M., & Sodeyama, C. (1999, October 12-15). Recognition of Arabic characters using Karhunen-Loeve transform and dynamic programming. In *Proceedings of the IEEE International Conference on Systems, Man, and Cybernetics* (Vol. 6, pp. 868-873).

Fakir, M., Hassani, M., & Sodeyama, C. (2000). On the recognition of Arabic characters using Hough transform technique. *Malaysian Journal of Computer Science, 13*(2), 39–47.

Fayek, M., & Al Basha, B. (1992). A new hierarchical method for isolated typewritten Arabic character classification and recognition. In *Proceedings of the 13th National Computer Conference*, Riyadh, Saudi Arabia (Vol. 2, pp. 750-759).

Fehri, M., & Ben Ahmed, M. (1994). A new approach to Arabic character recognition in multi-font document. In *Proceedings of the 4th International Conference and Exhibition on Multi-Lingual Computing*, London, UK (pp. 2.5.1-2.5.7).

Freeman, H. (1961). On the encoding of arbitrary geometric configuration. *IRE Transactions on Electronic Computers, 10*, 260–268. doi:10.1109/TEC.1961.5219197

Gillies, A., Erlandson, E., Trenkle, J., & Schlosser, S. (1999). Arabic text recognition system. In *Proceedings of the Symposium on Document Image Understanding Technology*, Annapolis, MD.

Goraine, H., & Usher, M. J. (1989, October 2). Recognition of typewritten Arabic characters in different fonts. In *Proceedings of the IEEE Colloquium on Character Recognition and Applications*, London, UK (pp. 1-5).

Goraine, H., Usher, M. J., & Al-Emami, S. (1992). Off-line Arabic character recognition. *IEEE Computer, 25*(7), 71–74. doi:10.1109/2.144444

Gouda, A. M., & Rashwan, M. A. (2004, July 14-16). Segmentation of connected Arabic characters using hidden Markov models. In *Proceedings of the IEEE International Conference on Computational Intelligence for Measurement Systems and Applications*, Boston, MA (pp. 115-119).

Hadjar, K., & Ingold, R. (2003, August 3-6). Arabic newspaper page segmentation. In *Proceedings of the 7th International Conference on Document Analysis and Recognition*, Edinburgh, UK (Vol. 2, pp. 895-899).

Haj-Hassan, F. (1990). Arabic character recognition. In Mackay, P. A. (Ed.), *Computer and the Arabic language* (pp. 113–118). New York, NY: Hemisphere.

Hamid, A. (2001, September 26). A neural network approach for the segmentation of handwritten Arabic text. In *Proceedings of the International Symposium on Innovation in Information and Communication Technology*, Amman, Jordan.

Hamid, A., & Haraty, R. (2001, June 25-29). A neuro-heuristic Approach for segmenting handwritten Arabic text. In *Proceedings of the ACS/IEEE International Conference on Computer Systems and Applications*, Beirut, Lebanon (pp. 110-113).

Hammami, L., & Berkani, D. (2002). Recognition system for printed multi-font and multi-size Arabic characters. *The Arabian Journal for Science and Engineering, 27*(1B), 57–72.

Harba, M. I. A., & Li, N. Y. (1996, November 28-30). Parallel digital learning networks for segmentation and recognition of machine printed Arabic text. In *Proceedings of the International Conference on Robotics, Vision and Parallel Processing for Industrial Automation*, Ipoh, Malaysia (pp. 228-232).

Hashemi, M. R., Fatemi, O., & Safavi, R. (1995). Persian cursive script recognition. In *Proceedings of the 3rd International Conference on Document Analysis and Recognition*, Montreal, QC, Canada (Vol. 2, pp. 869-873).

Hassibi, K. M. (1994). Machine-printed Arabic OCR using neural networks. In *Proceedings of the 4th International Conference and Exhibition on Multi-Lingual Computing (Arabic and Roman Script)*, London, UK (pp. 2.3.1-2.3.12).

Jambi, K. (1991). *Design and implementation of a system for recognizing Arabic handwritten words with learning ability* (Unpublished master's thesis). Illinois Institute of Technology, Chicago, IL.

Jambi, K. (1992, Nov). A system for recognizing Arabic handwritten words. In *Proceedings of The 13th National Computer Conference* (Vol. 1, pp. 416-426

Jin, J., Wang, H., Ding, X., & Peng, L. (2005). Printed Arabic document recognition system. In *Proceedings of the SPIE-IS&T Electronic Imaging Conference on Document Recognition and Retrieval XII* (Vol. 5676, pp. 48-55).

Kandil, A. H., & El-Bialy, A. (2004, September 5-7). Arabic OCR: a centerline independent segmentation technique. In *Proceedings of the International Conference on Electrical, Electronic and Computer Engineering* (pp. 412-415).

Khedher, M. Z., & Abandah, G. (2002, June 1). Arabic character recognition using approximate stroke sequence. In *Proceedings of the 3rd International Conference on Language Resources and Evaluation Workshop on Arabic Language Resources and Evaluation: Status and Prospects*, Las Palmas de Gran Canaria, Spain.

Khorsheed, M. S. (2002). Off-Line Arabic character recognition - a review. *Pattern Analysis & Applications*, 5(1), 31–45. doi:10.1007/s100440200004

Khorsheed, M. S., & Clocksin, W. F. (1999). Structural features of cursive Arabic script. In *Proceedings of the 10th British Machine Vision Conference*, Nottingham, UK (Vol. 2, pp. 422-431).

Khorsheed, M. S., & Clocksin, W. F. (2000, September 3-7). Multi-font Arabic word recognition using spectral features. In *Proceedings of the 15th International Conference on Pattern Recognition*, Barcelona, Spain (Vol. 4, pp. 543-546).

Kurdy, B. M., & AlSabbagh, M. M. (2004, April 19-23). Omnifont Arabic optical character recognition system. In *Proceedings of the International Conference on Information and Communication Technologies: from Theory to Applications*, Damascus, Syria.

Kurdy, B. M., & Joukhadar, A. (1992). Multifont recognition system for Arabic characters. In *Proceedings of the 3rd International Conference and Exhibition on Multi-lingual Computing (Arabic and Roman Script)*, Durham, UK (pp. 7.3.1-7.3.9).

LaPre, C., Zhao, Y., Schwartz, R., & Makhoul, J. (1996, May 7-10). Multi-font off-line Arabic character recognition using the BBN Byblos speech recognition system. In *Proceedings of the International Conference on Acoustics, Speech, and Signal Processing*, Atlanta, GA (Vol. 4, pp. 2136-2139).

Margner, V. (1992, August 30-September 3). SARAT - A system for the recognition of Arabic printed text. In *Proceedings of the 11th IAPR International Conference on Pattern Recognition Methodology and Systems*, The Hague, The Netherlands (Vol. 2, pp. 561-564).

Miled, H., & Ben Amara, N. (2001, September 10-13). Planar Markov modeling for Arabic writing recognition: advancement state. In *Proceedings of the 6th International Conference on Document Analysis and Recognition*, Seattle, WA (pp. 69-73).

Miled, H., Olivier, C., Cheriet, M., & Lecourtier, Y. (1997, August 18-20). Coupling observation/letter for Markovian modelisation applied to the recognition of Arabic handwriting. In *Proceedings of the 4th International Conference on Document Analysis and Recognition*, Ulm, Germany (Vol. 2, pp. 580-583).

Moalla, I., Elbaati, A., Alimi, A. M., & Benhamadou, A. (2002). Extraction of Arabic text from multilingual documents. In *Proceedings of the IEEE International Conference on Systems, Man and Cybernetics* (Vol. 4).

Mori, S., Nishida, H., & Yamada, H. (1999). *Optical character recognition*. New York, NY: John Wiley & Sons.

Mosfeq, R. (1996). Arabic character recognition using integrated segmentation and recognition. In *Proceedings of the 5th International Conference and Exhibition on Multi-Lingual Computing*, London, UK.

Mostafa, K., & Darwish, A. M. (1999). Robust baseline-independent algorithms for segmentation and reconstruction of Arabic handwritten cursive script. In *Proceedings of the SPIE Conference on Document Recognition and Retrieval VI*, San Jose, CA (Vol. 3651, pp. 73-83).

Mostafa, K., Shaheen, S. I., Darwish, A. M., & Farag, I. (1999, May 31-June 3). A novel approach for detecting and correcting segmentation and recognition errors in Arabic OCR systems. In *Proceedings of the 12th International Conference on Industrial and Engineering Applications of Artificial Intelligence and Expert Systems*, Cairo, Egypt (pp. 530-539).

Mostafa, M. G. (2004, April 5-8). An adaptive algorithm for the automatic segmentation of printed Arabic text. In *Proceedings of the 17th National Computer Conference*, Al-Madinah, Saudi Arabia (pp. 437-444).

Motawa, D., Amin, A., & Sabourin, R. (1997, August 18-20). Segmentation of Arabic cursive script. In *Proceedings of the 4th International Conference on Document Analysis and Recognition*, Ulm, Germany (Vol. 2, pp. 625-628).

Nawaz, S. N., Sarfraz, M., Zidouri, A., & Al-Khatib, W. G. (2003, December 14-17). An approach to offline Arabic character recognition using neural networks. In *Proceedings of the 10th IEEE International Conference on Electronics, Circuits and Systems* (Vol. 3, pp. 1328-1331).

Nazif, A. (1975). *A system for the recognition of the printed Arabic characters* (Unpublished master's thesis). Cairo University, Cairo, Egypt.

Nouh, A., Sultan, A., & Tolba, R. (1980). An approach for Arabic characters recognition. *Journal of Science, 6*(2), 185–191.

Nouh, A., Ula, A. N., & Edlin, A. S. (1988). Algorithms for feature extraction: a case study for the Arabic character recognition. In *Proceedings of the 10th National Conference*, Jeddah, Saudi Arabia (pp. 653-666).

Obaid, A. M. (1998). A new pattern matching approach to the recognition of printed Arabic. In *Proceedings of the Workshop on Content Visualization and Intermediate Representations*, Montreal, QC, Canada (pp. 106-111).

Obaid, A. M., & Dobrowiecki, T. P. (1997, September 15-17). Heuristic approach to the recognition of printed Arabic script. In *Proceedings of the IEEE International Conference on Intelligent Engineering Systems*, Budapest, Hungary.

Olivier, C., Miled, H., Romeo-Pakker, K., & Lecourtier, Y. (1996, August 25-29). Segmentation and coding of Arabic handwritten words. In *Proceedings of the International Conference on Pattern Recognition*, Vienna, Austria (Vol. 3, pp. 264-268).

Omar, K., Mahmoud, R., Sulaiman, M. N., & Ramli, A. (2000). The removal of secondaries of Jawi characters. In *Proceedings of the IEEE Region 10 Annual Conference*, Malaysia (Vol. 2, pp. 149-152).

Pal, U., & Sarkar, A. (2003). Recognition of printed Urdu script. In *Proceedings of the 7th International Conference on Document Analysis and Recognition*.

Parhami, B., & Taraghi, M. (1981). Automatic recognition of printed Farsi texts. *Pattern Recognition, 14*(1-6), 395-403.

Ramsis, R., & El-Dabi, S. (1988). *Arabic character recognition system* (Tech. Rep. No. KSC027). Kuwait: IBM Scientific Center.

Romeo-Pakker, K., Miled, H., & Lecourtier, Y. (1995, August 14-16). A new approach for Latin/Arabic character segmentation. In *Proceedings of the 3rd International Conference on Document Analysis and Recognition*, Montreal, QC, Canada (Vol. 2, pp. 874-877).

Sadiq-Hussain, & Sarsam, B. I. (1998, March 30-April 2). Development and evaluation of ANN algorithms for recognition of Arabic script. In *Proceedings of the ISTAED International Conference on Computer System and Application*, Irbid, Jordan.

Sakkal, M. (2002). *How to improve computer generated calligraphic designs*. Retrieved December 28, 2005, from http://www.sakkal.com/instrctn/computer_thuluth01.html

Sarfraz, M., Nawaz, S. N., & Al-Khuraidly, A. (2003, July 16-18). Offline Arabic text recognition system. In *Proceedings of the International Conference on Geometric Modeling and Graphics*, London, UK (pp. 30-36).

Sari, T., Souici, L., & Sellami, M. (2002, August 6-8). Off-line handwritten Arabic character segmentation and recognition system: ACSA. In *Proceedings of the 8th International Workshop on Frontiers in Handwriting Recognition*, Niagara-on-the-Lake, CA (pp. 452-457).

Simard, P. Y., Szeliski, R., Benaloh, J., Couvreur, J., & Calinov, I. (2003). Using character recognition and segmentation to tell computer from humans. In *Proceedings of the 7th International Conference on Document Analysis and Recognition* (Vol. 1, pp. 418-422).

Strange, C. L. (1993). Around the world in 80 days: Typesetting Arabic, Hebrew, Cyrillic, and Thai. In *Proceedings of the Professional Communication Conference on the New Face of Technical Communication: People, Processes, Products* (pp. 43-48).

Tellache, M., Sid-Ahmed, M., & Abaza, B. (1993, May 19-24). Thinning algorithms for Arabic OCR. In *Proceedings of the IEEE Pacific Rim Conference on Communications and Signal Processing*, Victoria, BC, Canada (Vol. 1, pp. 248-251).

Timsari, B., & Fahimi, H. (1996). Morphological approach to character recognition in machine-printed Persian words. In *Proceedings of the SPIE Conference on Document Recognition III*, San Jose, CA.

Tolba, M. F., & Shaddad, E. (1990, November 4-7). On the automatic reading of printed Arabic characters. In *Proceedings of the IEEE International Conference on Systems, Man and Cybernetics*, Los Angeles, CA (pp. 496-498).

Trenkle, J., Gillies, A., Erlandson, E., Schlosser, S., & Cavin, S. (2001, April 23-25). Advances in Arabic text recognition. In *Proceedings of the Symposium on Document Image Understanding Technology*, Columbia, MD.

Walker, R. F. (1993). *Spacio-temporal Arabic character recognition using polynomial contour fitting* (Tech. Rep.). Brisbane, Australia: Queensland University of Technology.

Ymin, A., & Aoki, Y. (1996, August 25-29). On the segmentation of multi-font printed Uygur scripts. In *Proceedings of the 13th International Conference on Pattern Recognition* (Vol. 3, pp. 215-219).

Zahour, A., Taconet, B., Mercy, P., & Ramdane, S. (2001, September 10-13). Arabic hand-written text-line extraction. In *Proceedings of the 6th International Conference on Document Analysis and Recognition*, Seattle, WA (pp. 281-285).

Zeki, A. M., & Ismail, I. A. (2002). A comparative study of five OCR systems. In *Proceedings of the National Conference on Computer Graphics and Multimedia*, Melaka, Malaysia (pp. 552-556).

Zeki, A. M., & Zakaria, M. S. (2004, April 5-8). Challenges in recognizing Arabic characters. In *Proceedings of the 17th National Computer Conference*, Al-Madinah, Saudi Arabia (pp. 445-452).

Zeki, A. M., & Zakaria, M. S. (2005, February 1-3). Determining the up/down orientation of Arabic documents. In *Proceedings of the International Conference on Modeling, Simulation and Applied Optimization*, Sharjah, UAE.

Zheng, L., Hassin, A. H., & Tang, Z. (2004). A new algorithm for machine printed Arabic character segmentation. *Pattern Recognition Letters*, *25*(15), 1723–1729. doi:10.1016/j.patrec.2004.06.015

Zidouri, A. (2004, October 20-22). ORAN - offline recognition of Arabic characters and numerals. In *Proceedings of the International Symposium on Intelligent Multimedia, Video and Speech Processing*, Hong Kong (pp. 703-706).

Zidouri, A., Sarfraz, M., Nawaz, S. N., & Ahmad, M. J. (2003, July 1-4). PC based offline Arabic text recognition system. In *Proceedings of the 7th International Symposium on Signal Processing and its Applications* (Vol. 2, pp. 431-434).

Zidouri, A., Sarfraz, M., Shahab, S. A., & Jafri, S. M. (2005, July 6-5). Adaptive dissection-based subword segmentation of printed Arabic text. In *Proceedings of the 9th International Conference on Information Visualisation* (pp. 239-243).

This journal was previously published in the International Journal of Technology Diffusion, Volume 2, Issue 4, edited by Ali Hussein Saleh Zolait, pp. 48-82, copyright 2011 by IGI Publishing (an imprint of IGI Global).

Chapter 17
Information Hiding Using Ant Colony Optimization Algorithm

Wasan Shaker Awad
University of Bahrain, Bahrain

ABSTRACT

This paper aims to find an effective and efficient information hiding method used for protecting secret information by embedding it in a cover media such as images. Finding the optimal set of the image pixel bits to be substituted by the secret message bits, such that the cover image is of high quality, is a complex process and there is an exponential number of feasible solutions. Two new ant-based algorithms are proposed and compared with other algorithms. The experimental results show that ant colony optimization algorithm can find the solution efficiently and effectively by finding the optimal set of pixel bits in a few number of iterations and with least Mean Square Error (MSE) comparable with genetic and genetic simulated annealing algorithms.

1. INTRODUCTION

Steganography (information hiding) is a technique to hide secret messages in a host media called cover media. In today's world of digital communication, this is accomplished by embedding the covert message in a carrier medium such as an image, video, or sound file. The goal of steganography is not only to ensure secret messages transferred secretly, but also to make the transferred secret messages undetectable. It is the art of invisible communication, and provides a plausible deniability to secret communication. Steganography takes advantage of the inherent weaknesses of human perception by subtly altering the characteristics of the carrier (Cheddad, Curran & Kevitt, 2010; Ge, Gao & Wang, 2007; Di et al., 2003).

DOI: 10.4018/978-1-4666-2791-8.ch017

The basic structure of steganography is made up of three components: the carrier, the message, and the key. The carrier can be a painting, a digital image, or an mp3; it is the object that will 'carry' the hidden message. A key is used to decode/decipher/discover the hidden message (Nabavian, 2010).

In image steganography almost all data hiding techniques try to alter insignificant information in the cover image. For instance, a simple scheme proposed by Lee and Chen (2000), is to place the embedding data at Least Significant Bit (LSB) of each pixel in the cover image. The altered image is called stego-image. Altering LSB doesn't change the quality of image to human perception but this scheme is sensitive a variety of image processing attacks like compression, cropping etc. The LSB insertion methods are common due to their simplicity and large capacity.

In order to overcome the problem of LSB technique of robustness, many researchers proposed different techniques to hide data in higher LSB layer (Chan & Chang, 2001; Chi-Kwong & Cheng, 2004; Chi-Shiang, 2009). Many other genetic algorithm (GA) based approaches to information hiding have been proposed (Chan & Lyu, 2005; Maity & Nandi, 2004; Wang, Yang, & Niu, 2010; Mazdak et al., 2009; Fard et al., 2006). Also, in 2010, Ching-Sheng and Shu-Fen utilized Ant Colony Optimization (ACO) algorithm to construct an optimal LSB substitution matrix.

All previous stego methods are homogenous, in which the same bit positions in the pixels of the cover image are used. For example in the LSB method, only least significant bits are used to hide data, but it has been shown that this method is weak in term of security. Also, using higher layers will affect the quality of the cover images. Thus, in order to overcome the problems of the previous methods, a new stego class has been proposed in by Awad and Jubori (2010), which is called non-homogeneous, in which the secret data can be hidden in different bit positions of different pixels. Also, a Genetic Simulated Annealing algorithm

(GSA) has been proposed for non-homogeneous information hiding. This algorithm, as has been shown by the experimental results, is effective but inefficient because of the need for long chromosomes, large population size, and large number of generations to find the optimal solution.

In this paper, different techniques are employed, and a number of algorithms are presented and studied for hiding secret information using images. The techniques used are GA and ACO, and three algorithms are proposed: GA-GA, Random-ACO, and GA-ACO. Thus, the objectives of this work are:

- Designing an efficient and effective algorithm for information hiding.
- To compare between GA and ACO in terms of efficiency and effectiveness in solving the information hiding problem.

2. PROBLEM FORMULATION

Given a cover image H of size *(imgsize* x *imgsize)* pixels, each pixel P_{ij} is of size n bits, thus, $P_{ij} = p^0$, p^1, ..., p^{n-1}. M is the secret message to hide which is of size *leng* bits. Therefore, we need *leng* pixels from H, P^0, P^1, ..., P^{leng-1}, to hide the message bits m^0, m^1, ..., m^{leng-1}. Each pixel is used to hide one bit from M, and any bit in the pixel can be used to be replaced by the message bit.

This problem can be formulated as directed graph $G = (V,E)$ as shown in Figure 1. This graph consists of the set of nodes (vertices) V; these nodes represent the bits of the cover image pixels selected to hide data, and E is the set of edges that represent the next possible pixel bits to be replaced by the information bits, i.e. it is a matrix representing the connections between nodes. The matrix $E_{leng,n}$ can be defined as follows.

E_{ij} is the difference between the original pixel P^i and the sego pixel, in which the bit p^{ij} is substituted by m^i, for all i = 0..leng-1, and j=0..n-1.

It is clear that:

Figure 1. Graph representation of the problem

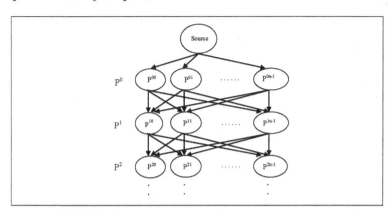

Number of nodes in the graph = $leng \times n + 1$

$$(1)$$

Number of edges in the graph = $n^{leng-1} + n$

$$(2)$$

Thus, the problem solution space size is equal to the number of edges, which is the number of possible sets of pixel bits that can be selected to hide data, i.e., the number of possible paths from the source node to the last pixel bit node in the graph G. The optimal solution for this problem is the set S of pixel bits (leng bits) to be substituted by the information bits, such that MSE value is the minimum and Peak Signal to Noise Ratio (PSNR) is the highest. Therefore, there are: n^{leng-1} $_{+n}$ feasible solutions, hence the search space grows exponentially when *leng* increases.

3. THE PROPOSED ALGORITHMS

This section is for describing the proposed algorithms for solving the underlying problem. These algorithms are:

- GA-GA
- Random-ACO
- GA-ACO

3.1. GA-GA Algorithm

This algorithm is presented in this paper in order to compare the performance of GA with ACO. Usually the cover image pixels are generated randomly, in this algorithm, GA (Goldberg, 1989; Holland, 1975) is used to generate the pixels by finding the optimal or near-optimal random number generator. Also, GA is used for finding the optimal or near-optimal random number generator that can be used for finding S. The random number generator considered here is Linear Feedback Shift Register (LFSR) (Golomb, 1976). The following is the description of the algorithm.

Representation Scheme

The GA population chromosomes are the candidate linear feedback functions of the LFSRs. Thus, each chromosome is a sequence of integer numbers, in the range 0..(imgsize x imgsize)-1. These numbers represent the coefficients of the feedback function of the LFSR. Fixed length chromosomes are used of length L integer numbers. For example, consider that the cover image is of size 300 x 300 pixels, L = 3, and the chromosome is: 2314 456 72980, thus, the feedback function of the LFSR will be: $g(x) = 1 + 2314X + 456X^2 + 72980X^3$

Fitness Evaluation

For the object of transmitting secret data, good approaches to information hiding must provide two attributes: high capacity and high quality. Thus to describe the quality of the stego-image precisely, MSE and PSNR can be used. The PSNR function is defined as follows:

$$PSNR = 10\,LOG\,\frac{255^2}{MSE} \qquad (3)$$

The MSE between the original image H and the stego-image H' is defined as:

$$MSE = \frac{1}{imgsize^2}\sum_{i=0}^{imgsize^2-1}(H_i - H_i')^2 \qquad (4)$$

Fitness function is used to evaluate each chromosome x. In this work, we use MSE in the measurement of the fitness as follows:

$$fit(x) = \frac{imgsize}{(MSE+1)} \qquad (5)$$

To evaluate each chromosome, GA is also applied, which is used to find the best LFSR used to generate S. Thus, the chromosomes are the candidate feedback functions of the LFSR, and each chromosome is a sequence of integer numbers in the rang 0..n-1. Also, fixed length chromosomes are used of length $L1$. The following is the algorithm (GA-eval) used to evaluate the chromosome x, presented in Box 1.

Box 1. Algorithm (GA-eval)

```
Input: The cover image pixels generated by the chromosome x, leng, and the se-
cret message M.
Output:  LFSR' for generating the pixels bits, i.e. S, and the fitness value
of the chromosome x.
Begin
  Generate the initial population (pop) of size popsize1 randomly;
  count ← 0;
  Repeat
    To evaluate pop, for each chromosome (candidate LFSR') in pop do the fol-
lowing:
      Use the chromosome to generate candidate S;
      Substitute the pixel bits of S by the information bits of M;
      Calculate the fitness value using Eq. (5);
    End for;
    Generate a new population by applying crossover and mutation, (pop1);
    pop ← pop1;
    count ←  count + 1;
  Until (count > Gen1);
  Return the best chromosome of pop and its fitness value;
End.
```

GA Parameter

The genetic operations used to update the population are 1-point crossover and mutation with probability 5%. The selection strategy, used to select chromosomes for the genetic operations, is the 2- tournament selection. The old population is completely replaced by the new population which is generated from the old population by applying the genetic operations.

Stopping Criteria

The run of GA is stopped after a fixed number of generations *Gen*. The solution is the best chromosome in the last generation.

The following, presented in Box 2, is the complete GA-GA algorithm.

Results

Table 1 presents the maximum fitness value (*MAX FIT*) obtained by running the algorithm for different parameter values (population size, chromosome length, and maximum number of generations). Obviously, the fitness values are very low, especially for long secret messages, and hence MSE is very high. Thus, this algorithm is not effective for solving the problem of this study. However, these results can be improved by increasing the population size and maximum number of generations yielding very long execution time.

3.2. Random-ACO Algorithm

In this algorithm, the pixels are generated randomly, and the set S of pixel bits is found by applying ACO algorithm.

Observations of the behavior of real ants have inspired the development of a large number of ant-based algorithms, used to solve combinatorial optimization problems. The first algorithm was developed by Dorigo (2004). Since then, a large number of ant-based algorithms were developed for different applications. According to Dorigo, ant system is composed of two parts:

- Tour construction.
- Update of Pheromone trails.

Box 2. Algorithm (GA-GA)

```
Algorithm (GA-GA)
Input: The cover image pixels, leng, and the secret message M.
Output: LFSR for generating the cover image pixels, and LFSR' for generating
the pixels bits.
Begin
  Generate the initial population (pop) of size popsize randomly;
  count ← 0;
  Repeat
    Evaluate pop using GA-eval algorithm;
    Generate a new population by applying crossover and mutation, (pop1);
    pop ← pop1;
    count ←  count + 1;
  Until (count > Gen);
  Return the best chromosome of pop;
End.
```

Table 1. The results of GA-GA algorithm

Leng in Byte	MAX FIT
8	300
16	299.481
32	295.431
64	257.368
128	153.51
256	93.8608
512	37.7603
1024	31.7924

By observing the behavior of ants, they discovered that ants can pass along the path of previous ants since they will leave chemical substances, called Pheromones, on their way. Following Pheromones, ants can find the optimal routs.

Several improvements of ACO have been devised as illustrated by Andries (2006). In this work, the ACO algorithm used is given below in Box 3.

3.3. GA-ACO Algorithm

In this method, GA is used to generate the pixels as described in section (3.1), and ACO algorithm is used to find the set S, as described in section (3.2). The following presented in Box 4 is the complete algorithm.

4. EXPERIMENTAL RESULTS

To implement the proposed methods, C++ programming language is employed. Moreover, to evaluate the fidelity of the method the MSE and PSNR are employed. In the experiments, we demonstrate the fidelity enhancing effectiveness of the proposed optimization process.

The performance of the algorithms is evaluated through several experiments with different parameter values. Then, the quality of the image is evaluated. In all experiments, a cover image of size 300 x 300 pixels is used, where each pixel is of size eight bits. Figure 2 presents the cover image used. Furthermore, the secret message bits used are generated randomly.

Experiment 1: The aim is to study the behavior of the proposed algorithms. Thus, this experiment has been carried out in order to investigate the effectiveness of Random-ACO algorithm. The results of applying this algorithm are presented in Table 2 that shows the MSE and PSNR for different values of *leng* and T_k. It is clear that there is no need for large number of ants to obtain high PSNR especially for short secret messages, and large number of ants yields better results for long messages, where $\rho = 0.1$, $\alpha=2$, $\beta=1$, and $\tau_0=0.05$.

Experiment 2: The aim of this experiment is to study the impact of *leng* on PSNR using Random-ACO algorithm, as shown in Figure 3. We can observe that PSNR is decreased as *leng* (in Byte) is increased, where gen=20, $T_k = 10$, $\rho = 0.1$, $\alpha=2$, $\beta=1$, and $\tau_0=0.05$. This is because, embedding longer message in the cover image means that the image is subjecting to additional noise.

Experiment 3: This experiment is to study the effect of ρ value of Random-ACO algorithm on PSNR. Two values have been tested: 0.5 and 0.1. The results are presented in Figure 4. As shown in this figure, the results are highly improved by using $\rho = 0.1$, where gen=20, $T_k = 10$, $\alpha=2$, $\beta=1$, and $\tau_0=0.05$.

Experiment 4: It is to assess the performance of GA-ACO as compared to Random-ACO. As shown in Figure 5 and Figure 6, using GA to generate the pixels improves the results of ACO algorithm. These results are obtained by running the algorithms 25 times and for different parameter values, and then considering the maximum and minimum fitness values obtained for different values of *leng*.

Box 3. Algorithm (Random-ACO)

```
Input:    leng, and the secret message M.
Output: The set S.
Begin
  Generate the cover image pixels randomly;
  Set up the parameters: T_k (number of ants), τ_0 (the initial value of Phero-
mones), α, β, ρ (evaporation rate), gen (maximum number of generations);
  count ← 0;
  Repeat
    For ant k in 0 .. T_k-1 do
      S_k ← ∅;
        Repeat
          Tour construction: Select the next vertex p^ij to visit by applying
the following random proportional rule:
```

$$prob_{ij} = \frac{[\tau_{ij}]^\alpha [\eta_{ij}]^\beta}{\sum_{l \in N_l^K} [\tau_{il}]^\alpha [\eta_{il}]^\beta} \tag{6}$$

```
        Where
            η_ij =
```

$$\frac{1}{1 + E_{ij}} \tag{7}$$

```
and it is the heuristic to visit the next pixel bit p^ij. τ_ij is the concentra-
tion of Pheromones on the path to the next pixel bit.
```
N_l^k is the set of neigh-
bors which are not visited by ant *k*, and α and β are adjustable parameters.
```
            S_k ← S_k ∪ { p^ij };
            Until visiting the last pixel;
    End for;
    Update of Pheromones Trails: Pheromones will be updated using the follow-
ing formula:
```

$$\tau_{ij}(t+1) = (1-\rho)\tau_{ij}(t) + \sum_{k=0}^{T_k-1} f^k \tag{8}$$

$$f^k = \begin{cases} \dfrac{1}{1+MSE^k}, & \text{if the arc to the pixel bit } p^{ij} \\ & \text{belongs to the tour of the ant } k. \\ \\ 0, & \text{otherwise.} \end{cases} \tag{9}$$

```
    count ← count +1;
  Until (count > gen);
Return best S_k;
End.
```

Box 4. Algorithm (GA-ACO)

```
Algorithm (GA-ACO)
Input:  leng, and the secret message M.
Output: LFSR for generating the cover image pixels, and S.
Begin
  Generate the initial population (pop) of size popsize randomly;
  count ← 0;
  Repeat
    For each chromosome in pop do
      Generate the pixels;
      Apply ACO algorithm to find S;
      Evaluate the chromosome using Eq. (5);
    End for;
    Generate a new population by applying crossover and mutation, (pop1);
    pop ← pop1;
    count ← count + 1;
  Until (count > Gen);
  Return the best chromosome of pop, and the best S;
End.
```

In these figures, the left bar in the chart is for GA-ACO algorithm, and the right bar is for Random-ACO algorithm.

Experiment 5: It is to study the effect of GA population size on the effectiveness of GA-ACO algorithm, as shown in Figure 7. We can see that increasing the population size of GA improves the fitness values. In this experiment, Gen=30, $\rho = 0.1$, gen=20, T_k = 10, α=2, β=1, and τ_0=0.05.

Figure 2. The cover image

Also, we need to assess the efficiency of the proposed ant-based algorithms. This can be accomplished by comparing the proposed ant-based algorithms with our previous work GSA algorithm (Awad & Jubori, 2010). GSA was used to find the optimal set S, where the pixels are generated randomly, and the GA chromosomes represent the candidate pixel bits sets. The efficiency is measured as number of iterations needed by each algorithm which is computed as (gen x T_k) for ACO algorithm, and (maximum number of generations x popsize) for GSA, where leng = 256 bytes. As shown in Table 3, we can obtain very high PSNR with a few number of iterations using ACO. The results are presented in this table as range of values.

5. DISCUSSION AND CONCLUSION

This paper is to consider an important and complex problem which is finding an effective informa-

Table 2. The results of experiment 1

T_k	gen	Leng in Byte	MSE	PSNR
10	10	8	2.2222E-05	94.66293
		16	4.4444E-05	91.65263
		32	6.6667E-05	89.89171
		64	8.8889E-05	88.64233
		128	0.00073333	79.47779
		256	0.00068889	79.74931
		512	0.00093333	78.43044
		1024	0.00226667	74.57692
		2048	0.00384444	72.28247
		5000	0.0134889	66.83104
		10000	0.0170889	65.80366
30	10	8	0	∞
		16	6.6667E-05	89.89171
		32	6.6667E-05	89.89171
		64	0.00044444	81.65263
		128	0.00015556	86.21194
		256	0.00048889	81.2387
		512	0.00064444	80.03895
		1024	0.00155556	76.21194
		2048	0.00364444	72.5145
		5000	0.0068	69.80571
		10000	0.0162889	66.01189
10	20	8	0	∞
		16	4.44E-05	91.65263
		32	6.67E-05	89.89171
		64	0.000133	86.88143
		128	0.000222	84.66293
		256	0.000356	82.62172
		512	0.001867	75.42013
		1024	0.0036	72.56778
		2048	0.006378	70.08411
		5000	0.011333	67.58724
		10000	0.019867	65.14955

tion hiding method that can be used to embed efficiently a large amount of information in a cover image without affecting the quality of this image. Information hiding is an important security technique used to protect the stored or transmitted private information and can be used in wide area of applications, such as web-based applications. Different algorithms for information hiding have been proposed, most of them are based on LSB technique which is of low level of security. Thus, to

Figure 3. Effect of leng on PSNR by using Random-ACO algorithm

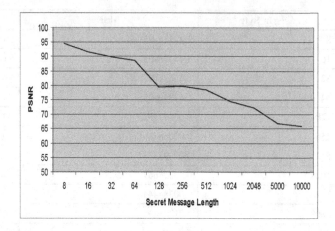

Figure 4. The results of experiment 3

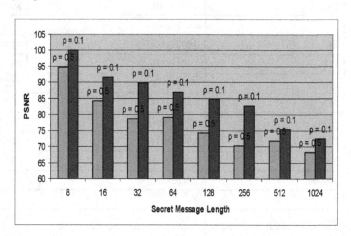

Figure 5. Comparison between GA-ACO and Random-ACO in term of maximum fitness value obtained

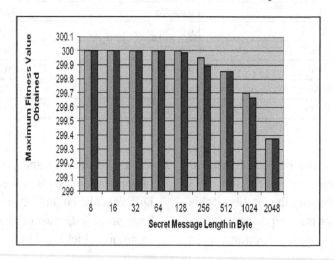

Figure 6. Comparison between GA-ACO and Random-ACO in term of minimum fitness value obtained

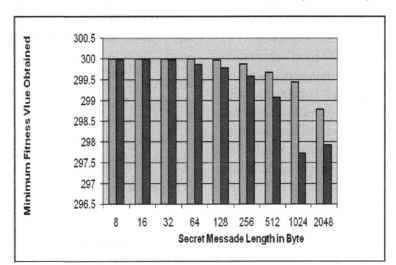

Figure 7. Effect of GA population size on the fitness values of GA-ACO algorithm

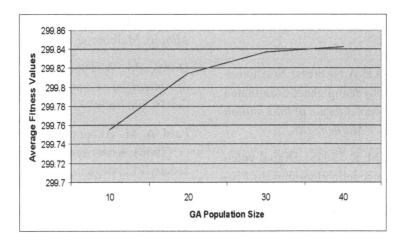

Table 3. Efficiency of Random-ACO algorithm

Algorithm	Number of Iterations	PSNR
Random-ACO	100-2500	82.6-76.6
GSA	25600-179200	61.23481-71.39866

overcome the weaknesses of the previous methods, the newly proposed class of steganography which is called non-homogeneous is considered the issue of the current research. A number of algorithms have been developed and presented in this paper, which are based on two techniques: GA and ACO. These algorithms can be applied to find the optimal set of cover image pixel bits to be substituted by the secret information. The experimental results show the efficiency and effectiveness of the ACO algorithms (Random-ACO and GA-ACO algorithms) in solving the problem of information hiding. The quality of setgo-image produced by these algorithms is very high comparable with GA and GSA. Furthermore, the efficiency of the proposed algorithms has been examined, and it has been shown that ACO outperforms GA and GSA. Thus, ACO provides a new promising direction in information hiding. However, other heuristic techniques may yield better results, therefore, studying other techniques and algorithms is recommended for future research.

REFERENCES

Andries, P. E. (2006). *Fundamentals of computational swarm intelligence*. New York, NY: John Wiley & Sons.

Awad, W. S., & Jubori, H. A. (in press). Non homogeneous steganography using genetic simulated annealing. *International Journal of Information Science and Computer Mathematics*.

Chan, P. W., & Lyu, M. R. (2005). Digital video watermarking with a genetic algorithm. In *Proceedings of the International Conference on Digital Archive Technologies*, Taipei, Taiwan (pp. 139-153).

Chan, Y. K., & Chang, C. C. (2001). Concealing a Secret Image Using the Breadth First Traversal Linear Quad tree Structure. In *Proceedings of the 3rd IEEE International Symposium on Cooperative Database Systems for Advanced Applications*, Beijing, China (pp. 194-199).

Cheddad, C. J., Curran, K., & McKevitt, P. (2010). Digital image steganography: Survey and analysis of current methods. *Signal Processing*, *90*(3), 727–752. doi:10.1016/j.sigpro.2009.08.010

Chi-Kwong, C., & Cheng, L. M. (2004). Hiding data in images by simple LSB substitution. *Pattern Recognition Letters*, *37*(3), 469–474.

Chi-Shiang, C. (2009). An information hiding scheme by applying the dynamic programming strategy to LSB matching revisited. In *Proceedings of the 3rd International Conference on Ubiquitous Information Management and Communication*, Suwon, Korea (pp. 246-250).

Ching-Sheng, H., & Shu-Fen, T. (2010). Finding optimal LSB substitution matrix using ant colony optimization algorithm. In *Proceedings of the Second International Conference on Communication Software and Networks* (pp. 293-297).

Di, Y., Huan, L., Liu, H., Ramineni, A., & Sen, A. (2003). Detecting hidden information in images: A comparative study. In *Proceedings of the IEEE/ICDM Workshop on Privacy Preserving Data Mining*, Melbourne, FL (pp. 24-30).

Dorigo, M., & Thomas, S. (2004). *Ant colony optimization*. Cambridge, MA: MIT Press. doi:10.1007/b99492

Fard, A. M., Akbarzadeh, T. M. R., & Varasteh, A. (2006). A new genetic algorithm approach for secure JPEG steganography. In *Proceedings of the IEEE International Conference on Engineering of Intelligent Systems*, Islamabad, Pakistan (pp. 216-219).

Ge, S., Gao, Y., & Wang, R. (2007). Least significant bit steganography detection with machine learning techniques. In *Proceedings of the International Workshop on Domain Driven Data Mining*, San Jose, CA (pp. 24-32).

Goldberg, D. E. (1989). *Genetic algorithms in search, optimization, and machine learning*. Reading, MA: Addison-Wesley.

Golomb, S. W. (1976). *Shift register sequences*. Walnut Creek, CA: Aegean Park Press.

Holland, J. H. (1975). *Adaptive in natural and artificial systems: An Introductory Analysis with Applications to Biology, Control, and Artificial Intelligence*. Cambridge, MA: MIT Press.

Lee, Y. K., & Chen, L. H. (2000). High capacity image steganographic model. []. Image and Signal Processing.]. *Proceedings on Vision, 147*, 288–294. doi:10.1049/ip-vis:20000341

Maity, S. P., & Nandi, P. K. (2004). Genetic algorithm for optimal imperceptibility in image communication through noisy channel. In *Proceedings of the International Conference on Neural Information Processing*, Calcutta, India (pp. 700-705).

Mazdak, Z., Azizah, A., Rabiah, B., Akram, M., & Shahidan, A. (2009). A genetic-algorithm-based approach for audio steganography. *World Academy of Science. Engineering and Technology, 54*, 360–363.

Nabavian, N. (2010). *CPSC 350 data structures: Image steganography*. Retrieved from http://www1.chapman.edu/~nabav100/ImgStegano/download/ImageSteganography.pdf

Wang, S., Yang, B., & Niu, X. (2010). A secure steganography method based on genetic algorithm. *Journal of Information Hiding and Multimedia Signal Processing, 1*(1), 28–35.

This journal was previously published in the International Journal of Technology Diffusion, Volume 2, Issue 1, edited by Ali Hussein Saleh Zolait, pp. 16-28, copyright 2011 by IGI Publishing (an imprint of IGI Global).

Compilation of References

Abandah, G. A., & Khedher, M. Z. (2004). *Printed and handwritten Arabic optical character recognition – initial study (Tech. Rep.)*. Amman, Jordan: University of Jordan.

Abd El-Gwad, A., Salem, M., Abou Shadi, F. E. Z., & Arafat, H. (1990, June 16-21). Automatic recognition of handwritten Arabic characters. In *Proceedings of the 10th International Conference on Pattern Recognition*, Atlantic City, NJ.

Abdelazim, H. Y., & Hashish, M. A. (1989, May 8-12). Automatic reading of bilingual typewritten text. In *Proceedings of the Conference on Very Large Scale Integration and Microelectronic Applications in Intelligent Peripherals and their Interconnection Networks*, Hamburg, Germany (Vol. 2, pp. 140-144).

Abdelazim, H., & Hashish, M. (1988). Arabic reading machine. In *Proceedings of the 10th Saudi National Computer Conference*, Riyadh, Saudi Arabia (pp. 733-743).

Abdelazim, H., Mousa, A., Salih, Y., & Hashish, M. (1989, October 21-24). Arabic text recognition using a partial observation approach. In *Proceedings of the 12th National Computer Conference*, Riyadh, Saudi Arabia (pp. 427-437).

Abelló, A., Samos, J., & Saltor, F. (2006). YAM2: A multidimensional conceptual model extending UML. *Information Systems*, *31*(6), 541–567. doi:10.1016/j.is.2004.12.002

Abo Samra, G., Jambi, K., Al-Barhamtoshy, H., Amer, R., & Al-Bidewi, I. (1997). A comprehensive algorithm for segmenting handwritten Arabic scripts in off-line systems. In *Proceedings of the 17th National Computer Conference*, Saudi Arabia (pp. 1-13).

Abu Dhabi Tourism Authority. (2011). *History & population*. Retrieved June 19, 2011, from http://www.visitabudhabi.ae/en/about.abudhabi/population.aspx

Abuhaiba, I. (1996). *Recognition of off-line handwritten cursive text* (Unpublished doctoral dissertation). Loughborough University, Loughborough, UK.

Abuhaiba, I. (2003). A discrete Arabic script for better automatic document understanding. *The Arabian Journal for Science and Engineering*, *28*(1), 77–94.

Abuhaiba, I. (2003). Arabic font recognition based on templates. *The International Arab Journal of Information Technology*, *1*(0), 33–39.

Abuhaiba, I., & Ahmed, P. (1993). Restoration of temporal information in off-line Arabic handwriting. *Pattern Recognition*, *26*(7), 1009–1017. doi:10.1016/0031-3203(93)90002-E

Abuhaiba, I., Holt, M. J. J., & Datta, S. (1998). Recognition of off-line cursive handwriting. *Computer Vision and Image Understanding*, *71*(1), 19–38. doi:10.1006/cviu.1997.0629

Abuhaiba, I., Mahmoud, S., & Green, R. (1994). Recognition of handwritten cursive Arabic characters. *IEEE Transactions on Pattern Analysis and Machine Intelligence*, *16*(6), 664–672. doi:10.1109/34.295912

Adamic, L., & Adar, E. (2005). How to search a social network. *Journal of Social Networks*, *27*, 187–203. doi:10.1016/j.socnet.2005.01.007

Adams, D. A., Nelson, R. R., & Todd, P. A. (1992). Perceived usefulness, ease of use, and usage of information technology: A replication. *Management Information Systems Quarterly*, *16*(2), 227–247. doi:10.2307/249577

Adrian, A., Norwood, S., & Mask, P. (2005). Producers' perceptions and attitudes toward precision agriculture technologies. *Computers and Electronics in Agriculture, 48*(3), 256–271. doi:10.1016/j.compag.2005.04.004

Aerschot, L., & Rodousakis, N. (2008). The link between socio-economic background and internet use: barriers faced by low socio-economic status groups and possible solutions. *European Journal of Soil Science, 21*(4), 317–351.

Agarwal, R., & Prasad, J. (1997). The role of innovation characteristics and perceived voluntariness in the acceptance of information technologies. *Decision Sciences, 28*(3), 557–582. doi:10.1111/j.1540-5915.1997.tb01322.x

Agarwal, R., & Prasad, J. (1998). The antecedents and consequents of user perceptions in information technology adoption. *Decision Support Systems, 22*, 15–29. doi:10.1016/S0167-9236(97)00006-7

Agrawal, P., & Famolari, D. (2006). Mobile computing in the next generation wireless networks. In *Proceedings of the 3rd International Workshop on Discrete Algorithms and Methods for Mobile Computing and Communications* (pp. 32-39). New York, NY: ACM Press.

Ajzen, I. (1991). The theory of planned behavior. *Organizational Behavior and Human Decision Processes, 50*(2), 179–211. doi:10.1016/0749-5978(91)90020-T

Akehurst, D. H., & Bordbar, B. (2001). On querying UML data models with OCL. In *Proceedings of the 4th International Conference on the Unified Modeling Language, Modeling Languages, Concepts, and Tools*.

Akour, I., Alshare, K., Miller, D., & Dwairi, M. (2006). An exploratory analysis of culture, perceived ease of use, perceived usefulness, and internet acceptance: The case of Jordan. *Journal of Internet Commerce, 5*(3), 83–108. doi:10.1300/J179v05n03_04

AlAmer, M. (2006). *Bahrain E-government Project*. Paper presented at the Govtec Exhibition and Conference.

Alampay, E. (2008). *Reporting Police Wrongdoing via SMS in the Philippines*. Retrieved December 12, 2008, from http://www.egov4dev.org/mgovernment/resources/case/text2920.shtml

Al-Badr, B., & Haralick, R. (1992). Recognition without segmentation: using mathematical morphology to recognize printed Arabic. In *Proceedings of the 13th National Computer Conference*, Riyadh, Saudi Arabia (pp. 813-829).

Al-Badr, B., & Haralick, R. (1998). A segmentation-free approach to text recognition with application to Arabic text. *International Journal on Document Analysis and Recognition, 1*(3), 147–166. doi:10.1007/s100320050014

Al-Badr, B., & Mahmoud, S. (1995). Survey and bibliography of Arabic optical text recognition. *Signal Processing, 41*(1), 49–77. doi:10.1016/0165-1684(94)00090-M

Albirini, A. (2006). Cultural perceptions: The missing element in the implementation of ICT in developing countries. *International Journal of Education and Development Using Information and Communication Technology, 2*(1), 49–65.

Alda's-Manzano, J. N., Ruiz-Mafe, C., & Sanz-Blas, S. (2009). Exploring individual personality factors as drivers of M-shopping acceptance. *Industrial Management & Data Systems, 109*(6), 739–757. doi:10.1108/02635570910968018

Aleke, B. (2003). *Up-take of e-commerce technologies by small and medium agricultural enterprises*. Unpublished doctoral dissertation, University of Northumbria, Newcastle, UK.

Aleke, B. (2010). *Developing a model for information and communication technology diffusion among small and medium sized agribusiness enterprises in Southeast Nigeria*. Unpublished doctoral dissertation, University of Northumbria, Newcastle, UK.

Aleke, B., Wainwright, D., & Green, G. (2009). Policy issues of e-commerce technology diffusion in Southeast Nigeria: The case of small scale agribusiness. *Northumbria Built and Virtual Environment Working Paper Series, 2*, 39-54.

Al-Emami, S. (1988). *Machine recognition of handwritten and typewritten Arabic characters* (Unpublished doctoral dissertation). University of Reading, Reading, UK.

Al-Faham, M. (2006, November 14-15). *Networks of international collaboration: key to research advancement*. Paper presented at the Arab World Conference on the Issue and Problems of Scientific Research, Alexandria, Egypt.

Al-Fakhri, F. (1997). *On-line computer recognition of handwritten Arabic text* (Unpublished master's thesis). Universiti Sains Malaysia, Penang, Malaysia.

Al-Gahtani, S. S. (2008). Testing for the applicability of the TAM model in the Arabic context: Exploring an extended TAM with three moderating factors. *Information Resources Management Journal, 21*(4), 1–26. doi:10.4018/irmj.2008100101

Al-Gahtani, S. S., Hubona, G. S., & Wang, J. (2007). Information technology (IT) in Saudi Arabia: culture and the acceptance and use of IT. *Information & Management, 44*, 681–691. doi:10.1016/j.im.2007.09.002

Al-Gahtani, S. S., & King, M. (1999). Attitudes, satisfaction and usage: factors contributing to each in the acceptance of information technology. *Behaviour & Information Technology, 18*(4), 277–297. doi:10.1080/014492999119020

Alherbish, J., & Ammar, R. A. (1998). High-performance Arabic character recognition. *Journal of Systems and Software, 44*(1), 53–71. doi:10.1016/S0164-1212(98)10043-2

Al-Khamayseh, S., Hujran, O., Aloudat, A., & Lawrence, E. (2006). Intelligent M-Government: Application of Personalization and Location Awareness Techniques. In *Proceedings of the 2nd European Mobile Government Conference,* Brighton, UK.

Allam, M. (1994). Arabic character recognition. In *Proceedings of the SPIE Conference on Document Recognition* (Vol. 2181, pp. 351-359).

Allam, M. (1995). Segmentation versus segmentation-free for recognizing Arabic text. In *Proceedings of the SPIE Conference on Document Recognition II* (Vol. 2422, pp. 228-235).

Al-Ma'adeed, S. (2001). An off-line cursive Arabic handwriting recognition system. In *Proceedings of the ACS International Conference on Computer Systems and Applications.*

Al-Ma'aitah, M. (2008). Impact of using electronic collaborative media on knowledge sharing phase. In *Proceedings of the 7ᵗʰ WSEAS International Conference on System Science and Simulation in Engineering*, Stevens Point, WI (pp. 152-158).

Almuallim, H., & Yamaguchi, S. A. (1987). Method of recognition of Arabic cursive handwriting. *IEEE Transactions on Pattern Analysis and Machine Intelligence, 9*(5), 715–722. doi:10.1109/TPAMI.1987.4767970

Al-Ohali, Y. (1995). *Development and evaluation environment for typewritten Arabic character recognition* (Unpublished master's thesis). King Saud University, Riyadh, Saudi Arabia.

Al-Rashdan, A. (2009). Higher education in the Arab world: hopes and challenges. *Arab Insight, 2*(6), 77–90.

Al-Sadoun, H., & Amin, A. (1995). A new structural technique for recognizing printed Arabic text. *International Journal of Pattern Recognition and Artificial Intelligence, 9*(1), 101–125. doi:10.1142/S0218001495000067

Alshebeili, S. A., Nabawi, A. A., & Mahmoud, S. A. (1997). Arabic character recognition using 1-D slices of the character spectrum. *Signal Processing, 56*(1), 59–75. doi:10.1016/S0165-1684(96)00150-8

Altuwaijri, M., & Bayoumi, M. (1994, May 30-June 2). Arabic text recognition using neural networks. In *Proceedings of the IEEE International Symposium on Circuits and Systems*, London, UK (Vol. 6, pp. 415-418).

Altuwaijri, M., & Bayoumi, M. (1995, December 17-21). A new recognition system for multi-font Arabic cursive words. In *Proceedings of the 2nd IEEE International Conference on Electronics, Circuits and Systems*, Amman, Jordan (pp. 298-303).

Altuwaijri, M., & Bayoumi, M. (1995. April 28-May 3). A new thinning algorithm for Arabic characters using self-organizing neural network. In *Proceedings of the IEEE International Symposium on Circuits and Systems*, Seattle, WA (Vol. 3, pp. 1824-1827).

Altuwaijri, M., & Bayoumi, M. (1998). A thinning algorithm for Arabic characters using ART2 neural network. *IEEE Transactions on Circuits and Systems II: Analog and Digital Signal Processing, 45*(2), 260–264. doi:10.1109/82.661669

Alvesson, M., & Deetz, S. (2000). *Doing critical management research*. London, UK: Sage.

Alwa, I. (2008). Scientific research in Arab countries- facts and figures (Web log post). *The MEMRI Economic*. Retrieved from http://memrieconomicblog.org/bin/content. cgi?article=91

Al-Waily, R. (1989). *A study on preprocessing and syntactic recognition of hand-written Arabic characters* (Unpublished master's thesis). University of Basrah, Basrah, Iraq.

Al-Yousefi, H., & Upda, S. S. (1992). Recognition of Arabic characters. *IEEE Transactions on Pattern Analysis and Machine Intelligence, 14*(8), 853–857. doi:10.1109/34.149585

Amin, A. (2001). Segmentation of printed Arabic text. In *Proceedings of the International Conference on Advances in Pattern Recognition* (pp. 115-126).

Amin, A. (2002, August 6-9). Structural description to recognizing Arabic characters using decision tree learning techniques. In *Proceedings of the Joint IAPR International Workshops on Structural, Syntactic, and Statistical Pattern Recognition*, Windsor, ON, Canada (pp. 152-158).

Amin, A., & Al-Sadoun, H. (1992, August 30-September 3). A new segmentation technique of Arabic text. In *Proceedings of the 11th International Conference on Pattern Recognition: Methodology and Systems*, The Hague, The Netherlands (Vol. 2, pp. 441-445).

Amin, A., & Masini, G. (1982). Machine recognition of Arabic cursive words. In *Proceedings of the SPIE 26th International Symposium on Instrument Display, Application of Digital Image Processing IV*, San Diego, CA (Vol. 359, pp. 286-292).

Amin, A., & Masini, G. (1986). Machine recognition of multifonts printed Arabic texts. In *Proceedings of the 8th International Conference on Pattern Recognition*, Paris, France, (pp. 392-395).

Amin, A. (1991). Recognition of Arabic handprinted mathematical formulae. *The Arabian Journal for Science and Engineering, 16*(4B), 532–542.

Amin, A. (1997). Arabic character recognition. In Bunke, H., & Wang, P. S. P. (Eds.), *Handbook of character recognition and document image analysis* (pp. 397–420). Singapore: World Scientific.

Amin, A., & Al-Fedaghi, S. (1991). Machine recognition of printed Arabic text utilizing natural language morphology. *International Journal of Man-Machine Studies, 35*(6), 769–788. doi:10.1016/S0020-7373(05)80160-9

Amin, A., Al-Sadoun, H., & Fischer, S. (1996). Hand-printed Arabic character recognition system using an artificial network. *Pattern Recognition, 29*(4), 663–675. doi:10.1016/0031-3203(95)00110-7

Amin, A., & Mari, J. F. (1989). Machine recognition and correction of printed Arabic text. *IEEE Transactions on Systems, Man, and Cybernetics, 19*(5), 1300–1306. doi:10.1109/21.44052

Anandarajan, M., Igbariam, M., & Anakwe, U. P. (2002). IT acceptance in a less-developed country: A motivational factor perspective. *International Journal of Information Management, 22*(1), 47–65. doi:10.1016/S0268-4012(01)00040-8

Anderson, A. (2003). Risk, terrorism, and the Internet. *Knowledge. Technology and Policy, 16*(2), 24–33. doi:10.1007/s12130-003-1023-7

Anderson, J. E., Schwager, P. H., & Kerns, R. L. (2006). The drivers for acceptance of tablet PCs by faculty in a college of business. *Journal of Information Systems Education, 17*(4), 429–440.

Andries, P. E. (2006). *Fundamentals of computational swarm intelligence*. New York, NY: John Wiley & Sons.

Antony, J., Kumar, M., & Labib, A. (2008). Gearing Six Sigma into UK Manufacturing SMEs: An empirical assessment of critical success factors, impediments, and viewpoints of Six Sigma implementation in SMEs. *The Journal of the Operational Research Society, 59*(4), 482–493. doi:10.1057/palgrave.jors.2602437

Antony, J., Kumar, M., & Madu, C. N. (2005). Six Sigma in small and medium sized UK manufacturing enterprises: some empirical observations. *International Journal of Quality & Reliability Management, 22*(8), 860–874. doi:10.1108/02656710510617265

Antovski, L., & Gusev, M. (2006). M-GOV: The Evolution Method. In *Proceedings of the 2nd European Mobile Government Conference*, Brighton, UK.

Arab Knowledge Report. (2009). *Toward productive intercommunication for knowledge.* Dubai, UAE: Alghurair Printing.

Arbanowski, S., Ballon, P., David, K., Droegehorn, O., Eertink, H., & Kellerer, W. (2004). I-centric communications: Personalization, ambient awareness, and adaptability for future mobile services. *IEEE Communications Magazine, 42*(9), 63–69. doi:10.1109/MCOM.2004.1336722

Arth, M. (1968). Ideals and behaviour: A comment on Ibo respect patterns. *The Gerontologist, 8,* 242–244. doi:10.1093/geront/8.4.242

Atici, A. A., & Yarman-Vural, F. T. (1997). A heuristic algorithm for optical character recognition of Arabic script. *Signal Processing, 62*(1), 87–99. doi:10.1016/S0165-1684(97)00117-5

Atkinson, R. (1999). Project management: Cost, time and quality, two best guesses and a phenomenon. *International Journal of Project Management, 17*(6), 337–342. doi:10.1016/S0263-7863(98)00069-6

Auda, G., & Raafat, H. (1993, September 14-17). An automatic text reader using neural networks. In *Proceedings of the Canadian Conference on Electrical and Computer Engineering* (Vol. 1, pp. 92-95).

Avison, D. E., & Myers, M. D. (1995). Information systems and anthropology: an anthropological perspective on IT and organizational culture. *Information Technology & People, 8*(3), 43–56. doi:doi:10.1108/09593849510098262

Avison, D., & Malaurent, J. (2007). Impact of cultural differences: A case study of ERP introduction in China. *International Journal of Information Management, 27,* 368–374. doi:doi:10.1016/j.ijinfomgt.2007.06.004

Awad, W. S., & Jubori, H. A. (in press). Non homogeneous steganography using genetic simulated annealing. *International Journal of Information Science and Computer Mathematics.*

Awoke, M., & Okorji, C. (2004). The determination and analysis of constraints in resource use efficiency in multiple cropping systems by small-holder farmers in Ebonyi State, Nigeria. *Africa Development. Afrique et Developpement, 29*(3), 58–69.

Azmi, R., & Kabir, E. (2001). A new segmentation technique for omni-font Farsi text. *Pattern Recognition Letters, 22,* 97–104. doi:10.1016/S0167-8655(00)00086-6

Baerenklau, K., & Knapp, K. (2007). Dynamics of agricultural technology adoption: Age structure, reversibility, and uncertainty. *American Journal of Agricultural Economics, 89,* 190–201. doi:10.1111/j.1467-8276.2007.00972.x

Bagchi, K., Hart, P., & Peterson, M. F. (2004). National culture and information technology product adoption. *Journal of Global Information Technology Management, 7*(4), 29–46.

Baldi, S., & Thaung, P. P. (2002). The entertaining way to m-commerce: Japan's approach to the mobile Internet – a model for Europe. *Electronic Markets, 12*(1), 6–13. doi:10.1080/101967802753433218

Ballon, P. (2004). Scenarios and business models for 4G in Europe. *Info Emerald, 6*(6), 363–382. doi:10.1108/14636690410568641

Bandura, A. (1986). *Social foundations of thought and action: A social cognitive theory.* Upper Saddle River, NJ: Prentice Hall.

Bannister, F. (2007). The curse of the benchmark: An assessment of the validity and value of e-government comparisons. *International Review of Administrative Sciences, 73*(2), 171–188. doi:10.1177/0020852307077959

Bannister, J., Mather, P., & Coope, S. (2003). *Convergence technologies for 3G networks.* New York, NY: John Wiley & Sons. doi:10.1002/0470860936

Barber, B. R. (2001). The uncertainty of digital politics: Democracy's uneasy relationship with information technology. *Harvard International Review, 23,* 42–47.

Barnes, S. J., & Huff, S. J. (2003). Rising sSun: iMode and the wireless Internet. *Communications of the ACM, 46*(11), 78–84. doi:10.1145/948383.948384

Barnett, T., Kellermanns, F., Pearson, A., & Pearson, R. (2007). Measuring system usage: Replication and extension. *Journal of Computer Information Systems, 47*(2), 76–85.

Baron, R., & Markman, G. (2003). Beyond social capital: The role of entrepreneurs' social competence in their financial success. *Journal of Business Venturing, 18*(1), 41–60. doi:10.1016/S0883-9026(00)00069-0

Basden, G. (1921). *Among the Ibos of Nigeria*. Dublin, Ireland: Nonsuch Publishing.

Bashshur, M. (2007, May 25-26). The impact of globalization and research in Arab states. In *Proceedings of the 2nd Regional Research Seminar for Arab States*, Rabat, Morocco.

Batelco. (2010). *O-net Mobile Broadband*. Retrieved August 21, 2010, from http://www.batelco.com.bh/portal/mobile/mobile_broadband.asp

Beamon, B. M. (1999). Measuring supply chain performance. *International Journal of Operations & Production Management, 19*(3), 275–292. doi:10.1108/01443579910249714

Bélanger, F., & Carter, L. (2008). Trust and risk in e-government adoption. *The Journal of Strategic Information Systems, 17*(2), 165–176. doi:10.1016/j.jsis.2007.12.002

Ben Amara, N., & Ellouze, N. (1995, August 14-16). A robust approach for Arabic printed character segmentation. In *Proceedings of the 3rd International Conference on Document Analysis and Recognition*, Montreal, QC, Canada (Vol. 2, pp. 865-868).

Benbasat, I., & Barki, H. (2007). Quo Vadis TAM? *Journal of the AIS, 8*(3), 211–218.

Bernier, E., Gosselin, P., Badard, T., & Bédard, Y. (2009). Easier surveillance of climate-related health vulnerabilities through a web-based spatial olap application. *International Journal of Health Geographics, 8*(18).

Berson, A., & Smith, S. (1997). *Data warehousing, data mining, and OLAP (data warehousing/data management)*. New York, NY: McGraw-Hill.

Bhattacherjee, A. (2001). Understanding information systems continuance: An expectation-confirmation. *Management Information Systems Quarterly, 25*(3), 351–370. doi:10.2307/3250921

Bhattacherjee, A., & Sanford, C. (2009). The intention–behaviour gap in technology usage: the moderating role of attitude strength. *Behaviour & Information Technology, 28*(4), 389–401. doi:10.1080/01449290802121230

Bianchi, G., Melazzi, N., Chan, P., Holzbock, M., Hu, Y. F., & Jahn, A. (2003). Design and validation of QoS aware mobile Internet access procedures for heterogeneous networks. *Mobile Networks and Applications, 8*(1), 11–25. doi:10.1023/A:1021163526385

Bimonte, S. (2010). A web-based tool for spatio-multi-dimensional analysis of geographic and complex data. *International Journal of Agricultural and Environmental Information Systems, 1*(2). doi:10.4018/jaeis.2010070103

Blackman, C. (2006). The public interest and the global, future telecommunications landscape. *Info, 9*(2-3), 6–16.

Bokhari, R. H. (2005). The relationship between system usage and user satisfaction: A meta-analysis. *The Journal of Enterprise Information Management, 18*(2), 211–234. doi:10.1108/17410390510579927

Booch, G., Rumbaugh, J., & Jacobson, I. (1999). *The unified modeling language user guide*. Reading, MA: Addison-Wesley.

Bouch, A., Bhatti, N., & Kuchinsky, A. (2000). Quality is in the eye of the beholder: Meeting users' requirements for Internet quality of service. In *Proceedings of the SIGCHI Conference on Human Factors in Computing Systems* (pp. 297-304). New York, NY: ACM Press.

Boudraa, A. A., Ayachi, B., Fabien, S., & Laurent, G. (2004). Dempster--Shafer's basic probability assignment based on fuzzy membership functions. *Electronic Letters on Computer Vision and Image Analysis, 4*(1), 1–6.

Boulil, K., Bimonte, S., Mahboubi, H., & Pinet, F. (2010). Vers la définition des contraintes d'intégrité d'entrepôts de données spatiales avec OCL. *Revue des Nouvelles Technologies de l'Information, B6*, 121–136.

Bourgeois, W., Hogben, P., Pike, A., & Stuetz, R. M. (2003). Development of a sensor array based measurement system for continuous monitoring of water and wastewater. *Sensors and Actuators. B, Chemical, 88*(3), 312–319. doi:10.1016/S0925-4005(02)00377-5

Bowman, J. (2008). *UAE flatly rejects citizenship for foreign workers*. Retrieved June 22, 2011, from http://www.arabianbusiness.com/506295-uae-flatly-rejects-citizenship-for-foreign-workers

Bremer, A. A., & Prado, L. A. L. (2006). Municipal m-Services using SMS. In *Proceedings of the 2nd European Mobile Government Conference*, Brighton, UK.

Brown, I., Letsididi, B., & Nazeer, M. (2009). Internet access in South African home: A preliminary study on factors influencing consumer choice. *The Electronic Journal on Information Systems in Developing Countries*, *38*(2), 1–13.

Brown, S. A., Dennis, A. R., & Venkatesh, V. (2010). Predicting collaboration technology use: Integrating technology adoption and collaboration research. *Journal of Management Information Systems*, *27*(2), 9–53. doi:10.2753/MIS0742-1222270201

Brown, S. A., Montoya-Weiss, M. M., & Burkman, J. R. (2002). Do I really have to? User acceptance of mandated technology. *European Journal of Information Systems*, *11*(4), 283–295. doi:10.1057/palgrave.ejis.3000438

Brown, S. A., & Venkatesh, V. (2005). Model of adoption of technology in households: A baseline model test and extension incorporating household life cycle. *Management Information Systems Quarterly*, *29*(3), 399–426.

Brue, G. (2006). *Six Sigma for small business*. Madison, WI: CWL Publishing Enterprises.

Burkhardt, J., Henn, H., Hepper, S., Rindtorff, K., & Schaeck, T. (2002). *Pervasive computing: Technology and architecture of mobile Internet applications*. Reading, MA: Addison-Wesley.

Burrow, P. (2004). *Arabic handwriting recognition* (Unpublished master's thesis). University of Edinburgh, Edinburgh, UK.

Burr, V. (1995). *An introduction to social constructionism*. London, UK: Routledge. doi:10.4324/9780203299968

Burton-Jones, A., Detmar, W., & Straub, J. (2006). Reconceptualizing system usage: An approach and empirical test. *Information Systems Research*, *17*(3), 228–246. doi:10.1287/isre.1060.0096

Burton-Jones, A., & Hubona, G. S. (2006). The mediation of external variables in the technology acceptance model. *Information & Management*, *43*, 706–717. doi:10.1016/j.im.2006.03.007

Bushofa, B. M. F., & Spann, M. (1995). Segmentation and recognition of printed Arabic characters. In *Proceedings of the 6th British Machine Vision Conference* (Vol. 2, pp. 543-552).

Bushofa, B. M. F., & Spann, M. (1997b, July 2-4). Segmentation of Arabic characters using their contour information. In *Proceedings of the 13th International Conference on Digital Signal Processing*, Santorini, Greece (Vol. 2, pp. 683-686).

Bushofa, B. M. F., & Spann, M. (1997). Segmentation and recognition of Arabic characters by structural classification. *Image and Vision Computing*, *15*(3), 167–179. doi:10.1016/S0262-8856(96)01119-5

Caballero, B. (2002). Ethical issues for collaborative research in developing countries. *The American Journal of Clinical Nutrition*, *76*, 717–720.

Calantone, R. J., Griffith, D. A., & Yalcinkaya, G. (2006). An empirical examination of a technology adoption model for the context of China. *Journal of International Marketing*, *14*(2), 1–27. doi:10.1509/jimk.14.4.1

Calì, A., Lembo, D., Lenzerini, M., & Rosati, R. (2003). Source integration for data warehousing. In *Proceedings of the Conference on Multidimensional Databases: Problems and Solutions* (pp. 361-392).

Caralli, R. A. (2004). *The critical success factor method: establishing a foundation for enterprise security management* (Tech. Rep. No. CMU/SEI-2004-TR-010). Pittsburgh, PA: Carnegie Mellon University.

Carcillo, F., Marcellin, L., & Tringale, A. (2006). BlueTo: a location-based service for m-government solutions. In *Proceedings of the 2nd European Conference on Mobile Government*, Brighton, UK.

Carney, J. G., & Cunningham, P. (1997). The Neural-Bag algorithm: Optimizing generalization performance in bagged neural networks. In *Proceedings of the 7th European Symposium on Neural Networks* (pp. 35-40).

Carpenter, J., Goldstein, H., & Rasbash, J. (1999). A non-parametric bootstrap for multilevel models. *Multilevel Modelling Newsletter, 11*, 2–5.

Carrizales, T. (2009). Critical factors in an electronic democracy: A study of municipal managers. *Electronic Journal of E-Government, 6*(1), 23–30.

Carrizales, T., Holzer, M., Kim, S. T., & Kim, C. G. (2006). Digital governance worldwide: A longitudinal assessment of municipal websites. *International Journal of Electronic Government Research, 2*(4), 1–23. doi:10.4018/jegr.2006100101

Carter, L., & Bélanger, F. (2005). The utilization of e-government services: Citizen trust, innovation and acceptance factors. *Information Systems Journal, 15*(1), 5–15. doi:10.1111/j.1365-2575.2005.00183.x

Castells, M. (2001). *The rise of network society* (2nd ed.). Oxford, UK: Blackwell.

Cavana, R. Y., Delahaye, B. L., & Sekaran, U. (2001). *Applied business research: Quantitative and qualitative methods*. New York, NY: John Wiley & Sons.

Central Intelligence Agency (CIA). (2005). *The CIA world fact book*. Retrieved December 3, 2005, from https://www.cia.gov/library/publications/the-world-factbook/

Cerf, V. G. (2003). Requirements for the Internet. In *Proceedings of the 11th IEEE International Requirements Engineering Conference* (pp. 1-2). Washington, DC: IEEE Computer Society.

Chakraborty, D., Joshi, A., Finin, T., & Yesha, Y. (2005). Service composition for mobile environments. *Mobile Networks and Applications, 10*(4), 435–451. doi:10.1007/s11036-005-1556-y

Chakraborty, I., Hu, P. J.-H., & Cui, D. (2008). Examining the effects of cognitive style in individuals' technology use decision making. *Decision Support Systems, 45*, 228–241. doi:10.1016/j.dss.2007.02.003

Chan, P. W., & Lyu, M. R. (2005). Digital video watermarking with a genetic algorithm. In *Proceedings of the International Conference on Digital Archive Technologies*, Taipei, Taiwan (pp. 139-153).

Chan, Y. K., & Chang, C. C. (2001). Concealing a Secret Image Using the Breadth First Traversal Linear Quad tree Structure. In *Proceedings of the 3rd IEEE International Symposium on Cooperative Database Systems for Advanced Applications*, Beijing, China (pp. 194-199).

Chang, I.-C., Hwang, H.-G., Hung, W.-F., & Li, Y.-C. (2007). Physicians' acceptance of pharmacokinetics-based clinical decision support systems. *Expert Systems with Applications, 33*, 296–303. doi:10.1016/j.eswa.2006.05.001

Cheddad, C. J., Curran, K., & Mc Kevitt, P. (2010). Digital image steganography: Survey and analysis of current methods. *Signal Processing, 90*(3), 727–752. doi:10.1016/j.sigpro.2009.08.010

Chen, L.-D., Gillenson, M. L., & Sherrell, D. L. (2004). Consumer acceptance of virtual stores: A theoretical model and critical success factors for virtual stores. *ACM SIGMIS Database, 35*(2).

Chen, J.-L. (2011). The effects of education compatibility and technological expectancy on e-learning acceptance. *Computers & Education, 57*, 1501–1511. doi:10.1016/j.compedu.2011.02.009

Chen, L.-D., Gillenson, M. L., & Sherrell, D. L. (2002). Enticing online consumers: an extended technology acceptance perspective. *Information & Management, 39*, 705–719. doi:10.1016/S0378-7206(01)00127-6

Cheung, A., Bennamoun, M., & Bergmann, N. W. (1997). A new word segmentation algorithm for Arabic script. In *Proceedings of the 4th Conference on Digital Imaging Computing, Techniques and Applications*, Auckland, New Zealand (pp. 431-435).

Cheung, A., Bennamoun, M., & Bergmann, N. W. (1997). Implementation of a statistical-based Arabic character recognition system. In *Proceedings of the IEEE Region 10 Annual Conference on Speech and Image Technologies for Computing and Telecommunications*, Brisbane, Australia (Vol. 2, pp. 531-534).

Cheung, A., Bennamoun, M., & Bergmann, N. W. (1998, October 11-14). A recognition-based Arabic optical character recognition system. In *Proceedings of the IEEE International Conference on Systems, Man, and Cybernetics*, San Diego, CA (Vol. 5, pp. 4189-4194).

Cheung, A., Bennamoun, M., & Bergmann, N. W. (2001). An Arabic optical character recognition system using recognition-based segmentation. *Pattern Recognition, 34*(2), 215–233. doi:10.1016/S0031-3203(99)00227-7

Chi-Kwong, C., & Cheng, L. M. (2004). Hiding data in images by simple LSB substitution. *Pattern Recognition Letters, 37*(3), 469–474.

Ching-Sheng, H., & Shu-Fen, T. (2010). Finding optimal LSB substitution matrix using ant colony optimization algorithm. In *Proceedings of the Second International Conference on Communication Software and Networks* (pp. 293-297).

Chin, W. W. (1998). Issues and opinions on structural equation modeling. *Management Information Systems Quarterly, 22*(1), 7–16.

Chin, W. W., Marcolin, B. L., & Newsted, P. R. (2003). A partial least squares latent variable modeling approach for measuring interaction effects: Results from a Monte Carlo simulation study and an electronic mail emotion/adoption study. *Information Systems Research, 14*(2), 189–217. doi:10.1287/isre.14.2.189.16018

Chi-Shiang, C. (2009). An information hiding scheme by applying the dynamic programming strategy to LSB matching revisited. In *Proceedings of the 3rd International Conference on Ubiquitous Information Management and Communication*, Suwon, Korea (pp. 246-250).

Choi, Y., Peak, J., Choi, S., Lee, G. W., & Lee, J. H., & Jung, H. (2003). Enhancement of a WLAN-based Internet service in Korea. In *Proceedings of the First ACM International Workshop on Wireless Mobile Applications and Services on WLAN Hotspots* (pp. 36-45). New York, NY: ACM Press.

Choi, T. Y., & Hartley, J. L. (1996). An exploration of supplier selection practices across the supply chain. *Journal of Operations Management, 14*(4), 333–343. doi:10.1016/S0272-6963(96)00091-5

Cho, S., & Sung, M. (2007). Integrative analysis on service quality and user satisfaction of wired and mobile Internet. *International Journal of Management Science, 13*, 79–97.

Chou, C., Condron, L., & Belland, J. C. (2005). A review of the research on Internet addiction. *Educational Psychology Review, 17*(4), 363–388. doi:10.1007/s10648-005-8138-1

Choudrie, J., & Dwivedi, Y. K. (2004, August). Investigating the socio-economic characteristics of residential consumers of broadband in the UK. In *Proceedings of the Tenth American Conference on Information Systems* (pp. 1558-1567).

Choudrie, J., & Dwivedi, Y. K. (2006). A comparative study to examine the socio-economic characteristics of broadband adopters and non-adopters. *International Journal of Services and Standards, 3*(3), 272–288.

Chu-Carroll, J., Prager, J., Czuba, K., Ferrucci, D., & Duboue, P. (2006). Semantic Search via XML Fragments: A high-precision approach to IR. In *Proceedings of the 29th Annual International ACM SIGIR Conference on Research and Development in Information Retrieval*, Seattle, WA (pp. 445-452).

CIA. (2010). *Nigeria- World Factbook*. Retrieved from https://www.cia.gov/library/publications/the-world-factbook/geos/ni.html

CIO. (2007). *The Statistics Collection 2007*. Retrieved February 21, 2009, from http://www.cio.gov.bh/StatPublication/02StatisticalAbstract/File/ABS2007/2007-CH02Population.pdf

Coad, P., & Yourdon, E. (1991). *Object-oriented analysis*. Upper Saddle River, NJ: Prentice Hall.

Cohen, J. A. (1960). Coefficient of agreement for nominal scales. *Educational and Psychological Measurement, 20*(1), 37–46. doi:10.1177/001316446002000104

Cohen, L., Duberley, J., & Mallon, M. (2004). Social constructionism in the study of career: Accessing the parts that other approaches cannot reach. *Journal of Vocational Behavior, 64*, 407–422. doi:10.1016/j.jvb.2003.12.007

Collis, J., & Hussey, R. (2003). *Business research: A practical guide*. New York, NY: Macmillan.

Compeau, D. R., & Higgins, C. A. (1995). Computer self-efficacy: Development of a measure and initial test. *Management Information Systems Quarterly, 19*(2), 189–211. doi:10.2307/249688

Computerworld. (2006). *New Zealand in top half of the information society index*. Retrieved from http://computerworld.co.nz/news.nsf/news/53F6C5B8FD111E42CC25716C001B8BFA?Opendocument&HighLight=2,mobile,broadband,new,zealand

Conway, M. (2006). Terrorist 'use' of the Internet and fighting back. *International Journal of Information Security*, *19*, 9–30.

Cook, S., & Daniels, J. (1994). *Designing object systems-object oriented modeling with syntropy*. Upper Saddle River, NJ: Prentice Hall.

Cooper, R., & Zmud, R. W. (1990). Information technology implementation research: A technological diffusion approach. *Management Science*, *36*(2), 123–139. doi:10.1287/mnsc.36.2.123

Cowell, J., & Hussain, F. (2001, July 25-27). Thinning Arabic characters for feature extraction. In *Proceedings of the IEEE Conference on Information Visualization*, London, UK (pp. 181-185).

Cox, S. (2002). Information technology: The global key to precision agriculture and sustainability. *Computers and Electronics in Agriculture*, *36*(2-3), 93–111. doi:10.1016/S0168-1699(02)00095-9

Crane, A., & Desmond, J. (2002). Societal marketing and morality. *European Journal of Marketing*, *36*(5-6), 548–560. doi:10.1108/03090560210423014

Dacin, M. T., Hitt, M. A., & Levitas, E. (1997). Selecting partners for successful international alliances: Examination of US and Korean firms. *Journal of World Business*, *32*(1), 3–16. doi:10.1016/S1090-9516(97)90022-5

Daniel, R. H. (1961). Management data crisis. *Harvard Business Review*, 111–112.

Dasgupta, S., Granger, M., & McGarry, N. (2002). User acceptance of e-collaboration technology: An extension of the technology acceptance model. *Group Decision and Negotiation*, *2*, 87–100. doi:10.1023/A:1015221710638

Davis, F. (1989). Perceived usefulness, perceived ease of use and user acceptance of information technology. *Management Information Systems Quarterly*, *13*(3), 319. doi:10.2307/249008

Davis, F. (1993). User acceptance of information technology: system characteristics, user perceptions and behavioral impacts. *International Journal of Man-Machine Studies*, *38*, 475–487. doi:10.1006/imms.1993.1022

Davis, F. D. (1989). Perceived usefulness, perceived ease of use, and user acceptance of information technology. *Management Information Systems Quarterly*, *13*(3), 319–339. doi:10.2307/249008

Davis, F. D., Bagozzi, R. P., & Warshaw, P. R. (1992). Extrinsic and intrinsic motivation to use computers in the workplace. *Journal of Applied Social Psychology*, *22*(14), 1111–1132. doi:10.1111/j.1559-1816.1992.tb00945.x

Davis, F. D., & Venkatesh, V. (1996). A critical assessment of potential measurement biases in the technology acceptance model: Three experiments. *International Journal of Human-Computer Studies*, *45*(1), 19–45. doi:10.1006/ijhc.1996.0040

Davis, F., Bargozzi, R., & Warshaw, P. (1989). User Acceptance of computer technology: A comparison of two theoretical model. *Management Science*, *35*(8), 982–1003. doi:10.1287/mnsc.35.8.982

de Lauwere, C. (2005). The role of agricultural entrepreneurship in Dutch agriculture of today. *Agricultural Economics*, *33*(2), 229–238. doi:10.1111/j.1574-0862.2005.00373.x

Deal, T. E., & Kennedy, A. A. (1982). *Corporate cultures*. Reading, MA: Addison-Wesley.

DeLone, W., & McLean, E. (2003). The DeLone and McLean model of information system success: A ten-year update. *Journal of Management Information Systems*, *19*(4), 9–30.

DeLorenzo, G. J., Kohun, F. G., Burčik, V., Belanová, A., & Skovira, R. J. (2009). A data driven conceptual analysis of globalization cultural affects and Hofstedian organizational frames: The Slovak republic example. *Issues in Informing Science and Information Technology*, *6*, 461–470.

Demuth, B. (2005). *The Dresden OCL toolkit and the business rules approach*. Paper presented at the European Business Rules Conference, Amsterdam, The Netherlands.

Demuth, B., Hussmann, H., & Loecher, S. (2001). OCL as a specification language for business rules in database applications. In *Proceedings of the International Conference on Unified Modeling Language, Modeling Languages, Concepts, and Tools* (pp. 104-117).

Demuth, B., Loecher, S., & Zschaler, S. (2004, September 15-17). *Structure of the Dresden OCL toolkit.* Paper presented at the 2nd International Fujaba Days MDA with UML and Rule-based Object Manipulation, Darmstadt, Germany.

Demuth, B., & Hussmann, H. (1999). *Using UML/OCL constraints for relational database design* (pp. 751–751). The Unified Modeling Language.

Devaraj, S., Fan, M., & Kohli, R. (2000). Antecedents of B2C channel satisfaction and preference: Validating e-commerce metrics. *Information Systems Research, 13*(3), 316–333. doi:10.1287/isre.13.3.316.77

Devaraj, S., & Kohli, R. (2003). Performance impacts of information technology: Is actual usage the missing link? *Management Science, 49*(3), 273–289. doi:10.1287/mnsc.49.3.273.12736

Di, Y., Huan, L., Liu, H., Ramineni, A., & Sen, A. (2003). Detecting hidden information in images: A comparative study. In *Proceedings of the IEEE/ICDM Workshop on Privacy Preserving Data Mining*, Melbourne, FL (pp. 24-30).

Diot, C., & Levine, B, N., Lyles, B., Kassem, H., & Balensiefen, D. (2000). Deployment issues for the IP multicast service and architecture. *IEEE Network, 14*(1), 78–88. doi:10.1109/65.819174

Dishaw, M. T., & Strong, D. M. (1999). Extending the technology acceptance model with task-technology fit constructs. *Information & Management, 36*, 9–21. doi:10.1016/S0378-7206(98)00101-3

Diso, L. (2005). Information technology policy formulation in Nigeria: Answers without questions. *The International Information & Library Review, 37*(4), 295–302. doi:10.1016/j.iilr.2005.10.006

Ditsa, G. (2005, May 15-18). *Issues of ICTs and development in less developed countries: A case of Africa and a view towards bridging the digital divide.* Paper presented at the Information Resources Management Association Workshop, San Diego, CA.

Ditsa, G. (2009). Trends and challenges facing developing world in adoption and use of ICTs: A view towards bridging the digital divide. *International Journal of Global Business, 2*(1), 78–100.

Dodourova, M. (2003). Industry dynamics and strategic positioning in the wireless telecommunications industry: The case of Vodafone Group. *Management Decision, 41*(9), 859–870. doi:10.1108/00251740310495919

Doll, W. J., & Torkzadeh, G. (1988). The measurement of end-user computing satisfaction. *Management Information Systems Quarterly, 12*(2), 259–274. doi:10.2307/248851

Donaldson, B. (1994). Supplier selection criteria on the service dimension. *European Journal of Purchasing & Supply Management, 1*(4), 209–217. doi:10.1016/0969-7012(95)00009-7

Dorfman, P. W., & Howell, J. P. (1988). Dimensions of national culture and effective leadership patterns: Hofstede revisited. In McGoun, E. G. (Ed.), *Advances in international comparative management* (Vol. 3, pp. 127–149). Greenwich, CT: JAI.

Dorigo, M., & Thomas, S. (2004). *Ant colony optimization.* Cambridge, MA: MIT Press. doi:10.1007/b99492

Drejer, A., & Skaue, K. (2007). Keys to the future: New business models in mobile organization. *International Journal of Mobile Learning and Organisation, 4*(1), 375–389. doi:10.1504/IJMLO.2007.016177

Dutta, A., Zhang, T., Madhani, S., Taniuchi, K., Fujimoto, K., & Katsube, Y. (2004). Secure universal mobility for wireless Internet. *Mobile Computing and Communications Review, 9*(3), 45–57. doi:10.1145/1094549.1094557

Dwivedi, Y. K., Khan, N., & Papazafeiropoulou, A. (2007). Consumer adoption and usage of broadband in Bangladesh. *International Journal of Electronic Government, 4*(3), 299–313. doi:10.1504/EG.2007.014164

Dyer, D. C., & Gardner, J. W. (1997). High-precision intelligent interface for a hybrid electronic nose. *Sensors and Actuators. A, Physical, 62*(1-3), 724–728. doi:10.1016/S0924-4247(97)01546-X

Easterby-Smith, M., Thorpe, R., & Lowe, A. (2003). *Management research – An introduction.* London, UK: Sage.

Efendioglu, A. M., Yip, V. F., & Murray, W. L. (2004). *E-Commerce in developing countries: issues and influences.* San Francisco, CA: University of San Francisco Press.

EGovernment Authority. (2007). *eGovernment Strategy*. Retrieved February 12, 2009, from http://www.e.gov.bh/pubportal/wps/wcm/connect/85203100 4b96f290b9dfbf13d8048f0c/eGov_Strategy-English. pdf?MOD=AJPERES

EGovernment Authority. (2010). *The eGovernment Portal*. Retrieved December 1, 2010, from http://www.e.gov.bh/

El Gowely, K., El Dessouki, I., & Nazif, A. (1990, June 21). Multi-phase recognition of multi font photoscript Arabic text. In *Proceedings of the 10th International Conference on Pattern Recognition*, Atlantic City, NJ (Vol. 1, pp. 700-702).

El-baba, J. (2006), *Networking research, development and innovation in the Arab countries*. Beirut, Lebanon: United Nation Economic and social commission for Western Asia (ESCWA).

El-Bialy, A. M., Kandil, A. H., Hashish, M. A., & Yamany, S. M. (2000). Arabic OCR: toward a complete system. In *Proceedings of the SPIE Conference on Document Recognition and Retrieval VII*, San Jose, CA (Vol. 3967, pp. 42-51).

El-Dabi, S. S., Ramsis, R., & Kamel, A. (1990). Arabic character recognition system: a statistical approach for recognizing cursive typewritten text. *Pattern Recognition*, *23*(5), 485–495. doi:10.1016/0031-3203(90)90069-W

Elgammal, A. M., & Ismail, M. (2001, September 10-13). A graph-based segmentation and feature extraction framework for Arabic text recognition. In *Proceedings of the 6th International Conference on Document Analysis and Recognition*, Seattle, WA (pp. 622-626).

El-Khaly, F., & Sid-Ahmed, M. A. (1990). Machine recognition of optically captured machine printed Arabic text. *Pattern Recognition*, *23*(11), 1207–1214. doi:10.1016/0031-3203(90)90116-3

ElSaid, G., & Hone, K. (2005). Culture and e-Commerce: An exploration of the perceptions and attitudes of Egyptian internet users. *Journal of Computing and Information Technology*, *13*(2), 107–122. doi:10.2498/cit.2005.02.03

El-Sheikh, T. S. (1990, March 19-22). Recognition of handwritten Arabic mathematical formulas. In *Proceedings of the UK Information Technology Conference*, Southampton, UK (pp. 344-351).

El-Sheikh, T. S., & Guindi, R. M. (1988). Computer recognition of Arabic cursive scripts. *Pattern Recognition*, *21*(4), 293–302. doi:10.1016/0031-3203(88)90042-8

Erdi, P., & Barna, G. (1991). Neurodynamic approach to odor processing. In *Proceedings of the Joint International Conference on Neural Networks*, Seattle, WA (pp. 653-656).

Erumban, A. A., & de Jong, S. B. (2006). Cross-country differences in ICT adoption: A consequence of culture? *Journal of World Business*, *41*(4), 302–314. doi:10.1016/j.jwb.2006.08.005

ESCWA. (2005). *Networking research development and innovation in Arab countries (Paper No. E/ESCWA/SDPD/2005/2)*. New York, NY: United Nations.

European Commission. (2007). *Improving knowledge transfer between research institutions and industry across Europe*. Brussels, Belgium: Author.

Eurostat. (2004). *E-commerce and the Internet in European businesses*. Retrieved from http://epp.eurostat.ec.europa.eu/cache/ITY_OFFPUB/KS-54-03-889/FR/KS-54-03-889-FR.PDF

Euzenat, J., & Shvaiko, P. (2007). *Ontology matching*. Berlin, Germany: Springer-Verlag.

Eze, C. C., Ibekwe, U. C., Onoh, P. J., & Nwajiuba, C. U. (2006). Determinants of adoption of improved Cassava production technologies among farmers in Enugu State of Nigeria. *Global Approaches to Extension Practice*, *2*(1), 37–44.

Fahmy, M. M. M., & El-Messiry, H. (2001). Automatic recognition of typewritten Arabic characters using Zernike moments as a feature extractor. *Studies in Informatics and Control Journal*, *10*(3), 48-51.

Fahmy, M. M. M., & Al Ali, S. (2001). Automatic recognition of handwritten Arabic characters using their geometrical features. *Journal of Studies in Informatics and Control*, *10*(2).

Fakir, M., Hassani, M., & Sodeyama, C. (1999, October 12-15). Recognition of Arabic characters using Karhunen-Loeve transform and dynamic programming. In *Proceedings of the IEEE International Conference on Systems, Man, and Cybernetics* (Vol. 6, pp. 868-873).

Fakir, M., Hassani, M., & Sodeyama, C. (2000). On the recognition of Arabic characters using Hough transform technique. *Malaysian Journal of Computer Science, 13*(2), 39–47.

Fard, A. M., Akbarzadeh, T. M. R., & Varasteh, A. (2006). A new genetic algorithm approach for secure JPEG steganography. In *Proceedings of the IEEE International Conference on Engineering of Intelligent Systems*, Islamabad, Pakistan (pp. 216-219).

Fayek, M., & Al Basha, B. (1992). A new hierarchical method for isolated typewritten Arabic character classification and recognition. In *Proceedings of the 13th National Computer Conference*, Riyadh, Saudi Arabia (Vol. 2, pp. 750-759).

Fehri, M., & Ben Ahmed, M. (1994). A new approach to Arabic character recognition in multi-font document. In *Proceedings of the 4th International Conference and Exhibition on Multi-Lingual Computing*, London, UK (pp. 2.5.1-2.5.7).

Feldman, M. S., & March, J. G. (1981). Information in organization as signal and symbol. *Administrative Science Quarterly, 26*(2), 171–186. doi:10.2307/2392467

Feng, H., & Zhou, Y. (2010). The discussion on building public information service system. *Information Studies: Theory & Application, 7*, 26–31.

Fishbein, M., & Ajzen, I. (1975). *Belief, attitude, intention, and behavior: An introduction to theory and research.* Reading, MA: Addison-Wesley.

Flanagin, A. J., & Metzger, M. J. (2001). Internet use in the contemporary media environment. *Human Communication Research, 27*(1), 153–181. doi:10.1093/hcr/27.1.153

Fleiss, J. L. (1971). Measuring nominal scale agreement among many raters. *Psychological Bulletin, 76*, 378–382. doi:10.1037/h0031619

Fodil, L. (2005). New generation network and services management for converged networks. In *Proceedings of the 1st International Workshop on Broadband Convergence Networks* (pp.1-3). Washington, DC: IEEE Computer Society.

Fornell, C., & Larcker, D. (1981). Structural equation models with unobserved variables and measurement error. *JMR, Journal of Marketing Research, 18*(1), 39–50. doi:10.2307/3151312

Forster, P. W., & Tang, Y. (2006). Mobile auctions: Will they come? Will they pay? In M. Khosrow-Pour (Ed.), *Proceedings of the IRMA International Conference* (pp. 779-783). Hershey, PA: IGI Global.

Fowler, F. J. (2002). *Survey research methods* (3rd ed.). London, UK: Sage.

Frederick, H. (2008). Introduction to special issue on indigenous entrepreneurs. *Journal of Enterprising Communities: People and Places in the Global Economy, 2*(3), 185–191. doi:10.1108/17506200810897187

Freeman, H. (1961). On the encoding of arbitrary geometric configuration. *IRE Transactions on Electronic Computers, 10*, 260–268. doi:10.1109/TEC.1961.5219197

Fuchs, C. (2009). The role of income inequality in a multivariate cross-national analysis of the digital divide. *Social Science Computer Review, 27*(1), 41–58. doi:10.1177/0894439308321628

Furrer, O., Liu, B. S.-C., & Sudharshan, D. (2000). The relationships between culture and service quality perceptions: Basis for cross-cultural market segmentation and resource allocation. *Journal of Service Research, 2*(4), 355–371. doi:10.1177/109467050024004

Gable, G., Sedera, D., & Chan, T. (2008). Re-conceptualizing information system success: The IS-impact measurement model. *Journal of the Association for Information Systems, 9*(7), 377–408.

Gallego, M. D., Luna, P., & Bueno, S. (2008). User acceptance model of open source software. *Computers in Human Behavior, 24*(5), 2199–2216. doi:10.1016/j.chb.2007.10.006

Gang, S. (2007). Transcending e-Government: a Case of Mobile government in Beijing. In *Proceedings of the 1st European Conference on Mobile Government*, Brighton, UK.

Garcia, J. A., Rousseau, F., Berger, G., Toumi, L., & Duda, A. (2003). Quality of service and mobility for the wireless internet. *Wireless Networks, 9*(4), 341–352. doi:10.1023/A:1023647311052

Gardner, J. W., & Bartlett, P. N. (1994). A brief history of electronic noses. *Sensors and Actuators. B, Chemical, 18*(1-3), 210–211. doi:10.1016/0925-4005(94)87085-3

Garrido, N., & Marina, A. (2008). Exploring trust on Internet: The Spanish case. *Observatorio Journal*, *2*(3), 223–244.

Ge, S., Gao, Y., & Wang, R. (2007). Least significant bit steganography detection with machine learning techniques. In *Proceedings of the International Workshop on Domain Driven Data Mining*, San Jose, CA (pp. 24-32).

Gefen, D., & Keil, M. (1998). The impact of developer responsiveness on perceptions of usefulness and ease of use, an extension of the technology acceptance model. *The Data Base for Advances in Information Systems*, *29*(2), 35–49. doi:10.1145/298752.298757

Gefen, D., & Straub, D. W. (1997). Gender differences in the perception and use of e-mail: An extension to the technology acceptance model. *Management Information Systems Quarterly*, *21*(4), 389–400. doi:10.2307/249720

Germanakos, P., Samaras, G., & Christodoulou, E. (2005). Multi-channel Delivery of Services: The Road from eGovernment to mGovernment: Further Technological Challenges and Implications. In *Proceedings of the 1st European Conference on Mobile Government*, Brighton, UK.

Ghosh, A., Wolter, D. R., Andrews, J. G., & Chen, R. (2005). Broadband wireless access with WiMAx/802.16: Current performance benchmarks and future potential. *IEEE Communications Magazine*, *2*(1), 129–136. doi:10.1109/MCOM.2005.1391513

Ghyasi, A., & Kushchu, I. (2004, June). m-Government Adoption: Cases of Developing Countries. In *Proceedings of the European Conference on e-Government*, Dublin, Ireland.

Gillies, A., Erlandson, E., Trenkle, J., & Schlosser, S. (1999). Arabic text recognition system. In *Proceedings of the Symposium on Document Image Understanding Technology*, Annapolis, MD.

Goldberg, D. E. (1989). *Genetic algorithms in search, optimization, and machine learning*. Reading, MA: Addison-Wesley.

Golomb, S. W. (1976). *Shift register sequences*. Walnut Creek, CA: Aegean Park Press.

Gome, A. (1996). Total quality madness. *Business Review Weekly*, *18*, 38–44.

Gong, W., Li, Z. G., & Stump, R. L. (2007). Global Internet use and access: Cultural considerations. *Asia Pacific Journal of Marketing and Logistics*, *19*(1), 57–74. doi:10.1108/13555850710720902

Goodhue, D., & Thompson, R. (1995). Task-technology fit and individual performance. *Management Information Systems Quarterly*, *19*(2), 213–236. doi:10.2307/249689

Goraine, H., & Usher, M. J. (1989, October 2). Recognition of typewritten Arabic characters in different fonts. In *Proceedings of the IEEE Colloquium on Character Recognition and Applications*, London, UK (pp. 1-5).

Goraine, H., Usher, M. J., & Al-Emami, S. (1992). Offline Arabic character recognition. *IEEE Computer*, *25*(7), 71–74. doi:10.1109/2.144444

Gouda, A. M., & Rashwan, M. A. (2004, July 14-16). Segmentation of connected Arabic characters using hidden Markov models. In *Proceedings of the IEEE International Conference on Computational Intelligence for Measurement Systems and Applications*, Boston, MA (pp. 115-119).

Gray, D. H., & Head, A. (2009). The importance of the Internet to the post-modern terrorist and its role as a form of safe haven. *European Journal of Scientific Research*, *25*(3), 396–404.

Grosan, C., Abraham, A., & Tigan, S. (2006). Engineering drug design using a multi-input multi-output neuro-fuzzy system. In *Proceedings of the 8th International symposium on symbolic and numeric algorithms for scientific computing*, Timisoara, Romania (pp. 365-371).

Grosan, C., Abraham, A., Tigan, S., Chang, T. G., & Kim, D. H. (2006). Evolving neural networks for pharmaceutical research. In *Proceedings of the International Conference on Hybrid Information Technology*, Korea (pp. 13-19).

Groucutt, J., & Griseri, P. (2004). *Mastering e-business*. New York, NY: Palgrave Macmillan. Henderson, R. (1966). Generalized cultures and evolutionary adaptability: A comparison of Urban Efik and Ibo in Nigeria. *Ethnology*, *5*(4), 365–391.

Guardini, I., D'Urso, P., & Fasano, P. (2005). The role of Internet technology in future mobile data systems. *IEEE Communications Magazine*, *38*(11), 68–72. doi:10.1109/35.883491

Gumussoy, C. A., & Calisir, F. (2009). Understanding factors affecting e-reverse auction use: An integrative approach. *Computers in Human Behavior, 25*(4), 975–988. doi:10.1016/j.chb.2009.04.006

Guo, Z., Zhang, Y., & Stevens, K. (2009, June). A 'uses and gratifications approach' to understanding the role of wiki technology in enhancing teaching and learning outcomes. In *Proceedings of the 17th European Conference on Information Systems*, Verona, Italy (pp. 2-13).

Guo, J. (2009). The status of the China government website accessibility. *Information Science, 27*(12), 1802–1805.

Gupta, B., Dasgupta, S., & Gupta, A. (2008). Adoption of ICT in a government organization in a developing country: An empirical study. *The Journal of Strategic Information Systems, 17*(2), 140–154. doi:10.1016/j.jsis.2007.12.004

Hadjar, K., & Ingold, R. (2003, August 3-6). Arabic newspaper page segmentation. In *Proceedings of the 7th International Conference on Document Analysis and Recognition*, Edinburgh, UK (Vol. 2, pp. 895-899).

Hahn, K., Sapia, C., & Blaschka, M. (2000). Automatically generating OLAP schemata from conceptual graphical models. In *Proceedings of the 3rd ACM International Workshop on Data Warehousing and OLAP*, McLean, VA.

Haidar, A. H. (1996). *Western science and technology and the needs of the Arab world.* Paper presented at the Joint Symposium on Traditional Culture, Science & Technology, and Development, Mito, Japan.

Haj-Hassan, F. (1990). Arabic character recognition. In Mackay, P. A. (Ed.), *Computer and the Arabic language* (pp. 113–118). New York, NY: Hemisphere.

Hamid, A. (2001, September 26). A neural network approach for the segmentation of handwritten Arabic text. In *Proceedings of the International Symposium on Innovation in Information and Communication Technology*, Amman, Jordan.

Hamid, A., & Haraty, R. (2001, June 25-29). A neuro-heuristic Approach for segmenting handwritten Arabic text. In *Proceedings of the ACS/IEEE International Conference on Computer Systems and Applications*, Beirut, Lebanon (pp. 110-113).

Hammami, L., & Berkani, D. (2002). Recognition system for printed multi-font and multi-size Arabic characters. *The Arabian Journal for Science and Engineering, 27*(1B), 57–72.

Hamner, M., & Qazi, R. (2009). Expanding the technology acceptance model to examine personal computing technology utilization in government agencies in developing countries. *Government Information Quarterly, 26*(1), 128–136. doi:10.1016/j.giq.2007.12.003

Harba, M. I. A., & Li, N. Y. (1996, November 28-30). Parallel digital learning networks for segmentation and recognition of machine printed Arabic text. In *Proceedings of the International Conference on Robotics, Vision and Parallel Processing for Industrial Automation*, Ipoh, Malaysia (pp. 228-232).

Harrison, E. F. (1987). *The managerial decision-making process.* Boston, MA: Houghton-Mifflin.

Harter, D. E., & Slaughter, S. A. (2003). Quality improvement and infrastructure activity costs in software development: A longitudinal analysis. *Management Science, 49*, 784–800. doi:10.1287/mnsc.49.6.784.16023

Hartwick, J., & Barki, H. (1994). Explaining the role of user participation in information system use. *Management Science, 40*(4), 440–465. doi:10.1287/mnsc.40.4.440

Hasan, H., & Ditsa, G. (1997). *The cultural challenges of adopting IT in developing countries: An exploratory study.* Paper presented at the Information Resources Management Association Workshop, Vancouver, BC, Canada.

Hasan, H., & Ditsa, G. E. M. (1999). Impact of culture on the adoption of IT: An interpretive study. *Journal of Global Information Management, 7*(1), 5–15.

Hashemi, M. R., Fatemi, O., & Safavi, R. (1995). Persian cursive script recognition. In *Proceedings of the 3rd International Conference on Document Analysis and Recognition*, Montreal, QC, Canada (Vol. 2, pp. 869-873).

Hassibi, K. M. (1994). Machine-printed Arabic OCR using neural networks. In *Proceedings of the 4th International Conference and Exhibition on Multi-Lingual Computing (Arabic and Roman Script)*, London, UK (pp. 2.3.1-2.3.12).

Hatfield, J. V., Neaves, P., Hicks, P. J., Persaud, K., & Travers, P. (1994). Towards an integrated electronic nose using conducting polymer sensors. *Sensors and Actuators. B, Chemical, 18*(1-3), 221–228. doi:10.1016/0925-4005(94)87086-1

Hennington, A., Janz, B., Amis, J., & Nichols, E. (2009). Information systems and healthcare XXXII: Understanding the multidimensionality of information systems use: A study of nurses' use of a mandated electronic medical record system. *Communications of the Association for Information Systems, 25*(25), 243–262.

Herden, O. (2000). A design methodology for data warehouses. In *Proceedings of the CAISE Doctoral Consortium,* Stockholm, Sweden.

Hernández, B., Jiménez, J., & Martín, M. J. (2008). Extending the technology acceptance model to include the IT decision-maker: A study of business management software. *Technovation, 28*(3), 112–121. doi:10.1016/j.technovation.2007.11.002

Hernandez, B., Jiménez, J., & Martin, M. J. (2009). Future use intentions versus intensity of use: An analysis of corporate technology acceptance. *Industrial Marketing Management, 38*(3), 338–354. doi:10.1016/j.indmarman.2007.12.002

Hesterberg, T., Moore, D. S., Monaghan, S., Clipson, A., & Epstein, R. (2003). *Bootstrap methods and permutation tests.* New York, NY: W. H. Freeman and Company.

Higgins, V., Dibden, J., & Cocklin, C. (2008). Building alternative agri-food networks: Certification, embeddedness and agri-environmental governance. *Journal of Rural Studies, 24*(1), 15–27. doi:10.1016/j.jrurstud.2007.06.002

Hill, C., Loch, K., Straub, D., & El-Sheshai, K. (1998). A qualitative assessment of Arab culture and information technology transfer. *Journal of Global Information Management, 6*(3), 29–38.

Hofstede, G. (1980). *Culture's consequences: International differences in related values.* Thousand Oaks, CA: Sage.

Hofstede, G. (1983). National culture in four dimensions. *International Studies of Management and Organization, 13*(1-2), 46–74.

Hofstede, G. (1983). Dimensions of national cultures in fifty countries and three regions. In Deregowski, J. B., Dziurawiec, S., & Annis, R. C. (Eds.), *Expiscations in cross-cultural psychology* (pp. 335–355). Lisse, The Netherlands: Swets and Zeitlinger.

Hofstede, G. (1983). National cultures in four dimensions. *International Studies of Management and Organization, 13,* 46–74.

Hofstede, G. (1985). The interaction between national and organizational value systems. *Journal of Management Studies, 22*(4), 347–355. doi:doi:10.1111/j.1467-6486.1985.tb00001.x

Hofstede, G. (1991). *Cultures and organizations: Software of the mind.* New York, NY: McGraw-Hill.

Hofstede, G. (1993). Cultural constraints in management theories. *The Academy of Management Executive, 7*(1), 81–94.

Hofstede, G. (2001). *Culture's consequences.* Thousand Oaks, CA: Sage.

Hofstede, G., & Bond, M. (1984). The need for synergy among cross-culture studies. *Journal of Cross-Cultural Psychology, 15*(2), 417–433. doi:10.1177/0022002184015004003

Hofstede, G., & Bond, M. (1988). The Confucius connection: From cultural roots to economic growth. *Organizational Dynamics, 16*(4), 4–21. doi:10.1016/0090-2616(88)90009-5

Hofstede, G., Neuijen, B., Ohayv, D. D., & Sanders, G. (1990). Measuring organizational cultures: A qualitative and quantitative study across twenty cases. *Administrative Science Quarterly, 35,* 286–316. doi:doi:10.2307/2393392

Holland, J. H. (1975). *Adaptive in natural and artificial systems: An Introductory Analysis with Applications to Biology, Control, and Artificial Intelligence.* Cambridge, MA: MIT Press.

Holsapple, C. W. (2003). *Handbook on knowledge management.* Heidelberg, Germany: Springer-Verlag.

Holzer, M., & Kim, S. T. (2004). *Digital governance in municipalities worldwide.* Newark, NJ: The E-Governance Institute, Rutgers University-Newark and the Global e-Policy e-Government Institute, Sungkyunkwan University.

Holzer, M., & Kim, S. T. (2005). *Digital governance in municipalities worldwide.* Newark, NJ: The E-Governance Institute, Rutgers University-Newark and the Global e-Policy e-Government Institute, Sungkyunkwan University.

Holzer, M., & Kim, S. T. (2007). *Digital governance in municipalities worldwide.* Newark, NJ: The E-Governance Institute, Rutgers University-Newark and the Global e-Policy e-Government Institute, Sungkyunkwan University.

Horton, R. P., Buck, T., Waterson, P. E., & Clegg, C. W. (2001). Explaining intranet use with the technology acceptance model. *Journal of Management Information Systems, 16*(2), 91–112.

Ho, S. Y., & Kwok, S. H. (2003). The attraction of personalized service for users in mobile commerce: An empirical study. *ACM SIGecom Exchange, 3*(4), 10–18. doi:10.1145/844351.844354

Hossain, L., & de Silva, A. (2009). Exploring user acceptance of technology using social networks. *The Journal of High Technology Management Research, 20*(1), 1–18. doi:10.1016/j.hitech.2009.02.005

Hossain, L., & Silva, A. D. (2009). Exploring user acceptance of technology using social networks. *The Journal of High Technology Management Research, 20*, 1–18. doi:10.1016/j.hitech.2009.02.005

House, R. J., Hanges, P. J., & Javidan, M. (Eds.). (2004). *Culture, leadership, and organizations: The GLOBE study of 62 societies* (pp. 239–281). Thousand Oaks, CA: Sage.

Huang, H., & Leung, L. (2009). Instant messaging addiction among teenagers in China: Shyness, alienation, and academic performance decrement. *Cyberpsychology & Behavior, 12*(6), 675–679. doi:10.1089/cpb.2009.0060

Humphrey, J., Mansell, R., Paré, D., & Schmitz, H. (2003). *The reality of e-commerce with developing countries.* London, UK: Media Studies. doi:10.1111/j.1759-5436.2004.tb00106.x

Hung, S. Y., Ku, C. Y., & Chang, C., M. (2003). Critical factors of WAP services adoption: An empirical study. *Electronic Commerce Research and Applications, 2*(1), 42–60. doi:10.1016/S1567-4223(03)00008-5

Hu, P. J.-H., Chen, H., Larson, C., & Butierez, C. (2011). Law enforcement officers' acceptance of advanced e-government technology: A survey study of COPLINK mobile. *Electronic Commerce Research and Applications, 10*, 6–16. doi:10.1016/j.elerap.2010.06.002

Husband, S. G., & Mandal, P. (1999). A conceptual model for quality integrated management in small and medium size enterprises. *International Journal of Quality & Reliability Management, 16*(7), 699–713. doi:10.1108/02656719910286215

Ifinedo, P. (2006). Acceptance and continuance intention of web-based learning technologies (WLT) use among university students in a Baltic country. *Electronic Journal of Information Systems in Developing Countries, 23*(6), 1–20.

Igbaria, M., Guimares, T., & Davis, G. B. (1995). Testing the determinants of microcomputer usage via a structural equation model. *Journal of Management Information Systems, 11*(4), 87–114.

Igbaria, M., & Livari, J. (1995). The effects of self-efficacy on computer usage. *Omega, 23*(6), 587–605. doi:10.1016/0305-0483(95)00035-6

Igbaria, M., Zinatelli, N., Cragg, P., & Cavaye, A. L. M. (1997). Personal computing acceptance factors in small firms: A structural equation model. *Management Information Systems Quarterly, 21*(3), 279–305. doi:10.2307/249498

Im, I., Hong, S., & Kang, M. S. (2011). An international comparison of technology adoption testing the UTAUT model. *Information & Management, 48*, 1–8. doi:10.1016/j.im.2010.09.001

Interact, U. A. E. (2009). *Top news stories.* Retrieved July 9, 2011, from http://uaeinteract.com/docs/Expat_numbers_rise_rapidly_as_UAE_population_touches_6m/37883.htm

Ip, W. H., Huang, M., Yung, K. L., & Wang, D. (2003). Genetic algorithm solution for a risk-based partner selection problem in a virtual enterprise. *Computers & Operations Research, 30*(2), 213–231. doi:10.1016/S0305-0548(01)00092-2

Isaacs, C. R., & Fisher, W. A. (2008). A computer-based educational intervention to address potential negative effects of internet pornography. *Communication Studies*, *59*(1), 1–18. doi:10.1080/10510970701849354

Jabbar, M., Ehui, S., & Von Kaufmann, R. (2002). Supply and demand for livestock credit in Sub-Saharan Africa: Lessons for designing new credit schemes. *World Development*, *30*(6), 1029–1042. doi:10.1016/S0305-750X(02)00021-9

Jack, S. (2010). Approaches to studying networks: Implications and outcomes. *Journal of Business Venturing*, *25*(1), 120–137. doi:10.1016/j.jbusvent.2008.10.010

Jambi, K. (1991). *Design and implementation of a system for recognizing Arabic handwritten words with learning ability* (Unpublished master's thesis). Illinois Institute of Technology, Chicago, IL.

Jambi, K. (1992, Nov). A system for recognizing Arabic handwritten words. In *Proceedings of The 13th National Computer Conference* (Vol. 1, pp. 416-426

Jang, J.-S. R., Sun, C.-T., & Mizutani, E. (1997). *Neuro-fuzzy and soft computing: A computational approach to learning and machine intelligence*. Upper Saddle River, NJ: Prentice Hall.

Jarvenpaa, S. (1989). The effect of task demands and graphical format on information processing strategies. *Management Science*, *35*(3), 285–303. doi:10.1287/mnsc.35.3.285

Jensen, C. S., Kligys, A., Pedersen, T. B., & Timko, I. (2002). Multidimensional data modeling for location-Based Services. In *Proceedings of the 10th ACM International Symposium on Advances in Geographic Information Systems* (pp. 55-61). New York, NY: ACM Press.

Jensen, O. W., & Scheraga, C. A. (1998). Transferring technology: Costs and benefits. *Technology in Society*, *20*(1), 99–112. doi:10.1016/S0160-791X(97)00031-6

Jessup, L., & Valacich, J. (2008). *Information systems today: Managing in the digital world*. Upper Saddle River, NJ: Prentice Hall.

Jin, J., Wang, H., Ding, X., & Peng, L. (2005). Printed Arabic document recognition system. In *Proceedings of the SPIE-IS&T Electronic Imaging Conference on Document Recognition and Retrieval XII* (Vol. 5676, pp. 48-55).

Jonason, A., & Eliasson, G. (2001). Mobile Internet revenues: an empirical study of the I-mode portal. *Internet Research: Electronic Networking Applications and Policy*, *11*(4), 341–348. doi:10.1108/10662240110402795

Jones, G. (1962). Ibo age organization, with special reference to the Cross River and North-Eastern Ibo. *Journal of the Royal Anthropological Institute of Great Britain and Ireland*, *92*(2), 191–211. doi:10.2307/2844258

Joseph, V. C., Lucky, K. K., & Mohan, R. (2006). SIP as an enabler for convergence in future wireless communication networks. In *Proceedings of the IFIP International Conference on Wireless and Optical Communications Networks* (pp. 5-10). Washington, DC: IEEE Computer Society.

Juell-Skielse, G. (2008). Pictures and Positioning in Mobile Complaint and Problem Management. In *Proceedings of the mLife 2008 Conference & Exhibitions*, Antalya, Turkey.

Julien, F. S., & Rivest, S. (2009, October 21-22). *Les analyses relatives au transport maritime: un exemple de géodécisionnel*. Paper presented at the Colloque Géomatique, Montréal, QC, Canada.

Kadushin, C. (2002). The motivational foundation of social networks. *Social Networks*, *24*(1), 77–91. doi:10.1016/S0378-8733(01)00052-1

Kallio, J., Tinnila, M., & Tseng, A. (2006). An international comparison of operator-driven business models. *Business Process Management*, *12*(3), 281–298. doi:10.1108/14637150610667962

Kandil, A. H., & El-Bialy, A. (2004, September 5-7). Arabic OCR: a centerline independent segmentation technique. In *Proceedings of the International Conference on Electrical, Electronic and Computer Engineering* (pp. 412-415).

Kanfer, R. (1990). Motivation theory and industrial and organizational psychology. In Dunnette, M. D., & Hough, L. M. (Eds.), *Handbook of industrial and organizational psychology* (pp. 75–170). Chicago, IL: Rand McNally.

Karahanna, E., Agarwal, R., & Angst, C. M. (2006). Reconceotualising compatibility beliefs in technology acceptance research. *Management Information Systems Quarterly*, *30*(4), 781–804.

Karahanna, E., Evaristo, J. R., & Srite, M. (2005). Levels of culture and individual behavior: An integrative perspective. *Journal of Global Information Management, 13*(2), 1–20. doi:10.4018/jgim.2005040101

Karahanna, E., & Limayem, M. (2000). E-Mail and v-mail usage: Generalizing across technologies. *Journal of Organizational Computing and Electronic Commerce, 10*(1), 49–66. doi:10.1207/S15327744JOCE100103

Kaspar, C., Seidenfaden, L., Ortelbach, B., & Hagenhoff, S. (2006). Acceptance of the mobile Internet as a distribution channel for paid content. In M. Khosrow-Pour (Ed.), *Proceedings of the IRMA International Conference* (pp. 68-72). Hershey, PA: IGI Global.

Keller, P. E., Kouzes, R. T., & Kangas, L. J. (1994). Three neural network based sensor systems for environmental monitoring. In *Proceedings of the IEEE Electro Conference,* Boston, MA (pp. 377-382).

Kerlinger, F. N. (1986). Survey research. In Kerlinger, F. N. (Ed.), *Foundations of behavioural research in education.* New York, NY: Holt, Rinehart, and Winston.

Kesh, S., Ramanujan, S., & Nerur, S. (2002). A framework for analyzing e-commerce security. *Information Management & Computer Security, 10*(4), 149–458. doi:10.1108/09685220210436930

Kevin, K. W., Byungjoon, Y., Seunghee, Y., & Kar, Y. T. (2007). The effect of culture and product categories on the level of use of Buy-It-Now (BIN) auctions by sellers. *Journal of Global Information Management, 15*(4), 1–19. doi:doi:10.4018/jgim.2007100101

Khedher, M. Z., & Abandah, G. (2002, June 1). Arabic character recognition using approximate stroke sequence. In *Proceedings of the 3rd International Conference on Language Resources and Evaluation Workshop on Arabic Language Resources and Evaluation: Status and Prospects,* Las Palmas de Gran Canaria, Spain.

Khorsheed, M. S., & Clocksin, W. F. (1999). Structural features of cursive Arabic script. In *Proceedings of the 10th British Machine Vision Conference,* Nottingham, UK (Vol. 2, pp. 422-431).

Khorsheed, M. S., & Clocksin, W. F. (2000, September 3-7). Multi-font Arabic word recognition using spectral features. In *Proceedings of the 15th International Conference on Pattern Recognition,* Barcelona, Spain (Vol. 4, pp. 543-546).

Khorsheed, M. S. (2002). Off-Line Arabic character recognition - a review. *Pattern Analysis & Applications, 5*(1), 31–45. doi:10.1007/s100440200004

Kijsanayotin, B., Pannarunothai, S., & Speedie, S. M. (2009). Factors influencing health information technology adoption in Thailand's community health centers: Applying the UTAUT model. *International Journal of Medical Informatics, 78,* 404–416. doi:10.1016/j.ijmedinf.2008.12.005

Kim, H., Kim, J., Lee, Y., Chae, M., & Choi, Y. (2002). An empirical study of the use contexts and usability problems in mobile Internet. In *Proceedings of the 35th Annual Hawaii International Conference on System Sciences* (pp. 132-142). Washington, DC: IEEE Computer Society.

Kim, K., & Prabhakar, B. (2000). Initial trust, perceived risk, and the adoption of internet banking. In *Proceedings of the Twenty First International Conference on Information Systems,* Brisbane, Australia (pp. 537-543).

Kim, B. G., Park, S. C., & Lee, K. J. (2007). A structural equation modeling of the Internet acceptance in Korea. *Electronic Commerce Research and Applications, 6,* 425–432. doi:10.1016/j.elerap.2006.08.005

Kim, D., Derrin, D., & Rao, H. (2008). A trust-based consumer decision-making model in electronic commerce: The role of trust, perceived risk, and their antecedents. *Decision Support Systems, 44*(2), 544–564. doi:10.1016/j.dss.2007.07.001

Kim, H.-J., Mannino, M., & Nieschwietz, R. J. (2009). Information technology acceptance in the internal audit profession: Impact of technology features and complexity. *International Journal of Accounting Information Systems, 10,* 214–228. doi:10.1016/j.accinf.2009.09.001

Kim, J., Lee, I., Lee, Y., & Choi, B. (2004). Exploring e-business implications of the mobile Internet: A cross-national survey in Hong Kong, Japan and Korea. *International Journal of Mobile Communications, 2*(1), 1–21. doi:10.1504/IJMC.2004.004484

Kim, S. H. (2008). Moderating effects of job relevance and experience on mobile wireless technology acceptance: Adoption of a smartphone by individuals. *Information & Management, 45*(6), 387–393. doi:10.1016/j.im.2008.05.002

Kim, T. G., Lee, J. H., & Law, R. (2008). An empirical examination of the acceptance behaviour of hotel front office systems: An extended technology acceptance model. *Tourism Management*, *29*, 500–513. doi:10.1016/j.tourman.2007.05.016

Kim, Y., Lee, J.-D., & Koh, D. (2005). Effects of consumer preferences on the convergence of mobile telecommunications devices. *Applied Economics*, *37*, 817–826. doi:10.1080/0003684042000337398

Kim, Y.-M. (2010). The adoption of university library web site resources: A multigroup analysis. *Journal of the American Society for Information Science and Technology*, 979–993.

King, W. R., & He, J. (2006). A meta-analysis of the technology acceptance model. *Information & Management*, *43*, 740–755. doi:10.1016/j.im.2006.05.003

Kirsten, J., & Sartorius, K. (2002). Linking agribusiness and small-scale farmers in developing countries: Is there a new role for contract farming? *Development Southern Africa*, *19*(4), 503–529. doi:10.1080/0376835022000019428

Klasse Objecten. (2009). *OCL tools and services web site.* Retrieved from http://www.klasse.nl/ocl

Kleijnen, M. H. P., Wetzels, M., & Ruyter, K. (2004). Consumer acceptance of wireless finance. *Journal of Financial Services Marketing*, *8*(3), 206–217. doi:10.1057/palgrave.fsm.4770120

Kleppe, A., Warmer, J., & Bast, W. (2003). *MDA explained.* Reading, MA: Addison-Wesley.

Knoche, H., & McCarthy, J. D. (2005). Design requirements for mobile TV. In *Proceedings of the 7th International Conference on Human Computer Interaction with Mobile Devices & Services*, Salzburg, Austria (pp. 69-76). New York, NY: ACM Press.

Knudson, W., Wysocki, A., Champagne, J., & Peterson, H. P. (2004). Entrepreneurship and innovation in the agri-food system. *American Journal of Agricultural Economics*, *86*(5), 1330–1336. doi:10.1111/j.0002-9092.2004.00685.x

Kole, E. (2000). *African women speak on the Internet: Research report of an electronic survey of African women.* Retrieved from http://www.eldis.org/assets/Docs/13200.html

Konradt, U., Christophersen, T., & Schaeffer-Kuelz, U. (2006). Predicting user satisfaction, strain and system usage of employee self-services. *International Journal of Human-Computer Studies*, *64*, 1141–1153. doi:10.1016/j.ijhcs.2006.07.001

Korgaonkar, P., & Wolin, L. (1999). A multivariate analysis of web usage. *Journal of Advertising Research*, *39*(2), 53–68.

Kosko, B. (1990). Fuzziness vs. probability. *International Journal of General Systems*, *17*(2), 211–240. doi:10.1080/03081079008935108

Kraemer, K. L., Dedrick, J., & Dunkle, D. (2002). *E-Commerce in the United States: Leader or one of the pack? Global B commerce survey, report of results for the United States Centre for Research on Information Technology and Organisations.* Irvine, CA: University of California.

KRG. (2011). *IT infrastructure Erbil.* Kurdistan, Iraq: KRG Department of Information Technology.

Kumar, M., & Antony, J. (2008, June 25-27). *Comparing the quality management practices between six sigma and ISO certified SMEs – a survey based approach.* Paper presented at the 13th International Conference on Productivity and Quality Research, Oulu, Finland.

Kumar, M. (2007). Critical success factors and hurdles to Six Sigma implementation: The case of a UK manufacturing SME. *International Journal of Six Sigma and Competitive Advantage*, *3*(4), 333–351. doi:10.1504/IJSSCA.2007.017176

Kumar, M., Antony, J., Singh, R. K., Tiwari, M. K., & Perry, D. (2006). Implementing the lean sigma framework in an Indian SME: A case study. *Production Planning and Control*, *17*(4), 407–423. doi:10.1080/09537280500483350

Kumar, S. (2004). Mobile communications: Global trends in the 21st century. *International Journal of Mobile Communications*, *2*(1), 67–86. doi:10.1504/IJMC.2004.004488

Kurdistan. (2011). *The other Iraq.* Retrieved from http://www.theotheriraq.com

Kurdy, B. M., & AlSabbagh, M. M. (2004, April 19-23). Omnifont Arabic optical character recognition system. In *Proceedings of the International Conference on Information and Communication Technologies: from Theory to Applications*, Damascus, Syria.

Kurdy, B. M., & Joukhadar, A. (1992). Multifont recognition system for Arabic characters. In *Proceedings of the 3rd International Conference and Exhibition on Multilingual Computing (Arabic and Roman Script)*, Durham, UK (pp. 7.3.1-7.3.9).

Kushchu, I., & Kuscu, H. (2003). From e-government to m-government: Facing the Inevitable. In *Proceedings of the European Conference on e-Government*, Dublin, Ireland.

Kwon, O., & Wen, Y. (2010). An empirical study of the factors affecting social network service use. *Computers in Human Behavior*, *26*, 254–263. doi:10.1016/j.chb.2009.04.011

Lairumbi, G. M., Molyneux, S., Snow, R. W., Marsh, K., Peshu, N., & English, M. (2008). Promoting the social value of research in Kenya: Examining practical aspects of collaborative partnerships using an ethical framework. *Social Science & Medicine*, *67*, 734–747. doi:10.1016/j.socscimed.2008.02.016

Landis, J. R., & Koch, G. G. (1977). The measurement of observer agreement for categorical data. *Biometrics*, *33*, 159–174. doi:10.2307/2529310

LaPre, C., Zhao, Y., Schwartz, R., & Makhoul, J. (1996, May 7-10). Multi-font off-line Arabic character recognition using the BBN Byblos speech recognition system. In *Proceedings of the International Conference on Acoustics, Speech, and Signal Processing*, Atlanta, GA (Vol. 4, pp. 2136-2139).

Lau, E. (2007). Electronic government and the drive for growth and equity. In Mayer-Schonberger, V., & Lazer, D. (Eds.), *Governance and information technology* (pp. 39–62). Cambridge, MA: MIT Press.

Lawrence, J. E. (2002). *The use of Internet in small to medium-sized enterprises.* Unpublished doctoral dissertation, University of Salford, Salford, UK.

Lawrence, J. E., & Tar, U. A. (2010). Barriers to ecommerce in developing countries. *Information. Social Justice (San Francisco, Calif.)*, *3*(1).

Lederer, A. L., Maupin, D. J., Sena, M. P., Zhuang, Y., & Abbasi, M. S. (2000). The technology acceptance model and the World Wide Web. *Decision Support Systems*, *29*, 269–282. doi:10.1016/S0167-9236(00)00076-2

Lee, D., Kwon, J., Yang, S. H., & Lee, S. (2007). Improvement of the recall and the precision for semantic web services search. In *Proceedings of the 6th IEEE/ACIS International Conference on Computer and Information Science* (pp. 763-768).

Lee, G. L., & Oakes, I. (1995). The pros and cons of TQM for smaller forms in manufacturing: some experiences down the supply chain. *Total Quality Management Magazine*, *6*, 413–426. doi:10.1080/09544129550035341

Lee, K. S., Lee, H. S., & Kim, S. Y. (2007). Factors influencing the adoption behavior of mobile banking: A South Korean perspective. *Journal of Internet Banking and Commerce*, *12*(2), 1–9.

Lee, M. S. Y., McGoldrick, P. J., Keeling, K. A., & Doherty, J. (2003). Using ZMET to explore barriers to the adoption of 3G mobile banking services. *International Journal of Retail & Distribution Management*, *31*(6), 340–348. doi:10.1108/09590550310476079

Lee, S. T., Kim, H., & Gupta, S. (2009). Measuring open source software success. *Omega*, *37*, 426–438. doi:10.1016/j.omega.2007.05.005

Lee, S., & Kim, B. G. (2009). Factors affecting the usage of intranet: A confirmatory study. *Computers in Human Behavior*, *25*(1), 191–201. doi:10.1016/j.chb.2008.08.007

Lee, Y. K., & Chen, L. H. (2000). High capacity image steganographic model. []. Image and Signal Processing.]. *Proceedings on Vision*, *147*, 288–294. doi:10.1049/ip-vis:20000341

Lee, Y., Lee, J., & Lee, Z. (2006). Social influence on technology acceptance behavior: Self-identity theory perspective. *The Data Base for Advances in Information Systems*, *37*(2), 60–75. doi:10.1145/1161345.1161355

Legris, P., Ingham, J., & Collerette, P. (2003). Why do people use information technology? A critical review of the technology acceptance model. *Information & Management, 40*, 191–204. doi:10.1016/S0378-7206(01)00143-4

Leidner, D., & Kayworth, T. (2006). A review of culture in information systems research: Toward a theory of information technology culture conflict. *Management Information Systems Quarterly, 30*(2), 357–399.

Leu, S.-J., & Chang, R.-S. (2003). Integrated service mobile Internet: RSVP over mobile IPv4&6. *Mobile Networks and Applications, 8*(6), 635–642. doi:10.1023/A:1026074309946

Levy, J. A. (1988). Intersections of gender and aging. *The Sociological Quarterly, 29*(4), 479–486. doi:10.1111/j.1533-8525.1988.tb01429.x

Liao, C.-H., & Tsou, C.-W. (2009). User acceptance of computer-mediated communication: The SkypeOut case. *Expert Systems with Applications, 36*, 4595–4603. doi:10.1016/j.eswa.2008.05.015

Lim, K.-S., Lim, J.-S., & Heinrichs, J. H. (2008). Testing an integrated model of e-shopping web site usage. *Journal of Internet Commerce, 7*(3). doi:10.1080/15332860802250336

Lin Yeb-Yun, C. (1999). Success factors of small and medium-sized enterprises in Taiwan: An analysis of cases. *Journal of Small Business Management, 36*(4), 43–56.

Lin, C.-H., Lin, S.-L., & Wu, C.-P. (2009). The effects of parental monitoring and leisure boredom on adolescents' internet addiction. *Adolescence, 44*(176), 993–1004.

Lin, C.-P. (2011). Assessing the mediating role of online social capital between social support and instant messaging usage. *Electronic Commerce Research and Applications, 10*, 105–114. doi:10.1016/j.elerap.2010.08.003

Lin, C.-P., & Anol, B. (2008). Learning online social support: An investigation of network information technology based on UTAUT. *Cyberpsychology & Behavior, 11*(3), 268–272. doi:10.1089/cpb.2007.0057

Lin, H.-F. (2007). Predicting consumer intentions to shop online: An empirical test of competing theories. *Electronic Commerce Research and Applications, 6*, 433–442. doi:10.1016/j.elerap.2007.02.002

Lin, M.-J. J., Hung, S.-W., & Chen, C.-J. (2009). Fostering the determinants of knowledge sharing in professional virtual communities. *Computers in Human Behavior, 25*(4), 929–939. doi:10.1016/j.chb.2009.03.008

Lin, T.-C., & Huang, C.-C. (2008). Understanding knowledge management system usage antecedents: An integration of social cognitive theory and task technology fit. *Information & Management, 45*(6), 410–417. doi:10.1016/j.im.2008.06.004

Liu, S. (2005). The current status, causes and reform of urban-rural dual structure in China. *Journal of Chengdu Institute of Public Administration, 13*(1), 72–74.

Livari, J. (2002). An empirical test of the DeLone-McLean model of information system success. *The Data Base for Advances in Information Systems, 36*(2), 8–27.

Li, X. (2008). The discussion on problems and measures of government public information service. *Business Economics (Cleveland, Ohio), 1*, 100–101.

Li, Z., & Hopfield, J. J. (1989). Modeling the olfactory bulb and its neural oscillatory processing. *Biological Cybernetics, 61*, 379–392. doi:10.1007/BF00200803

Loch, K., Straub, D., & Kamel, S. (2003). Diffusing the Internet in the Arab world: The role of social norms and technological culturaltion. *IEEE Transactions on Engineering Management, 5*(1), 45–63. doi:10.1109/TEM.2002.808257

López-Nicolás, C., Molina-Castillo, F. J., & Bouwman, H. (2008). An assessment of advanced mobile services acceptance: Contributions from TAM and diffusion theory models. *Information & Management, 45*(6), 359–364. doi:10.1016/j.im.2008.05.001

Lorange, P., & Roos, J. (1992). *Strategic alliances, evolution and implementation*. Oxford, UK: Blackwell.

Lo, S.-K., Wang, C.-C., & Fang, W. (2005). Physical interpersonal relationships and social anxiety among online game players. *Cyberpsychology & Behavior, 8*(1), 15–20. doi:10.1089/cpb.2005.8.15

Lu, Y., Deng, Z., & Wang, B. (2010). Exploring factors affecting Chinese consumers' usage of short message service for personal communication. *Info Systems Journal, 20*, 183-208.

Luarn, P., & Lin, H. H. (2005). Toward an understanding of the behavioral intention to use mobile banking. *Computers in Human Behavior*, *21*(6), 873–891. doi:10.1016/j.chb.2004.03.003

Lucas, H. (1973). A descriptive model of information systems in the context of the organisation. In *Proceedings of the Wharton Conference on Research on Computers in Organisations* (pp. 27-36).

Lucas, H. C., & Spitler, V. K. (1999). Technology use and performance: A field study of broker workstations. *Decision Sciences*, *30*(2), 291–311. doi:10.1111/j.1540-5915.1999.tb01611.x

Lu, J., Yu, C. S., Liu, C., & Yao, J. E. (2003). Technology acceptance model for wireless Internet. *Electronic Networking and Applications*, *13*(3), 206–222. doi:10.1108/10662240310478222

Lujan-Mora, S., Trujillo, J., & Song, I.-Y. (2006). A UML profile for multidimensional modeling in data warehouses. *Data & Knowledge Engineering*, *59*(3), 725–769. doi:10.1016/j.datak.2005.11.004

Luk, R. W., Leong, H. V., Dillon, T. S., Chan, A. T., Croft, W. B., & Allan, J. (2002). A survey in indexing and searching XML documents. *Journal of the American Society for Information Science and Technology*, *53*(6), 415–437. doi:10.1002/asi.10056

Luo, M. M.-L., Remus, W., & Chea, S. (2006, August 4-6). Technology acceptance of internet based information system: An integrated model of TAM and U&G theory. In *Proceedings of the Twelfth American Conference on Information Systems*, Acapulco, Mexico (pp. 1139-1150).

Luo, M. M., Chea, S., & Chen, J.-S. (2011). Web-based information service adoption: A comparison of the motivational model and the uses and gratifications theory. *Decision Support Systems*, *51*(1), 21–30. doi:10.1016/j.dss.2010.11.015

Lu, W. W. (2000). Compact multidimensional broadband wireless: The convergence of wireless mobile and access. *IEEE Communications Magazine*, *38*(11), 119–123. doi:10.1109/35.883500

Lu, Y., Zhou, T., & Wang, B. (2009). Exploring Chinese users' acceptance of instant messaging using the theory of planned behavior, the technology acceptance model, and the flow theory. *Computers in Human Behavior*, *25*, 29–39. doi:10.1016/j.chb.2008.06.002

Macmanus, J., & Wood-Harper, T. (2007). Software engineering: A quality management perspective. *Total Quality Management Magazine*, *19*(4), 315–327.

Mahboubi, H., Bimonte, S., Faure, T., & Pinet, F. (2010). Data warehouse and OLAP for environmental simulation data. *International Journal of Agricultural and Environmental Systems*, *1*(2).

Maity, S. P., & Nandi, P. K. (2004). Genetic algorithm for optimal imperceptibility in image communication through noisy channel. In *Proceedings of the International Conference on Neural Information Processing*, Calcutta, India (pp. 700-705).

Maldonado, U. P. T., Khan, G. F., Moon, J., & Rho, J. J. (2011). E-learning motivation and educational portal acceptance in developing countries. *Online Information Review*, *35*(1), 66–85. doi:10.1108/14684521111113597

Malinowski, E., & Zimanyi, E. (2006). Hierarchies in a multidimensional model: From conceptual modeling to logical representation. *Data & Knowledge Engineering*, *59*(2), 348–377. doi:10.1016/j.datak.2005.08.003

Malinowski, E., & Zimanyi, E. (2008). *Advanced data warehouse design: From conventional to spatial and temporal applications*. New York, NY: Springer.

Malinowski, E., & Zimányi, E. (2008). A conceptual model for temporal data warehouses and its transformation to the ER and the object-relational models. *Data & Knowledge Engineering*, *64*(1), 101–133. doi:10.1016/j.datak.2007.06.020

Mallick, M. (2003). *Mobile and Wireless Design Essentials*. Hoboken, NJ: Wiley.

Mandel, L., & Cengarle, M. (1999). On the expressive power of OCL. In *Proceedings of the World Congress on Formal Methods in the Developing of Computer Systems* (pp. 713-713).

Manyong, V. M., Ikpi, A., Olayemi, J. K., Yusuf, S. A., Omonona, B. T., Okoruwa, V., & Idachaba, F. S. (2005). *Agriculture in Nigeria: Identifying opportunities for increased commercialization and investment*. Ibadan, Nigeria: IITA.

Margner, V. (1992, August 30-September 3). SARAT - A system for the recognition of Arabic printed text. In *Proceedings of the 11th IAPR International Conference on Pattern Recognition Methodology and Systems*, The Hague, The Netherlands (Vol. 2, pp. 561-564).

Martin, S., & Jagadish, A. (2006, August 25-27). Agricultural marketing and agribusiness supply chain issues in developing economies. In *Proceedings of the New Zealand Agriculture and Resources Economics Society Conference*.

Martınez-Torres, M. R., Marın, S. L. T., Garcıa, F. B., Vazquez, S. G., Oliva, M. A., & Torres, T. (2008). A technological acceptance of e-learning tools used in practical and laboratory teaching, according to the European higher education area. *Behaviour & Information Technology*, *27*(6), 495–505. doi:10.1080/01449290600958965

Mathieson, K., Peacock, E., & Chin, W. W. (2001). Extending the technology acceptance model: The influence of perceived user resources. *The Data Base for Advances in Information Systems*, *32*(3), 86–112. doi:10.1145/506724.506730

Mazdak, Z., Azizah, A., Rabiah, B., Akram, M., & Shahidan, A. (2009). A genetic-algorithm-based approach for audio steganography. *World Academy of Science. Engineering and Technology*, *54*, 360–363.

Mazman, S. G., & Usluel, Y. K. (2010). Modeling educational usage of Facebook. *Computers & Education*, *55*, 444–453. doi:10.1016/j.compedu.2010.02.008

Mazon, J. N., & Trujillo, J. (2008). An MDA approach for the development of data warehouses. *Decision Support Systems*, *45*, 41–55. doi:10.1016/j.dss.2006.12.003

McClure, C. (2009). Reuse finds common ground - software reuse - Forum - Column. *Software Magazine*. Retrieved August 1, 2009, from http://findarticles.com/p/articles/mi_m0SMG/is_n6_v15/ai_17028302/

McFarland, D. J., & Hamilton, D. (2006). Adding contextual specificity to the technology acceptance model. *Computers in Human Behavior*, *22*, 427–447. doi:10.1016/j.chb.2004.09.009

McHugh, R., Roche, S., & Bédard, Y. (2009). Towards a SOLAP-based public participation GIS. *Journal of Environmental Management*, *90*(6), 2041–2054. doi:10.1016/j.jenvman.2008.01.020

Medina, I. G. (2009). SMS: a Powerful Tool for Mobile Marketing Communication. In *Proceedings of the mLife 2009 Conference & Exhibitions,* Barcelona, Spain.

Meek, C., & Arnett, E. (1938). Law and authority in a Nigerian tribe: A study in indirect rule. *Journal of the Royal African Society*, *37*(146), 115–118.

Melitski, J. (2002). *The world of e-government and e-governance*. Retrieved from http://www.aspanet.org/solutions/egovworld.html

Melitski, J., Holzer, M., Kim, S. T., Kim, C. G., & Rho, S. Y. (2005). Digital government worldwide: An e-government assessment of municipal websites. *International Journal of E-Government Research*, *1*(1), 1–19. doi:10.4018/jegr.2005010101

Melone, N. P. (1990). A theoretical assessment of the user-satisfaction construct in information systems research. *Management Science*, *36*(1), 76–91. doi:10.1287/mnsc.36.1.76

Mikhailov, L. (2002). Fuzzy analytical approach to partnership selection in formation of virtual enterprises. *OMEGA International Journal of Management Science*, *39*, 393–401. doi:10.1016/S0305-0483(02)00052-X

Miled, H., & Ben Amara, N. (2001, September 10-13). Planar Markov modeling for Arabic writing recognition: advancement state. In *Proceedings of the 6th International Conference on Document Analysis and Recognition*, Seattle, WA (pp. 69-73).

Miled, H., Olivier, C., Cheriet, M., & Lecourtier, Y. (1997, August 18-20). Coupling observation/letter for Markovian modelisation applied to the recognition of Arabic handwriting. In *Proceedings of the 4th International Conference on Document Analysis and Recognition*, Ulm, Germany (Vol. 2, pp. 580-583).

Miles, M. B., & Huberman, A. M. (1984). *Qualitative data analysis: A sourcebook of new methods*. Thousand Oaks, CA: Sage.

Minten, B., & Barrett, C. (2008). Agricultural technology, productivity, and poverty in Madagascar. *World Development*, *36*(5), 797–822. doi:10.1016/j.worlddev.2007.05.004

Minton, H. L., & Schneider, F. W. (1980). *Differential psychology*. Prospect Heights, IL: Waveland Press.

Mishili, F., Fulton, J., Shehu, M., Kushwaha, S., Marfo, K., & Jamal, M. (2009). Consumer preferences for quality characteristics along the cowpea value chain in Nigeria, Ghana, and Mali. *Agribusiness*, *25*(1), 16–35. doi:10.1002/agr.20184

Mishra, A. K., & Park, T. A. (2005). An empirical analysis of internet use by US farmers. *Agricultural and Resources Economics Review*, *34*(2), 253–264.

Miwa, H., Umetsu, T., Takanishi, A., & Takanohu, H. (2001). Human-like robot head that has olfactory sensation and facial color expression. In *Proceedings of the IEEE International Conference on Robotics and Automation*, Seoul, Korea (pp. 459-464).

Mizsei, J., & Ress, S. (2002). Chemical images by artificial olfactory epithelia. *Sensors and Actuators. B, Chemical*, *83*(1-3), 164–168. doi:10.1016/S0925-4005(01)01035-8

Moalla, I., Elbaati, A., Alimi, A. M., & Benhamadou, A. (2002). Extraction of Arabic text from multilingual documents. In *Proceedings of the IEEE International Conference on Systems, Man and Cybernetics* (Vol. 4).

Moghadam, A. H., & Assar, P. (2008). The relationship between national culture and e-adoption: A case study of Iran. *American Journal of Applied Sciences*, *5*(4), 369–377. doi:10.3844/ajassp.2008.369.377

Molla, A., Taylor, R., & Licker, P. S. (2006). E-Commerce diffusion in small island countries: The influence of institutions in Barbados. *Electronic Journal on Information Systems in Developing Countries*, *28*(2), 1–15.

Moncrieff, R. W. (1961). An instrument for measuring and classifying odors. *Journal of Applied Physiology*, *16*(4), 742–749.

Moody, L. D., & Kortink, M. A. R. (2000). From enterprise models to dimensional models: A methodology for multidimensional structure and data mart design. In *Proceedings of the International Workshop on Design and Management of Multidimensional Structures*, Stockholm, Sweden.

Moon, J.-W., & Kim, Y.-G. (2001). Extending the TAM for a World-Wide-Web context. *Information & Management*, *38*, 217–230. doi:10.1016/S0378-7206(00)00061-6

Moon, M. J. (2002). The evolution of e-government among municipalities: Rhetoric or reality? *Public Administration Review*, *62*(4), 424–433. doi:10.1111/0033-3352.00196

Moore, G. C., & Benbasat, I. (1991). Development of an instrument to measure the perceptions of adopting an information technology innovation. *Information Systems Research*, *2*(3), 192–222. doi:10.1287/isre.2.3.192

Mori, S., Nishida, H., & Yamada, H. (1999). *Optical character recognition*. New York, NY: John Wiley & Sons.

Mosfeq, R. (1996). Arabic character recognition using integrated segmentation and recognition. In *Proceedings of the 5th International Conference and Exhibition on Multi-Lingual Computing*, London, UK.

Mostafa, K., & Darwish, A. M. (1999). Robust baseline-independent algorithms for segmentation and reconstruction of Arabic handwritten cursive script. In *Proceedings of the SPIE Conference on Document Recognition and Retrieval VI*, San Jose, CA (Vol. 3651, pp. 73-83).

Mostafa, K., Shaheen, S. I., Darwish, A. M., & Farag, I. (1999, May 31-June 3). A novel approach for detecting and correcting segmentation and recognition errors in Arabic OCR systems. In *Proceedings of the 12th International Conference on Industrial and Engineering Applications of Artificial Intelligence and Expert Systems*, Cairo, Egypt (pp. 530-539).

Mostafa, M. G. (2004, April 5-8). An adaptive algorithm for the automatic segmentation of printed Arabic text. In *Proceedings of the 17th National Computer Conference*, Al-Madinah, Saudi Arabia (pp. 437-444).

Motawa, D., Amin, A., & Sabourin, R. (1997, August 18-20). Segmentation of Arabic cursive script. In *Proceedings of the 4th International Conference on Document Analysis and Recognition*, Ulm, Germany (Vol. 2, pp. 625-628).

Myers, M. (2009). *Qualitative research in business & management*. Thousand Oaks, CA: Sage.

Myers, M., & Tan, F. (2002). Beyond models of national culture in information systems research. *Journal of Global Information Management, 10*(2), 1–19.

Nabavian, N. (2010). *CPSC 350 data structures: Image steganography*. Retrieved from http://www1.chapman.edu/~nabav100/ImgStegano/download/ImageSteganography.pdf

Nabeshima, H., Miyagawa, R., Suzuki, Y., & Iwanuma, K. (2006). University of Yamanashi rapid synthesis of domain-specific web search engines based on semiautomatic training-example generation. In *Proceedings of the IEEE/WIC/ACM International Conference on Web Intelligence*.

Nakamoto, T., & Hiramatsu, H. (2002). Study of odor recorder for dynamical change of odor using QCM sensors and neural network. *Sensors and Actuators. B, Chemical, 85*(3), 263–269. doi:10.1016/S0925-4005(02)00130-2

Nakamoto, T., Nakahira, Y., Hiramatsu, H., & Moriizumi, T. (2001). Odor recorder using active odor sensing system. *Sensors and Actuators. B, Chemical, 76*(1-3), 465–469. doi:10.1016/S0925-4005(01)00587-1

Naruse, K. (2003). The survey of the mobile Internet, usage and awareness, study for m-commerce. In *Proceedings of the Symposium on Applications and the Internet Workshops* (pp. 127-130). Washington, DC: IEEE Computer Society.

Nawaz, S. N., Sarfraz, M., Zidouri, A., & Al-Khatib, W. G. (2003, December 14-17). An approach to offline Arabic character recognition using neural networks. In *Proceedings of the 10th IEEE International Conference on Electronics, Circuits and Systems* (Vol. 3, pp. 1328-1331).

Nazif, A. (1975). *A system for the recognition of the printed Arabic characters* (Unpublished master's thesis). Cairo University, Cairo, Egypt.

Ndou, V. (2004). E-government for developing countries: Opportunities and challenges. *Electronic Journal of Information Systems in Developing Countries, 18*(1), 1–24.

Ndubisi, N. O., & Jantan, M. (2003). Evaluating IS usage in Malaysian small and medium-sized firms using the technology acceptance model. *Logistics Information Management, 16*(6), 440–450. doi:10.1108/09576050310503411

Ngai, E. W. T., Poon, J. K. L., & Chan, Y. H. C. (2007). Empirical examination of the adoption of WebCT using TAM. *Computers & Education, 48*, 250–267. doi:10.1016/j.compedu.2004.11.007

Nguyen, T. B., Tjoa, A. M., & Wagner, R. (2000). An object oriented multidimensional data model for OLAP. In H. Lu & A. Zhou (Eds.), *Proceedings of the First International Conference on Web-Age Information Management* (LNCS 1846, pp. 69-82).

Nichols, L. A., & Nicki, R. (2004). Development of a psychometrically sound internet addiction scale: A preliminary step. *Psychology of Addictive Behaviors, 18*(38), 1–4.

Nikolaou, N., & Zervos, N. (2006). Wireless convergence architecture: A case study using GSM and wireless LAN. *Mobile Networks and Applications, 7*(1), 259–267.

Nilakanta, S., Scheibe, K., & Rai, A. (2008). Dimensional issues in agricultural data warehouse designs. *Computers and Electronics in Agriculture, 60*(2), 263–278. doi:10.1016/j.compag.2007.09.009

Ni, X., Yan, H., Chen, S., & Liu, Z. (2009). Factors influencing internet addiction in a sample of freshmen university students in China. *Cyberpsychology & Behavior, 12*(3), 327–330. doi:10.1089/cpb.2008.0321

Nnadozie, E. (2002). African indigenous entrepreneurship: Determinants of resurgence and growth of Igbo entrepreneurship during the Post-Biafra period. *Journal of African Business, 3*(1), 49–80. doi:10.1300/J156v03n01_04

Nonaka, I. (2007). The knowledge-creating company. *Harvard Business Review, 85*(7-8), 162–171.

Nonaka, L., & Takeuchi, H. (1995). *The knowledge-creating company: How Japanese companies create the dynamics of innovation*. New York, NY: Oxford University Press.

Norris, F., Fletcher, P. D., & Holden, S. H. (2001). *Is your local government plugged in? Highlights of the 2000 electronic government survey*. Baltimore, MD: University of Maryland.

Nouh, A., Ula, A. N., & Edlin, A. S. (1988). Algorithms for feature extraction: a case study for the Arabic character recognition. In *Proceedings of the 10th National Conference*, Jeddah, Saudi Arabia (pp. 653-666).

Nouh, A., Sultan, A., & Tolba, R. (1980). An approach for Arabic characters recognition. *Journal of Science*, *6*(2), 185–191.

Nysveen, H., Pedersen, P. E., & Thorbjornsen, H. (2005). Intentions to use mobile services: Antecedents and cross-service comparisons. *Journal of the Academy of Marketing Science*, *33*(3), 330–346. doi:10.1177/0092070305276149

Obaid, A. M. (1998). A new pattern matching approach to the recognition of printed Arabic. In *Proceedings of the Workshop on Content Visualization and Intermediate Representations*, Montreal, QC, Canada (pp. 106-111).

Obaid, A. M., & Dobrowiecki, T. P. (1997, September 15-17). Heuristic approach to the recognition of printed Arabic script. In *Proceedings of the IEEE International Conference on Intelligent Engineering Systems*, Budapest, Hungary.

Odedra-Straub, M. (2003). E-Commerce and development: Whose development? *Electronic Journal on Information Systems in Developing Countries*, *11*(2), 1–5.

OECD. (2003). The case of e-government: Experts from the OECD report: The e-government imperative. *OECD Journal on Budgeting*, *3*(1), 62–96.

OECD. (2004). Promoting entrepreneurship and innovative SMEs in a global economy: Towards a more responsive and inclusive globalisation. In *Proceedings of the 2nd OECD Conference of Ministers Responsible for Small and Medium-Sized Enterprises (SMEs)*, Istanbul, Turkey.

Ogunleye, O. S. (2009). Context and Capability: The Future of Small Screen Research and Development in Africa. In *Proceedings of the mLife 2009 Conference & Exhibitions*, Barcelona, Spain.

Oh, S., Ahn, J., & Kim, B. (2003). Adoption of broadband internet in Korea: The role of experience in building attitude. *Journal of Information Technology*, *18*(4), 267–280. doi:10.1080/0268396032000150807

Okazaki, S. (2004). New perspectives on m-commerce research. *Journal of Electronic Commerce Research*, *6*(3), 160–164.

Okazaki, S. (2005). How do Japanese consumers perceive wireless ads? A multivariate analysis. *International Journal of Advertising*, *23*(4), 429–454.

Olivier, C., Miled, H., Romeo-Pakker, K., & Lecourtier, Y. (1996, August 25-29). Segmentation and coding of Arabic handwritten words. In *Proceedings of the International Conference on Pattern Recognition*, Vienna, Austria (Vol. 3, pp. 264-268).

Olmstead, P. M., Peinel, G., Tilsner, D., Abramowicz, W., Bassara, A., & Filipowska, A. (2007). Usability Driven Open Platform for Mobile Government (USE-ME.GOV). In Kushchu, I. (Ed.), *Mobile Government: An Emerging Direction in E-Government* (pp. 30–59). Hershey, PA: IGI Publishing. doi:10.4018/9781591408840.ch003

Omamo, S., & Lynam, J. (2003). Agricultural science and technology policy in Africa. *Research Policy*, *32*(9), 1681–1694. doi:10.1016/S0048-7333(03)00059-3

Omar, K., Mahmoud, R., Sulaiman, M. N., & Ramli, A. (2000). The removal of secondaries of Jawi characters. In *Proceedings of the IEEE Region 10 Annual Conference*, Malaysia (Vol. 2, pp. 149-152).

OMG. (2007). *Unified modelling language: OCL, version 2.0*. Needham, MA: OMG.

OMG. (2009). *Unified modeling language (OMG UML), infrastructure version 2.2*. Needham, MA: OMG.

Oseni, G., & Winters, P. (2009). Rural nonfarm activities and agricultural crop production in Nigeria. *Agricultural Economics*, *40*(2), 189–201. doi:10.1111/j.1574-0862.2009.00369.x

Oxley, J. E., & Yeung, B. (2001). E-Commerce readiness: Institutional environment and international competitiveness. *Journal of International Business Studies*, *32*(4), 705–723. doi:10.1057/palgrave.jibs.8490991

Oyelaran-Oyeyinka, B., & La, K. (2005). Internet diffusion in sub-Saharan Africa: A cross-country analysis. *Telecommunications Policy*, *29*(7), 507–527. doi:10.1016/j.telpol.2005.05.002

Paeda, X. G., Melendi, D., Vilas, M., Garcia, R., Garcia, V., & Rodriguez, I. (2008). FESORIA: An integrated system for analysis, management and smart presentation of audio/video streaming services. *Multimedia Tools and Applications*, *39*(3), 379–412. doi:10.1007/s11042-007-0173-0

Pai, J.-C., & Tu, F.-M. (2011). The acceptance and use of customer relationship management (CRM) systems: An empirical study of distribution service industry in Taiwan. *Expert Systems with Applications, 38,* 579–584. doi:10.1016/j.eswa.2010.07.005

Paila, T. (2003). Mobile Internet over IP data broadcast. In *Proceedings of the 10th International Telecommunications Conference,* Espoo, Finland (pp. 19-24). Washington, DC: IEEE Computer Society.

Pal, U., & Sarkar, A. (2003). Recognition of printed Urdu script. In *Proceedings of the 7th International Conference on Document Analysis and Recognition.*

Palmberg, C., & Bohlin, E. (2006). Next generation mobile telecommunications networks: Challenges to the Nordic ICT industries. *Info, 8*(4), 3–9. doi:10.1108/14636690610676504

Pal, N. R., & Bezdek, J. C. (1999). Measuring fuzzy uncertainty. *IEEE Transactions on Fuzzy Systems, 2*(2), 107–118. doi:10.1109/91.277960

Pande, R. (2006). Profits and politics: Coordinating technology adoption in agriculture. *Journal of Development Economics, 81*(2), 299–315. doi:10.1016/j.jdeveco.2005.06.012

Papacharissi, Z., & Rubin, A. M. (2000). Predictors of internet use. *Journal of Broadcasting & Electronic Media, 44*(2), 175–196. doi:10.1207/s15506878jobem4402_2

Paré, D. J. (2002). *B2B e-commerce services and developing countries: Disentangling myth from reality.* London, UK: London School of Economics and Political Science.

Parent, M., Vandebeek, C. A., & Gemino, A. C. (2005). Building citizen trust through e-government. *Government Information Quarterly, 22*(4), 720–736. doi:10.1016/j.giq.2005.10.001

Parhami, B., & Taraghi, M. (1981). Automatic recognition of printed Farsi texts. *Pattern Recognition, 14*(1-6), 395-403.

Park, J., Yang, S., & Lehto, X. (2007). Adoption of mobile technologies for Chinese consumers. *Journal of Electronic Commerce Research, 8*(3), 196–206.

Paskaleva-Shapira, K. (2006). Transitioning from e-government to e-governance in the knowledge society: The role of the legal framework for enabling the process in the European Union's countries. In *Proceedings of the 7th Annual International Conference on Digital Government Research,* San Diego, CA.

Pavlou, P. A. (2003). Consumer acceptance of electronic commerce: Integrating trust and risk with the technology acceptance model. *International Journal of Electronic Commerce, 7*(3), 101–134.

Pavlou, P. A., & Fygenson, M. (2006). Understanding and predicting electronic commerce adoption: An extension of the theory of planned behavior. *Management Information Systems Quarterly, 30*(1), 115–144.

Pedersen, P. E., & Ling, R. (2003). Modifying adoption research for mobile Internet service adoption: Cross-disciplinary interactions. In *Proceedings of the 36th Annual Hawaii International Conference on System Sciences* (pp. 10-20). Washington, DC: IEEE Computer Society.

Pedrycz, W. (2005). *Knowledge-based clustering from data to information granules.* New York, NY: John Wiley & Sons. doi:10.1002/0471708607

Penny, A. J., Ali, M. A., Farah, I., Ostberg, S., & Smith, R. L. (2000). A study of cross national collaborative research: reflecting on experience in Pakistan. *International Journal of Educational Development, 20,* 443–455. doi:10.1016/S0738-0593(00)00019-5

Pérez, J., Arenas, M., & Gutierrez, C. (2009). Semantics and complexity of SPARQL. *ACM Transactions on Database Systems, 34*(3), 16–45. doi:10.1145/1567274.1567278

Pestana, G., da Silva, M. M., & Bedard, Y. (2005). Spatial OLAP modeling: an overview base on spatial objects changing over time. In *Proceedings of the IEEE 3rd International Conference on Computational Cybernetics.*

Peters, G., & McNeese, R. M. (2008). *Collaborative research in a post-Katrina environment: The facilitation communication and ethical considerations of university researchers.* Retrieved from http://creativecommons.org/licenses/by/2.o/cox.org/content/m17676/1.1

Petrova, K., & Huang, R. (2007). Mobile internet deployment in New Zealand. In S. Krishnamurthy & P. Isaias (Eds.), *Proceedings of the International Association for Development of the Information Society International Conference on e-Commerce* (pp. 337-34).Algarve, Portugal: IADIS.

Petrova, K., & Parry, D. (2008). Mobile Computing Applications in New Zealand. In Yoo, Y., Lee, J.-N., & Rowley, C. (Eds.), *Trends in mobile technology and business in the Asia-Pacific Region* (pp. 153–177). Oxford, UK: Chandos Publishing.

Petter & McLean. (2009). A meta-analytic assessment of the DeLone and McLean IS success model: An examination of IS success at the individual level. *Information & Management, 46*, 159–166. doi:10.1016/j.im.2008.12.006

Petty, R. D. (2003). Wireless advertising messaging: Legal analysis and public policy issues. *Journal of Public Policy & Marketing, 22*(1), 71–82. doi:10.1509/jppm.22.1.71.17627

Pfeiffer, S., Lienhart, R., & Efflsberg, W. (2001). Scene determination based on video and audio features. *Multimedia Tools and Applications, 15*(1), 59–81. doi:10.1023/A:1011315803415

Pijpers, G. G. M., Bemelmans, T. M. A., Heemstra, F. J., & Monfort, K. A. G. M. (2001). Senior's executive use of information technology. *Information and Software Technology, 43*, 959–971. doi:10.1016/S0950-5849(01)00197-5

Plucknett, D. L., & Smith, N. J. H. (2005). *The potential of collaborative research networks in developing countries.* Retrieved from http://www,fao.org/wairclocs/ilri/x5443e/x5443eo5.htm

Porter, C. E., & Donthu, N. (2006). Using the technology acceptance model to explain how attitudes determine Internet usage: The role of perceived access barriers and demographics. *Journal of Business Research, 59*(9), 999–1007. doi:10.1016/j.jbusres.2006.06.003

Prat, N., Akoka, J., & Comyn-Wattiau, I. (2006). A UML-based data warehouse design method. *Decision Support Systems, 42*(3), 1449–1473. doi:10.1016/j.dss.2005.12.001

Prescott, M. B., & Conger, S. A. (1995). Information technology innovations: A classification by IT locus of impact and research approach. *Journal of Data Base for Advances in Information Systems, 26*(2), 20–25.

Pynoo, B., Devolder, P., Tondeur, J., Van Braak, J., Duyck, W., & Duyck, P. (2011). Predicting secondary school teachers' acceptance and use of a digital learning environment: A cross-sectional study. *Computers in Human Behavior, 27*(1), 568–575. doi:10.1016/j.chb.2010.10.005

Rai, A., Lang, S., & Welker, R. (2002). Assessing the validity of IS success models: An empirical test and theoretical analysis. *Information Systems Research, 13*(1), 50–69. doi:10.1287/isre.13.1.50.96

Ramachandran, V., & Shah, M. (1999). Minority entrepreneurs and firm performance in Sub-Saharan Africa. *The Journal of Development Studies, 36*(2), 71–87. doi:10.1080/00220389908422621

Ramsis, R., & El-Dabi, S. (1988). *Arabic character recognition system* (Tech. Rep. No. KSC027). Kuwait: IBM Scientific Center.

Rao, N. (2007). A framework for implementing information and communication technologies in agricultural development in India. *Technological Forecasting and Social Change, 74*(4), 491–518. doi:10.1016/j.techfore.2006.02.002

Reference Framework Report, S. O. A. (2007). *Enhancing the enterprise architecture with service orientation.* CBDI Journal.

Ren, H. (2010).*Report on the work of the A town government in 2010.* Retrieved December 10, 2010, from http://www.humencn.com/news/info.asp?id=51495&classcode=200003

Reynolds, D., Thompson, C., Mukerji, J., & Coleman, D. (2005). *Digital Media Systems Laboratory: An assessment of RDF/OWL modelling.* Retrieved from http://www.hpl.hp.com/techreports/2005/HPL-2005-189.pdf

Rivard, S., & Huff, S. L. (1988). Factors of success for end-user computing. *Communications of the ACM, 31*(5), 552–561. doi:10.1145/42411.42418

Roberts, P., & Kempf, J. (2006). Mobility architecture for the global Internet. In *Proceedings of the First ACM/IEEE International Workshop on Mobility in the Evolving Internet Architecture*, San Francisco, CA (pp. 23-28). New York, NY: ACM Press.

Roberts, P., & Henderson, R. (2000). Information technology acceptance in a sample of government employees: a test of the technology acceptance model. *Interacting with Computers*, *12*(5), 427–443. doi:10.1016/S0953-5438(98)00068-X

Robichaux, B. P., & Cooper, R. B. (1998). GSS participation: A cultural examination. *Information & Management*, *33*(6), 287–300. doi:10.1016/S0378-7206(98)00033-0

Rodriguez, F., & Wilson, E. (2000). *Are poor countries losing the information revolution?* Washington, DC: World Bank.

Rogers, E. M. (1995). *Diffusion of innovations* (4th ed.). New York, NY: Free Press.

Roldan, J., & Leal, A. (2003). *Adaptation of the Delone and McLean's Model in the Spanish EIS Field*. Retrieved September 1, 2009, from http://business.clemson.edu/ISE/04chap.pdf

Romani, M. (2003). Love thy neighbour? Evidence from ethnic discrimination in information sharing within villages in côte d'ivoire. *Journal of African Economies*, *12*(4), 533–563. doi:10.1093/jae/12.4.533

Romeo-Pakker, K., Miled, H., & Lecourtier, Y. (1995, August 14-16). A new approach for Latin/Arabic character segmentation. In *Proceedings of the 3rd International Conference on Document Analysis and Recognition*, Montreal, QC, Canada (Vol. 2, pp. 874-877).

Ross, T. J. (1995). *Fuzzy logic with engineering applications*. New York, NY: McGraw-Hill.

Rouibah, K., Hamdy, H. I., & Al-Enezi, M. Z. (2009). Effect of management support, training, and user involvement on system usage and satisfaction in Kuwait. *Industrial Management & Data Systems*, *109*(3), 338–356. doi:10.1108/02635570910939371

Ruggiero, T. E. (2000). Uses and gratifications theory in the 21st century. *Mass Communication & Society*, *3*(1), 3–37. doi:10.1207/S15327825MCS0301_02

Rumbaugh, J., Balaha, M., Premerlani, W., Eddy, F., & Lorensen, W. (1991). *Object-oriented modeling and design*. Upper Saddle River, NJ: Prentice Hall.

Ryan, C., & Gonsalves, A. (2005). The effect of context and application type on mobile usability: An empirical study. In *Proceedings of the 28th Australasian Computer Science Conference* (Vol. 38, pp. 116-124).

Saab, S. S., & Kabbout, S. M. (2002). Map-based mobile positioning system: A feasibility study. *ACTA Press*, *5*(2), 50–59.

Sabo, E., & Zira, D. (2009). Awareness and effectiveness of vegetable technology information packages by vegetable farmers in Adamawa State, Nigeria. *African Journal of Agricultural Research*, *4*(2), 65–70.

Sadeh, N. (2002). *M-commerce: technologies, services, and business models*. New York, NY: John Wiley & Sons.

Sadiq-Hussain, & Sarsam, B. I. (1998, March 30-April 2). Development and evaluation of ANN algorithms for recognition of Arabic script. In *Proceedings of the ISTAED International Conference on Computer System and Application*, Irbid, Jordan.

Saeed, K. A., Abdinnour, S., Lengnick-Hall, M. L., & Lengnick-Hall, C. A. (2010). Examining the impact of pre-implementation expectations on post-implementation use of enterprise systems: A longitudinal study. *Decision Sciences*, *41*(4), 659–688. doi:10.1111/j.1540-5915.2010.00285.x

Sajjan, G. S., & Shala, L. A. (2008). Using semantic wikis to support software reuse. *Journal of Software*, *3*(4), 1–8.

Sakkal, M. (2002). *How to improve computer generated calligraphic designs*. Retrieved December 28, 2005, from http://www.sakkal.com/instrctn/computer_thuluth01.html

Sako, M. (1998). The nature and impact of employee 'voice' in the European car components industry. *Human Resource Management Journal*, *8*(2), 5–13. doi:10.1111/j.1748-8583.1998.tb00163.x

Sanchez-Franco, M. J. (2006). Exploring the influence of gender on the web usage via partial least squares. *Behaviour & Information Technology*, *25*(1), 19–36. doi:10.1080/01449290500124536

Sanchez-Franco, M. J., & Roldan, J. L. (2005). Web acceptance usage model: A comparison between goal directed and experiential users. *Internet Research, 15*(1), 21–48. doi:10.1108/10662240510577059

Sánchez, R. A., & Hueros, A. D. (2010). Motivational factors that influence the acceptance of Moodle using TAM. *Computers in Human Behavior, 26*, 1632–1640. doi:10.1016/j.chb.2010.06.011

Sanni, S., Ilori, M., Opaleye, A., & Oyewale, A. (2001). Nigeria's technology policy: Is it adequate in the globalizing world? *Technovation, 21*(4), 237–243. doi:10.1016/S0166-4972(00)00044-4

Santhi, K. R., & Kumaran, G. S. (2006). Migration to 4G: Mobile IP based solutions. In *Proceedings of the Advanced International Conference on Telecommunications and International Conference on Internet and Web Applications and Services*, Lisbon, Portugal (pp. 76-84). Washington, DC: IEEE Computer Society.

Sapio, B., Turk, T., Cornacchia, M., Papa, F., Nicolò, E., & Livi, S. (2010). Building scenarios of digital television adoption: a pilot study. *Technology Analysis and Strategic Management, 22*(1), 43–63. doi:10.1080/09537320903438054

Sarfraz, M., Nawaz, S. N., & Al-Khuraidly, A. (2003, July 16-18). Offline Arabic text recognition system. In *Proceedings of the International Conference on Geometric Modeling and Graphics*, London, UK (pp. 30-36).

Sari, T., Souici, L., & Sellami, M. (2002, August 6-8). Off-line handwritten Arabic character segmentation and recognition system: ACSA. In *Proceedings of the 8th International Workshop on Frontiers in Handwriting Recognition*, Niagara-on-the-Lake, CA (pp. 452-457).

Sassan, A. (2007, May 24-25). *Research and development in the Arab states: the impact of globalization, facts and perspectives*. Paper presented at the UNESCO Forum on Higher Education, Research and Knowledge, Rabat, Morocco.

Sassenrath, G. F., Heilman, P., Luschei, E., Bennett, G. L., Fitzgerald, G., & Klesius, P. (2008). Technology, complexity and change in agricultural production systems. *Renewable Agriculture and Food Systems, 23*(4), 285–295. doi:10.1017/S174217050700213X

Saugstrup, D., & Henten, A. (2006). 3G Standards: The battle between WCDMA and CDMA2000. *Info, 8*(4), 10–20. doi:10.1108/14636690610676513

Sboui, T., Salehi, M., & Bédard, Y. (2010). A systematic approach for managing the risk related to semantic interoperability between geospatial datacubes. *International Journal of Agricultural and Environmental Information Systems, 1*(2). doi:10.4018/jaeis.2010070102

Schein, E. H. (1984). Coming to a new awareness of organizational culture. *Sloan Management Review, 25*(2), 3–16.

Schepers, J., & Wetzels, M. (2007). A meta-analysis of the technology acceptance model: Investigating subjective norm and moderation effects. *Information & Management, 44*(1), 90–103. doi:10.1016/j.im.2006.10.007

Scheraga, C. A., Tellis, W. M., & Tucker, M. T. (2000). Lead users and technology transfer. *Technology in Society, 22*(3), 415–425. doi:10.1016/S0160-791X(00)00017-8

Schmidt, D. C., & Fayad, M. E. (1997). Lessons learned: Building reusable OO frameworks for distributed software. *Communications of the ACM, 40*(10), 85–87. doi:10.1145/262793.262810

Schneider, M. (2008). A general model for the design of data warehouses. *International Journal of Production Economics, 112*(1), 309–325. doi:10.1016/j.ijpe.2006.11.027

Schultze, U., & Carte, T. A. (2007). Contextualizing usage research for interactive technology: The case of car e- tailing. *The Data Base for Advances in Information Systems, 38*(1), 29–59. doi:10.1145/1216218.1216223

Schulze, C., Spilke, J., & Lehner, W. (2007). Data modeling for precision dairy farming within the competitive field of operational and analytical tasks. *Computers and Electronics in Agriculture, 59*(1), 39–55. doi:10.1016/j.compag.2007.05.001

Schwefel, H. (2002). Mobile Internet: Research toy or product vision? In *Proceedings of the IEEE International Symposium on Network Computing and Spplications* (pp. 267-268). Washington, DC: IEEE Computer Society.

Schwester, R. (2009). Examining the barriers to e-government adoption. *Electronic Journal of E-Government, 7*(1), 113–122.

Segars, A., & Grover, V. (1998). Strategic information systems planning success: An investigation of the construct and its measurement. *Management Information Systems Quarterly*, 22(2), 139–163. doi:10.2307/249393

Senturk, M. (2008). Transformation of Public Places and Social Life by the Impact of Mobile Phones. In *Proceedings of the mLife 2008 Conference & Exhibitions*, Antalya, Turkey.

Serenko, A. (2008). A model of user adoption of interface agents for email notification. *Interacting with Computers*, 20, 461–472. doi:10.1016/j.intcom.2008.04.004

Shan, A., Weiyin, R., Peishan, L., & Shoulian, T. (2008). Research of home information technology adoption model. *Homenet and Mobile Terminal*, 5, 10–16.

Shashidhar, A., Raman, S. M., & Moorthy, M. (2010). *Protégé RDF(s)-DB Backend Plugin*. Retrieved March 4, 2010, from http://protege.stanford.edu/

Sheikhzadeh, M., Trifkovic, M., & Rohani, S. (2008). Adaptive MIMO neuro-fuzzy logic control of a seeded and an un-seeded anti-solvent semi-batch crystallizer. *Chemical Engineering Science*, 63(5), 1261–1272. doi:10.1016/j.ces.2007.07.022

Shen, L. (2010). *Report on the work of the B town government in 2010*. Retrieved December 12, 2010, from http://www.lx.hh.gov.cn/InformationDisclosure.aspx?KindID=0001000300050010

Sheng, Z., Jue, Z., & Weiwei, T. (2008). Extending TAM for online learning systems: An intrinsic motivation perspective. *Tsinghua Science and Technology*, 13(3), 312–317. doi:10.1016/S1007-0214(08)70050-6

Shih, Y.-Y. (2006). The effect of computer self-efficacy on enterprise resource planning usage. *Behaviour & Information Technology*, 25(5), 407–411. doi:10.1080/01449290500168103

Shin, D., Kim, J., Ryu, S., Oh, D., Lee, J., & Kang, M. (2006). Scenario decomposition based analysis of next generation mobile services. In *Proceedings of the 8th International Conference on Advanced Communication Technology* (pp. 403-408). Washington, DC: IEEE Computer Society.

Shin, D.-H. (2009). Towards an understanding of the consumer acceptance of mobile wallet. *Computers in Human Behavior*, 25, 1343–1354. doi:10.1016/j.chb.2009.06.001

Shin, Y. M., Lee, S. C., Shin, B., & Lee, H. G. (2010). Examining influencing factors of post-adoption usage of mobile internet: Focus on the user perception of supplier-side attributes. *Information Systems Frontiers*, 12, 595–606. doi:10.1007/s10796-009-9184-x

Shore, B., & Vankatachalam, A. (1996). Role of national culture in the transfer of information technology. *The Journal of Strategic Information Systems*, 5(1), 19–35. doi:doi:10.1016/S0963-8687(96)80021-7

Simard, P. Y., Szeliski, R., Benaloh, J., Couvreur, J., & Calinov, I. (2003). Using character recognition and segmentation to tell computer from humans. In *Proceedings of the 7th International Conference on Document Analysis and Recognition* (Vol. 1, pp. 418-422).

Slangen, L., van Kooten, C., & Suchánek, P. (2004). Institutions, social capital and agricultural change in central and eastern Europe. *Journal of Rural Studies*, 20(2), 245–256. doi:10.1016/j.jrurstud.2003.08.005

Smagalla, D. (2004). Supply-chain culture clash. *MIT Sloan Management Review*, 46(1).

Smith, M. K., Welty, C., & McGuinness, D. L. (2004). *OWL Web Ontology Language Guide*. Retrieved November 12, 2009, from http://www.w3.org/TR/2004/REC-owl-guide-20040210/

Snee, R. D. (2004). Six Sigma: the evolution of 100 years of business improvement methodology. *International Journal of Six Sigma and Competitive Advantage*, 1(1), 4–20. doi:10.1504/IJSSCA.2004.005274

Soininen, M. (2005). Segments of the mobile Internet industry – examples from Finland and Japan. In *Proceedings of the International Conference on Mobile Busines*, Sydney, Australia (pp. 56-62). Washington, DC: IEEE Computer Society.

Soyer, A., Kabak, O., & Asan, U. (2007). A fuzzy approach to value and culture assessment and an application. *International Journal of Approximate Reasoning*, 44(2), 182–196. doi:10.1016/j.ijar.2006.07.008

Spielman, D., Ekboir, J., & Davis, K. (2009). The art and science of innovation systems inquiry: Applications to Sub-Saharan African agriculture. *Technology in Society*, *31*(4), 399–405. doi:10.1016/j.techsoc.2009.10.004

Srite, M., & Karahanna, E. (2006). The role of espoused national cultural values in technology acceptance. *Management Information Systems Quarterly*, *30*(3), 679–704.

Srivastava, S. C., & Teo, T. S. H. (2006, December). Determinants and impact of e-government and e-business development: A global perspective. In *Proceedings of the Twenty-Seventh International Conference on Information Systems*, Milwaukee, WI.

Srivastava, L. (2003). Boosting broadband in Iceland. *Info*, *5*(3), 8–26. doi:10.1108/14636690310698431

Stephenson, W. (1935). Technique of factor analysis. *Nature*, *136*, 297. doi:10.1038/136297b0

Stoel, L., & Lee, K. H. (2003). Modeling the effect of experience on student acceptance of web based courseware. *Internet Research*, *13*(5), 364–374. doi:10.1108/10662240310501649

Stojcevska, B., & Gusev, M. (2002). Mobile Internet concepts and mobile Internet TCP/IP. *IEEE Computer*, *12*(7), 97–105.

Stone, R. W., Good, D. J., & Baker-Eveleth, L. (2007). The impact of information technology on individual and firm marketing performance. *Behaviour & Information Technology*, *26*(6), 465–482. doi:10.1080/01449290600571610

Strange, C. L. (1993). Around the world in 80 days: Typesetting Arabic, Hebrew, Cyrillic, and Thai. In *Proceedings of the Professional Communication Conference on the New Face of Technical Communication: People, Processes, Products* (pp. 43-48).

Straub, D., Keil, M., & Brenner, W. (1997). Testing the technology acceptance model across cultures: A three country study. *Information & Management*, *31*(1), 1–11. doi:10.1016/S0378-7206(97)00026-8

Straub, D., Limayem, M., & Karahanna-Evaristo, E. (1995). Measuring system usage: Implication for IS theory testing. *Management Science*, *41*(8), 1328–1339. doi:10.1287/mnsc.41.8.1328

Straub, D., Loch, K., & Hill, C. (2001). Transfer of information technology to the Arab world: A test of cultural influence modeling. *Journal of Global Information Management*, *9*(4), 6–28. doi:10.4018/jgim.2001100101

Studer, R., Grimm, S., & Abecker, A. (Eds.). (2007). *Semantic web services concepts, technologies, and applications*. New York, NY: Springer. doi:10.1007/3-540-70894-4

Stuetz, R. M., Engin, G., & Fenner, R. A. (1998). Sewage odour measurements using a sensory panel and an electronic nose. *Water Science and Technology*, *38*(3), 331–335. doi:10.1016/S0273-1223(98)00559-9

Šumak, B., Polančič, G., & Heričko, M. (2010). *An empirical study of virtual learning environment adoption using UTAUT*. Paper presented at the Second International Conference on Mobile, Hybrid, and On-line Learning.

Sun Microsystems. (2004). *Java™ Remote method invocation specification*. Retrieved from http://java.sun.com/j2se/1.5/pdf/rmi-spec-1.5.0.pdf

Sundqvist, S., Frank, L., & Puumalainen, K. (2005). The effects of country characteristics, cultural similarity and adoption timing on the diffusion of wireless communications. *Journal of Business Research*, *58*(1), 107–110. doi:10.1016/S0148-2963(02)00480-0

Sun, T., Zhong, B., & Zhang, J. (2006). Uses and gratifications of Chinese online gamers. *China Media Research*, *2*(2), 58–63.

Sun, Y., Bhattacherjee, A., & Ma, Q. (2009). Extending technology usage to work settings: The role of perceived work compatibility in ERP implementation. *Information & Management*, *46*, 351–356. doi:10.1016/j.im.2009.06.003

Sydow, J. (2005). Managing interfirm networks. In Theurl, T. (Ed.), *Economics of interfirm networks*. Tübingen, Germany: J. C. B. Mohr.

Syeda-Mahmood, T. G., Shah, L. Y., & Urban, W. (2005). Semantic search of schema repositories. In *Proceedings of the Special Interest Tracks and Posters of the 14th International Conference on World Wide Web*, Chiba, Japan (pp. 1126-1127).

Sykes, T. A., Venkatesh, V., & Gosain, S. (2009). Model of acceptance with peer support: A social network perspective to understand employees' system use. *Management Information Systems Quarterly*, *33*(2), 371–393.

Szajna, B. (1996). Empirical evaluation of the revised technology acceptance model. *Management Science*, *42*(1), 85–92. doi:10.1287/mnsc.42.1.85

Takaaki, K., Kenji, F., & Yasuo, O. (2003). The MIAKO. NET public wireless Internet service in Kyoto. In *Proceedings of the 1st ACM International Workshop on Wireless Mobile Applications and Services on WLAN Hotspots* (pp. 56-63). New York, NY: ACM Press.

Talluri, S., Baker, R. C., & Sarkis, J. (1999). A framework for designing efficient value chain network. *International Journal of Production Economics*, *62*(1), 133–144. doi:10.1016/S0925-5273(98)00225-4

Taylor, S., & Todd, P. A. (1995). Understanding information technology usage: A test of competing models. *Information Systems Research*, *6*(4), 144–176. doi:10.1287/isre.6.2.144

Tellache, M., Sid-Ahmed, M., & Abaza, B. (1993, May 19-24). Thinning algorithms for Arabic OCR. In *Proceedings of the IEEE Pacific Rim Conference on Communications and Signal Processing*, Victoria, BC, Canada (Vol. 1, pp. 248-251).

Teo, T. S. H., Lim, V. K. G., & Lai, R. Y. C. (1999). Intrinsic and extrinsic motivation in Internet usage. *Omega*, *27*, 25–37. doi:10.1016/S0305-0483(98)00028-0

Teo, T. S. H., & Pok, S. H. (2003). Adoption of WAP-enabled mobile phones among internet users, omega. *The International Journal of Management Science*, *31*(6), 483–498.

Tessler, M., & Jamal, A. (2006). Political attitude research in the Arab world: emerging opportunities, *PSC Online*, *39*(3).

Theodoratos, D., Ligoudistianos, S., & Sellis, T. (2001). View selection for designing the global Multidimensional structure. *Data & Knowledge Engineering*, *39*, 219. doi:10.1016/S0169-023X(01)00041-6

Thomas, A. J., & Webb, D. (2003). Quality systems implementation in Welsh small-to-medium-sized enterprises: a global comparison and a model for change. *Journal of Engineering Manufacture*, *217*, 573–579. doi:10.1243/095440503321628251

Thomas, D. B., & Baas, L. R. (1992). The issue of generalization in q methodology: Reliable schematics revisited. *Operand Subjectivity*, *16*(1), 18–36.

Thomas, D. M., & Watson, R. T. (2002). Q-Sorting and MIS research: A primer. *Communications of the Association for Information Systems*, *8*, 141–156.

Thompson, R. L., Higgins, C. A., & Howell, J. M. (1991). Personal computing: Toward a conceptual model of utilization. *Management Information Systems Quarterly*, *15*(1), 124–143. doi:10.2307/249443

Timsari, B., & Fahimi, H. (1996). Morphological approach to character recognition in machine-printed Persian words. In *Proceedings of the SPIE Conference on Document Recognition III*, San Jose, CA.

Todd, N., & Szolkowski, M. (2003). Locating Resources Using JNDI (Java Naming and Directory Interface). In Todd, N., & Szolkowski, M. (Eds.), *JavaServer Pages Developer's Handbook*. Indianapolis, IN: Sams.

Todd, P. A., & Benbasat, I. (1989). *An experimental investigation of the impact of computer based decision aids on the process of preferential choice*. Kingston, ON, Canada: School of Business, Queen's University.

Tolba, M. F., & Shaddad, E. (1990, November 4-7). On the automatic reading of printed Arabic characters. In *Proceedings of the IEEE International Conference on Systems, Man and Cybernetics*, Los Angeles, CA (pp. 496-498).

TRA. (2008). *Telecommunications services indicators in the Kingdom of Bahrain*. Retrieved February 21, 2009, from http://www.tra.org.bh/en/pdf/Telecommunications-ServicesIndicatorsReport301008.pdf

Trenkle, J., Gillies, A., Erlandson, E., Schlosser, S., & Cavin, S. (2001, April 23-25). Advances in Arabic text recognition. In *Proceedings of the Symposium on Document Image Understanding Technology*, Columbia, MD.

Triandis, H. C. (1977). *Interpersonal behavior*. Monterey, CA: Brooke/Cole.

Trujillo, J., & Palomar, M. (1998). An object oriented approach to multidimensional database conceptual modeling. In *Proceedings of the 1st ACM International Workshop on Data Warehousing and OLAP*.

Trujillo, J., Palomar, M., Gomez, J., & Song, I. Y. (2001). Designing data warehouses with OO conceptual models. *IEEE Computer*, *34*(12), 66–75. doi:10.1109/2.970579

Tubiello, F., & Fischer, G. (2007). Reducing climate change impacts on agriculture: Global and regional effects of mitigation, 2000–2080. *Technological Forecasting and Social Change*, *74*(7), 1030–1056. doi:10.1016/j.techfore.2006.05.027

Turel, O., Serenko, A., & Bontis, N. (2007). User acceptance of wireless short messaging services: Deconstructing perceived value. *Information & Management*, *44*, 63–73. doi:10.1016/j.im.2006.10.005

UNESCO. (2010). *The current states of scientific around the world*. Paris, France: Author.

United Nations Department of Economic and Social Affairs. (2003). *e-Government readiness assessment survey*. Retrieved from http://unpan1.un.org/intradoc/groups/public/documents/un/unpan011509.pdf

United Nations Development Programme. (2009). *Human development report-Overcoming barriers: Human mobility and development*. New York, NY: Palgrave Macmillan.

Van der Weile, T., & Brown, A. (1998). Venturing down the TQM path for SME's. *International Small Business Journal*, *16*(2), 50–68. doi:10.1177/0266242698162003

van Deursen, A. J. A. M., & van Dijk, J. A. G. M. (2009). Improving digital skills for the use of online public information and services. *Government Information Quarterly*, *26*(2), 333–340. doi:10.1016/j.giq.2008.11.002

Van Raaij, E. M., & Schepers, J. L. (2008). The acceptance and use of a virtual learning environment in China. *Computers & Education*, *50*, 838–852. doi:10.1016/j.compedu.2006.09.001

van Velsen, L., van der Geest, T., ter Hedde, M., & Derks, W. (2009). Requirements engineering for e-government services: A citizen-centric approach and case study. *Government Information Quarterly*, *26*(3), 477–486. doi:10.1016/j.giq.2009.02.007

Vanbelle, S., & Albert, A. (2009). A note on the linearly weighted kappa coefficient for ordinal scales. *Statistical Methodology*, *6*, 157–163. doi:10.1016/j.stamet.2008.06.001

Varshney, U., & Jain, R. (2007). Issues in emerging 4g wireless networks. *IEEE Computer*, *34*(6), 94–96.

Vassey, I. (1984). *An investigation of the psychological processes underlying the debugging of computer programs* (Unpublished doctoral dissertation). University of Queensland, Brisbane, Australia.

Vatanasakdakul, S., Tibben, W., & Cooper, J. (2004). *What prevent B2B eCommerce adoption in developing countries? A socio-cultural perspective*. Paper presented at the 17th Bled eCommerce Conference eGlobal, Bled, Slovenia.

Veiga, J. F., Floyd, S., & Dechant, K. (2001). Towards modeling the effects of national culture on IT implementation and acceptance. *Journal of Information Technology*, *16*(2), 145–158. doi:10.1080/02683960110063654

Venkatesh, V., & Bala, H. (2008). Technology acceptance model 3 and a research agenda on interventions. *Decision Sciences*, *39*(2), 273–315. doi:10.1111/j.1540-5915.2008.00192.x

Venkatesh, V., Brown, S. A., Maruping, L. M., & Bala, H. (2008). Predicting different conceptualizations of system use: The competing roles of behavioral intention, facilitating conditions, and behavioral expectation. *Management Information Systems Quarterly*, *32*(3), 483–502.

Venkatesh, V., & Davis, F. D. (1996). A model of the antecedents of perceived ease of use: development and test. *Decision Sciences*, *27*(3), 451–481. doi:10.1111/j.1540-5915.1996.tb01822.x

Venkatesh, V., & Davis, F. D. (2000). A theoretical extension of the technology acceptance model: Four longitudinal field studies. *Management Science*, *46*(2), 186–204. doi:10.1287/mnsc.46.2.186.11926

Venkatesh, V., & Morris, M. G. (2000). Why don't men ever stop to ask for directions? Gender, social influence, and their role in technology acceptance and usage behavior. *Management Information Systems Quarterly*, *24*(1), 115–139. doi:10.2307/3250981

Venkatesh, V., Morris, M. G., Davis, G. B., & Davis, F. D. (2003). User acceptance of information technology: Toward a unified view. *Management Information Systems Quarterly*, *27*(3), 425–478.

Verdegem, P., & Verleye, G. (2009). User-centered e-government in practice: A comprehensive model for measuring user satisfaction. *Government Information Quarterly, 26*(3), 487–497. doi:10.1016/j.giq.2009.03.005

Vitell, S. J., Paolillo, J. G. P., & Thomas, J. L. (2003). The perceived role of ethics and social responsibility: A study of marketing professionals. *Business Ethics Quarterly, 13*(1), 63–86.

Von Hippel, E. (2006). Horizontal innovation networks: By and for users. *Journal of Research and Development Management, 36*(3), 273–294.

Waggoner, P. (2004). Agricultural technology and its societal implications. *Technology in Society, 26*(2-3), 123–136. doi:10.1016/j.techsoc.2004.01.024

Wainwright, D., & Waring, T. S. (2007). The application and adaptation of a diffusion of innovation framework for information system. *Journal of Information Technology, 22*, 44–58. doi:10.1057/palgrave.jit.2000093

Walker, R. F. (1993). *Spacio-temporal Arabic character recognition using polynomial contour fitting* (Tech. Rep.). Brisbane, Australia: Queensland University of Technology.

Wang, H.-C., Ku, Y.-C., & Doong, H.-S. (2007). Case study in mobile Internet innovation: Does advertising or acquaintances communication decide Taiwan's mobile Internet diffusion? In *Proceedings of the 40th Annual Hawaii International Conference on System Sciences* (p. 230). Washington, DC: IEEE Computer Society.

Wang, L. (2009). The study on public information service's supply mechanism of local government. *Information Studies: Theory & Application, 12*, 41–44.

Wang, S., Yang, B., & Niu, X. (2010). A secure steganography method based on genetic algorithm. *Journal of Information Hiding and Multimedia Signal Processing, 1*(1), 28–35.

Wang, W.-T., & Wang, C.-C. (2009). An empirical study of instructor adoption of web-based learning systems. *Computers & Education, 53*, 761–774. doi:10.1016/j.compedu.2009.02.021

Wang, Y.-S., & Shih, Y.-W. (2009). Why do people use information kiosks? A validation of the unified theory of acceptance and use of technology. *Government Information Quarterly, 26*, 158–165. doi:10.1016/j.giq.2008.07.001

Warkentin, M., D., Gefen, P. A., Pavlou, P. A., & Rose, G. M. (2002). Encouraging citizen adoption of e-government by building trust. *Electronic Markets, 12*(3), 157–162. doi:10.1080/101967802320245929

Warmer, J., & Kleppe, A. (1999). *The object constraint language precise modeling with UML*. Reading, MA: Addison-Wesley.

Warrens, M. (2010). Cohen's kappa can always be increased and decreased by combining categories. *Statistical Methodology, 7*, 673–677. doi:10.1016/j.stamet.2010.05.003

Wasko, M., & Faraj, S. (2005). Why should I share? Examining social capital and knowledge contribution in electronic networks of practice. *Management Information Systems Quarterly, 29*(1), 35–57.

Watts, C., & Ashcroft, L. (2005). ICT skills for information professionals in developing countries: Perspective from a study of the electronic information environment in Nigeria. *IFLA Journal, 31*(1), 146–153.

Watts, S., & Stenner, P. (2005). Doing Q methodology: theory, method and interpretation. *Qualitative Research in Psychology, 2*, 67–91. doi:10.1191/1478088705qp022oa

Weick, C. (2001). Agribusiness technology in 2010: Directions and challenges. *Technology in Society, 23*(1), 59–72. doi:10.1016/S0160-791X(00)00035-X

Weisfeld, M. (2009). *The object-oriented thought process* (3rd ed.). Upper Saddle River, NJ: Pearson Education.

Wessel, G., & Burcher, P. (2004). Six Sigma for small and medium-sized enterprises. *Total Quality Management Magazine, 16*(4), 264–272.

Wikipedia. (2011). *Kurdistan.* Retrieved from http://en.wikipedia.org/wiki/Kurdistan

Wikipedia. (2011). *United Arab Emirates.* Retrieved July 5, 2011, from http://en.wikipedia.org/wiki/United_Arab_Emirates#cite_note-6

Wilkens, W. F., & Hartman, J. D. (1964). An electronic analog for the olfactory processes. *Journal of Food Science*, *29*(3), 372–378. doi:10.1111/j.1365-2621.1964.tb01746.x

Wirfs-Brock, R., & McKean, A. (1999). *Objects design*. Reading, MA: Addison-Wesley.

Wixom, B., & Todd, P. A. (2005). A theoretical integration of user satisfaction and technology acceptance. *Information Systems Research*, *16*(1), 85–102. doi:10.1287/isre.1050.0042

World Bank. (1994). *Lending for industrial technology: Lessons from six countries* (Review No. 70). Retrieved May 20, 2011, from http://lnweb90.worldbank.org/oed/oeddoclib.nsf/DocUNIDViewForJavaSearch/55F1463FA43E535B852567F5005D8785?opendocument

World Gazetteer. (2011). *Abu Dhabi*. Retrieved August 2, 2011, from http://world-gazetteer.com/wg.php?x=&men=gpro&lng=en&des=gamelan&geo=-265&srt=npan&col=abcdefghinoq&msz=1500

Wu, I.-L., & Wu, K.-W. (2005). A hybrid technology acceptance approach for exploring e-CRM adoption in organizations. *Behaviour & Information Technology*, *24*(4), 303–316. doi:10.1080/0144929042000320027

Wu, J.-H., Chen, Y.-C., & Lin, L.-M. (2007). Empirical evaluation of the revised end user computing acceptance model. *Computers in Human Behavior*, *23*(1), 162–174. doi:10.1016/j.chb.2004.04.003

Xavier, P., & Ypsilanti, D. (2007). Universal service in an IP-enabled NGN environment. *Info*, *9*(1), 15–31. doi:10.1108/14636690710725049

Xiangdong, W. (2001). Mobile communications & mobile Internet in China. *IQTE*, *7*(5), 134–225.

Xia, Y. (2004). Socaity choice of public information service. *Journal of Library Science in China*, *3*, 18–23.

Yamakami, T. (2003). Toward understanding the mobile Internet user behavior: A methodology for user clustering with aging analysis. In *Proceedings of the Fourth International Conference on Parallel and Distributed Computing, Applications and Technologies* (pp. 85-89). Washington, DC: IEEE Computer Society.

Yang, D.-H., Kim, S., Nam, C., & Moon, J.-S. (2004). Fixed and mobile service convergence and reconfiguration of telecommunications value chains. *IEEE Wireless Communications*, *11*, 42–47. doi:10.1109/MWC.2004.1351680

Yang, H.-D., & Yoo, Y. (2003). It's all about attitude: Revisiting the technology acceptance model. *Decision Support Systems*, *38*(1), 19–31. doi:10.1016/S0167-9236(03)00062-9

Yang, K. C. (2007). Exploring factors affecting consumer intention to use mobile advertising in Taiwan. *Journal of International Consumer Marketing*, *20*(1), 33–49. doi:10.1300/J046v20n01_04

Yi, M. Y., & Hwang, Y. (2003). Predicting the use of web-based information systems: self-efficacy, enjoyment, learning goal orientation, and the technology acceptance model. *International Journal of Human-Computer Studies*, *59*, 431–449. doi:10.1016/S1071-5819(03)00114-9

Yi, M. Y., Jackson, J. D., Park, J. S., & Probst, J. C. (2006). Understanding information technology acceptance by individual professionals: Toward an integrative view. *Information & Management*, *43*(3), 350–363. doi:10.1016/j.im.2005.08.006

Yin, R. Y. (2003). *Case Study Research: design and methods*. London, UK: Sage.

Ymin, A., & Aoki, Y. (1996, August 25-29). On the segmentation of multi-font printed Uygur scripts. In *Proceedings of the 13th International Conference on Pattern Recognition* (Vol. 3, pp. 215-219).

Youngberg, E., Olsen, D., & Hauser, K. (2009). Determinants of professionally autonomous end user acceptance in an enterprise resource planning system environment. *International Journal of Information Management*, *29*, 138–144. doi:10.1016/j.ijinfomgt.2008.06.001

Yousafzai, S. Y., Foxall, G. R., & Pallister, J. G. (2007). Technology acceptance: a meta-analysis of the TAM: Part 1. *Journal of Modelling in Management*, *2*(3), 251–280. doi:10.1108/17465660710834453

Yung, W. (2007). *Bring existing data to the Semantic Web, Expose LDAP directories to the Semantic Web with SquirrelRDF*. Retrieved from http://www.ibm.com/developerworks/xml/library/x-semweb.html

Zadeh, L. A. (1965). Fuzzy sets. *Information and Control*, *8*, 338–353. doi:10.1016/S0019-9958(65)90241-X

Zadeh, L. A. (2008). Is there a need for fuzzy logic? *Information Sciences*, *178*(13), 2751–2779. doi:10.1016/j.ins.2008.02.012

Zahour, A., Taconet, B., Mercy, P., & Ramdane, S. (2001, September 10-13). Arabic hand-written text-line extraction. In *Proceedings of the 6ᵗʰ International Conference on Document Analysis and Recognition*, Seattle, WA (pp. 281-285).

Zain, M., Rose, R. C., Abdullah, I., & Masrom, M. (2005). The relationship between information technology acceptance and organizational agility in Malaysia. *Information & Management*, *42*, 829–839. doi:10.1016/j.im.2004.09.001

Zeki, A. M., & Ismail, I. A. (2002). A comparative study of five OCR systems. In *Proceedings of the National Conference on Computer Graphics and Multimedia*, Melaka, Malaysia (pp. 552-556).

Zeki, A. M., & Zakaria, M. S. (2004, April 5-8). Challenges in recognizing Arabic characters. In *Proceedings of the 17th National Computer Conference*, Al-Madinah, Saudi Arabia (pp. 445-452).

Zeki, A. M., & Zakaria, M. S. (2005, February 1-3). Determining the up/down orientation of Arabic documents. In *Proceedings of the International Conference on Modeling, Simulation and Applied Optimization*, Sharjah, UAE.

Zhang, J. (1999). Developing robust nonlinear models through bootstrap aggregated neural networks. *Neurocomputing*, *25*, 93–113. doi:10.1016/S0925-2312(99)00054-5

Zhang, L. (2008). The status analysis and measures of information divide in China. [Natural Science Edition]. *Journal of Henan Institute of Education*, *17*(3), 44–46.

Zhang, W., & Guitierrez, O. (2007). Information technology acceptance in the social services context: An exploration. *Social Work*, *52*(3), 221–231.

Zheng, L., Hassin, A. H., & Tang, Z. (2004). A new algorithm for machine printed Arabic character segmentation. *Pattern Recognition Letters*, *25*(15), 1723–1729. doi:10.1016/j.patrec.2004.06.015

Zhou, T., Lu, Y., & Wang, B. (2010). Integrating TTF and UTAUT to explain mobile banking user adoption. *Computers in Human Behavior*, *26*, 760–767. doi:10.1016/j.chb.2010.01.013

Zhu, Z., Li, Z., & Duan, Y. (2005). An active network based hierarchical mobile Internet protocol version 6 framework. In *Proceedings of the International Conference on Wireless Communications, Networking and Mobile Computing* (Vol. 2, pp. 1029-1033). Washington, DC: IEEE Computer Society.

Zidouri, A. (2004, October 20-22). ORAN - offline recognition of Arabic characters and numerals. In *Proceedings of the International Symposium on Intelligent Multimedia, Video and Speech Processing*, Hong Kong (pp. 703-706).

Zidouri, A., Sarfraz, M., Nawaz, S. N., & Ahmad, M. J. (2003, July 1-4). PC based offline Arabic text recognition system. In *Proceedings of the 7th International Symposium on Signal Processing and its Applications* (Vol. 2, pp. 431-434).

Zidouri, A., Sarfraz, M., Shahab, S. A., & Jafri, S. M. (2005, July 6-5). Adaptive dissection-based subword segmentation of printed Arabic text. In *Proceedings of the 9th International Conference on Information Visualisation* (pp. 239-243).

Zimmermann, H.-J. (1985). *Fuzzy set theory - and its applications*. Boston, MA: Kluwer Academic.

About the Contributors

Ali Hussein Saleh Zolait (Known Dr. Zolait) is the Assistant Professor of Management Information Systems (MIS) at the College of Information Technology – Department of Information System – University of Bahrain. Dr. Zolait is considered a prominent scholar and leader in the field of Innovation Diffusion and Technology Acceptance. He has published more than 30 articles on aspects of information security, internet banking, mobile application, supply chain integration, information systems performance in organization, Web maturity evaluation, information systems, performance analysis and instructional technologies, and e-commerce application. His work has been published in leading international journals such as *Government Information Quarterly, Behaviour & Information Technology, Journal of Systems and Information Technology,* and *Journal of Financial Services Marketing.* He is the Editor-in-Chief of the *International Journal of Technology Diffusion* (IJTD). Before coming to University of Bahrain, he was the Stoops Distinguished Assistant Professor of E-commerce and Management Information Systems at Graduate School of Business- University of Malaya - Malaysia which is ranked one of top 100 Universities in the world. Dr. Zolait also serves as the Visiting Research at the University of Malaya at Faculty of Business and Accountancy (2008). He has excellent communication skills, a collegial approach to faculty and student interactions, and a sincere appreciation of cultural diversity. He literally developed hundreds of students at all levels- undergraduate, MBA, MM, Executive Development, and Doctoral.

* * *

Ali AlSoufi earned his BSc in computer science from university of Bahrain, MSc in computer science from Aston University, UK and PhD in computer science from Nottingham University, UK. He worked for 11 years as lecturer at University of Bahrain, including 4 years as head of Computer Science department. Ali has 11 years of industrial experience out of which 8 years as a Senior Manager Application Programmes in IS department at Batelco, where he overlooked number of teams responsible for developing and supporting the company's critical applications systems such as SAP ERP, Oracle HRMS, NCR Teradata Data Warehouse, various billing systems, Oracle CRM, various Payment systems and number of web based applications such as Batelco's e-Shop. Between 2007-2010, Dr. Ali worked at Arab Open University as the head of IT and Computing Program and Assistant Director for Business Development. During the same period he was working as a consultant for Bahrain e-Government Authority (EGA). Currently he is a member of the EGA strategy development team. Dr. Ali is now working for University of Bahrain as assistant Professor. He has number of publications in various fields of Information Technology, and has regular contributions in both academic and industrial IT activities.

Wasan Shaker Awad is assistant professor of computer science at University of Bahrain, Bahrain. She did her PhD in 1998. She has been teaching at various universities in Iraq, Jordan, and Bahrain, and she has a teaching experience of more than 10 years. Her research interest covers computational intelligence, information security, and coding theory. She has published more than 15 papers in a number of international journals.

Amin A. Shaqrah is currently assistant professor of management information systems at Al Zaytoonah University of Jordan. He holds a PhD and MA in management information systems. He is a certified e-business consultants and a KM professional. He is affiliated with a number of international professional societies on KM, E-business, and a member of editorial review boards for a number of International journals. He had a leadership role in the design and implementation of MIS program at the undergraduate level. His research interests are mainly knowledge sharing and transfer, organizational knowledge theory, knowledge culture, CRM value strategies, data mining techniques, Innovative work environment, human and social implications of enterprise systems (ERP, CRM, SCM). His work appears in number of International journals and conferences.

Omar Shehab, Software Engineering (MSc), is a postgraduate student at Staffordshire University, Information Technology, Kuala Lumpur, Malaysia.

Ahmed Sowaileh has earned his BSc degree in CS from University of Bahrain and his master's degree from Arab Open University in IT. Currently he is the director of Information Systems Directorate of the Ministry of Justice, Bahrain. He has worked in the government sector for 13 years and he was involved in various e-government projects. His research interests are eGovernment services, m-services and IT management.

Jianbin Zhang is a PhD candidate in school of information management of Wuhan University, China. He is major in information resources management, and his research area of interest is government information construction.

Index